26

THE OXFORD HISTORY
OF ENGLAND

Edited by SIR GEORGE CLARK

THE OXFORD HISTORY OF ENGLAND

Edited by SIR GEORGE CLARK

These volumes have been published

THE REIGN OF
GEORGE III
1760–1815

BY

J. STEVEN WATSON
Student and Tutor of Christ Church, Oxford

OXFORD
AT THE CLARENDON PRESS
1960

Oxford University Press, Amen House, London E.C.4

GLASGOW   NEW YORK   TORONTO   MELBOURNE   WELLINGTON
BOMBAY   CALCUTTA   MADRAS   KARACHI   KUALA LUMPUR
CAPE TOWN   IBADAN   NAIROBI   ACCRA

PRINTED IN GREAT BRITAIN
AT THE UNIVERSITY PRESS, OXFORD
BY VIVIAN RIDLER
PRINTER TO THE UNIVERSITY

PREFACE

M Y debt of gratitude to many friends and guides working on eighteenth-century history will, I trust, be so clear in the following pages that it requires neither emphasis nor particularization here. Dr. F. L. Cross, in the catholicity of his interests, read my proofs to my great profit, and Dr. J. B. Owen did me the same service for part of them. The General Editor of this series, Sir George Clark, put his wisdom and experience most generously at my disposal. I am grateful also to those pupils, both in Christ Church and in my W.E.A. class at Headington, who clarified my ideas by forcing me to defend them. To Miss Elizabeth A. Livingstone I am most deeply obliged for her tireless labours in typing my manuscript, in working on the index, in pursuing references for verification, and in keeping me to a time-table. I must also thank my wife and family for bearing with me while I have been living with this book.

J. S. W.

August 1959

CONTENTS

IV. MINISTERIAL INSTABILITY, 1760–5

VII. THE ORIGINS OF THE AMERICAN REVOLT

VIII. LORD NORTH AND THE AMERICAN WAR
OF INDEPENDENCE

IX. THE FALL OF NORTH AND THE RISE OF REFORM MOVEMENTS

X. THE CONFLICT OF GROUPS, 1782–4

XI. PITT AND RECONSTRUCTION

XII. THE COLLAPSE OF THE OPPOSITION, 1784–93

XVI. FROM AMIENS TO TRAFALGAR

XVII. THE FAILURE OF THE TALENTS AND THE PROBLEMS FACING PORTLAND, 1806-9

I

THE ACCESSION OF GEORGE III

PERHAPS only George III, and his 'dearest friend' Lord Bute,[1] expected the accession of the twenty-two years old king in the autumn of 1760 to mark a sufficient break in English history to be called the beginning of an epoch. Politicians, it is true, expected changes, for the king was likely to appoint new ministers. His power to do so was a cardinal point in political theory, and was to remain so for at least another seventy years. Ministers in power under George II accordingly could hope to remain in place only by ingratiating themselves with the new master. They did not challenge his right to dismiss them. For the duty of the new king was to hold an administration together so that Britain might be governed. At all times ministers were likely to quarrel among themselves and to show their lack of any sense of collective responsibility or mutual good faith. The limits upon the king's freedom of choice were personal and fluctuating. The men he chose had to be able to serve together, and had to be able to see to business in Parliament. From the point of view of his own convenience it suited the king to work with someone popular in parliament. Otherwise his essential business would give trouble and necessitate great effort. Within such wide limits any king would choose ministers personally pleasing to him. It could surprise no one therefore if George III planned to employ some new men. But any such appointment would no more mark an epoch constitutionally than a change in Windsor coachmen marks a chapter in the history of locomotion.

The members of the small circle which was concerned with political authority either welcomed or dreaded (according to their interests) changes which would resemble those intended

---

[1] John Stuart, third earl of Bute (1713–92), a representative peer of Scotland, 1737; since 1747 a rising influence in the prince of Wales's court; secretary of state, 1761; first lord of the treasury, 1762, but resigned in 1763. Long disliked by politicians as a 'power behind the curtain' influencing the king. For further details see pp. 69, 70.

by George II in 1727,[1] a shuffling of the old pack of cards. Even less did ordinary men regard 1760 as a date from which historians might subsequently try to date the beginnings of revolutions in industry and in social life. No sense of a new world struggling to be born disturbed the solid and familiar certainties of mid-century life.

Contemporary opinion was more in the right of it than many later historians. Neither in the constitution nor in economic life is there any sharp break to be discerned in 1760. And yet in the political field the reign of George III had, almost from its start, a different climate from that of his predecessor. George III himself could not, whatever his intentions, produce this change. Great issues arose from the peace of Paris, from Wilkes's adventures, from America, from Ireland, which were different in intensity from those of the previous forty years. Fresh strain was put upon the old political system and so, in time, resulted in that system working differently. The Crown's selection of its servants, for instance, becomes a subject of more controversy when the candidates represent opposed principles than when the choice is merely of personalities. In the economic field the new developments were slower. The so-called industrial revolution cannot, by its nature, be pinned down to a date chart. But even the roughest dating of it cannot place its effective start before the 1780's. By the end of the reign, however, the atmosphere had changed both in the political salon and in the manufacturing shop. Only George III himself and his most prejudiced enemies—or distant Americans—could attribute to the king personally a major share in this alteration. Here, despite proverbs, there has been a great deal of smoke without any fire, if we except the *ignis fatuus* of George's own youthful and neurotic longings.

George did intend to make a significant change on his accession. He imagined that he would ride forth to kill dragons, the monsters of corruption and immorality. His father had, like all Hanoverian heirs, opposed the king.[2] A prince of Wales was the rallying point for opposition to government, opposition which aimed at remaining respectable by associating itself with

[1] See B. Williams, *The Whig Supremacy* (vol. xi of the present *History*), p. 193.

[2] See Mr. Romney Sedgwick's introduction to his *Letters of George III to Bute* in which the political consequences of this conflict of monarch and heir are studied as the 'Leicester House Cycle'.

the royal family, and which hoped for places and rewards when the prince came into his inheritance. So behind Frederick's contrariness lay impatience for power and personal animosity to his father. To maintain his importance any cry, any grievance, might be exploited. Frederick would even sometimes hope to pose as the moral man fighting the dirty methods and dirtier mistresses of George II. As methodism was the subject of sneers at court, Frederick attended the Moorfields tabernacle and hoped, he said, 'to seize the skirt of Lady Huntingdon's[1] mantle to lift me up to heaven'. To lift him up into prominence he would seize on some controversial issue, domestic or Hanoverian, and trail his coat before the king without further motive than the desire to annoy. Even his selection of Mercier as his chosen portrait painter was determined by his wish to flout more commonly accepted artists, whose offence was not their faults of composition but their favour at court.[2]

After Frederick's death in 1751 the twelve-year-old grandson of George II was heir to the prejudices, while not aware of the motives, of his father. In his adolescence he took seriously the cant phrases of opposition mouthed by his poor father. All men out of power during the century denounced the foreign entanglements entered into by their successful rivals; but if once themselves in the seats of authority they placidly continued in the old ways. All men in opposition exaggerated the corruption of government: few in office dreamed of changing the system. But George was neither old nor sophisticated enough to play this game as his father had. His feelings were the more intense because he was prevented from giving any practical and petty expression to them. Moreover he considered that his mother was shabbily treated by his grandfather and by ministers. His heart was full of spite and a longing for revenge; his resentment he interpreted as proof of his special mission to purify politics. For him a battle between right and wrong—not between 'court'

---

[1] Selina, countess of Huntingdon (1707–81), was converted by the methodists in her twenties. Her husband at first attempted to 'unconvert' her, employing for this purpose conversations with Bishop Benson. This failing she was left free to devote her wealth and energies to philanthropy and the encouragement of Calvinism within the church of England. She set up chapels registered as dissenting meeting houses, encouraged the revivalist activities of Whitefield, and endeavoured to bring to the ladies of the great social world a conviction that their hearts were 'as sinful as the common wretches that crawl on the earth'.

[2] Compare B. Williams, *The Whig Supremacy*, p. 381. Philip Mercier, born in Berlin in 1689, was appointed principal painter and librarian to the prince of Wales in 1727. He died in 1760.

and 'anti-court', 'ins' and 'outs'—was involved. With the exception of Lord Chatham, George III was probably the only man in the eighteenth century to believe absolutely in his own slogans about patriotism, purity, and a better system of conducting government soon to be ushered in. In fact, it will be argued below that the system was neither so corrupt nor so unified as George in his youthful ignorance imagined. On the other hand he was to find that the basis of 'influence', upon which all groups in politics had so far depended, was an element in the system which could not be dispensed with in normal conditions.

Despite the facts, George did imagine that he was born to cleanse political life. It is clear from his correspondence that he had suffered from earliest youth from a tendency to melancholia, a consciousness of his own inferiority, and a determination to correct these weaknesses by an effort of the will. This it is which explains his passionate devotion to Lord Bute, his 'dearest friend': Bute he accepted as a model for behaviour as a schoolboy accepts a favourite master. George II had to be cast for the role of devil, 'shuffling', 'unworthy of a British Monarch' —'the conduct of this old K. makes me ashamed of being his grandson: he treats me in the same manner, his knave and counsellor the D. of N. does all people'.[1] Any counsellor of George II was bound to be considered a knave. For Pitt, who had deserted the heir to serve the king, he felt particular hostility. He called him 'the blackest of hearts' and 'a true snake in the grass': this was in 1760 when Pitt's fame and powers were at their highest pitch of triumph. But Pitt had 'long shown a want of regard both of you my Dearest Friend and consequently of myself'. Young George did not condemn the war effort. He tried to find military employment in it. But because Lord George Sackville was abandoned by ministers and court martialled for cowardice and disobedience after the battle of Minden, the prince perversely set him up as an 'injur'd man'; Lord George's early connexions with the Leicester House[2] party and his bad reputation among George II's ministers, were sufficient to make George III retain sympathy with him for life.[3]

---

[1] These and the following quotations from George's letters are taken from R. Sedgwick, *Letters of George III and Bute*. The initials refer to the duke of Newcastle.

[2] i.e. the heir's party against the king, from the residence of the prince of wales.

[3] Lord George Sackville (1716–85), the third son of the first duke of Dorset; he took the name Germain in 1770. As a soldier and politician he had risen to be lieutenant general of the ordnance and colonel of the second dragoon guards by

George felt that his task on coming to the throne would be herculean, for 'as to honesty, I think all sets of men seem equaly [*sic*] to have thrown that aside', and he had to make politicians concentrate upon public rather than private interest. But he felt himself unsuited to the part. He moped to feel himself no hero. For compensation he elevated Bute to a pedestal for which the Scot had few qualifications. In 1758, when Bute indicated to the prince those failings of which the pupil was only too conscious, George replied:

'I now see plainly that I have been my greatest enemy; for had I always acted on your advice, I should now have been the direct opposite from what I am; nothing but the true love you bear me, could have led you to remain with me so long. . . . If you should now resolve to set me adrift, I could not abraid you, but on the contrary look on it as the natural consequence of my faults . . . if you shall ever think fit to take this step, my line of action is plain; for though I act wrong perhaps in most things, yet I have too much spirit to accept the Crown and be a sypher—'. He goes on to dream of abdication and retirement 'to some distant region' 'there to think of the various faults I have committed that I might repent of them'.

His only hope is that Bute, his strength, will forgive and sustain him. This is not serious thought. It is the abasement of a boy struggling to become resolute, who invests a hero with imaginary virtues and himself with odious vices.

It is clear that the obstinacy which was so marked a feature of George III as king was the product of effort: it sprang always from an inner distrust, a melancholy sense of sin, which he was too good a man to allow to master him. This was therefore his only means of facing the world. He lacked the pliability and easy virtue of less highly strung people. When his obstinacy encountered an immovable obstacle, all his resources were at an end and the black humour claimed him. Even in old age in such a situation he was back in a schoolroom mood. He would threaten abdication not in pique so much as in confession of absolute failure. Madness was but this mood in an extreme form.

Love and friendship were possible refuges for him. But in politics and around thrones friendship is not the solid oak of young men's dreams, but a willow moved by winds. And love

1757. After the disgrace of his court martial he was shunned in society. After George III's accession he returned to court and politics. He was secretary of state for the colonies, 1775–82 and was created Viscount Sackville, 1782.

has everywhere its disasters. Often trembling on the brink of melancholy mania, George was to be thrust from gloom to years of madness by the death of a favourite child.

It is clear that there never was any need to invent the legend that this young man was nourished on Bolingbroke or studied to revive past powers of the Crown, if we are to account for the sense of strain with which he approached the throne. For him to be a king, as his grandfather was, was effort enough. Bolingbroke he probably never read. There was no need to. For Bolingbroke's *Patriot King* contains only the hackneyed clichés of eighteenth-century politics, what oft was thought but which no one else thought worth explicit expression.[1] Young George aimed at no more power than his grandfather: but that was considerable, and he meant to use it to show the world that the reign of virtue had begun while proving to himself that he had subdued his weaker, wickeder, self.

George's character and his affection for Bute are revealed most strikingly by his letters in late 1759 about Lady Sarah Lennox. He protested that 'I have never had any improper thought with regard to her', but confessed that jealousy had reduced him to solitary despair. He therefore contemplated marriage with the fifteen-year-old beauty, but submitted the idea to Bute's judgement.

'I surrender my future into your hands, and will keep my thoughts even from the dear object of my love, grieve in silence, and never trouble you more with this unhappy tale; for if I must either lose my friend or my love, I will give up the latter, for I esteem your friendship above every earthly joy . . . tho' my heart should break, I shall have the happy reflexion in dying that I have not been altogether unworthy of the best of friends, tho' unfortunate in other things.'

Such sentimental language is not simply to be explained in terms of a prolonged adolescent affection. Bute was loved not only for himself but for what he represented to his young prince. In his heart George felt that marriage with Lady Sarah would be unfitting. And in Bute he had personified the highest standards of conduct which he aspired to reach. So, on receiving Bute's ban on such a marriage, George submitted with the reflection—'the interest of my country must ever be my first care, my own inclinations shall submit to it; I am born for the happiness or misery of a great nation, and must consequently often act

---

[1] For Bolingbroke, see B. Williams, *The Whig Supremacy*, pp. 395–6.

contrary to my passions'. Promptly he asked for a review to be made of all eligible German princesses—'to save a great deal of trouble' as 'matrimony must sooner or later come to pass'.[1] When he set down his resolution never to marry an English-woman, he said it was to please his dear friend: it was set down, clearly, just as much to strengthen himself.

It was in the same spirit of nailing his colours to the mast that on 31 October, a week after his accession, he issued a royal proclamation 'For the encouragement of piety and virtue, and for preventing and punishing of vice, profaneness, and im-morality'. This was the change in the old order that he planned.

The young king faced a political situation of extreme diffi-culty. But the difficulty was not of the kind which, in his in-jured innocence, he expected to encounter. He had anticipated a struggle to oust from their places the corrupt politicians who had slighted his parents and himself. He thought of them as the old gang, a united junta of aristocrats on the defensive. The truth was far different. Unity in common action was exactly what his grandfather's ministers lacked. The office holders were already on uneasy terms with one another before the change of sovereign. Their mutual suspicions were already threatening to split the ministry into fragments on the ground. The two great men, Pitt and Newcastle, said Lord Waldegrave, were agreed on one thing and one thing only—at no time again to endure the irritation of being linked with one another.[2] It was an un-certain team that George inherited. And a stronger substitute was not easily discernible.

The first ten years of the reign are a period of ministerial instability, of manœuvring by restless groups powerless to form an administration which can live in parliament. It is a period which is comparable only to the uneasy *va et vient* of the ministerial history of the fourth French republic. But this insta-bility does not, as has been sometimes thought, date from the accession of the new king. His share of blame must be that he approached this uneasy world of political makeshifts full of the idea that it needed a new broom, whereas in fact the need

[1] He married Princess Charlotte Sophia, second daughter of the late duke of Mecklenburg-Strelitz, in the Chapel Royal, St. James's, on 8 September 1761.

[2] James, second Earl Waldegrave (1715–63), had been the prince's governor from 1752 to 1756 and first lord of the treasury for four days in June 1757; his *Memoirs* (published in 1821) have many shrewd observations upon the leading figures of his time.

was for the soldering up of cracked friendships. The virtues required in a king in 1760 were the old-fashioned ones of tact and powers of conciliation: George III had only a fussy or brutal honesty. The instability of the political world probably may be dated from 1754 and the death of Henry Pelham.[1] Since that excellent man, full of commonsense policy and house of commons strategy, had been removed, it had been difficult to find a team to agree among themselves and to conduct business for more than a few months. No partner Newcastle could suffer could command the commons; no eminent man in the house would bear with Newcastle.

Temporarily, it is true, but only under the stress of a great war, it had been possible to arrange a partnership which masked these political facts. The Pitt–Newcastle combination was three years old when George III became king. It had been glorious without but quarrelsome within. It would stand only so long as an emergency, and lack of any other possible course, held its members together. Once it collapsed the true political position would be revealed. George's task would then not be that of preventing the political pieces from adhering together once more in some ugly pattern unpleasing to him; his problem would be to jam into place together sufficient of the usable, but mutually repelling, pieces to make some government which could live in the political conditions of the time.

Much has been written in the past about the organization of a government party.[2] Reading such accounts one is tempted to suppose that the most striking feature of eighteenth-century politics was the building up, through patronage and through corruption or even through bribery, of a disciplined ministerial body in the house of commons. Henry Fox, a politician of whom George III quickly had need, was a cynical manager, we are told, who was useful because he had learned from Walpole that every man has his price. This sounds as if the task of forming stable governments demanded no more than a purse and pimp. But while jobbery was an essential part of eighteenth-century government there never was a period when it could, alone, guarantee success. The important fact about the corruption of the century is that it produced so small a result after such intensive application. It enabled government to build up a body of

---

[1] See B. Williams, *The Whig Supremacy*, p. 325.

[2] See, for instance, B. Williams, *The Whig Supremacy*, p. 28.

practical and partly organized supporters in the house of commons. But while in times which lacked controversy, this group would attend successfully to day-to-day matters in the house, it was never large enough, or obedient enough, of itself to carry ministers through controversial periods, or to enable them to raise unpopular taxes. Corruption does not demonstrate the strength of pro-government forces, but their weakness. Without it there would have been no living in a climate so unfavourable to strong administration as prevailed in the eighteenth-century commons; with it business could be carried on provided the policy and the personnel of the ministry could appeal to the patriotism of country gentlemen or at least neutralize their anti-government bias.

It was the pride of the commons that they provided a constitutional balance by their innate suspicion of the executive. Lord Shelburne once defended freedom of the press on the grounds that it operated 'as a considerable check upon arbitrary power ... and though not so well calculated to build as to destroy, yet keeps the public awake and operates as a powerful negative, which in fact is the great requisite in all governments: for Providence has so ordered the world that very little government is necessary'. It was this feeling that provided the atmosphere of politics in 1760 and which made personal antagonisms, among the small circle of those capable of filling high office, of such disastrous consequence for the prospects of efficient administration. It was the cause of the hectic period of instability between the prosperous placidity of Walpole and the Pelhams and the ruinous but stable decade of Lord North. It was the basic fact of politics in 1760. As such its origins lie deep in the social and economic conditions of England in 1760, inexplicable unless these are understood.

II

THE ECONOMIC PATTERN IN 1760

ENGLAND and Wales in 1760 had a population of between 6½ and 6¾ million.[1] The steep rise in the number of Englishmen, which is perhaps the most striking feature of the reign of George III (by the end of the reign the population had almost doubled) had not yet begun in earnest. The birth-rate and the death-rate were both high and in proportion one to the other. An increase in deaths, from epidemic or such cause, would leave open farms and jobs to the young people surviving who might then marry earlier and produce children. Thus a rise in the death-rate was followed by a rise in the birth-rate: a lower death-rate, implying the retention of a place upon the earth, a share in its food and the sun by those who would previously have surrendered them, meant that young women would be denied opportunities to raise families at so early an age; in fact it would mean a fall in the birth-rate. This natural rhythm or equipoise of a stable agricultural society had not yet been drastically upset. Beginning soon after this date the death-rate was to decline without the hitherto inevitable consequence of a decline in births, indeed with an increase in births.[2] Of the many and controversial causes of this new phenomenon, some had already appeared in 1760. In Ireland the widespread cultivation of the potato, an eighteenth-century development,[3] made land which had previously supported one family capable of supporting two. In England, and to some extent in the lowlands of Scotland, an increase in productivity and wealth, both agricultural and trading, was providing an increased national subsistence

---

[1] The population of Scotland was about 1¼ millions; Ireland about 3¾ millions. (On the latter see K. H. Connell, *The Population of Ireland, 1750–1845*, p. 25.)

[2] The real decline in the death-rate may be dated from 1780. Between 1760 and 1780 there was a very slight rise in the death-rate compared with the previous twenty years. This may be attributed to harvest failures. The birth-rate was rising, as one would expect, in 1760–80. But it was not checked even after 1780. (See H. J. Habakkuk, 'English Population in the 18th Century' in *Econ. H. R.*, 2nd ser., vi (1953–4), pp. 117–33.

[3] For the argument that it was not until this century that the potato was a general crop in Ireland, see K. H. Connell, *The Population of Ireland, 1750–1845*.

though the expansion of industrial demand for labour had not yet added its stimulus to child-production.

The death-rate was beginning, but as yet only very slightly, to feel the effects of improved medical care. In Edinburgh the Medical School had been in existence for thirty-five years. In London the great hospitals, St. Bartholomew's, St. Thomas's, Bedlam, Guy's, the Middlesex, the Westminster, and the London Hospital, formed centres for the diffusion of medical methods. Vaccination had not yet been brought fully into the fight against the mortality bills. Jenner's[1] cowpox-inoculation became effective only from the end of the century. But already the idea of taking the disease in a mild form so as to escape its full consequences was being popularized, and George III himself, as a child, had had experience of this preventive method.[2] The most vigorously pushed line of medical research was that dealing with scurvy, because of its importance to the navy. In 1757 the admiralty ordered all pursers to supply 'roots and Greens to Seamen, with their Fresh Meat'. Dr. Lind had already tried the effect of oranges as an anti-scorbutic afloat. Cook's[3] trial of wort extracted from malt, of sauerkraut, of carrots, and of fruit, was only the most famous of a series of experiments which had already started in 1760. Fruit had been regarded until this time as dangerous and the cause of fever. But now doctors began to favour it as a valuable acid-producing balancer in the diet. Dietary experiments were being tried for the prevention of rickets. Within ten years William Stork was to kill himself by experiments to ascertain the nutritive value of various foodstuffs, ranging from water and sugar, to honey, black currants, and Cheshire cheese. Cod-liver oil, already used externally, was by 1780 administered internally to all the rheumatic cases at the Manchester infirmary. Jonas Hanway[4] was publicizing his views on infant welfare; in 1760 he was contending that artificial feeding on animal milk was better than reliance upon wet-nurses

[1] Edward Jenner (1749–1823), a doctor in Gloucestershire, 1773; first vaccinated from cowpox, 1796; published *Inquiry into Cause and Effect of the Variolae Vaccinae*, 1798; rewarded by parliament in 1802 and 1806; set up the National Vaccine Establishment in 1808.

[2] It was popularized by Lady Mary Wortley Montagu on her return from Turkey. See R. Halsband, *Life of Lady Mary Wortley Montagu*, p. 110.

[3] See below, p. 17, n.

[4] Jonas Hanway (1712–86), merchant in Russian trade and a commissioner of the victualling office remembered chiefly for his philanthropy, for his attack upon tea-drinking, and for his advocacy of the use of the umbrella.

of doubtful morals. At the Dispensary for Sick Children in London improved bubby-pots (feeding bottles) were, from 1769, being popularized. The Foundling Hospital had already asked the College of Physicians to investigate problems of weaning and the danger of giving opiates to restless infants. More immediately effective probably, in prolonging expectation of life, than any of this experimental medicine, would be the progress slowly being made in the paving of streets in towns, the decline in spirit drinking in favour of tea,[1] and better supplies of food. This latter might be expected to affect infantile mortality, the easiest area for improvement.

It is exceedingly difficult to generalize about nutritional levels in an age where statistics are wanting. In 1765, it has been calculated, a day's labour would buy a peck of corn: fifty years before it would have bought only two-thirds of a peck.[2] Rye bread had practically disappeared from the national diet, at least in the south of England. In London, it was alleged, the craze for white bread had encouraged extensive adulteration of the loaf with alum and other chemicals. The chief change for the better in the English diet was due to an increase in vegetable growing. In the north the potato was, with milk, the mainstay of the working man's table; in the south the potato was more slowly popularized and milk and butter were much less plentiful in ordinary homes: white bread and cheese were the staple foodstuffs. In all parts of the country, however, vegetables made a more varied menu possible. The cabbage had by now conquered the south as well as the north. A large dressed cabbage could be bought at Spitalfields for $1\frac{1}{4}d$. Even more important, the cultivation of the turnip, advocated by agricultural improvers, provided winter fodder for cattle. Oilcake was also increasingly used for this purpose. The swede was a new crop at the time, borrowed from Holland; not for another twenty years would it be joined by the mangel-wurzel. These new winter feeds increased the supply of fresh meat available. But it is difficult to calculate how often the workman's table saw meat. Bedford workhouse provided meat at four dinners in the week. On the other hand a Berkshire labourer's family of six persons expected

---

[1] This followed the increased duties imposed on spirits in 1751 and the rise in grain prices about this time.

[2] 1760 to 1780 were not years of good harvests, but the general movement of agriculture was towards improvement. See below, pp. 32 f.

only half a pound of bacon in the week and other meat only at celebration meals. A Westmorland labourer's family of three seem to have expected four pounds of butcher's meat a week; in their budget, unlike that of their southern contemporaries, oatmeal was the main item. In the 1770's Arthur Young was telling discontented working men that they should not expect to eat chicken—'and if they go without, *and eat mutton instead of it,* I desire to know of what consequence it is to the public?'[1] If mutton cost 5*d.* a pound (in the north) and the labourer's family was earning 11*s.* 6*d.* a week, the alternative italicized may seem optimistic. It is clear, nevertheless, that the variety of food had very much improved by 1760 and that the upper and middle classes were gluttons by later standards,[2] while even the working-class majority had grown accustomed to new standards of living which they were reluctant to abandon. The harvests up to 1760 had been exceptionally good for many years. The bad harvests between 1760 and 1780 raised the price of grain, producing great discontent, but it seems likely that vegetable prices did not rise in proportion. Improved farming was, by 1760, showing results; its full effects could be no more than delayed by the unkind weather of the early years of George III's reign.

The majority of the English subjects of George III were still employed in agriculture. There were only two cities in England with a population of over 50,000. London had 750,000 inhabitants and Bristol some 60,000. These two were quite different in size and character from the multitude of small market towns and little ports which made up the rest of the borough franchise in parliament, and which handled the commerce of the country. It is easy in the light of after events to exaggerate the contemporary importance of trade and industry in the national life in 1760. Even at the time the importance of trade was certainly recognized, perhaps even over-estimated. Men who knew the capacity of their estates and who took a realistic view of their future yields, only too easily were beguiled into expecting impossible gains from trade expansion. The most striking example is the wave of excitement with which people in 1760 looked

---

[1] *The Farmer's Letters to the People of England,* 3rd edn., 1771, vol. i, p. 148.
[2] The Goose, a Woodwardian Professor of Geology at Cambridge complained was 'a silly bird—too much for one and not enough for two' (H. Gunning, *Reminiscences of Cambridge.* Selections by D. A. Winstanley, 1932, p. 103).

forward to the exploitation of the riches of the East after Clive's victories. But in the same way, Spanish America, the West Indies, even the 'Greenland' fisheries, were given a place in the plans for national prosperity without much use of statistical sense in the assessment. No doubt, in the long run, this instinct of English gentlemen was sound: for they perceived the direction in which their destiny lay. Immediately, however, it was responsible for undue stress upon mercantile policy, for the pursuit of rash policies similar to those which had been advocated by the opposition to Walpole.[1] It was not only a West Indian pressure group in the house of commons, but a general belief that England's future prosperity could be built on Caribbean trade, which gives to debates on Guadeloupe, or indeed to all discussion of maritime strength, their excitement during the first years of George III.

The merchant tonnage to sustain these hopes was, in 1760, approximately 500,000 tons. The ships were small and ship-building was an industry widely dispersed along the coast. The new ships for the East Indian trade were larger than had previously been known, strong three-deckers for the long and dangerous run round the Cape to Bengal and China. They were built in the London shipyards. The system of shipping for the Indies is worthy of note as an example of a curious combination of monopoly and enterprise characteristic of the period. The East India Company had ceased to order its ships on the open market. Secure in their monopoly of trade between England and India they proceeded, logically enough, to try to ensure their shipping resources. A guarantee of use was given to certain ships specially suited for the trade. As these bottoms wore out (and the life of a ship on the Indian route was three round trips each taking a year and a half) the owner had the right to replace it. Thus there was maintained a minimum number of ships ready for the trade. In this way also there came into existence a shipping interest within the company, the managers and 'husbands' of these privileged bottoms, who resisted any attack upon the Company's trade monopoly the more fiercely because the monopoly gave them guaranteed freights. It was inevitable that the ships' husbands, with their guaranteed right to provide ships, should enter into business arrangements with the London yards where the ships were built. Thus the monopoly interest

[1] See B. Williams, *The Whig Supremacy*, pp. 196, 198.

extended backwards into the London wharves.[1] Yet at the same time within the monopoly the servants of the Company both in India and on the high seas practised the most ruthlessly individualistic methods of gaining their own fortunes. Ships' captains had the privilege of space being reserved on board ship for their private goods; this space they sold, as private traders, to opium or cotton merchants in India. But those altogether excluded, Liverpool shippers or textile manufacturers, increasingly as the reign went on, attacked the whole system.

The idea of a guaranteed and controlled trade and shipping was not a peculiarity of the East Indies. It was general. In 1760 war had, as ever, expanded the mercantile marine. It was never intended to allow a post-war slump to throw these ships out of work. The maintenance of the maximum number of ships and seamen in activity was a cardinal point of national defence. It was intended to secure this end by the Navigation Laws. And the Navigation Laws were the heart and crown of the whole mercantilist system. Enumeration of commodities which the colonies might manufacture or might import only from England, preferential rates of duty upon some colonial products exported to England, these were parts of an attempt to make a controlled economy, parts of a plan for imperial organization of economic activity. The whole of the old colonial system was, in theory, devised as much for the benefit of the colonists as for the mother country, or rather such a disjunction was not thought of as realistic. For it was considered essential to allow the merchants, manufacturers, and seamen, freedom to expand and experiment within the outlines of a general plan of control which should ensure that all this energy was deployed for the common good. The most obvious and pre-eminent point of common interest was national security in time of war. So while it was desirable that the people of New England should use Jamaican molasses and that the West Indians should use English manufactures and American grain, it was essential that the naval strength of the whole group, whose directing intelligence was in London, should be maintained. The commodities of inter-imperial trade must move in British bottoms. The supply of British sailors must never be wanting.

[1] These interests are explored in Lucy S. Sutherland, *A London Merchant, 1695–1774,* and in *The East India Company in Eighteenth Century Politics.*

A constant theme of debates in the eighteenth-century parliaments was therefore the need to keep up the navy and the merchant marine. The gentlemen of inland Oxfordshire or Warwickshire, as much as those of Northumberland or Somerset, were always ready to applaud expenditure on ships and deprecate the provision of a soldier's pay. In part this was a stock opposition cry. Soldiers were the instruments, it had been said for a century, of despotism. But sailor lads 'did the state maintain'. It went with the cry[1] for a 'deep-blue sea' foreign policy, that is a policy of expansion overseas with the minimum interest in continental Europe. But there was more to this preoccupation with shipping than that. At bottom it arose from a feeling that the future prosperity of the country lay upon the water and that the survival of Great Britain rested upon her superiority to France in naval war.

The old colonial system was mercantile rather than imperial. There is no more striking example of this than the treatment of Newfoundland. The purpose of English interest in Newfoundland in 1760, as it continued to be throughout George's reign, was not to paint the map red or to colonize, it was to find a base for fishermen hailing from the little West country ports from Poole to Falmouth. It was therefore forbidden for anyone to settle permanently in Newfoundland. It was not to be a settlement but a great centre for the drying of nets and the packing of fish, a safe harbour for those in temporary danger. It was regarded as part of the naval service and its governor was a naval commander who divided his time between a quarter-deck and St. John's, thinking of them in the same way. Strenuous attempts were made to prevent the 10,000 or 15,000 residents from being increased. Fishermen were entitled by right to their passage home whatever the circumstances of their captain. Bounties were (after 1775) given to those engaged in these fisheries, and bounties also helped to finance the building of larger ships for the round trip to the Banks and home.

In the Northern Whale Fisheries the object was similar, to keep in existence a few thousand hardy sailors working (after 1771 with bounties) in British bottoms. To receive bounty three-quarters of the crew had to be British. In the waters covered by Southern Whale Fisheries the South Sea Company

---

[1] Reckoned as a 'tory' cry by the historical accident that it had been most vociferously expressed by tories under Queen Anne.

and the East India Company had vested interests. The South Sea Company resented outsiders sailing round Cape Horn, and the East India Company obstructed free enterprise in the area of New Holland, the New Hebrides, New Caledonia, and New Zealand. But the need for encouraging a hardy race of fishermen triumphed over vested interests.

The government was prepared to encourage Byron, Wallis, Carteret,[1] and Cook[2] to explore in the South Pacific. And in doing so they had applause at home from gentlemen who had never done more than cross the Channel, when making the Grand European Tour in youth, but who put into their libraries Dampier's *Voyages round the World* and his *Voyages and Discoveries*.[3] Nor did they read these works purely with romantic enthusiasm. They, like Dampier himself, had an eye to business. When the explorers set off in their tough little 300- to 500-ton vessels they went looking for better bases from which England might break into the Pacific trade; they were also searching for the conjectural great Southern Continent. In each case they were seeking customers not colonies. Many people regarded the penetration of India by Clive and the Company with suspicion. They did not like the problems of conquest and of government to interfere with the trading interest. Of political complication it was hoped the great Southern Continent would be free. No greater troubles would be caused by the inhabitants, it was hoped, than those which arose from the excessive cordiality of the natives of

---

[1] John Byron (1723–86) sailed round the world 1764–6 and became governor of Newfoundland and a rear-admiral. Samuel Wallis (1728–95), a captain in the navy, explored Polynesia 1766–8. Philip Carteret (d. 1796) sailed with Byron and then in 1767–9 circumnavigated the globe making many discoveries in the Pacific.

[2] James Cook (1728–79) was the greatest of these both by his sustained effort and his scientific care. The son of a labourer: a common seaman in the navy, he rose to be a master and as such surveyed the St. Lawrence (1759). As a lieutenant he sailed in 1768 for Tahiti and went on round the world charting the coasts of New Zealand, east Australia, and part of New Guinea as he went. In 1772 he looked for a Southern Continent and found the Antarctic icefields. In 1776 he attempted to sail round North America from the Pacific. He was murdered by natives in Hawaii in 1779 after a further voyage along the Pacific coast of North America and an exploration of further islands in the Pacific. His interest in medical improvements for the health of his crews has already been mentioned (p. 11). All voyages of exploration were much assisted after 1772 by his development (using the work of John Harrison, 1693–1776, the clockmaker and winner of the prize for determining longitude at sea) of the chronometer. Cook took for his ideal vessel the types normally used in the Newcastle coal trade along the east coast. They were strong and handy.

[3] William Dampier (1652–1715), a pirate who became a captain in the navy.

Tahiti—which was named 'King George III's Island' by its discoverer Samuel Wallis. The search was for harbours and for collection or storage points. Once found they would open up trade and absorb manufactures while greatly increasing the shipping and the seamen, which were the true and natural strength of the country.

The strength of the feeling in England in favour of mercantile expansion can be tested by the case, once more, of the Southern Whale Fisheries, which involved journeys down beyond Cape Horn and into the Pacific. These fishermen could count upon support from London in conflicts with France, or Spain, in spite of the fact that very few ships from home ports were able to take part in the trade. It was the preserve of some hundred boats from Nantucket, an island with no natural resources but the sea and the character of its fishermen. These men were regarded as imperial assets. No doubt it would have been preferable, in a perfect world, to have the trade based on Bristol. But the interests of Nantucket were always to be defended against foreign attack, for they were part of the resources of the British marine.[1]

In the same spirit colonial shipping in general was fostered as part of the empire's most valuable resources, in spite of the fact that English shipbuilders feared their competitive power. By the period of the American War 150 vessels a year were coming from Massachusetts shipyards alone. The cost of a 200-ton ship built on the Thames was about £3,000, while in Philadelphia it could be built for £2,600. Here again, while the gentlemen of England preferred to see vessels built at home, this feeling hardly counted in face of their overmastering desire for the expansion of shipping and the numbers of seamen within King George's territories. Permanently worried, as they were, about their dependence upon the Baltic for naval supplies and stores, they were bound to smile upon the expansion of an alternative source under their own influence and (imperfect) control across the Atlantic.

The great objective was the defeat of France in a war of trade. Colonies were important in that they promoted trade. If France lost Canada, her naval strength would eventually be damaged by a decline in her fur trade. If France lost the West Indies, British ships would replace hers on the South Atlantic. Like a

[1] Independence therefore obliged some Nantucket men to emigrate.

tree without roots, she would then begin to wither. This was a popular argument in 1760. It remained popular until the hard experience of war at the end of the reign showed it to be untrue. It is this reasoning which lies at the back of the Navigation Laws. European commodities could be imported into England, in general, on payment of the appropriate duties. But about one-half of the imports from Europe were subject to a further regulation. Corn, grain, wines, salts, sugar, fruits, olive-oil, timber, and naval stores, could be admitted to British ports only if they were brought either in ships of the producing country or in British ships. Further, by the Staple Act (1663) Britain was made the staple for all European commodities destined for the colonies, that is they must be taken by way of England and pay English duties. They must moreover be transported to the colonies in ships of England or of the colonies.[1] Aimed originally against Dutch rivals in the carrying trade, the Navigation Laws had by 1760 become part of an Englishman's faith in the destiny of his country on the seas. Even radical economists such as Dean Tucker[2] and Adam Smith[3] were to acknowledge that, on grounds other than economic, the Navigation Laws might be defended. Most members of parliament did not distinguish between the economic and the strategic aspects of commercial regulation. For them shipping and security went together but so did shipping and trade.

The total value of imports into England in 1760 was officially estimated at approximately £11 million. Exports were about £16 million. To appreciate the significance of such figures one can compare them with the national budget;[4] £15½ million was the total of supplies voted in 1760, and this was a war year of exceptional high cost. In the previous reign the average supplies voted amounted to some £7 million a year, and by 1774 the figure had been reduced once more to some £11½ million for an average year. It is clear, therefore, that country gentlemen would, though ignorant of precise figures, see in international trade a most important section of the strength of England. Moreover many gentlemen were obsessed by the horrors of the mounting national debt which, within three years of George's

---

[1] For a further discussion of policy with regard to the colonies, see below, pp. 180 f.
[2] See below, p. 329. [3] See below, p. 329.
[4] The word 'budget' is used for convenience here. There was no annual stock-taking, no full budget, until the nineteenth-century innovations of Addington. The total amounts have to be collected from several returns.

accession, had reached some £130 million with an annual charge on revenue of £4¾ million. But the debt was not consolidated and most of it existed as debts to whose service particular taxes were specifically and exclusively devoted. Thus by 1760, 222 separate heads of revenue had to be kept in distinct accounts in public offices because these revenues were appropriated to particular charges. But most of the revenues which serviced the public debts were drawn from customs or excise, were charges, that is, upon trade. Two-sevenths of the excise, for example, serviced the pre-1743 life annuities, while it was perfectly orthodox for the new Grenville customs duties in 1763 to be statutorily pledged to meet the cost of American government. It follows that while an annual charge of almost £5 million was frightening to members of parliament they usually thought of it not as a whole, but as a series of charges upon trade, and therefore looked to trade expansion as a necessity of solvency.

Great Britain in 1760 exported textiles, metal goods, tin, pottery, and cured fish. She re-exported tobacco, sugar, Indian calicoes, and leather. The export of woollen goods was the largest single item, rather more than a quarter of the whole. She imported mainly consumable goods such as wines, spirits, sugar, tea, coffee, furs, and silk. In addition she imported raw materials such as wool, linen, and hemp, and naval stores from the Baltic. Holland still had the largest trade with Britain, followed in order by the British West Indies, the American colonies, Germany, the East Indies and China, and Russia. The tendency was for trade with the West Indies and with the East Indies and China to increase much more rapidly than that with Holland. The Dutch trade was declining in comparative importance rather as that with Spain and Portugal had already done.

The most interesting, and soon the most important, section of trade was that of the Atlantic triangle. England exported manufactured articles to Africa, and bore from West Africa the black slaves for the West Indies and for the southern mainland states. From the West Indies she imported sugar. In part this sugar had to be paid for by provisions from the American mainland. North America was paid by the West Indies in bills on London and in rum. Finally, obligations to the Americans were settled, both as regards these bills and for tobacco and for timber, by the export of manufactures to them. This was, so to speak, a natural triangular relationship, which the commercial code of the old colonial system merely emphasized or reinforced. The mercantilist system did not, in this area of the world, begin to run against natural channels of trade, contrary to popular belief in America at the time and since, until after the Americans had obtained their independence. After that the British system involved an attempt to exclude the Americans, now that they were aliens, from this partnership, an attempt which was as vain as it was doctrinaire.

Linked with this Atlantic interchange between the colonies and England, was the persistent though surreptitious attempt to penetrate into the Spanish islands and colonies to the south. This contraband trade was less inflammable as an issue between England and Spain than it had been twenty years previously, nevertheless it was the source of incidents between them still. British manufactures and slaves sent to the West Indies were re-exported to the Spanish colonies in return for gold and for dyestuffs. With these the West Indies were assisted in paying for the foodstuffs they needed from America. The importance of this contraband trade became clear in the decade following 1760 when the British government, in its efforts to enforce new duties, imposed regulations which assisted the Spaniards in throttling the smuggling. The effects were immediately apparent in the legitimate triangle of trade. The West Indies' capacity to absorb British exports was damaged. Between 1763, the beginning of the enforcement policy, and 1765, British exports to Jamaica alone fell by £168,000. Soon after this, in 1766, the policy was reversed. The illicit trade was made legal, from the British side, and was brought under control, by the establishment of free ports in the West Indies. The object was to bring both Spanish and French colonies of the Caribbean area within the British West Indian *bloc*. Single-decked vessels of foreign origin—that is small and local craft, which could not be potential rivals on the high seas—might import articles of local growth[1] into four designated ports in Jamaica and two in Dominica. This, it was hoped, would enable the British West Indies to become slave suppliers to the whole Central American area; the slaves would be fetched to the central market in

---

[1] But tobacco was banned, in order to safeguard the interests of Virginia, and any sugar had to be marked to prevent its re-export to Britain to the detriment of the British West Indies.

British ships. Thus British trade to the West Indies would benefit, and ships would no longer be sailing partly in ballast from England to the Caribbean.[1]

This triangular trade across the Atlantic, then, was not only important in 1760 but increasing in importance. Moreover it was intimately connected with some of the most controversial issues in politics of the next twenty years. The American mainland side of this trade will therefore have to be considered further in connexion with the War of Independence.[2] At the accession of George III it seemed, to most of those concerned with economic problems, a less valuable and less interesting aspect of Atlantic trade than the West Indies. In addition the West Indies had already produced at Westminster a group of members with personal knowledge of the islands and with business connexions there. The returned West Indian, with his fortune made, like the returned East Indian, sought a country house and a seat in parliament. On the whole the climate of Jamaica did not encourage permanent migration from England. Once in parliament such a man, together with those actively engaged in the sugar trade, could make vocal the interests of West Indian trade. The American mainland absorbed settlers for good. The mainland trade had a few professional spokesmen. Burke was to serve New York: cities such as Bristol[3] which traded with the mainland might defend American interests if they coincided with those of the city; but the mainland point of view was less well represented, and seemed less bound up with Great Britain, than that of the islands.

Another great and expanding trade pattern in 1760 was that with India and the Far East. The East India Company had the monopoly of the trade. Its activities came under fire from many with exaggerated ideas of the profit it made. In fact the trade was hedged about with difficulties. It was easy to find in India cargoes for supplying Europe. The big ships of the company brought back Indian muslins and cottons, and also 4 million pounds of tea for home consumption, in addition to some of the spices of the East. Efforts were being made constantly to penetrate the area of the Dutch and Portuguese influence in the

---

[1] The policy was continued and developed after the loss of America. See below, p. 289.

[2] See below, pp. 180 f.

[3] Also represented between 1774 and 1780 by Edmund Burke.

spice islands so as to increase this profitable trade. The Company was just beginning to force its way into a real share of the trade with China, hedged about as that was by the regulations and prohibitions of the Chinese authorities who confined trade to certain areas and a few persons. It was more difficult to find cargoes to exchange for these Eastern products. The cotton industry at home was not yet come of age, and England imported rather than exported cotton cloth. The great woollen industry had as its enemy the climate of India. The Chinese trade could be balanced by opium exports from India: this, however, simply increased the urgency of finding cargoes for Indian consumption. For some manufactured goods consumers could be found in India, but, in general, the import of Far Eastern articles had to be balanced by the export of bullion (from the profits of the resale of imports in Europe), and by what may be called services in India. This latter does not only mean the profits of government which Clive's victories had opened up, profits which were often illusory as far as the Company was concerned though enormous for a few of its luckier servants personally. The conduct of business and trade within India, or from India to other Eastern markets, yielded profits which formed an invisible balance for imports into England. But these profits might balance the account as between India and England: they did not balance the Company's books, for they disappeared into the pockets of individual Englishmen. Thus at the moment of its greatest triumph, after Clive's victories, the East India Company in 1760 was on the threshold of a period of misleading accounts, of speculation, and of political intrigue.[1]

Trade with the Far East and to the West was thus expanding. That with the Levant was declining in face of French competition. The trade with Portugal and the Spanish homeland was also diminishing. It still continued to be a valuable source of raw wool and a market for woollen manufactured goods and cured fish. Except in Scotland the life of gentlemen of fashion would have been drastically altered if anything had disturbed the import of wine from Portugal, for Portuguese table wines as well as port were popular. The trade with the Iberian peninsula had long been valued because it had showed an export surplus. Thus while Indian trade was often reviled because it led to bullion exports, that with Spain was praised

---

[1] See a fuller account of this below, pp. 158 f. and 305 f.

because England had to be paid, in part, in gold. Nevertheless more direct contacts with the gold sources in the New World were replacing this trade. With most of the rest of Europe the direction of activity was determined by the sea and rivers. Holland, with its river mouths, was a valuable link with distribution centres such as Frankfurt-am-Main.

The importance of Holland did not end with her part as a customer and as an agent for the rediffusion of the goods. Placed at a nerve-centre of trade, and with her capital accumulated as one of the oldest carrying nations, she had been the first in Europe to develop, from her intimate knowledge of world trade, a financial service to which England was indebted. The Amsterdam stock exchange was still the most important centre of its sort in 1760, though London was making great advances. In the provision of capital, in advances by way of taking up government loans, in arranging for the payment of troops, the Dutch were the financial leaders of the world. It was estimated that over one-third of the British government's total debt was held in Holland or under Dutch names and agents. To the detriment of their own trading and manufacturing interest, in the long run, Dutch investors supplied capital to England, no doubt because they had a respect for the soundness and potentialities of her position in world trade. Lower interest-rates, arising from a good supply of capital, were a stimulus to inventiveness, to new enterprise, and to industrial as well as commercial expansion. In 1760 it was a source of rejoicing in England that the war had already damaged French credit so much that London, through the agency of the Dutch, would have the command of all money in Europe which sought investment.[1]

One other area of British trade deserves special mention. Imports of naval stores, wood, and hemp, from the Baltic were difficult to pay for; in trade with Russia, for example, England exported only £70,000 worth of goods but imported £950,000 worth from her. Part of the urgency with which bullion payments were sought in other parts of the world had its origin in the need to pay in specie for these indispensable imports. American supplies would not suffice to maintain a navy. Thus one comes full circle to a paradox in considering the mid-century mercantilist view of trade. It was, after all, in order to increase

[1] See C. Wilson, *Anglo-Dutch Commerce and Finance in the 18th Century.*

England's strength as a world power that a favourable trade balance was sought. Yet the trade most unfavourable from the point of view of the exchanges was that above all others vital to her strength and security.

The key to understanding the whole economic system is to realize that trade and war-potential were regarded as one. For this reason there had to be an imperial pattern of trade imposed from Westminster by means of trade laws, embargoes, and duties. But within such a framework there was great scope for free enterprise. Government was able to exercise less supervision over the conduct of either trade or industry at this time than in the later period of theoretical *laissez-faire*. Many old systems of control of economic activity were moribund. The old organization by Trading Companies was decaying. The Hamburg, the Russian, and the Eastland Companies had become useless. The Turkey Company was considered oppressive, and trade in the Mediterranean was in decline. The South Sea Company had, in practice, become a financial house, managing part of the national debt; its interest in the far southern waters was a matter of prestige, more arrogant than real. The Hudson Bay Company nursed hopes of reaping the advantage of Wolfe's victory in the form of an expanded fur trade. But only the East India Company remained as a major example of the control of commerce by a national and statutory monopoly. Yet while the East India Company was in danger of becoming a government agency, ruthless individual enterprise flourished under its mantle.

A multitude of small local interests and small ports struggled for trade. On the east coast in the coal trade, for example, ships from Newcastle, Sunderland, Scarborough, Sandwich, Yarmouth, Shields, Stockton, Bridlington, Aldborough, London, Rochester, Broadstairs, Margate, Ramsgate, Whitby, Ipswich, and Poole all took part. Here, from time to time, attempts were made to regulate the trade by combinations of the most important interests to exclude competitors. On the west the city of Bristol, dominated by vested interests in its corporation, was the leader of trade with America. Liverpool, oligarchic in local government but enlightened in policy, had all the advantages and disadvantages of the parvenu in its fight for advancement. It was not restricted by conservative practices or regulations: on the other hand Liverpool men were not on good terms with the East India Company and in their slave trading wished to avoid dependence on the Company's muslins. They had a motive therefore to encourage English printed-calico production; for the time being, however, the slowness of the Lancashire cotton industry to expand handicapped Liverpool in the Atlantic race.

The growth of trade is obviously linked with the rise of industry. The capital accumulated in trade expansion, for instance, helped to launch the new productive processes which were soon to be dramatically important. On the other hand an increase in the production of textiles was a stimulus to the search for new markets, and because of Yorkshire's output ships searched the coasts of Australia and sailors bargained with the mandarins of South China. But though production was increasing, it is important not to exaggerate the extent to which industry was expanding in 1760. In the politics of the time, certainly, members of parliament were much more interested in the problems of trade than in those of industry. The latter chiefly came before them when pressure groups, such as the Newcastle coal-producers, attempted to regulate production to the detriment of other areas, or when protection was demanded against foreign imports. Industry was taken for granted by most people, as a comparatively static and undramatic part of the national life. Nor were they much at fault. In France not only was the government more active in patronage of industry, but the rate of expansion was faster than it was in England. This was true of iron and steel, of textiles, even of coal. Yet England had certain advantages by 1760. The population was smaller than that of France, but it was more easily reached as one market. There were, in the first place, less internal checks and dues to impede the movement of goods within the country. The tax on sea coals entering London was a comparative rarity.[1] Furthermore the movement of goods was physically easier to all parts of England. The canal age was only just about to begin. The improvement of road surfaces and maintenance had not, as yet, reached its heights, and the coach or van in consequence had driven the pack-horse off only the important roads. But nature favoured England. Except in the north and west few

---

[1] It was part of the income of the duke of Richmond: see Sir G. N. Clark, *The Later Stuarts* (O.H.E., vol. x), p. 8.

places in England at this time were more than a long day's
journey by cart from navigable water. And once on the water,
transport was cheap. The small ports and rivers all over England flourished as trade channels, in the years between 1760
and the railway age, as never before or since. The roads
themselves were the responsibility of the parishes through which
they ran, except where the maintenance of them had been
handed over to turnpike trusts. Good stretches were followed
by bad.

Even on the main road from Newcastle to the south, the future
A1, Arthur Young had to hire men to prevent his coach from
overturning; on a turnpike stretch itself he found that, after
fearing compound bone fractures as he bounced over broken
stones, he came to the worse peril of being buried alive in
muddy sand. The concave road north from Oxford to Wood-
stock was a trough filled with sand whose foamy surface was
scraped off from time to time. In the whole of benighted Devonshire the sledge competed with the pack-horse in the absence of
wheeled carriages. On the fashionable road from London to
Bath, on the other hand, a fast service of coaches was already
running. It was quite common for villages to be cut off entirely
from the rest of the world by mud and water for the whole of
the winter. Even so, the roads were thought the best in Europe.
The canal age may be said to begin in 1759 with the duke of
Bridgewater's canal from Worsley coalfield to Manchester,
which halved the average price of coal in that growing urban
area.

The growth of industry was thus encouraged by an effective
home market which, by the standard of the times, was large.
The coal trade[1] of Newcastle, for instance, had from time
immemorial supplied London because the pits were near the
sea. Glamorgan, to take a contrast, was not yet opened up
because, though it is bounded by the Bristol Channel, the
streams which flow down its valleys from the present coalfields
are torrents, rapidly flooding in rainy weather and useless
for transport, while roads did not exist: the first road from
Merthyr to Cardiff was being made when George III came to
the throne. The other requirement for expansion, capital, was

---

[1] In mining one great mechanical invention had already affected the whole
scope of the industry, Newcomen's pumping-engine (B. Williams, *The Whig
Supremacy*, p. 111).

being provided from the profits of commerce. When Boulton[1] began to sell his Birmingham brass buttons over the world, he required great resources if he was to ride the difficulties of credit and risk involved in such a trade. But the profits accruing enabled him to invest in new factories and to venture on new partnerships, such as that with Watt. And Boulton, it is worth remarking, was enabled to begin his expansion on the savings of his father's lifetime in trade. But the full employment of capital required greater banking facilities than were available in 1760. In 1750, according to Burke, there were only twelve 'bankers' shops' outside London. By 1793 there were nearly 400. Credit in 1760 was organized in a small and local way. Banking was a by-product of commercial capitalism. The biggest local merchant, or perhaps the local collector of the land taxes, had from time to time funds to adventure, but the area of operations was limited to the scenes and characters around their homes and the transfer of capital from a backward area to a progressive one was still slow and difficult.

English industry, in such conditions, was not standing still, but neither was it in any revolutionary gallop. The Society of Arts (of 1754) had for its full title 'The Society for the Encouragement of Arts, Manufacture, and Commerce' and it, together with the Royal Society, did give active encouragement to men with new scientific ideas. But even here, once more, the French tended to anticipate England. Only in the application of ideas, the eradication of difficulties in practice, did England show signs of superiority. Kay's flying shuttle[2] was supported by government aid in France; nevertheless its use there died out. In England the defects of this shuttle were by 1760 being slowly but finally overcome.

Even at this date, well before the advent of steam, certain prerequisites of mechanized mass production were—it is clear to eyes wise after the event—coming into existence in England. In the first place larger units of production, particularly in iron and steel, were emerging. In textiles also, even under a domestic system, the centralizing of control over cloth production in the hands of capitalists had been growing for a century. Next, one may note the increased use of machines however crude. In

---

[1] Matthew Boulton (1728–1809), engineer and manufacturer. See also below, p. 334.
[2] Invented about 1733.

Birmingham the use of the rolling mill and the stamp for producing cheaply and by unskilled labour was already common by 1760. In the sixties water frames and home jennies were, similarly, to bring mechanized aids into textiles. Most important of all is the increase in standardization which is a marked feature of these years. Boulton studied classical designs until he picked a favourite and then impressed it upon all his buttons in an attempt to produce a uniform popular line for a world market. The very similar action of Wedgwood[1] in fixing upon a best-selling pattern for his pottery is even better known. These movements towards standardized shapes preceded mass production and were essential for its coming. Furniture-making is perhaps an even better example of the point, for there mass production was a much later development. But even in furniture, though the craftsman's skill was not to be rivalled by machine in George III's reign, there was already a movement towards set styles and standards. The great names of Chippendale, Hepplewhite, and Sheraton,[2] are known to everyone not for what they made but for the books of designs and styles which they published, and which in time affected the work of the humblest market-town furniture carver. Hence the name of Hepplewhite is used by any antique dealer to describe a type rather than to name a maker, and in this his historical judgement marches with his commercial acumen.

These features—standardization, and larger scale production particularly—reflected a growing market. But they do not denote an 'industrial revolution'. The greatest and oldest of English industries, textile production, was not yet concentrated in factories. Problems of bleaching and dyeing were unsolved. The advantage of Lancashire was its free labour supply untrammelled by guild regulations or old traditions. It had also

---

[1] Josiah Wedgwood (1730–95) opened a pottery of his own at Burslem, Staffordshire, in 1759, and opened his new works at Etruria (where he had built a village for his workpeople) in 1769. Inventive in improving both ware and design in pottery. F.R.S. 1783, F.S.A. 1786. Active in the operation of the Chamber of Trade of British manufacturers in the 1780's. The greatest figure in the expansion of Staffordshire pottery manufacture.

[2] Thomas Chippendale (1718?–79) published the *Gentleman's and Cabinet Maker's Directory*, 1754.

George Hepplewhite (d. 1786), *The Cabinet Maker's and Upholsterer's Guide*, published by his wife 1788–9.

Thomas Sheraton (1751–1806) published *The Cabinet Maker's and Upholsterer's Drawing Book*, 1791; *The Cabinet Directory*, 1803.

For further discussion of furniture see below, p. 340.

adventurous capitalists, particularly in Liverpool. Manchester was expanding as a centre for cotton-making, but the units were still small and partly domestic. Woollens were far more important. But though there were some factories the typical method of production was still the domestic system. The capitalist employed families living in the Yorkshire villages to spin and weave on piece-work in their own cottages the cloth which his agent collected at the appointed time. The increasing use of machines did not at first end this dispersal of labour. For the streams of Yorkshire were used for water-power and woollen goods remained the product of the riverside villages. Some employees lived a village life entirely dependent upon their earnings in the industry: others were part-time weavers, part-time labourers in the fields. The handloom was easy to master, and it provided work for all the family. If the loom was operated on credit, or belonged to the capitalist, it could tie the operative to his master. In any case the labour force was easily expanded in prosperity and contracted in times of little demand. The most one can say of changes taking place in 1760 is that the East Anglian area of production was losing ground to Yorkshire, as swiftly flowing water became of more importance to the process of production.

A similar dispersal of the labour force can be seen in the Midland nail industry. A family in a small workshop would take from the capitalist a certain quantity of iron and engage themselves to turn it into a given quantity of nails for him on the domestic hearth. In pottery, sub-contracting of this sort also prevailed even though, for convenience, the closer together the small potters' houses were grouped the better pleased the master. Thus a row of houses tended to become a sort of factory in departments. The important pottery producers imposed their patterns but not their discipline upon those they hired. Even in the metal industries, which because they demanded more heavy equipment tended to be organized upon a factory plan, this small independent unit within a central control was prevalent. Boulton at the beginning of 1761 decided to manufacture 'various articles of the Birmingham hardware and toy trades in which a water mill was essentially necessary', and built his famous Soho works; this has been thought a full factory in the modern sense, but study of its layout shows that it was a halfway house between the old domestic system and the new order. It was a honeycomb of small shops. It was as though the sub-contractors, the specialists in some branch of the productive process, had been brought in under the one factory roof but not thoroughly incorporated into the organization. Water again, it will be noted, determined the location of production. This was true also of the main iron and steel works.

Water for working bellows and woods for charcoal were still the first needs for an ironworks in 1760. It is true that the Darbys at Coalbrookdale, in Shropshire,[1] had discovered how to use clod coal for iron some time about 1710. But more than half a century had to pass before the use of coal became general, owing to the need for special kinds of coal and to the secretiveness of the Darbys about their discovery. The use of coal for smelting cast iron was not general before 1770. Coal was, however, generally used in the smithies, with the result that the Warwickshire coal supplies had attracted a population of some 500,000 dependent on metal trades to the area ten miles or so around Birmingham. Coking ovens for producing coke were, in 1763, being started. Since the 1740's Huntsman's[2] steel crucible had opened up an expansion of steel in Sheffield: Walkers was already an important firm there. Cast iron was entering new fields as improvements in the moulds, again the result of experiment at Coalbrookdale, enabled manufacturers to extend the range of goods they made. The expansion of wrought iron had to wait some thirty years and the exploitation of Henry Cort's[2] processes. Swedish iron was still considered better for wrought-iron work, or for steel, than home-produced. It had just been decided in 1757 to encourage the import of American pig-iron through any British port (and not just to London). At the same time America was forbidden to manufacture iron goods. In 1764 iron was added to the list of enumerated commodities which had to be bought from or through Great Britain. In 1761 3,000 tons of pig-iron were imported from the colonies and 44,250 tons, usually in bars, from foreigners. Though full development of iron and steel had to wait for Watt's engines, the units of production were already large. The Carron works (near Falkirk), opened by Roebuck and Garbett the year before George III came to the throne, started with a capital of £12,000. Soon after this the Coalbrookdale works

---

[1] For them see B. Williams, *The Whig Supremacy*, pp. 112, 113.
[2] See below, pp. 505 f.

were said to be employing a thousand people, including miners producing for the furnaces; the annual output from each Shropshire furnace was approaching a thousand tons. War had, in fact, already stimulated iron production: the new Wilkinson works, for instance, opened in 1762 and destined to play a leading role within thirty years in the production of metal machines and parts, were born of the stimulus of war.

British industry, then, in 1760 was prosperous but not revolutionary. It had affected the way of living of thousands of people on Tyneside, Shropshire, Warwickshire, Yorkshire, Lancashire, and Staffordshire, but it was not drawing to itself the country population; it had not sapped the institutions nor affected the political attitude of Englishmen. To the industrialists the only interest of politics was that by judicious pressure they might secure protective duties or government orders for the benefit of their business. Among leading social and political figures of George III's world a few had already tapped these new sources of wealth. The second Viscount Dudley and Ward, for example, found his rents increasing from ownership of twenty pits around Stourbridge, while the Wortley Montagu coal fortune was a useful adjunct to the power of Lord Bute. But this inflow of wealth to the aristocracy came mainly from their position as landowners. It did not alter, but emphasized, their attachment to broad acres as a title to power. The industrial areas of the country were governed on the pattern of the agricultural: coal, or iron, or glass, could be regarded as, so to speak, a rather special local crop which made possible larger rent rolls.

Agriculture itself was undergoing great changes, but generalizations cannot be made which will hold true of the whole country. The work of Jethro Tull, in drilling in rows and growing more cleanly, was still spreading very slowly over the country. The same is true of Townshend's exploitation of marl, of artificial grasses, and of crop rotation.[1] The only counties where agricultural progress was marked in 1760 were Essex, Hertfordshire, Leicestershire, Norfolk, and Suffolk. In Essex chalk fertilizers were being used and hollow drainage improved. In Hertfordshire London refuse—soot, horn-shavings, ashes, and rags—was bought for manure. It points the picture of

[1] See B. Williams, *The Whig Supremacy*, pp. 102 and 260.

contrasts that in Middlesex, even more conveniently placed for such enlightened farming, there was no such progress; one-tenth of that county was still common, its roads were bad, and its farmers unenterprising. The East Anglian improvers had already revolutionized their agriculture. There large landowners were applying scientific methods long before Coke began to plan the improvement of his properties.[1] Their main achievement was in wheat growing. The ports of Yarmouth, Lynn, Wells, and Blakeney handled half the corn exported from the whole of England. With its textile industries still flourishing East Anglia was thus at the height of its prosperity and power. In another of the progressive areas the social order was different. Instead of the large proprietors talking agricultural 'shop' in their large country houses, in Leicestershire a great number of small and middling tenant farmers slowly improved on the ways of their grandfathers. The most famous of these farmers, Robert Bakewell,[2] had been experimenting with stock-breeding for fifteen years when, in the year of George III's accession, he succeeded to the complete management of his father's farm. The improvements in stock-breeding travelled more slowly than those in arable farming. Yet by 1760 the appearance and use of horses, sheep, and cattle had been changed in Leicestershire. Bakewell replaced the old breeds of sheep, which had been of use mainly for producing wool and providing manure, with new breeds selectively reared for meat. They were animals of shorter fleece but heaviest in the best butcher's joints. They came to their peak in two seasons instead of in three or four. In life they throve better and in death they weighed heavier. Within a half century the average weight of sheep at Smithfield rose from 28 lb. to 80 lb. Bakewell's Leicester horses had clean short legs and a thick body; they were produced not for looks but for labour, so that they soon replaced oxen for ploughing at least in the Midlands and south of England. With cattle Bakewell was less successful than his rivals at Burton-on-Trent and Coventry. The supply of meat was rapidly increased. But the improved longhorns gained fat at the expense of milk; for the local industry in Leicestershire

---

[1] Thomas William Coke of Holkham, earl of Leicester (1752–1842). The monetary gains made by Coke have been grossly and almost universally exaggerated. He was the best-known example of a general tendency already established in Norfolk. See R. A. C. Parker, 'Coke of Norfolk and the Agrarian Revolution' in *Econ. H.R.*, 2nd ser., viii (1955–6), pp. 156–66.

[2] R. Bakewell (1725–95).

of cheese-production this was a serious defect.[1] Later in George's reign the shorthorns of Durham were to outdo Bakewell's longhorns. Though stock improvers were secretive, for good business reasons, nevertheless by 1760 the rebuilding of the animal stock of farmers was under way.

The stock-breeding improvements of the Midlands were linked with the earlier crop experiments of East Anglia, for the new breeds needed the turnip and clover crops if they were to be fattened early. By 1760 the cultivation of clover had been taken up as far afield as Cumberland. But both kinds of improvement demanded time and money. It was not to be expected that farmers with short leases would undertake drainage or install new equipment. The need for improvement and for expenditure was most obvious in the south and east Midlands, roughly in that area from Gloucestershire to the Wash which had not experienced the enclosure movement of earlier centuries. For here the open-field system made proper crop rotation, selective stock-farming, or drainage, impossible. As far south as the Vale of Aylesbury cultivation was in arable open-fields, lying in ridges, on a rotation of fallow, wheat, and beans. Each plough required five horses to scratch three inches deep; the beans were sown broadcast and were therefore not hoed. The ridges did not allow drainage but kept this fertile soil in a state of swamp. The only solution to a problem of this sort was to consolidate holdings and to make each farm big enough to justify expenditure on drainage and new buildings. Up in Lincolnshire the fen area around Boston presented a more difficult drainage problem; it could not be solved until those who were to put up the money could have security for a return on it. Small-scale cultivation was unimprovable and in Northamptonshire, for instance, valuable cow-dung was commonly used for fuel. The movement for enclosure, with all the social evils accompanying it, was a necessity if wheat production was to increase, or sheep or cattle to be fed according to the new standards. This movement was already in progress in the Midlands and was accelerating year by year after George III came to the throne. In those parts of the country already enclosed the need was for the spread of information and the application of

---

[1] The first Stilton cheese is said to have been produced at Melton Mowbray, and in the early years of George III's reign its fame was being spread along the Great North road with an understandable rapidity.

capital. But in the north the general backwardness of the
country discouraged scientific farming. There was no excuse
but inertia for the inefficiency of farmers in Kent and Middlesex.

Revolutionary change was apparent, then, in the countryside
sooner than in industry. Before 1760 the yeomen of England had
ceased to exist as an important class in the community. In the
village there were small tenant farmers who also held freeholds:
these were men struggling to exist on a few acres and grazing
rights. But even gentlemen landowners, with rent rolls of say
£400 a year, had experienced difficulty in holding up their
heads in face of the great men with their thousands a year.
The smaller country houses built at this time, with classical
façades and formal libraries, imitations in miniature of the
style of Houghton or Holkham or the immense Wentworth
Woodhouse, were difficult to pay for, though essential for self-
respect. In each stratum of rural society the bigger men were
pushing their smaller companions hard. Yet in spite of this the
society remained stable: change was accompanied by groans
and grumbles but not by resistance. The small proprietor cursed
the extra shilling on the land tax, the tenant abused rising rents
and falling rain, and the labourer could only ventilate his feelings to a wife and to God. The reason for this placidity is, of
course, that changes happened piece-meal, and were seen in a
local and not a national context.

III

THE SOCIAL AND POLITICAL
STRUCTURE IN 1760

THE economic conditions which have been reviewed in the
last chapter produced a society which was stable and in
which the landed interest was dominant. Too much stress,
however, can easily be laid upon the distinction between
country interest and that of urban commerce. Many landed
proprietors, more particularly the wealthiest, had interests in
the city of London or in the trade of their particular locality.
Great lords might dabble, like, for example, Lord Verney or
Lord Shelburne,[1] in the stock market: squires' families could
often be enriched by a judicious marriage with a city alderman's
daughter: the territorial aristocracy were often glad to find
openings for younger sons in the service of the East India
Company. The landowning upper classes were not an unap-
proachable breed apart. Nevertheless the class structure was
more fixed than has sometimes been supposed. The squire
looked upon his business acquaintances in town—as he did
upon his solicitor, his parson, or his steward—as members of a
different order with whom it was possible to be on good terms
because they knew and did not question their places: easiness
of manners, in fact, was the consequence of unquestioned social
distinctions.[2] Nor was it easy to follow the upward path from
trade to the ruling landed gentry (the path to the very top, to
the house of lords, was hardly open at all until the very end of

---

[1] Sir William Petty, second earl of Shelburne and first marquis of Lansdowne
(1737–1805): for his career as one of the most important politicians of the day see
the political narrative below.

Ralph Verney, second Earl Verney and third Viscount Fermanagh (1712?–91),
was a patron of Edmund Burke and a powerful politician in Buckinghamshire, who
was ruined by his speculations in the 1760's: see below, pp. 165, 166. For the evidence of stock exchange speculation see L. S. Sutherland, *The East India Company in
Eighteenth Century Politics*, p. 206.

[2] 'The Englishman', wrote Jean Rouquet in 1755, 'always has in his hands an
accurate pair of scales in which he scrupulously weighs up the birth, the rank, and
above all, the wealth of the people he meets, in order to adjust his behaviour
towards them accordingly.' I am indebted for this quotation to Mr. C. Mitchell
of the Warburg Institute.

the century). The evidence suggests that the process of promotion would require three generations. Edmund Burke, whose title to advancement was genius and not trading wealth, was typical at least in his acceptance of the leadership of the ancient landed families, and typical again in preparing for the advancement of his own family by the purchase of a country seat (at Beaconsfield in Buckinghamshire) and by sending his son to Christ Church, Oxford, to be educated for the world of political affairs. The most insistent of the social climbers were the East and West Indian adventurers returning with their fortunes to find a place as quickly as possible in the countryside from which they had been exiled in their youth. Even here the most famous example is likely to be characteristic. Pitt, earl of Chatham, more a grand seigneur than many of the blue-blooded, was the grandson of a piratical fortune-maker.

Even though the busy merchants of the towns might affect to despise the lordling in silks they were content to accept his leadership. Most Englishmen still lived in villages or very small towns. Here, of course, the dominance of the squires was even more marked, was indeed inevitable. The village lived very much unto itself in this age of slow communications and undeveloped industry. The multitude of small producers—blacksmiths, clockmakers, furniture-makers, and so on—who added to the variety of life would find their best patron in the local lord or squire. To offend him was desperately bad for business. The squire was the centre of authority and of culture. He returned from his occasional visits to London with new ideas; his wife came back with dresses and fine manners. If improvement was going forward in the fields then he would be its leader. If he was a small proprietor then his acres would be the first to see new ploughs or crops; if many tenant farmers depended upon him then he would encourage more efficient production either by his benevolent interest or by the simpler stimulus of keeping rents high. Only he could understand the legal procedure in connexion with enclosure or had the money to embark upon it. Villagers who thereby lost their grazing rights were but the more dependent upon the chief local employer. Thus to most people the plan of the universe seemed sufficiently evident from daily experience and the authority of the gentry inevitable and reasonable.

In some areas, such as parts of Somerset, or Yorkshire, where devotion to one trade, mining or wool, had destroyed the harmony of the typical village, there were certainly no natural leaders to be found. The sheep were without a shepherd. But this did not produce an onslaught on the pillars of society. In such areas men turned not to revolution but to Wesleyanism. Full of potentialities of radicalism for the future the methodist movement at this stage was a preservative of order. John Wesley[1] was in 1760 negotiating with the Calvinists and his preachers were beginning to celebrate the eucharist: he was set on the process which by 1784 was to carry his church outside the Anglican fold. But the effect of his activities, and even more those of George Whitefield,[2] was to introduce enthusiasm into religion, to the disgust of those with ordered lives and ordered minds: a feeling of purpose, a trust in Providence, was thus given to those who might otherwise have been filled only with the violence of despair.

Violence there was in plenty in the settled England of 1760. Riots and disorders were part of the way of life, a regular distraction from the drabness of the life of the poor, a release of emotion and energy; and as such they were taken for granted by the upper classes and did little to weaken the system. That system was at once easy-going and brutal. Much crime went unpunished. Yet when punishment came it was savage. It was taken for granted that the roads should be infested with robbers and also that the death penalty should be inflicted for a theft of five shillings from a shop or of forty shillings anywhere; while some debtors rotted in prison others escaped all obligations by a timely trip abroad. Some philanthropists were horrified by the mixture of inhumanity and inefficiency; they laboured to relieve the ignorant bestiality of the poor and the unthinking cruelty of the powerful. John Howard[3] devoted his life to informing the public of the foul and degrading state of the prisons. When he became, though a dissenter, high sheriff of Bedfordshire, he was able to effect sanitary improvements and to alter the basis of payment to jailers in at least one part of

---

[1] For Wesley see Basil Williams, *The Whig Supremacy*, pp. 92–97.

[2] For Whitefield, ibid., and also above, p. 3.

[3] John Howard (1726–90), captured and imprisoned in France in 1756. Afterwards visited English jails and described the horrors he discovered. Published his translation, *Historical Remarks on the Bastille*, 1774, his own *State of the Prisons*, 1777, *Appendix on the State of the Prisons* 1780, and a new version with further evidence *State of the Prisons* 1784. Travelled abroad to survey foreign prisons.

England. From time to time others would be stirred to action about some particular long-standing example of brutality. Edmund Burke, for example, called attention to the useless rigours of the penalties imposed upon offenders against morals.[1] Yet at the end of George III's reign, as Sir Samuel Romilly and Mrs. Fry[2] took up their reforming missions, the situation was not perceptibly better than in 1760. Attack upon one area of barbarism was unlikely to succeed without a raising of the standards of society as a whole.

The philanthropy of the age was extensive: it was often tinctured with the utilitarian motive of promoting social order by teaching the duty of obedience to social superiors. Elementary education was conducted on a haphazard and charitable basis. If there was a school in the village or market town it would probably be run either under the rules of the church of England's Society for the Promotion of Christian Knowledge or by a methodist committee; it would be maintained by the voluntary subscriptions of the upper class. Robert Raikes, from 1780 onwards, organized a successful movement for providing education on Sundays for the children of the labouring classes.[3] On a higher level grammar schools, with independent endowments, many originating in the sixteenth century but with a considerable number of new foundations in the eighteenth, provided a thorough but narrow mental education. Their system depended upon the unremitting training of the memory, using exclusively the works of Greek and Roman authors for that purpose. For those lucky enough to live near a school like Burford, or to have parents capable of sending sons to such places as Winchester, this thorough training opened up an entry into scholarship and the professions. Among the grammar schools some, the future public schools, were already rising in prestige by reason of their teaching and the boys they attracted. In training the leaders of the country Eton, particularly with the patronage of George III, began to excel Westminster. At

---

[1] After the death in the pillory of a man convicted of unnatural practices.

[2] For Sir Samuel Romilly see below, p. 437, and also Sir E. L. Woodward, *The Age of Reform* (O.H.E. vol. xiii), p. 451: for Mrs. Fry see Woodward, pp. 449, 598, 599.

[3] Robert Raikes (1735–1811), a printer and newspaper owner in Gloucester, is often incorrectly described as the originator of Sunday schools. His achievement in putting the movement on a workable footing, and expanding it, is important enough without the claim to invention.

the top of the educational ladder were the universities of Oxford and Cambridge. The decadence of the universities has perhaps been exaggerated by nineteenth-century reformers.[1] Though for a great many undergraduates the time they spent there was devoted only to learning the ways of the world without much discipline or the check of examinations, the universities did continue to produce some scholars whose learning was deep if narrow, and men of affairs capable of decorating their speeches with classical quotations. Cambridge, with its tripos examination, was better organized for teaching the young than Oxford: but in both places everything depended upon the character of particular tutors and pupils. The drunken don and his studious colleague lived side by side within the tolerant academic shades.

This educational world was narrow both in its membership and its subject matter. In contrast the dissenting communities in England had built up their own academies whose curriculum was wider and more modern: in consequence dissenting scholars, of whom Richard Price and Joseph Priestley[2] are leading examples, were prominent in the fields of science and sociology. In Scotland the universities were more vigorous and more various in their interests, while a more sustained effort had been made to put elementary education within the reach of the majority of the population. Despite the defects of the English educational picture, however, the standard of literacy seems to have been high by comparison with the rest of Europe. This is a subject on which, in the absence of statistics, it is impossible to make sure generalizations. But it is perhaps significant that there was an active provincial press and that one of its managers, John Newbery,[3] found profit as well as fame in producing a series of books for children.

[1] Edward Gibbon (for whom see below, pp. 347 f.), by his account of his unprofitable year at Magdalen, Oxford, is responsible for the sweeping condemnation of the university by most secondary works.

[2] Richard Price (1723–1791), a nonconformist minister and writer on political questions from a radical viewpoint; influential in his advocacy of financial schemes to reduce the National debt; see also below, p. 291.

Joseph Priestley (1733–1804), educated at Batley Grammar School and a Dissenting academy at Droitwich; a Presbyterian minister; a philosophical radical in his politics; a student of chemistry and electricity noted for his isolation of oxygen and his theory of electric attraction.

[3] John Newbery (1713–67), a maker of patent medicines, journalist, and publisher; in books such as *Mrs. Margery* (or *Goody*) *Two Shoes*—which he probably wrote and certainly published—he quaintly introduces commendations of his medicines (particularly the famous Dr. James' Powders) into the narrative. He was

At the centre of any consideration of the state of manners, as well as of the stability of society, must be an assessment of the church of England. That church in 1760 was the target for methodist criticism and later generations have regarded it as lifeless and shameful. Full of abuses it was, yet it was not utterly nor universally decadent. It suffered, most obviously, from the rationalistic spirit of the times. Its virtues at the best were those of common sense. The best men in it did their duty faithfully but without fervour: the worst were free from the tumults of conscience.[1] The upper dignitaries of the church, bishops, deans, canons, were appointed by the Crown and the bishops were an important voting force on the government side in the house of lords: necessarily therefore these high ecclesiastics had a large proportion of the worldly wise in their ranks, those who knew how to make powerful friends and to please the government of the day. The lower clergy had more often a grumbling dislike of it. The High Church party of the period was so called not for its spiritual doctrines, or its ceremonies, or its vestments, but for its conviction that the church was superior to the state, was in fact independent (except formally and in official temporal affairs) of the state. But suspicion of the executive did not imply being at odds with the social system. On the contrary it was the ownership by the gentry of the right of presenting to so many livings which sustained the parish clergy against authority. The squire would often appoint a relative or his own old tutor, but always someone in sympathy with his own views, to the parish living.[2] The dependence of the parson not upon the royal government or the bishop but upon the squire was of particular importance at a time when the pulpit was unrivalled as a propaganda agency and when the church was the only centre of village life and of village politics.

The upper ranks of the hierarchy were often well paid and able to enjoy leisure. If they preferred scholarship to pastoral activity they were able to indulge their taste. William Coxe left his fellowship at King's College, Cambridge, in 1768, but he never deserted research: as a pluralist rector or as archdeacon

the friend as well as the patron of such writers as Oliver Goldsmith, Dr. Samuel Johnson, and Christopher Smart. For him see Austin Dobson, *Eighteenth Century Vignettes*, i. 118.

[1] For the rebirth of a more intense feeling in Anglican circles see below, p. 353.

[2] And the squire's views were more often than not contemptuous of central authority; see below, p. 51.

of Wiltshire he was at all times the historian.[1] Bishop Warburton wrote on Moses and on Milton but earned most fame by his learned notes in his edition of Pope's poems. Warburton, if he preached against Wesley, to his credit also attacked the slave trade.[2] The incomes of country clergy varied enormously, but they were sometimes scandalously poor. A low standard of living does not seem to have inclined humble clerics to express the grievances of the agricultural poor but rather to have made them the more anxious to defer to the lay controllers of better livings and free meals. Among the clergy there were many absentees and pluralists. In many parishes confirmation and communion services were very rarely held. Bishops such as Secker[3] deplored the failure to feed the hungry flock. But for such failures beggarly emoluments were sometimes an excuse. If even holding two livings did not suffice to support a horse for the vicar and he had to travel on foot across the fields it is not surprising that he was tempted to be infrequent in his ministrations. Slackness there certainly was: but at the same time many a parish priest unnoticed and unremarkable, soberly served his people. With all its faults the church brought an element of cultured dignity to a hard-headed world. It was neither contentious nor missionary in spirit. It was rational and respectable. Its task, as it saw it, was to invest the ordinary ways of life at the time with decency, not to attempt their reformation. It is this which made it so strong a supporter of the power of the landed gentry.

The social leadership of the squires was matched by their administrative and political predominance. It was the strength of the landowner's control of local government in the counties which gave him his self-confident independence. It is an error to think of local government in 1760 as a subordinate authority operating within defined limits. On the contrary the effective government of England was, as far as concerned everyday things, conducted on a county or borough basis with little

---

[1] William Coxe (1747–1828), author of *The House of Austria, Sir Robert Walpole, Marlborough*, and other works of great and careful research.

[2] William Warburton (1698–1779), author of *The Divine Legation of Moses*; ridiculed Bentley's *Milton*; Pope's literary executor and brought out an edition of his works; bishop of Gloucester, 1759–79.

[3] Thomas Secker (1693–1768) had been bishop of Bristol and Oxford. He was archbishop of Canterbury from 1758 to 1768.

interference from London. In 1760 the only effective authority
in the counties was the commission of the peace, the justices,
working through the parish units. At their head was the lord-
lieutenant. He was the leading man of the justices, the head of
the armed forces (the militia) of the county, and his position
was one of honour. His duties, in practice, rarely amounted to
more than nominating the clerk of the peace and keeping the
king informed of the views of county society whenever a justice's
place had to be filled. When one family was not clearly the
leader in the county for wealth and repute the choice of a lord-
lieutenant by the king might be made on political grounds. But
the king's freedom in distributing this honour was narrowly
limited by a general sense of the fitness of things, or, in other
words, the necessity of recognizing the claims of great landed
property. Another royal appointment was the high sheriff, who
was head of the county court, which was limited to cases involving no more than 40s., and in which an under-sheriff
usually did the work. Coroners were elected by freeholders to
present criminals for trial and to inquire into deaths: this was
an undistinguished but profitable post. The high constable of
the county had become simply an agent of the justices and saw
to the levying of rates. But the real power was in the hands of
the justices of the peace. They had to be men of an estate of at
least £100 a year.[1] They were, in fact, in all counties except
Middlesex, drawn from the class of squires.

In the hands of these country gentlemen lay great power. A
single justice could punish the village poacher or deal with
other minor offences. He was usually able to judge from his
local knowledge as well as from evidence given before him; for
his paternal supervision of the village assisted him in his work
on the bench. Meeting together in twos or threes at petty
sessions the magistrates dealt summarily with a great variety of
matters. At quarter sessions, finally, they heard appeals and so
supervised the whole working of county government. They
were, in fact, the government of the county. For the efficient
conduct of affairs they needed the co-operation of the parishes and
boroughs within their jurisdiction. The extent to which boroughs
had emancipated themselves from county control depended
upon the charters they had secured. London, Haverfordwest,

[1] By the Act 5 Geo. II, c. 18, 1732; see W. C. Costin and J. S. Watson, *The Law
and Working of the Constitution*, i. 130.

and Berwick-upon-Tweed had escaped even from the authority of the lord-lieutenant as head of the militia. Many others remained only nominally within the county, having secured for their mayors and aldermen the functions of justices of the peace, and enjoyed self-government within the borough boundaries. But there were other small towns who had not secured this privilege and more closely resembled the parish.

The parish indeed was, in great areas of England, the only surviving unit of government with popular meetings: its vestry meeting took action as a public body, putting the wishes of the justices into effect. This was as true in areas of Lancashire given up to industry as it was in rural Buckinghamshire. The vestry had the power of raising a tax for local purposes. It raised the money for the poor in the form of a rate. Though the main administrative officers of the parish were not elected but were compulsorily appointed by the justices, a lively vestry could at least examine their spending. Upon its initiative depended the efficiency or slackness with which local public services were operated. The vicar, if he cared to attend, was usually chairman of the vestry, but there were great varieties of vestry meeting. In some places it was an oligarchy which co-opted fresh members at need; in others it was open to all the local inhabitants, and the choice of the churchwardens might be a riotous democratic process. It is impossible to relate efficiency to democracy. Some oligarchic vestries, like St. George's, Hanover Square, or Brighton, were efficient and enterprising, taking on new duties and appointing special officers of their own initiative: other oligarchies were slack and corrupt, incapable even of maintaining the village street or keeping the churchyard clean. The same contrast may be discovered among open vestries.

The lack of control by the parishes over the officers appointed by the justices was a source of muddle. The parish of Manchester —having within it several townships, a manorial court, and tens of thousands of inhabitants—had a vestry which did not even check the accounts of officials. As a result the rates were in arrears and it was not certain how many people were being maintained in the poorhouse. Such urbanized parishes, however, show the system in its worst light. In a country village the natural leaders of village society would co-operate with their own friends who were on the commission of the peace. The parson (who, when of sufficient standing was sometimes himself a justice) was a sobering influence in the vestry.

Attempts had already been made in 1760 to remedy the shortcomings of the system of county government. Various bodies for special services had been set up by special acts of parliament. In Middlesex a special corporation, for instance, had been established to deal with the care of the poor. Turnpike trusts were in existence to maintain some sections of important road;[1] their income came in part from tolls and in part from the rates of parishes affected. In addition voluntary organizations might, in public-spirited communities, charge themselves with improving river navigation, or lighting the streets, or paving them. The Westminster magistrate, sitting at Bow Street, in 1760 was the blind Sir John Fielding[2] whose efforts (together with those of his deceased brother the novelist) had already brought a special police force into existence to check highway robbery; this force of theirs extended its operations beyond Middlesex or Westminster over the whole country. But special organizations did not destroy the ultimate authority of the justices of the peace: justices supervised a turnpike trust's work as they did that of a parish surveyor.

The system operated by the justices was based upon the idea of universal obligation, the common law duty to maintain the king's peace, carried into administration. It also depended upon a conception of a settled, perfect, and unchanging order. It was assumed, for instance, not that government should have a 'road policy' but that all roads and bridges should be in complete repair. If one was found to be not in repair that was an offence, a nuisance, and the parish on whom the obligation to maintain it rested, should be presented before the magistrates for a failing in duty. The parish would then be ordered to set its inhabitants to work on unpaid road labour, or to pay, in the form of a rate, for hired men to do the job for them. Pigs straying in the churchyard, the failure of a poor law surveyor to find a willing successor, the collapse of a local town hall, all these might be grouped together as nuisances, that is things contrary to that proper order and peace which all had a duty to maintain. Administrative action was thus taken under a judicial form. As, moreover, everyone had an obligation to preserve public order, most jobs—from overseeing the poor to appre-

---

[1] See above, p. 27.   [2] He was knighted in 1761 and died in 1780.

hending burglars—were unpaid and compulsory; the justices named those upon whose shoulders they were to fall, and local scores could sometimes be paid off in doing this. While their main strength lay in their knowledge of the county, for legal guidance the justices had their clerk of the peace—or rather his deputy, for he usually left the work to be done by the leading firm of local solicitors, with whom he shared the emoluments.

The justices sometimes attempted to enforce standards of production by punishing shabby or fraudulent work. They continued to bind boys as apprentices to chosen trades. The whole poor law depended upon them: they compelled parishes to support the helpless and employ the able bodied. The parish submitted names from which the justices chose an overseer of the poor. Rates for their support were decided on appeal to quarter sessions. The justices enforced the resettlement of the destitute in the parishes of their origin under the act of Charles II's reign. The sessions also controlled the constables of the watch, and were responsible for catching malefactors; they licensed fairs and drinking, which they rightly thought closely connected with crime.

It is clear that in addition to their judicial work the justices at the sessions had to take charge of all the miscellaneous functions of government. And in the use of their discretion they were legislators as well. The most striking example of this came thirty years after when the change in the poor law, known as the Speenhamland system,[1] the supplementation of wages from the rates, was effected not by an act of parliament but by an *ad hoc* decision of the Berkshire justices and was imitated by magistrates in other counties. One may instance also the ban on itinerant trading by the Kent justices, or the Berkshire justices' prohibition of Sunday drinking except by bona fide travellers,[2] or the rule that there could not be an ale house in any Dorset village without the assent of the parson,[3] or, in many counties, alteration of the basis of assessment for rates. Or again, negatively, the Elizabethan statutes for the fixing of fair wages did not require repeal, for country gentlemen simply

[1] See below, pp. 527, 528.
[2] Both these examples are from the 1780's. On this subject see S. and B. Webb, *English Local Government, The Parish and the County*, pp. 536 f.
[3] In 1752.

decided to cease to enforce them. These gentlemen were not in receipt of grants from a national exchequer. The funds needed were raised locally by the rates they authorized. Nor were they supervised by any national department. There was no agency for doing so. Their independence was only limited by the possibility of having an information filed against them, or by a mandamus being issued, in which cases they would have to appear before the king's bench judges, to answer a charge of breaking the law or of failing to carry out their legal obligations, respectively. Squire Western[1] was told by his clerk ('who has some understanding of the law of the realm') that he 'could not legally commit anyone to Bridewell only for ill-breeding'. He heeded the advice for as he 'had already had two informations exhibited against him in the King's Bench he had no curiosity to try a third'. Nevertheless such control was clumsy and intermittent. It was difficult to bring up every breach of the rules in the royal courts, and only those with money and some education would attempt it. Provided no one of importance in the county was offended, the magistrates were almost immune from interference.

It was uncommon for magistrates to be removed. The idea that the social status of the magistracy must be maintained prevented any king from purging the county. This idea was sound. Magistrates varied in character, but their position in local society was a guard against the worst kind of corruption, for it brought out their sense of paternal responsibility. Where men of low social status were put in the commission of the peace the results were disastrous, for they were tempted to make a profit from fees. 'A mercenary magistrate who is rewarded in proportion not to his integrity but to the number he convicts', Oliver Goldsmith justly wrote in 1760, 'must be a person of the most unblemished character, or he will lean on the side of cruelty'. In Middlesex[2] the standing of magistrates had generally declined, probably because in that urbanized area men of property refused to face the difficulties of the position. Goldsmith probably was thinking of the 'Trading justices' of Middlesex when he describes the corrupt magistrate as 'a human hyena'. Burke twenty years later referred to them as 'the scum of the earth—carpenters, brickmakers, and shoemakers . . .

[1] In Henry Fielding's novel, *Tom Jones* (published in 1749), bk. VII, chap. ix.
[2] For Middlesex see G. Dowdell, *A Hundred Years of Quarter Sessions*, passim.

unworthy of any employ whatever'.[1] The situation of Middlesex was a stage worse than that in Staffordshire or Lancashire, where the country gentlemen allowed the special problems of pottery, mining, or cotton, areas to drift. Even in the country areas its evils became evident when landowners who promoted enclosures can be found punishing, in their capacity as magistrates, the sufferers who rioted in protest. In 1760, however, the weakest points of county government had not yet been exposed. Country gentlemen as yet felt themselves fully capable of running the county without assistance and would indeed brook none. In this England may be contrasted with Scotland: there the Presbyterian kirk kept its control of much of social life, but in England the squires answered for everything in the countryside from morals to markets.

Life in a town was more intense than life in the villages: but it was almost as self-contained. The cities and towns cherished, as an inheritance from the revolutions of the seventeenth century, their freedom from outside interference. The government of urban communities was complex and most varied. Independence was most real when the corporation possessed the powers of justices of the peace and had the right to make local regulations for their citizens. It might be expected that the possession of parliamentary representation by many boroughs would make the inhabitants deeply concerned with national issues. But the ordinary merchant or craftsman at most times gave what energy was left over from the shop or the workshop to local squabbles and intrigues, matters which obviously affected his daily life and income. In Newcastle-upon-Tyne the radical party made the preservation of the town moor the only issue which could excite the citizens; around this question local government turned and upon it elections to parliament for Newcastle had to be fought. Similarly in Coventry the embezzlement of Sir Thomas White's bequest was the topic which filled all minds and was the cry of electioneers. In Bristol the failure of the corporation to maintain docks and the tolls charged by the Merchant Venturers for harbour facilities were at least as important as policy towards America, even though in that case Bristol had a special stake in a trade which had become a subject of parliamentary discussion. Thus the politics of boroughs were inextricably involved with petty squabbles, and

[1] S. and B. Webb, *English Local Government, Parish and County*, p. 325.

the great names of Whig and Tory, like the lesser labels of King's Friend, Newcastle's man, Scotch interest (Lord Bute's supporters), were all of them used to fit, however inappropriately, over the various factions fighting engrossing battles of purely local concern.

Of the 200 or so municipal corporations some were hardly more than villages and the chief importance of these was therefore their possession of parliamentary representation. Even the most rotten borough might sometimes revolt against control. Even a handful of voters, exercising rights in virtue of holding a little cluster of houses, sometimes demanded more than beer and puddings, might seek to wring substantial local advantages for their community out of parliamentary nominees. But it is among the boroughs of some size that one must seek to find the distinctive contribution of urban communities to social and political life in 1760.

The government of towns was sometimes in the hands of an oligarchy; this was the case in Penzance, Leeds, Coventry, Bristol, and Leicester. In small but prosperous Penzance, the mayor and eight senior aldermen had all positions of local importance in their hands. They owned the pier, paved the streets, maintained the jail, and all other services. They operated at a profit and needed to levy no rates. With the twelve junior aldermen they formed the corporation which was replenished by co-option of new members when required. In Coventry the mayor and aldermen, as justices of the peace, chosen by a co-opting grand council, absorbed all executive authority and used it corruptly. Public services (paving, watching, lighting, and watering) in the city were transferred (in 1763) at the request of the corporation to special commissioners, who levied a rate for these purposes. On the other hand the closed oligarchy which governed Liverpool, less than forty in number (and once more co-optive), showed vigour and enterprise. It had, since 1715, been building docks and increasing the wealth of the city. Liverpool was progressive in lighting its streets and widening them. It led the way in every urban improvement.

There were less than forty democratically governed boroughs in the whole country, but among them was the greatest, the city of London. Norwich, at the heart of the most thriving provincial area of the country, may be taken as an example of a democratic but unhappy city government. There the electorate consisted of all the freemen, upon whom service in the old guilds of the city was a duty. But this democracy had been rendered inefficient by a deadlock between the competing powers of the annually elected council and the aldermen (who were chosen for life); by 1759 vain attempts were being made to reshape the whole constitution of the city. Competing groups promised salaried appointments or free beer to gain support both in city and parliamentary elections. In some other open boroughs civic services were delegated to special bodies of commissioners, sometimes statutorily established, sometimes the result of voluntary co-operative effort by enlightened citizens.

London is the supreme example at once of the independent spirit and the complex politics of the boroughs. In it, from its situation, importance, and history, however, national issues played a large part. Its municipal government had remained democratic and its parliamentary franchise was open to all ratepayers. London was the sounding board and leader of independent radical opinion in the country as a whole. In Common Hall it passed resolutions on matters of national policy, its lord mayor could demand audience of the king and the city had the right to be heard at the Bar of the house of commons. Its voice was frequently raised, in the earlier part of the reign, against the policies of those in authority at court. This voice, in a mixed constitution with ideas of the virtual representation of interests, counted for more than just the votes of its four members of parliament. There were, indeed, in London many wealthy financiers and merchants in whose interest it was to stand well with ministers who would dispense favours. These affluent figures therefore tried to rein in the radicalism of the city. But the majority of shopkeepers had no such motive to keep them from going 'agin the government'. They looked on the government as a nuisance attributing the bad, and not the good, years of trade to ministerial policy. The wealthier Londoners were already tending to live outside the city boundaries in such outlying villages as Islington or Clapham. But the key to power lay in the elections by wards to the Court of Common Council. The resident citizens over their shops or counting houses were cultivated by active ward politicians whose political machines thus came to express the small man's radical point of view. Wilkes's career[1] was to prove the power of these organizations. Lordly

[1] See below, pp. 131 f.

politicians, like Lord Shelburne, who had friends, such as Alderman Sawbridge,[1] to intrigue for them in London found that the game was easier to play when they were in opposition than when they were in office. The city electorate was too large to be bribed. The treasury could only hope to moderate London's civic pride.

The political consequences of this system of local government in county and borough are not difficult to see. When a member of the local squirearchy was returned by the general feeling of his neighbours, as a member of parliament for the county, he went as the spokesman for what was almost an independent and self-governing community:[2] this it was which made him so redoubtable, albeit lethargic, a figure at Westminster. In his eyes the central government contributed little to the real business of life. What was important was done locally by his own class. Ministers were concerned with running a foreign policy, with the 'fiddle faddle' of court life, and in consequence with the collection of taxes. It is little wonder that such a member looked with suspicion upon increases in ministerial power and instinctively believed that the less government (in the sense of national government) a country had the better it would prosper. Men of this cast of mind were often useful and conscientious justices of the peace, good landlords, and popular figures at a county ball. They were rarely men of high political ambition or of ministerial capacity. To them therefore local affairs were real and Westminster rather a bore. When they bothered to attend a debate it was often only to scotch some dangerous suggestion for change. They were easily aroused by the cry that the power of the executive was increasing. They honoured the king and watched his servants with suspicion.

There were, however (in England and Wales), only 92 members for counties as against 417 for borough seats.[3] Any conclusion that the urban outlook was therefore over-represented as

---

[1] John Sawbridge (1732?–95), M.P. Hythe, 1768; a member of the Society for the Defence of the Bill of Rights (for which see below, p. 139); lord mayor of London 1775; M.P. for London 1774, 1780, 1784, and 1790.

[2] Sir James Lowther, later earl of Lonsdale (1736–1802), a great borough patron, once, when sitting as member for Cumberland, incautiously spoke of his county as though it were a separate state, declaring that, if certain proposals became law, they would reserve their position.

[3] The total membership of the house of commons was 558, including 45 Scottish and 4 University members: 100 Irish members were added after the Act of Union.

compared with the countryside is mistaken. For the majority of
borough seats were not held by members of a trading middle
class. They were controlled either by the great landowning
peers, or by the squires of the county, or by treasury managers,
or, finally, by an arrangement between local people and such
interests.[1] Thus the borough of Stamford was entirely controlled
by the Cecils, its expansion prevented and its point of view
expressed entirely by the lord of the manor. In Grantham
the Cust family co-operated with the greater interest of the
dukes of Rutland to share the representation. Banbury was,
through its corporation, at the disposal of Lord North. In
Surrey the Onslows, as leading gentlemen, usually had a member
of the family sitting for Guildford or for Haslemere. In Sussex
the duke of Newcastle used government patronage to secure the
election of borough members acceptable to himself. In the north
a Lambton (the family of the future earls of Durham) represented Durham city without a break up to 1813, a continuity
excelled in the west by the Whitmore family's tenure of the
Bridgnorth seat for two full centuries from 1660. As landlord
or customers the greater gentry might affect a borough's prosperity. It has been calculated that 111 patrons influenced or
determined 205 of the borough seats in England.[2]

Some borough members, therefore, had the same presupposi-
tions as their more honoured friends who sat for counties. There
were boroughs in which the urban classes did make their point
of view felt; London and Westminster, conspicuously, would
accept none but members pandering to, if not springing from,
the *bourgeoisie*.[3] But what, politically, was this point of view?
The more vigorous the local life of a borough the greater its
sense of self-sufficiency. To the inhabitants of a seaport the best
known agent of the Crown would be the collector of customs
duties, to the merchants of an inland town the agents of the
excise and the receivers of the land tax. They enjoyed few

[1] As a further complication it must be remembered that even where a local
trading interest might force itself to the fore, its leading representative would seek
to rise in the social scale. In Newcastle-upon-Tyne the Blacketts and the Ridleys
who so often held the seats were half-way on the change from local tradesmen to
country gentlemen.

[2] By Sir Lewis Namier, *The Structure of Politics at the Accession of George III* (2nd edn.),
p. 150. He estimated that thirty in addition were more or less under the immediate management of the government.

[3] For variations in the franchise in boroughs see A. and E. Porrit, *The Unreformed
House of Commons*, and also B. Williams, *The Whig Supremacy*, p. 27.

services in return for their money. A prejudice against central authority was the result. But this was tempered in the case of the towns, as it could not be in the counties, by several counter-attractions. Bristol (oligarchically governed for local affairs) had a wide and popular parliamentary franchise. Robert Nugent, for twenty years one of their members, was elected to support the government because 'a commercial city such as theirs, stood in continual need of the interposition and assistance sometimes of the Treasury, sometimes of the Board of Trade and sometimes of the Commissioners of the Customs and the Excise . . . to moderate and mitigate the *letter* of the law in contingent cases'.[1] A friend of the king's ministers might, in other words, secure aid for the trade of the whole town. Nugent looked after the interests of Bristol by adhering to each government in turn (except Rockingham's precarious twelve-month ministry) regardless of politics. Yet it is significant that the other Bristol member at this time was as tory as Nugent was whig, the nominee of a Bristol club of spirited independence.

In all urban communities moreover there were, as there were not in the counties, people anxiously looking for government jobs as a source of livelihood. This was most evident in the small seaports. In Rye (Sussex) the mayor and corporation wished to maintain their pre-eminence by building up a clientele among the lesser citizens. For this purpose it was useful to be able to nominate the commander of the boat employed to inspect ships on behalf of the customs. It was advisable for the mayor of Rye therefore to stand well with Whitehall and to offer the parliamentary seat to the government of the day. Yet this was not a complete surrender. In 1762 Rye could battle against the treasury because the neighbouring (and hated) town of Winchelsea had been favoured. The strength of local unity in a place like Rye might make it difficult for the Crown to find possible rivals to the ruling families. In such cases a compromise would have to be reached. In a port like Harwich two government departments, the post office and the treasury, had posts to fill. Local interests could thrive amid departmental competition. Moreover the chief government agent in managing the borough—in the case of Harwich it was Mr. Roberts[2]—could

---

[1] Dean Tucker (1775), quoted Namier, *Structure of Politics* (2nd edn.), p. 88.
[2] John Roberts (1712?–72) had been Henry Pelham's private secretary and had continued as a manager for Newcastle when the latter was at the treasury. He

use his position to build up a following for himself. The local clients knew the agent rather than his employers. If he then joined in a rebellion he might force the government to make concessions to him or to the town for the sake of having a friendly member of parliament elected.

A further adulteration of the natural bias of the towns against central control arose when they were dominated, either for parliamentary or local government purposes, by any particular citizen of ambition. Such a man might well have business favours to ask of ministers. Thomas Fonnereau, the member for Sudbury in Suffolk in 1760, was a financier on a great scale whose prosperity depended on doing business with the government. He set himself therefore to tame this 'naturally anti-ministerial borough' (as he himself described it).[1] In Tiverton (Devon) the serge-making trade was financed by a Mr. Peard whose capital in part depended on his use of government tax-collections. By lending capital he secured a stranglehold upon local government which it used to return the member of parliament.[2] A merchant anxious to get a government contract to clothe or feed our armies in war, would find it useful to have a seat in parliament to use as an argument. To get this seat he had to secure support in a borough and influence its local concerns. The simplest way was to buy all the houses in a rotten borough and so control all the votes. But often the rich adventurer had to join in the politics of the corporation and offer to an extending circle of interests some solid reason for allowing him to vote for the court. It is not possible to state precisely the extent to which any given borough, with real municipal life, had fallen from its natural independence into the position of a client of an active politician or of the treasury. It varied with local politics and with the needs of the hour. Where ministers had influence it was often only enough to tip the balance in a battle of local interests. As a result such influence would be ineffective unless it was exceedingly skilfully managed by someone who mixed with, or at least consulted, the local politicians

became M.P. for Harwich in 1761 and continued to hold the seat until his death in spite of Newcastle's loss of power.

[1] Against him a leading dissenter, Thomas Fenn, led the resistance, even though Fenn himself owed his importance to his post as a receiver of the land tax for the government.

[2] Until his suicide in 1764 Peard controlled the elections in the interest of the Ryder family. See W. R. Ward, *The English Land Tax in the Eighteenth Century*, p. 172.

of the corporation, and was prepared to interest himself in its welfare. The management, in turn, of such agents was a work which demanded all the attention of a minister assisted by treasury clerks to keep lists and file begging letters. This tedious and tricky attention to local problems was indeed the major part of any sound national government's domestic policy.

It will be apparent that though their ways of life were so different, country squires and borough tradesmen were alike in their solid, self-assured, self-governing independence, and consequently both had an initial dislike of outside interference. In this their practical experience and their constitutional theory marched together. The conflicts over sovereignty which had made seventeenth-century history had been settled by the demonstration in the years following 1688 that parliament, the king, lord, and commons in parliament assembled, was a legally sovereign body.[1] But this sovereignty was not intended for everyday use. Parliament was thought of as the final umpire in a dispute between established groups if they should conflict, not as an active ruler. It was the liberties of the groups within the state which were considered to be the secret of English blessedness. That parliament would not exceed its proper activity was, in practice, to be made certain by the predominance in parliament of one of the major groups with a vested interest in freedom from interference, the landed gentry. This low view of the functions of government could be supported by quotations from Locke, with whose work every educated mind was saturated. The idea of liberty by the balance of many powers had earned the laudatory comments of Montesquieu. The interlocking of the executive and legislative powers—which Montesquieu is often accused of overlooking—was in fact productive not of a stronger executive but of a more effective negative upon it, because deference to the prejudices of parliament was thereby a matter of daily necessity.[2]

In practice England was not a unitary state but a collection of corporations and groups, each with a life of its own, cohabiting with ease of long experience within the framework of the

---

[1] On this consult G. N. Clark, *The Later Stuarts*, passim, for the historical events and A. V. Dicey, *The Law of the Constitution*, for its legal consequences.

[2] The work of a Swiss commentator, J. L. de Lolme, *Constitution de l'Angleterre*, which was published in 1771, best makes clear this combination of the final and limitless sovereignty of parliament with social and political conservatism.

Revolution Settlement. The church of England, as has been pointed out, had its higher dignitaries appointed by the Crown but went its own way without paying them much heed. Even the dissenters had a place established for them by custom, a custom of ignoring the letter of the law which penalized them.[1] The universities of Oxford and Cambridge lived unto themselves. The university of Oxford, in particular, was comically 'tory', with its politics often a struggle between high tories and Jacobites, repudiating, apparently, the whole Hanoverian world. This 'toryism' under analysis turns out to be merely a cant phrase to express its hatred of royal interference.[2] The regius professors, as royal appointees, were left in leisure, impotent to corrupt the self-centred contrariness of the college fellows. Only Merton and Christ Church were 'whig' colleges; and Christ Church with its Crown-appointed dean and canons was a pocket of government influence of an exceptional kind producing cabinet ministers from its aristocratic undergraduates and bishops from its dons. The self-perpetuating governing bodies of other colleges, in both Oxford and Cambridge, damned the government and went eventually to college livings to continue, in obscurantist sermons, to demonstrate their independent ways.[3] Inside the two autonomous worlds of learning there were, from time to time, political struggles of enormous intricacy: as in the boroughs, national labels were used to cover local issues.

In a world of such vested interests, balanced with one another, lawyers were bound to play a prominent part. Conflicts of authority would be resolved by the application of the traditional principles of law rather than by appeal to the ultimate

[1] See below, p. 156.

[2] This 'tory' spirit was therefore in reality a fanatical devotion to the gains which had been made when the Hanoverians displaced the Stuarts, the right to run their own affairs, to elect fellows or presidents, without royal participation.

[3] St. John's College, Oxford, may be cited to illustrate this point and also a further one, the similarity of urban radical independence and high tory conservatism. Merchant Taylors' School had its intake of boys from radical London. These boys went by closed scholarship to make up the great majority of St. John's, usually reckoned a high tory college. Many then went on, being in holy orders, to college livings. At each stage of their lives, at father's counter, at company school, at college, and at the vicarage, they could grumble away in independent security against central authority. Only exceptional ambition could make them suppliant. It is thus not surprising that President Fry of this society could be a friend of the radical Wilkes or oppose the disciplining of Methodist scholars. For details (but not my interpretation of them) see W. C. Costin, *St. John's College, Oxford, 1598–1860*.

court of parliament. The Inns of Court, despite the importance of Crown patronage in the legal profession, cherished
their black-letter traditions as a specialist mystery which
heightened their importance and their independence. It was
professional *esprit de corps* rather than statutory enactments
about the security of a judge's tenure of his position which
guaranteed the independence of the judiciary.[1] As parliament
had little legislative activity, as the perfection of existing law
was assumed, the interpreters of that law had, in practice, the
power to make adjustments to fit new problems. The great earl
of Hardwicke had just completed his transformation of the law
of equity and was to die in 1764.[2] But William Murray, earl of
Mansfield, only entered on his real period of greatness when he
became a lord chief justice in 1756. From then until his death in
1793 he dominated legal discussion. His exposition of the law
about seditious libel in the cases of Wilkes, Junius, and the dean
of St. Asaph[3] aroused great anger because it so severely limited
the responsibility of juries. Amid general applause, on the other
hand, he established the doctrine (in Somersett's case)[4] that
slaves enjoyed the benefits of freedom while they stood on English soil. More quietly—but with consequences important in the
future—Mansfield incorporated into the Common Law of
England a set of principles for commercial cases which were to
be the basis of a legal code. There is no other lawyer of the reign
of comparable stature until John Scott, first earl Eldon, became
lord chancellor in 1801.[5] But such was the deference paid to
lawyers as constitutional pundits that men like Thurlow, Ellenborough, Loughborough, Erskine had an importance in public
life greater even than their talents might have been expected to
earn. Thus secure in their power the judges interpreted the
law with 'a leaning towards liberty', a bias against the hand of
power.

This bias was the secret of England's unique constitution. It
appears even in the procedure of the house of commons. There

---

[1] The final step in giving judges security by statute was, however, taken at the
accession of George III by 1 Geo. III, c. 23 which continued the judges in office
despite the demise of the Crown.

[2] For him see B. Williams, *The Whig Supremacy*, pp. 63–65.

[3] See the cases arising out of Wilkes's arrest and the case of the Dean of St. Asaph
in W. C. Costin and J. S. Watson, *The Law and Working of the Constitution*, vols. i and ii.

[4] Ibid., vol. i, p. 314 and vol. ii, p. 257.

[5] See below, p. 284 n. 1.

were at least thirteen stages for full debate on any bill: the rules operated always in favour of delay, always against anyone desiring change. With undercurrents of feeling of this sort (and as half a century of torpor had suffocated the old controversial issues) the labels of whig and tory served little purpose. These labels had become traditional in certain families and in certain parts of the country. At most it may be said that anyone calling himself a tory was glorying in his lack of political common sense and lack of ambition for office. Whigs were those who aspired to ministerial status, but also included all those who—even if as anti-court as any tory—gladly accepted the existing order. The tory cries of Anne's reign had become the stock phrases of any in opposition, whigs included. With the formal return to court of a few obstinate tory families on George III's accession, the old names became of even less use for distinguishing ideas. They lacked party organization even to keep them alive as bodies of friends. At the centre of things ministerial whigs contended for power: outside this circle of great men the moderate whigs kept a judicious balance, supporting their ministerial friends if they seemed to keep within trodden bounds, but swift to join in resistance to any innovation such as a new tax. The country whigs cannot be logically distinguished from tories.

Certainly whigs had no particular link with an urban middle class or even with dissent. As practical politicians the great whig lords had, as has been shown, to concern themselves with conciliating corporations and making friends among aldermen. As practical politicians, again, they were prepared to leave the laws against dissent in abeyance. Roman catholic squires in the country were left in peace as eccentrics, even when they might make papists out of their social inferiors in the village. But they played no part in politics. In the towns the protestant dissenters had no particular programme, save the desire to see the laws which nominally put them outside the constitution abolished. But as they were not as a rule of the highest or wealthiest class such things as standing for parliament were in any case outside their range. They were like an unfashionable social club, whose votes, where they had them, could be secured by decent civility to their leaders.[1]

The chief problem of the servants of the Crown in conditions

---

[1] The duke of Newcastle bade his candidate in Lewes (Sussex) begin his campaign by making certain of nonconformist support.

such as these was that of holding in check the disruptive forces so as to carry on the essential tasks of government. For this they needed some body of support more dependable than the whims of country gentlemen. It was by the management of boroughs that the treasury might build up this support. As has been seen,[1] by judicious intervention and compromises, members could be returned whose seats, in part, depended upon official help; their votes, therefore, could, within limits, be commanded by ministers. The skill required of a minister was to deal separately with each borough not so much to win an election but to avoid a contested one. The duke of Newcastle might agree to allow one fierce independent to be unopposed if he could be accompanied by a staunch government man, in double-member constituencies.[2] The exact bargains struck differed from borough to borough and year to year. It was this work, and not vulgar bribery, which built up the government interest. The government had little money available. It had spent some £30,000 on election expenses for its candidates over the whole country in the election of 1754; but this was at a time when one side could spend £20,000 in one county (Oxfordshire) for one contest, and when it was estimated that gentlemen in Bristol spent £60,000.[3] In the election of 1761, upon George III's accession, the government, to satisfy the new king's pure conscience, avoided spending cash. But even if the government had little money, it had many jobs. All the posts in revenue collection, in the customs, in the post office, and other departments, the promotions both in the army and the navy, and every conceivable post of honour or profit, whether active or sinecure, might be used to reward faithful service. It was not just that a member of parliament might desire a post for himself or his relatives; the security of his seat might depend upon his satisfying the desires of the key figures among his supporters. The small jobs— the sort of place a Sussex fisherman might covet in harbour administration or that which a Cheshire gentleman might wish

---

[1] Above, p. 53.

[2] In the same spirit of compromise Lord North avoided starting contests in Oxfordshire if he could be left in peaceful control of Banbury.

[3] Sir Lewis Namier's examination (*The Structure of Politics*, chap. 4) of the secret service accounts of the duke of Newcastle has shown that this money was spent on espionage and diplomatic service in the main. Some part went in eleemosynary pensions without real political significance. Less than one-fifth, roughly £8,000 a year, was spent on electoral work, while about another £9000 a year was devoted to pensions (of all kinds) to Members of Parliament.

his younger son to occupy in the salt tax inspectorship—were as
important as the large ones, such, for example, as the sinecure
ushership in the exchequer which Horace Walpole enjoyed for
life thanks to the services of his great father. In the collection of
the land tax parliament named the country gentlemen who had
to assess their own shares in the fixed quota of the county. But
the receivers of the money were appointed by the treasury. As
these receivers might easily be two years behindhand in sending
in their collection, they might have perhaps £50,000 of government money in their hands; this could be used like private
capital. With it they could build a clientele.[1]

The use of government posts to maintain a political connexion
probably did not reduce efficiency in the civil service as much
as has sometimes been supposed. The post office, in addition to
its normal duties, industriously intercepted and read the letters
of foreign ministers. The admiralty took the lead in copper-
bottoming ships, a scientific advance. It was the vigilance and
pertinacity of excise inspectors which made them unpopular.
The cost of tax collection in England was the lowest in the
world. The income tax, when it came to be introduced, was
made more efficient by making use of the files and the expertise
of the land tax office. In all offices, in short, hard work was
done, even if it was not done by those who held the titular and
highly paid responsibility. Deputies might be working for a
fraction of the salary nominally attached to a post (as was certainly the case in the clerks' department of the house of commons), but they did the work. Nor, though appointments were
made on influence and not merit, were there usually wholesale
purges of serving officials on a change of minister, one of the
chief defects associated with the 'spoils' system. The usual im-
pairment of efficiency was, indeed, continuity of service. Once
appointed, a civil servant seems to have possessed, in practice,
a right to hold his place, short of scandalous misbehaviour,
though he might grow too aged to write or to attend the
office.

The attempt to increase the treasury's control of the staff of
other offices under Walpole had failed—but it had not been so

[1] In Suffolk the collector quarrelled with the government and was found guilty
of bribery. He was not dismissed though his whole political position depended upon
his holding this position. The treasury often failed to exploit its power. It was
limited by slackness and also by the need to appoint someone of real local standing.
In this, the position was comparable to that affecting the commission of the peace.

much an effort to increase patronage as to stir departments
from the sleepy acquiescence in the rights of agents to a free-
hold in the service.[1] A change in government usually only
meant that new appointments would be filled from the ranks
of friends of the new administration. Even in 1763, when there
was a purge in the tax office, it was only after the victims had
been given a chance to demonstrate their loyalty to the new
order and seems to have been as much an opportunity to clear
out dead wood as to remove Newcastle's spies.[2] Offices might
be monopolized by one family. In the post office, once Anthony
Todd had (in 1752) become a secretary, he found places for
two nephews who in turn succeeded their uncle so that the post
office was a Todd domain for about half a century. A whole
tribe of the Willes family similarly combined posts as decipherers
with others in the bishopric of Bath and Wells for the whole
eighteenth century.[3]

Parliament felt, at George III's accession, no responsibility
for the efficiency of the executive service. They still regarded
the whole civil administration as the king's government (or
'family') which the king should not only run for himself but for
which he should pay. Parliament provided George III, who
surrendered the hereditary revenue for his lifetime, with an
income fixed at £800,000 a year. Out of this he had to provide
not only for his court but for the civil and foreign services. The
salaries of diplomats abroad were not under the eye of parliament. They were paid by the master for whom they worked,
the king. As long as he lived within his fixed income he could
manage his services as he pleased. The idea of public money
was not yet fully developed. Hence the eighteenth-century
prevalence of the fee system. Those who took the king's shilling
became his men and suffered in the general estimation of their
independence. It was preferable to serve the king without
depending mainly upon his wages, deriving instead an income
from fees for services rendered to individual members of the
public. A clerk who charged the public for particular services
was earning his living by serving it, and was not a kept man of
the Crown. As he met a public need he prospered. Thus in

---

[1] For contrasting views on this point see E. Hughes, *Studies in Administration and Finance*, and W. R. Ward, *The English Land Tax*. I here follow Dr. Ward's arguments.   [2] See below, pp. 88 f.

[3] I am indebted here to the researches of Dr. K. L. Ellis of the university of
Durham.

many public offices the official salary was negligible: the emoluments were great. Even the land-tax collectors were paid by poundage at skinflint rates and, as has been stressed already, really made the position worthwhile by their independent activities.[1] To perform private services in an official position was less degrading than to be a salaried and controlled cog in a machine. To come under the patronage of some great lord—as Burke did with Lord Rockingham or Calcraft with the Fox family, or Rigby with the duke of Bedford—was less injurious to one's independent status than to work in the greater service of the Crown. Parliament's concern with the civil service was only to watch jealously lest it sapped the independence of members of parliament and to lament its drain upon the royal pockets which, in the last resort, had to be refilled from the taxes of the country. In normal times, however, the working of the executive offices was not a topic for parliamentary discussion.

The perennial subject of debate there was the encroachment by the executive upon the independence of members. Yet even the members in whose election the treasury played a part could rarely be bought outright by ministerial favours. The extent of their loyalty to ministerial patrons (like that of the nominees of private patrons to their leaders) fluctuated in a way which baffles exact listing. It was their acknowledged independence which gave county seats their great honour in the world. Yet independence in a member of parliament must always be personal rather than institutional: even the county member ceased to enjoy his proud immunity from political intrigue if he had ambitions and abilities. Sir George Savile[2] deservedly had the highest repute for integrity among Yorkshire gentlemen. But friendship with Rockingham bade fair to make a professional of him: this would threaten the confidence of Yorkshire freeholders. Dowdeswell,[3] from independent Worcestershire, once

[1] For example Fordyce, the Scottish receiver of Crown rents, in 1766 had a salary of £650 a year while expenses were £700 a year. He paid for the post. But it was worthwhile because he had £80,000 of public money in his hands and was thus a great banker.

[2] Sir George Savile, eighth baronet (1726–84), M.P. Yorkshire, 1759–83. He promoted bills to secure the rights of electors, the relief of clerics from the weight of the Thirty-nine articles, and the abolition of certain antiquated disabilities of Roman catholics. He was accepted in the inner circle of the marquis of Rockingham's friends and supported the cause of the rebellious Americans.

[3] William Dowdeswell (1721–75), M.P. Tewkesbury, 1747–54 and M.P. Worcestershire, 1761–75; chancellor of the exchequer under Rockingham in 1765 and

he dreamed of office could no longer avoid the practical bargains of professional politicians. But few county members were men of such ability. In Somerset even lords or the sons of lords were anathema to a sturdy squirearchy who sought a good backbench man not of the front rank socially or politically.

To some extent the influence of London and its cultural predominance sweetened the asperity of the representatives of the independent squirearchy. To come to Westminster and be cajoled by lords and secretaries of state must have made some backwoodsmen less wilfully blind to the needs and desires of the executive. In the long run the spread of ideas from London society sapped that provincial-mindedness and self-sufficiency which lay at the back of political resistance to the central government. The most 'unpolitical' counties were those which lay farthest to the west and north from London. A Surrey county member was more aware of political reality, lived less in Uncle Toby's world of half a century back, than his colleague from Lancashire or Westmorland. Nevertheless this process made slow progress against the everyday experience of ruling one's own world at the sessions.

No amount of analysis of the electoral structure will reveal the complete secret of how governments succeeded in living in the conditions of 1760. The working of the constitution at that time depended upon ideas which their holders would have found it difficult to define but upon which they nevertheless acted. They took for granted that there should be a balanced system with spheres of action for the executive, the federative (that is the executive in its external aspect) and for the legislative powers. They assumed, blandly, that the proper limits for each of these powers were evident to men of good will and common sense. They believed, that is to say, that there was 'a patriotic line' of conduct, avoiding both factious opposition and subservience, which men of honest character could recognize and follow. Opposition as a consistent thing, formed opposition, opposition organized on grounds of principle or personal rivalry, was frowned on as improper. Equally, while the king's service should be carried on, power tended to make its holders greedy of more and so to shake the balance of the constitution. It was the duty therefore of the independent member to be

acted closely with Rockingham's group thereafter, refusing to join Chatham in 1766.

vigilant against extensions of executive authority: but he had to do his duty as an individual: he had to avoid becoming the tool of ambitious men who would obstruct wilfully.

It was not to be supposed that such conduct could be consistently maintained in practice, however general the theory. Nevertheless, as a standard of behaviour, as an objective, it was pre-eminently important. It accounts for the way politics worked: for the success of some ministers and the failure of others. It explains the paradox of the respect felt for the king's government and the distaste for active (particularly for innovating) ministers. Arthur Onslow, the greatest Speaker of the house of commons of the century, was in the autumn of 1760 preparing to retire. He was the personification of this patriotic line. He had used his voice sometimes against ministers, sometimes to flay an opposition, and yet he had retained his reputation as an impartial man above politics. This was because whenever he entered the melée he expressed the line which in their hearts men felt was the agreed patriotic one. It was characteristic of Onslow to deplore the taking of divisions because votes in the house emphasized differences, and the object of debate should be to induce ministers to follow a course universally felt to be right. The Excise Bill thirty years earlier[1] had been instinctively regarded as an undue extension of power. The cider tax, within three years of George III's accession, was felt to be another. Equally the Wilkite opposition was, at times, considered by ordinary men to be vicious and destructive of the basic minimum of courtesy necessarily extended to the royal administration. It was not easy to dragoon even those who owed their seats to influence to support for long measures which ran counter to a common feeling for the just middle course. In 1760 there was still an agreement, produced by war, that enthusiastic support should be given to the government which had fought it successfully: at the same time there was a suspicion that war ministers might fight on unnecessarily for prestige. Pitt's failure to appreciate this was a weakness in his position.

It was found more and more difficult as time went on to discover or agree on the proper middle course between tyranny and faction. When issues of principle arose they naturally produced parties and conflict. But simple country gentlemen, after half a century barren of such issues, were slow to admit it must

[1] See B. Williams, *The Whig Supremacy*, p. 182.

be so. They still sought the patriotic line and assumed it must be there. Their king agreed with them. For George III, in this as much else, shared the feelings of back-bench gentlemen. He too believed there was a simple correct course to be followed by men of good intentions. He knew his own heart to be innocent. It followed that those who opposed him were knaves. He could appeal to the past in support of his claim to make up a ministerial team as he pleased and to receive the support of independent men so long as it followed a national and patriotic policy. But he was bound to suffer disappointment because such ideas came from a settled era, while he had to rule in a period of great issues, issues on which any two men equally honest, equally independent, equally English, might arrive at diametrically opposed conclusions, and might fight one another not just for office but for the principles of their belief.[1]

The number of those who could put forward such principles and engage in such a contest for power was not great. In the small class of potential ministers there were two categories. On the one hand were the great men whose borough influence or family connexions made them political captains: in this category George III had to reckon with Newcastle, Bute, Bedford, the Grenvilles, Rockingham, Devonshire, Mr. Thynne,[2] Shelburne, Grafton, or North. These men had the outlook of commanders in affairs: the following which they derived from private influence was increased by their periods of ministerial service when they attracted a wider circle around their banners. On the other hand there were a number of able and ambitious men of smaller fortune who aspired to better themselves in political service, whether of the Crown or of a great captain: in this class were such as young Jenkinson,[3] Rigby,[4] Calcraft,[5] Edmund

---

[1] The outbreak of the war with France in 1793 produced a movement of opinion in the country which made George III more successful in representing a patriotic general will in the latter half of his reign than at its beginning. See below, p. 356.

[2] Later third Viscount Weymouth, and (in 1789) first marquess of Bath (1734–96).

[3] Charles Jenkinson, first earl of Liverpool (1727–1802), a protégé of Lord Bute and under-secretary of state in 1761; secretary to the treasury 1763–5; out of office under Rockingham, but under North rose to be secretary-at-war (1778); under Pitt president of the board of trade, chancellor of the duchy of Lancaster, and created an earl.

[4] Richard Rigby (1722–88), the manager of the duke of Bedford's parliamentary group; paymaster of the forces (1768), and died immensely rich.

[5] John Calcraft (1726–72), originally patronized by the duke of Rutland; appointed a regimental agent by Fox and made a fortune; deserted Fox for Pitt and supported the reform cause.

Burke, or John Robinson;[1] they were reinforced by the ambitious lawyers who used politics as a professional aid (such as Mansfield, Hardwicke, and Camden had done), men such as Fletcher Norton, Wedderburn, or Thurlow.[2] Men in this class did not usually aspire to the highest places, but were capable of hard work and clear administration.

All these active politicians, like the king, had to work out their struggles, manœuvres, and intrigues before the jury of independent men produced from a stable and static England. They could not defy the strong if incoherent feeling of ordinary members about proper political behaviour. If once an administration was out of sympathy with the general sense of a proper constitutional course, its days would be few and difficult. Equally once the small number of possible ministers were too deeply divided by quarrels to assemble a government on a broad enough basis to rule confidently in a suspicious house, then again chaos would follow. In the autumn of 1760, as previously, no government could survive which did not possess three pillars: the support of the king, ability to manage a government party by all the arts of patronage and flattery, and—not least important—the power to set forth a case in parliament which would at best arouse support because it was patriotic and moderate, and would at worst neutralize that latent opposition spirit upon which factious men out of place sought to play. In the autumn of 1760, however, as has been explained, ministers were at odds with one another and the king was intolerant of all political arts. As a pupil of Bute it seemed to him that there were three practical problems upon which there could be no doubt as to the correct course: the war, finance, and the personnel of government. He soon found how difficult it was to practise what Bute preached.

---

[1] John Robinson (1727–1802), secretary of the treasury (1770–82) and North's chief organizer of his supporters.

[2] For them see below, pp. 150, 151.

IV

MINISTERIAL INSTABILITY, 1760–5

OF the topics which occupied the mind of the new king in October 1760 two at least, the duration of the war and the drain on the national finances, disturbed his subjects also. It may be doubted whether many of his people were as deeply perturbed as their master by the prevalence of vice and low standards of personal integrity. But the king, as he thought, found this evident in high places. The ministers who kissed his hand were all under suspicion. Lord Bute was to keep a censorious eye upon their proceedings. The suspect team was a ragged one. Pitt, at the height of his glory, was secretary of state, a great hawk-nosed tyrant of a minister. The other secretary, Holderness, was unassuming but useful and experienced. The duke of Newcastle was first lord of the treasury, with the pushing but second-rate Legge in the office, as yet the junior office, of chancellor of the exchequer. Lord Anson controlled the admiralty and Henry Fox looked after his own investments as paymaster of the forces.[1] So far this administration had seemed to have every requirement for stability. In Pitt it had not only an organizer of victorious war but a parliamentary speaker able to excite and intimidate the country squires and so command support from the most independent. More-

[1] William Pitt (1708–78), created earl of Chatham 1766, had risen to prominence as a spokesman of the opposition to the court. Then the Pelhams had forced George II to include him in their administration in which he proved insubordinate. He had flirted with Leicester House but since the spring of 1757 he had combined with Newcastle as joint leader of the ministry.

Thomas Pelham-Holles, duke of Newcastle (1693–1768), had been in high office with only minor breaks since 1724. Since the death of his brother, Henry Pelham, he had monopolized the control of patronage but had found difficulty in choosing partners to lead the house of commons.

Henry Bilson Legge (1708–64), fourth son of the first earl of Dartmouth, was approaching the end of his third term of office as chancellor of the exchequer.

Henry Fox (1705–74), created Baron Holland 1763. A man of great parliamentary abilities who had allowed Pitt to get ahead of him in race for honour in 1756.

George Anson (1697–1762), a professional naval officer who had circumnavigated the globe in 1744; married to Lord Chancellor Hardwicke's daughter and drawn into the circle of Newcastle's friends; created Baron Anson in 1748, and became first lord of the admiralty in 1751.

over, with the great majority of people 'out of doors' (that is
with the reserve of opinion not necessarily enfranchised but
powerful as a second line of pressure on government) Pitt was
popular as a patriot and an honest man. In Newcastle the
ministry had the greatest electioneer and manipulator of personal allegiances of the century. His voluminous correspondence
testifies to his sleepless care to make friends and influence
people, his fussy pre-occupation with every member's interests
and attachments, his unwillingness ever to offend by a cold
answer to a possible supporter. It also shows his need to be
constantly reassured about political decisions and about his
health. He often appeared a figure of fun, as at the funeral of
George II, when he was equally determined to make a list of
absentees and to stand on someone else's train so that the cold
of the floor should not strike up through his feet. But behind
this superficial old-maidishness he had a shrewd mind. Opponents easily underrated him because they saw only the fuss and
missed the patient hours of labour which he devoted to politics.

These two ministers were complementary halves of a perfect
whole. And they had had full royal support. George II was as
anxious as Pitt to win the war, and more ready to forget his
personal feelings to that end. Therefore he tolerated the masterful ways of one minister and the petulance of the other. By
1758 the king had spent £2½ million of his own Hanoverian
money and borrowed £¼ million in Germany in furtherance of
a war for which Pitt became the great organizer.

But the contrast between the two ministers, though they
depended upon one another, was a source of danger. Pitt boasted
of his honesty, by which he meant a refusal to bother about the
details of holding a group together by the distribution of places;
this refusal would prove politically suicidal in normal eighteenth-
century circumstances. Newcastle saw to this mundane but vital
work. Pitt talked of using Newcastle's majority for carrying
out operations beyond Newcastle's comprehension. Naturally
Newcastle and his friends found Pitt's contemptuous use of
them aggravating. To win a war it is permissible to move armies
and assemble fleets, correspond with kings, and celebrate victory with rhetoric, while giving no thought to tomorrow's bills.
But the treasury had to think of how the bills were to be met.
Newcastle had the duty of counting the cost of operations: he
had, in consequence, his own views on European policy. Pitt

lived always on the level of splendid gestures and of clashing forces. For some years events had at last risen to his level and made his melodrama into drama, his rhetoric into the voice of a nation. Newcastle, by duty as much as by inclination, lived in the cold light of a sober day, adding up his friends and his treasury receipts anxiously, with a lifetime of practical experience. Pitt had admirers, but he had few friends in the ministry except his brother-in-law, Lord Temple. Newcastle's friends were as many as artful patronage would make them—and as unreliable.

George II had devoted himself to preventing rupture between these opposed characters because he knew both were necessary to success in the war against France and Austria. George III and Bute represented an uncertain third element in the balance of forces. George III also was a patriot, who wished to bring the war to a successful conclusion, but he was younger, more innocent, and less aware of the political dangers ahead. After four months of settling on the throne, the king decided upon minor changes in his administration. In March 1761 Bute was given a position where he could use his good influence officially. He displaced Holderness as secretary of state and became Pitt's twin; Barrington replaced Legge at the exchequer and then in April Halifax became lord-lieutenant of Ireland.[1] There was no outcry of ministers against this move. It was a natural one. It was desirable, in everyone's eyes, that the king's personal adviser should have an official status and be brought fully into co-operation with other ministers. Nor was Bute an unnatural choice for high office, quite apart from his friendship with the king.

Lord Bute was then forty-eight years old. As a connexion of the duke of Argyll he had been a Scottish representative peer from 1737 to 1741. Then he had spent ten years in obscurity, devoting himself to botany and to his family, a man with a cultivated mind and a well-turned leg.[2] But by making a fourth

---

[1] William Wildman Barrington, second Viscount Barrington (1717–93), a privy councillor since 1755; secretary at war 1765–78 and therefore notorious for his share in the loss of the American colonies.

George Montagu Dunk, second earl of Halifax (1716–71), had made his reputation while president of the board of trade (since 1748) by extending American commerce. For his less happy subsequent career see narrative that follows.

[2] His interest in letters was later to be shown by his securing a pension for Dr. Johnson: the development of Kew Gardens was to owe much to his direction of George III's attention.

at cards when rain stopped a cricket match in which the prince of Wales was engaged, he edged into court favour. When Frederic, prince of Wales, suddenly died in 1751 Bute became the mainstay of the fatherless family. But it was not royal favour alone, nor one death only, which made Bute a leading politician. The death of the duke of Argyll in 1761 left the Scottish interest of forty-five members of parliament and sixteen peers (which was always well organized and almost invariably in support of the existing government)[1] to Bute's command as a family inheritance, for the Argyll heir was 'non-political'. Moreover Bute had married Mary Wortley Montagu in 1736. She was the daughter of the miserly Edward Wortley Montagu who by 1761 had amassed a fortune of £1½ million, mostly from his ownership of coalfields, and who in 1761 died leaving his daughter a life interest in this treasure. Of this Bute therefore had the control.[2] In addition, in August 1761 his daughter Mary married Sir James Lowther, who devoted some of his great fortune and much of his time to collecting parliamentary boroughs as a hobby; he certainly could count upon three seats at this time and later had the reputation of controlling nine. This gave Bute the opportunity to add an English group to his Scottish vote. Thus in the course of a year Lord Bute had emerged from the seclusion of the heir's court to stand forth as a parliamentary group leader in his hereditary right, with the beginnings of a family connexion in the commons, and with sufficient wealth to undertake the expensive role of electioneer on Newcastle's scale. If he had desired to push these claims no set of politicians could have ignored his claim to office. Crowning all, the accession of George III had given him the warmest support of the king. No politician of the century had more trumps suddenly thrust into his hand. None showed less character in playing them.

Though his natural right to a secretaryship of state had to be admitted, his activities would inevitably be watched with anxiety by the uneasy allies, Pitt and Newcastle. Pitt was willing

---

[1] For the reasons for this, and for discussion of Scotland generally, see below, pp. 280 f.

[2] Lady Mary's brother Edward had been disinherited by his father for excesses, bizarre even for the eighteenth century. They included sporting buckles and buttons worth £2,500, wearing a wire wig, becoming a Mohammedan, marrying first a lady of easy virtue and then a Nubian, and having to run to escape jail in Paris. In 1776 Edward Montagu, anxious to provide an heir to the money so long in his sister's care, but short of time and energy, advertised in Italy for a pregnant bride. This nefarious plot was ruined by his death from choking on a chicken bone.

to make a parade of elaborate courtesy, provided he was left with the control of the war. Newcastle was worried that applicants for favours might seek the new power rather than himself: as usual he fretted jealously about trifles, for his whole system depended upon a multitude of trifling attentions.

That spring and summer of 1761, however, the government still seemed outwardly stable. Bute and George III were at one with the old hands in saying that the war must be won. They agreed that to achieve this the allies must be kept in good heart. The subsidy to Prussia, of just over £600,000, had therefore to be continued. Pitt was left in control of operations. As for Newcastle, he complained that he was allowed no secret service money for conducting the general election in March 1761. But the election was fought in much the usual way, by bargains mostly directed towards settling the representation of boroughs without the expense of a contest. And Newcastle shared in the arrangements. Lord Bute took part in discussions of electoral manœuvre, as many another of Newcastle's colleagues had done, but the old man was not dislodged from the centre of the web. As a result there were rather fewer contests than usual and the new parliament was very like its predecessor.[1]

Nevertheless in these early months of the reign there was growing a feeling, of which ministers could not be unaware, that it would not be enough to continue policy as in 1759. In 1760 Mauduit's[2] book *Considerations on the War* had achieved some success by pointing out the ruinous cost of the war in Europe and by arguing that only the colonial war could ever show a profit to this country. The king was sincere in his argument that the war must be pushed through to final victory. But many felt that that was already won. Those who disliked entanglement in Europe could point to gains in India, the West Indies, and America as evidence of victory. The confused situation of the fighting in Europe was no concern of England, though it might matter to Hanover.[3] It was evident that the king himself inclined to this way of thinking: that was why, in

[1] The price of a seat had risen somewhat, to £2,000, in the usual private bargaining between aspirants and borough owners. Sir L. Namier, *Structure of Politics at the Accession of George III* (2nd ed.), p. 164.

[2] Israel Mauduit (1708–87), a woollen draper who became agent for Massachusetts in England in addition to preaching in protestant chapels and pamphleteering.

[3] For a detailed account of the military events of the years 1760–3 see the narrative already published in B. Williams, *The Whig Supremacy* (O.H.E. vol. xi), pp. 343–52.

his speech from the throne, he laid emphasis upon being born and educated in Britain and upon his 'glory in the name of Britain'. It meant that he did not care much for Europe or for Hanover, that he belonged to the school of thought (from which Pitt was reckoned a deserter) which put overseas interests above the continent of Europe. More than twenty years later he was of the same opinions: 'I would wish if possible to be rid of Gibraltar and to have as much possession in the West Indies as possible.'[1] From such a viewpoint it did seem that England had won all that mattered to her and only remained under arms for the sake of continental friends. Here the question of the cost became all-important. All the ministers, except perhaps Pitt, were conscious of a growing intolerance of war burdens. They all agreed that peace was desirable. But how urgently peace was needed, what sacrifices they would make for it, what could consolidate victory, all these were questions on which there was disagreement. In the cabinet there was a dispute whether a reference in the king's speech to our desire for victorious peace should be accompanied by a reference to an 'expensive and bloody war' or to an 'expensive but just and necessary war'.

In the previous reign the average annual supplies which had to be raised were about £6½ million. In 1754-5 the figure had been as low as £4 million. By 1759, owing to the war, the year's bill was £12¾ million. In 1760 the amount to be raised was £15½ million and in 1761 £19½ million. An annual charge risen to more than three times the pre-war level was frightening to ordinary members and frightening to Newcastle. Moreover, it revealed the weakness of the financial structure of the country. There was no elasticity in the revenue collecting system. The normal method of dealing with war was to increase the land tax to the 4s. level: as every 1s. of the land tax, on its stereotyped quotas, produced £½ million, this meant a yield of £2 million. In 1761 £2 million was raised from the land tax, £4¾ million from the normal taxes and customs; the yield of the new 3s. a barrel tax on beer was a matter for speculation: £12 million had to be found in annuities, that is by borrowing. What clearly was needed was a new and large source of revenue. The increased trading wealth of the country was not being efficiently tapped to supply the national exchequer. Ever since 1755 Newcastle had been collecting schemes from advisers, inside the

[1] *Letters of George III*, ed. Fortescue, vi. 183, 11 Dec. 1782.

office and out, for new taxes on this and that. But the fatal fear of eighteenth-century governments of offending a public known to be suspicious of all innovation made Newcastle draw back from the dangers of any proposal radical enough to make a real difference. Public feeling was that a 4s. land tax had gone on long enough: the reception of new taxes would have been stormy. So Newcastle relied upon the miserable expedient of increasing the national debt. It seemed to follow from all this that the only course was to make peace quickly before the country was ruined by victorious war. With the consent of all ministers peace negotiations with France, begun in 1759, were resumed at Augsburg.

Pitt, though assenting to the desires of his colleagues, was more concerned with the conduct of operations. The capture of Belle Isle, off the French coast, was some compensation for a miserable year in Germany. There Frederic the Great was at his lowest point. The invading Russians occupied Pomerania and Prussia seemed on the point of extinction. Against this dark picture could be contrasted the bright colonial prospect. For in 1761 the French station of Pondicherry in India was captured, Dominica in the West Indies was taken, and the Cherokee Indians on the American mainland were forced to submit. In negotiations with France, therefore, it was agreed, as a basis for peace, that each power should hold those colonial territories of which it was actually in effective possession at the moment. At first the only hitch in the conversations seemed to be the French proposal that all captures made by the British at sea before the formal declaration of war should be returned. The negotiations took a less happy turn in July 1761 when the French, to settle all outstanding dangers to a peace settlement, urged that British disagreements with Spain (as yet a neutral) should be discussed and settled at the same time and embodied in the same general pacification. This was unacceptable and in September the peace talks were broken off.

These events abroad, however, had made active the latent disputes among members of the cabinet. Pitt had agreed that peace was desirable but emphasized that it was to be peace with complete victory. He now believed that the French, while widening the gap between Britain and her ally Prussia (though Frederic at this stage in desperation approved of the negotiations), were intriguing to bring Spain actively into the conflict as their ally. He favoured fighting more vigorously to bring the war to a better end. He was already a convert to the need to have a vigorous effort in Europe to prosper the fighting overseas. He now favoured extending the war by an attack upon Spain. Intercepted letters left him in no doubt that war with Spain was inevitable. He wanted to take the initiative, to capture the treasure fleet sailing from the River Plate and to cut the connexion between Spain and her colonies. So he would open up new areas for colonial conquest. Newcastle disliked this renewal of Pitt's money-no-object strategy. He did not dare contemplate an extension of so expensive a war. He was not convinced that, whatever their eventual advantages, he could afford to embark upon further conquests in the New World. On the other hand he resisted the peace-at-any-price arguments of those who supported the duke of Bedford. Newcastle was convinced that firm friends on the continent were necessary. He would favour support of Prussia and care for Hanover, therefore, until general peace could be made. He was in a middle position between the extreme peace and economy party and that of Pitt. Lord Bute was equally firm against Pitt's heroic measures and not far from Newcastle's position. Pitt, unable to endure contradiction, resigned in disgust on 5 October 1761.

Pitt's fall from power was not the work of the king. It was caused by a disagreement on policy with colleagues, old as well as new, and by his own imperious attitude. The most that can be said for the king's responsibility is that he had little love for Pitt and little appreciation of the consequences of his retirement. He therefore failed to make the efforts to conciliate the minister which prudence would have counselled. On his retirement Pitt's services were marked by the grant of £3,000 a year and by his wife's becoming a baroness. He carried with him out of office only his brother-in-law Earl Temple. His other brother-in-law, George Grenville, remained in place and rose in importance; Egremont[1] (whose sister married George Grenville) succeeded as secretary of state. Pitt therefore did not even carry

---

[1] Charles Wyndham, second earl of Egremont (1710–63), came of a Somerset family which had long retained their tory sympathies for the house of Stuart.

Richard Temple Grenville (1711–79) succeeded to his mother's peerage in 1752; lord privy seal since 1757; lord-lieutenant of Buckinghamshire and chief of a political group which included his brother George.

George Grenville (1712–70) was treasurer of the navy and was now drawn into cabinet discussions. His subsequent career appears in the narrative below.

with him the group with which he was connected by marriage. Nevertheless his loss was a threat to the future of the government. He was a past master of the art of playing upon the feelings of independent men in the house and of riding upon popular excitement outside it. The trust which he had won in such circles by his remarkable cleanhandedness he had reinforced as an architect of victory. His personal glory was worth more in the house of commons than an organized *bloc* of votes; his eloquence, his record, and his conviction of his own superior talents, were a force of which any administration might be afraid.

The new parliament met a month later. Newcastle showed no sign of grief at the loss of Pitt. On the contrary, in his summons to friends to meet him at the Cockpit the night before the first day of the session, he bade them 'show their strength in support of the King and the present administration': his disputes with Bute about such points as the lord lieutenancy of Shropshire had not yet reached any point of crisis. Nor did the king's speech show any weakening of resolve to pursue peace through honourable victory. But ammunition for Pitt was in the making. The earl of Bristol had been negotiating in Madrid about Anglo-Spanish differences.[1] Richard Wall, the Spanish minister of foreign affairs, had proposed to submit points of difference to the arbitration of France, a power with whom England was at war. The suggestion of such a referee was taken as a sign of hostility. It was followed by rumours of the signature of an alliance of France and Spain. Upon Spain's refusal to deny her compact with the enemy, Bristol left Madrid in December and on 4 January 1762 war was declared against Spain. Thus what Pitt had advocated had come to pass, with this difference that a chance of taking the initiative and of seizing the treasure fleet had been lost.

Ministers were encouraged, however, by further colonial successes in 1762. In January an expedition took the French West Indian island of Martinique and this was followed by the seizure of Grenada and the Grenadines, St. Lucia, St. Vincent, and Tobago. In June the French took St. John's, Newfoundland,

---

[1] George William Hervey, second earl of Bristol (1721-75), envoy to Turin, 1755-8; ambassador extraordinary to Spain, 1758-61; later lord privy seal in the Grafton administration, 1768.

but this was promptly recaptured. In August Havana was taken from Spain. In October an expedition fitted out at Madras forced the Spanish Philippines garrison at Manila to surrender. The extension of the war, even if half-heartedly undertaken, could be said to have been profitably pursued and bargaining power increased. Meanwhile the general dislike of the European war had been heightened by fresh complications arising in that theatre. It was with great difficulty that Brigadier-General John Burgoyne[1] finally foiled the Spanish attack upon Portugal; it was an undramatic and tedious campaign by which Prince Ferdinand of Brunswick re-established his hold upon most of Hesse.

A dramatic change of fortune in Europe was the death of the Czarina Elizabeth of Russia on 5 January 1762. Her successor Peter III (from Holstein) was a German enthusiast. In February he declared that Russia intended to return all the conquests she had made in the war. In March he suspended hostilities against Prussia. In May, such was his devotion to the great Frederic, he agreed to help Prussia expel the Austrians—so recently Russia's close allies—from Silesia. This happy turn of events took Prussia from desperation to opportunity. However, in July Catherine the Great overthrew her husband Peter and assumed power. But while she promptly countermanded the scheme of fighting alongside the Prussians yet she did not return to co-operation with Austria. Russia kept to an armistice with Prussia, restoring posts previously conquered, and seemed content with an enigmatic isolation.

These events, on the face of them, seem likely to rejoice British hearts. In fact they produced a divergence of views between Prussia and Britain and consequently brought into prominence the differences in the government with regard to this alliance and to the war in Europe generally. The general feeling of ministers was that the Russian somersault made peace more easily obtainable because Prussia could enter negotiations on a firmer footing. Why should they not profit by the dismay of

[1] John Burgoyne (1722–92) was a man of most various talents who has the misfortune to be remembered chiefly for the disaster of his surrender at Saratoga during the American war. He was both a soldier of ideas who frequently clashed with his superiors and an active politician who took a leading part in attacking corruption in Indian affairs. He was also a playwright. With his wife Charlotte (the daughter of the earl of Derby), with whom he had eloped, he was prominent in social and artistic circles in London.

Austria to clinch a bargain? They might restore the *status quo ante bellum* in Europe and retain all colonial acquisitions. It was natural that this should be the British view. It was equally natural that Prussia should not share it. After six years of frantic efforts, after the devastation of her territory and the impoverishment of her people, Frederic's Prussia must regard a restoration of a territorial *status quo* as the equivalent of defeat. Frederic saw in Russian changes an opportunity to fight the war with renewed activity and to win victories which should compensate for past losses. There was a world of difference between the views of a power which had conquered sub-continents and wanted to relax, and one which had only just kept a footing on its own soil and which still needed to conquer. Thus the peace party in England was strengthened at the very time when Prussia ceased to contemplate a cessation of hostilities.

This inevitable divergence was made worse each week by minor quarrels and instances of lack of trust. Frederic negotiated with the Russians behind the back of his British ally. His complaint, later, of British duplicity in keeping him in the dark about arrangements with his foes was matched by the equally valid, though less well publicized, complaints of Bute that Prussia had deserted Britain for an alliance against her interests. In return for Russian aid against Austria, Frederic was prepared to support an attack upon Denmark on the Schleswig-Holstein issue. Britain had no particular love for Denmark, which had shown itself rather pro-French, though nominally maintaining neutrality. But Denmark's integrity had been guaranteed, while she remained neutral, in return for a guarantee that Bremen and Verden should not be wrenched from Hanover. Behind this legal point was a more substantial one. Britain, thinking of her naval stores, was bound to oppose the plans of any power capable of dominating the whole of the Baltic. In the past she had worked with Russia against Sweden. It was a recognition of a changed balance of force which now made some statesmen apprehensive of Russian designs in the area.

It is true that Frederic might argue that Britain was at war with France, Spain, and Austria but not with Russia, and that therefore he had a right to make his own terms with her. But the same argument applied to Britain's negotiations with France, for with her Prussia was not formally at war. In each case the answer was the same: such negotiations were bound to affect the course of the war, the relations of both powers with the common enemy Austria, and their own security and alliance. It is difficult to see how the contrary aims of Prussia and Britain could have been reconciled. Perhaps an alliance of Prussia, Russia, and Britain to reduce France and Austria to submission, followed by common action by Prussia and Britain against Russia, would have been the ideal course from a British point of view. But Frederic would legitimately have refused to be made use of in such a way when he could derive greater advantage from monopolizing Russian friendship. Moreover, even if Peter would have joined in such an action, Catherine certainly would not, for her eyes were on Poland and Turkey. The situation by May 1762 was therefore extremely difficult. It was clear that Prussia would not willingly end the European war as Britain desired.

It was argued by George Grenville, who was already making himself felt as a preacher of economy, that to renew the treaty with Prussia and to pay her a subsidy was worse than a waste of money; it was to give Prussia the means of doing what was most disliked, extending the war. Newcastle for his part had let it be known to the Austrian court that he was so set upon peace with her that he could contemplate her taking Silesia back from Prussia. This, of course, gave Frederic a further source of complaint; it was certainly foolish in that it could not but give encouragement to the Austrian war party. Newcastle grumbled about Prussian bellicosity yet he believed the subsidy must be renewed. He held it to be a cardinal point of policy, essential to the colonial struggle with France as well as to general security, that Britain must have a point of strength, an ally against the French, in Europe. Until there could be a change back to the system of the 1740's, that is to the Austrian alliance, ties must be kept with Prussia, even with a self-willed and recalcitrant Prussia, to avoid isolation. On this issue Newcastle was defeated by George Grenville both in debate in the cabinet and in the struggle for the king's ear. On the crucial issue of whether, in the spring of 1762, a vote of credit for £2 million or £1 million was needed (the difference being the cost of maintaining subsidies), Newcastle and Devonshire[1] alone argued in the cabinet for the higher figure. Lord Mansfield, with typical lack of fighting spirit, was silent. The rest all opposed.

[1] William Cavendish, fourth duke of Devonshire (1720-64), had been lord-

Newcastle was already on edge because he thought those who sought favours were going to Bute rather than to himself. Now, on this vital financial point, he found that not only his ministerial colleagues but two working members of his own treasury board, Messrs. Elliot and Oswald, opposed him. This was rebellion in his own department. He declared that he and George Grenville 'cannot jointly have the conduct of the Treasury'. From 7 May he was offering his resignation, and on 26 May 1762 it was accepted and announced. The second of the twin pillars of the ministry in power at George's accession was removed. It may be that Newcastle hoped that his resignation would not be accepted and that his strong action would enable him to coerce his colleagues. But George III was no hypocrite and could not disguise his relief that Newcastle should go. Both the tyrannical and the corrupting minister had now been removed from among his servants. Yet it is clear that George III had not removed them, though he constitutionally might have done: he had failed to support them when, separately, they fell foul of their colleagues on major issues of policy.

Newcastle did not intend his departure to be final or to sever his links of more than twenty years with the controlling of business and the organization of the supporters of government. He hoped his friends would continue in office, supply him with information and would, both by tactful advocacy and by showing themselves difficult on his account, finally draw him back into place again. Bute now became first lord of the treasury and George Grenville the new secretary of state. But there was no trust between them. The king advised that Grenville should be 'narrowly watch'd and sifted' for perhaps he had upset Newcastle for his own purposes. Bute was so unhappy trying to replace Barrington as chancellor of the exchequer at this time of personal intrigues that he fell ill of nervous exhaustion.

The way should now have been clear for a more united cabinet to take a firmer line with Prussia and to make peace. The subsidy indeed was dropped but this did not dispose of the European problem. For Grenville now held out for higher peace demands than Bute believed possible. Bute was so irritated

lieutenant of Ireland in 1755 and partner of Pitt in the short-lived administration of 1756–7. He was now lord chamberlain.

with Prussia that he was only willing to stipulate that France should evacuate the Rhenish provinces, leaving a vacuum into which either Prussia or Austria—who might still be at war— might enter. Grenville contended that the French evacuation must be so arranged that Prussia should be able to safeguard her security by denying them to Austria. Bute and Egremont nego- tiated with France, behind the backs of their colleagues, on the basis of concluding peace with France while leaving all Spanish questions on one side. On 26 July 1762 Bute suffered the humi- liation of being in a minority of one in the cabinet, for Egremont deserted him on this question. The capture of Havana only intensified ministerial difficulties. Whereas Bute believed this might be exchanged for Florida, George Grenville, Egremont, and Charles Townshend[1] all argued that they must have Porto Rico as well.

Discord among ministers was made more feverish by their fear of their opponents in parliament. For while the inarticulate majority of the country ardently desired peace, and ministerial policy had therefore great potential support, there were now two great politicians anxious to pick holes in any settlement which was made. So great had been success in war that any treaty could be made to seem unworthy of the efforts. Ministers trembled to find how little sympathy they could command in influential political circles. In the effort to meet criticism in advance and to escape responsibility, ministers manœuvred against one another. For the same reason it seemed likely any time between May and October of 1762 that Newcastle might be brought back into place again.

Almost as soon as Newcastle had retired there was talk of his return. In June he was unable to decide whether he would oppose or not. He was aware of the common feeling that opposition, if formed and personal, was a dirty game: so 'I would not put it into the power of any man living to say I intended opposition'.[2] On the other hand, if it was known he would not oppose, how could he be of sufficient nuisance value to blackmail the king into taking him back again? Once he had declared that he would not oppose then 'my lord Bute's next

[1] Charles Townshend (1725-67), the son of the third viscount Townshend, was at this time secretary at war. He was soon to earn a reputation of brilliance by always doing the opposite of what was expected of him and of what, for that matter, was sensible.

[2] Sir L. Namier, *England in the Age of American Revolution*, p. 387.

levée would be twice as full as any he had yet had'. Newcastle was caught between the conventional decencies and the practical necessities of the politics of that age. The government feared that the king's uncle, the duke of Cumberland, would make opposition respectable by giving it his patronage, and make it formidable by bringing Pitt and Newcastle together under his wing. Pitt rendered that impossible. At Bath for the waters in July he let it be known that he scorned Newcastle personally and did not understand his views.

Nevertheless, in their fear of an opposition onslaught ministers hesitated and bickered. In July Bute made overtures to Newcastle in order to rid himself of dependence upon George Grenville, and because he hoped Newcastle would support his pacific attitude. In September George Grenville, in his turn, was believed to be in favour of bringing Pitt into the administration to support his own views on the peace and to defend the treaty in parliament. In October Halifax and Egremont were actively engaged in coaxing Newcastle back into office. All such flirtations with the two ex-ministers were bound to fail. Pitt would not join with men who had thwarted him to help them patch up a peace he thought botched. Newcastle often appeared to be wavering and in his worried way enjoyed being courted, but he wanted power without making himself responsible for the peace and so becoming a target for Pitt's thunderbolts. In addition he did not want to share power and patronage with anyone. He had therefore none of the qualities necessary in an ally in face of attack.

It was clear in such circumstances what Bute had to do. He had to demonstrate how strongly based was the government, on the support both of the king and of all independent men desiring immediate peace. For this he had to publicize his case and organize its presentation in parliament. The former was attempted through the press. But Smollett's *True Briton* was hardly a match for the invective of Wilkes's *North Briton*.[1] The

---

[1] Tobias George Smollett (1721–71), a surgeon turned novelist and journalist. His novels (particularly *Roderick Random*, 1748, *Peregrine Pickle*, 1751 and *Humphrey Clinker*, 1771) have a coarse vigour in the picaresque style which won him fame. The same qualities in his journalism earned him imprisonment for libel.

John Wilkes (1727–97) had so far been notorious for his dissipation in such circles as the fraternity of Medmenham Abbey. Under Lord Temple's patronage he was now entering on the extraordinary career which appears in the narrative below, particularly pp. 98 f.

organization of support in the house, in defiance of Newcastle, demanded a great deal of care for very small details, as well as a groundwork of extensive information about members' tastes, local difficulties, and relations one with another. Here the administration had been weak since Newcastle left. Bute and his brother-in-law, Stuart Mackenzie, did keep account of Scottish affairs and were competent to manage that vote. But none of the ministers, not Bute, nor Halifax, nor Grenville, nor Egremont, possessed enough experience to make full use of the power they had in England. They dealt perforce with little men who were creatures of Newcastle and could not discipline them for lack of knowledge of their local rivals. Moreover, they suffered from the dispersal of authority among themselves. There was no minister with the power of a manager-in-chief of patronage and personnel. Perhaps also Bute and George III handicapped themselves by being loath to admit that the grubbing methods of Newcastle were necessary. But by October 1762 they were convinced that even the best causes need organized exposition. On 13 October Henry Fox was made the leader of the court party in the house of commons. He had both the knowledge and the taste to counter Newcastle: in his very different style he could even make a speech to answer Pitt.

Henry Fox knew his own drawbacks. With the country gentlemen, as with the king, his reputation was not good. George and the gentry thought him an evil, covetous man. So he was not advanced in official position. He remained in his lucrative but minor post of paymaster while managing the house; it was no part of Bute's plan to gain professional politicians' support at the cost of that of the back-benchers. It was desirable not 'to scare the Tories'. At the same time as a master of tactics was appointed the high command in the cabinet was reorganized. George Grenville was demoted to the admiralty as well as losing the lead in the commons. Halifax took his place as secretary. Even so Bute was not complete master, for Halifax supported Grenville's ideas about the peace and continued to scheme to bring in Newcastle to co-operate with Fox. Nevertheless, there was a new air of business in the management of affairs. Fox had formerly been attached to the duke of Cumberland. Now that Cumberland was opposing the peace Fox left him. Not content with that he detached others from that camp. Lord Sandwich had control of three members of parliament but was financially embarrassed.[1] He now took the job of ambassador to Spain, explaining to Cumberland that he was forced to do so because 'my affairs being in the most confused condition . . . I could never have any peace of mind if I was to throw away the means of making some reparation to the family, for the damage they have suffered from my indiscretions'.[2]

In other words he needed the salary and allowances which came from an official post. It was not bribery except in the sense that power and position are always a bribe to the ambitious. It may serve as one example of Fox's political management. Another is his letter to Sandwich asking him to arrange for Mr. Major, Mr. Henniker, and Mr. Stephenson (all merchants and all members of parliament) to come and talk to him: also Lord Clive was to be approached for 'I am told Lord Clive's great love to the D[uke] of D[evonshire] is new and not fix'd. To your Excellency it is neither new nor weak. And I hear the whole family were, not long ago, vastly pleased with a letter Lord Bute wrote to his Lordship'.[3] The three merchants were gained for the court: Lord Clive was not, for the proposed settlement of India did not satisfy him. But he made it clear that once this was out of the way he was ambitious to serve and be honoured. Fox in all this was quite simply taking trouble about personal relations which had been neglected for the past six months. He was removing obstacles which might have come between the minister and public opinion, not creating that opinion.

Newcastle was now in a very difficult position. All through the summer he had continued to debate whether he should oppose or be reconciled. If he was to be feared he must fight against the peace terms. But the duke of Devonshire reminded him, as a candid friend, that he had been a most pacific counsellor in office and had joined in ejecting Pitt. How could he now play the part of a glory-seeker? Was it possible, apart from consistency, to fly in the face of a general desire for speedy peace without destroying his own group? 'I find people in general',

---

[1] John Montagu, fourth earl of Sandwich (1718–92), had already had important military posts and had had an important period of office as first lord of the admiralty. As will appear in the narrative his real administrative talents have been obscured by the misfortunes of the American war.

[2] Namier, quoting Sandwich MSS., *Structure of Politics on the Accession of George III*, p. 355, 10 Nov. 1762.

[3] Namier, *Structure*, p. 355, 12 Nov. 1762.

his friend Hardwicke told him in November, 'even our most
particular friends, most inclined to peace . . . you instructed
them that it was absolutely necessary.' The king himself
accused him of contradicting his previous advice. It was true
that the king's reproaches were blunted by his confusing the
Ganges with the Mississippi, but Newcastle, even so, was put on
the defensive. He could only deny that he had ever been in
favour of letting Santa Lucia be returned. Such a line of argument would not impress the back-benchers. Moreover, he had
now no one of leading rank to put his case, whatever it was, in
the house of commons. It would not be enough to hold his
professional politicians together if their case could not be
authoritatively expounded in debate. The great figure in a
commons debate would be Pitt. Newcastle had no mind to lend
his organization to serve the purpose of Pitt's advancement.
His position was thus hopelessly self-contradictory. Threatening
a fight he still hoped to recover the king's favour, while yet
again he hoped to avoid responsibility for the king's peace
policy. Unwilling to share authority he yet felt the need of a
collaborator in the commons. The policy which was to be
attacked was largely that which he had helped to frame.

By the end of October 1762 the duke of Bedford,[1] as chief of
the British negotiators, had concluded preliminaries of peace
with the French. It was decided to force those of Newcastle's
friends who remained in office to declare themselves for or
against them. It was hoped to associate as many as possible of
the leading public men in responsibility for the peace which
was to go before parliament. So the duke of Devonshire was
summoned to attend the privy council. On his declining to
attend he was insultingly put out of his office of Chamberlain.
Henry Fox, characteristically, approved of the ejection of this
prominent follower of Newcastle while regretting the manner
in which it had been done. Lord Hardwicke[2] followed Devonshire into retirement. As Bute had shown his teeth Newcastle
was forced to fight. He reversed his advice to his more important friends: instead of remaining they were to resign and so
make the court feel his displeasure. He lamented the incon-

[1] John Russell, fourth duke of Bedford (1710–71), had been associated with the
opposition in the previous reign but had become lord privy seal in 1761. As will
appear, however, he had not the temperament for outstanding success in politics.

[2] Philip Yorke (1690–1764), first earl of Hardwicke, the great lord chancellor
(see above, p. 57) who had for years been Newcastle's counsellor and friend.

stancy of those who, like Lord Powis and the Shropshire group, which he had specially favoured, refused to come into the wilderness to gratify him. The ambitious sons of Newcastle's most faithful Hardwicke would not come out. Thinking of their careers in the law they would not offend the court and lose places for a speculative investment in the favour of the old and erratic duke. Even his nephew and heir Lord Lincoln tried to make apologies to the court while he grudgingly did as he was bid by Newcastle. This, clearly, was nothing like a resignation by a modern political party. George III was right to think it a factious game, a personal squabble among the leading politicians of whig views and ministerial calibre. No matter how much Newcastle tried to inflate the issue it remained simply whether the offence given to Devonshire, after he had been an absentee servant, should be resented. So the defections from Newcastle were numerous. Notably the marquis of Granby, the popular commander in the wars.[1] and his father the duke of Rutland, refused to desert the court. By December 1762 when the Preliminaries of Peace came before parliament for approval, it was clear that Bute and Fox had defeated the plot against them, at least as far as the leading politicians were concerned.

The signing of peace preliminaries by French and English plenipotentiaries had forced Prussia and Austria to conclude peace also on the basis of the *status quo* of 1756. But for England the terms of the peace arranged at the end of 1762 (and finally proclaimed in March 1763) were a recognition of victory, even if some people were disappointed in the gains. Great Britain gained from France the entire province of Canada, all Louisiana east of the Mississippi river, Cape Breton, and all the islands in the St. Lawrence. The French retained fishing rights in the St. Lawrence with the islands of St. Pierre and Miquelon as a base. In the West Indies Britain gained Tobago, Dominica, St. Vincent and the Grenadines, but returned Guadaloupe, Martinique, Mariegalante, Desirade, and St. Lucia, to France. On the African coast Senegal was retained and Goree returned. In India all French factories, that is trading stations, were restored to her on the condition that she, in effect, admitted the supremacy of the British East India Company; for France was not to fortify

---

[1] John Manners, marquis of Granby (1721–70), whose military exploits are still remembered on many inn signs; he succeeded Earl Ligonier as master general of the ordnance.

any point in Bengal, and was to recognize the British-supported rulers in the Carnatic and the Deccan. The eclipse of France as an expansionist power in India was complete and final. Britain was given back Minorca in exchange for Belle Isle, thus keeping her base in the western Mediterranean. France was to demilitarize Dunkirk. Spain was to restore to Portugal all conquests and to cede east and west Florida to Britain. Farther south, the attack upon Buenos Aires having ended in disaster, Britain asked only for the right to cut wood in Honduras, making no military installations. In return for all this Havana and other conquests were restored.

There were several lines of attack upon these peace terms. There were those who felt that it was a bad bargain to take Canada and return Guadeloupe. In the first place, Canada was not a great market for Britain nor a supplier of goods she needed to import, as were the West Indies. Canada involved the expense and nuisance of government without the profits of trade. A further extremely acute criticism was made by the duke of Bedford. It was only the fear of the French to the north and west of our New England colonies which had made the colonists amenable to any sort of control. The removal of the French administration from Canada would therefore increase the chances of American revolt: his aim would rather have been to master, without removing, the French menace in the New World. France gained more from her sugar plantations than from her fur trade. Guadeloupe was therefore on two further counts preferable to Canada as an acquisition. On the other hand, West Indian interests, vocal in the house of commons, were on the whole against the acquisition of any more French sugar plantations, for this meant bringing them inside the protective fence and into competition with the old possessions. But whatever the arguments, it was not in any case really practicable, politically, to prefer Guadeloupe to Canada. No event has probably ever been more celebrated on canvas than Wolfe's capture of Quebec. Wolfe died in every style from the classical to the naturalistic to suit all tastes and rouse one general emotion. The conquest of a whole province had impressed the public imagination. Pitt talked of 'winning Canada on the banks of the Elbe' as the summary and justification of his whole career. Canada was, superficially at least, one of the major causes of the whole war. Bute and Halifax were bound to exhibit an annexed Canada as their major trophy of peace.

Another way of criticizing the peace was for its manner rather than its substance. Pitt accused Bute of sacrificing imponderables, the future security of this country based upon the friendship of other powers. Prussia, it was contended, had been antagonized without the compensation of a reconciliation with Austria; the continued hostility of both France and Spain must assuredly be expected. It was no profit to this country to gain new worlds but lose every friend in the old. In any future struggle every power would be against her. As a description of the position this was not far wide of the truth. A lack of European allies was to weaken the English position for the next thirty years. But the break in the Prussian alliance had arisen from a real divergence of aims. At the most Bute had by gaucheries exacerbated sore places which were there already. The continuance of isolation was the result of the recrudescence of the Polish question and of French astuteness, not of any failings of King George's ministers.[1] For a popular cry against the peace it was more effective simply to complain in the most broad and general terms that it was not glorious or grasping enough. Once more this was an emotion which Pitt could best exploit. Before public opinion he stood as the hero who had achieved miracles in turning a mismanaged war into a string of victories. At the height of the triumph he had been jostled to the back. Lesser men, it might be, had proved incapable of turning his conquests into the solid coin of peace at the best rate of exchange. However difficult it was to substantiate such a claim when the splendid gains of 1762–3 were analysed in detail, the acknowledged greatness of Pitt moved men towards at least a suspension of their critical faculties and a feeling that he might miraculously be right. It was certainly true that peace had been made by those who had not disguised their avidity for it.

Yet all such arguments collapsed before the general feeling that immediate peace was a financial necessity. Of the support of ordinary members the court had always been sure, provided they were not left leaderless to be confused by Newcastle's machinations. It is important not to exaggerate what Henry Fox had done. There is no evidence of bribery or intimidation being used to persuade members to support the peace. Histo-

[1] On this see below, particularly p. 108.

rians have repeated stories of corruption which rest on nothing but falsehoods put out by disgruntled opposition groups. The truth was that Pitt and Newcastle had let themselves appear less single-minded in the pursuit of peace than their opponents. Pitt took pains in his speech on the preliminaries to declare that he had 'no connection with others'. This was a bid for independent sympathy by a denial of factious scheming. But it condemned Newcastle, by implication, as a plotter. If he was a plotter, he was an inefficient one. Charles Townshend,[1] who had been thought most likely to give a lead to Newcastle's friends, did not himself oppose the preliminaries. His friends therefore opposed without being able to clear themselves of inconsistency. The vote in favour of the peace was 319 against 65, a very large attendance and division because country gentlemen hurried up to town to rejoice that there was peace, and a glorious one, at last. Pitt could bide his time. Newcastle's friends had been led, or allowed to drift, into the position of being found guilty of going against the general patriotic line of the country. It was bad to swim against the current: it was worse to do so on several different courses.

At Christmas 1762, therefore, Bute was strengthened in his control of the career politicians by his victory in parliament. It was to profit by a success and not to gain it, that it was next decided to remedy the indiscipline within the executive. Those who opposed the king's government while holding places at pleasure were given the choice either of giving loyal service in future or of losing their profitable jobs. In high place one may select as an example Thomas Robinson, M.P., the son of Lord Grantham, who was holding the sinecure position of secretary of the defunct Augsburg congress: though this was not likely to meet again, Robinson still drew his salary of £2,800 a year. He had voted against the peace preliminaries. He therefore lost his sinecure. The noted Newcastle manager John Roberts[2] similarly was deprived of his sinecure post of inspector of the accounts of the collectors at the out-ports. It was even more serious for Newcastle when the attack was switched on to his more lowly placed agents in the customs, excise, land tax receipts, surveyor's office, audit, stamps, salt, and alienation offices.

[1] He had resigned the secretaryship at war (see above, p. 80) in 1762; he accepted the presidency of the board of trade in March 1763.
[2] For him see above, p. 53 n. 2.

Newcastle did not yet realize that he had committed himself
to opposition. Though his friends of standing had either broken
with him or come out, he still expected to gain information
from the many clerks he had placed in government employment. He still thought of himself as their chief and patron. For
forty years he had attached adherents to himself because he
had places and promotions to give. He had come to look on
such followers as his personal supporters. But in truth they
adhered to him as controller of the treasury and not as a person
and certainly not as a policy-maker. Once it was certain that he
was out for good, that he would not be back again after a month
or two to punish Judases, these seekers after patronage would
adhere to the head of the treasury for the time being. No
change of view or principle or policy seemed as yet to be involved in such a change of masters. Thus the real calamity for
Newcastle of Fox's appointment and of the vote for the peace
preliminaries was that it supplied the evidence that he was out
for good. The purge of 'Pelhamite Innocents' (or supporters of
Newcastle) in 1763 merely accelerated the change of loyalty in
government service which was starting to happen anyhow.
Some few for personal reasons, or slowness of understanding, or
jealousy of rivals, did remain faithful to Newcastle and lost their
honours, to swell Newcastle's begging-letter bag from then on.
But the extent of the slaughter of placemen can be overestimated.
The government left in peace any who did not defy it by working for their old master against the new. The important managers for the most part showed themselves willing to accept the
new order. As examples of different courses the case of Mr.
Milward and Mr. Lamb may be taken. Milward had £250 a
year as a surveyor of riding officers in the Kent customs. His
real service was to run the parliamentary representation of
Hastings, by influencing the forty-two voters there. Among
these forty-two he had given out government places which cost
£1,580 a year. It was too much to expect the treasury to continue to help Mr. Milward if he devoted himself to the return
of Newcastle-men against the treasury. Milward decided he
could not run the borough if the treasury were unkind, and he
came to heel. Mr. Lamb had a customs post but his main task
was to return the members for Rye. For adhering to Newcastle
he lost his sinecure: elections in Rye were now more difficult,
but in the end, years later, the Lamb interest was found so well-

knit in Rye that the treasury had to patch up peace with them. In most working executive offices continuity was not broken: civil servants, like the bishops, forgot the Lord who had created them, because once snugly in office they could easily have security of tenure.

What was unusual in all this was simply Newcastle's blindness in believing that the troops were still his to command: this blindness was the result of his exceptionally long period in power. It followed also that in opposition he would be tempted to organize a party among those whom, as a great landlord, he could still influence, and among those who had suffered for him; it was possible he might do this to an extent hitherto unknown in the eighteenth century. The old wire-puller was too old to learn new tricks. Yet for a while, in 1763, he was so disheartened that he seemed inclined to give up. His young and ambitious friends had to spur him on. They began to meet in an opposition circle and to inform him of their views. And these young men insisted that it was necessary to join up with Pitt. They saw that Newcastle alone could not come back in glory, for his system had had its weakness exposed.

Bute seemed triumphant in January 1763. He was, however, already weary of the political struggle: he was talking of resignation. Winning was not worth the mortification of the spirit. Henry Fox—that dirty fellow—was always thinking of his own interest, his future place in the house of lords, and the paymaster's accounts. George Grenville, playing to the gallery in March 1763, supported an inquiry into the way money had been spent in the war. This terrified Newcastle, but it equally angered Henry Fox, the paymaster and now Grenville's colleague. Besides the perpetual squabbles of his colleagues, Bute had a more serious trial of his endurance to face. For in the court's victory at the end of 1762 there was a danger concealed. So strong was the popular desire for peace and a reduced land tax that it was not enough for ministers to conclude the war; they were expected to get at once on to a peace-time financial footing. This was an impossibility.

The tapering off of war costs is not a rapid matter. Moreover the increase in indebtedness, without corresponding innovation in taxation, had permanently burdened the treasury. The financial system called as clearly for change as it had done when Newcastle was in control. Ministers still faced the problem, at which he had glanced nervously, of finding some new fruitful tax. But country gentlemen expected not new taxes but less of the old. In 1762 the national bill had been reduced by £1 million to £18½ million. In 1763 it proved possible in the end to make a further reduction of £5 million to £13·6 million. Even this was twice a pre-war total. It was met by finding £2 million from the sinking fund (i.e. from general unassigned taxes), raising £1¾ million on exchequer bills, almost £¾ million by a lottery, £2¾ million by further annuities, in addition to normal taxation. Normal taxation, that is, in the sense that war-time taxation remained. The land tax had still to provide £2 million and remained at the top rate of 4s. in the £. The malt and beer tax was continued. The only new idea introduced was a tax upon cider. This was the occasion for a violent political conflict.

Bute's predecessors had taxed beer. Was it not logical to put a comparable burden upon cider? The government introduced proposals for a charge of 4s. a hogshead upon cider and 4s. a bin upon wines. No tax could have been better chosen to arouse eighteenth-century passion. For it was an excise, and the excise was collected under a system of inspectorship which was both efficient and oppressive. The excise inspectors sometimes resided with their victims, keeping a day-to-day watch upon the operations they taxed. They pried into a man's business as no one else dared before the invention of an income-tax. Moreover in cases of dispute the excise cases could be heard before either justices of the peace or the commissioners for excise. It was said that in excise cases the justices were 'arbitrators with large discretion between the Crown and the subject' and that there was 'a large discretion in mitigation' in excise cases.[1] The proceedings before the commissioners were likened to Star Chamber for their secrecy; the commissioners were free to bargain with the parties, accepting equitable arrangements when they chose to do so, and this resembled a power of dispensing with the letter of the law and compounding offences. After thorough inquiry the commissioners, if they arrived at no bargain, might push the alleged offender before the court of exchequer where costs were always high. Moreover, the onus of proof lay upon the subject who might have to pay triple costs if he lost and could not recover costs from the Crown if he succeeded. All excise

[1] The attorney general in 1789, 1790, quoted in E. Hughes, *Studies in Administration and Finance*, p. 332.

therefore was, as Walpole had found, regarded as tyrannical. But an excise upon cider had peculiar points of unpopularity. For the beer excise could be collected at comparatively few points of supply, the maltsters and breweries. To collect a cider excise meant investigating the affairs of every apple-grower in the west country. It aroused an outcry against increasing the number of government agents and so increasing the power of government by adding to its patronage and influence. It also aroused the cry against invading the privacy and the independence of Englishmen's homes.

The government was not happily placed to beat off such an attack. Their chancellor of the exchequer, Dashwood,[1] was probably the least competent minister ever to hold that office. He clearly never understood the figures with which he had to deal. Moreover no one seemed to have made any calculation of the anticipated yield of the new tax and it was not therefore easy to prove that it would play a vital part in making ends meet. Further, the resolution with which arguments were advanced from the government side was weakened by the fact that Bute and George Grenville were, inside the cabinet, at variance about the needs of the year. George Grenville was still arguing for drastic economies in outlay in Europe, while Bute (like Newcastle before him) felt that economy should not be pushed to the point of abolishing European activities altogether. Lord Halifax was not a strong man and was in the lords. In the commons Henry Fox was not satisfied that his services were appreciated by the court and worried about future rewards for his work.

The government was therefore nervous. To save face they fought the taxes through both houses. The ambitious men out of office naturally arranged their speeches to appeal to the prejudices of independent members. It was at this time that the legend of George III's and Bute's plan to subvert the constitution and bring in a more despotic régime began to find wide acceptance—on no more evidence than might have been scraped together against George II and Walpole for promoting the Excise Bill of 1733, except that now this ministry persisted where Walpole had abandoned his reform. But the need for

---

[1] Sir Francis Dashwood, baronet (1708–81), fifteenth baron le Despenser; a member of the reputable Dilettanti Society and of the disreputable Hell-fire Club; he ended his career as joint postmaster-general, 1770–81.

money was now greater nor was there any alternative comparable to Walpole's revival of the salt tax. The opposition made
the most they could of Bute's Scottish blood. Scots, it was said,
were happy to see tyranny destroy English independence. Their
almost invariable support for the administration of George II
was pointed out and, quite inconsistently, they were vilified as
Jacobites alien to whig traditions. Bute was personally slandered,
in addition, by the rumour that he owed his position not to
George's affection alone, but to the intimate favours of the
king's mother. An attempt, in short, was made to exploit every
prejudice of independent gentlemen so that they could be
brought up to vote in a passion. Given the background of anti-
executive feeling and the emotive nature of a cider excise, the
wonder is that the campaign failed. The cider tax passed the
commons, after six divisions, by a vote of 106 to 55[1] and then
went through the lords by a vote of 83 to 49. Even then the
resources of the opposition were not at an end. It was usual for
determined opponents of a government to play upon discontent
among the public at large and not only among members of
parliament or voters. A few good riots, as in 1733, brought
home to ministers the danger of pursuing unpopular courses.
The city of London[2] as usual acted as banner-waver for radical
feeling in the whole country otherwise unexpressed except by
disorder. The city of London petitioned both houses of parliament against the innovation of a cider tax and when that
availed nothing, they defiantly, and for the sake of a gesture,
petitioned the king to refuse his assent to the measure.

Though the storm had been high it was weathered. There
was now, in March 1763, some hope that the excesses of their
opponents in the late debate might bring ministers a reaction
in their favour. The country gentlemen might well consider
that an attempt had been made to enlist them in a factious plot
of overmighty subjects. George III, feeling this himself, hoped
that moderate men would come to feel it too. But Lord Bute's
nerve was now quite gone. On 8 April 1763 he resigned, and
was succeeded at the head of the treasury by George Grenville.
In August the death of Lord Egremont led to a further rearrangement of the ministry. Lord Sandwich came in to the

---

[1] This was the last division; earlier the numbers voting had been as high as
188 to 84.
[2] To understand its radicalism see above, p. 50.

office of secretary of state, and Lord Egmont[1] was put at the head of the admiralty. A new infusion of life into the administration was effected by promoting the duke of Bedford to be lord president of the council and so attaching the whole Russell connexion more firmly to its support.

The character of the king's administration had thus changed in 1763. By April 1763 the peace was made and new problems were coming forward: Bute's withdrawal when he seemed to have won the game can be accounted for only in terms of his failings of character. That stiffness of self-conscious rectitude which aroused George III's admiration prevented his mixing easily with colleagues. His high-souled morality accompanied an excessive sensitiveness. He could not bear abuse. He enjoyed power but not enough to endure criticism. In a court he might succeed: 'Caress the favourite, avoid the unfortunate and trust nobody', advised his wife Lady Mary: all this her husband could do. But in the forum of debate, unlike the chambers of intrigue, it was necessary to disregard abuse, clamour, and misrepresentation. Bute had every advantage for winning except the will and the fortitude. He retired, clearly hoping to enjoy the role of adviser and critic from without, for it is not only easier to see problems as a whole from outside but also less strain on the nerves.

Fox for his part had no such thin skin. But he was a man of curiously limited ambition. He did not want to improve the world or even to dominate the house of commons. He wanted to be rich. He wanted a peerage. Riches he obtained from the office of paymaster. He did not misappropriate public money. In an age when public and private accounts were not clearly kept apart he accumulated in his hands public money which, eventually, would be used for public purposes. But while the capital was returned to the public, interest earned upon sums he controlled went into his private fortune. He had the loan of all the money intended for war payments, and the control also of the allotment of some contracts. Moreover as a minister and a sociable fellow he had advance information of events useful to a speculator. To enrich himself in this way he had accepted subordinate place under Pitt and Newcastle and borne his reputation, among ordinary men, of a shifty schemer. To win a

---

[1] Sir John Perceval, second earl of Egmont (1711-70), a former leader of the prince of Wales' opposition to George II.

peerage he had agreed to come forth for Bute and organize the government party until peace was finally achieved. It had been a bargain for a temporary service.

Now the time was up; Fox wanted his place in the lords and his leisure for private affairs. In the spring of 1763 he claimed his release therefore. It now transpired that there was a misunderstanding about the exact terms of his agreement of service. Fox meant to run the pay-office from the lords. The king and Bute had understood, through their intermediary Lord Shelburne, that Fox would resign the post in the commons and the paymastership simultaneously. A very nasty little dispute took place. Fox even threatened that if he had to give up his paymastership he might not take the lords but devote his talents in the commons to making life unpleasant for former colleagues. In the end he went to the lords and retained his paymastership for two more years;[1] this episode added further to the atmosphere of chicanery which its opponents attributed to the Bute administration: it also helped to give Lord Shelburne a reputation for fraud and deception. Lord Shelburne already suffered by having risen too rapidly under Bute.[2] By this time blunt ordinary men were already calling him slightingly 'that genius': from 1763 onwards the whole Fox family spread the story of his alleged duplicity in trapping Henry Fox into agreement to resign his place. Fox's own reputation for cunning added to the enormity of such a success of manœuvre.

With Bute and Fox leaving the ship the poor young king was in an awkward plight. He had affronted both Pitt and Newcastle. Pitt would not serve with anyone having responsibility for the peace treaty. To take either of them back on their own terms would have been a humiliation and a confession that politics could not be run on honest simple lines. Anti-administration feeling still ran high after the cider-tax debates and could therefore be aroused the more easily by the discontented chieftains. If the executive was to hold its own in the balanced constitution a minister had to be found acceptable both to parliament and the king; one who would persuade the king of what was needful to quiet the commons and who would persuade the

---

[1] It took a further twenty years, until 1782, to disentangle the accounts of his office and to separate government funds from the Fox family fortune.

[2] He had taken his seat in the house of lords, aged 24, in 1761, and had immediately been offered an office. Though he had refused this he was known to have influence in high places.

commons to agree to the necessary measures of the king's government. But there seemed now no such minister or combination of ministers. George Grenville was chosen as the least bad of possible alternatives. He had been as troublesome as a stubborn mule, but at least he was not one of the corrupt old gang and he was a devoted lover of the house of commons.

George Grenville was nicknamed 'The Gentle Shepherd' by Pitt in contemptuous allusion to a song of the time. The name is misleading. He was not gentle but domineering, more like a rather unimaginative schoolmaster than a shepherd. His mind had no great depth, his speeches no eloquence, his methods no finesse. He had a great memory and posed as an expert on house of commons' procedure. But his procedural views were usually those of the antiquarian rather than the practical statesman. His greatest strength lay in his businesslike methods, his care for detail, and the clarity of his mind. This clarity, it is true, was the result of a lack of vision of anything but the point nearest ahead of him, but it did, with his strength of will, enable him to defeat men with greater natural talents.

George Grenville decided, on assuming the control of the treasury, that the first thing necessary was to control the squabbles between ministers which had been so deleterious to the king's affairs for the past two years. Moreover, for any régime to be strong, it must be believed to have the future in its hands. It must have the confidence of the king if it was to attract the support of the politicians and then, in turn, enjoy the respect of the general body of parliament. Grenville therefore must control colleagues and events by his recognized primacy in the king's favour. This Walpole had enjoyed by his co-operation with the queen, the Pelhams by making themselves indispensable in parliamentary management, Lord Bute by his domination of a royal pupil. Characteristically Grenville tried to command favour by regulations and to order by hard and fast rule what could only be won by cunning, patience, and success. From the first he feared that Bute still enjoyed more of the king's confidence than he did himself. It was not enough for Bute to retire from town. He wished to prevent all correspondence. When in the summer of 1763 it was rumoured that Bute was seeking alliance with Pitt through friendship with Beckford,[1] Grenville saw in it a sinister attempt to eject him.

[1] William Beckford (1709-70), a wealthy West Indian trader who was M.P. for

He was afraid everyone would look on him as a stopgap, for all knew he had been reluctantly entrusted with power. In the end Grenville imposed a novel control on king and colleagues. His aim was that no one should consult with the king unless Grenville knew of, and agreed to, the negotiation. He would not serve if even the royal surveyor (Mr. Worsley) was allowed to see the king without his knowledge. Such dictatorial rules were 'necessary for carrying on His Majesty's Government'. Even Walpole had never dared to suggest such censorship: he had relied on his own talents for intrigue to negative the whispers of hostile colleagues. Grenville, however, tried to attract all loyalty to himself. Patronage was to be dealt with, even on its mechanical and clerical side, by his secretary Lloyd, rather than by Charles Jenkinson, for Jenkinson had served Bute. In September 1763 Grenville tried to prevent the king from giving the privy purse to Sir William Breton on no ground but that he had been connected with Bute and 'would still serve to increase the jealousy and the reports industriously spread about the short duration of the present government'.[1] When the king protested his faith and loyalty to Grenville he was, in effect, told that the substance was not enough: it must appear in every trifle to all men that he had the king's backing. Accordingly Bute was not only pledged to rusticate in the country but it was made known that Grenville had extorted the promise.

Grenville also insisted that 'he could never consent that any of the House of Commons's offices should go through any channel but his own'; 'he must be known to have the patronage, or the whole must break'. He had perforce for the first three months to allow Egremont a share in patronage. But he had no intention of making the same concession to the two secretaries Halifax and Sandwich, or to the duke of Bedford. He went so far as to say that in matters of management he could not 'look upon them as his colleagues', for they had family groups behind them to make them formidable politically, while he had as a single, lonely man, to make himself powerful if he was to be respected. His cabinet was kept small in number, as fitted

the city of London, and lord mayor in 1762 and 1769. He was a great admirer of Pitt and had a house in the country near Bute's.

[1] On this occasion the king's wishes for Breton prevailed. The quotations are from *The Grenville Papers*, ed. W. J. Smith.

his plan of centralized control; four or five ministers at most
normally came. In September 1764, for instance, Grenville,
Halifax, Sandwich, Northington, and Egmont took decisions
on major issues of foreign policy. Under this tight discipline the
king chafed along for two years because there was no other
possible arrangement.

To consolidate his government, Grenville judged it necessary
to cow those who had stirred up such violence in the country
against Bute. Pitt and Temple were the leading exponents of
this covert demagogy, and Temple's most effective agent, because the most violent, had been John Wilkes. At this time
thirty-eight years old, Wilkes was the son of a wealthy distiller,
educated fashionably at Leyden university, who had purchased
a parliamentary seat (for Aylesbury) and obtained a colonelcy
in the Buckinghamshire militia. His career up to the separation
from his wife in 1757 was that of a new man climbing the usual
ladder of promotion in the world. But from then on his life,
among women of easy virtue and men of studied vice, involved
him in financial difficulties. With no son, but only his much-
loved daughter, to follow him, orthodox advance perhaps
ceased to allure him. Wilkes lived more and more upon his wits,
which were ready but by no means rough,[1] and distinguished
himself by always going to the ultimate extreme in all adventures. In the Hell-fire Club or in politics his recklessness was
apparent, for he scorned the decent concealment, the hypocrisy,
the cloudy phrases in which weaker men sought safety. In 1762
he was known as a man of fashion, the friend of Dashwood and
Sandwich; he was a cross-eyed ladies' man, a cheerful gambler,
and a frequenter of literary circles. In 1762 he had started,
under Temple's encouragement, the *North Briton* paper. 'How
far', asked Mme de Pompadour, 'does liberty of the Press extend
in England?' 'That', Wilkes replied, 'is what I am trying to
find out.'

His attacks upon the court were eagerly read in the city of
London. His comparison of the times of Edward III and
George III—with stress upon the amours of the royal mother
and the favourite—made Horace Walpole squeal delightedly,

---

[1] But they could be appreciated by the populace as well as the elegant. Canvass-
ing in the election in Middlesex five years later, Wilkes begged a vote only to
meet the response 'I'd rather vote for the Devil'. 'Naturally,' retorted Wilkes, 'but
if your friend is not standing, may I hope for your support?'

'It is wormwood!' Ably abetted by the poet Churchill[1] and occasionally restrained by Lord Temple, on whose loans he now depended, Wilkes went on to new heights of slander on ministers and the peace. In number 45 of the *North Briton*, on 23 April 1763, he described the king's speech where the peace was referred to as 'honourable to my Crown and beneficial to my people' as a falsehood. Grenville, Halifax, and Egremont considered that this was the point at which they could profitably strike. A general warrant was issued: it was not directed, that is, to a named person but ordered the arrest of all concerned in the production of the *North Briton* and the seizure of their papers. It was issued by the secretary of state in a magisterial capacity, and executed by treasury agents on 30 April 1763. A writ of habeas corpus was evaded for a time by putting Wilkes into the custody of the secretary of state and holding him incommunicado in the tower, while his papers were ransacked. Though parliament was not sitting the Speaker (Sir John Cust) was informed of the arrest of a member of the house. Lord Temple was ordered, as lord-lieutenant of Buckinghamshire, to remove Colonel Wilkes from his position. Upon the publication of insolent letters in reply from himself and from Wilkes, Temple was dismissed from his lord lieutenancy.

Wilkes on his appearance in the court of common pleas on 3 and 6 May 1763 took his stand upon three arguments. First general warrants were illegal: second, the secretary of state had no power to act as a magistrate: third, as a member of parliament he claimed the privilege of being free from arrest. The chief justice of common pleas, Sir John Pratt (later Lord Camden) was a friend of Pitt's and therefore was not inclined to strain the law in favour of the ministers. The chief justice ruled that the secretary of state could exercise magisterial powers: the legality of general warrants had later to be thrashed out; but in any case he found that the offence charged against Wilkes was not treason, nor felony, nor a breach of the peace (the offences which lay outside parliamentary privilege) and that therefore as a member of parliament he was privileged and must be set at liberty. Characteristically Wilkes had already contrived to widen the quarrel and heighten emotions. In his speech to the judge he had said, 'The liberty of all peers and gentlemen and,

---

[1] Charles Churchill (1731–64), a curate at St. John's, Westminster, made celebrated by his savage satirical works *Rosciad* and *Apology* in 1761.

what touches me more sensibly, that of all the middling and inferior set of people . . . is in my case this day to be finally decided upon'. He portrayed what was in fact a bungled attack by ministers upon the violence of their political opponents as a plot against the liberty of the citizen. His release he pictured as a shock to tyranny. It is clear also that though he had involved himself in this affair as Lord Temple's journalist, the excitement of conflict was already tempting him to seek other and more desperate allies among those who were not borough-owners, who did not even have votes, but who would enjoy a little rioting to the accompaniment of rhetoric. He was once more flying instinctively to the most extreme and dangerous course.

On his return to his house Wilkes wrote to accuse the secretaries of state of stealing his possessions. He tried to take out a search warrant to enter their houses to recover his papers. The secretaries were unwise enough to answer him and Wilkes printed the exchanges and circulated them through London as a pamphlet. For the next few months legal actions by Wilkes (and those arrested with him) against Halifax, the secretary of state, and all his agents put the legality of general warrants to the test in the court of common pleas. Pratt ruled against their legality and Wilkes recovered £1,000 damages against the under-secretary of state, Robert Wood. His printer, Mr. Leach, was awarded £400. The government was stung and humiliated. London radicals rejoiced. A 'Rose and Crown' club at Wapping swore to feast on Wilkes's birthday and then had to beg to be told when it was, for otherwise they must be drunk every day or else forsworn.

There were, however, signs that some members of the parliamentary opposition did not regard Wilkes's extreme courses as an acceptable aid to them. The duke of Grafton,[1] for instance, had refused to go bail for him (though he visited him in prison) for fear of involving himself too closely with a man of bad character who had insulted the king directly. Lord Temple commanded Wilkes not to reprint the offending articles. But Wilkes, finding no printer brave enough, set up his own printing press to republish his libels. In so doing he provided the full proof of his responsibility for them. So on 15 November 1763,

---

[1] Augustus Henry Fitzroy, third duke of Grafton (1735–1811), at this time was one of Newcastle's energetic young friends. For his later career see the narrative below.

when parliament reassembled, the government counter-attacked. The house of commons, by a majority of 237 to 111, voted that number 45 was a seditious libel and it was ordered to be publicly burned. Meanwhile in the house of lords a further effort was made to frighten moderate men away from Wilkes and to discredit those who had used him as their agent. Lord Sandwich and the bishop of Gloucester produced an obscene poem[1]—*The Essay on Woman*—which Wilkes had been privately printing at his press. An accusation of publishing pornography was thus added to the charges against him, though it had not been published and a copy had been obtained by bribing men of the lowest moral character to supply evidence. Accordingly, when on 23 November 1763 the house of commons debated whether parliamentary privilege should protect a member accused of seditious libel, it was not easy to commend Wilkes to country squires by portraying him as an outspoken champion of their liberties who had been set upon by ministers with a gag. Pitt, who had in 1759 encouraged his visits, now deserted Wilkes. He denied any connexion with him. He described him as 'a blasphemer of his God and a libeller of his King'. The house voted that parliamentary privilege did not cover his case. Wilkes had not only to face attacks in parliament but also in the courts—on an ordinary warrant—for his repeated offence. He avoided appearance in parliament for a while on a plea of ill health; he had, indeed, been painfully wounded in a duel, which Horace Walpole described as a plot against Wilkes's life. Then in December he slipped away to his daughter and to safety in France. On 20 January 1764 he was expelled from membership of the house of commons. He remained jaunty and provocative— asked to play a hand at cards he excused himself, 'Dear Madam, do not ask me. I am so ignorant that I cannot tell a King from a knave'—but his cause and his fortunes seemed ruined. In February 1764 his trial for seditious libel and for obscenity came on; as he did not appear he was (nine months later) outlawed.

The only way in which the opposition in parliament could still hope to use the incident to discredit the administration was by drawing attention back to their first blunder in the issue of a

---

[1] The poem seems to have been written by Wilkes's dead friend Thomas Potter, the son of a former archbishop of Canterbury, and to have been brought up to date with topical allusions by Wilkes.

general warrant. This, it might be argued, whatever the personal shortcomings of Wilkes, showed the high-handed methods
of the court party. The legal case was doubtful in spite of
Camden's pronouncements. That old follower of Newcastle
and great lawyer, Lord Hardwicke, had thought such warrants
legal though it might be inexpedient to use them. But in any
case it was an issue on which appeal might be made against
Grenville to the scruples of country gentlemen. Accordingly,
on 15 February 1764 Sir George Savile and Sir William
Meredith,[1] as members of the opposition whose reputation for
honest independence was high, moved to declare general warrants illegal. The attorney general, Sir Fletcher Norton,[2] tact-
lessly but correctly told the house that their opinion on a point
of law was worth no more than that of a lot of drunken Covent
Garden porters. Despite such *gaffes* the government won the
division, but only by a majority of fourteen—234 to 220. The
government was saved by the Welsh and Scottish members.
The majority of members for counties and for boroughs with
large electorates voted against them. Even among the 269
members present who sat for boroughs with small electorates
their majority was only 17. It is clear that support for the
government among the English politicians who sat for pocket
seats was not overwhelming, while there was a small anti-
government majority among men of independent election. It
seemed that the king might find it expedient to replace ministers
who brought his affairs to this crisis in parliament. Outside
parliament feeling in favour of Wilkes among humbler classes
was so strong that the foreman who had betrayed him over the
Essay on Woman could find no employment and committed
suicide.

But Grenville and the king showed courage. They trusted
that general warrants was an issue that would be forgotten,
and that Wilkes, if he returned, would drag his cause into
further disrepute. Grenville hoped that other aspects of his
policy would regain the confidence of the squirearchy. It was a
mark of courage that the court dismissed General Conway[3]

---

[1] For Savile see above, p. 62. Sir William Meredith (d. 1790) was M.P. for
Liverpool, sympathizing with the Newcastle–Rockingham point of view.

[2] Sir Fletcher Norton (1716–89) was a lawyer noted for his vigour and his naked
ambition. He became Speaker of the house of commons in 1770 and was created
Lord Grantley in 1782.

[3] Henry Seymour Conway (1719–95), the brother of the earl of Hertford, and a

from his post in the bedchamber and from his military command, as a punishment for voting against the government on general warrants. It is a sign of the rapid melting of opposition unity that no great outcry against this dismissal was aroused. At most it increased Grenville's unpopularity among the 'professional' men of Westminster.

Among the gentlemen of England Grenville could use strength drawn from his popular financial policy to offset any ill effects of his brush with Wilkes. Grenville's leading idea was to avoid unpopular new taxation by means of the most rigorous economy. Within a year of his gaining control the supplies were reduced from £13½ million to just over £7¾ million. He was, of course, helped by the disappearance of the extraordinary costs of war. The army was reduced from 120,000 men to some 30,000.[1] But he powerfully aided this process, watching both trifles and the major sources of expenditure. He called attention to a twenty-year-old treasury minute which limited the expense allowance of ambassadors, and thereafter these representatives abroad lived either more modestly or at their own cost. Sir John Fielding knew when he advocated a horse police patrol of the Tottenham Court Road that it would run counter to Mr. Grenville's 'resolution not to lay any permanent expense on the Crown'.[2] More important was his treatment of the navy. The frustrated first lord of the admiralty (Egmont) complained, by April 1764, that 'we have not now (guardships included) in Great Britain seventeen ships of the line complete'. Ships returning from the wars to Plymouth, Portsmouth, and Chatham had not a shilling spent on them. To make them serviceable would require the spending of half the original cost of production upon the repair of their hulls. The dockyard workers were reduced to the low level of 1748. Egmont concluded that the navy would be ruined and the country endangered if hostilities were to break out again. Grenville's reply was to insist that economies should be possible out of £1½

cousin of Horace Walpole. He had progressed as a young politician of the Pelhamite group, sitting for boroughs controlled first by Rockingham and then by Falmouth. At this time he sat for Thetford, a borough controlled by Grafton. His dilemma in choosing between friends and office was not unusual save in the importance (see below) that his decisions came to assume.

[1] The number of regiments was not reduced below 70, but the strength of all these was ruthlessly cut. This meant, said Pitt, dooming 'the bravest men the world ever saw . . . to be sent to starve in country villages and forget their prowess'.

[2] This was in June 1764.

million of naval bills: he retained in the king's speech a sentence that ample money was being provided 'for maintaining the Fleet in a respectable state'. Grenville's attitude was applauded at the time. But he must take a major share of the blame for the failure of the navy at the start of the American War.

With all his cheese-paring economy, Grenville could not reduce the land tax below 4s. His provision for the year 1764 allowed for £2 million from the land tax, £2 million from the sinking fund, £1 million from exchequer bills through the Bank of England, £¾ million from the malt and cider taxes. It was still a budget where the major burden rested upon landed property, though a new duty was placed upon foreign coffee. This change was followed by a more drastic bid for applause. The cause of all financial difficulties Grenville could show was the cost of the war to defeat France overseas. Eventually it was supposed that this war would pay for itself in an increase in trade. Was it not therefore most unjust that not only the burden of war debt but even the cost of maintaining the services and defences essential to this trade should all fall upon the English landowner, who could not, as such, hope to reap the benefits?

In the case of India the Company did not expect free services from the taxpayer: it administered the new acquisitions, paid for its civil staff, and maintained its own armed forces for its security. All this it paid for from the profits of the trade. It was self-contained except that some surplus eventually accrued to England from the retirement to England of Englishmen with the fortunes made in India. In complete contrast America failed either to provide such an accession to the national stock by the return of Englishmen who emigrated or, and more strikingly, by financing the cost of maintaining the bases from which trade was pursued. Settlement on the mainland of the American colony was not, in any case, a policy which accorded with general mercantile ideas,[1] but it had gone too far to be halted or discouraged by 1763. At least, however, these unsatisfactory outposts of England, devoted to their own interests rather than the national plan, should be expected to cover their own maintenance cost. Provision for this already existed on paper. Walpole's molasses duty of 6d. on foreign sugar should, as well as controlling the pattern of the mainland's trade with

---

[1] See above, p. 22; and for a fuller discussion of the origins of the American war, below, pp. 174 f.

the Caribbean islands, have provided funds for American expenses. But no one in America relished paying duties any more than the English did. Whereas in England the government took some pains to enforce payment, in America the duties had been 'executed for some time in a most negligent and shameful manner', as Jenkinson reported. Grenville's orderly soul was shocked by such disorder. In 1764, therefore, he reduced the duty to one-half (3*d*.) and proceeded to tighten up all the machinery of enforcement, making use of the navy to that end. At the same time the proceeds were earmarked for American purposes. In such a course he had the full support of public opinion at home and of the theory on which colonial expansion was buttressed. Even in America it was difficult to work up feeling against regulations which were a reduction in the old rate of duty. Nor was it easy to attack the idea that laws should be enforced rather than evaded. In the long run, however, 'the beginning to execute them afresh made them have the appearance of new laws', as Jenkinson again commented. But Grenville's eyes were not on the long run but on the daily reports on his desk and the obvious and immediate decencies of administration.

This policy of making ends meet by making every separate account balance was continued into 1765. In the accounts for that year Grenville at length stopped the process of increasing the national debt each year. War finance was finished. Expenditure stood at about the same level as the previous year. The floating debt for the navy of about £1½ million was converted into annuities so as to be fixed and in time extinguished. He could not yet reduce the land tax but was convinced that his economic policy was going on the right course to that end. So he reduced the coffee duty and made arrangements for stricter enforcement of it, in imitation of his own Molasses Act of the previous year. Grenville, indeed, made much of his twelve months' achievement. He claimed that his vigilance in the enforcement of duties had produced an extra £400,000 of revenue from tea. He had seized the opportunity of the renewal of the Bank of England's charter to compel the Bank to provide a £100,000 contribution to the nation and to take up Exchequer bills at a low rate of interest. All this self-praise was couched in terms to attract the country members. They rejoiced in the hard bargains with the city; they were glad that the financiers this year had no profitable loan to take up. After dealing with a new tax on gum arabic, Grenville, in March 1765, made a much more important innovation. To meet the cost of military defence in the New World he imposed an American stamp duty—a tax, that is, on papers required in official transactions. This duty he had outlined twelve months before: he had allowed a year in which the colonists might make suggestions of other means of raising the required sums. None being forthcoming, the duties now were pushed through both houses by the government.

The main point of controversy about the stamp duties was that they were a direct tax upon the colonies. Hitherto England had collected from them by indirect taxes which were part of the general system of regulation of trade. The twelve months' delay had given time for the colonists to instruct their agents and for those trading interests in this country whose prosperity was bound up with the well-being of America to concert their opposition. There was, moreover, a case in theory to be made out against them; the cry of 'No taxation without representation' was heard. All the stress was laid upon its naked, direct, revenue-collecting purpose. If such a tax was needed it should be imposed upon themselves by American assemblies. Moreover, though stamp duties were old in England, in America they were an innovation. It was suggested, in the characteristic idiom of the times, that the purpose of the minister was to increase his staff of collectors, swell his power through patronage, and make the executive more tyrannical. In such emotive arguments did the friends of America vainly try to win the body of the house away from their respect for an economical minister who aimed at relieving the burdens upon English land.

Lord Rockingham, the leader now of Newcastle's friends, declared opposition to the stamp duties. Pitt was also against them. But the only strenuous parliamentary campaigning against the duties was conducted by Isaac Barré, a colonel dismissed from the army for political reasons, who had personal knowledge of the American scene. For the most part the opposition mustered their constitutional arguments without faith in their power to produce a political change. Pitt, indeed, was ill and could excuse his failure to fight hard. But it was significant that it was rumoured that Mr. Pynsent—who had determined to leave his fortune to Pitt as a reward for his attacks upon the government—was considering whether Pitt's recent lack of spirit in opposition was not a reason for altering his will in favour of Wilkes.[1]

George Grenville's firm hold of the idea that nothing should be done to increase the charge upon the English taxpayer had inevitably its consequences not only for policy towards America but also for foreign policy generally. Sandwich, as secretary of state, was worried about England's isolation in Europe. To escape this England could seek alliance with Prussia or with Austria or with Russia, so as to concert measures against France. Austria at this time showed no signs whatever of leaving her alliance with France. Sandwich, like Newcastle, in his heart always seems to have hankered after the 'old system', that is, the alliance with Austria, and in January 1765 he had hopes of rebuilding it and adding Russia. But Austria had nothing to gain by aggravating France and rated the use of England to her interests in central Europe at a correctly low level. With Russia negotiations began in 1763 and were very protracted. The envoy, the earl of Buckinghamshire, was incompetent. But even his successor, Sir George Macartney, could aim only at a commercial treaty.[2] For Catherine of Russia was most interested in expansion into Poland. She wished to keep Turkey and Sweden quiescent while she achieved this. So in 1763 Russia proposed that Great Britain should find funds to aid Russian intrigues in Poland, should find money for bribing the Swedes, and should support her against Turkey. Until this was done Russia could not take part in an alliance against France. While Britain did not fear Russian influence in Turkey, for it was a counterpoise to that of France in the Mediterranean, any idea of an alliance which involved subsidies was abhorrent to George Grenville. The most that he would do was to restore relations with Sweden (broken in 1748) and to support the anti-French party there, the Caps. He refused to give a subsidy to Sweden to replace that given her by France.

Russia therefore in 1764 made an alliance with Prussia: the two powers agreed that they should push the Russian candidate,

---

[1] Mr. Pynsent came from that resolutely independent county Somerset. In 1765 he did leave Pitt £3,000 a year.

[2] John Hobart, second earl of Buckinghamshire (1723–93), a lord of the bedchamber and later (1777–80) viceroy of Ireland.

George Macartney (1737–1806) began in these Russian negotiations a career which was to lead to the governorship of Madras and the Cape of Good Hope as well as an Irish earldom.

Poniatowski, for the Polish Crown, that Prussia should aid Russia against any Turkish attack, while Russia should give Prussia help in the event of a French attack. In addition Sweden should be kept weak under her constitution of 1720. This treaty emphasized England's lack of importance in Europe: it was optimistic to hope that it might become the basis of a great northern league against France, and the danger was clear that it might drive Austria further into France's arms. Poniatowski was placed on the Polish throne without a European upset. For France wisely had decided to avoid entanglement in eastern Europe and to hoard her strength for a revenge upon England. Thus it could not pay any of the other powers to embroil themselves with her. So long as their eyes were on Poland and Turkey England was irrelevant to their plans.

Relations between Prussia and England were marked by petty quarrels. In July 1764 ambassadors were withdrawn, leaving only secretaries of embassies in Berlin and London. With this the opposition made great play. Pitt declared that an alliance with Prussia was vital and that he could make it. For he ignored Poland and believed that Frederic's admiration for him was stronger than his self-interest. By 1765 the Rockingham group, in an effort to please Pitt, paid lip-service to the idea of the Prussian alliance. George Grenville of necessity concentrated his attention upon defensive measures against danger from France and Spain. He was averse to running any risk of a collision in the Mediterranean. Therefore no aid was given to Paoli and his Corsican rebels against Genoa. Even when France agreed to aid Genoa, this non-intervention was maintained.[1]

In general, however, George Grenville was determined to take a firm defensive stand against France, though his colleagues thought that, with the fleet weakened by his economies, this was hazardous. In pressing France for payment for prisoners maintained in the late war and for bills issued in Canada, Grenville was resolute. He forced the French to make restitution when one of their privateers seized English vessels at Turk Island in the Bahamas. Equally he stood up to the Spaniards in the inevitable quarrels about cutting logwood in Honduras.

[1] The upshot was that France conquered Corsica in 1768. Shelburne at that time wished to respond to Paoli's appeals and go to war to force France out. He was outvoted in the cabinet, with the result that Corsica became French and Napoleon Bonaparte a Frenchman.

Foreign policy in these two years was, in short, limited in its aims but productive of friction between the ministers. Sandwich, in particular, felt little sympathy with Grenville. By the spring of 1765 George III could justly complain that the jealousies of his servants gave him little peace, while in the general warrants issue they had disturbed the quiet of the whole country. No sooner did he show signs of fretting than the conduct of ministers became even more trying; for Grenville was aware how much he depended upon the king's favour. Like a lover fearing he is losing his mistress's favour he could not check those demands for reassurance which, because they irritate, help to bring on the dreaded revulsion. Fears of Bute's secret influence were increased by the king's coldness. Certainly Bute was sending advice to the king, but he was no more capable of playing the great minister than he had been in 1763.[1] The king was cooler towards him: he did not deserve the complaints with which Grenville, Bedford, and Halifax teased him. George III said that he 'had found himself too much constrained, and that when he had anything proposed to him, it was no longer counsel, but what he was to *obey*'. Yet he saw no political escape. Melancholia seized him. He had an illness which seems probably to have been the first attack of his madness, though dismissed as a cold by Grenville. This illness made the king decide to have a council of regency appointed in case he should collapse in future. Grenville at this time was resisting demands for increased allowances by the king's brothers. He declined to advise on the membership of the regency council. This did not prevent both Grenville and Bedford seeking audiences, separately, in which they took the king to task for not consulting them more fully about this project.

Lord Halifax, who was willing to help instead of merely lecturing his master, felt that to put the king's mother in the regency council was to expose the government to all the scandalous mud-slinging that had broken Bute's spirit. By a judicious form of words defining the royal family eligible for the council, the princess could be excluded. The king agreed to this, perhaps without fully understanding the point or perhaps convinced that his mother was too unpopular to be accepted by parliament. Having sacrificed his mother for fear of the parliamentary opposition, it was particularly mortifying to find two

[1] R. Sedgwick, *Letters of George III to Bute*, introduction, p. lxv.

members,[1] friends of Bute, moving an amendment to put the princess into the council, while the opposition applauded, and ministers put themselves in the hands of the house. Thus the king was made to appear as an undutiful son. It seemed to him that his ministers were less of his own way of thinking than was the house of commons. The king was therefore prepared to sacrifice his own pride if only he could be rid of them. But his first fumblings after a new ministry were unsuccessful. Grenville had to be retained. Grenville now made new demands if he was to go on. Lord Bute was still the bogy. Therefore his brother-in-law, Stuart MacKenzie, was to be dismissed and excluded from all Scottish patronage. Lord Weymouth,[2] or any other person ministers might choose, should be made lord-lieutenant in Ireland. Lord Granby was to replace the duke of Cumberland as commander-in-chief.[3] This last proposition was made void by Granby's refusal to consider the promotion. But to all the rest the king eventually replied, 'I see I must yield. I do it for the good of my people'. It was a true reason. The alternative to Grenville seemed to be no government at all, political chaos. It was not that Grenville stood at the head of a great body of parliamentary opinion or party. There was no such opinion, no such party. The situation was simply that parliament was difficult to control. The men capable of leading parliament were divided among themselves and only the king could give them the centre for unity. Yet in the troubles of these first five years he had allowed a breach to arise between himself and so many leading politicians that only Grenville appeared as a possible leader. Grenville, finding himself indispensable, but feeling insecure, inflicted new humiliations on his master to bolster up his own confidence.

In this moment of defeat the king found aid from his uncle the duke of Cumberland. The king delegated to Cumberland the task of making some other ministry which could give him peace and be acceptable to parliament. The duke's very sensible view was that the obvious and only practicable team was still a combination of Pitt with the friends of Newcastle. Their rupture with the king over the peace was past history, and Wilkes was

---

[1] Mr. Morton and Mr. Martin. Lord Bute gave out that he did not approve of their manœuvre.

[2] One of the Bedford group; see above, p. 65, and below, p. 213.

[3] Even Henry Fox, Lord Holland, was put out of the way, losing his paymastership at last.

an exile. Newcastle's friends, now led by the marquis of Rockingham,[1] welcomed this suggested alliance. It was what the younger members had been urging for the past two years. But Pitt had terms to make. He insisted upon a foreign policy based upon friendship with Prussia, upon a damnation of general warrants, upon a more conciliatory attitude to Americans, and upon the repeal of the cider tax. All this was granted him. But he also insisted upon office being given to his brother-in-law Lord Temple. He clearly feared that, surrounded by the friends of Rockingham, he might find himself forced back in the position of 1761, unable to insist upon his will prevailing. Lord Temple complicated the position with his private schemes. He desired to serve as an equal with Pitt and not just as an echo. He therefore hoped to heal the breach with George Grenville and make a ministry with himself at its head and Pitt and Grenville giving it strength. He could not, however, expect Grenville to swallow Pitt's programme, for it was a vote of censure on his record. Temple therefore would not serve. Pitt's refusal was the necessary result. To the king and to Cumberland Pitt pleaded his gout.

In the eyes of some of the Rockingham group, such as Grafton, Pitt's refusal made it unlikely that their own efforts could succeed. If they came into office, they would have Pitt's eloquence stirring the independent men against them. To this would be added George Grenville's cold and stiff hostility, after his dismissal. The times were bad and offered scope for agitation. The silk weavers were riotous and the harvest unpromising. Something would have to be done about American discontent. Nevertheless they told Cumberland that they were willing to serve the king.[2] In July Rockingham became first lord of the treasury, Grafton and Conway[3] secretaries of state, Lord Winchelsea president of the council, and Dowdeswell chancellor of the exchequer. Newcastle, in his old age, was content to become privy seal.[4] As a friendly gesture to the Pittites, Lord Chief

---

[1] Charles Watson Wentworth, second marquis of Rockingham (1730–82), had been a lord of the bedchamber until his dismissal in 1762.

[2] Charles Townshend refused to come in—whether on calculation of chances or because he was moving towards Pitt it would require a psychoanalyst to decide.

[3] So recently dismissed from his minor place for voting against general warrants.

[4] He died in 1768, aged 75.

Justice Pratt was raised to the peerage as Lord Camden. The earl of Northington continued as lord chancellor.[1]

[1] This was no surprise. Robert Henley, first earl of Northington (1708?–72), had been made lord keeper in 1757 and lord chancellor in 1761, but he had been on uneasy terms with his late colleagues. Moreover, the office of lord chancellor was, and continued to be, regarded as peculiarly a personal service to the king. Chancellors were 'keepers of the king's conscience', managing his ecclesiastical and legal appointments—almost his personal agents inside the cabinet.

V

CONTINUED MINISTERIAL DIFFICULTIES, 1765–70

LORD ROCKINGHAM was not a man of great energy or talent. But he was honest, well-connected, a great landlord, and full of common sense. His approach to his task in July 1765 was eminently reasonable. He was ready to forget most of the quarrels of the past five years, and to oblige the king whenever it could be done without jeopardizing the strength of his administration. He refused to grant the duke of Newcastle's requests for the reinstatement of all who had suffered for his sake in 1762–3 because this could only be done by a new purge of those who had succeeded them. He wished to end the vendetta. Yet Rockingham knew that government functioned best when there was the mutual confidence which comes from men working together who are accustomed to live on terms of friendship with one another. The ministry had therefore to be a 'party' one in this very restricted sense that the holders of all the principal posts were to be approved by Rockingham and should regard themselves as a team. The duke of Newcastle's arts of management should be employed to cement and consolidate the group and then to pacify the house of commons, which had been too much agitated of late. There would be no need of the dictatorial rules employed by Grenville. If the ministry was one of friends, or at least cordial acquaintances, Rockingham would be able not to command the king but to discuss matters with him from a position of strength. He would be able to admit into office not only Pitt and his allies but those also of Bute or Bedford or Grenville, provided they would be absorbed into the team without an attempt to impose a new order upon it. For this it was essential that they should recognize the mild captaincy of Rockingham himself. To persuade them he could depend only on his own acknowledged fairness. For as Burke said of him by way of epitaph: 'His virtues were his means.'

This combination of 'party' with willingness to receive

recruits, of tolerance with organization, marked an attempt to rebuild the sensible system of the Pelhams. In this spirit Lord George Sackville, for whom the king had still a soft spot, was restored to the privy council and made vice-treasurer of Ireland. In this spirit also negotiations were kept up, throughout the twelve months of the administration, to bring Pitt in. But Pitt was not to be won. At bottom this was because he refused to accept even that mild degree of restraint upon him which was involved in accepting the fact that the Rockinghams believed in operating as a group. He said that he must safeguard his own honour and therefore could not recognize Rockingham's reinstatement of Lord George Sackville, for he regarded it as a censure on his own action in 1760. Pitt demanded that Newcastle should be excluded from the cabinet because of his jealousies. More important than this, he required a 'transposition' of the chief office-holders. The meaning of this is clear. Pitt would only serve with Rockingham after some considerable slight had been put upon that marquis, sufficient to lower his prestige and to alarm all his group, so leaving it disorganized before Pitt's personal ascendancy. Even before Rockingham kissed hands, his ally the young duke of Grafton had lost faith in the group which had dined together in opposition under Newcastle's banner. Grafton had succumbed to Pitt's personal magnetism and served only with the hope of a speedy entry of Pitt into the leadership.

In matters of national policy little divided Rockingham from Pitt: much therefore cut him off from the Grenville and Bedford groups. The new ministry abolished the cider tax, amid general approval. It carried a resolution in the house of commons declaring the illegality of general warrants for the seizure of persons or of papers except so far as was expressly permitted by statute. These moves might be regarded as condemning acts of both the previous administrations. But they were generally popular, for in each case they reversed decisions where previous ministers had prevailed against the instincts of independent members. Moreover, Wilkes himself was cold-shouldered. Away in Paris he now hoped for favour. He would have liked to come back to England. If this was impossible he would have liked the post of ambassador at Constantinople. But all he was offered by the friends either of Rockingham or Pitt was £1,000 a year, privately subscribed, to stay quietly where he was. The Rock-

ingham administration further pleased ordinary members of
parliament by its decision to open free ports in different parts
of the West Indies[1] so as to stimulate that trade. The trade
treaty with Russia, so long discussed, was at length concluded.[2]
A modification of the window tax made it less burdensome upon
the middle and lower classes, and this, it was hoped, would
help to lessen hardship in a year of bad harvest. An increase in
naval expense, with a further cut in money devoted to the
army, was a further example of Rockingham's attempt to follow
a line which would not antagonize the independent country
gentlemen.

It was in their dealings with America that the weakness of
the administration became apparent. The opposition to the
Stamp Act in the colonies was being organized. Many colonists
bound themselves to refuse imports from Britain so as to make
England feel their resentment in her pocket. Englishmen who
lived by American trade were anxious to get back to normal
conditions; they therefore supported Pitt in his high constitutional line against the tax. Rockingham, Conway, Grafton, and
Newcastle all agreed that the Stamp Act should be repealed.
Nevertheless they realized that most country gentlemen were
strongly in favour of America paying for itself and were for the
maintenance of imperial control from Westminster. The stamp
tax might not in this view be perfect, but its imperfections should
not be exploited so as to destroy England's ability to exact from
America the cost of its security. George Grenville, the stern
author of this tax, would not fail to point out to the commons
that he had been prepared to accept other means of raising
money but that none had been put forward. Inside the ministry
Northington, the lord chancellor, and Barrington, the secretary
at war, insisted that Americans must pay. In considering how
to carry through the commons a repeal unpalatable to many,
the Rockingham group were conscious of one great weakness in
their organization—they had no outstanding spokesman in the
commons. Rockingham, Grafton, and Newcastle were in the
lords. Conway was a man of hesitant moods and no more than
a competent speaker. It is true that Pitt, on this issue, was sure
to loose his most echoing thunders. But Pitt would do this without close consultation on tactics. He would be liable to shake
friend as well as foe.

[1] See above, p. 21.   [2] See above, p. 107.

In these circumstances the cabinet attempted to close its ranks and to conciliate opponents by a compromise.[1] A bill to declare the right of parliament to tax the colonies was passed through both houses of parliament. Only Pitt in the commons and his friend Camden in the lords opposed the bill: the resolution upon which it was founded passed without division against it. This assertion of power was followed at once by a bill repealing that most recent exercise of it, the Stamp Act. This repeal, backed by Pitt from his lonely eminence, was carried by 108 in the commons (275 to 167) in a crowded house. In the lords more than 200 peers attended and the Rockingham majority was 30. On the face of it the administration had done well. The active politicians sitting for boroughs had given their support. County members were probably fairly evenly balanced, showing that the case for repeal, when prefaced by assertion of the right to tax, had won tolerance from independent back-benchers.[2]

Appearances were deceptive: ministers were at their last gasp. Their right wing had heard with alarm Pitt declare that 'I rejoice that America has resisted: three millions of people so dead to all feelings of liberty as voluntarily to submit to be slaves, would have been fit instruments to make slaves of all the rest.' The duke of Grafton, on the other wing, had been more than ever convinced that the administration could not go on unless it was reinforced, as had originally been intended, by the accession of Pitt. Thus Pitt, out of office, was splitting the ministers into two groups. At the same time the friends of Lord Bute also gave trouble. In a committee considering an address to the crown which asked that governors might be told to 'recommend' to the provincial assemblies some way in which losses sustained in the colonies might be made good, Lord Bute successfully moved an amendment substituting the word 're-quire' in the place of 'recommend'. This was a call for a more imperious tone in dealing with the colonies, emphasizing the opposite side of the compromise to that favoured by Pitt's

---

[1] The duke of Newcastle thought this a solution of 'boys' and sapiently foretold that it would widen and not heal their divisions.

[2] County members against the government were 36% of the whole: how many were absent is doubtful; a reasonable guess would be 20%, which would leave 44% in support of repeal. The corresponding figures for large boroughs would be 21%, 20%, and 59%, and for the smaller ones 27%, 20%, and 53%. See Namier, *Structure of Politics at the Accession of George III* (2nd ed.), pp. 154, 155.

friends. Some office-holders voted for it. Rockingham's ministers asked the king to dismiss the more prominent of them. Though the king had not encouraged the revolt, he was not willing to punish the rebels. This seemed to indicate that Rockingham did not enjoy the favour of the crown.

George III had not plotted against his ministers. He had accepted them as the best Cumberland could provide him with in 1765. He did not enjoy seeing the reversal of measures taken in the past three years, but he seems to have appreciated the necessity for it. What perplexed him in April 1766 was how he should act now that his servants were openly at odds with one another. The duke of Cumberland had died in November 1765. He had acted as an unofficial leader of the ministry, using his prestige to support Rockingham. Rockingham thought they could go on: he refused to advise the king to send for Pitt: he believed moreover that the king must make it clear that 'people in office were to hold their posts at the good will of the ministers'.[1] But they could not go on as they were, for Grafton had decided to resign if Pitt was not called in to take charge, and Conway was inclined to agree with this decision. Grafton resigned in April 1766 and his place was filled by the duke of Richmond.[2] In July Lord Chancellor Northington, claiming that he had been kept out of the confidence of his colleague, in his turn resigned. Nothing daunted, Lord Rockingham proposed that he should be replaced by Charles Yorke, the son of the former Lord Chancellor Hardwicke.[3] But the situation was hopeless; now both the left- and the right-wing leaders had gone, and attempts to gain reinforcements had been abandoned. It was obvious that the Rockingham ship would sink, for all considered it sinking and therefore no one would work it.

Both the king and the country were worried about the political future. So many administrations had broken up in so few years, with personal feeling becoming more bitter at each

---

[1] Grafton, *Autobiography*, p. 71.

[2] Charles Lennox, third duke of Richmond (1735–1806), had distinguished himself in the army and was now entering political life. He was to prove a difficult man to work with. His radical views gradually became more pronounced. In spite of enjoying high office under the younger Pitt (see narrative below) his career was strangely disappointing.

[3] This would have meant that the 'anti-American' side of the ministry would have been strengthened.

break, that it was difficult to see how any administration could be formed to deal with America. The need for a firm executive team was the more pressing just when it seemed less possible. Ordinary members of parliament were losing their normal antagonistic attitude to the executive because they feared that the king would soon have no government capable of maintaining his interests abroad. The balance of the constitution might now require support of the executive and the choking of ill-timed factious opposition. Such a movement of opinion, slowly appearing among backwoodsmen, was more vocal among minor but businesslike politicians in the house. In the spring of this year, 1766,[1] a group of such politicians met to discourse in confidence on the disordered state of their world. The need they saw was for the king to assert himself more than of late and give the country a stable government—'His Majesty should have the free choice of his own servants and that he should not put the management of his affairs unconditionally into the hands of the leader of any party.' For in party lay, in their view, the origin of discord. The parties they distinguished were that of Lord Rockingham (still in power), that of the duke of Bedford (with whom Lord Temple and George Grenville now seemed to be working), and that of Mr. Pitt; this last was 'merely ideal', for 'it rests on no settled attachment'—that is, had only Pitt's personality instead of interest to unite it. There was, in addition, a fourth party; it consisted of gentlemen such as those at this meeting, who 'have always hitherto acted upon the sole principle of attachment to the Crown'. They thought themselves the most numerous party. They felt they were capable of maintaining an administration but for one sad defect. They consisted entirely of subalterns and had no great leader. And without a great name no cabinet could easily be assembled, nor, if assembled, endure for long.

This analysis of the situation was accurate in 1766. There were a considerable number of men anxious to serve any cabinet which knew its mind and was certain of its future. They were practical men with ambitions and administrative ability. These were the 'King's Friends' who have been so often referred to by historians but never properly described. They were not in fact a group organized even as that century knew organiza-

---

[1] For the dating and documentation of this meeting see N. S. Jucker, *The Jenkinson Papers*, pp. 404 f.

tion. 'King's Friends' was a term to describe an attitude of mind, not a connexion with the court: it was used by those who rejoiced in it as a description like 'patriot' or 'non-party man'; by those who belonged to Rockingham's group it was a term of abuse, like 'placeman' or 'careerist'. But there never was a time when they were organized as a political force. The names recorded of the leaders at this special gathering of gentlemen in 1766 were Lord Granby, Lord Strange, Mr. Stanley, and Sir Fletcher Norton. Lord Granby, the heir of the duke of Rutland, was a friend of Grenville's who had stayed in office with the Rockinghams, and had behind him the Rutland borough influence; Hans Stanley was also a Grenvillite, a diplomat, a governor of the Isle of Wight, a man of smaller fortune.[1] Lord Strange, the son of Lord Derby, appears to have taken the line of country gentlemen and to have supported Grenville's firmness towards America. Sir Fletcher Norton was a very ruthless lawyer 'on the make'; though reckoned a friend to the king, later he was, when disappointed of promotion, to make a most fierce attack upon the court. In all this there is nothing to suggest that a new force had arisen in politics. There is here only patriotic desire to see firmer government, mixed up with the personal ambition of those not irretrievably committed to the great political groups of the day.

It was, after all, an eighteenth-century commonplace to profess support of the crown, as the embodiment of unity, against faction. At this time the platitude seemed to need reiteration. Charles Townshend, that weathercock, said in September 1765 that he was not connected with ministers 'but that his attachment is solely to the King'. Stuart Mackenzie declared that Rockingham relied for his rule upon the 'King's firmest friends', among whom, of course, he reckoned himself. But such friends were not specifically those with whom the king had communication,[2] but rather those who hoped he would restore some order to politics. Such the 'King's Friends' remained, those who from dislike of party or from determination to serve

---

[1] Hans Stanley (1720?–80) had had a part in the peace negotiations in Paris in 1761 and had been made a privy councillor in 1762. He became governor of the Isle of Wight in 1764 and cofferer of the household in 1766. He was a trustee of the Sloane bequest and interested in learning.

[2] Direct communication with the king on important issues was, in these early years, an important part of Bute's special influence; later, in the troubles following the fall of North, Jenkinson too enjoyed this privilege. See below, p. 258.

with all parties, supported administration as such. To call them 'embryo civil servants'[1] is enlightening in so far as it emphasizes their concern for the executive and in so far as it calls attention to that thirst for jobs which inspired some of the most prominent of them. But it is confusing, on the other hand, in that some men of talent in this group became great politicians, like Jenkinson, with fixed political standpoints (on America, or later on the catholic question);[2] moreover, the lesser men supported the court in an unofficial, independent, and patriotic way, being true-blue rather than bureaucratic.[3]

The gentlemen in support of the court who met in 1766 were right in perceiving that their chief need was a leader of major status. Bute still thought of himself as such a leader. He was the friend of the king in a full sense. But his measure had been taken by the country and by the king. George III, feeling his need for new ministers, yet reluctant to lose the existing ones, did, by letter, consult Bute. Bute told him that this was an emergency in which he had a duty to call on Pitt while rousing patriotic sentiment. Undoubtedly Bute expected to be summoned forth himself as the embodiment of patriotic feeling. George III was realist enough to know that if he put himself in Pitt's hands he must do so on Pitt's terms without reserving any part of his favour. Pitt, though his views on America were at variance with those of many of the 'friends' of the court, though he had only six years before been a black-hearted man in George's estimation, was at last summoned to save his king and country. Instead of gratifying Rockingham by appointing Yorke as chancellor the king sent for Pitt.

Pitt, who now became the earl of Chatham, had at length obtained power on his own terms. He had refused to serve with any combination of men because thus his own will would be

---

[1] The phrase, or its equivalent, has been used by several historians who have developed the analysis made by Sir Lewis Namier.

[2] And a 'King's Friend' like Norton could factiously turn into a Rockingham peer (Lord Grantley).

[3] The *London Chronicle* in June 1770 expressed this in sympathetic terms, calling them those who 'have not enlisted themselves under any of those parties, which the discontent of some and the disappointed ambition of others, have formed to distress the King and impede government. They are almost the only persons . . . who having received favours from the Crown, have never flown in H.Majesty's face, nor repaid his kindness with reproaches and ingratitude. . . . In short they have been the same men in power and out of power.' This, of course, was a partisan reply to Burke's innuendos against 'King's Friends', for which see below, p. 125.

countered by an alliance within the ministry. He no longer
needed to insist upon Temple serving with him, for he had been
called to power with the right to select his own colleagues and
to carry out his own policy. His aim was to pulverize the groups
and then select pieces to his own taste from the wreck. From the
Rockingham connexion he had already detached the hero-
worshipping Grafton, who became first lord of the treasury.
Now Conway was also persuaded to join him and stay as secretary of state. This defection cut Rockingham's friends to the
heart.[1] Lord Shelburne, formerly an adherent of Bute but now
almost more Pittite than Chatham, was the other secretary of
state. Charles Townshend could hardly be said to have been
detached from anyone, so erratically had he always rolled
about, but he was pinned down for the moment to being chancellor of the exchequer. Lord Granby was the commander-in-
chief. Camden, as a personal friend, was made lord chancellor.
Chatham himself was lord privy seal, a position free from departmental labour, whence he might inspire the great enterprise.
Chatham thus took up again the work of using Newcastle's men
for his own purposes: but this time he had detached the men
and had not to keep on terms with a jealous Newcastle. Indeed,
a deliberate slight was inflicted on the Rockingham whigs. Lord
Edgcumbe, a Rockingham whig with four Cornish boroughs at
his command, was dismissed from his post of treasurer of the
household in order to give that place to Sir John Shelley.
Shelley's merit was that he was a relative of Newcastle's who
made himself particularly odious to the old duke.[2] The result
of this insult was unfortunate. The Rockinghams appealed to
the common spirit of all their adherents. All those of them who
had been willing to serve with Chatham now resigned,[3] with
the exception of Conway and, of course, Grafton. Conway was
peculiarly unhappy, feeling himself scorned by his old friends
while his new ones failed to appreciate the sacrifice he made for
them.

[1] Among those whom Chatham could not win over were Dowdeswell, Rockingham's chancellor of the exchequer, who refused the offer of the board of trade, and
Egmont, who resigned from the admiralty not so much from loyalty to Rockingham
(he had first served Grenville in that office) as from dislike of Chatham.

[2] Another of Newcastle's relatives, one in favour with him, Thomas Pelham, was
also slighted in this reshuffle.

[3] The duke of Portland, the earl of Scarborough, the earl of Bessborough, and
Lord Monson, plus the admiralty board of Sir Charles Saunders, Augustine Keppel (later Viscount Keppel), and Sir William Meredith.

Chatham wished to deal with the Bedford group as he had dealt with Rockingham. He tried to persuade Gower[1] to take office as an individual. This failing, he negotiated, but in vain, to attract some other members of the group to himself. But the Bedfords, guided by Rigby, asked too many places and put too high a price on their services.

Negotiations had collapsed by November 1766. Thus by the end of that year Lord Chatham had met with only small success in his attempt to split the groups and form a new structure round his own personality. Most of the Rockinghams, the Bedfords, the Grenvilles, were outside and critical of his ministry. On the other hand he had behind him some independents who admired his record; he had the confidence of those who felt that this was the last chance of a settled government; he had the support of the crown. Moreover, Chatham promised that measures would justify what men had too little faith to trust. His programme of action would command support. He set himself to end isolation in Europe and to pacify America.

Chatham believed that it was easy to recover one European friend. Frederic the Great of Prussia had professed himself an admirer of Pitt ever since the war. Hans Stanley[2] should therefore go on a special embassy to renew the alliance with Prussia. This project collapsed even before Stanley could set out. Frederic made it clear that he did not propose to run the risk of conflict with France or Spain or Austria. His eyes were on Poland and his ally was Russia. Anything which distracted him was folly. Chatham found that Europe would not reshape itself to honour his glory. This was the first blow to his haughty will. The second was the misbehaviour of the Americans. It was true that Pitt's resumption of power was hailed with joy in America. But the colonists were no more willing than the Prussians to surrender their interests to satisfy Chatham's pride. Since the Stamp Act had been repealed, since Chatham was not likely to implement the declaratory act, Americans, particularly in New York, began agitation against a new grievance. This was the Mutiny Act of 1766 which authorized military leaders to com-

---

[1] Granville Leveson-Gower (1721–1803), second Earl Gower and (1786) created marquis of Stafford, had been lord privy seal 1755-7 and lord chamberlain of the household 1763-5. He came back into office, as lord president of the council, in 1767.

[2] See above, p. 119 n.

mand the local inhabitants to supply accommodation, fuel, and victuals for the troops. Massachusetts refused to make any such provision; New York refused co-operation unless the order were made not under statute but by a royal requisition under prerogative. Chatham and Camden, the staunchest champions of America hitherto, both condemned this attitude. Chatham, while blaming Grenville for it, declared that Americans were now out of their senses.[1]

At the outset, therefore, Chatham's promise of achievement was made to look ridiculous. To complete his mortification a bad harvest produced a domestic crisis. The export of corn had to be prohibited by order in council. In seeking a bill of indemnity for this interference with the normal law of the land, the government asked for indemnity only for those who executed and not for those who advised the measure. On this they suffered the humiliation of being defeated in the house of lords, where their bill was amended to cover both cases. In some gloom therefore Chatham retired to Bath to nurse his gout and his feelings. In his absence the 'infelicity which', in his own phrase, 'ferments and sours the councils of His Majesty's servants' grew more bitter. For Chatham had not been content to detach men of many different views and join them in his government, he had refused to organize them when he had them enrolled. He knew that the only unifying force for this team was its common deference to his talents. He knew also that his talents appeared not in private intercourse—the tactful letter, the careful adjustment of points of view, the circulated summary of a case—but in great decisions announced without argument and in great speeches which moved parliament to fear and admiration. Therefore he wasted no time on cabinet conferences. He refused even to tell his colleagues what was in his mind. He would promise to declare only in parliament what was to be done. But by the autumn of 1766 this technique was already losing its magnetic force. On foreign policy and America the decisions had been wanting: there was nothing to declare. Moreover, Chatham was now in the house of lords and not in the commons where his power had been felt.

---

[1] In 1767 an act was passed by the Chatham administration which, while it avoided inflicting penalties on America, prohibited the Assembly of New York from passing any act whatsoever until they had complied with the requisitioning orders.

Much has been written of the loss Chatham suffered in popular esteem by taking a peerage. But this was much less important than the loss he suffered in leaving his proper audience. He rarely commanded the upper house as he had the lower. Already, too, the commons was more important for the initiation of policy than the lords.[1] Many of the pressing problems of the day were financial and here the commons was the forum in which decisions had to be arrived at. Thus, at the same time that Chatham's fallibility of judgement became plain, his voice was less resonantly clear. There was no substitute for him in the house of commons. There the affairs of the ministry were handled jointly by Conway and Charles Townshend, the former trying to reconcile himself with old friends by neglecting present ones, and the latter making his bid for personal glory. Neither agreed with Chatham on the next issue that arose. This was the renewal of the East India Company's charter.

The East India Company had gained great territories from the war and the victory over the natives of Bengal.[2] To Chatham it seemed that the moment had arrived for one of his most striking gestures. He wished to claim that all Indian territory must be under the sovereignty of the crown: it might then be leased out to the Company. But he was not willing to negotiate with the Company on the main issue. He would assert the rights of the crown and make grants from grace. On the other hand, Charles Townshend had already taken part in the inner politics of the court of the Company. Influence there might increase his political strength and even bring him a profit. In the course of these intrigues he had committed himself to the idea that there should be bargaining between Company and government. Conway's concern was to get the best possible financial settlement with the Company to aid the straitened national budget and do so with the minimum of political fuss. Accordingly he wanted to accept the propositions which the Company put forward as a basis of agreement. Chatham was angered by such rebellion. His name and fame had failed to move Prussia or America; now it was ignored even by the underlings whom he had chosen as his instruments. He tried in vain to find a substitute[3]

---

[1] Albeit most of the cabinet continued to be drawn from the peers; the few commoners in the cabinet were accordingly important.

[2] See below, pp. 161 f.

[3] An offer was made to Lord North, who declined it.

for Townshend as chancellor of the exchequer. He refused to argue or to compromise. He simply retired from the fray. The gout from which he had been suffering was succeeded by mental illness. He could not bear to look on human faces. He denied his door to colleagues. He employed Lady Chatham as his only link with the outside world. His imperious will had never yielded, but now it dissolved into gloomy incoherence: he refused to accept the facts.

The East Indian business was patched together by the duke of Grafton in June 1767. The Company agreed to pay the sum of £400,000 a year to the state out of the administrative and trading profits of Bengal. At the same time there was a statutory limitation of the Company's dividend to 10 per cent. This was only a solution for the moment, to be reviewed at the end of two years. But for the Chatham experiment in heroic, partyless, and patriotic government it was the final collapse.

In 1770 Edmund Burke[1] pronounced judgement upon this experiment in ruling by the force of one man's genius. In his *Thoughts on the Present Discontents* Burke examined this 'tessellated pavement without cement'[2] along with other unstable combinations of the past decade: it proved, he said, the need for 'party' unity in government and indeed in opposition. Of the three requisites for success by an eighteenth-century ministry, the support of the crown,[3] ability to explain a policy persuasively to the commons, and skill in managing a group of supporters, the last was by no means the least important. But in theory most men disapproved of faction and of party combinations. Burke, in condemning Chatham, gave theoretical justification to the practice of men of common sense. His pamphlet was approved in advance by most of Rockingham's group. To achieve any result in politics, the arts of the party organizer, however

---

[1] Edmund Burke (1729–97), the philosophical statesman and publicist, was at this time M.P. for Wendover and acting as secretary to Lord Rockingham. For the importance of his career see the narrative below.

[2] This famous phrase occurs not in the *Thoughts* but in a speech of Burke's four years later.

[3] The choice of a ministry was, in orthodox theory, the king's within certain limits set by parliament's having an eventual veto. As Chatham said (reported by Richmond) in 1771: if the king 'were to ask his opinion of Rockingham for the Treasury he would reply "Sir, you cannot have a more proper man in every respect nor indeed so proper a one." But on the other hand if the King should name another person, B. instead of A, equally a Whig of known principles, honour and abilities, he would not break off for A. instead of B.' (See Miss A. Gilbert's forthcoming edition of Richmond's correspondence, *The Radical Duke*.)

mundane or even dirty, were essential. In no other way could a consistent policy be followed. 'Good men must combine or fall one by one the unpitied victims in a contemptible struggle.'

Paradoxically Chatham's experiment in pulverizing the groups ended by provoking a theoretical defence of party action. In this way he helped to speed the decline of royal initiative. For in the face of the united action of men who would only serve together and on lines which they had previously agreed, either a patriot minister or a patriot king in the end found himself impotent. The process was a very slow one—and marked by ups and downs according to political conditions—all through the reign of George III, but Chatham's dramatic failure was the writing on the wall for the old eighteenth-century system of monarchy. Burke's pamphlet could be read as a personal attack on the monarch himself. Its explanation of ministerial instability was that there were secret machinations at court, a cabinet within the cabinet, an intrigue behind the backs of ministers. Though phrased, perhaps, to exculpate George III personally this could not but cast suspicion on the king's honesty and so poison his relations with the Rockingham group for the future. Moreover it made Chatham appear rather like another, but less well-loved, Bute.

Though Chatham, in the spring of 1767, might take refuge from reality in a darkened room in Hampstead, his unfortunate colleagues had still to struggle on, meeting crises as they arose. They did so with the handicap of one legacy from their chief. It was part of the no-party system that the ministry should be a departmental one, that is that ministers worked independently at the head of departments without co-ordination among themselves. The supreme chief having collapsed, this chaotic system was seen at its worst. The financial needs of the country remained, as had been the case ever since 1756, the source of the most trouble. It is true that an income was extracted from the East India Company, but the slackening of the painful drive for cheese-paring economy started by Grenville more than absorbed this. Whereas in 1765 Grenville had balanced his accounts, under Rockingham expenditure had gone up, and in 1766 the increase was £½ million. It made matters worse that the cider tax as well as the American stamp duties had been abolished. In 1767, under Chatham, expenditure rose by a further £¼ million. To make ends meet the debt was increased by more loans. A further £1½ million had to be found from annuities at 3 per cent. The opposition, led on this point by George Grenville, were able to make the life of the chancellor of the exchequer, Charles Townshend, most uncomfortable. In February 1767 George Grenville and Rockingham's former chancellor, Mr. Dowdeswell,[1] made a joint attack. They carried against the ministry a proposal to reduce the land tax from the 'war time rate' of 4s. to 3s. Thus at a blow £½ million was lost to the exchequer. This was not only a sign that the opposition were playing to the back-benches: it marked the inefficiency of the leadership of the ministerial team. They were often to be found speaking and voting against one another.

The reduction of the land tax intensified the need to find new sources of revenue or to reduce expenditure. Charles Townshend had boasted in January 1767[2] that he knew of a method to obtain revenue from America without causing offence. To this boast he was held by insistent questions from Lord George Sackville. The cabinet had no such plan. Nor had Townshend, whose excuse was simply that opinion in the house was in favour of some such experiment. The promise having been given, the plan was afterwards vamped up. The scheme, which was introduced in May, was to impose new customs duties on America. The colonists had said they accepted the regulations of trade but rejected direct taxes. Townshend's scheme was to devise duties which would bring in revenue while appearing to be part of the regulatory system and beyond constitutional cavil. Duties were imposed on lead, glass, paper, painters' colours, and tea imported into America from Britain. As might have been foreseen, the consequence was to arouse a colonial agitation against all forms of taxation for English revenue, including indirect taxation.

It had been the mark of Chatham's government not only that it was made up of many individuals selected without party allegiance, not only that the whole was commanded by an imperious captain, but that the policy which this ministry was to

---

[1] William Dowdeswell (1721–75) came from a county, Worcestershire, noted for its dislike for paying taxes (see A. W. Ward, *The English Land Tax in the 18th Century*, p. 76 n.). In 1766 he had received the thanks of the mercantile interest for his work as chancellor of the exchequer under Rockingham. Though the motion to reduce the land tax was made by Dowdeswell in February, it had been prepared by activities of Thomas Whateley, acting for Grenville, since the previous October.

[2] On 26 January 1767 in a debate on army estimates.

pursue ran counter to the general prejudices of most members of parliament. Chatham had hoped to command support from patriotic men by his name even when, as in American affairs, he pronounced that their ordinary views were wrong. He hoped to beat down the feeling that America must be taxed—a feeling which had been too strong for the arts of practical politicians under Rockingham—by his acknowledged authority on colonial affairs. With the Townshend duties it is clear that a second step had been taken in the disintegration of this plan. The leaderless team took, as might be expected, the decision to swim with the stream and not against it. It was natural to do so. It is what 'friends to the King and his administration' expected. It was the course which seemed right to the king himself.

The change of direction also marked a move forward by Charles Townshend to fill the shoes of Chatham. To the duke of Grafton and General Conway, on the other hand, the anti-American policy was still abhorrent. Everyone agreed that if Chatham was not able to return, the ministerial team would need reinforcements. In 1767, therefore, overtures were made to Lord Rockingham and to the friends of the duke of Bedford. The latter were in sympathy with the new policy of firmness towards America but their demands for places were once more high. The king, in any event, would not treat with the Bedfords if that involved any chance of a return of George Grenville, that bullying prig, to his personal circle. Lord Rockingham, sympathizing in view with the Grafton wing of the cabinet, was not willing to join the existing administration in order to alter its balance. He demanded that there should be a new administration formed by himself from those with whom he was in agreement and with whom he could work. This neither the king nor the ministers who had accepted Chatham's system, or lack of it, could accept.

Lord Rockingham's opposition was not strong enough to shake the ministry decisively. He failed to produce a plan for common action with the Bedford group partly because he objected to their contact with Grenville and partly because they could not tolerate his friendship for Conway. So the cabinet remained as it was throughout the rest of 1767. Lord Shelburne was busy with schemes of his own for America, devising the Quebec Act[1] for the settlement of Canada, working along lines

---

[1] See below, p. 198.

indicated by Chatham. He ceased to attend cabinet meetings. His policy was as purely his own as was that of Charles Townshend.

Townshend died of inflammation of the bowels in the late summer.[1] To his place succeeded the conciliatory and able Lord North. This change did not immediately compose the quarrels within the cabinet. Their only positive and agreed action lay in Ireland. The lord-lieutenant was Lord Townshend. He forwarded to London proposals to avoid yet further 'colonial' disputes by making concessions to the Irish parliament.[2] The cabinet agreed to limit the duration of an Irish parliament to eight years, to grant Irish judges security of tenure, to cut down pensions, and to introduce habeas corpus in Ireland. But this was not part of any move towards a more 'liberal' policy. It was decided, as most things were, under the influence of one particular, strong, departmental officer, and without regard to anything but the needs of the moment.

In 1768 the ministry at last gained the reinforcement for which it had so long negotiated. The Bedford group came in, increasing the support for government in both houses of parliament, but particularly in the house of lords. Gower became lord president while Weymouth became secretary of state in Conway's room.[3] This increase of voting strength also meant a further shift in the balance of power inside the ministry. Those who still believed that Chatham's colonial policy was correct were now in a minority at each successive crisis. Lord Shelburne was the most brilliant of Chatham's disciples. He was also the most disliked. His influence was particularly damaged by the cabinet reshuffle. For out of his department was carved a third secretaryship of state, that for the colonies. From this time, therefore, Viscount Hillsborough replaced Shelburne as the minister for imperial affairs.[4] Nor did the attack upon Shelburne stop there. He was vulnerable because even those who, like Grafton, might in general be expected to agree with his principles, disliked and distrusted him personally. Shelburne

---

[1] Having only secured, by way of rewards, the grant of the peerage of Greenwich to his wife.   [2] See below, pp. 221 f.

[3] Conway stepped down to become lieutenant general of the ordnance.

[4] Wills Hill (1718–93), second Viscount (Irish) Hillsborough and Baron (English) Harwich, was to be conspicuous for his harsh attitude towards the Americans. He was secretary of state for the Southern Department, 1779–82, and was created marquis (Irish) of Downshire.

was too clever, too reticent, and too unbending. He relied often upon private sources of information and upon the studies of unorthodox but clever men. He built up for himself not a connexion like ordinary politicians, but a private 'brains-trust' of economists who furnished him with 'briefs' for his rather arrogant pronouncements. Even in his private business affairs he used a manager (Macleane)[1] notorious for being 'too clever by half'. Shelburne came to be suspected of stock-exchange manipulation as of every clever and ungentlemanly trick.[2] His unpopularity was not fully grown by 1768, but already men thought of him as 'the Jesuit'. A decision to dismiss Shelburne was therefore popular.

Lord Chatham was at length stirred to action by the evident intention of reversing his policies. Every principle for which he had stood in 1766, with the single exception of departmental unco-ordinated cabinets, was now being denied. 'Measures not men' might still be inscribed on the standards of the administration, but they were the opposite measures from those he had planned. He arose from torpor, but only to resign. He used as a pretext the decision to dismiss Sir Jeffrey Amherst[3] from his post as absentee governor of Virginia. His real reason was that the Bedfords were getting their way in questions of policy and their way was anti-American.

It would have been well for Grafton if he had decided to leave with Shelburne and with Chatham,[4] for their departure left him as the incompetent captain of a mutinous crew. But he remained in office for two years more, partly from a sense of duty to the king, partly because he was too obtuse to realize how rapidly he had become a prisoner of the Bedfords, but partly because his pride was involved in winning a great battle in domestic affairs for which he felt personal responsibility.

[1] Lauchlin Macleane emerges from obscurity in 1759 as a doctor in India; an acquaintance of both Bute and Wilkes; governor of St. Martin's in the West Indies 1765; secretary to Shelburne and M.P. 1768–71; agent for Warren Hastings; drowned on his way home to England from India, 1777; see L. B. Namier, *Structure of Politics*, p. 316 and K. Feiling, *Warren Hastings*, passim.

[2] L. S. Sutherland, *The East India Company in Eighteenth Century Politics*, p. 206.

[3] Jeffrey Amherst (1717–97) had been made governor of North America and knighted after his victorious conduct of operations 1758–9. He had returned to England and had been made governor of Virginia in 1763. He was created Baron Amherst in 1776.

[4] Weymouth took Shelburne's place as secretary of the Southern Department and the earl of Rochford filled the vacancy in the Northern Department. The earl of Bristol became lord privy seal.

The domestic struggle arose out of the general election in the spring of 1768. The election as a whole was quiet and normal, that is to say it was fought, in those constituencies where there was any contest at all, on local issues and between local interests. But John Wilkes, reappearing from France, stood first for the city of London and then for the county of Middlesex. Wilkes's return was the last fling of a broken man, but it recovered all he had lost. He realized by this time that those he had called his friends, from Temple to Rockingham or Grafton, would let him rot out his days abroad. Rather than expire in this way the outlaw threw himself once more into English politics. His first choice was the city of London.

In 1768 the trading classes in general blamed ministers for interruptions in commerce with America. Both Lord Chatham and Lord Shelburne had their personal allies among leading city politicians who were at odds with the respectable ministerial men. The East India Company, whose enormous financial power should have been used to reinforce the 'court side' in city life, was itself riven by political conflicts and reproduced the personal rivalries of Westminster.[1] Such a scene was made for Wilkes's reckless talents. Yet in 1768 he failed. He was admitted into a city company to qualify him to stand. At the election Harley, the lord mayor and a court supporter, topped the poll with 3,729 votes. He was followed by Ladbroke, also a court man, by Beckford,[2] and by Barlow Trecothick. These four were elected. Sir Richard Glyn, John Paterson, and John Wilkes were defeated. Wilkes was bottom with 1,247 votes. Wilkes had had too little time for a campaign. Further he had no friends among great politicians. In future it was to be possible for him to establish his own interest. Among the shopkeepers of small means who lived inside the city (which was already by this time no more than an eighth of the metropolitan area) it was possible—by assiduous organization and by always taking the wildest line—to build up a machine capable of defeating at once court, independent political patrons, and the financial cliques. But Wilkes could not build this up in a day.

Rejected in London, Wilkes stood for Middlesex whose election was a little later and where there were less organized interests to contend with. The county of Middlesex was already

---

[1] For radicalism in the city of London see above, p. 50.

[2] For him see above, p. 96 n.

partly urbanized. Its local government system had broken down, for the local squires were incapable or unwilling to deal with the problems of a shifting, violent, population.[1] It followed that the forty-shilling freeholders, the county electorate, which in an ordinary county voted obediently as the leading gentry ordered, were in Middlesex a restless and radical body. They were not even organized in groups as were the voters of London and Westminster. For them, therefore, the name of John Wilkes, enemy of the established order, outlaw, had great attraction. In addition Wilkes had gained two very valuable allies in his London adventure. John Horne, better known as Horne Tooke, the radical parson from Brentford, was a natural rebel and a fluent committee man. His father was a poulterer and his eldest brother a noted market gardener who was said to have introduced the strawberry to English tables.[2] Horne himself had wished to be a lawyer and had subsided into the church. His delight was to show his natural legal talents in conducting his own cases against professional lawyers. He was also a scholar with eccentric ideas on philology.[3] For Wilkes his charm was his roystering tastes, his knowledge of Brentford, his violent oratory, and his taste for committee work. The other ally was Mr. Serjeant Glynn, a man of very different character. Glynn was an upright, slightly pedantic man, an antiquarian whose legal knowledge was extensive, but who had fallen foul of Chief Justice Mansfield. He liked to talk at length of the Anglo-Saxon origins of our free institutions. Glynn and Horne together supplied organization to turn Wilkes's notoriety into votes.

Lord Temple gave Wilkes land in Middlesex to qualify him as a country freeholder. He stood, quite simply, as the independent man, persecuted by an inefficient and expensive government. He challenged arrest as he canvassed for votes. In a disorderly drunken election he had 6,000 Spitalfields weavers, the victims of hard times, to help him keep some sort of order. The

---

[1] See above, p. 47.

[2] A. Stephens, *Memoirs of John Horne Tooke*, i. 6.

[3] These were set out in *The Diversions of Purley*, the title being taken from Horne's country residence in later life. He changed his name to Horne Tooke on acquiring by bequest the estate of the eccentric Mr. Tooke whose interests he had safeguarded against an Enclosure Bill after a characteristic piece of agitation which involved libelling the Speaker of the house of commons and escaping the consequences on a legal technicality. Horne Tooke was the last Anglican clergyman to sit as a member of parliament. The Clerical Disqualification Act of 1801 was a declaratory act of which he was the occasion.

figures in the end (28 March 1768) were Wilkes 1,292, Cooke 827, and Sir William Proctor 807. Wilkes then insisted upon being arrested (20 April). The government up to this stage had shown every desire to avoid a direct struggle with so obstreperous a character. Once Wilkes was in prison his power to arouse excitement as a martyr was much increased. His partisans excited all the anti-ministerial passion of the time. On 10 May 1768 troops round the prison in St. George's Fields were involved in a skirmish with crowds who had come to draw Wilkes in triumph from his cell to parliament. In this a spectator, a Mr. William Allen, was killed. It was unfortunate that the troops were the Scots Guards—countrymen of Bute. At the inquest the jury found Private Maclane guilty of murder and Private Maclauray and Captain Murray guilty of abetting him. The grand jury (at Guildford) subsequently threw out the charges, but nevertheless Wilkes had scored one more success. He proceeded to publish letters on the riots, accusing the ministry of using Scottish butchers to intimidate free Englishmen.

When Wilkes had appeared (27 April) before Mansfield, that learned and cautious judge had cancelled the outlawry on the grounds that the writ had been made out 'at the County Court for the County of Middlesex' instead of 'at the County Court of Middlesex for the County of Middlesex'. But Wilkes had still to face (on 20 June) the original charges, of publishing the *North Briton* and the *Essay on Woman*, from which he had fled five years before.[1] He was fined £500 for each publication and sentenced to ten months' imprisonment on the first charge and twelve months on the second. He was also bound over for seven years on recognisances of £1,500. But he was M.P. for Middlesex. His fellow member Cooke died and Wilkes's ally Glynn was triumphantly elected to replace him. At this election disorder was, if anything, worse. To meet Wilkite weavers the other side organized the Irish chairmen, whose arms were presumably muscular from carrying the gentry round London streets. In fights between these gangs a Wilkite (G. Clerke) was killed by an Irishman M'Quirke. M'Quirke was convicted of murder but, to the indignation of the radicals, was pardoned.

These months of disorder had to be taken into serious account by the government. The secretary of state, Weymouth, wrote to the chairman of the Lambeth quarter sessions bidding him

---

[1] See above, p. 101.

show no hesitation if military aid were needed. This letter, which he obtained and published, Wilkes called 'a hellish project, brooded over by some infernal spirits'. In reality it was merely an elementary precaution in a time of real danger. For 1768 and 1769 were years of distress in London. A wave of strikes (without the restraint of trade union machinery, for this did not exist) had thrown London into disorder. The weavers of Spitalfields left work in protest against the master weavers reducing rates by 5*d*. a yard. Four thousand sailors left their ships for higher pay and roamed about cheering for Wilkes. In quick succession there were stoppages among the hatters, the Thames watermen, the tailors, the glass grinders, and the coal-heavers. These discontented workmen were prominent in crowds around Westminster when parliament met again in the autumn. That winter the Southwark joiners and hat-dyers had also left their work. To all these men, needy and angry as a result of economic conditions, Wilkes became a sort of symbol: he had no economic programme, but he was in revolt, and they were in revolt also.

To contain such explosive forces it must be remembered that the authorities could call only on the magistrates, the inefficient watch, the efforts of private citizens, and upon the troops. It was because their means of maintaining order was so clumsy that they called for swift, strong coercion. The Gordon riots[1] twelve years later were to demonstrate how difficult it could be to restore control once the mobs were loose. The Gordon riots were also a further demonstration that the sporadic disorders of the London area only became menacing when some leader drew them together and prolonged them. So in the summer and autumn of 1768 Grafton believed it essential to crush Wilkes. Prison did not cage him sufficiently. His election for Middlesex must be quashed. Grafton emphasized that this decision was not taken to punish Wilkes for his past offences (for in 1763 Grafton had been counted his friend) but in order to extinguish the 'spirit of riot which . . . threatened to bring on a disrespect to all government and lawful authority'.[2]

In April 1768 the cabinet were united in their belief that Wilkes must be expelled; their ground was that he was an out-

---

[1] See below, pp. 236 and f.

[2] Grafton's words in his *Autobiography and Political Correspondence*, ed. W. R. Anson, p. 195.

law when he stood as a candidate. A meeting of junior official men[1] advised Lord North that Wilkes's expulsion was necessary if the authority of government was to be upheld. It was only in the winter, after Chatham and Shelburne had left office, that any division of opinion appeared among ministers. Dunning,[2] for instance, the solicitor general, resigned early in 1770 because he felt that Wilkes should be heard in his own defence before his letter on the government's repression of riots was voted a libel. Lord Chancellor Camden began to wonder whether expediency might not dictate a retreat from the firm position which he had at first advised; he soothed his nerves with a careful academic study of the famous Douglas case.[3]

[1] With one dissentient, Richard Hussey, who thought Wilkes had already been punished enough.

[2] John Dunning was thus one more liberally minded man to leave Grafton. He soon played a leading part in the opposition to North (see below, p. 232 and n.).

[3] Lord Camden had a professional interest in the Douglas case which had reached the house of lords on appeal from the Scottish Court of Session. The rest of London society had been enjoying it, without such excuse, ever since 1761. Archibald Douglas, third marquis and first duke, lived under the domination of servants for most of his life. For his last three years he had exchanged their rule for that of his headstrong cousin—'Peggy Douglas of Mains'—whom he had married: but he had no children. She was eccentric, as witness her returning from Europe with the embalmed body of a servant or the popular story that she had burned down the castle (in 1758) to clinch an argument with her husband. He was more than eccentric and lived in fear that his sister might have him locked up as a lunatic or for the murder of her reputed lover, Mr. Ker. With an admirer of his sister, the duke of Buccleugh (then Dalkeith)—'a man of mean understanding and meaner habits'—Douglas was content merely to fight a duel. This only sister, Lady Jean, secretly married an adventurer, Colonel (later Sir John) Steward of Grandtully. She claimed that in 1748 in Paris, at various addresses, and at the age of fifty, she had given birth to twins. Of these the elder, and sole survivor, claimed the estates on the death of his presumed uncle in 1761. The case took eight years to decide and a thousand quarto pages of testimony exposed the whole domestic life of the Douglas family. The Hamiltons, the other claimants to the estates, alleged that Lady Jean had no children but that the two boys were the sons of destitute French peasants bought for a few louis apiece in order to acquire the estates by fraud. Lady Jean, after a life spent in living on her wits, had died in poverty, debt, and a cloud of pious letters. Her husband, who never could distinguish truth from falsehood, had passed a good part of his life in prison, but was also dead before 1769. Everyone relished the revelation of mad and bad life in high places. Dr. Johnson argued with Boswell about it. The Bedford connexion took up the Hamilton side, under the influence of the dowager duchess of Hamilton, herself a colourful character, who had come to London as Miss Elizabeth Gunning, and on the strength of her beauty married three dukes and gave birth to four. Eventually in 1769, Lady Jean's son, or pretended son, won his case and inherited the Douglas estates. Camden and Mansfield for once agreed, voting in his favour. Though he begat eight sons, every one of these was childless and the estates eventually passed through his daughter to the earl of Home.

In January 1769 Wilkes petitioned the house of commons complaining that Lord Mansfield had been guilty of bias against him in proceedings arising out of his libel on Lord Weymouth's conduct at the time of the St. George's Fields 'massacre'. The commons voted his attack upon Weymouth scandalous and seditious. On the motion of the secretary at war, Barrington, seconded by Mr. Paymaster Rigby, Wilkes was, in February 1769, expelled from his seat in parliament.

Though it was on the government initiative that Wilkes was expelled it should not be supposed that the majority against him was difficult to collect. Many gentlemen naturally shared Grafton's view that a debt-ridden ex-outlaw was not eligible to represent even the popular voice in the constitution. But Wilkes was determined to raise a more exciting constitutional point. He flourished on grievances. He attracted to his defence all those who, for whatever reason, disliked Grafton or the Bedfords. In the city of London two important politicians, Alderman Townsend (M.P. for Looe) and John Sawbridge (M.P. for Hythe), who were adherents of Shelburne and Chatham, were free, now that their patrons were in opposition, to join Wilkes's committee. Though the court party in London tried to veto it, Wilkes was accordingly elected by the united radical vote as alderman for the ward of Farringdon-Without. More immediately offensive to the house of commons was the fact that Wilkes was re-elected for Middlesex unopposed and at no expense to himself.

Grafton had had no thought of the constitutional consequences of Wilkes's expulsion for he had not foreseen this re-election. But if the house had been right to expel him the first time, would it not be ridiculous to suffer his immediate re-election? Accordingly Wilkes was expelled again. A third time he was elected and expelled. In the fourth election candidates were found to stand against him. The result of the poll was Wilkes 1,143, Luttrell 296, Whitaker 5, and Roche 0. In May 1769 the house of commons carried its views to their extreme conclusion and resolved that, as Wilkes was ineligible, Colonel Luttrell had been elected.[1] This decision was denounced

---

[1] Henry Lawes Luttrell (1743-1821) combined an army career with politics. He gave up a Cornish seat (Bossiney) to fight Middlesex. He eventually rose to be master general of the ordnance in 1797 after succeeding his father in the Irish earldom of Carhampton in 1789.

by the whole 'popular' party as a violation of the rights of the electorate. John Wilkes had at length achieved his aim. He had raised a real constitutional point of substance with which to associate his fortunes. Out of his personal adventure he had brought into being a division on principle which split politicians into camps and which remains debatable ground.

The case of Grafton, North, and the court may best be put in the terms in which it commended itself to the young Charles James Fox[1] who entered parliament at this time. The future leader of liberal causes was a hearty supporter of the ministry against Wilkes and the Middlesex agitators. For he believed, as he was always to do, in the virtues of the mixed and balanced constitution. The house of commons to play its proper part in this scheme had to be independent both of the court above it and of the people below. It might legitimately respect and be influenced by either the king or the people, but it must be subject to neither. Members should be men of free judgement. In this view riots, as over the cider tax, might be reckoned a fair method of impressing on members the unpopularity of a measure and might, as one factor in the argument, help members to make their decision, just as knowledge of the king's desires or comfort might be taken into account. But these were factors in a problem decided by members. They still made up their own minds. What was illegitimate was to pass from conventional pressures to absolute coercion, for then members lost their powers of decision. This a king would do if he were to persecute opponents. This Wilkes was doing in refusing to accept the decision of the house and trying to force them by violence to eat their words. That this was Wilkes's intention Fox had no doubt. In this very year, 1769, the court of common hall of the city of London began to draw up instructions for their elected members of parliament and to demand that they should pledge themselves to carry them out. Such a system of a mandate would have the effect of making the member a cipher by denying him authority to do anything on which the public have not been explicitly consulted.

The guard against such a destruction of the house of commons lay, in the ministry's view, in the exercise of its privileges. It had

---

[1] Charles James Fox (1749–1806) was the third son of Henry Fox, Lord Holland. He had been elected for Midhurst when he was still a minor. His support of the anti-popular side was to continue until 1774.

fought the Stuarts and the law courts successfully to obtain sole control over its membership and over election disputes. Thus privilege, which in 1763 Wilkes had invoked to protect himself against prosecution, was now used against him. In each case the upholders of privilege talked of the necessity of preserving the independence of members of parliament from outside pressure. From the government side in 1769 the difficulty lay in defining exactly how much influence upon a member of parliament from outside, whether from a patron or a mob, was legitimate and where unconstitutional coercion began. It was a difficulty, at least, in theory. In practice Grafton, for instance, was sure that Chatham's use of forces out of doors had been fair and that Wilkes had crossed an invisible line. To many men this line was clear beyond argument and sanctified by traditional practice.

Those who, without being Wilkites, were stirred to protest against the decision on the Middlesex election, also based their case upon the need to preserve the balance of the constitution. Montesquieu, who, twenty years earlier, had eulogized the balanced English system, had prophesied its ruin when the executive should grow too strong and control the house of commons. The opposition to Grafton maintained that the troubles of the whole reign had been due to the excessive influence of the court. It was vital therefore that the commons should be protected against this upper weight. The commons should increase its strength by playing off the people against the ministers. Followers of Chatham refused to see in the vote of the house to seat Luttrell a free expression of opinion. Degenerate members had weakly submitted to the executive in expelling Wilkes. As they accounted for the fact that they were themselves out of office by alleging that the Bedfords flourished on corruption, so they saw in the commons excluding Wilkes further evidence that the house had ceased to decide for itself. They wished to strengthen the house against degeneration. They maintained that the decision on Middlesex meant that a corrupt majority claimed to nominate new members. But the strength of the legislature was rooted in the rights of the electorate.

After every election there were some seats which were still disputed, on petitions alleging malpractice being presented to the house. These disputed elections were decided not on merit but from partisan grounds. Often these cases were taken as a test of strength in a new parliament to see how the groups were aligning themselves. This open scandal was not entirely removed even later when George Grenville's Controverted Elections Act of 1770 delegated the discussions to special committees. But while this remained an acknowledged evil, could it be safe to extend the powers of the commons beyond the discussion of electoral qualification right up to the naming of the member for an independent county? It could not: it would make it possible for a corrupt majority, bought by favours from the crown, to stifle the voice of the country. It was by arguing that the house of commons would lose its significance in this way that the opposition hoped to arouse the latent fear of the executive among unattached members and so to offset the general revulsion from the character and methods of Wilkes.

John Wilkes himself was not content with so traditional a technique of opposition. He was happy to blacken the repute of Weymouth and Grafton, but he had more to do if he was to put himself beyond the restraints of prison and debts. With the aid of Parson Horne he introduced a new element into eighteenth-century politics. He did not propose simply to excite opinion out of doors. He organized it and gave it a lasting shape; in so doing he turned the popular opinion which had been an episodic but normal feature of politics into a force capable of growth which might alter the system. In February 1769 the Society for the Defence of the Bill of Rights had its first meeting. Horne rightly defined its objects as primarily to get Wilkes into parliament and to defend his cause as a symbol of opposition to the government. To this end it paid the £3,000 Wilkes owed for election expenses, compounded with his creditors for the £12,000 of debt with which he was previously burdened, and gave him £1,000 to start him off again.[1] These sums in themselves are evidence that it was not a club of poor men. It drew support from traders and shopkeepers who were dissatisfied with colonial and economic policy and who, in addition, resented the smallness of their part in the political life of the nation.

In the course of 1769 supporters of Wilkes toured Yorkshire, Wiltshire, and Bedfordshire. The excitement was sufficiently well guided for petitions requesting the king to dissolve his

---

[1] In 1769 also Wilkes obtained £4,000 damages against Lord Halifax (defrayed by the crown) in his long postponed action arising from the use of general warrants.

corrupt parliament to be voted at many public meetings throughout the kingdom. The city of London, in 1770, excelled all others in the offensiveness of the terms of its petition. When both houses of parliament censured the corporation and when the king showed his displeasure to Lord Mayor Beckford, the reply of the city was to put a statue to Beckford in the Guildhall to commemorate his presentation of their attack on the ministers. In the days before the invention of the parliamentary question this concerted attack by petitions was the best expression of a roused public opinion.

By 1770 Wilkes was not only out of prison and financially patched up, he was also admitted as an alderman of the city, master of the Joiners Company, and the head of something like a political party. For the Wilkites by 1770 had a central committee, provincial contacts, and a programme. The six points they reiterated were: (1) Improvement in the system of trial by jury so as to reduce (particularly in libel cases[1]) the power of judges like Mansfield. (2) An inquiry into the St. George's Fields Massacre. (3) An inquiry into Clerke's death in the riots. (4) An inquiry into justice in Middlesex with reference to the notorious justices of the peace. (5) The right of the public to the whole revenue of India. (6) Justice for Wilkes. To this, as a seventh point, should be added rather vaguely, support for the Americans. But though this was a programme, it has only to be listed for its inadequacy to be revealed. The organization was of more significance for the future than the doctrine. It was an innovation to have any platform at all, but this platform was too ephemeral, too personal to Wilkes. Indeed Wilkes was always the *franc tireur*. In 1770 the Society of the Bill of Rights split. Wilkes regarded the society as his backers. Horne and Shelburne's agents were willing to use Wilkes as a figurehead, but they believed that there was more to the movement than his fortunes. Mr. Bingley, who had printed Wilkes's attacks on the courts, refused to answer Mansfield's interrogation and to give information about his employers. For contumacy he went to prison for three years. Wilkes declined to allow money to be used for Bingley as he needed it all himself. This was the signal

---

[1] In cases of libel the jury could only decide (a) whether the words complained of had been the work of the defendant, (b) whether these words had the meaning alleged. Whether that meaning constituted libel was left to the judge until Fox's libel act in 1792 (see below, pp. 302 f.) gave this decision also to the jury.

for Horne, in protest, to leave the Bill of Rights Society and to found a new Society for Constitutional Information into which he attracted the wealthier of the radicals and the more theoretical.

The effect upon Wilkes of this split was to make him at once more violent and less seriously radical. He lost his backbone of principle while he was forced to turn more desperately to arousing the passions of the most needy of the population. In 1771, when he was elected sheriff of London, he fought not only against conservatives but against the progressives supported by Horne and by the parliamentary opposition. He advocated the abolition of impressment for the navy and a public control of bread prices in the interests of the indigent. The radicals' ranks were only temporarily closed again in 1771.

It was part of the traditional doctrine of the independence of the house of commons against pressure from below that its debates were nominally secret. It was part of standing orders that no report should be made of proceedings. This order was habitually ignored. But as a result of the campaign against Wilkes, renewed efforts were made to enforce it. What more effective means was there of protecting members from societies for political information than to keep secret what was said in parliament? So, in 1771, Messrs. Thompson of the *Gazetteer*, Wheble of the *Middlesex Journal*, and Miller of the *Evening Post*, were summoned, under parliamentary privilege, to answer to the house for their presumption in giving reports of parliamentary debates. This was a challenge the radicals gladly accepted. Horne rather than Wilkes seems to have planned their strategy. Miller failed to appear before the house. The messenger of the commons was then sent into the city to arrest Miller, on a warrant being issued by the Speaker. But the city authorities were united in resisting this invasion of their own privileged immunities. The house of commons messenger was himself arrested in the city. Alderman Wilkes, as a magistrate of London, took a copy of his warrant and compelled the deputy sergeant of the house of commons to go bail for him before he would release him. In this way the whole issue of the commons versus the people was reopened; on the popular side stood the city of London whose privileged position was accepted by the most conservative constitutionalists.

The house of commons, however, did not fail to continue the battle on this wider front. The city authorities, Lord Mayor

Brass Crosby, M.P., Alderman Oliver, M.P., and Alderman Wilkes, were ordered to attend the house to answer for their insolence. Wilkes took this opportunity to reopen his personal grievances. He would only accept a summons made out to him as member of parliament for Middlesex. Lord North, wiser than Grafton, declined to traverse yet again this treacherous ground. The summons to Wilkes was made out for a day on which the house would not be sitting; action was taken only against Crosby and Oliver who, after defiant replies, were sent to the tower.

The printers' case marks the point at which the engagement with Wilkes was broken off. It is not true that a clear victory had been won for the publicity of parliamentary debates.[1] Lord North continued to have reporters excluded from the galleries whenever he wished to keep a debate quiet and to leave them open when the government had a good case worth publicity.[2] He did this quite simply by telling the Speaker when to enforce the standing orders against admitting strangers. The process by which the reporting of debates grew more and more respectable was a very slow one: it was helped on by the practice of some members of parliament of giving the text of their speeches to the press. But the 1771 case does mark the end of the attempt to prosecute those who tried to resist the wishes of the house. Wilkes was thereby robbed of opportunities for agitation.

Wilkes retreated from the national stage and made London his theatre. He tried to get the office of city chamberlain, a profitable one, for himself or for his brother. In 1772, 1773, and 1774 he was put forward to the Court of Aldermen as a candidate to be lord mayor. His opponents among the aldermen vetoed his nomination twice, but on the last occasion were obliged to grant him the highest place in London. In the general election of 1774 Wilkes was elected, with Glynn, for Middlesex, and this time was allowed quietly to take his seat. In that parliament there were twelve Wilkite members of parliament. Their programme looked serious. They wanted shorter parliaments, a bill against placemen, and another against the acceptance of money from the Crown, as well as the redress of grievances in Britain, Ireland, and America. But Wilkes did not really have

[1] I do not know any evidence to support this often repeated view except that given in the remainder of the paragraph.

[2] The middle 70's are a period of very faulty records of debates in consequence. Our knowledge of 1768–71 is fuller and more reliable.

his heart in the dull business of doing propaganda for ideas. His parliamentary activity was limited to agitation for the erasure of the records of his expulsion from the records of the house. He did introduce a bill for parliamentary reform in 1776 only to withdraw it without a division. By his inertia he surrendered his influence among serious reformers in London to Chatham and to Shelburne. In 1773, for instance, Common Hall in London pressed all members of parliament to support the idea of shorter parliaments: in 1774 that reform was a leading idea in a celebrated speech of Chatham's.

In the long run Wilkes's achievement was to have brought the popular element in the constitution into active and developing life. But this effect was not immediately obvious. In the short run his efforts seemed only to be to exacerbate the tone of political life and to distract attention from the more important colonial issue. The last eighteen months of Grafton's administration (1768–70) were hag-ridden by Wilkes. With great issues about America dividing him from his colleagues in the cabinet, Grafton was obliged to labour every day to counter Wilkes's manœuvres. It was hard to get a seat in the house of commons when Wilkes was under discussion; it was sometimes difficult to raise half the number among exhausted members to debate a purely American question.[1] The ingenuity shown by Wilkes in bringing up his case on all sorts of occasions—in connexion with the right of members of parliament to present petitions, by slandering the Speaker and so on—disrupted the time-table of the commons. It became commonplace for the House to sit until three or four in the morning and to divide time and time again. The unfortunate Speaker, Sir John Cust, who, in those days before there was a deputy Speaker, was bound to remain in the chair often for fourteen quarrelsome hours at a stretch, developed as a result internal disorders of which, in 1770, he died, another victim of Wilkes.

Yet decisions about America were made, decisions whose importance was not sufficiently noticed at the time. The Americans, particularly those of Massachusetts, had been goaded by the Townshend duties into a denial of the right of parliament to bind them with such laws. The cabinet decided, on the instance of Grafton and Camden, to repeal the Townshend duties, except that on tea, though they refused to admit that parliament's

[1] So Colonel Barré complained—Cavendish *Debates*, ed. J. Wright, i. 126.

power was limited. This was a compromise not unlike that of the Rockingham administration's combination of a declaratory act with the repeal of stamp duties. But once more the compromise foretold the collapse of the cabinet. Grafton's supporters were in favour of repealing the tea duty along with the rest, and thought its retention useless as a symbol of legal right and pernicious as a source of future quarrels. The forthcoming changes in policy were announced in a circular letter from Lord Hillsborough to colonial governors. Camden and Grafton accused Hillsborough of leaving out the conciliatory sentences to which they had secured cabinet assent and of strengthening the passages about 'legislative authority' and 'execution of the laws' in a way designed to wound American feelings. Grafton would have resigned as a protest against the unwarrantable action of Hillsborough except that the public would have assumed that he was running away from Wilkes's petitions. Camden said he felt 'silent indignation' at the 'arbitrary measures' which his 'avowed opposition could not prevent'.[1] He prepared to follow Chatham towards opposition.

While Grafton was fighting in the cabinet a losing battle for a liberal policy towards the colonies, he was being vilified in public as the deviser of arbitrary government. Wilkes alone did not foist this reputation on him. In 1768 the duke of Portland's title to his lands in Cumberland first came before parliament. Though the Portland family had had the forest of Inglewood and the manor of Carlisle (as part of the honour of Penrith) peacefully in their possession since William III's grant seventy years before, Sir James Lowther applied to the treasury for a lease from the Crown of these lands. A defect in the Portland title was discovered and the treasury granted Sir James his lease, despite a promise to Portland that no action should be taken while he was pursuing necessary research into past deeds. Therefore Portland had no remedy but to demand legislation to extend the provisions of the act of James I barring claims of the Crown against any title which had been quietly enjoyed for sixty years before the passing of that act. The government had this 'Nullum Tempus' Bill postponed in 1768. That the treasury should be behaving so high-handedly towards a property owner, that the intended beneficiary should be Lowther, Bute's son-in-law, turned this Cumberland struggle into a national one, with

[1] These quotations are from Grafton's *Autobiography* (ed. W. R. Anson), p. 246 n.

the opposition denouncing arbitrary royal power. In 1769 an act was passed to convert the fixed into a moving limitation, so that sixty years' possession would be for all future time an answer to Crown claims.

Further denigration of Grafton came from the pen of Junius. Junius, whoever he may have been,[1] was an enemy quite unlike Wilkes. In his letters in the press appearing between 1767 and 1772 (though only from 21 January 1769 is the signature Junius used) Junius wrote as a member of the inner ring of the political and fashionable world. In balanced but hysterical prose, he savaged those in authority. Burke said that he excelled the *North Briton* in strength, wit, and judgement, but also in rancour and venom. His aim was to catch the attention of a sophisticated audience by removing the polite shams screening public men; he thus aroused the curiosity of his readers and then gratified their malice. He used the gossip of the offices to embarrass ministers and the details of their private lives to discredit their policies. In his world all men were venal and degraded. The fascination of his attacks is that they are couched in the artificial style of the time and yet strip away all conventional decency from their victims. Junius's own views, it appears, were in favour of triennial parliaments but he defended rotten boroughs. He supported the popular side in the Middlesex election quarrel while he maintained an authoritarian view against the Americans. He was, therefore, in policy, exactly the opposite of Grafton, liberal where he was illiberal and vice versa. For Grafton, Bedford, Sir William Blackstone,[2] and Mansfield he seems to have felt a personal antipathy. His attacks upon the govern-

---

[1] The identity of Junius is still a puzzle. The names of those with whom he has been identified are legion, including Edmund Burke, John Wilkes, George Grenville, Henry Grattan, Lord Temple, Chatham, Alexander Wedderburn, and Edward Gibbon. Attributions to either Lord Shelburne or Philip Francis have, however, commanded most support recently. In favour of the theory of Philip Francis (for whom see below, p. 170 n.) there is handwriting testimony, the coincidence of absences, Francis's sudden promotion in 1772, and the considerable knowledge shown by Junius of the war office in which Francis served. The arguments against this and in favour of Shelburne are set out in C. W. Everett, *The Letters of Junius*.

[2] Sir William Blackstone (1728–80), the first professor of English law at Oxford. His *Commentaries on the Laws of England* had appeared 1765–9 and established his fame as the greatest expositor of the revered legal tradition. He had entered parliament in 1761 and gave his expert opinion in favour of Wilkes's disqualification. He became a judge in Common Pleas in 1770. Even legal reformers had to admit his greatness as an historian of the law.

ment helped to convince the literate classes that Grafton's administration really constituted a threat to English liberty.

Amid accusations of overthrowing the constitution, Grafton muddled miserably along to the end of 1769, timid without caution, despairing in face of danger yet confident when all was lost. In January 1770 Chatham, in revived vigour now that he was free of office and frustration, opposed the address to the Crown. Lord Camden, though nominally still lord chancellor, then attacked his colleagues in the government. He was accordingly dismissed. Lord Granby, under pressure from Chatham to do so, followed Camden into opposition. Grafton's position was thus further weakened by the withdrawal of all those with whom he was in confidential agreement. As a last effort to maintain himself he offered the lord chancellorship to Charles Yorke, Hardwicke's son. Yorke, it is true, had been of the school which believed in treating the Americans firmly; but he had, through his family, maintained his friendship with Rockingham's group. He and Grafton dreamed of bringing back members of the Rockingham circle into government and redressing the balance, by broadening the bottom, of the administration. This was an impossible hope. Yorke declined office. Then the king, and his own ambitions, prevailed upon him to change his mind. He would, after all, become Lord Morden and sit on the woolsack, whatever his friends thought of him. It is evidence of the intensity of political feeling at this time that, before he could act upon this decision, Yorke in a frenzy of anguish and excitement cut his own throat and died. After a few half-hearted attempts to find an alternative chancellor, the duke of Grafton at last retired himself. It was the end of the experiment in high-minded, impractical, unprincipled, government into which Chatham had inveigled him. Surprisingly enough it was also the end of the period of ministerial instability and the beginning of twelve years of a settled administration recalling the days of Walpole and George II.

VI

LORD NORTH ESTABLISHES HIS POWER, 1770–4

LORD NORTH, when he became first lord of the treasury, was thirty-seven years old. He had been educated at Eton, Oxford, and on the grand tour. He was, all his life, not only a good scholar in the classics but a proficient master of French, German, and Italian. As the son of the earl of Guilford he naturally came into parliament for the family borough of Banbury and, as naturally, into junior office at the treasury under Newcastle in 1759. There he had contrived to remain through the ministries of Bute and Grenville. Having retired at the start of the Rockingham 'party' government, he had been brought back by Chatham as joint paymaster of the forces in 1766. From that post he had advanced to the chancellorship of the exchequer on the death of Charles Townshend. In 1770 he took on, with general consent, the leadership of the ministry relinquished by Grafton. It was not intended to make a dramatic change. North stood for no new course in policy and was not even the head of a clan of supporters. He took over from Grafton his secretary Mr. Bradshaw; he took over also the problems of leading a ministry of departmental, unbanded, ministers.

Lord North might be described as a Chathamite in his views upon the organization of government but he disapproved of the vagaries and ignored the genius of that great man. A more informative description might be simply that of an easy-going man of business who, lacking both long-term plans and close party attachments, therefore met all problems separately and as they were forced upon him. For his chief virtues were his good sense and his good temper. These were enough, in ordinary eighteenth century conditions, to reproduce the calm of another Walpole era: they kept North in power for twelve years.

Ever since 1760 the jealousies of ambitious politicians had been able to produce crises and changes of government because positive and unpopular lines of policy had been pursued. Bute fell because he was a Scot and yet a coward; Grenville because of his narrowness of mind; Rockingham perished on the repeal of the Stamp Act; and Chatham promised miracles he could not perform. But all this time the forces of the Rockingham opposition were wasting away: only friendship among leaders, obstinate devotion to the clan, or dependence for a parliamentary seat upon a patron, could keep the inner core of the party together. The outer fringes, the clientèle of Newcastle, had rapidly shifted their allegiance. After ten years even those who had first chosen the wrong horse had had time to correct their error and approach the source of power, the throne. What worked against this process was the repeated revival of political warfare as fresh issues arose on which politicians might rashly commit themselves, or on which they might hope to break the government with a frontal assault, backed by popular opinion. Thus in 1768, despite the opposition of Chatham and Rockingham, Grafton might have had good prospects if he had not allowed his colleagues to pursue their American policy uncorrected and if he had not given battle to Wilkes and put himself constitutionally on the aggressive.

Lord North believed in government more than in his own ideas. He was therefore acceptable to the king. He had no intention of forcing any new policy on the commons. He too believed that sleeping dogs should be left alone. He was therefore acceptable to the ordinary member of parliament. He believed in conciliating as many leaders of importance as possible. He was therefore acceptable to any politicians except those who demanded the first places for themselves. In foreign affairs he believed in non-intervention in Europe and a firm but quiet colonial policy. In home affairs he believed that good economical housekeeping was all that was required. He endeavoured, in short, to find that patriotic agreed course which would commend itself to all but the factious. If he could do so, then the natural forces decimating opposition would be free to have their effects. He deserved that the great issues—which Burke was discovering in his pamphlet in 1770—should disappear as they had between 1720 and 1760.

The American issue, which has obscured Lord North's virtues in the records, did not in 1770 seem very much alive, at least viewed from Westminster. Between 1770 and 1774 Lord North successfully re-established a stable administration, not on the king's influence so much as on his own tact. He had an advantage over every first lord of the treasury since Grenville in that he was in the house of commons himself. He did not, as Newcastle, Rockingham, Chatham, or Grafton did, have to fear an insubordinate leader there who might use the position for his own ambition. Moreover, he could speak with ease and persuasiveness. The outstanding house of commons men may be divided into two categories: those who command and declaim, like a Chatham or a Churchill, and those who control by appearing dull but trustworthy, like a North or a Walpole or a Baldwin. Once when Isaac Barré[1] was castigating the minister for losing an empire, mismanaging the fleet, and ruining the people, he concluded with a cry that while all this was going on the Noble Lord was asleep on the treasury bench. North shifted uneasily, and opened his eyes only to interject, 'I wish to God I were'. The deflating joke, the soft answer to turn away wrath, these were the trusty weapons of Lord North in parliament. In cabinet he was perhaps less effective. He avoided whenever possible the face-to-face argument. He preferred to keep a very loose rein, to damp down enthusiams, and by dilatoriness to let problems have every chance of solving themselves. The most showy of Lord North's accomplishments was his grasp of finance: in this field both king and public applauded his dexterity.

When North took the first place in 1770 he had still Grafton's troubles to conclude. The office of lord chancellor was, for the time being, put into commission. Eventually in 1772 Lord Apsley,[2] an inferior but inoffensive man, was made lord chancellor. The problem of Wilkes and the Middlesex election was a further legacy. North put Sir Fletcher Norton into the speakership of the house of commons in order to have a man of firmness and character there who would stop the abuse of procedure by which, under Sir John Cust, Wilkes's friends had been able to monopolize the attention of the house. In 1771, when Sir George

---

[1] Of Barré and Lord North another anecdote is told which illustrates North's humour. When both were in retirement they both went blind and employed men to lead them. In Tunbridge Wells Lord North's attendant saw Barré approaching and asked his master if he should lead him quickly past. North insisted upon being brought alongside Barré and said, 'Colonel Barré, though you and I have had quarrels in the past I wager there are no two men in England who would be happier to see one another to-day.'

[2] Henry Bathurst (1714–94), created Baron Apsley 1771 and succeeded as second Earl Bathurst 1775; he had been attorney general to the princess of Wales in 1754 and then a judge of Common Pleas.

Savile moved his annual motion to declare the rights of electors, Lord North did not throw himself into the quarrel. He successfully moved the previous question, that is, he refused to allow the issue to be fought out. From 1770 to 1774 he declined on grounds of expediency to go over this stale ground. In 1774 he opposed no obstacle to Wilkes's entry as member of parliament for Middlesex.

It is true that in 1771 the opposition did contrive to bring the commons into conflict with the city of London over the printers' case.[1] But here it is probable that Lord North was carried along by enthusiasts among his own supporters, particularly George Onslow, the member of parliament for Surrey (who claimed, as nephew of the great Speaker Onslow, to be a guardian of the constitution), by Sir James Turner and by Charles James Fox. The king recommended 'that every caution may be used to prevent its becoming a serious affair' and prophesied that punishment would only give Wilkes new life. North heeded the latter part of this advice by refusing to proceed against Wilkes himself even though action was taken against the other city authorities. In this he had the majority of members behind him; Lord Mayor Crosby did not succeed in arousing sympathy among moderate men. Moreover in future Lord North avoided even such minor battles with popular forces. He had occasion, indeed, to rebuke Fox for taking notice of provocation from the radicals.

North worked quietly in these four years (1770-4) to broaden the base of his administration. He already had in his ranks the old Bedford connexion. The death of George Grenville in 1770 removed the chief reason why the Grenvillites should not drift back into office. In 1771 their new leader, the earl of Suffolk, became a secretary of state.[2] There was no reason why he should refuse. Lord North's policy of economy was that most dear to Grenville. His attitude of quiet firmness towards America was that which Grenville always claimed to have maintained himself. Another recruit was the young Alexander Wedderburn who came in as solicitor general. This pushing lawyer had attached himself to Lord Clive who was an ally of Grenville's. Wedderburn's adhesion greatly increased the debating strength of the

---

[1] See above, pp. 141 f.

[2] Even earlier, in 1770, William Knox, one of the most capable men of business round Grenville, had accepted the post of under-secretary for the colonies, with George Grenville's blessing.

ministry in the house of commons. It was a sign that the Wilkes affair was dead. For Wedderburn had been an outspoken opponent of American claims but a champion of those of Wilkes. An even greater addition to the ministerial strength in debate came with the appointment of Thurlow to be attorney general. Lord North was soon to form the habit of sitting somnolently between his two legal colleagues, the one, Wedderburn, thrusting, quick-witted and eloquent, the other, Thurlow, sturdy, menacing, and graceless. Thurlow was to be fourteen years in high places, but he owed this not to his knowledge of the law, which was scanty, nor to his political principles, which were unknown, but to his power as a personality, his rough and always ready judgement. Dr. Johnson admitted that he liked to prepare for a conversation with Thurlow for 'I honour Thurlow, Sir; Thurlow is a fine fellow, he fairly puts his mind to yours'. Thurlow's mind, in conversation or debate, was brought alongside others to fire in a broadside which smashed opposition by its weight. 'No one', said C.J. Fox, 'could *be* as wise as Thurlow *looks.*' He had the assurance of a practical man who only sees those problems to which he has an answer. Lord North (when despite all his efforts there had to be a battle in the house) used Thurlow as his heavy artillery.

In addition to reinforcing his Bedfordite colleagues with the Grenvillites, and with the followers of that lost leader Bute,[1] Lord North also persuaded Grafton to resume office as lord privy seal[2] in June 1771. Grafton took a place partly to show 'a resolution to support Government as long as it could be supported',[3] and partly because Lord North seemed to have curbed those tendencies in the cabinet which had led to his own resignation. The adhesion of Grafton, that is to say, was an indication that Lord North was unlikely to harry America any more than he would hound Wilkes. This sign was confirmed when in 1772 Lord Dartmouth became secretary for the colonies. For William Legge, earl of Dartmouth, who was Lord North's half-brother, had been a trusty adherent of Lord Rockingham and the

[1] Lord Sandwich, for instance, by now a political power in his own right but associated with Bute in 1763, became secretary of state in 1770 and first lord of the admiralty in 1771.

[2] Grafton would have preferred the admiralty, but that was given to Lord Sandwich.

[3] The phrase is Bradshaw's, formerly his secretary, who became North's Treasury agent, see Grafton, *Autobiography*, p. 263.

spokesman of that 'Old Whig' group on matters of colonial policy. North, by placing him in charge of America, seemed to promise to pursue the Rockingham policy of 1766, the policy of compromise. Just as in 1766 the declaratory act went hand in hand with repeal of stamp duties, but from a practical point of view the emphasis was intended to be on the repeal, so in the early 1770's the emphasis was to be upon the abolition of most of Townshend's duties not upon the maintenance of that on tea.

It was not only because his colonial views were known to be liberal that Dartmouth was a valuable acquisition for the ministry. Dartmouth was a man of probity; his conscience was correct and his manners courteous. His acceptance of a place endorsed North's claim to have built up a broad and acceptable coalition of all the respectable points of view. The opposition were in despair. It seemed to most people that when Chatham returned to politics he did so only to attempt the destruction of the edifice he had vainly tried to construct himself, a national government. He stood condemned as factious in the eyes of many uncommitted men: in the eyes of those committed to the Rockingham group he was still, on the other hand, the man who refused to work to a reasonable plan. To Chatham or Shelburne the Rockingham group were a self-opinionated dull set who were too unimaginative to recognize their own inferiority.

All Lord North had to do, it seemed, was to avoid giving this disgruntled and diminishing opposition any great political issue on which to reunite and revive. Being less power-greedy than a Walpole he was able to attract more talent to his team. Being less commanding than Chatham but more subtle than Grafton, he was able to keep this talent from intrigue against him by his skill in playing off one man against another while remaining affable to all. Moreover, as time went on, his hold upon the king's affections increased his standing in the cabinet and in the commons. Sometimes North's apathy irritated the king and he would criticize his first lord; sometimes he egged on another minister in the hopes of forcing North to action. But at bottom he knew North was honest, reliable, and necessary. Therefore he was loyal and grateful to him. The able men of business, who were strongly attracted to a prospering enterprise, shared the king's feelings for North. Experts in particular branches of policy, full of their office schemes, they were often frustrated by North's slowness to implement their ideas. But in the last analysis they were loyal to him because his talent for keeping the system stable was the prerequisite for any consistent administrative action at all. Thus, for instance, Jeremiah Dyson,[1] an expert on the procedure of the house of commons, of which he had been a clerk, sometimes gave the king more definite advice than that received from North; but both the king and Dyson aimed at giving North motive power, not at overthrowing him. He had to balance the Bedford group against the rest and produce a workable compromise. By the time a general election came on, in 1774, Lord North had established an unshakeable position both at court and in the house of commons: furthermore he devoted care to the details of personal relations, to the local affairs and squabbles, which made the difference between success and failure in elections: Robinson prepared the lists for every constituency and North applied his personal persuasion on the basis of this information.

These four years of political consolidation, 1770–4, were barren of excitement. Lord North quietly pursued his aim of restoring financial stability, neglected since Grenville fell. The land tax remained at 3s. (except for the year 1771, when it rose to 4s.) not because that was a safe level but because North found that raising it alarmed the country gentlemen. He warned the house that an extra £½ million annually was needed for proper policy, and then contrived to manage without it. He was forced to look for new taxes on luxuries. In 1771 he raised £7¼ million, in 1772 £7¾ million, in 1773 £7½ million. Out of these moderate sums he aimed to put a small surplus to debt redemption in any quiet year. In the war scare of 1771–2, he could only pay for rearmament out of new loans. But by a pacific policy he hoped to find £1 million to £1½ million each year for redemption of the national debt. After 1772 this ambition led him into optimistic views. He refused to take any interest in European politics; he would not anticipate trouble in America. Despite Sandwich[2] he tried to cut expenditure on the Navy. He seriously impeded, at least, the first lord's programme for arresting the post-war decay of our naval force. When payments from the East India Company to the state

---

[1] Jeremiah Dyson (1722–76) had, as clerk of the commons, discontinued the sale of posts in his office. He had become a member of parliament in 1762 and a lord of the treasury in 1768.

[2] After Sandwich became first lord of the admiralty (succeeding Sir Edward Hawke) in January 1771.

ceased,[1] North simply cut naval and military expenses the more ruthlessly. By 1774 it seemed to most country gentlemen that Lord North had achieved what no one else had been able to do since 1763: he had ended the period of war-finance and was well on the way to paying off the burdens left by the last War of Empire. From this they expected, in the end, a permanent reduction in the burden of taxation upon them. It is not easy, remembering the importance of this question ever since the accession of George III, to exaggerate how greatly this achievement increased North's hold upon independent members of parliament.

The only real threat to North's financial retrenchment had come in 1770. Since 1764 there had been a British post at Port Egmont in the Falkland Islands. Slightly earlier the French had set up a post in another part of the islands. In 1766 the French had handed over their settlement to the Spanish. The two isolated flag stations on the desolate islands had for a while gone on in ignorance of one another; but in 1769 the British had informed the Spaniards that they should leave these possessions of King George III. At the beginning of 1770 the Spaniards replied by bringing overwhelming force against the handful of men Britain maintained there, compelling their surrender, and —after removing the rudder of their only ship to impose humiliating delay on them—obliging them to sail home. For a time in the summer of 1770 it seemed that war with Spain must be the result of this news. The opposition sharply criticized the poor state of the navy which, in fact, made immediate hostilities impossible. But Lord North did not despair of peace. His Bedfordite secretary of state, Weymouth, had gone so far in bellicosity that he had to be replaced by the earl of Rochford.[2] North sought a bargain with Spain and in 1771 it was made. The British government protested to Spain against the conduct of the Spanish governor of Buenos Aires (that is to say it chose to regard the offence as the responsibility of a wild underling rather than the fault of the king of Spain). Spain for her part disavowed the violence used and engaged to give orders for the restoration of the British post. The question of the sovereignty

---

[1] See below, pp. 167f.
[2] William Henry Zuylestein, fourth earl of Rochford (1717–81), was prominent among those who wished a firm line to be taken with the Americans. He now transferred from the Northern department (where Sandwich filled the gap) to the Southern.

of the Falkland Islands was to be left unaffected by any of these transactions and open to be decided in the future. In secret both sides agreed to evacuate the islands and so to avoid any immediate reopening of the squabble.

The dispute had interrupted North's financial plan. It had revealed the deplorable state of the navy after eight years of neglect. It had resulted in the increase of the land tax for one year and a spate of activity in the dockyards (to bring the naval strength up to eighty ships of the line), and vigorous impressment to find 25,000 more seamen. But when at the end of it all Chatham called the convention 'worse than war' he only swung the opinion of the country against him and into support of North's characteristically quiet settlement.

The political stage was taken up, once Spain had been disposed of, by two domestic matters. One was the Royal Marriages Act of 1772. The marriage of the duke of Gloucester, brother to the king, to Lady Waldegrave[1] had been answered by a refusal to receive the lady at Court. When another royal brother, the duke of Cumberland, married a widow, Mrs. Horton,[2] the king demanded action to preserve the dignity of the royal family. By the Royal Marriages Act, members of the royal family, as defined in a royal message, were unable to contract valid marriages unless they had the king's consent declared in council and signified under the great seal, or unless they were over twenty-five years of age and had given twelve months' notice to the privy council. This act was used by the opposition to whip up feeling against ministers for being too subservient to the Crown. But as an issue it fell very flat. It passed easily and quickly through both houses. Its chief interest for the politics of the time is that it provided an occasion for C. J. Fox to show his volatility: he chose on this issue to attack his colleagues and affront the king.

Even less could be extracted to comfort an opposition out of another domestic issue of these years. Some clergy of the Established Church were irked by the bond upon conscience imposed by the necessity for university graduates and ordinands to declare their belief in the Thirty-nine Articles. At a meeting at the Feathers Tavern they drew up a petition to parliament in favour of a relaxation of the law. It was perhaps a mistake that

---

[1] An illegitimate daughter of Sir Edward Walpole.
[2] Sister of Colonel Luttrell, the member for Middlesex. See above, p. 136 and n.

in this petition they appeared to attack not particular difficulties in the articles but the whole idea of imposing such a test. In any event the house of commons refused, by 217 votes to 71, to receive the petition. But out of their discussion of the articles of the established church there arose a movement among the dissenters to seek greater social liberty. As had happened almost forty years earlier under Walpole,[1] a London committee approached parliament for this purpose. It was alleged as a hardship that, while protestant dissenters had freedom of worship, their ministers and schoolmasters had to subscribe the doctrinal articles of the church of England. It was admitted that they did not comply with the law and that the law was not normally enforced against them. But it was urged that this merely proved the injustice of driving worthy men outside legality. The case of the dissenters was well argued to the house of commons by Sir George Savile, whose character commanded respect from independents as well as the Rockingham group. The house of commons passed the Relief Bill in 1772 but it was rejected in the house of lords. The same story was repeated in 1773.

The government had no very clear policy on this issue. On the whole they opposed it, for as the king said they felt 'in this mixed Government, it is highly necessary to avoid novelties. . . . Are we to have no other object but to be altering every rule our ancestors have left us? Indeed this arises from a general disinclination to every restraint.'[2] Thurlow put this purely conservative attitude most frankly to the deputation of presbyterians who waited on him, 'Why gentlemen, if your old sour religion had been the Establishment, I might have complied; but as it is not, you cannot expect me to accede to your request': 'they retired', it is said, 'smiling, and probably less dissatisfied than if he had tried to reason them into a conviction of the justice of the Test and Corporation Acts'.[3] Yet though resisting

---

[1] See Wolfgang Michael, *Englische Geschichte im Achtzehnten Jahrhundert*, iv. 473 ff.

[2] *Correspondence of George III*, ed. J. Fortescue, iii. 70 (where the letter is wrongly dated 1774: it should be placed in 1772). The king also said 'it is the duty of Ministers . . . to prevent any alterations in so essential a part of the Constitution as everything that relates to religion, and there is no shadow for this petition as the Crown regularly grants a Noli prosequi if any over-nice Justice of Peace encourages prosecutions' (ibid. iii. 335). The avowed aim of the bill was only to relieve one class of dissenting officials from an obligation on points of doctrine. It was clearly intended, however, to begin the repeal of the whole system of Test Acts.

[3] John, Lord Campbell, *Lives of the Lord Chancellors*, v. 662.

the innovation Lord North and his colleagues characteristically chose not to make a party fight of it in the house of commons. They preferred to allow the bishops in the house of lords to organize successful resistance.

Apart from financial consolidation the only major achievement of these years was the regulation by government of the affairs of the East India Company. To understand North's Regulating Act it is necessary to appreciate the position in which the Company now found itself both in India and in English politics.

The East India Company had a statutory monopoly of trade between England and India. It had, by 1763, ousted all rivalry of any real significance by other European states in India. But it was not purely a trading company. In the East it was assuming powers of government. At home part of its importance lay in its work as a great finance house, or private banker. It was ready to take up government loans and to raise money itself in the financial market by the issue of bonds. Its strength in performing these functions of a financial middleman in part depended, naturally, upon the credit which it enjoyed as a trading company. It was, in consequence of its other activities, a dispenser of patronage with all the political complications which followed from that. If one had a son to provide for, a director of the East India Company could find him a place in the service which, though miserably paid, offered a chance of making a fortune in private commerce in India.[1] To get to India one needed, as it were, the permit of the company given in the form of a clerkship in their service. This made it inevitable that the directors of the Company would be courted in city circles and that the government should seek to use the directors to further government influence in London. A man might, therefore, be a shareholder in the East India Company simply because he thought it an investment of money which would bring large dividends, or because he wished to buy his way into a monopoly which had permits for fortune-seeking in its gift, or because he was an active politician.

---

[1] See for an example how poor William Hickey's father finally disposed of his son as an attorney in India. *Memoirs of William Hickey*, ed. A. Spencer, i. 253, and iv. 39. (The details in these Memoirs may be of disputable authenticity, but this episode appears to have verisimilitude.) Writerships, it was said, could be purchased at £1,500 to £2,000.

No English government could afford to ignore the dangerous situation into which the East India Company had drifted by the time of Lord North's entry into power. Underlying other difficulties was the problem of a balance of trade which has been noted earlier.[1] The Company found that because English exports to the East were always in danger of falling short of the value of the imports from the East its purchase of goods in India (known as 'the investment'), made by much use of credit and bills drawn on London, involved it in recurring financial crises. Invisible exports, in the form of the activities and services of Englishmen in India, which helped to maintain the economic balance,[2] were the source of much of the inefficiency, corruption, and hence political conflict which dogged the Company's policies. But the difficulties of trade were accompanied by the more dramatic complications of war and expansion; complications which could not be avoided in the conditions of the 1760's.

In India the Company had been conducting their trade in a world which was changing and which they imperfectly understood. Everywhere in India was change, revolution, and violence. The collapse of the old Moghul Empire at Delhi opened the way to a Hindu revival and to many adventurers who conquered thrones by the sword. By 1770 there was hardly an Indian prince to be found whose family had more than fifty years of history behind it. To the east of the Company's trading post at Bombay, in the western Ghauts between the Deccan and the coastal strip, fighting Hindu chiefs had established their independence of Delhi. These Mahratta powers had taken the port of Bassein and the island of Salsette from the Portuguese (whose settlement at Goa overshadowed the English in Bombay). They had marched at times across the Deccan, where one of the viziers from Delhi had set himself up as nizam of Hyderabad, as far as Tanjore near the second British post at Madras. To the north-east they had raided into Bengal, taking Orissa and disturbing the third and last English 'factory' at Calcutta.

While the Mahratta powers were thus asserting themselves there had been established the rule of a Tartar adventurer as nawab of Bengal; of a Persian as nawab of Oudh; Afghan chiefs dominated Rohillakund on the edge of Oudh, and the grandson

---

[1] See above for fuller details, pp. 22 f.
[2] For more details see above, p. 23, and below, pp. 305 f.

of a Punjab dervish, Haidar Ali, revived the Hindu state of Mysore. Delhi itself was taken by the Afghans. Trying to trade in this welter of war and assassination the British Company had faced a further peril in the cunning with which the French had joined in the struggle of Hindu and Moslem and had used their few trained native troops to build trade upon thrones. Thanks to the enterprise of Clive[1] the French had, by 1763, been beaten at their own game. The Company's instinct after this was to concentrate upon business. But they were not able to disinterest themselves in Indian intrigues. They had ejected, to take an example, the Chanda Sahib, and put Muhammed Ali into his place as ruler of the Carnatic: but so long as his throne was not secure, their factory at Madras and trade along the Coromandel coast was always in danger.

The Company post at Bombay in the sixties was less in the forefront of affairs than either of the others: men lived quietly there though in some apprehension of Mahratta power. At Madras the situation was much more complicated. It was difficult, for one thing, to show a profit on operations in that area. Particularly sordid but lucrative financial deals were done in this part of the south-east. For Muhammed Ali, the polite and shifty prince of the Carnatic, had many fears. He feared the arms of Hyderabad, of the Mahratta confederacy,[2] and of the upstart Haidar Ali, among external forces. He wished, inside his ramshackle state, to destroy the independence of the ruler of Tanjore which the British had guaranteed. He was haunted by fears and his palliative was military preparations. But for troops he needed money. Among the Englishmen in Madras there were many who, as Company agents, pressed him to be well armed and who, as private money-lenders, found him the credit for this, while as contractors they sold him equipment. The nabob pledged revenues in advance to meet his obligations. Adventurers like Paul Benfield[3] soon began to grow rich as the nabob's accounts grew incomprehensible. This in itself involved

[1] For Robert Clive (1725–74), created Baron Clive in the Irish peerage 1762, see the narrative below and also B. Williams, *The Whig Supremacy* (O.H.E. vol. xi), p. 309.

[2] The Mahrattas had indeed been shattered by the Afghans at Panipat in 1761, but their recovery was swift.

[3] Paul Benfield (d. 1810) went out to India in the service of the Company 1764; proceeded to make a fortune in private business; ordered home 1774; M.P. Cricklade 1780: denounced by Burke and others; restored to his position in India but returned to England 1793; died in poverty as a result of speculation.

the English more deeply in the local politics of Madras. By the settlement Clive made in 1765 the Company acquired an increased territorial stake in this area, the five Northern Circars and the coastal strip from Madras to Orissa. In such circumstances it was impossible for the Madras presidency to follow Clive's advice—which was in contrast to his example—to take no part in the struggle of the princes of Hindustan.

The most prosperous of the Company posts was that in Bengal. Here open political control had gone the farthest. The Company had been forced into the open by Seraj-ud-daulah's massacre of their servants. They had replaced him as nawab by Mir Jaffir. In 1760 on Clive's initiative they had plotted with the native bankers and set up Mir Kassim. Yet Clive protested that all the Company wanted was a stable and quiet régime under which it could trade. Mir Kassim certainly offered the possibility of such a new order. On his accession he rewarded the Company by ceding to them Burdwan, Midnapur, and Chittagong. He also made handsome presents to the Company's servants. These included the grant of a jaghir, or payment for a nominal office of honour worth £25,000 a year, to Clive.

Mir Kassim though open handed in gifts was also anxious to have his hands upon real power. He paid his arrears of debt to the Company and obtained from them artillery and 25,000 trained soldiers. He ventured to remove the deputy governor of Bihar from his office even though the deputy governor was a Hindu banker, a member of the class with whom the English in Bengal had their closest ties. Next he attempted to control the English themselves. Ever since 1715 the nawabs had exempted their cargoes under the Company's flag from the internal duties which lay heavily upon the native population. This exemption was intended only for the Company's official trade. But the certificates of exemption (*Dustchucks*) were used by every unscrupulous Englishman for his private trade. In the internal trade in tobacco, grain, and betel, such an Englishman could undercut his native rival, or force that rival into partnership with him to share in the privilege. Vansittart,[1] the governor in

---

[1] Henry Vansittart (1732-70) went to India in the Company's service in 1746; became friendly with Clive; governor of Bengal 1760-4 and quarrelled with military and civil officers; returned to England in 1764; M.P. Reading 1768; director of East India Company 1769; lost at sea when on his way to India for a mission of investigation.

Bengal, supported by Warren Hastings,[1] was willing to allow Mir Kassim to examine goods under the British flag: the governor's council at Calcutta, however, was suspicious of the intentions of the nawab, and refused to authorize this.[2] Thereupon Mir Kassim simply abolished all internal customs duties in his country and so put all traders upon a footing of equality. Unfortunately Ellis, the overbearing one-legged chief of the Company's trading post at Patna, took matters into his own hands, disregarding his superior Vansittart, and tried to teach the nawab a lesson by launching an attack on Patna city. In the fighting he and his entire force were slaughtered.

Ellis's provocative insubordination had the result of appearing to justify all the English critics of Mir Kassim had said. For the nawab was driven, as the English rallied to defend and then to avenge Ellis, to contract an alliance with the independent neighbouring state of Oudh, and also with the nominal overlord of all the Indian princes, the Moghul emperor at Delhi and his Afghan ancillaries. Thus in 1764 the Company was at war with a coalition of Indian princes. In that year Major Hector Munro[3] won the decisive battle of Buxar against the Indian coalition and destroyed their armies. This victory marks a new development in the history of the Company. No longer were they using puppet Indian governments to beat down European rivals in competition for trade. They had now overwhelmingly defeated Indian forces struggling for independence of European control. The Company had become a government as well as a trader. After Buxar, Bengal was entirely under its control, Oudh was at its mercy, and the emperor at Delhi sought its protection. The Company clung to the idea that it was still only a trading company and refused to admit that it had territorial responsibilities. By the peace settlement Mir Jaffir came back a second time to the Bengal throne. But he no longer had to pay the divani, or tribute, to the Delhi emperor. Instead the divani was paid to the Company. The Company restored Korah and Allahabad

---

[1] Warren Hastings (1732–1818) went to India 1750; member of Calcutta council 1761; second in Madras council 1769; governor of Bengal 1772–85; an inspirer of Asiatic studies; for his greatness as a ruler in India and for his vilification see the narrative below.

[2] The abuse of the *Dustchuck* system was brought to an end later (1772–4), when Hastings had become governor of Bengal.

[3] Sir Hector Munro (1726–1805), later a major general, was in command at Madras and captured Pondicherry 1778; served under Coote 1781; captured Negapatam 1781; M.P. Inverness burghs 1768–1801.

to the emperor (whose capital was now in Afghan hands) in return for his formal assent to their having the divani and over-lordship of Bengal, Bihar, and Orissa.[1] Oudh was left independent to act as a buffer state, but its ruler, Shuja-ud-doulah, had to pay an indemnity to the Company.

It should have been recognized that the Company on taking the divani of Bengal had become its government. But Clive, back in India, preferred the so-called dual system, and did so with the approval of the London directors. This meant that the Company looked only to take the surplus profit of the administration of Bengal, leaving responsibility for just government with the feeble old nawab and his unscrupulous servants. The result was bound to be the oppression of the people. Clive's attempts to forbid Englishmen to take presents or to engage in inland trading were ineffective, but had they been successful would only have scratched the surface of the new grievances of Bengal. In 1767, when Clive returned to England again, he was under the delusion that he had given the English ultimate power without the nuisance of day-to-day administration, and that he had increased both the profits and the purity of the Company in India.

This conviction Clive shared with city business men and with Westminster politicians. In 1767 everyone was talking of the great riches which control of Bengal would bring to the Company. Chatham, as has been seen, was inclined to dispute their title to it.[2] Grafton compromised by mulcting them of a payment of £400,000 a year to the state as the price of being left undisturbed. Yet all the while most of these profits were imaginary. Even in India it was difficult to run war as a paying proposition. The responsibilities which they were refusing to face in Bengal were in fact to produce a bill which had to be met.

The common delusion that profits of the Company were snowballing was inspired by a quite different phenomenon, the great profits made by some individual company servants. The number who lived to enjoy wealth in England was a small part of those who went abroad, but though few, they were spectacular: they were the 'nabobs'. Their wealth was made in a variety of ways. They did not regard themselves as a superior race to the Indians but entered with gusto into Indian commercial life.

---

[1] These terms were agreed in Clive's treaty of Allahabad, 1765.
[2] See above, p. 124.

Not only, as in the scandal of the *Dustchucks*, did this mean exploiting internal trade: they undertook the coastal trade between Bombay and Persia and adventured towards Malacca and China. They countered attempts to prohibit such activities by Company servants with the simple device of secret partnerships with native merchants. Moneylending to Indian rulers has already been instanced as another way to fortune.[1] Money was also lent to their own Company. When the Company offered bills redeemable in London in exchange for cash with which to make 'the investment' its own servants found this a convenient method of getting their own fortunes back to England for their retirement. Since they thus as officials negotiated terms with themselves (or with agents of themselves) in a private capacity, the bargain was not likely to be to the Company's advantage. In times of war the equipment and transport needed by the Company might often have to be bought from native dealers who, in reality, were the employees of Company servants. Any such contract offered scope for fleecing the Company.

On their return home the 'nabobs' often bought estates and a seat in parliament, thus increasing the importance of the Indian 'interest' in national politics.[2] In the 1760's, therefore, the Company's policy was involved in a curious cross-entanglement of interests. On the one hand the Company's shareholders wanted as high a dividend as possible. This meant reforming the system in India so as to prevent money leaking into the pockets of Company servants. On the other hand those directors who had friends or relatives still labouring in the Indian heat had a vested interest in allowing the bad old system to continue. When Laurence Sulivan, a returned Indian servant of the Company, rose in 1758 to the control of the board of direction in London, his first object was to make the Company's books balance. Part of his own fortune was sunk in its shares. But he had to meet resistance from those still making their fortunes. In later stages of the conflict inside the direction of the Company he found himself allied with interests which were against reducing the perquisites of the Company's servants: then he appeared therefore as an enemy of reform. Similarly Clive, the recipient of enormous presents from Indian princes, tried to prevent such

[1] See above, p. 159.
[2] Clive became the leader of a Shropshire group of members of parliament.

presents being given in future: but his zeal varied according to the alliances he made in the complicated politics of the Company. It is not possible to simplify and to label men as corrupt or as reformers in this battle of interests, in which a man might be at once a shareholder and a representative of servants on the make.[1]

Such complications in themselves made extreme variations in policy and financial speculation only too likely. But the danger was increased by political manœuvre. The government and the opposition fished for friends in East India House waters. The government sought to influence London through its contacts with the direction of the Company: it also had to calculate the effect upon votes in parliament of any course it might take in Company affairs. There was a two-way traffic in influence between the Company and the ministry. In 1763, for instance, when Bute was seeking to line up the city in defence of his peace policy, Henry Fox and Lord Sandwich took part in the Company elections. The directors were elected annually by shareholders' votes, anyone with £500 of stock being entitled to vote. It was possible therefore to create votes for an election, either by purchasing blocks of stock for the occasion, or by splitting one's holding into £500 units in the hands of nominees instructed to vote as their master told them. Henry Fox had used the public funds of his paymaster's office to buy stock. Sulivan, in the event, was elected against the votes of Clive's friends and so the directorate of the Company supported the peace. Clive, in revenge, sought a political ally and found one in George Grenville. By 1765 he had turned the tables on Sulivan; Clive's second visit to India[2] to reorganize Bengal was the proof of his victory. He had in all this a personal and confusing motive. For while he professed to stand for a more efficient Indian service which would check official jobbery, he wished at the same time to preserve his own jaghir,[3] against the threat that his enemies among the directors would confiscate it. The opposition to Clive by 1767 consisted of those who attacked his own fortune-hunting as well as of those who resented his curtailment of their own lucrative sidelines.

[1] It is worth stressing these considerations if the difficulty of evaluating the career of Warren Hastings (see narrative below) is to be fully appreciated.

[2] 1765-6.

[3] His present from Mir Kassim worth £25,000 a year, see above, p. 160.

Once the Company had the divani of Bengal the price of shares rose. Chatham's government had not only extracted £400,000 a year for the government; it had simultaneously limited the dividend to 10 per cent., while if the dividend fell below 6 per cent. the Company were not obliged to pay the annual subsidy to the state. All speculators who thought it should be possible to pay more than 10 per cent. had an interest in courting politicians who might lift the ban. They also had an interest, less keenly felt at this stage, in purifying the administration in India so as to benefit the Company's treasury. Before the Company elections of 1769 friends of Lord Rockingham in opposition had united themselves with the pressure group agitating inside the Company for high dividends. Burke's friends, particularly Lord Verney, were buying stock, in part for a stock-exchange profit and in part for political advantage in the election of directors. Development of stock exchange technique made it possible to buy on credit. The group of Sulivan and Vansittart (with whom Lord Verney and Lord Shelburne were at this stage associated) built up a fund of £100,000 stock, promising to pay at a higher price (280) than it had ever reached before.[1]

This feverish buying was matched by the directors then in power, aided by £25,000 of the government's money. For in 1769 Grafton's provisional regulation of the Company's affairs had to be put on a permanent basis or modified. In the event Sulivan returned to the court of directors with Vansittart, but the friends of the government held about half the seats on the direction.[2] The position of East India stock was now highly artificial. A boom had been proceeding since 1766. A fall was only to be expected unless the news from India aroused fresh expectations of profit. On the contrary, news arrived in May that the Company was involved in war.

The politicians of Madras—and it must be remembered that each of the three Company stations ran their own separate foreign policies—had plotted with childish Machiavellianism to unite Hyderabad and the Mahrattas in a league against Haidar Ali of Mysore. Their plot had backfired. The Mahrattas,

---

[1] See L. S. Sutherland, *The East India Company in Eighteenth Century Politics*, chap. vii and appendix 1.

[2] It was then decided that the payment of £400,000 should continue. The dividend ceiling was raised to 12½ per cent.

the real enemy of all three British settlements, were hostile: Haidar Ali had invaded the Carnatic. He had reached Madras and Fort St. George. The French, it was rumoured, were preparing forces at Mauritius to assist this offensive against the Company's hold on southern India. Though such messages exaggerated the danger and Haidar Ali was pacified, the false optimism about Company affairs was destroyed. The shares fell to 239. Lord Verney was ruined. Lord Shelburne lost £3,000 of his own and a further £30,000 given to help his agent Lauchlin Macleane. Sulivan's whole fortune disappeared.

This dramatic result of a struggle for control pointed the argument for a reform of Indian organization. At home Lord North used his talents for diplomacy in an effort to conciliate all important groups in the Company. Lord Sandwich persuaded (in 1771) the directors to limit its shipbuilding both for the sake of the navy (for there was a timber shortage) and to cut the capital commitments of the Company. Sulivan sent three supervisors, headed by the experienced Vansittart, to bring back peace and order into the three presidencies in India. These supervisors were lost at sea. The government also sent an agent, Sir John Lindsay, to investigate relations with the Indian princes.[1] The collapse of confidence in the Company was also marked by a propaganda campaign against Lord Clive as the outstanding example of the corrupt 'nabob'. Books by publicists such as Alexander Dow reopened all the old complaints against his jaghir.[2] This might have passed, an exciting episode, had it not been that news from India continued to be bad. Famine devastated Bengal between 1770 and 1772. One-sixth of the population died. As a result the territorial revenues accruing to the Company declined by £400,000. At the same time its military costs rose by over £160,000. For as the Company gradually absorbed the Carnatic, it roused the fears of independent Hyderabad and fighting Mysore. The Mogul empire having collapsed, the resurgent Hindu states, the Mahratta confederacy of Central India, and the princes of all other states, had to be faced. For the Company, even if it denied it, seemed to be the main contender for succession to the Delhi empire. It looked as

---

[1] This direct intervention in Indian affairs by the state was probably due in part to complaints reaching Whitehall from Indian rulers, such as the nawab of Arcot, through their English advisers and agents.

[2] Alexander Dow (d. 1779), a historian and dramatist who was also a lieutenant-colonel in the Company's armies in India.

if it must either fight or be driven out by more resolute native princes. Though it had no positive wish to expand, it had at least to prepare for the defence of what it had gained since Buxar.

The Company was thus facing increased administrative costs with declining administrative profits. It still had the chance of remedying the situation by expanded trade. Whereas in 1765 it had invested £437,000 in the annual cargoes for England, in 1770–1 it sank £900,000 in Indian purchases. It could do this only by an increase in the bills drawn on London which would eventually be presented for payment at headquarters. Optimistically the directors contrived to raise the dividend, anticipating profits. But their servants in India were drawing bills on them on a scale for which they could not provide. In 1771 they realized that bills amounting to £1½ million would have to be met over the next three years. Nevertheless they announced a dividend of 12½ per cent., the maximum. At this awkward moment, in June 1772, the great Scottish banker, Alexander Fordyce,[1] failed and fled from his creditors. There was at this time a loss of commercial confidence, a great credit crisis with economic stagnation and trade depression in the whole of Western Europe. This meant that the East India Company could not dispose of its Indian goods as well or as quickly as it had hoped. It was brought near to bankruptcy. It could not repay the £320,000 it had borrowed from the Bank of England to meet normal needs in the summer. It had to ask Lord North to allow it to postpone payment of £203,000 it owed to the Customs.

The situation which Lord North, however disinclined to controversial action, was forced to meet, was a paradoxical one. Here was a great Company which in ten years had become the most potent force in India, whose trade was increasing, which ruled provinces, whose servants were among the wealthiest Englishmen (or Scots) of the day, but which was on the brink of bankruptcy and riven by internal feuds. With posts in its gift for which men intrigued, with a private army, with financial stature second only to the Bank of England, the Company was driven to ask help of parliament; and in parliament government supporters and opposition were poised ready to fight over and

---

[1] Alexander Fordyce (d. 1789), a receiver of the land tax; partner in London firm of Neale, James, Fordyce, & Down: see also above, p. 62 n.

against it. In 1767 the government had been demanding a share of a power and of a profit thought too great for subjects to monopolize. In 1772 the Company was begging loans: yet all its structure and potentialities remained intact.

Lord North hoped at first to settle this problem quietly and by agreement with the Company. At East India House it was accepted that reform was necessary. A bill was introduced into parliament to set up a new judicial system in Bengal, to prevent the governor and council there from indulging in private trade, and to increase control over the activity of the Company's servants. Unfortunately these reforms were not put forward at once. While they were being formulated General Burgoyne voiced the general feeling of the house of commons that the situation of the Company at home, and the evils reported from India, were so serious as to demand public inquiry by parliament. A select committee was set up to ferret out the corruption, to which humanitarians attributed the sufferings of Bengal and on which shareholders blamed the slump in Lombard Street. Lord North, as usual, went along with the current of opinion, but not heedlessly or hopelessly. He tacked a little and tried to divert rather than dam the current of popular opinion. He gave up the provisional settlement which he had agreed with the Company. He set up a committee of secrecy from among his own friends in the house to examine all the papers of the Company and draft a workable solution for parliament to enact. Thus two committees studied India in the winter of 1772 and the spring of 1773. Burgoyne's Committee persuaded the house to vote that all territorial acquisitions rightly belong to the Crown but had, in India, been wrongfully appropriated by private persons. They then gave body to this general resolution by moving that Lord Clive had been guilty of promoting his private fortune 'to the dishonour and detriment of the state'. In this they failed. The house voted that while Lord Clive had possessed himself of £234,000 he had at the same time rendered 'great and meritorious services to this country'.

The Burgoyne committee had, in effect, attempted to suggest that all the troubles of India were due to the rapacity of a few conspicuous individuals: Clive's enemies had used this to follow up a vendetta against him. Clive had fought back with a ferocious candour. He was 'amazed at his own moderation' in picking so little for himself in the making of an empire. Ordinary members, it may be surmised, agreed that the rapacity of its servants helped to produce the weakness of the Company. But a solution of Indian problems asked more than spiteful retribution. They had a revulsion of feeling when Clive, a great soldier as well as a money-grubber, was selected for martyrdom. Lord North, as an honest man, voted for Clive's condemnation,[1] but as a minister he rejoiced to find himself in a minority: for so Burgoyne's meddling with India came to a dead end.

The government was now free to offer its own solution based on facts rather than rancour. They saw that there must be a firmer control of the administration in India. They were convinced that authority must come from outside, because the Company's direction was too easily influenced by its richest servants and its greediest shareholders. Yet at the same time the government could not itself take over Bengal, Madras, and Bombay, for the stake in India was still a trading one to which complicated problems of administration were, so to speak, fortuitously tacked on. Therefore Lord North's solution was a compromise. A loan of £1,400,000 was compulsorily made by the state to the Company to put it on a sound financial footing. Its tea trade was assisted by freeing it from customs duties on re-export. The mayor's court at Calcutta was to be limited to mercantile cases and a new judicial system with a chief justice and three puisne judges, appointed by the Crown, was to be set up. Most important of all, it was intended to bring a new discipline into the Indian service by making the presidency of Bengal supreme over Madras and Bombay. This supreme presidency was to be ruled by a governor-general and a council of four.[2] General provisions for eliminating abuses were incorporated in North's Regulating Act, but the detailed reform of the service—in matters such as the collection of revenue, for instance —was left to the discretion of this new supreme Bengal Council working on the spot. The first holders of these offices were nominated in parliament at once. They were Warren Hastings as governor-general, a choice agreeable to the Company; Richard Barwell also represented the Company interest; Colonel Monson and Philip Francis were appointed from outside the

---

[1] Ministers voted as their consciences dictated. Thurlow was against Clive, Wedderburn for him. Clive had just been appointed lord-lieutenant of Shropshire, not so much to show confidence in his integrity as to dissuade him from joining the Rockingham opposition.

[2] For the ambiguities in these provisions see below, pp. 171 and 307.

Company; General John Clavering was appointed as commander-in-chief of the Indian forces and a royal representative on
the council, on which he ranked next to Hastings.[1] Vacancies
on the council were to be filled, until 1778, by the East India
directors subject to the king's veto. After 1778 this veto would
cease, but the whole plan was to operate only until further
thought could be given to the Company on the expiration of its
charter in 1780. The king's ministers were to be shown all in-
coming dispatches so that they might know the general tendency
of policy.

The opposition in parliament were divided. The Rockingham
group, lamenting the wanton and wasteful record of the Company, still maintained that a change in persons but not in
principles was all that was required. They were conscious of the
immense field of patronage that existed in India. They accused
Lord North of trying to get his hands on this source of political
influence. They defended the sanctity of the chartered independence of the Company because it was the only means of keeping
trade and patronage out of the grip of the Crown. They wanted
an independent Company to run its affairs better without
ministerial interference. They did their best both in East India
House and in the commons to prevent North's scheme from
receiving a fair trial. That section of the opposition associated
with Chatham and Shelburne could not take the same line of
principle, for they had already, in 1767, declared their belief in
the Crown's right to territory, as distinct from trade, won by
the Company. Though they criticized details of the scheme they
therefore accepted it in general.

Lord North's plan found favour in the commons. A sad record
of abortive reorganizations seemed to prove that the govern-

[1] Richard Barwell (1741–1804), born at Calcutta; on the establishment of the
Company 1765; the most faithful of Hastings's supporters; retired with a fortune,
1780, and entered parliament 1784.

George Monson (1730–76), son of first baron Monson; a soldier distinguished in
fighting at Pondicherry 1760; aide-de-camp to George III, 1769; an opponent o
Hastings; died in India.

Philip Francis (1740–1818), the most able and bitter of Hastings' enemies in
India; a clerk in the war office who was forced out by Barrington just before his
appointment to the Indian council; often supposed to be the author of *Junius* (see
above, p. 145); left India with a fortune 1780; member of parliament 1784, and
pursued his vendetta with Hastings; knighted under the regency.

John Clavering (1722–77) served as a professional soldier in Europe and the
West Indies, becoming lieutenant-colonel; an opponent of Hastings; knighted
1776; died in India.

ment must intervene to supervise the Company. At the same time Lord North was felt to have shown moderation. He seemed to have insisted upon the minimum of authority and to have resisted the temptation to interfere in Company affairs beyond what was required to make the trade stable and to put Indian acquisitions in order. He was generally acquitted of the crime charged against him, of endeavouring to increase the patronage of the Crown.

Thus North's acts passed and initiated a new era in English relations with India. The co-operation of the Company was not easy to secure. It had to be intimidated by public opinion. Along with the other reforms the voting qualification in elections for directors was raised from £500 to £1,000 of stock. From this time forward the choice of the direction was not quite such an unpredictable scramble. North's assistant, John Robinson, made it his duty to cultivate friendship with the leaders in Company affairs, so as to ensure that a party in sympathy with the king's government was in control at East India House. This control of policy at headquarters, by influence and diplomacy, was as important as the nomination of a governor-general in Bengal. Yet it did not imply that there had been a dangerous increase in the powers of the Crown. For the directors were in a strong position once they had recovered from the shame of the financial crisis. They had to be wooed. To influence them required the using up of some of the government's ordinary political patronage, which was thus diminished and not increased by Robinson's management of East India House. The directors kept the gift of favours in India under their own control and accepted English douceurs as the price of keeping their general policy in line with ministers' idea of the national interest. On the whole, North's manipulation had as its aim consolidation of the position in India and the stability of the great finance house which depended upon it. In this sense he lived up to his professions in passing the Regulating Act.

The working of the Regulating Act in India was to reveal its many shortcomings, some of which were the direct consequence of Lord North's compromising spirit. In practice the presidencies in Bombay and Madras were often successful in evading control by the governor-general in Calcutta. There were also conflicts in that governor-general's council; but at least the two parties there, that of Hastings and that of Francis, were moved by a sense of duty to their own country and to the Indian population, which had first found expression in North's acts. Therefore 1773 marks the point at which, reluctantly, it came to be realized that England could not confine her interest in India merely to trade.

Lord North's manipulation of this Indian crisis, the most important positive result of his first four years as first lord of the treasury, reveals his characteristic abilities at this time. He successfully hit on that line of compromise and moderation which commended itself as 'non-party' to independent members of parliament and to the king. He appeared unambitious, sensible and devoted to the preservation of a broadly based administration which could serve the king while respecting parliamentary opinion. In contrast the opposition were made to seem factious. In 1773 Horace Walpole thought that the 'Opposition had in a manner given up the contest in Parliament'. That contest was only reopened by a decisive new stage in relations with America. Contests of principle suddenly grew more bitter. For a time the authority of North's government was thereby made more powerful, but eventually the American question was to wear him out and to erase his years of success from the memory of posterity.

VII

THE ORIGINS OF THE
AMERICAN REVOLT

A SUPERFICIAL view might suggest that Lord North had his catastrophic encounter with America because the East India crisis led him to push the sale of the Company's tea abroad. The empire might seem to have been lost, not gained, in a fit of absence of mind. This resembles the shallow judgement from the other side that it was the failure of men like Samuel Adams and Patrick Henry[1] to run a store successfully that fired them with ambition to run a new nation, that great public principles issued from small private humiliations. But when the issues are analysed the loss of America takes on an air of inevitability and it is apparent that personal and accidental griefs were pregnant with issue only because they aroused latent antagonisms.

The deep-seated causes of the American struggle were not, in the normal sense, economic. The argument about the laws of trade, about enumerated commodities and prohibited industries, is almost as superficial as that about the importance of Lord George Germain's desire to re-establish his own reputation as a military chief. The fundamental cleavage between England and the thirteen colonies was, in a broad sense, social. The difference in ideology on the two sides of the Atlantic was the natural product of a difference in their ways of life. Thus both Englishmen and Americans regarded Locke as their political Bible: that they gave such different interpretations of the *Treatise on Civil Government*—the English conservative, the American revolutionary—was to be expected from the circumstances in which they lived and which they took for granted.

[1] Samuel Adams (1722–1803) dissipated inherited wealth by incapacity in running a brewery; heavily in arrears with taxes; from 1764 devoted himself to Boston politics; a leading figure in the 'Boston tea party'; a member of congress; governor of Massachussets 1794.

Patrick Henry (1736–99) twice failed in keeping a shop in Virginia; turned to law with brilliant success; took leading part in resistance to Stamp Act and in revolutionary upheaval in Virginia; governor of Virginia, showing clemency to loyalists; a federalist.

Englishmen declared that the revolution of 1688 had established a government subject to the will of the people. 'The people' they interpreted not as a mass of individuals each counting for one and no more, but as a family with natural ties, affections, and superiorities, so that the squire could speak for his villagers as a father for his dependants. The sovereignty of parliament—a doctrine in harmony with Hobbes's teaching rather than Locke's—was accepted as a practical necessity. Chatham was old-fashioned in declaring that above parliament was the spirit of the English Common Law, for this doctrine smacked of the seventeenth century; the last trace of it was to disappear under Benthamite common-sense argument as the eighteenth century came to an end. But in any case there was no need to discuss the possible theoretical limits to the sovereignty of parliament. For, as has been argued above,[1] parliament could not in practice do more than was acceptable to the unchallenged leaders of English society. The English gentry had ceased to bother about Locke's theory that government might be discharged for abuse of power as soon as they had entrenched themselves in the legislative branch of government and could prevent any such abuse arising. It was convenient therefore to consider parliament as absolute. It would then be the final arbiter between executive and judiciary in any dispute such as had wrecked seventeenth-century constitutional experiments. As arbiter it would be safe because it was dominated by those with most to lose. This, then, was why Englishmen read Locke's defence of the revolution of 1688 as a conservative work.

Englishmen did not look on the colonists with hostility in 1760, nor would they have admitted that they wished to exploit them. The English attitude would more properly be described as one of perplexed resignation. For, as has been explained earlier,[2] Englishmen at this time were traders and not imperialists. Resident English communities abroad, self-sufficing imitations of England, did not fit into this picture; they were not so much inimical to it as alien. Englishmen desired the American continent and islands taken as a whole to serve as a market for their manufactures and a source for products which could not be found at home. In the development of this interchange they wished above all to develop a maritime supremacy over France.

[1] See p. 55.   [2] See above, pp. 16 f.

Indeed the whole purpose of trade seems at times to be thought of as the defeat of French and Spanish power. From this point of view the fur trade from Canada and down from the Lakes to the Ohio and Tennessee, still unsettled country, was very valuable. The naval stores supplied by the northern colonies were useful. Tobacco, rice, and sugar from the West Indies and the southern colonies were indispensable. With this stress on trading values it was nevertheless appreciated that Americans had institutions and a life of their own to lead; for this aspect Englishmen felt the same sort of tolerant indifference as for the presbyterian discipline of the Scots in Scotland. It was desirable that this American life should be on a comprehensible and regular basis, but its details were no concern of England's. Thus by 1763 eight out of the twelve mainland colonies had been made royal colonies, subject to the prerogative of the Crown: Pennsylvania and Maryland were still proprietary colonies: in Rhode Island and Connecticut the governors were still elected instead of being appointed by the king. But there was certainly no English plan to monopolize control of political life in the colonies.

The chief evil was felt to be the inter-colonial jealousies: as a result of these England in war received inadequate aid from those on the spot. Even Pitt had only gained American assistance by promising to reimburse the colonists for their expenses. In 1763 there was a bill on this account of £1 million. In Virginia, while war with France should have engaged attention, Patrick Henry drew all interest to his attack on the payment of Anglican priests in free tobacco. New England merchants had traded with the enemy. The Albany plan for united colonial action had failed. The colonists had seemed engrossed in their own petty interests and businesses, their competitive fortune-hunting, while the foundations of their whole world were being defended by England. Therefore there was a general feeling at Westminster when peace was restored that this must not continue. Just as an English landowner or merchant paid, albeit complainingly, for the few common services provided by the state, for the foundations of a civilized corporate existence, so should the feckless Americans. If they could never pay for the cost of French expulsion, they ought at least to meet the bill for defence against any future French menace and for control of the Indians.

The American attitude to England was deceptive. On the surface most of the colonists were grateful for English activity. Chatham was a hero, England was home, and George III the best of monarchs. But these were cant phrases which meant little to those who, in all sincerity, mouthed them. Not that the majority of Americans felt sentiments the opposite of these. They were simply engrossed in the affairs of their particular colony in a way which shut out either British or American loyalty. The political prejudice which was real and active in most of them was one known also in England but in a less fierce form, that is a resistance to interference by an executive government. To the majority of the population, the farmers, the rules of governors were an irritating interference: for the frontiersmen there was, except at rare crises, no effective government. To the merchants of the seaboard the government was something which tried to stop the smuggling by which fortunes were most quickly made.

In England classes were settled and accepted; social promotion was a slow game with conventional rules. In America fortunes were more swiftly made and lost. There were no fixed ranks and classes. Enterprise made money and this meant power. Of course Americans in Massachusetts as well as Virginia took their social graces, along with their wives' finery, from England. But in reality it was already an egalitarian society in the sense that Jack was hoping to be better than his master within his own lifetime. Titles, which to an Englishman recorded grades in power, in America were only geegaws. It was a loose and competitive society, even in the old-established seaboard, while along the frontiers men were stripped down to Indian cunning in the battle for existence and new lands. The frontier was indeed already becoming the safety-valve of a dynamic society. The Appalachians still stood as a boundary line, but already the misfits were beginning to go west. Thither too, particularly in Pennsylvania, the less acceptable immigrants from Europe were pushed out to build a new world. And this movement to the west took Americans all the time, in sympathy as in geography, farther away from Europe.

This individualism accounts for the difficulty of making the colonists unite, of enforcing law and order, or of getting Americans to assume financial responsibility for their share of the common problems of the empire. But there were, of course,

great differences between colonies. Up in Canada a minority of
Britons with a conquered French majority were anxious for
help from London to maintain themselves. In the New England
colonies, the individualist spirit was still channelled, in ordinary
life, by the stern spirit of puritanism. Puritanism, however, was
not in alliance with government. Observing godly rules of private conduct did not dispose a man to make obeisance to those
set in authority by the state. It might, on the contrary, make
rebels. Otis[1] and Adams whipped up the feeling of the less
fortunate but equally self-esteeming majority against families
like the Olivers and the Hutchinsons[2] who had, by 1763, established themselves in local political life as monopolists. Otis
accused them of 'grinding the faces of the poor' to put 'a cruel
yoke on the people who are so near to the state of original
equality'. It was language which appealed to the farmers and
small tradesmen.

In New York, Jersey, and Pennsylvania, the merchants of the
coast and the farmers struggled with the pioneers of the interior.
Here again radicals appealed to egalitarian instincts against the
few great families. In New York the Delanceys had only to fear
the Livingstons in political influence.[3] But politics counted for
comparatively little in social struggle. Even the monopolizing
of the best land near the coast was of comparatively little
moment in a developing continent. In Pennsylvania the eastern
Quakers feared the Scottish, Irish, and German men of the
frontier. In 1764 the frontiersmen marched on Philadelphia. It
was to reinforce their power that the Quakers sent Benjamin
Franklin[4] to England in 1764 to bring their colony under a
royal governor: but political barriers (and under a limited

---

[1] James Otis (1725–83), lawyer and member of Massachusetts legislature; supplied legal arguments against Stamp Act; condemned violence but was accused of
causing it; insane from 1770.

[2] Olivers—Peter Oliver (1713–91) was a great landowner as well as a judge in
Massachusetts. As a loyalist, he became a refugee in England.

Hutchinsons—for Governor Hutchinson, see below, p. 178.

[3] The Delanceys were descended from Huguenots. Oliver Delancey (1749–1822)
became a brigadier-general of the loyalist forces; after the war he went to England,
sat in parliament, and became a general in the regular army.

Livingstons—Peter Von Brugh Livingston (1710–92), a wealthy trader who
nevertheless took part in the anti-British campaign but was a moderating influence;
retired from politics 1775.

[4] Benjamin Franklin (1706–90), famous as an author, scientist, inventor, philanthropist, and diplomat; after business success became agent for Pennsylvania (and
later Massachusetts) in England. For his later career see narrative below.

franchise only 2 per cent. were enfranchised) could not stand against the facts of the social situation.

In the south things had certainly more of an aristocratic air. The great plantation owners of Virginia or Carolina, producing their tobacco or rice with black-slave labour, tried to behave like English country gentlemen. But they had little real sympathy with an English way of life. They were members of the Anglican church,[1] had fine manners, and drank deeply. This apart, what was there similar in the life of the despot over black labour and the English nobleman? Moreover the Virginian had basically the outlook of the primary producer: self-centred and proud he yet felt himself the booby victim of unscrupulous middlemen. He hated the resident moneyed men, all Scots, in Norfolk, Virginia, who were his agents.[2] He was a producer where his English model was an administrator. In the Carolinas and Virginia the problem of the western frontier was acute, both because the frontiersmen menaced the settled well-to-do of the coast and because of the inducements it held out to men of property to invest their capital adventurously. George Washington was one of many Virginians to plan the profitable exploitation of the Indian lands.

There were thus, among the 2½ million Americans on the east of the Continent, many stresses and divisions. But such divisions, while they seemed to afford opportunity for English initiative, in truth made an English control unthinkable. Englishmen could not hope to appreciate the complexity of, say, the quaker struggle to keep Pennsylvania respectable. In the struggle against 'democratic' forces a man like Governor Hutchinson[3] could hope for little aid from distant Westminster. He could hope that opening opportunity across the mountains would draw off the malcontents; he could strive to make himself feared for his own power; he could conceivably try to make

---

[1] Though the Anglican church, that sign of social order, was established in Virginia, an act of parliament would have been required to complete it with an American bishopric. Discussion of such a move aroused Americans because it would have emphasized the English right of interference.

[2] One-third of all property confiscated in Virginia after the War of Independence was taken from these businessmen of Norfolk.

[3] Thomas Hutchinson (1711–80), a graduate of Harvard and member of a family famous in America; chief justice of Massachusetts 1760; carried out Grenville's policy; acting governor of Massachusetts from 1769, formally appointed 1771; his correspondence with London was published by Benjamin Franklin; left America 1774; deplored penal measures against Boston 1776.

himself a leader against a common enemy; but he could not hope to make those in London understand his position nor could he improve it by their aid. For the number of lucrative jobs to use as patronage in America was small. The colonies consistently refused to grant a fixed civil list out of which rewards might have been paid to followers of the ministerial policy. Only in Virginia, Maryland, North Carolina, Georgia, and Nova Scotia, were any officials independent of the financial control of local assemblies. And—this point must be made again—even the few official rewards available had little attraction to men of ambition compared to the open prizes of an expanding society. Places of profit and honour could be found only for a small part of the aristocracy of the coast: this class was divided thereby into a few with pride of place and the envious remainder who tended to become contemptuous critics of the government. Yet this class, even as a whole, was a small minority. The farming majority observed the seasons and ignored politics.

A farmer and a merchant could agree on two points. They believed in the virtues of their free enterprise: they knew that decisions in this New World had necessarily to be made by men on the spot who took the consequences. It was unthinkable to regulate their adventurous lives by decisions taken 3,000 miles away across the Atlantic. To send a question to London and wait for a reply might easily take six months. Indian raids could not be dealt with, nor sowings decided, nor ships loaded, with such delay for each decision, especially when those at a distance were ignorant of the detailed facts. So long as the French had been in Canada, the American had felt himself, for all his boldness, at the mercy of great powers and combinations beyond his comprehension. Some French interest in Prussian Silesia, which he did not understand, might mean that the king of France would encourage his Canadian subjects and their Indian friends to organize a war which only distant England knew how to resist. But when the French were tamed, the American had only the Indians, the elements, and other Americans to face, all of them enemies whom he could tackle without English aid.

In short, where Englishmen saw, and despised, the disunity and lawlessness of America, the colonists were filled with a pride in making a new life for themselves. They congratulated themselves on the vigour of their minds and bodies, on the superiority of their birth-rate, and on their natural common-sense. But the meanest Englishman, said the radical Richard Price,[1] took for granted his superior understanding and his power to regulate colonial affairs.

With two societies so different in habits and situation it was impossible for one to interfere consistently with the other. Moreover the disunity of America might give way to a temporary unity if a real attempt was made at interference. They could unite, like the Sects under Cromwell, to defend their right to live discordantly. Any irritant might be the occasion for animating the difference between colonists and the home country. The regulation of imperial trade was one of such irritants. The British theory of a planned and mutually co-operative economic community has already been explained.[2] To achieve it, all imperial trade had to be conducted in British or colonial ships, a great advantage to the shipbuilders of New England. All European and East Indian goods had to be imported into America by way of Great Britain. The exports of the colonists were classed as enumerated or non-enumerated. The non-enumerated goods were free to move into southern Europe (i.e. south of Cape Finisterre) or other parts of the world, but if destined for northern Europe had to be taken by way of Great Britain. The enumerated goods had always to be exported by way of Great Britain. The list of enumerated goods had been slowly increasing since 1661; but George Grenville more than doubled the number of enumerations in the course of one year, 1764. Thereafter they included tobacco, cotton, indigo, dyes, molasses, copper, furs, hides, skins, pitch, tar, turpentine, masts and arms, coffee, whale fins, raw silk, and potash. Sugar was allowed to be carried to southern Europe and rice to southern Europe or to foreign settlements in America. The purpose of the English was to get valuable raw materials and deny them to European rivals. They could be paid for with English manufactures. It was a consistent extension of this policy therefore when Americans were forbidden to trade in manufactured woollen goods from one colony to another, when they were ordered not to erect any further plating or slitting mills for an iron industry, and when, in 1767, iron was added to the list of enumerated commodities. This prohibition of some industries damaged America, in the conditions of the time, but slightly. But the few who did suffer harm whipped up latent

[1] In his *Observations on the Nature of Civil Liberty*, 1776, p. 19.   [2] Above, p. 15.

hostility to the system. There was also a psychological consideration. Colonies in economic difficulties felt that the possibility of relief by new enterprises was being closed to them.
America deplored the prohibition of industry which she was in
no position to undertake.[1]

Along with the regulations and the prohibitions went bounties
on commodities much needed in England, particularly naval
stores, pitch, silk, and wine. The system was not so artificial as
has sometimes been thought. Great Britain was the natural
market for most of these American products and the cheapest
supplier of finished articles to her. This can be proved by the
fact that after separation, with prejudice existing on both sides
against such trade, it continued to increase. Whereas British
exports to America amounted to £2 million a year in 1760, by
1793 they were approaching £3 million. Eleven out of twelve
inhabitants of New York in the 1760's were dressed in English
clothes. Even after European war had dislocated shipping in
1793, they continued to buy such products. The colonial system
of trade was, in a sense, unnecessary, as it made obligatory
what would have happened anyway. Its champions could claim,
however, that it gave security of expectation to the parties on
either side of the Atlantic.

The system might be justified on a broad view. But merchants
narrowed their view to their own particular interests; there were
admittedly awkward corners which did not fit into the pattern.
New England colonies, for instance, were bound to experience
difficulty in working within the controlled economy. They
bought English manufactures but had few primary products to
use in payment; indirectly they redressed the balance of payments by manufacturing for the southern colonies and by acting
as middleman in the trade to the interior. Even so they found
it hard to square the account; so cheap French sugar instead
of dear colonial sugar was smuggled in. The middle colonies
balanced accounts more easily, but they too found it necessary
to trade, in defiance of law, with the foreign West Indies, exporting food to them as well as to British plantations. The
southern colonies fitted the most comfortably into the British
system. Their tobacco, cotton, rice, and indigo, were guaranteed
the British market; the British consumer was denied cheaper

---

[1] It was one advantage of the moving frontier in British eyes that it diverted
American energies from urban manufacture to further agricultural enterprise.

foreign products. The problem of the southerners was a shortage of liquid capital. Their production was made possible by loans made to them by those who marketed their goods, mainly English merchants. Crops had to be pledged in advance for debt. In the 1760's the Virginian planters were £2 million in debt to British agents, and this was half the entire American indebtedness to the home country.

These chafings of the controls on American necks were of small significance at normal times. But America, like England, experienced a trade recession at the end of the war in 1763. When times were bad all those who worried about their future were liable to abuse the system as the cause of trouble. In Virginia, for instance, George Washington[1] and moderate men of his stamp began to talk of the tyranny of their creditors. Washington contemplated growing corn to be free of the restrictions on tobacco export. Tobacco was an export particularly depressed. Though snuff was fashionable in England, no one with any pretensions to gentility there smoked any longer. Even a free and easy army officer serving abroad in India might feel that good manners obliged him to sneak away privately to indulge in the dirty habit of smoking.[2] So England's consumption of tobacco was disappointing. At the same time Virginian soil had been cultivated carelessly in a way that exhausted it and made production harder. Delaney of Maryland believed the only hope for the tobacco trade was free export. England re-exported 82,000 of the 96,000 hogsheads she imported; she thus took a cut from the inadequate profits in addition to the £400,000 she collected in customs. Yet so long as the commercial pattern was imposed only in outline and so long as infringements of the law were allowed to give relief, it is unlikely that there would have been much agitation against it even in years of depression.

It was, of course, during George Grenville's administration that American malcontents were brought into the open.[3] Grenville's policy for America was coherent: it was based upon a settlement of the frontiers. Something had to be decided about the future of that area of the American interior where the interests of new Canadian subjects, Indian tribes, and American colonists intermingled, the area of Detroit, Illinois, the Ohio,

[1] For Washington see p. 198 and general narrative following.
[2] *Memoirs of W. Hickey*, ed. A. Spencer, iv. 158.
[3] For further details see above, pp. 104 f.

Cumberland, and Tennessee. The object of the board of trade, over which young Shelburne presided, was to keep to the original purpose of Britain, that is increased trade with light administrative costs. Therefore it was decided to keep this vast area roughly as it was. A frontier line was to be drawn at the back of all the old colonies and beyond this they were not, 'for the present', to expand territorially. In the West the fur traders from the north and east were to be encouraged to pursue their valuable enterprise. Meanwhile efforts were to be made by the colonists, acting as middlemen, to push the sale of British manufactures to the Indian tribes. From this policy were expected the advantages of trade and the reduction of military cost. The need to reassure the Indians against the aggressiveness of the eastern colonies was given point by Pontiac's Conspiracy in 1763 which was with difficulty, and little colonial help, suppressed by General Amherst.

The fixing of frontiers was not intended to be rigid. But expansion by colonies should be brought under control from London. It was pointed out that the unsystematic advance across the Appalachians led to injustice even to the colonists themselves, for it allowed powerful groups to monopolize virgin territory to the exclusion of land-hungry farmers. Admittedly the intention of the British government was to slow down, if not prevent, any trek to the west. For they intended to divert the pressure of American migration northwards up to Nova Scotia and southwards into Florida. The new northern colony which would thus be formed could produce timber; that to the south would increase the sub-tropical resources of the empire. They were both preferable to the farmlands of the interior. To implement this policy, Halifax and Hillsborough in 1764 set up a service of superintendents to protect the Indians and supervise the frontiers. This service was to cost £20,000 a year. Supporting them 10,000 troops, in forts along the lakes and mountains, would cost £350,000 a year to maintain.

George Grenville's assistants had thus provided a comprehensive policy which should guide settlement and allow trade to develop in peace. It was directed to the welfare of colonists as much as to the home government. To meet part of the cost of it George Grenville, as has been seen, brought in the Stamp Act and the Sugar Act.[1] The Stamp Act was an attempt to raise

----

[1] These have been discussed from the English point of view above, pp. 104 f.

revenue (perhaps £60,000 a year) by a tax on legal transactions and on newspapers. The so-called Sugar Act was part of a policy of enforcing the system of trade while making it more reasonable. It meant the suppression of smuggling and tightening the pressure on the merchants at a time of adversity. It did not agitate the majority of the population on their farms, but it rankled with a very vocal minority.

The Stamp Act produced a much greater outcry, not because it was really more important, but because it was a novelty. It was, after all, very unconvincing for men of Massachusetts to say—as they did—that they honoured the trade laws as a beneficial system, but at the same time to protest against the navy being used to arrest smugglers.[1] It was difficult to attack the admiralty courts on the ground that they punished smugglers who would have escaped under trial by jury. But it was perfectly possible to attack the Stamp Act because it had never been known in the colonies before. This was taxation for the sake of revenue and not for the sake of trade regulation. The greatest cry of all—'No taxation without representation'—could be used to inflame farmers, as well as merchants, into a defence of that independence which was bred in their bones. The people who were most hit by the Stamp Act were the classes most effective in propaganda. For tavern keepers needed to register (for £1 a year) and newspapers to be printed on stamped paper. Thus over the bar counter and from the editor's desk the feelings of ordinary Americans could be aroused. It was useless to argue that imperial policy demanded expenditure on their behalf. For the policy of shutting up the west as an Indian reserve had only to be clearly stated to be rejected by the acquisitive colonies. To contend that unless this were done there would be expensive wars and quarrels, though true, was not going to carry conviction to men of self-confidence.

The constitutional position of the several legislatures of the American colonies was open to dispute. All that practical men had so far cared about was having effective power in local affairs. But now it became necessary to decide whether they were (as Patrick Henry in Virginia was the first to claim)

---

[1] When Grenville began to make the system more efficient it was said that the administrative cost of collecting c. £2,000 of customs was c. £8,000. *Grenville Papers*, ed. W. J. Smith, ii. 114. It was popularly supposed that the value of the goods smuggled was as much as £700,000 annually.

separate and sovereign legislatures under the Crown, or whether they were subordinate not only to the Crown but to that other legislature in Westminster. Dr. Johnson was quite certain they were under the authority of Westminster. He compared them to 'the vestry of a large parish which may lay a cess [i.e. tax] on the inhabitants and enforce payment' but which did so subject to the overriding power of Parliament 'like any other Corporation in England'.

Americans were too proud to accept this comparison. They felt that Lord Camden was in the right when he said: 'It is impossible that this petty island can continue in dependence that mighty continent, increasing daily in numbers and strength.' They did not, for ten years more, even begin to question royal supremacy. George III was still lauded in America. He only came under any criticism by obstinately espousing the cause of the full sovereignty of parliament over the colonies. So little foundation is there for the legend that George III lost America by being an unparliamentary king. In 1764, however, it is clear that the majority of Americans were not even hostile to the British parliament. It was only in a rump session of the Virginian legislature that Patrick Henry's resolutions, affirming independence under the Crown, were carried. But once a lead had been given, other legislatures joined in the agitation. These legislatures were controlled by a wealthy minority which was in favour of resisting the Stamp Act as the thin end of the wedge, and which, in addition, saw in an agitation a method of diverting discontent. The colonial leaders fought at once against control by George Grenville and against revolt from below. Personal scores were at the same time paid off. The wealthy John Hancock of Boston was hand in glove with the rioters in demonstrations against the Stamp Act. Hutchinson, on the other hand, was smeared by Adams and Otis with the stain of supporting the act. Benjamin Franklin suffered in esteem, for a while, by counselling submission.

When an anti-stamp congress met it put forward, as American beliefs, that the king was their supreme head, that under him the parliament at Westminster was sovereign to manage affairs of imperial concern, but that it was not competent to impose taxation for revenue in America. There began to emerge the American interpretation of Locke. The revolution of 1688 was not one decisive event, but one illustration of the principle on which society was regulated. All governments and legislatures were the agents of the people and could be dismissed if they failed to perform the services for which they were appointed. Principal among such services was the protection of property. So valuable was this service that no government might use power to take property away. Consent was therefore essential to taxation. The consent of the British parliament was not sufficient. For on this vital matter Americans had their own assemblies to represent their wishes. In a sense this was to beg the question. It implied that Americans were already a separate and distinct society, a contention which was contradicted by their admission of parliamentary sovereignty over the rest of the field.

The distinction between taxation for revenue and duties imposed for control was an untenable one, though it had Chatham's endorsement. In truth, the Americans were beginning slowly to feel their own separateness and to reject any sort of control. Many of them hated Grenville's efficient exclusion of foreign sugar, particularly now that the French had been handed back their West Indian islands. But even the minority could not yet bring themselves to cast off traditional loyalty or to realize the full implications of their situation. The history of American grievances for the next ten years shows that as one was removed another came into prominence; none was the root cause of unrest, but all were symptoms, and once the fear of English interference had been roused, almost anything could be construed as a threat. The Stamp Act itself proved unenforceable. The stamps were burned by rioters. Stamp master Zachariah Hood rode so hard from Massachusetts for protection in New York that he killed his horse under him. There was no effective force in any of the colonies to restrain the rioters. Such conservative reaction as there was, was timorous and ineffective.

In England the news of the Stamp Act disturbances and the theory produced at the Congress came as a shock. There was great surprise that American protests could be co-ordinated. The merchants trading with America were alarmed for the future of their business. As creditors of America they appreciated the difficulties. The colonies were chronically short of ready cash for business. Their attempts to keep the wheels turning with paper money had been obstructed by another act of Grenville's, the prohibition of colonial paper currency in 1764. With an enforced commercial code hindering New England enterprise, with a deflationary discouragement of new business, it was the height of folly to create alarm and despondency with a new tax. Their compromise of repealing the Stamp Act while passing a declaratory act to state England's right of sovereignty,[1] the Rockingham ministry hoped would prove an acceptable solution to Americans, for it took them, all that is but a very few extremists, at their word. At the same time Rockingham tried to deal with what was thought to be the root cause of unrest, the economic difficulties of New England. New England, it was tacitly admitted, could not balance her trade without French sugar to make into rum.[2] The duty on foreign molasses was therefore reduced to 1*d.* a gallon. At the same time a free port was opened in Dominica to aid New England and England herself, to push goods into the Spanish colonies and to extract specie in return.

On the face of it, this solution was both ingenious and bold. Its boldness lay in its defiance of the West Indian pressure group in the house of commons.[3] But the downfall of the Rockinghams did not originate in West Indian antagonism. Nor did it arise from American feeling. It is true that the colonists were unsatisfied. They congratulated themselves that the home government would always give way before a small show of force. But the leaders of agitation also asked what could be the reason for a declaratory act, if it was not to bring in another Stamp Act, or worse, once the colonies were quiet again? They declared—a further step into the dangerous air of abstract principles—that they opposed the 'Rights of Nature' to the British declaration. This was, however, only the speech of a small minority. Most colonists, though more conscious of politics than ever before, were prepared to get on with the daily round with a feeling of satisfied honour.

The disintegration of the Rockingham plan was due, as has already been explained[4] to the failure of the delicate

---

[1] For a fuller account see above, pp. 115 f.

[2] French molasses were cheap because the French government, to protect home brandy, forbade their manufacture into rum by Frenchmen. 85 per cent. of the molasses used in Rhode Island were foreign.

[3] For this group see above, p. 22.

[4] See above, p. 116.

compromise at home. To many politicians it seemed that the Rockinghams had meekly surrendered to rioters and that there would be no longer any method of maintaining order or of controlling expansion in the colonies. The governors would fall into the hands of the assemblies. Yet though the Rockinghams fell from power and never outlived the reproach from the 'strong-arm' party, the government of Chatham was equally, or more, pro-American. Chatham indeed agreed that America must meet some of her own costs. But he denied that she should do so on British lines or by a British tax. The Chathamites, unwarned by war experience, would have liked Americans to make a voluntary contribution, taxing themselves through their assemblies. Thus Chatham clung to 'no internal taxation without representation' and simultaneously to the idea of imperial action. Britain must be sovereign to decide the issues of peace and war, of continental politics, but she must allow free men to subscribe freely.

The difficulty in front of the policy of 'free subscription' was that there was no united American assembly or point of view. Chatham could not say 'here are American problems: to solve them will cost so much: American people, will you foot part of the bill? Raise the money among yourselves as you see fit'. For there were no American people, only thirteen divided colonies. The unity shown in the Stamp Act Congress was purely negative and revolutionary. George Grenville could make them unite, but their friend Chatham had already tried and failed. The only solution was to break up the total sum required from Americans into appropriate quotas from the various colonies and make thirteen demands. This was the system of 'requisition'. It had the advantage that it did not involve the exercise of the power of the Westminster parliament, for the requisition was made in the king's name under prerogative. But it had the overwhelming disadvantage that it took the power of decision right out of colonial hands. It increased the power of the king's executive both in America and in England in a way which every legislative assembly would resent because it was contrary to parliamentary control of the purse.

Chatham's financial ideas were still-born. In 1766 Boston refused to supply troops with candles and creature comforts: New York, for a time, until its assembly was suspended, refused to heed a similar requisition to maintain troops under the

Mutiny Act. If the colonies boggled at a trifling demand of this nature, they would certainly not answer a bigger demand. For if they did, they would not control the way money was spent; it might be claimed for the Indian frontier but used to keep order in Boston. In the other colonies there was certainly a growing feeling that New York and Boston had behaved badly, but there was no disposition to give up their own immunities. Thus the financial problem remained. In 1767 the charges for America amounted to £428,000 or the equivalent of a shilling on the English land tax. After Chatham's collapse, two members of his administration produced, independently, schemes for escaping from the deadlock.

The second in time to be produced, but by far the more interesting and radical, was that of Lord Shelburne. Shelburne had two aims, to reduce expense and to conciliate American opinion while retaining the outlines of an imperial system centred in London. He went back to the problem he had studied when at the board of trade before he had become a Chathamite, and he revised all his previous conclusions. The plan for turning expansion to north and south while keeping the hinterland for Indians and fur-traders had not worked. The superintendents had been unable to prevent the colonists from threatening the Indians (and each other) while the bill for their work was a large part of those American costs which England had not been able to recover from the colonies. He proposed to decentralize control of the hinterland. He would withdraw the troops and superintendents and allow the colonists to expand over the continent. If there was blood, it would be on their heads, if there were expenses they would see them to be their own and pay them without a requisition from London. This expansion was not to be a race between the existing colonies: three new colonial units, agreed with colonial land companies, should be established, one at Detroit, one on the Illinois, and one on the lower Mississippi. These new colonies for a while would require some military assistance, but were to be encouraged to provide their own forces and, along with the older colonies, to garrison the forts in the unsettled areas.

Shelburne claimed many advantages for his plan. The new colonies would be more strongly governed than the old. It would relieve the pressure inside the colonies and also the conflicts between them. It would help to keep America agricultural by drawing off the population to the interior. The colonists in their expansion would be better customers for English goods than the Indians could be. Finally Shelburne hoped, by another feature of his plan, to obtain financial relief and to increase executive strength at one blow. The lands granted to settlers should pay quit-rents to the Crown. As the system was organized in the new areas, it should be overhauled in the old. Thus from land grants a revenue might be obtained, as a normal commercial bargain not as taxation, which would be free of the interference of colonial legislatures. From this fund a body of devoted servants of the Crown might be paid.

Of all the schemes for meeting England's needs while pacifying America, this is probably the most ingenious. Yet against it was the argument that England could not allow quarrels between colonists to arise out of exploitation of the west, or allow colonists to endanger security by their treatment of the Indians. Shelburne was forced by his colleagues to modify the scheme and to admit more supervision by English agents. Again it is unlikely that the collection of quit rents could have been made efficient at that distance and through colonial servants. With the movement to the west, Americans would, furthermore, have become more alien and averse to interference anywhere. In any case Shelburne's plan was not put into effect. He was forced out of office. The version of his scheme to be adopted was one which allowed for some extensions by the old colonies subject to permission from Whitehall acting on the advice of the Indian superintendents.

The other scheme devised by Chatham's colleagues was the more famous but less profound device of Charles Townshend[1] of imposing indirect taxes managed by a board of commissioners for the whole American coast, free from pressure inside individual colonies. The proceeds were to be used for the armed forces in America and, if adequate, for the cost of civil government so as to free the governors and their executive from the stranglehold of the colonial assemblies. As an economy, military forces were to be cut to a skeleton on the frontiers. As Townshend's estimate of receipts was only £40,000, such economy was essential; it was lunacy to think that there would be any money available for paying a civil list.

Townshend's duties were disastrous in a multitude of ways.

---

[1] The details of which have been discussed above, p. 127.

By talking of a civil establishment maintained on their yield he excited fears in America of that complete control from England which he was always powerless to impose. The smart lawyers' trick of gathering revenue from indirect taxes because the colonists had in words acknowledged their validity, merely caused Americans to attack the whole idea of a regulation of trade which they had hitherto taken for granted. The colonists saw in Townshend's plan not the *jeu d'esprit* of a clever fool, but an indication of the real intentions of all Englishmen. This, they said, was why Rockingham passed a declaratory act. It was not enough to fight abuses, the whole system would have to be attacked from the ground up or the danger would remain. Finally Townshend's duties adversely affected British merchants, for it was a tax on the goods they exported; there was therefore discontent at home.

The American reaction came first from Massachusetts. There Samuel Adams drafted a circular letter to send to the other colonists calling for common resistance to the duties. From Pennsylvania John Dickinson[1] stirred opinion with his *Farmer's Letters*. The argument in each case went back to constitutional first principles. It was admitted, once again, that under the English constitution the English parliament was the sovereign power. But it was argued that there were certain laws of nature, certain assumed limits, which kept even this sovereign power from some actions; Townshend's duties went over these limits. It was an argument not without appeal to Englishmen of the eighteenth, and later, centuries. For the sovereignty of parliament is, in practice, limited by the unstated bounds which the body of citizens put to it in their own minds. It is the shifting of this agreed but invisible boundary in the minds of Englishmen which has permitted parliament to increase its range without any change in constitutional law. In the 1760's Englishmen would have ejected a parliament which interfered with their private lives as it calmly might even a century later. The American resistance to government, to any government (even, after independence, to their native one), was but an exaggeration of an English squire's attitude. But unfortunately the boundaries set in the common mind were not the same on

---

[1] John Dickinson (1732–1808) studied in Middle Temple 1753–7. In Pennsylvanian politics took the conservative side against Franklin; fought against England but voted against the Declaration of Independence.

either side of the Atlantic. Englishmen accepted, even then, rules rejected as contrary to nature by the individualistic Americans. Again the Americans put their case in terms of 'Natural Law' and so aroused the deepest suspicions of practical Englishmen.

The Massachusetts Circular was answered by Lord Hillsborough's circular letter to colonial governors instructing them to ignore this appeal to revolt. The Massachusetts assembly was suspended. This turned the Massachusetts protest, which had seemed a doubtful success, into a rallying point of colonial opinion. It was at this stage that George Washington became convinced that the English government was set on complete domination and that it must be steadfastly resisted. The Customs were, meanwhile, more efficiently collected by the new board, after the dismissal of corrupt agents. Payment was demanded in specie, which increased the currency difficulties of the colonies. Smuggling was not stopped, however. Philadelphia in the next years was recorded as having imported a negligible amount of tea. Yet its inhabitants were drinking 2,000 chests of it a year.

The colonies were not content to evade the law. They hoped to kill it as they had killed the Stamp Act, by economic pressure on English merchants. Non-importation agreements were made and Americans agreed to abstain from consumption of English goods. In New England, which was now prosperous again in spite of its exchange difficulties, a further advantage of this idea was that it would compel a return to the simple life and the renunciation of English frippery. In all this period the English troops were criticized by Americans for corrupting colonial manners (and colonial girls) with their riotous, free-spending ways. American women to be patriotic had to dress in homespun, decline tea, and follow simple paths of virtue. The campaign had some effect on marts as well as morals. The port of Boston was particularly hard hit, and economic distress naturally led to bigger gangs of roughs behaving with bolder insolence. The newspapers laboured to convince the farmers that they should feel sympathy rather than aversion for the population of the ports. Intimidation of authority was widespread. No colonial magistrate, no colonial jury, would punish disorder.

The Non-importation agreement was a failure in the long

run despite appearances. In England the merchants did not rise unanimously to the help of Americans as they had on the Stamp Act crisis. Partly they were, like most Englishmen, contemptuously weary of American disorder: as business-men they had begun to look on the American market as too uncertain in these conditions; many of them were struggling, with some success, to force their way into alternative markets where conditions were more stable. They were convinced also that America could pay; for prosperity had returned. Nevertheless when Lord North, in coming to full power in 1770, abolished all the Townshend duties with the exception of tea,[1] English trading opinion thought this a sound common-sense settlement. Lord North's wish for peace was clear; it was only unfortunate that, in appealing to the Grenville and Bedford groups among his supporters, he used the phrase 'the colonists must lie at the feet of Great Britain'.

In America, non-importation put an even greater strain on the businessmen of the ports. In 1770, as North was repealing the more stupid duties, two events brought on the collapse of American resistance. In Boston, Grafton had stationed four regiments of troops to prevent complete chaos. Their commanding officer, Colonel Dalrymple, confessed that his men were not saints, but he justly praised their restraint in face of jeering attacks; no soldier could venture out by himself into the streets of Boston. Now half the forces were withdrawn and sent to Halifax. Encouraged by this, the Boston mob proceeded to an attack on a company of men under Captain Preston (on 5 March 1770) who were standing guard round the customs house with its receipts inside. The soldiers stood steady under blows, until one was knocked down; then someone gave the order to fire and five Bostonians were killed. The troops withdrew under stoning to avoid further bloodshed. This 'Boston Massacre' was used in the radical propaganda of Sam Adams to put fresh heart into colonial agitation. The effect was, however, to convince ordinary colonists that the Bostonians were going too far. 'Property will soon be very precarious', declared the *New York Gazette*, foreseeing social revolution, so, 'It's high time a stop was put to mobbing.'

In New York distress had produced a new radical leader,.

---

[1] In addition to its value as a symbol of sovereignty the tea tax yielded £11,000 to £12,000 a year.

Alexander McDougall,[1] who sedulously aped the antics of John Wilkes. The leaders of the New York Assembly feared it might be ground out of existence between the hostility of the English government and the reckless demagogy of McDougall. Amid a general conservative reaction of feeling New York broke the agreement and threw open the port in the later summer of 1770.[2] This was the end of the non-importation campaign, though individual Americans continued to abstain from tea.

It seemed therefore as if there was a good chance in 1770 of the American question going quietly to sleep unsolved, insoluble, but no longer serious. Lord North for his part was no more ambitious than statesmen before 1763 to direct American affairs. In asking support from those who condemned colonial impudence he could claim to have broken non-importation, to have kept a revenue from tea, and to have defended the principle of the Declaratory Act. But to sympathizers with America he could point out that he did not intend to oppress colonists, that the frontier had been partially opened to them, and that many Americans themselves approved of his quiet policy. Moderate Americans were content to have taught interfering Englishmen a lesson and wanted to avoid further excitement. In the next three years the colonies relapsed into their former quarrelsome disunity. Connecticut contended fiercely with Pennsylvania for the control of the Wyoming valley: New York disputed with New Hampshire for authority in the western mountain lands. In the Carolinas the untoward consequences of the late excitements were seen in the rebellion of the 'Regulators'. The regulators were the vigilantes of the frontier, an unofficial government of the pioneers. They marched, 6,000 strong, against their own state government with a cry of 'No Taxation without Representation', claiming that they were oppressed by a coastal aristocracy. They were defeated with the loss of fifteen lives.

Of course the hostility to England, once aroused, did not die away even in these three years. In 1772 the revenue ship *Gaspée*,

---

[1] Alexander McDougall (1732–86) emigrated from Scotland as a child; seaman then merchant; represented New York in the Continental Congress.

[2] New York had been very thorough: it cut its British imports from £482,000 in 1764, to £74,000 in 1769. In the same period Boston cut its imports by about half. Rhode Island never reduced its imports. Portsmouth (New Hampshire) was profiting by the stand made by rival ports. In Virginia, Maryland, and Georgia, non-importation was never really effective.

aground off Rhode Island, was burned and its young commander, Lieutenant Dudington, treated in a dastardly way. There
was also the affair of Hutchinson's letters. By revealing the
contents of private letters—obtained in some mysterious way—
between Hutchinson and a member of parliament, Benjamin
Franklin restored himself to favour with the radicals and destroyed Hutchinson's career. The new governor of Massachusetts was General Gage.[1] The attempt, too, to set up a civil list
in Massachusetts on customs' revenues gave fresh ammunition
to Sam Adams. But on the whole it may be said that British
control had become a sort of bogy: the colonists had more real
and immediate difficulties to occupy most of their time.

[1] Thomas Gage (1721–87), a soldier who had served under Amherst in the
conquest of Canada; commander-in-chief in America 1763–72; governor of
Massachusetts 1774–75; superseded by Howe.

VIII

LORD NORTH AND THE AMERICAN
WAR OF INDEPENDENCE

LORD NORTH's four years of success at home were also therefore years in which a working arrangement seemed to have
been found in America. Their end came suddenly. It is
testimony to the complete gulf between the two worlds that the
immediate cause seems out of proportion to its results. In his
rehabilitation of the East India Company,[1] North included an
ingenious provision for disposing of their surplus stock of tea,
tea which still came under Townshend duties and which was
still regarded in America therefore as the drink of renegades.
The East India Company was to pay the 3*d.* duty on its entry
into America, but they were excused reimbursing the English
customs for the 1*s.* English duty which would previously have
fallen on it. They were also permitted to send the tea direct and
on their own account to America, instead of having it handled
by middlemen in England. The consequence, it was said, was
that tea would sell at 10*s.* a lb. in America instead of the 20*s.*
which it had fetched only a short while ago. This would increase its consumption even among rebels and so the East India
Company would be helped out of its financial difficulties. Two
hundred and ninety-eight chests of tea, worth £10,994, were
quickly dispatched to Boston. Further, the Company aided the
government by taking measures against smuggling now that it
was delivering direct to America. The tea was consigned in
known quantities and to authorized merchants acting as Company agents.

There was great excitement in radical circles in America.
The smuggling centres of New York and Philadelphia (for Boston was now too well policed to smuggle in quantity) were outraged. All those in the trade who were not chosen as agents by
the Company were also indignant at this monopolization. There
is, however, some evidence that the excitement was confined to
a minority. For the logical answer was an inter-colonial league

[1] See above, p. 169.

to refuse to buy tea. Yet the radicals aimed at preventing tea being landed for fear that once on shore it would be bought and drunk by most Americans. At Boston, where efforts to prevent tea being accepted seemed likely to fail, it was thrown into the harbour. This was the famous Boston Tea Party of 16 December 1773. The radical leaders in Boston by direct action once more provoked the English government to retaliation. Lord North, it is arguable, might have treated this as he had treated the Rhode Island pillagers of the *Gaspée*: he might have appointed an inquiry which would not have found anyone willing to turn king's evidence against those who, in the disguise of Indian braves, had consigned the tea to salt water. Then he could have hoped for some abatement of excitement. But Lord North, and even more his colleagues in office, believed that it was dangerous to overlook lawlessness in Boston. English conservatives believed that one stern punishment would end the trouble.[1]

The punishment selected by North was to close Boston as a port until the tea had been paid for and the revenue officers compensated. A change was also made in the constitution of Massachusetts to bring it into line with more orderly colonies. The councillors (that is the upper house of the legislature) were to be nominated by the Crown instead of being elected by the house of representatives. Justice was to be made firmer by allowing the governor to transfer trials to England if he thought it necessary. By a Quartering Act Boston was made to make barracks available for royal troops inside the town.

It was expected in England that Massachusetts would once more be disowned by the other colonies, and that other ports would gladly absorb business diverted from Boston. On the contrary, however, there was a general movement to support Boston. For many feared that if England were permitted to suspend a constitution and close a port in this way, there would be no safeguards left for any colonial legislature, no corporation sacred to such an executive, and that all that had been gained since 1763 would be in danger. As in England under James II, it was anticipation of a revolution from above which provided a rallying ground for resistance. It is a symptom of the apprehensive state of American opinion that the Quebec Act, which

---

[1] Some, even, of Rockingham's friends felt indignation at the conduct of Boston and Lord John Cavendish, for example, agreed with the government in its punitive policy.

North's government had had in preparation long before the 'tea party', was interpreted across the Atlantic as further retribution for colonial resistance to tea.

The purposes of the Quebec Act were to provide for the juster administration of Canada, now that it had been in English hands for ten years, and to make another attempt to settle the question of the interior of the Continent. Under the first head Canada was given a legislative council to rule her, appointed by the Crown, on which the Roman catholic majority were to have a place. At the same time French laws, without a jury trial, were recognized in civil cases. The French Roman catholic priests, not being regulars, were allowed to enjoy estates and to receive tithes from their own communion. Under the second head the boundaries of Canada were to extend down to include Illinois, Vincennes, and Detroit, in which areas there were scattered French settlements. Thus 'the old north west' would be brought under a Canadian council and kept as a fur traders' happy hunting ground. In the south-west the government probably intended to allow freer expansion than in the past. Taking the act as a whole, it may be considered a realistic and tolerant attempt to deal with an alien population in a conquered territory. It was to prove acceptable to Canada for twenty years.[1]

The Quebec Act aroused bitter feelings in the thirteen colonies, however. In the first place the extension of Canada down to the Ohio barred the sort of westwards expansion which, since 1768, had been accelerating from the seaboard colonies. The Vandalia Company, in which George Washington,[2] Patrick Henry, and a group of Philadelphia speculators were interested, was made valueless. The British conception of a trading empire was brought into sharp opposition to colonial expansionism. In the second place the colonists saw in the fostering of Canada an attempt to hold them down by military force. They imagined, not without a basis in speeches at home, that the English government were trying to re-create the threat of a French disciplined autocracy to the north and west of them. King George was taking the place of King Louis and reversing

[1] See below, p. 302.
[2] The future commander-in-chief and first president of the United States, Washington (1732–99) had served with the British forces against the French and in 1759 had settled down to be a gentleman-farmer and politician.

the decision of 1763. Thirdly, the act roused religious passion. To the New England colonies, predominantly puritan, the Roman catholic religion was still associated with tyranny and their reactions to it were as emotionally direct as those of all Englishmen had been in 1688 or as those of the Gordon rioters were to be in 1780. Excitement was heightened by the proposal, being discussed at this time, of appointing an American bishop: this was regarded in Harvard, Yale, and Princeton, those nurseries of dissent, as proof that the English government had an unholy alliance with the pope. For though Englishmen cherished the church of England as a middle way between dissent and popery, in the New England scheme of things the church of England was taken as the offshoot of Rome.

In 1774, therefore, Americans were convinced that Lord North intended to enslave them by inches. He, on the other hand, thought he had only to restore order in Massachusetts and the inexplicable effervescence would subside. Conservatives in America did not accept the radical proposal for a solemn league and covenant which implied a fight to the death with England: instead they successfully proposed a pan-colonial Congress to meet in Philadelphia in 1774. In that congress, however, the radicals inevitably took the lead. It was agreed to work for the repeal of all British colonial legislation passed since 1763; it was decided neither to export nor import from England (with significant exceptions to allow the southern states to dispose of their crops) until they had satisfaction: the congress endorsed the resolutions passed in Suffolk county, Massachusetts, to pay no taxes to Britain and to prepare to defend themselves if British troops attacked. One conservative scheme, produced by Franklin's assistant, Joseph Galloway of Philadelphia, was allowed to collect dust on the table. This was a proposal that the colonies should federate and, under congress, negotiate a reasonable financial settlement with London for America as a whole. This scheme supplied the constitutional machinery which might have enabled Chatham's financial ideas of seven years earlier[1] to be worked. But it was too late. British ministers naturally now looked on a congress as an illegal body which had no purpose but to foment feeling against them.

In Boston, meanwhile, General Gage pursued a cautious

[1] See above, p. 188.

policy of avoiding incidents. He nevertheless gave the sound advice to his superiors—'If you think ten thousand men enough, send twenty; if a million is thought enough, give two; you will save both blood and Treasure in the end.' At home the government was irresolutely poised between deciding on stern punishment and endeavouring to conciliate the colonists. North, characteristically, tried both, though his own leaning was clearly to clemency and peace. The opposition made hopeless motions for conciliation. Even among the merchants there was a conviction that customers and debtors on the other side of the Atlantic needed to be whipped before they could be relied on to do business quietly. Nevertheless, in 1775 Chatham proposed that troops should withdraw from America to create the better atmosphere in which a request for supplies could be made. He never budged an inch from his insistence upon sovereignty over their assemblies, but he was equally insistent that the collection of money was in a special category and must be freely rendered by the colonists. This was now too superficial a proposal. It was in this year, too, that Burke made his celebrated and moving speech for conciliation. He too maintained the ultimate sovereignty of the British parliament. He swept aside as ridiculous the Chathamite attempt to limit sovereignty as regards money with some vague line. For as he had said two years before: 'If it be true that the complicated bodies which make up this complicated mass are to be preserved as one Empire, an authority sufficient to preserve that unity and by its equal weight and pressure to consolidate the various parts that comprise it, must reside somewhere: that somewhere can only be in England.'[1] But while Burke believed that England had a natural and inevitable claim to over-riding power, he believed that this power should not be regularly exercised. He would have had it held in the background for use only in a crisis such as an attack by a foreign power. He contended that the empire was like a family in which the father, no doubt, had legal authority but which was ruled and held together not by law but by a union of hearts, the unconscious give and take of daily action together. A family in which the father cites the law is bound for destruction because the father must have neglected the affections. 'Magnanimity in politics', declared Burke, 'is not seldom the truest wisdom and a great Empire and little minds

[1] Letter to Sir C. Bingham, 1773.

go ill together.' If the Americans were offered freedom, they
would cleave to the mother country in gratitude: if they were
allowed to grow rich, even by evasion of just demands, so much
the greater would be the resources and power which they could
bring to the common effort in case of another war with France
and Spain.

All this was lacking in detail. Cynics could point out that
Burke was only stating, in fine long words poorly spoken, the
Rockingham compromise—a declaratory act but no exercise
of power. Yet Burke had, in the mysterious alchemy of his
mind, turned this practical compromise into a great and
living principle of a commonwealth. He had done so, however, for the admiration of posterity and not for use in 1775.
Neither English nor Americans were in a mood where his
speech could be opportune. Burke's practical work in 1775
was to advise his New York clients, who were dragging their
feet in the colonial movement, not to trust any of the acts of
the British government.

After the two conciliatory motions of the opposition, Lord
North, in spite of grumbling on his own side, made his official
proposition for re-establishing harmony. North's proposals were
that each colony which should return to its obedience and
acknowledge English sovereignty and show itself willing to raise
its just part of common expenses, should be allowed to decide
for itself the ways and means of finding the money. On the
American side, John Dickinson, now a conservative, persuaded
congress to approach London with an olive-branch petition
setting out their grievances and asking for redress of them. But
these two gestures showed only how men on each side wished
for agreement which attitudes of mind now habitual made
impossible. In April 1775 shots had been fired at Lexington.

Massachusetts had armed its militia to resist attack from
General Gage. They had stored arms at Concord up the Charles
river from Boston. It was likely in such a situation that any
chance event would start the firing. On 19 April 1775 Gage
sent a party to Concord to confiscate the rebel arms. At Lexington, on their road, they were engaged in a small skirmish with
a body of the militia. The stores at Concord were destroyed at
their approach and the troops then made their way back under
skirmishing attacks to Charlestown near Boston. The American
losses were believed to be 60, the wearied troops had lost in

killed, wounded and cut off, about 273. It was enough. The whole country rushed to arms, boasting of the skill of their frontier marksmen. General Gage proclaimed Sam Adams and John Hancock to be rebels whose crimes could not be pardoned. In the early summer three generals, Howe, Burgoyne, and Clinton, arrived in Boston with reinforcements.[1] In June the colonists attempted to construct earthworks across the neck of the peninsula at whose end Charlestown stands so as to isolate the troops there. On 17 June 1775 General Howe forced the rebels away, but only after several attacks and at the loss of 1,054 men killed or wounded, half his force engaged. This was the battle of Bunker or Breed's Hill.

Sporadic fighting broke out in the south later in the year. The Governor of Virginia, Lord Dunmore, had the same thought as Gage, to secure the gunpowder of the militia. He secured it without bloodshed. Upon a demand for its return being made, the governor threatened to restore his colony to order by force. He committed the unforgivable crime, in the eyes of the liberty clubs, by threatening to enfranchise all the negroes, and lead them in the king's name against their upstart masters. It is perhaps significant of English restraint and hope of restoring all to normal, that Dunmore alone made use of this weakness in the American position and of this startling contradiction in their beliefs about the equality of man. Dunmore was soon after compelled to evacuate his house. He retired to a man-of-war and conducted a private marauding campaign along the coasts of Virginia, burning down Norfolk, the centre of commerce.

By the end of July 1775 North's propositions had been rejected, and George Washington appointed commander-in-chief of American forces. By the end of August a colonial invasion of Canada, under Schuyler, Montgomery, and Benedict Arnold was well under way. Though this attack failed at Quebec

---

[1] Sir William Howe, fifth Viscount Howe (1729–1814), a soldier who served in the conquest of Canada; member of parliament Nottingham, 1758–80; lieutenant-general, 1775; succeeded Gage as commander in America; resigned his command in the American war, 1778; lieutenant-general of the ordnance; succeeded his brother in Irish viscountcy, 1799.

(For Burgoyne see above, p. 76 n.)

Sir Henry Clinton (1738?–95), soldier in Germany, 1760–3; major-general, 1772; member of parliament, 1773; knighted, 1777; commander-in-chief in America, 1778; quarrelled with his second in command, Cornwallis, and resigned, 1781; governor of Gibraltar, 1794.

(Montgomery was killed and Arnold[1] maimed), it was decisive in its effects on English opinion. The opposition found that their friendship for America brought them great unpopularity. 'The generality of the people of England are now led away by the misrepresentations and arts of the ministry, the court, and their abettors; so that the violent measures towards America are freely adopted and countenanced by a majority of individuals of all ranks, professions, or occupations, in this country', Rockingham despairingly wrote to Burke in September. Stephen Sayre (an American but formerly sheriff of London) was sent to the tower on the charge of plotting to seize the king. Radicals of Wilkes's stamp faced charges of disloyalty. There was indeed a massive strengthening of Lord North's political position. The suspicion, long felt, that the Rockinghams were factious received confirmation from across the Atlantic. Instead of a general desire for 'a negative upon government' which had so long prevailed in men's minds, there was now a general conservative impulse which led independents to support the throne and the ministry against all enemies of order. Lord North's majorities were larger than expected. Only inside his cabinet did he lack support. There there was discord. Grafton retired to opposition, ever the ineffective sympathizer with the colonies. Dartmouth stepped out of the cabinet, though taking the office of lord privy seal. Rochford was persuaded that he was too infirm and must go. To fill these places Lord George Sackville Germain[2] became American secretary, and Weymouth southern secretary. It was now a cabinet for war, presided over by a champion of peace and economy.

While the cabinet prepared for war, North tried always to whittle down costs and think out plans for conciliation. The secretary at war, Barrington, gloomily maintained that there were not the forces available for a land war and advocated a naval blockade. Lord Sandwich at the admiralty had been doing good work within the limits of North's retrenchment budgets. What ships there were were up-to-date in such modern improvements as copper-bottoms. But a shortage of seasoned timber made a quick expansion difficult, even if North could be

---

[1] Benedict Arnold (1741–1801), a rebellious son of very strict New England family; a captain in the Connecticut militia; for his subsequent career as patriot and traitor see narrative below.

[2] He had taken the name of Germain in 1770 on succeeding to the estates bequeathed to him by Lady Elizabeth Germain.

brought to sanction expansion. Further, Sandwich thought that the great danger was an attack by France. Therefore he struggled to maintain naval strength in home waters and was loathe to see his ships go off to the distant naval war proposed by Barrington. Graves, commanding in American waters, had only twenty-seven ships of which only three were ships of the line: a further ten ships reinforced him in September 1774. But he had to contend with scattered American privateers. Lord George Germain was both optimistic and bellicose. He wished to win the war quickly with decisive blows. He criticized impartially North, Sandwich, and Barrington, for lack of military vision.

North failed to control his cabinet. He had little confidence in his senior ministerial colleagues. He worked mostly with Eden[1] (the under-secretary to Suffolk), with Jenkinson, and Cornwall (junior lords of the treasury), and with Robinson (the secretary to the treasury). North constantly tried to compromise where, for the sake of strategy, he should have commanded. When compromise failed then he shuffled off responsibility. When Eden complained of Barrington, North replied, he 'may perhaps not be so active in promoting measures which he does not approve as we could wish. I do not know that we have any particular neglect to lay to his charge, and without that I am sure that no application for removing him will succeed. The reasons must be very cogent which can carry that point: I speak from knowledge.'[2] Such excuses are lamentable. George III would naturally retain his power to control ministers so long as North ran away from an argument. From the military point of view there was need of a strong controlling planner; it would have been better if the king had been either less or much more the master of the cabinet. But North allowed several policies to be followed at once because he refused to believe that the time for action had arrived.

There was no retreat possible as the spring of 1776 came on. Congress had been loath, for all its military preparations, to break the link with Britain finally. It was a stranger, who had

---

[1] William Eden (1744–1814), first lord of the board of trade, 1776; vice-treasurer of Ireland, 1783; negotiated the commercial treaty with France, 1786; created Baron Auckland in the Irish peerage, 1789; served Pitt and Addington; president of the board of trade under ministry of all the talents.

[2] 18 September 1775 (Auckland Papers: Add. MS. 46490 unbound). My attention was drawn to this letter by my former pupil Mr. Lawrence Brown.

been only two years in America, Tom Paine,[1] who shattered the silence of restraint, awe, and caution. In his *Common Sense* he boldly declared that the only logical end of their course was independence: their link with the king was a delusion, for the king was not better but, if possible, worse than his English ministers. The rapid sale of his book from January 1776 proved that he had said what many thought but had not liked to say. Paine indeed had a rough, shrewd, commonplace mind. He solved all problems by neglecting complexities. He went always to first principles, often so simplified as to bear no relation to the real world. But in 1776 it was an advantage to see the end without being confused by local considerations or past history. Congress took up the project he had dared to name. In February 1776 Silas Deane was sent to negotiate aid from the French. On 4 July America declared her independence and unity, prefacing it with a précis of John Locke on the rights of peoples and Thomas Jefferson[2] on the offences of George III. Jefferson also wrote into the declaration the aims of the new republic, transcending the record of quarrels which occasioned it. The revolutionaries pledged their faith in a new form of government which would guarantee equality and liberty at the same time for all conditions of men.

Even at this date, however, Maryland, New Jersey, and Pennsylvania, were reluctant to declare for independence, and New York abstained for eleven days. Pennsylvanian conservatives resisted so strongly that they provoked a revolution inside their own state. Tom Paine and Benjamin Franklin drew up a new constitution for Pennsylvania which was a victory for the western settlers over both the quakers and the moneyed men of the coast; it was a constitution with annual parliaments, manhood suffrage, and an executive without much power. Such radicalism might well cause alarm in the south; in England

---

[1] Thomas Paine (1737–1809), an excise officer dismissed for leading a movement for increased pay; emigrated to America, 1774; served with American armies; secretary to the committee on foreign affairs; propaganda writer for American cause; invented an iron bridge; published *The Rights of Man*, 1790–2 in London; fled to France and made a French citizen; member of the convention but imprisoned under Robespierre; published *The Age of Reason*, 1793; returned to America, but unpopular there for his extreme opinions on politics and religion.

[2] Thomas Jefferson (1743–1826), Virginian leader in independence movement; philosopher of the revolution. Later leader of an agrarian anti-Federalist party; president of the United States.

there was hope that these levelling doctrines would alarm and divide the other colonies.

No greater mistake—and there were many mistakes—was made by English ministers in their conduct of the war than their excessive reliance upon a split in American ranks and upon active large-scale aid from the loyalists. It might be true that many did not approve of the extreme course steered by the leaders: but they were never prepared to strain every nerve to aid Britain. They were conservative but also quiescent for a long time. In Carolina, truly, the frontiersmen rose under the leadership of M'Donald in 1776 to fight against congress. They were beaten. This was, however, more a continuation of an old internal feud than a sign of enthusiasm for King George or Lord North. In 1776 Clinton took 2,000 men and a naval squadron to an attack on Charleston, hoping for a simultaneous rising in South Carolina. It seemed a cheap way of waging the war. The attack failed because no local forces attacked the town from behind. The loyalists were very poorly organized.

The difficulties of English arms became plain in the course of 1776. In essence these were that a small number of trained soldiers, many hired from Hesse, had to suppress a great number of partially trained men who had the whole eastern seaboard in which to make themselves a nuisance. All British forces had to be maintained and supplied across 3,000 miles of ocean and this not just for a campaign, as in 1759–60, but over a period of years. General Howe at the beginning of the year had to evacuate Boston in face of large numbers hemming him in there. He retired for a while to Halifax, Nova Scotia. The full British effort came into play when Lord North sent Admiral Lord Howe[1] to act with his brother, the general, to conduct war and offer peace. The terms they offered were much the same as North's conciliatory propositions:[2] the threat with which they accompanied them was an offensive backed by 20,000 troops. When they brought their full force into operation, on the rejec-

---

[1] Richard Howe (1726–99), fourth (Irish) Viscount Howe, distinguished service at sea from 1740; member of parliament for Dartmouth, 1757–82; treasurer of the navy, 1765–70; rear admiral, 1770; resigned command in America, 1778; first lord of the admiralty, 1783; created Earl Howe, 1788; won a great victory over the French 1794; pacified mutineers at Portsmouth, 1797. The code of signalling was perfected by him.

[2] See above, p. 201. They were able to concede, in addition, security of tenure for colonial judges, but they demanded the dissolution of congress and all revolutionary assemblies, and compensation for loyalists.

tion of the overtures, they captured Long Island at the end of August and New York, which the Americans evacuated, in late September. General Howe moved on to the mainland and confronted Washington on the high ground of White Plains. Washington continually withdrew, constantly facing Howe across rivers at which the British prepared for action, but as constantly slipping away without battle. Clinton meanwhile captured Rhode Island and Carleton[1] destroyed American ships on Lake Champlain. By the end of December the British were established on the coast from Rhode Island through Jersey to the Delaware. At this point General Howe put his troops into winter quarters and desisted from the campaign. His difficulty was that he had won without conquering and nowhere was his lodgement permanent. His troops gained control wherever they appeared, but on their moving on, the territory was exposed to attack from the unmastered interior.

To master the interior no means had been found but to encourage the Indians to press down from the rivers and mountains on the back of the Americans. But by the end of 1776 the Virginians had almost exterminated the Creek and Cherokee tribes, whose attacks had been the most severe. Nor were the Indian attacks easily co-ordinated with the strategy of the British commander. A consequence of adopting this forlorn expedient, however, was to diminish yet further the hope of a massive loyalist rising. For Americans complained of the unnatural ferocity of a king who exposed his countrymen to the wildness of the savage and the unfeeling thoroughness of the German mercenaries (who, as usual, made up a large part of British armies). All the same, at the end of 1776 Washington was in sore difficulty. Howe appeared to have done enough to cause the enemy to disintegrate. Loyalists in New York and Long Island pressed forward to make submissions. Once congress had left Philadelphia for Baltimore pro-British tendencies showed themselves so strongly in the former city that Washington had to remind them of their revolutionary zeal with three regiments of the colonial army. The militia began to melt quietly away.

[1] Guy Carleton (1724–1808), served in army in America, 1758–62; governor of Quebec, 1775–7; commander-in-chief in America, 1782–3; created Baron Dorchester, 1786; in Canada as governor, 1786–91 and 1793–6; advised Grenville in making of new constitution for Canada, 1791.

Washington arrested this decline with an action small militarily but great in psychological effect. On 26 December 1776, when the professional army opposed to him considered action out of the question, he made a surprise attack across the Delaware at Trenton, where three battalions of Hessians held the post with the assistance of British light horse. Their commander was killed and 918 Hessians surrendered. At this American hopes rose mercurially and Washington's numbers ceased to shrink. In Howe's headquarters and in London it was realized that the American cause would not now collapse on its own. Sixteen more ships of the line were put into commission to meet the American privateers fitting out in French and Spanish ports. For France and Spain were increasing their aid to the revolution.[1] It was essential to win the war in America quickly before this aid became open intervention by England's European rivals.

Howe demanded 20,000 more men for 1777. He received only 2,500, and despaired of a decisive campaign. Sandwich refused to send Admiral Howe more ships in view of the European danger. The financial situation at home was bad. Lord North lamented the increase in debt; his land tax was up to the wartime level of 4s. He thought Hessians too dear in the market. Unfortunately, also, the king had to confess to parliament in 1777 that he was £600,000 in debt on the civil list. Parliament settled his debts and increased the civil list to £900,000 a year; but North knew that his position had been built up on his reputation as the economical minister. Already over-anxious rats began, too quickly, to get over the ship's sides. Sir Fletcher Norton, with all the prestige of his position as Speaker of the house of commons, went over to the opposition. He told the king, in an official speech presenting the year's accounts for 1777, that revenue had been given 'great beyond example; great beyond your Majesty's highest expense', and went on to preach better management. North, his cabinet colleagues began to think, was a liability if he could not even steer their business through the commons quietly.

It was a matter of great urgency, therefore, in view both of the world situation and of home politics, to end the war in 1777. Germain, prompted by General Burgoyne, completed a master plan which by the early summer of 1777 was in operation. The design was to end American resistance by splitting New Eng-

[1] In December 1776 Franklin was in Paris negotiating for French intervention.

land apart from the rest of the colonies with a movement from the interior. This could be done by bringing forces down from Canada, from the St. Lawrence through the Hudson gap. At the same time a movement northwards from Howe's camp at New York would link up with this thrust. The whole New England area would be sliced away from the south. Accordingly Burgoyne in June was with his army of about 7,200 men, plus artillery, in camp on Lake Champlain; by the end of July he had taken Ticonderoga (between the Adirondacks and Vermont) and was preparing to come down the Hudson to a point of junction for the British armies at Albany.

General Howe was, of course, informed of the strategy and his part in it. The defect he saw in the plan was that, on his information, there could be no hope of Burgoyne reaching Albany before September at the earliest. If he sat waiting six months while the northern expedition got under way, the tonic effect upon Americans of seeing Washington take the initiative might lose him the Atlantic seaboard. In the early months of 1777 reinforcements reached Washington and permitted him to overrun New Jersey. Cornwallis,[1] under Howe, thought it dangerous to be spread out in isolated posts and gradually withdrew his forces until they were cramped but collected at Amboy, near Sandy Hook. Howe once again failed to draw Washington into an action. He decided therefore to shake American confidence (and fill in the months of waiting) by an attack on Philadelphia. This was authorized by Germain. Howe left New York by sea in July, having had news that Burgoyne was arrived confidently at Ticonderoga. It was a fatal move.

Howe had a very bad passage along the coast. He did not arrive at Chesapeake Bay until 25 August. He proceeded to defeat Washington, whom he had drawn into battle at last, at Brandywine, and to take Philadelphia. This was a barren success. For he acknowledged that he could not return to the Hudson area to help Burgoyne. The latter had reached Saratoga and

---

[1] Charles Cornwallis, first Marquis and second Earl Cornwallis (1738–1805), had seen service under Granby in Germany 1758–9; sent with reinforcements to America 1776; second in command to Clinton 1778; directed operations in the south; capitulated at Yorktown 1781; from 1786, as governor-general in India, he opened a new era of reformed administration there; master-general of the ordnance 1795–1801; viceroy and commander-in-chief in Ireland where he put down the rebellion and helped effect the Union; resigned with Pitt in protest against the failure to grant catholic emancipation; died on returning to restore peace in India.

camped. He was short of food. A party sent to capture colonial supplies at Bennington was totally destroyed. St. Leger, who was advancing down the Mohawk valley, to bring a third army to the intended junction at Albany, was checked at Fort Stanwix.[1] Burgoyne had to decide whether to retreat to Ticonderoga or to press on to Albany. He had received no messages at all from Howe. Both courses were hazardous. He felt obliged to adhere to the plan sanctioned at home. He went on. Clinton, left in New York with weak forces, could not force his way far or quickly up the Hudson. So, by October 1777, Burgoyne was hemmed in at Saratoga and on the 17th surrendered his whole army to the American force under General Gates.

The Saratoga surrender changed the whole character of the war. For everyone had been waiting to hear the result of Burgoyne's decisive blow. On the news of its failure, Lord Rockingham wrote, 'My heart is at ease.' The opposition confidently prepared in 1778 to launch an attack against the purpose and planning of the war. But this idea was out of date, for in 1778 there was a new war. The French had also been waiting on events. With the certainty now of a long and grievous struggle for England, the French came out openly on the American side. In March they signed a treaty of friendship with the Americans. This was inevitably followed by war between Great Britain and France with her ally Spain. Thus Chatham's predictions came true. France had fired with American guns and the fight that had ended in 1763 had now to be taken up again. A wave of patriotism produced men and money from places like Manchester, Liverpool, and even from London.

While the feelings of the country became, if anything, more anti-American, Lord North, Germain, and the majority of the cabinet reacted more realistically. They were advised at the end of 1777 that it was impossible to crush America without 80,000 more men. Before the French declaration they had already decided upon a new course in America. This was to use troops only to keep footholds on the American coast and to revert to the idea of a naval war. The advent of France into hostilities confirmed them in this intention. As the defeat of France had to be the major objective, the less effort diverted to America the better. Even now the cabinet lacked co-ordination. A decision to make a great naval effort had been taken without counting

[1] Later called Fort Schuyler.

the ships. Sandwich could not get authority for rapid ship-building until March. Sir Henry Clinton, the new commander-in-chief in America, was instructed in March to try to bring Washington to a decisive action. If that failed he should be content to harry American ports and destroy American shipping. He should also launch an attack, in co-operation with the navy, on the French West Indian island of St. Lucia. This meant that he had to evacuate Philadelphia. If need be he was also to quit New York, then Rhode Island, and divide his 14,000 troops between the West Indies and Halifax, Nova Scotia. At the very time that these drastic orders were being given, fresh peace commissioners were being sent to treat with congress. These plenipotentiaries, Lord Carlisle, Johnstone, and Eden, were not told of the changes imminent in military action in America.

Lord North felt as vividly as anyone how inadequate he was as a war-minister: he begged to be allowed to resign. The king, seeing no other man who could hold together a cabinet to prosecute the war, answered his lamentations with appeals to his loyalty and courage. It was difficult, certainly, to find a possible successor within the cabinet, while a look at the opposition showed nothing but feuds. The Rockingham group had reached the conclusion that they must abandon their old recipe for American ills, the principle of the declaratory act. They now argued that the only safe solution was the most thorough one. They advocated the prompt acknowledgement of American independence. They thus hoped to win Americans away from the French cause. To this neither Chatham nor Shelburne could agree. Both protested passionately against the total abandonment of the empire that Chatham had won. On 7 April 1778 Chatham made his famous last speech in the Lords, in the midst of which he collapsed, to die a month later. But that valedictory speech was not in the main an attack upon coercion of the Americans. It was a fierce protest against the motion of Rockingham's friend, the duke of Richmond, to recognize the United States as a new country. Chatham was for conciliation and not capitulation.

The offer which the peace commissioners made to America was that England would recognize congress, she would give up the claim to tax the colonies, and she would allow civil officers to be elected; consideration would be given to the possibility of seating American representatives at Westminster.[1] In return they demanded that the British parliament should regulate trade, that loyalists should be restored to their property, that all military commands should be in the king's name and subject to his authority, and that all debts due to Englishmen should be honoured. These terms did not tempt the Americans. Their spirits were rising: for they saw Clinton evacuate Philadelphia and take, as instructed, a negative course in military operations. English eyes were not, for the moment, fixed upon the movement of men and ships but upon the reception given to the peace commissioners; upon that depended the last hope of patching up differences with the colonies in face of a hostile world. They were coldly received. By October 1778 it was clear that talks could achieve nothing at all. The disgruntled commissioners recommended Clinton not to fight any longer as against subjects whose loyalty the king might hope to regain, but to campaign ruthlessly, bitterly, as against a foreign and malignant foe. This advice the British commander ignored as it conflicted with orders from home. Some of his allies did not need it. In this year Butler, a loyalist leader, and the Indian tribes utterly destroyed Wyoming on the Susquehana river: Americans soon, with equal savagery, plundered and decimated the country of the Indian 'five nations'.

The French fleet under D'Estaing arrived off the American coast and Lord Howe, lacking the promised reinforcement of Byron's[2] ships (whose sailing had been delayed), had to restrict his activities. Indeed it argued incompetence on the French side that the British were not overwhelmed on Rhode Island. As it was, the St. Lucia expedition was delayed until late in the year. When it did sail it took St. Lucia, St. Pierre, and Miquelon, but the French captured Dominica.

The same slackening of effort that had been a feature of 1778 was evident in 1779. English ministers were plunged into ever deeper difficulties at home. Spain, on entering the war, laid

---

[1] The idea of answering the cry of 'No Taxation without Representation' by giving America representation at Westminster had been championed by Francis Mesenes, attorney-general of Quebec: Adam Smith gave it his support. It was impracticable because a member of parliament living three months' distance from his supporters and in a strange atmosphere very speedily would lose their confidence and his own strength.

[2] John Byron the circumnavigator (see above, p. 17 and n.) was at this time in command of the West Indies Fleet.

siege to Gibraltar. Invasion of England herself was threatened.
The navy was particularly strained. It had to keep ships con-
tinuously at sea if it was to supply America across the ocean,
fight the French in the West Indies, supply Gibraltar, guard the
channel, and endeavour to keep the French fleet bottled up.
And at this critical juncture Admiral Keppel's court martial
marked the climax of political squabbling in the higher ranks
of the navy itself. Keppel had charge of the home fleet and, in
the intervals of quarrelling with Sandwich at the admiralty, was
a formidable admiral against the French and conducted the
blockade of Brest. He had had under him, in an indecisive battle
off Ushant in July 1778, another capable and skilful officer, Sir
Hugh Palliser. The recriminations between the two admirals
reflected their political views. Palliser was court-martialed for
insubordination but acquitted: Keppel was court-martialed for
failing in his duty and acquitted. The whigs hailed the news
that the charges against Keppel had been dismissed as 'malicious and ill-founded' as a blow to the ministry.

On his return home, Lord Howe had advised that it was impossible to hold America. The Bedfordites Gower and Weymouth
resigned from the ministry, arguing that it was North who made
victory impossible. Suffolk died. It was not easy to fill the vacant
places, particularly as North confessed his agreement with the
views of his retiring colleagues. Many other worries (about
Ireland,[1] for instance) distracted the cabinet. Therefore little
initiative could be expected in America. Indeed, England was
losing heart rather than losing battles, and her lack of determination was to be the chief factor in the final stages of the
American war.

George III showed himself more of a bulldog than most of
his people. He argued to North in June 1779 that peace was of
course desirable. He agreed that the war was not profitable;
indeed, in the terms of a 'tradesman behind his counter', it
rarely was. But he denied that the question of peace with
America, on which Sir William Meredith was bringing forward
an opposition motion, was just a question of money. 'Whether
the laying a tax was deserving all the evils that have arisen from
it, I should suppose no man could allege that without being
more fit for Bedlam than a seat in the Senate, but step by step
the demands of America have risen—independence is their

[1] Considered below, pp. 221 f.

object'—and he argued that if they were to get their independence, then the West Indies would follow them, tied as they were to the American market. After the West Indies would come Ireland. And the final result would be the ruin of Great Britain economically. Therefore nothing could be worse than to give in. He begged his ministers to fight the good fight, without lingering glances to the past, in the knowledge that it was a fight for survival.[1]

In America Clinton and Cornwallis must have been encouraged by reports of American disputes to think that in time they might still win. Prices, owing to the over-issue of paper money, had risen fantastically in America: examples are to be found of things costing 150 times their pre-war cost. The colonial army was complaining to congress that in these conditions it could neither feed nor clothe itself properly. By 1781 this discontent did, in fact, produce a mutiny. In 1779 Clinton continued the new policy of sporadic expeditions and attacks along the American coast. He chose to make his main sallies in the south. Success in them led the home government to agree that he should make the southern states the centre for British activity, establishing his power there with the assistance of the local loyalists whose military effort had increased in importance. Accordingly a small raiding force under Campbell[2] and Hyde Parker[3] took Savannah at the turn of the year, and by the end of January the whole of Georgia had come under British control. In these circumstances, the evacuation of Rhode Island, so long held and to so little purpose, could be represented to be a strategical redeployment and not a retreat before the French.

This southern campaign prospered in 1780. The proximity of British forces had roused the loyalists of the Carolina frontiers. Though they were defeated, Clinton was encouraged to move troops from New York for the attack upon Charleston. In the game of hide and seek which British and French forces played round the Caribbean and up the American coast, the British for the moment had the advantage. D'Estang had returned

[1] *Correspondence of King George III*, ed. J. Fortescue, iv. 350 f.

[2] Sir Archibald Campbell (1739–91) had been a prisoner of war in 1775, but released and promoted brigadier-general 1776; governor of Jamaica 1785.

[3] Sir Hyde Parker (1739–1807) was later to be commander-in-chief at Jamaica and later still the commander at Copenhagen (1801) to whose signals Nelson turned a blind eye.

home and Guichen was outmanœuvred by Rodney,[1] the new British commander in West Indian waters. The American general Lincoln at Charleston was therefore caught without hope of relief. In May he surrendered with 5,611 soldiers and 1,000 seamen. On the face of it, this was not a bad revenge for Saratoga. But of course such a defeat had neither the psychological nor the strategic importance of Burgoyne's débâcle. The capture of Charleston was followed by a further victory (won by Colonel Tarleton[2] of Cornwallis's force) at Waxhaws on the North Carolina border. By June the British had left no enemy in armed resistance in the whole of South Carolina. These successes had their expected effects upon the loyalists of the neighbouring colony. The North Carolina loyalists rose, but as usual they failed to co-ordinate plans with the British. So their defeat preceded Cornwallis's advance, a repetition of the story of South Carolina. However, Cornwallis came up to attack Gates, who had 6,000 men for the defence of North Carolina, and found him at Camden. An attack at dawn on 15 August 1780 put the militiamen in Gates's army to flight. The steadfast remainder, some 2,000 men, were killed or taken prisoner. Though raids farther north were unsuccessful, the record of southern successes was impressive.

It was as well Lord North had some consolation. For the situation in Europe had deteriorated still further. The northern powers had formed a league of armed neutrality to resist the British search of vessels on the high seas for contraband. It was with heavy hearts that ministers made all the usual local bargains and arrangements to maintain their friends in the general election of this year. No one, except the king, seemed any longer to have any hope of eventual success in America. Yet it may be asked whether the facts imposed such gloom. In Europe, it is true, the fight went on in a spasmodic and inefficient way against augmenting foes. In India, too, Hastings needed all his genius to bring British power through unshattered. But in

[1] George Rodney, first Baron Rodney (1719–92), the most enterprising of the admirals of the time; returned to service 1778 after three years spent evading his creditors by residence in Paris; defeated Spanish fleet 1780 and posted to the West Indian station; resigned command to Hood 1781; rejoined Hood 1782 and defeated the French off Dominica; rewarded with peerage and the thanks of parliament.

[2] Sir Banastre Tarleton (1754–1833), accompanied Cornwallis to America; author of *History of the Campaigns of 1780 and 1781*; M.P. Liverpool 1790–1806 and 1807–12.

America substantial victories had been won and the number of loyalists fighting for the king was showing an increase. Intercepted letters, in addition, revealed that relations between the French and the Americans were bad. These intercepts even suggested that the French were no more happy about the cost of the war than the English were: that they would have to give up if they could not quickly gain some material acquisition to set against their expenditure, while the search for such a trophy would finally embroil them with Washington.[1]

Yet depression persisted, and it had real causes. None of the successes were easy to turn into conquests. Clinton himself had returned from Charleston to New York from which base he sent men raiding up-river. He seemed not to have made up his mind whether he was to organize local raids or whether he was to conquer all the south. The effect of this was seen in 1781 when Cornwallis, though defeating Greene at the battle of Guildford Court House, had no reserves and no contact with Clinton. Lacking supplies, with Gates raising the country against him, he had to retire exhausted instead of forcing on success. The loss of prisoners meant less to Americans than to the professional British armies. And above all these military considerations was the political one, that every Englishman knew that victory left unsolved the problem of how to govern estranged and remote colonists, even if their armies laid down their arms. The public at home and generals in the field felt that they were fighting for an end which could not be visualized, for war aims which had melted away once the struggle had ceased to be police action and become war. There was an unreality therefore in military operations and success in them was only a mirage.

By 1781 Benedict Arnold[2] had deserted the Americans and become a British commander. Arnold was used by Clinton to enlarge the scope of the southern campaign, now incomparably the most important part of his strategy, with an invasion of Virginia. It can be argued that this ambitious plan was a mistake and that it would have been better to consolidate a hold on a few bases such as Charleston. Arnold with 1,700 men, however, swarmed up the rivers spreading ravage and terror,

---

[1] I am indebted to Dr. K. H. Ellis's work on the secret office in the post office for knowledge of these intercepts.

[2] See above, p. 203.

for he fought not according to the rules of professional captains but with the ferocity of a man who must win or end in death and execration. The Virginian invasion caused Washington to detach a force under La Fayette (a French volunteer with the American forces) to hold Arnold. The French tried in vain to send further help by sea. Clinton sent 2,000 more troops to extend the British hold on the James river. Cornwallis meanwhile had drawn back to Wilmington in North Carolina; American authority seeped back to cover the Carolinas as his tired but successful troops withdrew. Cornwallis, prudently, felt the dangers of the many separate enterprises which meant that isolated bodies of British troops were contending amid a sea of irregular American guerrilla fighters. He therefore marched to Virginia to effect a junction with Arnold's forces. This he did and the combined forces were strong enough to compel La Fayette to avoid them though never strong enough to end American resistance in Virginia.

Disaster now, in the late summer and autumn of 1781, came quickly to the British. Cornwallis decided to establish a Virginian base in which his army could restore its energies and which would serve for future operations. He chose a spot between the rivers York and James, a point on the peninsula near the mouth of the Chesapeake called Yorktown. Here he made a station for his 7,000 picked men; he intended it to serve the same sort of purpose as New York did farther north. But Washington decided to meet his enemies while they were stationary and separate. He made a feint attack on New York, then marched down by Trenton, Philadelphia, Baltimore, and Annapolis to hem Cornwallis in. Sir Samuel Hood[1] arrived in late August with 14 British sail of the line at Sandy Hook and added these to the 5 sail of the line and the 50-gun ship which Admiral Graves had under his command.[2] But by 28 August the French admiral de Grasse was at the Chesapeake with the stronger force of 24 sail of the line. After an indecisive engagement on 5 September yet further reinforcements reached de Grasse from the fleet at Rhode Island: the British fleet sailed back to New York.

---

[1] Sir Samuel Hood, first Viscount Hood (1724–1816), entered navy 1741; commander on North American station 1767–70; under Rodney at victory of Dominica in 1782; member of parliament 1784; commander in the Mediterranean 1793; occupied Toulon and captured Corsica, but recalled 1794.

[2] Rodney was for the time being unwell and at home preparing to defend his conduct in the West Indies in angry debate in the house of commons.

From New York Clinton strove to get 7,000 men away by sea to the aid of Cornwallis. The latter now lay at Yorktown looking out to sea at the French fleet. Inland two armies ringed him round, 8,000 French troops and 5,000 Americans. Cornwallis's men put up a stout resistance until 19 October 1781: then the entire camp surrendered. On 24 October the British fleet arrived with Clinton's reinforcements. Seeing that it was too late it sailed sadly back without any encounter with the triumphant French.

A second British army had thus been lost in America. Yet the total of men surrendered was not unmatched by losses of the Americans. The most worrying feature of Cornwallis's calamity, the loss of sea control, was remediable. In February next (1782) Rodney brought 12 more sail of the line to unite with Hood in the West Indies. With a combined fleet of 36 sail of the line he began searching for the French and for the Spanish fleets. At 7 o'clock on the morning of 12 April Rodney and Hood forced de Grasse with 34 sail of the line into a decisive action. The French flagship, the 112-gun *Ville de Paris*, after suffering horrible carnage in a most determined fight, at length surrendered. In the action and its aftermath, the French lost some 9 major ships. This, the battle of 'The Saints', ended the French naval threat to the West Indies and won back control of the Atlantic for England. For the rest of the war the most the French fleet attempted in this theatre was surprise attack upon convoys. Meanwhile on land the British held on to New York and to Charleston. At the very time of Cornwallis's surrender Arnold, lately returned from the south, had been raiding successfully into Connecticut. The opposed forces on the mainland watched one another in 1782 inactive and equal. The true significance of Cornwallis's surrender was not to be seen by an eye exclusively naval or military. Its effect was to be observed in the house of commons where Sir James Lowther's motion for a declaration that no more force should be used in America was defeated by only 220 to 178 votes. The revival of the opposition to North was, of course, not only fed by American reverses: but Yorktown was at least final proof that a speedy victory was impossible. In February of 1782 193 members of the house of commons voted for a speedy surrender: North's majority had shrunk to 1. His twelve years of continuous power were over. Politics under the impulse of the American war had taken new directions: a new conservatism in feeling faced a revived radicalism. By the time peace with the United States was reached on 30 November 1782 fresh issues were actively disturbing the English political world. These issues make necessary closer examination of the years from 1778.

IX

THE FALL OF NORTH AND THE RISE OF REFORM MOVEMENTS, 1778–82

LORD NORTH had been secure in power up to 1774 because he aimed at being comprehensive in the personnel of his ministry and economical in its policy. He created an atmosphere in which back-bench members lost their suspicion of 'the hand of power' and inclined to support the court more consistently than usual: disgust at the antics of Wilkes and at the factious quarrels of the opposition pushed them further in this direction. Patriotism, on the outbreak of war with America, could only reinforce this movement of opinion. Young men like William Hickey and Lord George Gordon[1] who drank success to America and confusion to North were, not unnaturally, considered by most of their seniors to be little better than traitors. Leading politicians, whose only hope of power rested upon British defeat, fell into the same category. Only Chatham, secure in his record of achievement, could assault his own country's government in time of war without forfeiting respect.

The popularity of North's government melted away as news of misfortune came across the Atlantic. He was himself aware of the contradictions in his position. He was lauded at once as the leader of a government which was going to teach the rebels a lesson and as an exponent of Walpolism—the art of saving money by leaving sleeping dogs in peace. This was a contradiction inherent in the minds of ordinary Englishmen. North lived uneasily after 1774 on the horns of a dilemma: either the new loans raised for the war would be substantial, in which case there would eventually be an outcry against the heavier taxes required to service them, or costs would be ruthlessly kept down, with the result that the conduct of the war would arouse the anger of those who expected total victory. In fact it was his fate to suffer both attacks: there were contradictions in his black days as there had been in the sunny ones. North, after Saratoga,

[1] Hickey, *Memoirs*, ed. A Spencer, ii. 72. For Lord George Gordon see below, p. 235.

was being criticized for lacking vigour and also for increasing the debt.

Not only America harassed North after 1774. The Regulating Act for India never worked smoothly; two sections in the Bengal Council intrigued for his support, while wars with Indian states forced ministers to consider what the future of English power in the subcontinent should be.[1] The opposition in parliament badgered North about the case of Pigot,[2] governor of Madras, who was imprisoned by his own council. Irish problems were even more insistent. Full consideration of them must be postponed until later.[3]—Lord North himself would always have preferred postponement of the Irish problem!—but some account of the Irish question is vital to an understanding of North's position and his gloom.

Ireland bade fair to become a second America. The Irish parliament was subordinate to the legislature at Westminster. The Irish executive was appointed by George III on the advice of English ministers. Irish commerce was corseted in English commercial regulations. Unlike America Ireland was close at hand and controlled by great landlords, many of them resident in England. Patronage, moreover, was a very considerable force by which to hold a pro-English interest together. The Irish parliament had long been managed by 'undertakers' whose means were corrupt and whose aims were to earn favours from English viceroys. Since 1760, however, the undertakers had been unruly. When they chose to raise their demands they were in a powerful position, so long as they maintained a united front. They could not only block business in the Dublin parliament. Behind the parliament were all the discontents of a poor and alien population which an unscrupulous politician could soon rouse to riot. The question of a tax on absentee English landlords, for instance, would always bring out the distressed on the streets. An attack on bishops would excite the presbyterians up in Ulster. Commercial restrictions were the *bête noire* of every trader who found it difficult to pay his bills. The Roman

---

[1] For India from 1773 to 1793 see below, pp. 305 f.

[2] Sir George Pigot, first (Irish) baron. Pigot (1719–77), as governor of Madras, conducted a skilful defence against the French 1758–9; in his second term of office, 1775–7, his efforts to restore the ruler of Tanjore (on orders from home) aroused the anger of his own council, who put him in prison, where he died. Opinion on the merits of the case was divided in the directorate of the East India Company. In parliament the opposition espoused Pigot's cause against the ministry.

[3] See below, pp. 387 f.

Catholic peasantry were quiescent but certainly no friends to the powers of London.

The American war had produced economic depression in Ireland. The normal peacetime export of woollens and provisions from Ireland to America or to France became illegal. None the less the landed Protestants, who dominated Ireland, wished to assist England in her hour of need. So there began a movement to provide England with troops from the Irish military establishment and to replace them for home defence by volunteers. The need of a home guard seemed evident enough when the American privateer captain Paul Jones[1] was cruising off Carrickfergus Bay. By May 1779 there were some 8,000 men in the volunteer movement. Despite its original intentions it was clear that this force might well endeavour to replace authority from England. It was almost from the start used as a powerful threat to support those Irish politicians who quarrelled with the lord lieutenant.

Ever since 1776 North's lord lieutenant for Ireland, Lord Buckinghamshire, had been anxious to put Irish affairs on a more stable footing. He had tried to form an administration which should have broad support from men of property in Ireland and which should depend less upon corruption. To do this he had to go outside and beyond the 'undertakers' in parliament. Yet this naturally set the undertakers against him; they showed a disposition to ally with the merchants and with the volunteers in a joint attack on the lord lieutenant. The best way he could prevent such an extraordinary alliance was to show himself liberal to Irish opinion and prevent the political jobbers from masquerading as reformers. In 1778 Lord North, under Buckinghamshire's pressure, moved five resolutions dealing with Irish commerce. They aimed at lifting the restrictions which kept Irish enterprise—already sufficiently impeded by the poverty of the country's resources—shackled. Lord North had to meet opposition from England. Traders in England protested against freeing their competitors; solid squires sympathized with their protests because they did not approve of knuckling under to disloyal Irishmen; some of the greatest political lords of the day feared that the next step would be a tax on their Irish rents sent to England.

[1] John Paul Jones (1747–92), slave-trader, smuggler, and, latterly, commander in the American navy, made prizes off Carrickfergus in 1778.

Lord North foresaw trouble in the end if something was not done for Ireland, but he saw trouble at once if anything was done. He did not push his resolutions, and the lord-lieutenant's letters received no attention. In 1779, in consequence, the Irish formed non-importation agreements to punish England as the Americans had done. When Gower promised to collect more information on Ireland and do something for her, his pledge was repudiated by Lord North. The opposition were delighted to have North in a cleft stick. By their speeches they encouraged the Irish to believe that they would be supported by Rockingham even in courses the most desperate. And once a rousing campaign against the government was begun, Irish politicians were driven to extreme courses if they would continue to control the excitement. C. J. Fox at this time talked of the natural rights of man which no statute, not even Poyning's law, could take away. This was an invitation to Ireland to proclaim revolutionary independence in the name of John Locke. Yet Fox's friends with Irish property were opposed to the suggestion, made by the lord lieutenant at this point, that absentee landlords should be taxed.[1]

Through 1779, distracted with the nightmare of a French invasion and with news from America, North let Ireland drift without leadership. The volunteers filled this vacuum. They were capable of doing so. For they were drawn from well-to-do and protestant circles. The cost of their uniform alone was sufficient to exclude the needy. In the Irish parliament two great orators from among the old governing class, Flood and Grattan,[2] gave the movement something at which to aim. They declared for freedom of Irish trade. At a rally of volunteers, when a French invasion still threatened, the domestic aims of the movement were plainly declared. In military formation

---

[1] He also proposed the establishment of a national bank for Ireland.

[2] Henry Flood (1732–91), the illegitimate son of a chief justice, educated at Trinity College, Dublin and Christ Church, Oxford. Irish M.P. 1759; in opposition until appointment as vice-treasurer of Ireland, 1775; a leader of the volunteer movement but retained office; co-operated with Gratton in movement for the independence of the Irish parliament but quarrelled with him; a member of the English house of commons, 1783.

Henry Grattan (1746–1820), a graduate of Trinity College, Dublin; barrister; won, by the brilliance of his oratory, the leadership in the campaign for the independence of the Irish parliament in which he sat from 1775; after the attainment of independence refused office, 1783; supported parliamentary reform and catholic emancipation; ally of Fox against Pitt; opposed the union; M.P. for Dublin, 1806–20.

they assembled to the cry of 'Free Trade or Else——' and the Irish house of commons voted thanks to them. Landowners like Charlemont[1] called their tenants up pretty smartly to protest-meetings against the English government's restrictions.

In London only Robinson and Jenkinson showed much activity, reading all the papers in their offices and pulling all the strings outside them.[2] But paper-and-string expedients would not satisfy the Irish. It seemed to Irish leaders that England was stiff with her loyal Irish while she made concessions to rebel Americans. The moral was clear. The Irish parliament (its members being intimidated by the mob and the attorney-general having gone into hiding) refused to underwrite government loans and threatened to pass only a six months' money bill instead of the normal one for two years. In Westminster C. J. Fox said, 'he approved of that manly determination which, in the *dernier ressort*, flies to arms in order to obtain deliverance—they will recur to first principles, to the spirit as well as the letter of the constitution'. He was speaking of English as well as Irish discontent, but for the moment Irish problems forced their way to the front in Lord North's mind.

North now (1780) granted to Ireland the right to trade freely with the colonies, freedom of wool and glass exports, participation in the trade with the Levant, and the restoration of the bounty on her coarse linen sent into England. Grattan and Flood were still discontented, arguing that economic concessions could be withdrawn as easily as England had made them. They called for legislative security, for constitutional changes to cement their gains. But the majority of the Irish parliament accepted North's plan. They passed a mutiny bill which was to be perpetual. In England the opposition were angry at the ease with which Irish agitation had, apparently, been bought off. Burke, who approved the economic concessions, found himself cast off by his Bristol constituents who did not; at the same time he disagreed with those Irishmen who thought that no more concessions were needed. The most North can be said to

---

[1] James Caulfeild, fourth Viscount Charlemont (1728–99), created earl of Charlemont, 1763; a liberal-minded man of literary tastes who was well known in London society. He followed the political line of Gratton and Flood.

[2] These two men of business despaired of North's inactivity and would have liked the king to spur him on. They pressed the viceroy's letters upon North's attention. Jenkinson himself was given an Irish reward in 1779—the clerkship of the Pells at emoluments increased from £2,800 to £3,500.

have done, however, was to baffle and enrage his English enemies. His supporters were not encouraged nor was the Irish issue settled.

Difficulties within the government were growing. North was well aware that the old Bedford group had no confidence in him. This seemed to increase his irresolution. He worried as much as Newcastle had ever done about trifles of cabinet management. He alternatively boasted that he never interfered with the work of his colleagues and complained that he was not allowed to be the grand co-ordinator of effort. Thurlow said 'nothing can goad him forward, he is the very clog that loads everything'. On Suffolk's death he could not make up his mind who should succeed to the vacant secretaryship. It took Lord North from March to November of 1779 to decide that Lord Stormont[1] should have the office. In November also he had to replace Weymouth (with Hillsborough) and Gower (with Bathurst) for these two Bedfordites left the distressed ship.

All this time Robinson and Jenkinson tried to patch North up. They warned him of Wedderburn's disloyalty and Eden's rancour. They acted like able private secretaries to a weak minister, trying to infuse energy into him and intriguing, behind his back but in his interest, with all those who might help his tottering steps forward.[2] The greatest push of this sort was given by the king. Declaring that 'if others will not be active I must drive', he himself presided at the cabinet on 20 June 1779 and begged ministers to fight together for their own futures and that of the country. Yet at this time Thurlow was proposing not to fight but to buy off opposition: he wanted coalition with their critics.

The only sure way out of North's troubles was victory. Alas, the European war went worse than the American. In the summer of 1779 the combined fleets of France and Spain, some 60 or 70 ships of the battle line, lay off Plymouth. It is difficult to understand why they were content to cruise from the beginning of June until the end of August when, at last, owing to illness

[1] David Murray, Viscount Stormont, second earl of Mansfield (1727–96), the nephew of the great chief justice, the first earl; after a diplomatic career he now entered the cabinet; lord president of the council 1783 and 1794–6.

[2] This seems to me the obvious interpretation of their actions and I think Professor Butterfield, *George III, Lord North, and the People*, pp. 119, 149, 150, has put the wrong emphasis on them.

among their crews, they returned home. Certainly the garrison of Plymouth, with ammunition that did not fit their guns, was not likely to offer much resistance, while Hardy's[1] home fleet (about 38 sail) could only watch from a discreet distance. Gibraltar, too, though its defence was splendid, had to endure three years of siege with only an annual convoy of supplies flitting through to it. Even as late as 1781 the superiority of the French and Spanish fleets was such that, after landing a force to take Minorca, they could sail north to form a line barring entrance to the Channel from Ushant to the Scilly Isles. Once again sickness, aided this time by the faintheartedness of Don Luis de Cordova, the Spanish admiral, saved the English coast and the inferior English naval forces from attack.

Victory was thus far from Lord North's grasp. Nor did he subordinate all else to its pursuit. Throughout the war attacks were made upon the expenditure of the ministry. North, in view of his past triumphs, was peculiarly sensitive to accusations of waste and squandering. In 1776 he had formally declared himself pledged to making the machinery of administration give better value for money. His treasury minute announced that promotion was to be by merit and not by seniority. In 1777 he had announced a plan for consolidating the collection of customs and then of excise and stamps. This would have reduced the expensive administration of the revenue services but, owing to the appropriation system honoured by time,[2] it required negotiation with many interests. It was not until 1781 that North had meetings with public creditors involved: the scheme never came to anything. In 1779, to counter parliamentary attack upon his financial policy, North set up the expert Committee for Examining the Public Accounts whose reports were later to be the basis of Pitt's reforms. But the unfortunate North gained little credit by it. His enemies pointed out that he had set up the expert committee to avoid the demand for a parliamentary inquiry which might have exposed corruption.

North had not the time, in the midst of a disastrous war, to reduce the costs of government by pruning its luxuriance. Therefore he had to raise loans and invent taxes. Taxes were

---

[1] Sir Charles Hardy (1716?–80), a commander most of whose active service had been in the period 1744–60; M.P. Portsmouth, 1774; given command of Channel fleet, 1779.

[2] See above, p. 20.

put on inhabited houses and upon non-profit-earning male servants in 1778. It was the beginning of a fiscal crusade for taxation of business and for charges assessed upon means. However fruitful for the future they were not popular at the time. North, at least, tried to arrange that the burdens should not have to be borne for ever. One-eighth of the whole debt was self-liquidating in 1774 as compared with one-tenth eight years before. But even his floating of loans earned North unpopularity. His loan of 1780–1 was issued, in the ordinary way, to contractors 'on the list' after a meeting at the treasury. But after issue the premium on the omnium (i.e. the loan as a whole including extra annuities given as a *douceur*) was 8½ to 11 per cent. It was widely believed that the profit accruing to the contractors thereby was designed by the government: certainly many treasury clerks were on the list of loan contractors.[1]

In short, from 1778 onwards Lord North was seen to be as incompetent in war as he had been capable as a peace-time politician. As country gentlemen lost their faith in him the hopes of the opposition rose. Their main handicap was that they still seemed unpatriotic. Against this they pleaded that it was true patriotism to attack an unnecessary and unsuccessful war. They declared that things would never have come to this pass if the power of the executive had not grown so strong that criticism had been brushed aside. They talked of corrupt majorities, an excessive influence by the Crown, and in short did their best to revive all that suspicion of government which had of recent years been lulled. The argument of Burke's associates was a simple one—'Why is the Country in its present crisis? Because we are out of power. Why are we out of power? Because too strong an executive has corrupted the self-righting forces in the constitution. Therefore let the legislature reassert itself to put us in power.' This was a line of reasoning made for the consumption of back-bench independents. It was a vaguely reforming argument, but lacked definite shape and body.

In 1779 all this parliamentary rhetoric was given significance by a force which emerged from outside the circles of the politicians. Wilkes's old companion, the upright Glynn, died in 1779. To fill the vacant seat for Middlesex the government favoured Mr. Tufnell who was an opponent of theirs but a reasonable

[1] For this, as for all other fiscal details of this period, see J. E. D. Binney, *British Public Finance and Administration, 1774–92.*

one. The utmost pitch of their hope was to have Middlesex represented by a steady and not a hysterical radical. As Tufnell was already a member of parliament he had to be given the Chiltern Hundreds to enable him to stand for Middlesex. The Wilkesite radicals wanted to put up George Byng, who also had a seat already and therefore asked for the Chiltern Hundreds. North explained that Tufnell's application had been first received and Byng could not be accommodated.[1] Out of this trivial squabble the Wilkesites—though Wilkes was quiet—tried to revive their movement. Dr. Jebb,[2] an academic constitutionalist patronized by Shelburne, addressed a meeting in Middlesex at which he developed their case. The exclusion of Byng by trickery was, he said, a minor instance of power muzzling the voice of the people; it showed that those who had excluded Wilkes and decreed the representation of Middlesex,[3] were still at their old games. He denied that these were isolated instances: the whole system was wrong and to put it right it was not enough to petition parliament. The people needed an organized association which should make the pressure of popular feeling outside parliament a steady instead of a fluctuating force, until finally it was brought properly into the formal machinery of the constitution. In other words Jebb advocated an extension of the popular side of the old constitution, more Westminster and Middlesex seats.

While Wilkesism revived and became more theoretical in the south, an even more important movement began in the north. In Yorkshire at the end of 1779 a county meeting aired the traditional view that the counties—particularly those at a distance from London—were the soundest parts of the constitution. Dr. Jebb urged the freeholders to make their feelings potent by appointing committees to act for them. Under the influence of the Rev. Dr. Christopher Wyvill[4] the men of Yorkshire put their complaints into more definite form. They con-

[1] In the end the radicals put up Thomas Wood who was returned unopposed after Tufnell withdrew in fear of disorder.

[2] John Jebb (1736–86), rector of Ovington (Norfolk); oriental scholar: showed unitarian views in lectures at Cambridge; active in promoting Feathers petition (see above, pp. 155f.); resigned preferments; became physician in London, 1777; canvassed for Fox, 1780.

[3] See above, pp. 136 and f.

[4] Christopher Wyvill (1740–1822), a rector in Essex, 1779; after organizing the Yorkshire movement, published many works advocating toleration and parliamentary reform.

tended that taxes grew ever heavier and yet all Lord North bought with the money he raised was defeat and disorganization. Yorkshire was, on the century-old basis of assessment for the land tax, actually less heavily taxed than the south. So in the course of time Wyvill shifted his emphasis from complaint of high taxes to complaint of excessive executive power. Independent Yorkshiremen, it was contended, would not have bungled affairs as the king's minister had done. But independent Yorkshiremen in the commons were outvoted by mercenary borough representatives. Wyvill's remedy was the obvious one, to increase the relative importance of independent men of standing in the commons against the executive's vote. In this he could count on the support of Sir George Savile as a member of parliament for the county of Yorkshire. Savile's support brought the Yorkshire Association into touch with the Rockingham group to which he belonged. But the squires were chary of becoming tools of any political faction.

Wyvill persuaded Yorkshiremen to put their arguments in a petition to the house of commons. To support the petition (and to make it a driving-force and not a safety-valve) the county set up a committee of action. Other counties joined in with similar committees and petitions. Between the county committees there was correspondence and consultation. Soon there was an informal central committee sitting in London, where it disputed for authority in the movement with a committee which had been set up by the Westminster electors.

What was new and threatening in this movement was that, though in its machinery it resembled the Wilkesite campaign, it had behind it, in contrast to the earlier movement, many men of great respectability and property. It really did seem to do what it claimed to do, to speak for the honoured but hitherto ineffective men of county influence. Such an energizing of squires was made possible only by the almost universal feeling of mingled shame and doubt which the collapse of national prestige had brought about. It follows that their certainty that their healthy influence on affairs was what was needed, was only equalled by their uncertainty about the practical steps that should be taken. They knew taxes were too high, the executive too strong, and members of parliament too venal. But for practical suggestions their indignation movement was dependent upon the organizers and committee men. These organizers, men like Wyvill or Granville Sharp,[1] had to balance theoretical principles against the realities of politics. Early in 1780 the organizers had decided, without consulting the local committees, to have a general assembly to guide the movement, with the prospect of such an assembly becoming something like a rival parliament. It was also decided that this assembly should be free from party connexions and that members of parliament should be excluded from it. In the end members of parliament were admitted and there never were more than twelve counties and four cities represented in it. Their programme was, first, a drive for rigorous economy, second, the addition of 100 more independent county members to parliament and, third, annual parliaments. It was further decided to oppose all candidates at the next election who would not support the programme. Such a national political issue at a general election was a startling innovation: in fact it was not very effective.

This great movement of opinion attracted the opposition politicians whom it ignored. Shelburne's men and Rockingham's pressed forward to use it and if possible to get the leadership of it. Even the restrained Rockingham himself almost quoted Locke in his enthusiasm when he said that parliament would surely not reject their petition, for then it would appear to have broken its trust with the people. The young William Pitt, a disciple of his father and of Shelburne, had himself elected a member of the Kent committee which was under Lord Mahon's[2] influence. In Cambridge the dissenters were very active in the movement, but so was Dr. Watson, the regius professor of divinity. The duke of Manchester, the duke of Rutland, the duke of Richmond, Charles James Fox, and John Wilkes, all pushed themselves forward in the committees. It was, after all, traditional for an opposition to try to rouse forces out of doors to intimidate a minister securely supported within parliament. This time the force out of doors had roused

---

[1] Granville Sharp (1735–1813), grandson of an archbishop of York; civil servant; humanitarian opponent of the slave trade and pamphleteer in defence of the Americans.

[2] Charles Stanhope, Lord Mahon, and later third Earl Stanhope (1753–1816), an eccentric radical peer; known as 'Citizen Stanhope' for his sympathy with the French Revolution; also a man of science writing on canals, musical tones, electricity; invented a microscope lens and a stereotyping process acquired by the Clarendon Press; disinherited all his children.

itself. But the opposition chiefs could at least rush to the front of
it. There was indeed, as ever, discord among the major opponents of North. Fox was very wild in words. It was at this time
that he discovered how well he could sway a popular meeting
and he was a little intoxicated with his own oratorical powers.
But he, and his Rockingham associates, were for moderation.
The mention of sanctions if parliament should ignore the movement was deplored by this group. They wanted the petitioners
to limit themselves to noisy and boisterous backing of Burke's
motions against North. Lord Shelburne was more acrimonius
and more radical. He distrusted the abilities and intentions of
Rockingham's friends. He himself employed Price, Priestley,
and Jebb to sketch a reforming programme for him. He had
schemes for reform of civil service rules and salaries, for debt
payment, and for making peace with America without complete
surrender. His ruthlessness was the greater for his habit of
having few political friends and many skilled advisers. A third
element within the Petitioning movement, that led by Wyvill,
cursed all politicians.[1]

Lord North met the petitions with conciliatory and cautious
phrases. He acknowledged the right of the freeholders to petition about grievances but insisted that the petitions must be
taken not as the voice of the counties, or of England, but of a
few individuals. He uttered some dark warnings about the
danger to property if this excitement out of doors continued.
But with America, Ireland, and his budgets damning him, and
with bad news from India coming in to fill his cup, he was on
the defensive. The Rockinghams moved up to a formal assault
upon his ministry. After Savile had spoken on the Yorkshire
petition in January 1780 Edmund Burke attempted to destroy
the ministry by constructive proposals in February. In his best
vein of eloquence he introduced five bills for the redress of the
grievances complained of. They were bills to abolish sinecure
places, and to refloat the civil list. Their general object he
defined as securing 'the independence of Parliament and the
economic reformation of the civil and other establishments'.
He was followed up by Savile's demand for the publication of
pension lists to reveal government influence. He was rivalled

---

[1] Wyvill, however, was much criticized by Sharp for accepting triennial in
place of annual parliaments in the programme, for this was a compromise with the
politicians.

by the Shelburnite Colonel Barré who successfully called for a commission of accounts. In March Burke's own plan, particularly that part which would abolish the board of trade altogether, took up much of the time of the house, though they had enough left to pass a bill, subsequently rejected by the Lords, to bar government contractors from the house. The government's only sign of life was their resolution giving notice of ending the charter of the East India Company. The initiative had completely left them. In every debate the cry went up against corruption and influence. Forces in the house were excitingly even. On 8 March 1780 the government only outvoted the proposal to abolish the third secretaryship of state by 208 to 201. On 13 March Burke carried his motion to abolish the board of trade by 207 to 199. When he turned from this success to attack the civil list he found himself defeated by 211 to 158. The reason is plain. The squires joined with some gusto in abolishing government departments in the interest of economy and weakening the influence of ministers. But they respected the idea of the balanced and divided constitution. Some of them felt that the civil list could be cut back, but the details of its administration fell outside the legislature's sphere of interest: to interfere at least with the more private parts of it was an insult to the king and a usurpation of power.[1]

It was Dunning,[2] by now the legal star of the whole opposition, who put them back into sympathy with the independents and so regained leadership of discontent. On 6 April he moved his famous resolutions, a rough summary of the case of the opposition and of the petitioners, 'that the influence of the Crown has increased, is increasing, and ought to be diminished'. This was in truth a very dubious proposition. Dunning was of course correct when he said that war, by increasing the number of contracts, by giving more openings for promotion, by requiring more subscriptions to loans, inevitably increased the number of those who could seek favours from the government. He was right also in saying that patronage in India—though not directly in the government's hands—had increased enormously in twenty years. But the conclusions drawn by him, and by

[1] Speaker Norton, though a Rockingham adherent by this time, made this clear. He attacked North and the public uses of the civil list but said that the king should be asked and not ordered to make economies in his household.

[2] John Dunning (1731–83), first Baron Ashburton: solicitor-general, 1768–70; prominent in the discussion of the rights of juries in libel cases; M.P. for Calne.

historians, from this evidence were not valid. It was not true that George III had sustained a government against the real will of the country. Indeed, within the month the true strength of North's position was to be revealed. North had been the favourite of all but malcontent groups, his policies those of the country as well as the king. Now that the policies had resulted in ruin, the country, less loyal and a great deal less plucky than the king, wanted to disown them and blame North. George III had exercised less royal authority in keeping North, up to 1780, than George II in keeping Walpole from 1739–42, when that peace minister fell on evil days of war.[1] But North fostered the idea of the supremacy of royal influence by lamenting all the time that he was forced to stay in office against his will—Walpole at least knew he wanted to be in power.

Dunning's general resolution was carried by 233 to 215. Next the house approved unanimously the principle of investigating the civil list. In the rising excitement the country members, Horace Walpole noted, had changed their minds on this. On 10 April the government meekly accepted a motion to publish accounts of all sums received by members of parliament from the civil list. On the same day, however, Dunning found his majority reduced to two (215–213) when he moved that the subordinate officers of the king's household should be incapable of sitting in parliament. On 13 April Crewe's Bill to disfranchise revenue officers was defeated by 221–195. On 24 April Dunning attempted to bring the house back to his original triumph: he moved that until the balance of the constitution was restored (and the grievances set out in petitions were dealt with) the house should not be dissolved or prorogued. This echo of the seventeenth century alarmed the house. Dunning was defeated by 254 to 203. Lord North once more had the situation under control. In anger Fox threatened to absent himself from debates. He attributed the failure of his side to push home their attacks to the backsliding of independent members. 'The defection which he had alluded to originated chiefly among the county members, many of them of great weight and respect.' Yet it was these very county members whose numbers all the reformers proposed to increase in order to re-balance the constitution.

Fox's explanation was that the wobbling members were base.

[1] See Dr. J. B. Owen, *The Rise of the Pelhams*, chap. i.

They had voted on 6 April for Dunning's resolution only so that they could face the county associations with credit at a general election: on 24 April they were currying favour with the minister and the court. The real explanation would seem to be more interesting and more important. Independent gentlemen agreed with Dunning's general proposition, for it was inconceivable that affairs should be so ruinous unless unfair influence had been used in parliament. They believed that North should go. Yet in the days that followed they had to face the practical problem: if he went who should succeed him? It must be either the Shelburne group, or, more probably, that of Rockingham. Yet both these were factious cliques. The gentlemen of England still hankered after the broad-based, easygoing régime North had once given them. Every step the Rockingham group took to force home their initial victory over the government paradoxically weakened their position, for it alarmed the independents. The climax was the proposal to resolve against the king's right to dissolve or prorogue. For this was revolution. No ordinary squire wanted to exchange the inefficient government by departments under North for a revolutionary régime under Rockingham; the violence of C. J. Fox, while it never affected his personal popularity, was already destroying confidence in his judgement. In May the Westminster subcommittees, where he had support, declared for adult male suffrage, complete separation of the executive and the legislature, and annual elections to parliament by parishes. This was not what most members of parliament, or even most petitioners, were after.

The strength of Lord North, it became clear, lay not only in his hold on the king. It really consisted in the fact that there was no alternative to him acceptable to that great body of gentlemen who wanted quiet unambitious government. It was hoped he might be bullied into being more efficient, that he might increase the number of independent members in parliament. But it was impossible to remove him so long as the other leaders were wild, oppressive, and factious. Once the conservative reaction began in mid-April every effort to whip up excitement out of doors became evidence for caution. Yet if the Rockinghams did not whip up excitement then the petitioners would lose heart or at least lose confidence in the politicians. The whole movement began to subside.

This particular campaign of the opposition was finally ex-

tinguished, strangely enough, by the intervention of the eccentric
Lord George Gordon. For his use of forces out of doors was so
much more striking and more dangerous that it frightened
North's most ardent critics away from further experiment with
them. In 1774 the Quebec Act had, in the interests of justice
and stable Canadian government, granted an official position
to the Roman church there. For long enough the laws against
Roman catholics had been allowed to slumber unused in England. It was desirable, in the search for manpower for the
armies, to remove the prohibitive oaths technically required of
those who served in the king's forces. Sir George Savile and
Rockingham favoured, on general grounds, the relaxing of intolerant laws. So in 1778 a relief act passed easily through both
houses to allow military recruits simply to take an oath of
fidelity to the Crown.[1] When it was proposed to extend this
moderate toleration to Scotland in 1779, however, riotous
presbyterian lowlanders induced ministers to relinquish the
project of relieving the Highlanders. In imitation, though belatedly, of Scotland the extreme protestants in England then
formed an association. Of this movement Lord George Gordon,
the third son of the duke of Gordon, was the leader.

Lord George Gordon was twenty-nine years old. He had left
the navy when he was twenty-one because he refused to wait
for promotion from his rank of lieutenant. At twenty-three he
had come into parliament for a Wiltshire borough controlled
by Fox's witty friend, Selwyn. He had not had great political
success. But he was gay, wild, and dashing, a friend to the
American cause and a believer in the black-heartedness of Lord
North. He had attacked the house of Hanover and even so the
king had received him in audience. His personal ambitions,
which he was incapable of defining or achieving, obviously
became confused in his mind with a religious fervour and with
an obsession against North's 'system'. He had been well received, as a protestant and a Scot, by leaders of the Kirk. The
English opposition leaders clearly held him of little account. In
the spring of 1780, after he had seen the king, he poured out his
complaints to Speaker Norton. The Speaker advised him to tell
his tale to the king and to co-operate with the opposition

---

[1] Papists were then instructed by Bishop Challoner (Roman Catholic bishop in
charge of the London district) that, in gratitude, it was their duty to pray for the
royal family.

leaders. Gordon replied that he did not believe men such as Burke were real reformers or true protestants. Gordon, in the end, copied not the political leaders but the independent petitioners. In the early summer of 1780 petitions against Roman catholic influence—a purely imaginary influence—began to pour into the house every day. Yet few of the opponents of the administration took the movement seriously. Lowther, who had become a violent opponent of North but lacked brains to win the position which his boroughs would seem to have made possible for him, was almost alone in encouraging Gordon. Lord George, however, had none of the inhibitions about the use of pressure felt by Fox, or Pitt, or even Wyvill and Sharp. On 2 June 1780 it was announced that the protestant petition would be presented to the house backed by a procession to impress upon members the force of opinion behind it.

The organization of this movement is still difficult to explore. In the radical ward politics of the city of London any protest meeting was a good excuse to display the traditional anti-executive spirit of the city. The aldermen, risen by ward politics themselves, were chary of annoying even the least intelligent of the tradesmen at a time when many merchants were experiencing the difficulties of war-time dislocation of trade (unlike the capitalists who flourished on war-time loans). Anti-Irish feeling, emotionally though not logically linked with the protestant association, was also strongly aroused by North's trade concessions. A city leader, Alderman Bull, M.P., gave aid to Gordon, seconding his resolutions in the commons. A linen-draper in the Minories, Mr. Jackson, also took an important share as a sort of mob director when the crowds had begun to riot. Determined and earnest chapel-going shopkeepers, who saw in popery the root of every evil, from adultery in high society to the weakness of the British fleet, gave a hard core to the movement: in front of them all strutted Gordon.

On 2 June a decently dressed and sober crowd blocked the entrances to parliament while inside Gordon, Bull, Lowther, and six others moved to take their petition into immediate consideration. Lord George was transported with excitement, addressing the commons one moment, then darting away to harangue the crowds outside, then back to address the commons again. Some ministers were unable to reach the house and others were roughly handled as their coaches tried to penetrate the crowd. For it was impossible to clear away the people. The only guardians of order, the magistrates, were conscious of their lack of means, at this stage, to back orders with force. After dark the crowds grew rougher and were swelled by wilder elements. The Sardinian chapel in Lincoln's Inn Fields was destroyed. The riot began to lose its political if not its protestant purpose. It began to find a centre in London rather than West-minster and in arson rather than shouting. This shift had two consequences. The troops were called out and the actions of the mayor and common council of London became all-important. For a mistaken view of the constitutional law on the subject of riot prevailed even among ministers. This was that the troops could not fire on a mob until the riot act had been read. The riot act would have to be read by the magistrates of the city of London. This gross error in law alone can account for the way in which the riot was allowed to grow bigger over the next few days. Secretary of state Lord Stormont did not issue orders; he only called the attention of the lord mayor, Kennett, to the likelihood of more tumults within his jurisdiction. Charles Jenkinson told Stormont, 'It is the duty of the Troops, My Lord, to act only under authority and by direction of the Civil Magis-trate. For this reason they are under greater restraints than any other of His Majesty's subjects. . . .' He said they should be cautious even in defending themselves.

The city magistrates were nowhere to be found whenever the troops sought their sanction. In part this was because they did not want to rank themselves with those who repressed the ebul-lience of a free-spirited city; in part also it was because they feared reprisals from the mob against their own personal pro-perty. The lord mayor said, 'there are very great people at the bottom of the riot': Kennett was a wily city politician and no hero. He had risen from being a waiter at the notorious King's Arms to owning a tavern, becoming a wine merchant, and so to be a radical alderman and lord mayor. Lord John Cavendish, an opposition Whig, condemned the lord mayor's cowardice in standing by while buildings burned. By 5 June private houses were being looted as well as foreign chapels: Burke's was threatened and Sir George Savile's was attacked. On 6 June a new element of violence was added. After burning the house of Sir John Fielding (the Middlesex magistrate who had attempted to use his powers) the mob exploded the distilleries in Holborn and burst open Newgate prison: those released were choice recruits for the rioters.

At last, however, it began to be realized how serious the breakdown of order had become and at last a proper view of the law of riot was taken. At the privy council, attended by Rockingham as well as ministers, the king and the attorney-general stoutly defended the true legal doctrine. In the words of Markham, the archbishop of York, 'a fatal error had prevailed among the military that they could not in any case act without the orders of a civil magistrate which is the case when a great mob has assembled but has not yet proceeded to acts of violence. But when they have begun to commit felonies any subject, and the military among the rest, is justified in Common Law in using all methods to prevent illegal acts.' The king insisted that there must be a proclamation calling on all to restore public order; the troops should be ordered to suppress the riot whatever city magistrates might do. The magistrates had, in fact, just released some of the rioters previously arrested.

On June 7 common council of the city agreed to petition the house of commons against toleration for Roman catholics. On that day, however, common council received the royal proclamation. Wilkes was rash enough to propose that it be committed for consideration but he found no seconder for such insulting delay. Within an hour he had changed his own tactics and was talking of urgent action to restore order. Wilkes had up to this time been passive in discussion of city policy on the disturbance, claiming that his own ward of Farringdon Without engrossed all his time. But now, after his false move, he realized that opinion among city rulers was prepared to follow the lead of the privy council. Certainly it was no longer an amusing display of London's nuisance value. On this same day, 7 June, more distilleries were sacked: the streets ran spirits (so that the water supply of Lincoln's Inn became alcoholic) and rioters were burned as they lay inebriated in the ruined buildings. The troops began firing that evening. Captain Holroyd (later Lord Sheffield, Gibbon's friend) distinguished himself by his defence of the Bank of England.

In this time of war, however, troops were scarce in London. It was not until the militia came in to relieve the guards of some duties that there was any mobile reserve which could be rushed to danger-points. Other volunteers, the barristers of the Inns of Court, the coalheavers, and Wilkes's old enemies, the Irish chairmen, were organized for defence. Even so on 8 June the governor of the New Gaol in the Borough was compelled to avoid an attack by releasing his prisoners. On 9 June the lord mayor still pleaded with Amherst, in command of the military, to appease the mob by releasing those taken prisoner. But by 9 June the mob was beaten. Lord George Gordon was taken and put in the tower. London was not brought back to normal until 12 June. The number of people killed or wounded was 458, and 59 rioters were sentenced to death though only 21 actually suffered the penalty. Lord George Gordon himself was found not guilty of high treason. When the petition of common council against the papists was presented to the house of commons by Aldermen Bull and Sawbridge on 19 June members were diverted by the spectacle of Wilkes, now firmly on the right horse, opposing it and reproaching his fellow aldermen for being less active than he in fighting for law and order.

The Gordon riots had among their minor effects the transformation of John Wilkes into a respectable subject. They also involved an increase of rates in London parishes who had actions for damage brought against them, with the backing of the insurance companies, for the negligence in preserving property. Lord George Gordon's career was blasted. He was afterwards converted to Judaism: then in 1788 he was imprisoned for a libel on the queen of France, failed to find sureties for his future good behaviour, and died of jail fever after five years in prison. But the riots had more general and important results than these. They destroyed the easy confidence of city politicians that disorder in London was their safe weapon against a tyrannical government. They had seen the mob out of all control of civic leaders. If it had had any real purpose and had not begun on a fantastically small issue (and then simply turned to riot for rioting's sake) it might well have been as sinister as the 1789 Bastille demonstration in Paris. The Rockingham opposition, too, realized that agitation out of doors was no longer a traditional and safe reserve weapon in their armoury. The country gentlemen were horrified and damned all who could be made to appear responsible for such a spirit in the nation.

In this way the swing of opinion back to Lord North as a safe man, which had been evident in the commons at the end of April, was, by mid-June, increased in speed and weight. On

1 September parliament was unexpectedly dissolved. The general election was unusually quiet and expensive contests very few. Some opposition members lost their seats and at the reassembly in October the old Speaker, Sir Fletcher Norton, was replaced by C. W. Cornwall[1] to suit ministerial convenience. It says something for the courage of Shelburne, Rockingham, Fox, and Pitt, that they did not give up the game in despair.[2] Their cause was saved, not by any domestic enthusiasm for them or their ideas, but by general alarm about foreign affairs. The American losses were only the last straw, a sort of symbol of the calamities which befell the country. For these calamities abroad North, however unfairly, had to take responsibility.

The hostility of France, Spain, and Holland was the immediate cause of the abandonment of the attempt to coerce America. This hostility was decisive because Britain was still, as she had been since 1763, without a friend in Europe. North had made no effort to escape this isolation because to have no allies was the cheapest foreign policy. The difficulty of finding allies had, in any case, increased since Chatham had grappled with it.[3] Russia was fighting Turkey from 1768 to 1774 and scorned the small assistance in Greece which was all Britain could proffer. On the other hand she needed, and had, the benevolent neutrality of Prussia. This co-operation led on naturally to the first partition of Poland (1772, 1773), in which Austria joined. Britain was as irrelevant to it as she was to the Russian suppression of Pugatcheff's rebellion in 1774. In the Baltic there was no greater opening for British power. Sweden's energies were consumed in the *coup d'état* carried out by her king in 1772: Denmark also experienced a revolution which ended the régime of Struensee and Brandt whose patron the queen— a sister of George III—was locked away in prison. Nor could British statesmen find aid in renewing the old contacts with Austria. Joseph II relied upon alliance with France as the background to his internal reforms and to his expansion.[4] The ill

---

[1] Charles Wolfran Cornwall (1735–89), a businesslike man who had succeeded in minor offices but was to prove a lethargic Speaker.

[2] As it was, Pitt's reforming proposals had all their stress on increasing the county and not the urban representation. Burke and Fox concentrated upon economical reforms to cut out corruption. Even the old radical Horne made himself conciliatory by proposing to compensate holders of rotten boroughs with places in the house of lords. [3] See above, p. 122.

[4] In 1777 the dauphin of France was married to Marie Antoinette, l'Autrichienne.

feeling between Prussia and Austria aroused by Joseph's designs upon Bavaria in 1778 was dispersed not by British influence but by the mediation of France and Russia. Joseph, leaving Prussia securely in position as a champion of the petty German states, veered away towards the idea of an alliance with Russia and the penetration of the Balkans.

In all these twists of European affairs France held herself still to the resolve to avoid involvement in war on a central European question; she was aloof from Poland and Bavaria; she took no part in Swedish or Turkish changes. The reason was clear. She was keeping her hands free for revenge upon Britain. While she did this Britain could escape isolation only by forcing her way into some dispute in the hope that France would then come in too. Such British intervention could be arranged by pushing the interests of Hanover. In the Bavarian war, for instance, Hanover might have stood forth for Prussia or for Austria and have put forward demands of her own likely to lead to a war in which Britain could use her as a base. No policy can be imagined less likely to command support in England, more repugnant to George III, or more destructive of the financial position of the country.

The result of this continued isolation was seen in Britain's friendless state when things went badly in America. In 1780–2, as has been seen above,[1] France was trying to recapture the West Indies and India. Spain was besieging Gibraltar and raiding convoys. Holland joined in to get her share of the spoils from the apparently inevitable collapse. The Baltic powers, also concluding that Britain was impotent, seemed likely to carry their objection to her naval supremacy to the point of war. Prussia welcomed any difficulties which drew the attention of other powers from Europe and left her free to pursue a programme of internal reconstruction. Austria wished her ally France well and hoped that she too might gain time for domestic rebuilding. So Britain fought solitarily and ingloriously against western Europe. In 1781 an engagement between Hyde Parker and the Dutch off the Dogger Bank was an expensive draw. All the time the naval resources were inadequate to meet a combined French and Spanish fleet.

Peace had to be bought and forced, bought by concessions to America and then forced on Europe by the use of the resources

[1] See pp. 212, 213.

thus set free. Lord North could not with honour carry out this manœuvre. In 1780, 1781, and 1782 the fate of the government hung on this balance of dissimilar considerations—Was safe government at home less important than an end to the disastrous war? The end came in the spring of 1782. But though North resigned because there was no confidence in his foreign policy, it seemed that it would be difficult to expect support for the new ministers in anything but ending the war. Yet on this, the one issue on which they had general approval, the new ministers proceeded to quarrel among themselves. For the ministry was a coalition of the Rockingham and Shelburne groups: their views on a settlement with America did not coincide: their personal jealousies added fire to differences of policy. When there is added to this the fact that their ideas on domestic reform had still to be popularized or even defined, it might well seem that ministerial chaos had returned after twelve years. The king might well anticipate a repetition of the instability of his first ten years, made worse by the infusion of emotional cries and great principles into differences once merely personal.

X

THE CONFLICT OF GROUPS, 1782-4

THE ministry which succeeded Lord North in March 1782 was made up of members of the Rockingham and Shelburne groups. Rockingham himself was the first lord of the treasury, Fox and Shelburne secretaries of state, Lord John Cavendish chancellor of the exchequer, and Burke paymaster of the forces. Pitt's inclusion, though supported by Shelburne, was vetoed on grounds of age and inexperience. From the start the king showed a preference for the Shelburne rather than the Rockingham wing. For Shelburne at least reverenced Chatham's ideas (including that of a broad non-party administration), and respected the position of the Crown. Rockingham was too fond of his friends, in the king's view, to be a true patriot; the most prominent of those friends Charles James Fox had given personal offence to George III by his speeches and by his ripening friendship with the prince of Wales. The anger of a father seeing his son led into dissolute habits reinforced the pride of a monarch whose deepest convictions were set at naught.

The known preference of the king for Shelburne in turn augmented the dislike which the Foxites already felt for their colleague. It was true that the duke of Richmond (master general of the ordnance) and Earl Camden (president of the council), and even the duke of Grafton (lord privy seal), admired his clarity of mind and ruthlessness of purpose. In the disputes inside the ministry Conway (commander-in-chief) might be, as ever, a doubtful quantity. Lord Thurlow (lord chancellor), as the sole survivor from the North régime, could stand outside the squabble of the two groups, claiming to represent the king and through him an interest above such factions. But the rest, Keppel (first lord of the admiralty), the duke of Portland[1] (lord-lieutenant of

---

[1] William Henry Cavendish Bentinck, third duke of Portland (1738-1809), brother-in-law of the duke of Devonshire, and one of Rockingham's friends, but hitherto of small importance; became first lord of the treasury 1783; home secretary 1794-1801, and then lord president of the council; first lord of the treasury 1807; a dull but reasonable politician.

Ireland), with Fox, Lord John Cavendish,[1] and the marquis of Rockingham, looked on him as an outsider who had played them false in the past and would do so again. They insured against this by pushing their own trusty nominees, regardless of the king's feelings, for all junior places. Fox said that he perceived 'the Administration was to consist of two parts, one belonging to the King, the other to the public'. He soon added his hope of giving 'a good stout blow to the influence of the Crown', which he thus identified with Shelburne.

Yet this 'influence of the Crown' was at the lowest ebb. The king had given up North. All recent policy was going to be reversed. Even military and naval appointments, a sphere never openly invaded by ministers before, was to be left to these ministers who condemned the war.[2] The strength of the Crown was always in its embodiment of agreed national causes and the preservation of them against the uncertain turns of political and personal fortune. But this only worked when there was a common-sense agreement under the surface of politics and among the leaders of opinion in the country. In 1782 the king was powerless because he was brave. He believed France was near bankruptcy and would crack first if the war went on. He believed a surrender to America would involve surrender in Ireland and the ruin of trade. He believed that a revolutionary spirit was abroad and would, unless resisted, convulse England as it had New England. But public opinion was unashamedly for a quick peace. A large section of those of ministerial calibre, having been associated with the conduct of the war, were out of service so long as the peace spirit prevailed. The king had no alternative but to accept the Rockingham and Shelburne men with their peace policy and reforming intentions. It was clear that the help he could give to the Shelburne wing, in his weakened position, was very slight. It was more than offset by Shelburne's handicap in day-to-day politics. For he had few spokesmen in the commons apart from Isaac Barré. The eloquence of Fox and Burke enabled them to count on support in that house. This was a strong argument in the divided cabinet.

[1] Lord John Cavendish (1732-96), fourth son of the third duke of Devonshire; chancellor of the exchequer 1782 and again in 1783; a friend of Edmund Burke.

[2] Rodney was recalled from his successful command on grounds purely political.

It was not only personal dislikes which kept the new ministers from working as a team. They had differences of policy also. But on the first issue confronting them they were united. Irish commotions were a legacy from North's administration. Eden, lately Irish secretary, forced the Irish question before the house of commons within a month of the new ministers taking their offices, and he did so from a radical standpoint. The Irish volunteers had been brought to believe that economic questions were dependent upon constitutional ones. So long as Westminster could override the parliament in Dublin, no Irish trade, no Irish liberty, was safe. In February 1782 a convention of volunteer delegates at Dungannon voted that Britain should not legislate for Ireland or burden Irish trade: they claimed for the Irish parliament the right to pass a mutiny act annually and not in perpetuity: they demanded of the Crown an independent judicature.

Both sections of the new ministry agreed with Eden that the demand for Irish legislative independence, at least as far as concerned her internal affairs, must be conceded. Both sections were anxious about the regulation of relations between the two independent legislatures thus set up; both felt that those matters which were not of domestic but of imperial concern—defence, trade, and foreign affairs—must have a central direction which had to be in London. Yet experience with America had shown the folly of imposing such a direction, the difficulty of dividing it from domestic affairs, by dictation from London. The ministers worried about the proper solution of this difficulty at the same time as they had to conclude a war and to reorganize the administrative machine which they found in chaos.

It was agreed that the foundation of all true policy in this matter was to win Irish goodwill. This was the lesson from America as preached by the Rockinghams. Therefore the problem of the future relationship of the two countries was relegated to some future conference and agreement. The immediate action was to repeal the Act of 1719 (5 George I, c. 5) which declared the right of the British parliament to make laws binding Ireland. Thus it was hoped the Irish would feel free and then, out of common interest, they would agree to a trade policy which would benefit both countries. In rapid succession both the right of the British privy council to alter Irish laws and the perpetual mutiny act were abolished. For a time this seemed successful.

The Irish parliament rejoiced in its independence and voted to raise 20,000 Irish seamen.[1]

Ireland was only shelved and not settled. Within the year suspicion arose that independence was only a fraud. The British parliament had to pass another special act to declare the independence of the Irish parliament and to declare that there was no appeal from Irish courts to English ones. Even when that was done, the problem of co-ordinating the two parliaments had not been faced. The only link after 1782 was through the king and through the lord-lieutenant in Ireland who was head of the Irish executive but also a member of the British cabinet. To this executive connexion Grattan had assented by agreeing that the acts of Irish parliaments needed the great seal. Such a connexion was not enough unless there was also agreement on broad issues. But in 1782 the larger problem could not yet be worked out.[2]

After Ireland, ministers had to fulfil their promises of domestic reform. Shelburne and his group believed in reform of the principles of representation and at the same time in the reform of administrative methods. The first was not to be produced in a few weeks. The second was begun at once but yielded slow results. A committee was set up to consider the financing of the American war and abuses in the raising of loans. Another inquiry was instituted into the increase of smuggling. The sixth report of North's committee inquiring into public accounts was received; it recommended that the system of paying public servants by fees should be changed to that of salaried service. In the treasury a fee fund was started out of which the joint secretaries to the treasury were each to be paid £3,000 a year. Next year (1783), under Shelburne, this salaried system was carried further in the treasury. Cavendish felt unable to destroy sinecures by a stroke of the pen because they represented pensions for past services for whose reward he had as yet no alternative source. Another reform was a clearer division of departments. One secretary of state was to be concerned with home and colonial affairs (Shelburne), the other (Fox) with foreign relations. There was no need for a third secretaryship.

More dramatic than such measures of reform were those produced by Burke and his friends. Crewe's Act disfranchised the

---

[1] At the same time they settled an estate, by way of thanks, upon Grattan.
[2] See below, p. 389.

revenue officers of the Crown, removing the vote from those who, by their service, were reckoned most open to government pressure. On the same day Clerk's Act disqualified those holding government contracts from sitting as members of parliament. These were strong knocks at the influence of the court, because they removed steady support which had been at the command of whoever was chosen to head the king's treasury. In the previous eight years of war, forty-nine members of parliament had held direct treasury contracts, seven of these had won their contracts after gaining parliamentary seats in 1774 for that purpose, and ten of them were contractors before they came into the house. Two of them[1] now chose to renounce their contracts and retain their seats.

Burke's Acts were undoubtedly the most important of the session. The less controversial of them made a valuable reform in financial administration. The paymaster of the forces had never distinguished between his own private cash and the official moneys in his hands. As a result all government accounting was years in arrears and most intricate. Henry Fox's accounts were, even as Burke spoke, still being disentangled: even Chatham's official accounts—and he had abstained from making profit— took more than a decade to clear. In future, Burke enacted, the paymaster's accounts were to be kept at the Bank of England as an official, non-personal, account from which drawings were to be made only for official purposes. Within the next three years this sensible but—as experience was to show[2]—not fraud-proof system was extended to the navy and other accounts.

Burke's other Act was more exciting. He professed to supply the final answer to the growth of executive extravagance and of executive influence. This was the purpose of his Civil List Act. But its very completeness was a sign of its weakness. For it came fully fledged from Burke's fertile brain. It had not been tested and tried practically. It was too much the product of theoretical first principles. It was more thoroughgoing than anything produced by his rivals and at the same time a great deal less effective. It enforced efficient economy on the king, and simultaneously struck at influence, by a very simple device.[3] The debts

[1] Harley and Drummond.

[2] See the impeachment of Melville (Dundas), below, p. 418.

[3] Sir David Keir has argued (see *Law Quarterly Review*, l (1934), 368–85) that Burke was only interested in curtailing influence and believed that the executive's efficiency was outside his interest: on this argument Burke believed the king should

which the king had contracted on his civil list were funded and interest due on this fixed debt was to be charged annually on the civil list in future. The total sum granted by parliament for the king's civil list was fixed at £900,000 a year, its level at that time. For the spending of this sum the various services and benefits paid out of the civil list were divided into classes in order of priority. In the bottom category came the salaries of his majesty's ministers who looked after his finances. Therefore these ministers were provided with the best of all stimulants to economy, for if they spent too much there would be no money for their own salaries. In 1786, to take an example, the total sums paid to those in Burke's categories came to £897,000. There was only a margin of £3,000. So it was impossible to undertake corruption or bribery on any appreciable scale. From the same motive the amount allowed for home secret service—money always regarded with suspicion—was cut even below a reasonable level. While all ministries were cut to the minimum, two were even abolished: the third secretary of state and the board of trade were removed as unnecessary.

Burke prided himself upon having discovered an automatic control of royal lavishness. But one item in the civil list accounts, which he had refused to allow for, in fact ruined the whole scheme. Occasional payments, payments for special purposes which were irregular, were not allotted a place. Yet they amounted to some £138,000 in a normal year. They were paid as they arose in advance of the careful categories. Thus the civil list entered the new era not with a slight surplus but with a heavy deficit. Special parliamentary grants to cover the occasional charges were required if the civil list was to be balanced. But once ministers realized that the special charges had to be met without regard to Burke's Act, they only too rapidly came to regard the whole act as a dead letter. Almost from the beginning its order of priorities for payment was neglected and ministers particularly did not wait their turn for their wages. In 1786 Pitt was obliged to resettle the civil list by appropriating money for particular sections of it. Even its influence upon patronage was slight. For patronage had never been borne mainly upon

'live off his own' and manage his staff as he pleased within the financial limits fixed by the act. Neither Burke's own words, nor the text of the act, nor Dr. Binney's research into public finance of the time, seem to me to support so clear-cut a view, however.

the civil list. Burke was the victim of a delusion in believing that George III had wasted great sums of his own upon supporting a political machine. The real curbing of patronage lay in the day-to-day scrutiny of the working of the public offices, conducted by Pitt in ensuing years, and not in Burke's over-simplified plan.

Nevertheless the new ministry had so far shown enterprise and energy in living up to its promises of reform. Their attempts to live up to the promises of peace as well divided and destroyed them. For peace with America fell into Shelburne's colonial department while peace with France was the province of Fox. Both sets of negotiations were to be conducted in Paris, and they were not easily separable. Fox and Shelburne each had their agents in Paris. Each had their own ideas of how best to conclude the war swiftly. Fox's scheme may be simply put. He believed that it was essential to make peace with America first and then to use American retirement from the fray to force France to terms; these should be roughly the restoration of the position before the war. To conclude quickly with America he believed, from what Benjamin Franklin said, that it was necessary to begin by recognizing the independence of the United States and only to bargain about boundaries and trade afterwards. He wished to offer the United States a gesture of goodwill so as to convince them of English sincerity and good intentions. To Shelburne this was defeatism. For, even at this late date, he stood where Chatham had done in 1777. He saw that America could not be kept by force. But he hoped that the Americans might be content with independence in the sense of running their domestic affairs but would voluntarily unite their foreign policy and co-ordinate their trade policy with that of the king. All that was valuable in the old connexion would then be preserved. Shelburne therefore wished to recognize American independence only when he had persuaded the Americans to accept his interpretation of it. He thought Fox was proposing to give away the trump cards. In boundary drawing, Shelburne was prepared to be more generous to America than Fox was. He was fighting not for territories but for a conception of British world policy and trade for which the Rockingham group had neither understanding nor sympathy.

Fox accused Shelburne of using his Paris representative, Richard Oswald, to undermine the work of the other agent,

Tom Grenville, to such an extent that cabinet policy was set at naught.[1] This he urged made it impossible to win American confidence with the result that America refused to abandon her allies France and Spain. This quarrel about priorities—whether the treaty should follow or precede the acknowledgement of independence—acted as the focal point for all the suspicions felt for Shelburne. Fox decided that the only safeguard was to make Tom Grenville the agent for peace negotiation with America as well as (separately but simultaneously) with France. At the end of June 1782 the majority of the cabinet, viewing this question on its merits, were against Fox, who then decided to retire. His departure was hastened by the death, on 1 July, of Lord Rockingham. The Rockingham group hoped he would be succeeded by Portland, one of themselves, who was sufficiently dull to lead clever men. But the king used his constitutional right to offer the lead to Shelburne, who accepted it. This was enough to make Fox's petulant, personal resignation appear in retrospect like the action of a group leader. Several minor office-holders followed Fox into retirement: only Lord John Cavendish, of cabinet ministers, came out with him.

In the new administration Lord Shelburne had seven of his own following in the cabinet. It was calculated (by Gibbon) at this time that Shelburne would be able to reckon on the support of 140 votes in the commons: against this Fox would have 90 and Lord North 120. These were now the three main groups. In addition, it must be remembered that over a hundred members had given no man their confidence: on important debates about peace or constitutional reform these independent voters might be expected to attend. Shelburne's 140 were made up of the few who respected him as the political heir of Chatham, those who thought him the true reformer of the day, those who adhered to anyone who held the treasury, and those who expected him to win the political battle. Fox's 90 were those who for years had faithfully kept together in opposition under Rockingham, those who thought that he was bound to win power and influence soon, and those who found the magic of

[1] Richard Oswald (1705–84), a merchant turned diplomatist; introduced to Shelburne by Adam Smith.

Thomas Grenville (1755–1846), third son of George Grenville; M.P. Buckinghamshire, 1780; a friend of Fox; subsequently, 1806–7, president of the Indian board of control and first lord of the admiralty. A famous book collector.

his eloquence overwhelming. Lord North's 120 consisted, in the main, of those who, during the considerable space of twelve years, had bound themselves so openly to his cause that it was impossible to 'rat', and those who, in alarm at all the talk of change in the constitution, looked to North as the sensible conserver of the good old ways.

As no group had enough support to be sure of managing the commons, it might be expected that Shelburne, to hold power, would unite with Fox or North. But Shelburne still believed in Chatham's non-party system. He was averse to bargaining with organized groups. He was anxious to bring Foxites and Northites into his fold, but as individuals and without their chiefs. Shelburne deplored a weak executive and a divided legislature. He proposed to remedy it by building on the king and on that underlying 'patriotic' agreement which he represented. Shelburne felt that if he announced an intelligent programme of reform and made a constructive peace—showing the while his freedom from party spirit—he would rally to his ministry the votes of the independent gentry. Once it had been seen that, thanks to the support from Crown and counties, his administration was a stable one, the professional politicians would begin to leave Fox and North and jump on the ministerial waggon. This melting of their forces would, in its turn, compel the leaders of the groups to adopt a reasonable tone, perhaps even to consent to serve on a non-party basis. Thus a government of a united country would emerge. As, also, it would be part of his programme to increase the number of independent members of parliament he could hope that from that time on the strength of the factions would be for ever weakened.

Shelburne, unlike royal favourites such as Bute or North, had the serious intention of making changes in the spirit of the constitution and these might involve raising the standing of the Crown. Stress on the royal prerogative, which was shown in Shelburne's acceptance of appointment, was therefore associated in this period not with reaction, but with reform. At this stage, however, the king personally had no more to do than to show confidence in Shelburne. This he did. It gained for Shelburne the support of some who sought careers through court favour. Dundas had already transferred from Lord North; Jenkinson slowly made up his mind that he too might find a secure foothold in this combination. Eden and Lord Loughborough (as Wedderburn had become) were alarmed at Shelburne's growing security and nagged Lord North to do something before it was too late. John Robinson, the expert on voting and seat-management, predicted that Shelburne could make his place safe. All these reactions were influenced by routine calculation. Shelburne, nevertheless, chose to stand or fall by an appeal to those outside day-to-day political management.

In the summer of 1782 Shelburne announced a programme, such an announcement being in itself an innovation. He would repair public finance by converting loans to lower interest-rates and operating a scheme for debt redemption. Taxes, to make this possible, would be simpler and more justly distributed. The sinking fund to redeem the debt would be in the care of impartial public trustees. Trade would be revived, not by restoring as much as possible of the old protective system but by a general revision of customs to make trade freer on the lines suggested by Adam Smith.[1] Finally, Shelburne promised to bring forward a scheme for a reform of parliament which should make it more truly expressive of the spirit of the country by an increase in the number of members representing large county electorates.[2]

Shelburne had clearly decided not to bid for the support of North's conservative friends, but to defy them. He chose instead to appeal for the applause of the people with the support of the king. The fault in his calculations was to suppose that the independent squires—who, with the radical middle-class town politicians, are intended by the loose word 'people'—were enthusiastic for radical reform. In truth they were still in the same mood as during the debates of 1780 following Dunning's resolution.[3] That is to say that they were as distrustful of radical reformers as they were disillusioned about North's competence. This radical plan was therefore not likely to resolve the political deadlock. But Shelburne, in any case, sealed his fate by the terms on which he negotiated the peace.

Shelburne's plan for a peace settlement was far-reaching, imaginative, and misunderstood. He had seemed less radical in this field than Fox because he wished to delay recognition of American independence and to retain some link with the new

---

[1] See below, p. 329.
[2] This intention was so unpopular with North's friends that it was not included in the king's speech, though it remained Shelburne's policy.
[3] See above, pp. 232 f.

country. But—as Fox pointed out when he wished to excite the country—Shelburne really favoured much more sweeping concessions to the United States. For Shelburne was not thinking along traditional lines at all. He saw the settlement not as a surrender to America under French pressure, nor even as a reversal of North's blunders, but as the opening of a new and more glorious period of British history. This view of it he was unable, however, to make clear either to his contemporaries or even to historians. Yet to the making of fruitful peace he brought patient care, clear arguments, exciting theory, and audacity.

Shelburne believed that America might yet be kept within the British area of influence even though he was obliged to cede her independence. To a reader of Adam Smith and Dean Tucker the old economic sovereignty was out of date. All that British traders required was security along their trade routes with sound credit arrangements. The more territory the new United States possessed, the more British manufactures they would be capable of absorbing, provided always that their goodwill had been assured. Shelburne had a vision of the Atlantic as a great co-prosperity sphere in which two self-governing units, Britain and America, were partners in commerce. While Americans penetrated the open lands of the Mississippi and assumed fresh responsibilities of government there, the British, free from all such expensive tasks, should be free to act as the natural centre of trade, linking the expanding western world with Europe and the East. Closely connected with this economic dream there also lingered in his mind the unrealistic hope that, in time, the Americans might yet come to see that London, their link with the rest of the world, should be the place where decisions could be taken concerning the relations of this Atlantic alliance with other countries. He had, putting it bluntly, the hope that the king would control a foreign policy common to both countries. This was vain; yet the idea of a free America becoming more truly complementary to Britain was not so visionary. To make it possible it was essential that Americans should concentrate their attention on the interior of their continent and that they should feel goodwill towards Britain.

Shelburne believed that both these prerequisites of partnership were to be secured by granting America all that she could reasonably desire in the way of territory. Canada, Newfoundland,

and Nova Scotia were to be retained by Britain: otherwise
Shelburne had no bargains to make about American soil.
He freely gave to Franklin, Jay, and Adams, the American
negotiators in Paris, the interior of the continent. Canada had
a very good claim to the 'Old North West'—the area between
the St. Lawrence and the Ohio, lands south of the Great Lakes.
But with a good grace Shelburne granted all this away to the
United States. Let them explore, civilize, settle, and import
British manufactures. Again, though he retained Newfoundland, he gladly agreed to let Americans fish off its banks, provided only that colonists were not to follow the fish. So once the
technical point about the timing of recognition of their independence had been settled—and settled as they wished but with
devices for saving British pride—Shelburne's only disputes with
America arose over the treatment of loyalists and the honouring
of debts due by Americans to Englishmen. The interests of
those who had been loyal to King George had to be protected
for the sake of our national honour: the debts had to be paid
for the sake of commercial confidence. The latter end was better
served than the former. The loyalists' losses were recommended
by Congress to the attention of the individual states, naturally
without effect; they were eventually given compensation in
Canada and Nova Scotia by the British governments.[1] The
debts due to Britain previous to 1775, on the other hand, were
definitely acknowledged by the American Government to be
valid.

Shelburne's open-handedness towards America was not to
the taste of France. Vergennes, the French minister, wanted to
make great gains for his country in the West Indies. He also
hoped to keep America as a client state. Therefore he was
willing to help Britain in resisting American claims. As France,
not America, had really brought Britain to her knees it was a
reasonable assumption that she should gain the most. The
French disliked American penetration to the Mississippi because
a satisfied, expanding, America would not be in their pocket.
Moreover, once America was satisfied, she would not squeeze
concessions to France out of Britain. The French could, at the

---

[1] The development of British Canada, indeed, may be said to date from this
movement of loyalist refugees from the United States into virgin territories. This
development produced tension between French and British Canadians, on which
see below, p. 302, and also Sir E. L. Woodward, *The Age of Reform*, pp. 361 f.

most, threaten Britain with one more campaign. Their schemes
in India had been so well countered by Warren Hastings, their
supremacy in the Caribbean had been so effectively ended by
Rodney, that on their own they had few bargaining counters.
In the West Indies therefore France only gained Tobago and
had St. Lucia handed back to her. She restored to Great Britain
her conquests, Grenada, the Grenadines, Dominica, St. Christopher's, Nevis, and Montserrat. France was, farther north, given
fishing rights along the west coast of Newfoundland and unrestricted possession of the islands of St. Pierre and Miquelon.
In Africa, France took the river Senegal for a slave-trade base
and England took the river Gambia. In India, France abandoned all hope of re-establishing that influence with native
states which had been hers in 1756 and was satisfied with the
restitution of her trading posts; as a sop to French opinion the
administration of a few villages around Pondicherry and Kari-
kal, worth in all but £30,000 a year, was made over to her.
This may be summed up as the restoration of the situation
before the war. France had fought to establish a new state whose
first action, thanks to Shelburne's manœuvres, had been to
leave her in the lurch.

With the second European enemy, Spain, Shelburne used the
French to moderate the impracticable demands made in Madrid. Both he and George III played with the idea of exchanging
Gibraltar for valuable overseas possessions of Spain. But Spain,
fiercely as she had fought for Gibraltar, had fought in vain,
and would not now give away her American empire to gain it.
So, after argument, Britain gave up East and West Florida to
Spain, relinquished her claims to Minorca, but held on to
Gibraltar, recovered her islands in the Bahamas, and asserted
her claims to cut wood in Honduras. The cession of the Floridas
was regretted because it prevented the development of British
trade up the Mississippi, but at the same time it substituted
friction between Spain and the United States for that which
would have troubled Britain. With the third European enemy,
Holland, Britain proceeded on the basis of a restoration of all
conquests made during the war, refusing to discuss the rights of
neutral shipping, rights which had been the occasion of the
Dutch entry into the fight. Britain was reluctant to restore
Trincomalee (in Ceylon) because of its usefulness on the route
to India. The restoration was made, however, when it was clear

that France was not planning to retain that other Dutch post on the route, the Cape of Good Hope. From the Dutch Britain obtained Negapatam, an unimportant town near Madras, and the right to navigate in eastern seas among the Dutch spice islands.[1]

The peace which Shelburne negotiated was incomplete. Territorially Britain had restored the *status quo* with her European enemies and renounced colonization on the mainland of America. At the same time, in all sets of negotiation, strategic points important to her own sea power had been safeguarded. For the meaning of Shelburne's plans was his search for revived greatness through trade across the seas. It followed from this, however, that to complete the treaties he needed economic agreements immediately with America and, less urgently, with France. Both were promised in the appendages to the agreements he signed in February 1783. His young chancellor of the exchequer, William Pitt, had charge of a bill to make possible a new trading agreement with America. By this bill Americans were to enjoy all the rights of Englishmen in matters of trade. In return Canadian fur-trappers would have been free to penetrate to the Ohio, and British ships welcomed at Boston. This economic union was to be the natural result of generosity towards American territorial demands. Though this, to Shelburne, was the idea which justified his settlement, it was bound to be unpopular in England. For few Englishmen had Shelburne's faith in the advantages of large areas of unrestricted trade; most traders still put their trust in mercantile restriction. They would fear, for example, to allow Yankee sailors freely into the West Indies and would prefer to shut America out from the empire she had quit.

When Shelburne presented his treaties in parliament, he had to face an outburst of dissatisfaction. We wanted, grumbled back-benchers, an end to a stupid war but not this humiliating surrender. Was there any need to let the United States engross a continent? Shelburne was hamstrung in his own defence. He could only hint at his purposes in making the treaty. For he knew that his project of a revision of the whole trading policy of the empire would, if anything, be even more enraging than

---

[1] Peace with Holland was not finally concluded until May 1784, but its shape was decided in January 1783 when the French and Spanish agreed to it, thus leaving the Dutch without allies if they chose to object to these terms.

the abandonment of the Ohio. So his great project was never properly explained or understood. His defence, with its stress upon the smallness of concessions to European powers, and upon Britain's military exhaustion, was too negative to quiet the general fury. Indeed Shelburne had worked so much on his own that even his cabinet colleagues had not had his confidence nor understood his purposes. Some of them were on the verge of resignation in the spring of 1783. Shelburne's hints and asides about a master plan only worsened the position. They confirmed the general suspicion that he was a dangerous schemer, always indirect, never to be trusted. Shelburne played the part of prime minister too domineeringly at a time when good constitutionalists still denied that there ought to be any such office as prime minister. Shelburne's attempt to win his way by a *tour de force* was fatal.

In February 1783 it was clear that Shelburne was likely to fall. The country would accept peace because it needed it, but then condemn the man who had made it. No one political group could command general support to maintain a stable government. For Shelburne would bear the stigma of losing the peace, North of losing the war, and Fox of losing self-control. Any two of these groups in coalition would have enough organized support, however, to hold on until they could outlive the reproaches of the past. The most natural alliance was that of Shelburne and Fox, a reknitting of the government which had existed until the death of Rockingham. This was blocked by Fox, who would only serve if Shelburne himself resigned. A coalition begun by the surrender of their leader could offer little security to those, like Dundas, who had transferred their allegiance to Shelburne and therefore depended on his protection. Coalition of Shelburne with North was impeded by memory of Shelburne's attacks upon North and by the intransigent attitude of young Pitt.[1] He declared that North's followers should support the government and receive minor places, but that North himself was unclean and untouchable. North had no personal ambition left, but he was in duty bound to do his best for those who had given him faithful support. His followers felt about Pitt's offer, as those of Shelburne did about Fox's ultimatum: that there was no security for them in a bargain which began with the proscribing of their leader. All overtures failed

[1] The chancellor of the exchequer. He was twenty-three.

and Shelburne was left to challenge parliament trusting only to the prestige of being the king's minister and to the disunion of his critics.

This disunion had, however, become union. The critical debate on the peace treaties took place on 17 February 1783. Four days before Fox and North had entered an alliance to bring Shelburne down. North's motives are clear. He saw that there must be a coalition of two groups if there was to be any government at all. He believed that Fox could easily come to terms with Shelburne. The reunited reformers would then have a general election in which, backed by the king and by popular agitation, they might in many constituencies destroy the hopes of North's friends. If he was not to be annihilated he must unite with Shelburne or Fox. The former offered him only a menial role. Fox was willing to take him in as an equal partner. His choice was obvious. Fox's thoughts are equally clear. He too saw the need for some bargain. Under a Shelburne coalition he believed he would be kept in the dark while the prime minister used his hold on the king to disrupt Foxite unity. Shelburne might succeed where Chatham had failed in 1766. North was an easygoing man who would yield first place to Fox, provided the prejudices of his friends were respected.

On 24 February 1783 Shelburne resigned after defeats of 224 to 208 and 207 to 190 in the house of commons. Shelburne and Pitt had done well in attracting independent support and in inducing Fox's friends to desert him; but they were still in a minority. Shelburne himself most unjustly believed that the king had failed to give him full support. The king felt that Shelburne was faint-hearted and had deserted him. The king refused to believe that so 'unnatural' an alliance as that of Fox with North could last for long. So strong was his sense of the unholiness of their union that from 24 February to 2 April he refused to summon the duke of Portland (the nominal head of the coalition of Fox and North) to take office. He marked the chaos in public affairs after a muddled war, an outburst of radical projects for reform, and a misunderstood peace, by allowing a political void to continue for almost six weeks.[1] Then with a bad grace he bowed to the inevitable. It was a victory of the

---

[1] This was the only period in which the so-called King's Friend, Jenkinson, admitted that he had ventured to give the king advice in person on general politics. Compare above, p. 119.

leaders over the king which was unprecedented in its brutal frankness.

The unnatural character of the Fox–North coalition has, nevertheless, been exaggerated. It is true that Fox had denounced North. But that was in the main over American policy and the war. Both were dead issues. The new ministers of necessity ratified the peace treaties in March 1783, after the ruin of their author. It is true, also, that North's friends feared reform movements because they believed they would undermine the whole social system, while Fox had acted as the chairman of radical committees to lead popular forces against North. But Fox, as he later confessed, was not aiming at a radical change in the constitution, but only to redress its balance, to weaken the executive and make the legislature more independent: the same ideas about the constitutional balance which, at the time of Wilkes, had made him unpopular[1] had since made him the mob hero. With the passage of acts disfranchising revenue officers, with the exclusion of government contractors from the house, and, above all, with the mechanical severity of Burke's Civil List Act, Fox might well feel that his reforming ambitions had been achieved. Or at least he might feel that the reforms so far made needed time to show their effects. Furthermore it was impossible to drive on with reform regardless of the conservative feelings of the squires, when the object of reform was to make squires count for more. Far better, then, to demonstrate the value of what had been done while co-operating with the official men and the frightened men who clung to North. So Fox promised North—as none of Shelburne's men would do—that he would push no further reform schemes in England for the time being.[2] There were plenty of problems outside England waiting solution. The union, in short, was not unnatural, but only a marriage of convenience and necessity. As such there was no reason why it should not have been fruitful.

The king would not see the need for this change in government. The ideas of Chatham upheld by Shelburne still made their appeal to him. Nor could George easily forget Fox's

---

[1] See above, p. 137.

[2] This acceptance of the inevitable by Fox, explicitly declared, may usefully be compared with Pitt's implicit acknowledgement of the same political necessity. See below, pp. 275 f.

exuberance in opposition and his clannishness in friendship: North, he felt, had betrayed the country in choosing to work with Fox rather than Shelburne. It remained to be seen, however, whether this time the king justly represented the feelings of private gentlemen. Fox certainly hoped that he could smooth over all difficulties by *bonhomie*. He forgot how deep an impression his rhetoric had made upon his audience. What to him were words, conveying at most the general feelings of his heart, seemed to those who heard him threats of action, fierce and resolute. To the king, Fox was all humility, but George remained suspicious. The only way Fox could kill suspicion was by years of quiet routine government. Unfortunately the same extraordinary and urgent problems faced the new administration as had faced the old: Ireland, India, consolidation of the peace, and questions of reform. Everyone waited expectantly to see how they would be tackled.

North agreed with Fox that the evils of the day originated in his own lack of 'vigour and resolution to put an end to' slipshod government by departments. Their new administration was to be co-ordinated 'independent of the King' (in Fox's phrase) by Fox, who should yet avoid going against the vested prejudice of North's supporters. On the reform issue accordingly, the path was clear. When Pitt, from an opposing bench, brought in a measure to increase county representation, it was resisted and defeated by 293 to 149; there was no great agitation out of doors against this decision. Economical reform, on the other hand, continued, though gently.[1] At the treasury Lord John Cavendish continued Pitt's work of substituting salaries for fees. It was his policy—as in a stronger form it was to be Pitt's again later—to cut out abuses as places fell vacant, thus reforming by the inexorable efflux of time. The prince of Wales was given a private establishment of £50,000 a year, but this was all to be found out of the existing civil list without any increased charge (once he had been equipped at the outset) on

---

[1] One incident tarnished the record of this ministry as far as administrative purification was concerned. Two officials in the pay office, Messrs. Powell and Bembridge, who had served there since the days of Henry Fox (and were executors of his estate), were suspected of gross financial irregularity. Barré, who was paymaster under Shelburne, had dismissed them. Burke, on the argument that it was unfair to dismiss them so long as their guilt was unproved, restored them. The subsequent proof of their irregularities brought upon Burke the charge of conniving with friends to cover up corruption.

parliament. This meant that the king would have to scrape along even more carefully. Reform was thus kept alive, but without alarming any of the independent gentry.

Shelburne's peace was ratified though the implications in its author's mind were lost to sight. On Ireland Fox and North agreed with their predecessor that the consequences of the grant of independence would have to be skilfully worked out. In the nature of this case, however, they could have no plan ready until they had negotiated with the Irish leaders.

It was India on which the coalition was both willing and able to take prompt action. Such action was needed. The East India Company was once again[1] in financial difficulties. It was receiving aid from the treasury and struggling to meet an abnormal number of bills drawn on London. Its trading position had seemed to recover after 1773, in part because of the trade from India to China. But trade had then been adversely affected first by the Mahratta wars and then by the incursion of Haidar Ali of Mysore into the Carnatic.[2] War not only upset the balance of the Company's finances. It was a further argument for the intervention of the government. The fighting in India and on its seas had been part of the late international conflict. It seemed unwise to leave so vital a part of national security either in the infirm hands of a quarrelling directorate, or in those of their self-willed servant Warren Hastings, the governor in Bengal.

Hastings's government under North's Regulating Act had been marked by bitter and perpetual disputes within the Bengal Council, and between the council and the chief of the Judiciary. That North's Regulating Act had not worked well was as plain as the onus of responsibility was obscure. In addition to all such reasons of state in favour of a new system of Indian control there was the argument of humanitarianism. Many men had come to feel that amid the wrangles of Englishmen in India the welfare of the native population was forever sacrificed: all men by 1783 had come to pay lip-service at least to the need to combine the happiness of the Indians with the balancing of the Company's books.

So strong were these arguments for reform in India that Fox's

---

[1] See above, pp. 165 f.

[2] For fuller details of Indian history in these ten years see the account given below, pp. 305 f. in connexion with the career of Warren Hastings.

bill had several predecessors. Robinson in 1778 had sketched a plan for North which that bewildered man had had no time to discuss. This plan had been redrawn by Jenkinson in 1781 only to be shelved in its turn. Since 1781 a select committee, inspired at every stage by Burke, had been reviewing Indian history and issuing reports; though nominally considering the judicial system it had been sketching reform of the whole pattern. Over the same period another committee, the secret committee (led by Dundas with great assistance from Jenkinson), had, while nominally considering the origins of the war in the Carnatic, been working on rival general schemes of reform. Dundas had, while serving in Shelburne's administration, already put before parliament a bill for future Indian government which, though then rejected, sketched a system very like that which finally came about.

Not only was the coalition spurred on by arguments of weight and by knowledge of recent moves, but they had within their midst a minister who had come to interest himself passionately in the matter. Edmund Burke had, no doubt, been first impelled to study India by the misfortunes of his friends. They had lost money in the stock exchange disasters preceding North's act. Worse still William Burke was not as fortunate as he had expected when he betook himself to India. Through these ignoble connexions, Burke was brought into contact with many returning Indian adventurers with axes to grind. But to explain how Burke came to absorb himself in Indian affairs is not to explain away the spirit with which he expounded them. Many of his facts, when derived from Philip Francis, can be shown to be twisted out of true shape: but this does not discredit the principles which Burke so eloquently illustrated from them. Burke at this time was convinced that the Company was in the hands of corrupt men who oppressed India, ignored honest merit, and failed to give a return to the state or to the shareholders. One further element enlisted Burke's imaginative mind. He felt the importance to the English way of life of the great corporations independent of the state, the sacredness of chartered independence within the community. This appeal to his philosophy of history not only made Burke more active in pressing for an Indian bill, but it also determined some of the characteristics of the bill which Fox introduced in November 1783.

It had been a common feature of all reforming schemes since

1773 that they involved a greater degree of government regulation of the East India Company. In part this was defended on
the ground that the state had a just interest in administrative
revenues in India, in part that the stability of the Company
was essential to the London money-market, in part that sound
administration and peace were the concern of the public.
Robinson had argued that the king's government should have
the legal right to appoint half the directors of the Company. He
had quietly tried to influence the election of as many as possible.
But all such action, all such proposals, ran up against the great
prejudice of the eighteenth century. They involved an increase
in the powers of the executive. All such proposals could be
pilloried by their opponents—of whom there were necessarily
a great number within the ruling circle of the Company—as a
barefaced attempt to steal the patronage of the sub-continent
for royal use. Burke had held forth in his most elevated style in
defence of chartered corporations when Lord North or Chatham
laid fingers on the wealth of the East. All the whigs of Fox's
circle had joined in voting that the influence of the Crown
'ought to be diminished'. How then could the evils of India be
righted?

The solution pronounced was ingenious and elaborately
articulated. Fox proposed that the whole management of the
territorial possessions of the Company, with all the powers
hitherto enjoyed by the directors and Court of Proprietors, was
to be given to a board of seven commissioners who were named
in the bill before parliament. These seven were to enjoy their
office for four years. They were to be removable by the king on
the address of either house of parliament, a tenure only a little
less secure than that of judges. Vacancies were to be filled, and
a new board named after four years, by the king. Under this
supreme council, nine assistant commissioners were to manage
the commercial business of the Company. These assistants,
chosen from among shareholders who had £2,000 of Indian
stock, were also named in the bill, though subsequent appointments were to be made by open voting by the shareholders
(Court of Proprietors). This measure removed supreme control
from the old clique in the Company but avoided giving power
to the executive. Instead it placed it in the hands of a public
board outside the fluctuations of political power, an experiment
with a familiar sound to twentieth-century Englishmen. Even

though future appointments were to be with the Crown, they would resemble appointments to the bench rather than to cabinet office. Something like a new East India corporation was thus proposed. At the same time the interests of the existing Company were balanced against public control by the stipulation that the commercial assistants were to be elected from among stockholders by stockholders.

This reorganization at the centre did not, in itself, deal with the insubordination and excesses alleged at Bombay, Madras, and Calcutta. Here Burke's second bill[1] rejected the wishes of Hastings (and other advisers) for an increase in the powers of one man on the spot. Instead of making a dictator out of the governor in Bengal, Fox proposed to make all authorities in India more tightly subservient to the new home commission. The seven commissioners were to root out abuse, control all action, and build up a new tradition of clean administration.

In all these arrangements there is a theoretical skill matched only by blindness to practical considerations. The last point, for instance, could be easily argued: having set up a new guardian of the common interest of India and England, it was surely logical to give it all power. It was logical but impossible. For how could the most enlightened of commissioners in London govern India when information and decisions took months to cross the seas and a crisis might be over before the rulers had heard of its existence?

This was the most glaring fault in the scheme from the Indian point of view: from the point of view of the coalition government, on the other hand, it was the method of appointing commissioners which was the fatal miscalculation. For Burke and Fox had respected the contemporary suspicion of the Crown but had not allowed for general distrust of themselves. It was in vain that they extolled the merits of security of tenure in producing enlightened control. All that contemporaries noted were the names of the happy sixteen who were given this security. The senior seven were chosen from the supporters of North and Fox; the nine business men were all selected from among Foxites in the old Company. Was it to be supposed that they would prove impartial when they had earned their places by party loyalty?

[1] The authorship of the bills has been shown to be Burke's. L. S. Sutherland, *The East India Company in Eighteenth Century Politics*, p. 397.

The very crown of Burke's scheme, the security of tenure, was interpreted in a sinister light. Fox claimed to have invented public control unmixed with executive corruption. It was said that in practice this meant that the whole vast patronage of the Company was given, unalterably, to Fox's own friends; not just 'jobs for the boys' but jobs for the boys to distribute for years to come. For the old division of power of the Regulating Act between the Company and the state was now destroyed. Fox would be a more powerful corrupter than the king, and might buy himself a permanent majority following in the house of commons. The indignant Company played on the fear of that overmighty subject 'Carlo Khan' more effectively than the government could on fears of King George. All the suspicions of Fox and the Rockinghams, who had gloried in their clan spirit, were at once aroused. In the house of commons Pitt, Dundas, and Jenkinson fought battle after battle, through nights stale with oratory to unprofitable dawn, in which the purpose was always to exploit this appeal to popular prejudice. Yet together Fox and North had enough loyal followers to prevail in the commons. The decisive vote was taken in their favour by 208 to 102.

Outside parliament a great effort was made to arouse opinion. Many pamphlets were rushed out from the press, for money to subsidize them was not wanting to the interests threatened. This too was a climax in the new warfare of satirical prints. Since Hogarth had discovered the commercial possibilities of the wide circulation of prints among all classes, the propagandists had learned the lesson for political purposes. The fat, gambling, greasy Fox, with smiles too wide to be trusted, with all the gold of the East at his back, was a subject to adorn any tavern wall or middle-class study. On the other hand, the East India Company was everywhere admitted to be both scandalous and insolvent. Another practical point must have counted with men of good intent. This was the third administration in eighteen months: if it were torn down, could there be any government at all? If Shelburne, Fox, and North, with three distinct followings, were all rejected, would it not be proved that no ministry could be formed? And would not this show an ignorance of fundamental political sense and their duty to 'the King's government'? Fox might, in the domestic chaos which had followed war with America, hope paradoxically enough

to gain strength from the instinct to preserve some government at the very time when he gloried in reducing executive
influence. This hope, if such it was, was destroyed by the king
himself.

There is no evidence to support the view put forward by some
historians that George III schemed to destroy the coalition
from its formation. Clearly he disliked it, for he had resisted its
assumption of power as long as possible. But, like everyone else,
he despaired of finding any alternative arrangement. He had
sullenly acquiesced in the government's actions for six months.
It was likely that he would feel the full force of the objections to
Fox's India Bill. Personal mortification would make him more
acute to discover a plot against the public. If he failed to respond
instinctively there was Thurlow, forced out of office by the
coalition, to arouse his feelings. Even so, the king could not, as
a responsible man, wreck the only possible ministerial combination. It was therefore of the very first importance that some of
North's men had, since 1782, begun to detach themselves from
him. Dundas, as has been seen, had linked himself with Shelburne and an Indian policy of his own. After the Fox–North
coalition, Robinson surreptitiously deserted his old master:
Jenkinson also was now an enemy of North. But all these were
able minor politicians; what was required to give their sympathies practical effect was some commanding figure. Few of
North's friends, besmirched by the American calamity, were
capable of leading. Fox's friends were loyal to their side. Lord
Shelburne had forever ruined what hopes he had had by his
arrogance in office. A new man of ministerial calibre, a man of
no past errors or old friendships, was needed to rally deserters
from North. When Dundas came down from Scotland during
the debates on India in the commons, he persuaded the twenty-
four-year-old Pitt that the time had come for him to step forward
in this role. To Dundas's arguments were added Robinson's
calculations. Between 5 and 9 December Robinson prepared an
analysis of how members of the commons would react to a
change of government, and calculations of changes if there
were a general election.

At the moment when the bill passed the commons, it was
therefore possible to tell the king that if he would dismiss his
ministers there was a successor willing to serve and an alternative government with hope of surviving. Thurlow wrote a note

which the king handed to Temple for use in the house of lords. George declared 'that he should consider all who voted for it as his enemies'.[1] It was an indirect method of dismissing the coalition. When it was known in the lords, the Fox–North government was beaten first by 87 to 79 and then (on 17 December 1783) by 95 to 76. On 18 December ministers were dismissed (without audience) and Pitt became first lord of the treasury. His cabinet colleagues (as they were assembled in January 1784) were Earl Gower, Lord Sydney, the marquis of Carmarthen, Lord Thurlow, the duke of Rutland, Viscount Howe, the duke of Richmond. As a team, it had more blue blood than strength.[2]

This extraordinary exertion of the royal power was marked at once by motions of reproach in the house of commons. That house declared by 153 to 80 that it was a scandalous breach of privilege to report the king's personal opinions upon legislation. But George III had his constitutional ground to stand on. It was not constitutional but practical impediments which had prevented his quarrelling with Fox ere this. Now it seemed that he had not only the opportunity but even the duty to dismiss him. George III staked all upon winning general assent to the proposition that the India Bill was an abuse of power and that, in consequence, the blameless Pitt should be assisted to maintain some sort of administration. Certainly since 1780 many men had lost all confidence in North without gaining much for the new ideas of Fox. Pitt was an alternative to either, a man at once a reformer and a friend to his king, one neither committed to a faction nor subservient to courtly ideas. He was moreover the son of a great father.

Pitt's aim was to do what Shelburne had failed in. He had to attract to himself the followers of North and, if possible, some of the old Rockingham group also. As compared with Shelburne he had the advantage of not having borne the responsibility for the terms of peace.[3] Even more important, perhaps, was the

---

[1] Lord John Russell, *Memorials of C. J. Fox*, ii. 220.

[2] Thomas Townshend, Baron Sydney, later Viscount Sydney (1733–1800), served under Chatham, Rockingham, and Shelburne; resigned 1789.

Francis Osborne, marquis of Carmarthen, fifth duke of Leeds (1751–99), had been dismissed from the lord lieutenancy of the East Riding of Yorkshire for opposition to North and then rewarded by Rockingham with the post of ambassador in Paris; he resigned from Pitt's government in 1791, see below, p. 297.

[3] It might be added that Pitt also had the advantage that he was spared the complications of having to work with Shelburne. For with more sense than gratitude

history of crises through which politics had passed. Opposites had met in coalition and the king had denounced his ministers. To many Northites Pitt seemed a last, and a desperate, chance of some decent government. Against this, however, must be set the fact that the circumstances of Pitt's appointment had enraged and embittered men of Fox's circle. Pitt in these circumstances could only hold on against hostile majorities, to give time for stragglers to desert to him and time for the irreconcilable opposition to be branded as men of ambition whose conduct would justify the most sinister interpretation of their India Bill. Pitt's ministerial team might therefore be reckoned a stopgap: to it converts would be welcomed.

Pitt, through the king's speech, told the commons that the use of the prerogative to dissolve was not immediately contemplated. In January (1784) the commons, nevertheless, resolved that if they were dissolved and elections were held it would be a crime to attempt to raise supplies. They then proceeded to postpone the discussion of the second reading of the Mutiny Bill, essential to the discipline of the armed forces, until 23 February. This amounted to a threat to counter the use of the prerogative by an exercise of parliamentary independence, to produce a head-on collision of king and commons unknown since the revolutionary seventeenth century. It was a sign of weakness, however, that Fox should have been so hostile to the idea of a general election, whether his reasons were fear of public opinion or fear of the influence of the executive in the constituencies. For Fox professed still to speak for the nation. His majority in the house of commons which had been 106 in December was still 39 in January. On this he stood, a champion of the independence of the commons.

It was agreed by all that though Fox's scheme had been defeated, some regulation of the East India Company was essential. Here again Pitt profited by the disorders of the last half year. The East India Company, its very foundations shaking from Fox's assault, co-operated with Pitt in putting forward a control scheme which but a year before they would have regarded as outrageous. The powers of the governor-general in Bengal over the other governors were to be strength-

---

he refused to offer Shelburne office, though he had once been his protégé. Pitt not only knew that others would object to serving with Shelburne; he himself testified to the misery of being his colleague.

ened. Measures were proposed to check oppression in India and
to punish the Company servants who enriched themselves out-
rageously. Most important of all, the political and military
affairs of the Company were put under a board of control
appointed by the Crown. This differed from Fox's bill in that
the controllers were to be ministers, like other ministers of the
Crown, changing with the wishes of the king and the fluctuations of politics. At the same time it was intended that this
executive should not gain power through jobbery, for the patronage of the Company was to remain, in theory at least, with
the East Indian elected directors and not to fall within the
scope of the board of control. This bill Pitt commended to the
house as a reasonable attempt to correct the abuses of the past
without either inflating the king's power or creating a private
patronage fund. The commons rejected it by 222 votes to 214.
Fox's majority was down to 8, one-fifth of what it had been
earlier in the month.

Deadlock in the commons was viewed with alarm. At a
meeting at the St. Albans Tavern moderate politicians expressed
their wish that a government of national union should be
formed. Pitt had formerly agreed with Fox: Fox and North had
come together under Portland's leadership. Surely it should be
possible for Portland to take office with Pitt. When these views
were represented to Pitt, he professed himself willing to act with
Portland and Fox. In the house of commons he made clear,
however, that he could never sit at council with North. That
amiable though execrated man promptly declared his willingness to sacrifice his own ambitions to bring about a general
reunion. What was not clear in Pitt's professions of co-operation
was who should lead any reunited reform ministry. Pitt declared for 'equality': with men of such qualities as Pitt and Fox
equality is impossible except in an equal contest and a fair fight.
But Pitt, characteristically, did not explore this question, leaving it to the other side to define and impose conditions. Portland
and Fox would not serve unless Pitt first resigned and an entirely new ministry was formed. By this they, in part, meant to
censure the king and Pitt for the way in which the government
had been set up: more usefully, they meant to force the question
of leadership to the front. Fox was not prepared to kiss the rod,
attach himself to Pitt's staff, and add his numbers to Pitt's
policies. He announced his willingness to consider a new India

Bill and serve with an entirely new administration. Pitt equally always refused to resign before union, for this would mean accepting the dominance of Fox. Both therefore in mid-February 1784 expressed willingness to serve together but both set limits to their co-operation which prevented action. Yet Pitt appeared the more amenable. Portland and Fox seemed vindictive, petty, and unyielding. When Portland declined to meet the king unless he was sure his preliminary condition would be met, he was widely considered captious. When, at the end of February, Pitt was welcomed by Wilkes at a banquet in the city of London it was as the friend of independent voters (as well as of the king) against the old gang. The house of commons meanwhile postponed the voting of supplies (by 208 to 196) and voted an address to the king to remove his ministers. On the king's reaffirming his desire for a broader administration on a fair and equal basis but refusing to dismiss his ministers as a preliminary to that, the house voted a second address which met with the same answer. Finally the commons voted a representation, full of reproaches, to the king. This was carried by a majority of only one (191 to 190). It was a signal for Pitt to bring forward the Mutiny Bill and for the Foxites to allow its passage. It was obvious now that Pitt had, in three months, impressed the backbench members of parliament with the fact that, despite his youth, his was not a government of flippant gamblers, but a serious attempt to establish a stable system on the basis of the patriotic consensus of opinion which had been obscured of late by personal issues. The passage of the Mutiny Bill (10 March) was therefore a confession that the house of commons allowed the ministry a *prima facie* case for its existence. It was time to explore the right of that house to speak for the country. On 25 March the parliament was dissolved.

In the general election which followed the power of the treasury was naturally felt. For three months Robinson and George Rose[1] had been busy making the usual bargains with local interests to secure the return of members likely to support the government. It was not a matter necessarily of finding new members: the old member might be persuaded to become

---

[1] George Rose (1744–1818) served in the navy, then in the exchequer and the board of taxes; made secretary to the treasury by Shelburne; Robinson's pupil and successor as a manager of the government interest in elections; M.P., 1784; subsequently a vice-president of the board of trade, paymaster general, and treasurer of the navy; a writer on financial subjects.

friendly if he could be convinced that otherwise the Crown's favours, which cemented his local position, would be denied him. As well as treasury influence there was available to Pitt's cause the money of private persons, particularly those in the East India Company, who had been frightened by the plans of Fox. Thus there can be no doubt that Pitt's victory was, on normal eighteenth-century calculations, to be expected. No government ever lost an election in that century. But equally no government ever won so striking a victory as this one. This points to a further and novel element in Pitt's success. The forces of public opinion were roused as never before on a public issue —except perhaps on Walpole's Excise Bill, but that was not at election time, and then the excitement was against and not for the ministers. The excitement in 1784 was not shown in contested elections—there were no more than usual—but in decisions behind the scenes. Sitting members, identified closely with Fox's plans, went home to their neighbours to find that they were regarded as corrupt men on the make, burglars surprised in the act of raiding Indian patronage for their own purposes: very often rather than defend themselves, at heavy expense, they simply made way for some new local representative, unspotted by controversy and sympathetic to Pitt. Thus in the county of Yorkshire, where the great friends of Fox—the Cavendishes, the Fitzwilliams, the earl of Carlisle—could bring voters to the poll, and where a contested election in 1807 was to cost Wilberforce[1] £58,000 and the other candidate some £200,000, there was no full contest on this occasion. The eloquence of little Wilberforce aroused so strong a passion of support, so many hands were raised in his favour, that the great lords conceded him the day without a poll. The old petitioning movement, founded in Yorkshire, rallied to him. Burke said that Wilberforce, a shrimp mounted on a table, seemed to grow into a whale, and carried all before him. So it was, less dramatically and openly, in many constituencies.

Pitt won the election of 1784 with a triple alliance: public opinion, even among the voteless, was with him; the moneyed men, many of them believing their chartered privileges at stake,

---

[1] William Wilberforce (1759–1833) had been M.P. for Hull since 1780; M.P. Yorkshire, 1784–1812; a devout evangelical; the parliamentary leader of the campaign against the slave trade; supported foreign missions; a friend of Pitt and a powerful independent force in the house of commons.

backed him; with such encouragement added to the intelligent use of treasury bargains the cause of Pitt was irresistible.[1] One hundred and sixty of Fox's friends failed to reappear at Westminster. This was therefore a vote of confidence in George III. He had correctly interpreted the resentment against Fox, North, and Burke.[2]

---

[1] The election of 1784 has been a subject of dispute between historians. W. T. Laprade, *Parliamentary Papers of John Robinson*, argued that victory came because Treasury influence was used intensively; Mrs. E. George, 'Fox's Martyrs' in the *Transactions of the Royal Historical Society*, vol. xxii, produced evidence to support the older view of the importance of popular feeling. Contemporary evidence seems to me to support Mrs. George. For instance, the second Viscount Palmerston, a sensible observer and friend of Fox at this stage, prophesied that Pitt would gain 'a large majority' . . . 'from the epidemical kind of spirit that has gone about the country in favour of the King's Prerogative against the House of Commons' (B. Connell, *A Whig Peer*, p. 152). This is supported, from the other side politically, by Lord Eldon (see *Life*, by H. Twiss, i. 162 f.).

[2] The election of 1784 may therefore be compared with that of 1835 (Sir E. L. Woodward, *The Age of Reform*, pp. 96, 97), when William IV misjudged the feeling of the country (it was indifferent) and when he no longer had much treasury influence to use.

XI

PITT AND RECONSTRUCTION, 1784-9

PITT's victory was not a triumph for a party or even for his policies. By contrast with Fox and North he had been acclaimed as being a patriot before he was a politician. Fox's disastrous mistakes had driven into the background all fears of the influence of the Crown, all suspicions aroused by Pitt's training in Shelburne's school of reform. The Foxites, by striving to bring in party government, had reduced themselves to a clique in opposition. So long as Pitt seemed to aim at the extinction of faction, his retention of office was secure. But he could not count on carrying particular measures dear to him. His aim was to broaden the bottom and quicken the head of his administration. The Northites slowly moved across to him as the strength of his position as *the* government became evident. Yet until 1789 Pitt remained the only member of the house of commons who was in the cabinet. His assistants in the lower house, particularly Dundas, were able men, but his influence there remained a personal *tour de force*. This heroic single struggle also gave, despite talk of the extinction of party, something like party unity and solidarity to his cabinet. For his lordly colleagues there acknowledged that his was the burden and his the inspiration. Therefore obedience to Pitt's will, when it was exerted, became the important unifying factor. Pitt was too ambitious and his colleagues too light-weight for the system of 'government by departments' to arise again. Yet Pitt's control of policy was not always exerted. It was essential to his role as non-party saviour of the state that he should consent to put forward some schemes as his own without compelling colleagues to do more than abstain from opposition.

Pitt's relations with the king were on the same pattern. If Pitt deserted him the king would lie powerless to decline the service of Fox and bondage. Both Pitt and the king knew this. It was obviously a strong card for Pitt to play if the king proved recalcitrant. Yet it was not a card easy for Pitt to lead, given the conventions which he accepted. For his standing in politics always depended on his being the man who put administration above pet projects. Unless he was sure of as much general approval of his arguments as existed in March 1784, therefore, he could not threaten resignation on any particular issue. Pitt's strength in battle with the Crown grew naturally as the years went by and consolidated his authority. But it was always subject, as in 1801,[1] to the qualification that he must remain true to the picture of himself accepted by the country; he could be right or wrong but never obdurate except when the king was universally felt to be perverse. As each claimed to represent a patriotic policy, much depended upon their skill in assessing the general will. Thus it is foolish to talk of the relations of king and minister as though they were independent authorities; they were as necessary to one another as husband and wife, and consequently their relations depended upon compromise whose precise form was settled not by a code but by character.

In 1784 the compromise was clear. The king would give full support to Pitt as an administrator: Pitt's more theoretical plans of reform would be ventilated but no pressure was to be exerted from the throne to cow opposition. The position of ordinary members of parliament was much the same as the king's: they would keep Pitt in government provided he left them free to decide on the merits of his legislation (as distinguished from his administration) for themselves. Thus it arises that Pitt's government at first presented an appearance of weakness in the commons in spite of the overwhelming victory in the elections.

Pitt's reforms of the customs were accepted in principle.[2] His regulation of India was, despite vehement attacks, passed into law. His India Act was a great reform, but it represented the inevitable conclusion of the conflict initiated by Burke. After the events of the past twelve months, even the most diehard conservative vested interests had to accept it as the most reasonable settlement of the problem. Much of it was a repetition of his previous bill.[3] A board of control was set up consisting of six privy councillors nominated by the king, changing as ministers changed. This ministerial board was to have sight of all the papers of the Company and was to issue orders to the directors of the Company, which they were bound, in practice, to obey.

[1] See below, pp. 401 f.   [2] For these see below, pp. 286 f.
[3] See above, p. 268.

Moreover the board of control could, in case of emergency, transmit the orders direct to India. On the other hand patronage, the appointment to offices in India, was retained by the Company subject to the king's overriding power to veto or remove. The governor general in Calcutta was, with his council, given absolute power over the other presidencies with regard to foreign policy. The weakness of the act here was that it did not deal with the relations of the governor to his council. It was not until the passage of an amending act in 1786 that the governor was given power to override his council. Then only was despotic rule in the East combined with parliamentary check at home. Then only would a statesman of the calibre of Cornwallis contemplate accepting the post. By a final section of the 1784 Act, British subjects were made amenable to English courts for wrongs done in India. All returned 'nabobs' were to declare their fortunes. An attempt was to be made to limit money-grubbing to a figure consistent with honesty and dignity in the Company's service. This was to be the system upon which a new and more austere life in India was imposed upon Company servants.

This victory was merely the closing of a chapter in a way made inevitable by recent disputes. The weakness of Pitt's control of the commons was soon demonstrated, and repeatedly. Early in the parliament he was personally rebuffed. The election for Westminster had shown Fox and Lord Hood above the Pittite, Sir Cecil Wray. But no return was made; instead a prolonged scrutiny of the votes kept Fox from appearing as the representative for this 'popular' constituency[1] with all the prestige it carried. It did not keep him out of the house as he had also been returned for the Orkney and Shetland islands. Fox accused Pitt of conspiring with the high bailiff maliciously to injure him. For nine months Pitt supported the scrutiny which kept Westminster unrepresented. But in the spring of 1785 the government was defeated by 162 to 124, the scrutiny was ended and Fox and Hood took their seats. In effect the house of commons had found Pitt guilty of ungenerous and personal intrigue against an opponent, a charge, considering the circumstances

[1] The popular vote had been 'got out to the polls' for Fox by a beauty chorus of aristocratic ladies: Georgina, duchess of Devonshire, Viscountess Duncannon, the countess of Carlisle, the countess of Derby, and Lady Beauchamp, all bought votes with smiles.

of his coming to power, particularly dangerous to him. In the next year (1785) the country gentlemen, as ever enthusiastic for cheap government, refused to rally to Pitt when he proposed to set right, at the cost of £760,000, the worst gap revealed in the national defences in the late war. The duke of Richmond, as master general of the ordnance, brought to parliament a plan for the fortifying of the dockyards at Plymouth and Portsmouth. After a tie (169 on each side) Speaker Cornwall gave his casting vote against the government.

More important aspects of Pitt's plans suffered similarly in these first two years of his power. Pitt had accepted Shelburne's economic policy with regard to America. But in the circumstances of 1784 it was impossible to discuss the integration of the economy with that of the United States. It was not until 1794—and then abortively—that conversations were opened for an Atlantic trading community. Instead in 1784 a new committee for trade, drawn from privy councillors, was set up to do the work of that board of trade which Burke had abolished. And this committee from the beginning tended to take a more mercantilist view of trade than Pitt himself, a tendency greatly increased when, in 1786, Jenkinson was made its president[1] and driving force. Pitt set this committee to work to help him solve the problem of Ireland. The acknowledgement of Irish legislative independence had made it urgent to co-ordinate the policies of the two countries. How was Ireland to be guaranteed her separateness and yet kept from conflict with the external and economic interest of Great Britain? The problem was now the more urgent because it became clear that legislative independence had not quieted the revolutionary movement in Ireland. The Irish were experiencing economic troubles for which they would, if left to themselves, seek remedies little to England's taste.

Pitt brought before parliament in Dublin (through the lord-lieutenant, Rutland, and the Irish secretary, Orde[2]) economic proposals designed to increase prosperity and prevent a conflict of legislatures. His plan was to fuse the economies of the two countries into one by admitting Ireland into the whole colonial trade and by adopting a system of trade between Ireland and

[1] And given the title of Lord Hawkesbury.
[2] Thomas Orde, first Baron Bolton (1746–1807), M.P., 1780; appointed treasury secretary by Shelburne; later governor of the Isle of Wight; a friend of the painter Romney.

England which should either be that of complete free trade or at least that of identical duties by the adoption in each case of the lower prevailing duty. In return for this privilege Ireland should bear part of the cost of maintaining the avenues of trade along which she was now to be free to proceed. The surplus product of the Irish hereditary revenue[1] (over £656,000) was to be paid to the account of naval expenditure. The Irish parliament was satisfied with the proposal after it had been amended to exempt Ireland from any payments until her overall account showed a profit. But in England an outcry was organized against Pitt. The merchants organized a 'Great Chamber of Manufacturers' led by Josiah Wedgwood to conduct the war of pressure and propaganda. It was alleged that freer trade would ruin English manufacturers, for Irish labour costs were 20 per cent. cheaper. Cotton, calico, and sugar were prominent in the discussion. It was said that the Irish would import foreign sugar and ruin both the British West Indies and those middlemen who observed the Navigation Laws. The propaganda was unrealistic but the panic was real. Members of parliament were moved by the widespread apprehension and the argument was never rationally conducted. Fox and others openly confessed their ignorance of the arguments of economists; it was enough for them to echo English traders. Pitt attempted to refute their case with argument. He then gave way to their obstinacy. He was not prepared to try using the authority of his office to subdue the wrongheadedness of obscurantism. The West Indies were to be protected against foreign sugar in Irish ships; the monopoly of the East India Company was reaffirmed; the Navigation Laws were to bind both countries. Furthermore, there was to be no duty on inter-island commerce lower than $10\frac{1}{2}$ per cent.: the Irish were to contribute to the navy even when their national budget might show a loss. Once more Pitt had put forward a favourite scheme to find the house elected under his banner unwilling to consider it. On this occasion his concessions availed him little. The Irish commons now arose in fury. Their benefits were decreased and yet they were expected to creep obediently into the English navigation system and pay for the privilege even when their accounts showed a deficit. Fox, hoping his words would be heard in

---

[1] Which were customs duties in the main so that increased prosperity under the new system might therefore justify an imperial charge.

Dublin, described this as 'bartering English trade for Irish slavery'. So great was the resistance in Ireland that Pitt abandoned the whole project.

It is in the light of these humiliations that Pitt's pursuit of parliamentary reform should be considered. He remained, he assured Wyvill, faithful to those arguments for the necessity of a reform of parliament which had brought him to a leading position as an opponent of North. Yet he knew that many who supported him as a necessary bar to Fox's faction regarded his reforming ideas as at best youthful folly and at worst a bomb under the pillars of order. The king agreed that Pitt should bring in a bill, but he could not pretend to hope it would succeed. So for all his promises to introduce the measure 'as a man and as a minister' Pitt could put no mention of it in the king's speech in 1785. None the less in April 1785 Pitt moved for leave to bring in his bill. He proposed to disfranchise thirty-six rotten boroughs, paying compensation to those who suffered thereby, and to transfer these seats to the counties.[1] In the counties he suggested the widening of the franchise by adding 40s. copyholders and some leaseholders to the established 40s. freeholders. This modest measure was ill received. Fox assailed the suggestion that they should buy a purer constitution by compensating corruption. This feature was the only one, on the other hand, that Dundas could praise. Pitt had forced the king to allow him to introduce his scheme, but he had no power to compel the cautious commons to pass it. They might talk of reform up in the counties when they despaired of seeing Lord North's incompetent hand removed. But with Pitt in power there was less need to heed Pitt's arguments. He was defeated (18 April 1785) by 248 votes to 174.

It must be emphasized that few of those who defeated him wished him to resign. He was still the corner-stone of national government, but the house insisted upon its right to reject his legislation. These terms Pitt accepted. He put aside thoughts of parliamentary reform as too partisan for the present. His attitude was understood by ardent reformers. Until the outbreak of the French Revolution Pitt was held to be a stauncher friend

[1] It is probable that Pitt also intended to enfranchise Manchester, Birmingham, Leeds, and Sheffield, the great new towns, as well as to extend the vote in Edinburgh, Glasgow, and Winchester. Such intentions were, however, only vaguely indicated in his speech in the house of commons.

to parliamentary reform than Fox. A measure could be introduced when time had made it less contentious. Yet time was to make it more and not less alarming. Electoral reform was shelved in Whitehall for half a century, advocated only by enthusiasts, revolutionaries or, very spasmodically, by an unhopeful opposition.

This was indeed a record of defeat for the energetic and masterful young man fresh from electoral victory. Yet already by 1786 Pitt was quietly gathering strength. He showed from the first those personal qualities which were to give him such ascendancy in politics for twenty years. In the Irish fiasco, for instance, his strongest characteristics as a minister were seen. He worked on a basis of precise information. His appetite for figures was great. His use of sources of information was catholic. His arguments were factual, clear, and cogent. His vision was both wide and calm. He was neither a pedant with eyes for nothing but the day's business, nor a man of excited imagination like Burke. He saw far, but calmly; to listen to him was like enjoying the luminous and detailed, flat but far-reaching, canvas of a Canaletto. He was at every point the practical man of politics. Above all, those who worked with him appreciated his patience and his loyalty to them. His method was not to reveal all that was in his mind. He was always a man of few intimates, who contrived to get his way in private conversations rather than in cabinet debate or genial symposium. But to those in whom he confided he adhered. These were qualities which won at once administrative assistance and house of commons respect.

The second element in Pitt's growing power was the attachment of men of business drawn from both Fox and North. The longer Pitt sat at the treasury, the more permanent his administration was seen to be, the stronger it became by the natural gravitation of men of ambition and ability to the seat of power. By 1786 the support of Eden, of Jenkinson, of Grenville, and of Rose was already evidence that the routine work of government was in capable hands. The art of managing man in normal eighteenth-century style was not to be neglected. Pitt used the reward of seats in the house of lords to buy waverers to his side.[1] The most efficient aid to this part of his system was provided by

---

[1] Details of the increase in peer-creation under Pitt in A. S. Turberville, *The House of Lords in the Age of Reform*, pp. 42 ff.

Dundas. Dundas, in his mid-forties at this time, was the earliest of the deserters from North to Pitt. He was not yet in the cabinet. But he was already the controller of patronage both in Scotland and in India, as well as being treasurer of the navy.

The solid support of the Scottish parliamentary vote, under Dundas, for Pitt, was not, of course, an abnormal phenomenon. The Scottish vote was usually to be counted on the government side in the game of eighteenth-century politics. The Scottish members of parliament supported authority in the time of Pitt as in that of Bute.[1] Dr. Johnson would have it that this was the sign of the national character of a Scot—'as abject to those above him as he is insolent to those below him'—or alternatively of the poverty of the northerner forcing him to scrape for jobs. The explanation is in fact more complicated. Scotland had been ruled, in fact, since the Act of Union by her presbyterian established church. The kirk was democratic in the sense that laymen were represented by election in all its governing committees.[2] At the same time it was authoritarian: each section of each parish was under the eye of an elder, with the penalties of public shame and excommunication to enforce obedience to a moral and social code. Moreover the kirk retained the power which in England had slipped from the church to the state. The kirk punished immorality and faithlessness: it conducted education both at the lowest and the highest levels. In short, real power in Scotland lay in the elective authoritarian councils of the church and not in the hands of the state. The law relating to customs, the taxes imposed upon land, these were generally scorned and intermittently enforced. The phrase in which the Scottish infant learned, at mother's knee, to sum up the relations of church and state, 'equal authority with co-ordinate jurisdiction' was in practice interpreted to the benefit of the church.[3]

This meant that Scotland was going her own ways in in-

---

[1] See above, p. 70.

[2] In schismatic branches of the church ministers were chosen by congregations, but the established church had had to allow the right of patrons to appoint to livings.

[3] It is only fair to add that the intellectual atmosphere in the higher ranks of the kirk was becoming less rough and fierce in the eighteenth century. There was a mild, almost latitudinarian, spirit in the universities which produced Principal Robertson, Hume, and Adam Smith.

dependence of Westminster. So, in fact, did the English counties under the justices of the peace. But the English counties relied upon their members of parliament to maintain this independence for them in parliament. The Scottish member of parliament equally was expected to watch with an eagle eye to prevent any administrative interference with Scotland. But his role was less important. In the last resort Scotland and her church would preserve themselves by force, as in the anti-catholic riots of 1779;[1] she rested on the guarantees of the Act of Union and her own self-will. It followed from all this that while the English member of parliament was a leading figure in the social life of his county, the Scottish member of parliament had no such status; he was an addendum not a local leader. The real use of the member of parliament was to get what he could for Scotland in a practical way from the rich English offices. The Scottish member of parliament was chosen not by the kirk or the people (even to the extent that an English member of parliament was) but he was chosen by a few aristocratic houses. This was one means by which the great chiefs of Scotland kept their authority high despite the competition of the direct democracy of the kirk. There was a balance of Scottish society in which patronage rested with the aristocracy and the fixing of a way of life with the presbytery.

The aristocracy were enabled to control this inessential luxury of parliamentary representation because the state of the franchise was so corrupt and little heeded. Out of a population of some one and a half millions there were 2,662 voters in the counties (with 30 members of parliament) and 1,301 in the burghs (with 15 members of parliament). The burghs were the ancient—and sometimes decayed—Scottish towns; their representation was effected through a system of grouping which still further lessened the chance of the expression of any real 'urban' sentiment.

'When we look', said Fox, 'to the Kingdom of Scotland, we see a state of representation so monstrous and absurd, so ridiculous and so revolting, that it is good for nothing except perhaps to be placed by the side of the English in order to set off our defective system by the comparison of one still more defective. In Scotland there is no shadow even of representation. There is neither representation of property for the counties, nor of population for the towns.'[2]

---

[1] See above, p. 235. [2] *Parliamentary History*, xxxiii. 730 (1797).

But then, we may comment, the purpose was not to represent Scotland (which was very effectively done in the kirk) but to run an employment agency for the benefit of her surplus men of talent and the preservation of her great family connexions.

Until Dundas, the grouping of the Scottish interest had been done either by the duke of Argyll or by no one. Dundas, one of a solid legal and landed family, set himself to organize Scottish representation as it had never been done before. It was a task calling for the patience of a Newcastle and for great local knowledge. When in 1775 Dundas agreed with the Stuart family that Mr. Henderson should be elected for Fife, he knew he would have to reckon with Argyll's support of a Mr. Skene and the backing of the rest of the county for a Mr. Oswald. When Oswald won the election he was promptly made auditor of the exchequer for Scotland so as to vacate the seat; when Skene was elected to succeed him, he had to be unseated on a petition.[1] This was an early and arduous experiment. By 1780 Dundas had so wormed his way into the heart of every Scottish bargain that he was the indispensable link in every choice of members. In the Scottish north-east, for example, the interests were many: the duke of Gordon, Lord Fife, Mr. Brodie of Moray (using a fortune made in India), Mr. Findlater, and Mr. Grant. None of these could succeed alone. The terms of their agreements were devised by Dundas; he gave some regard to each claim: he sugared every compact with his patronage. In the result, therefore, all the five seats in this area were held by men who would act only in consultation with Dundas who was, for them, the head of government.

After 1784 Dundas used all the skill he had acquired, plus the authority of the board of control, to induce the East India Company to distribute the jobs in the East as he desired. The thirsty plains of India absorbed the stream of Scotland's young men of energy. Moreover, with years of experience in managing men, Dundas was well fitted to build up disciplined support for Pitt in England as well as Scotland. That Pitt should rely upon this skill was natural. Dundas did not often interfere, in these early days, with policy decisions except when they involved India and the slave trade. Pitt might busy himself with projects while Dundas saw to it that the men were there. His complete absorption in his job and his loyalty to his bright

[1] For this incident see H. Furber, *Henry Dundas, First Viscount Melville*, pp. 192 f.

young chief elicited a confidence and—as far as that emotion moved in Pitt—an affection in return.

When all allowance has been made for the routine and pedestrian arts of politics in the consolidation of Pitt's hold upon power, it must nevertheless be admitted that a greater factor was the triumph of his own work on post-war reconstruction. In 1784 Pitt was in power as the champion of the Crown and the independents against faction: this meant that he could remain in power only if he succeeded in at least administrative reform. For this was intimately linked with the cause of financial solvency and fairer taxes. In 1784 the total national income was £18 million. £6 million of this was derived from the customs, £7 million from the excise (including salt), and £3 million from direct taxes. The war with America had cost some £100 million. The national debt imposed a charge of close on £9 million a year. In such a situation Burke and Fox had sapiently insisted that every extravagance should be eliminated from the king's service. But they had taken a partial view of the source of waste. They had been content to limit money for the civil list, and leave to others the task of making economies so as to keep within the specified sum. But the civil list made up less than one-seventeenth of the total annual expenditure, or less than one-eighth even of expenditure excluding debt charges. Pitt set himself the task of examining every item in the annual expenditure and he concerned himself not with totals or categories—even those with emotional political significance—but with the individual items, the work of every clerk in the machine of government. Thus to back-benchers seeking economy he was the man who knew how; at the same time economy arrived at by the reduction of sinecures had constitutional significance for it lessened the powers of corruption.

The work of daily scrutiny and improvement in government offices was the unremitted labour of Pitt's life. On this his reputation rests. It is a mistake to see the young Pitt as a reformer, the middle-aged Pitt a reactionary; to him, the law on habeas corpus or on public meeting was always of less interest than the great cause of efficient administration. Come war or peace, petitioning crises or anti-Jacobin coercion, Pitt steadily improved the system of Whitehall. He aimed at making executive government carry weight not by corrupt inducement but by its service, its stability, and its good sense. In his constancy to this aim he stood outside the fashionable way of framing the issues of politics as much in 1784 as in 1794. His strength consisted in his refusal to accept the ideas either of the Foxites or the Eldonites.[1]

In pursuit of reform as he understood it, the first task was to reduce expenditure and overheads. For this task he had ready to hand the work of the committees set up by North to examine the working of government. He continued to abolish sinecures. Characteristically, however, he preferred to avoid those pronouncements, those strokes of the pen and hand, beloved of Burke, with their necessary accompaniment of argument and strife. He chose, whenever possible, to mark down a sinecure and, on the death of its holder, he would refuse to appoint a successor. Thus quietly waste withered. It was a weeding operation spread over years, undramatic, visible only when comparison is made by decades rather than years, but the more complete for that. One of the few acts of positive legislation he used in this labour was the abolition of the sinecure offices of the auditors of the imprests. In 1785 the gentlemen enjoying these useless posts were replaced by a working board of five auditors. The new board did the work for a third of the sum the old had drawn from the State for not doing it. But, to avoid wounded feelings, the dismissed sinecurists were to be paid £7,000 a year each for life in compensation. This illustrates one reason, the expense, for avoiding whenever possible so decisive a method of proceeding: the other, the political excitement created, is attested by Pitt's failure to carry his bill abolishing sinecures in the customs service. In general, therefore, he chose to allow death to smooth the reformer's path. He waited for old Horace Walpole's death in 1787 before ridding the country of the costly and useless office of usher of the receipt of the exchequer: Pitt set up in its place the stationery department, which was designed to supply materials to all offices at wholesale prices.

A further method of reforming public offices was admitted to be that of replacing the old fee system by a salaried official class. In the treasury both Shelburne and Cavendish (under Fox) had

---

[1] John Scott, first earl of Eldon (1751–1839), a brilliant lawyer but a politician identified with the most extreme form of reactionary conservatism; solicitor-general, 1788; lord chief justice of common pleas, 1799; lord chancellor, 1801–6 and again 1807–27.

carried out schemes of this sort. In this matter Pitt made slower progress than might be expected. The reason is that while the saving to the community was great when moderate salaries superseded fantastic fees, nevertheless in the short run such developments increased the bill the government had to pay. In 1788, for instance, Pitt made Mr. Todd of the post office surrender his private profits on the packet boat service[1] but to effect this he had to add £400 a year as a compensation to Todd's £1,000 a year salary. In general, therefore, Pitt's support for a salaried system was evident only fitfully and when back-benchers in the commons agitated the subject. In every innovation[2] Pitt had to pacify vested interest or antagonize some of his supporters in the commons. In consequence he often appeared dilatory.

Yet while he moved slowly when the rights of individuals were in question, Pitt showed an admirable thoroughness in reorganizing the pattern of civil service work. The civil servants in the tax office (responsible for the land tax) were not deprived of their desks: but they found that the work they had to do there was inexorably increased. Pitt was determined to collect the arrears of tax on which provincial receivers grew fat and for want of which the government was in debt. Nine receivers were removed in 1784. In 1787 a treasury letter to collectors warned them of a new urgency. A system of inspection gave them no peace. As a result the outstanding balance due to Whitehall was sharply reduced. At the same time the tax office clerks were informed that they were expected to work on drafts of new taxes as well as collecting the established ones. Then in 1785 came a reorganization of work. Four offices employing eighteen commissioners had been required to collect a paltry £¾ million in assessed taxes. These were brought into one consolidated tax office, which had to administer also the taxes on carriages and on stage coaches and on horses. The excise board was relieved of some duties (but took over tobacco duty from the customs) and the tax office found its labours sharply increased. Nor was

---

[1] Mr. Todd had accumulated a fortune of £100,000 out of his life work at the post office.

[2] A further example might be the use of fast mail coaches on the proposal of John Palmer (1742–1818) for post office work; though these coaches increased post office revenue from 1785 onwards their introduction led to quarrels and difficulties in the office, and Palmer had eventually to be paid £50,000 compensation and retired from the service.

there hope of relief. For Pitt made it clear that he believed that as in the treasury (with an effective staff of 44) and the exchequer (with 300), so in all offices, fat would be slimmed away with the passage of time. He blankly refused any increase in pay to compensate for an increase in work. This, then, was yet another example of reform without purges, the reconditioning of government in the process of making it work.

A more famous consolidation was that of the customs duties. Here the saving was not only in the amalgamation of offices but in the ending of the old system of charging every loan upon separate items of duty.[1] Instead of keeping separate ledgers for every increase in duties and holding public money in a multitude of separate funds, the customs and excise were to be paid into one consolidated fund from 1787 onwards. The security of the public creditor was to rest upon the good faith of government as a whole and not upon his claim to some particular portion of some tax. Thanks to this reform the number of folios kept for records was reduced from sixty to twelve, with all the saving in hours and men's labour automatically flowing from this.[2] A new public security was given, moreover, to those whose official salaries were charged upon this consolidated fund. It was no new idea. North had proposed it. Fox would have had to consider it. But Pitt, as in so many spheres, earned praise because in fact he did it.

As part and parcel of this financial work Pitt took constitutional points in his stride. In 1786 the civil list, so long regarded as the king's private concern and kept so even by Burke, was reviewed by parliament: henceforward money was annually appropriated by parliament to serve particular purposes under the old civil list. Thus the modern conception of the civil list, that small portion of the king's money which he needed only for private purposes, began to emerge. Pitt, in taking further responsibility for public money from the king, brought to the task his zeal for economy. So also in the administration of Crown lands and woods he intensified the drive to make them profitable by the appointment of special commissioners in 1786.

---

[1] For details of this see above, p. 20.

[2] Unfortunately, new duties after 1785 were not always put to the consolidated fund. By 1797 there were eight new separate accounts being kept. They had to be reconsolidated in 1803.

In the negotiation of loans Pitt was not a great innovator. Outcry had been raised against Lord North for favouring financiers friendly to the government in the allocation of state loans. Pitt did not, except for the loyalty loan of 1796, attempt to raise money by an appeal to the country at large. He continued to use the accepted channels, the financiers on the treasury list, as agents. But he strengthened the competitive element by requiring offers to be made by sealed tender. The attempt to raise money by the offer of life annuities (in 1789) was a failure, only two-fifths of the required sum being raised. The national lottery, launched in 1784 (and only abolished in 1824) was Pitt's attempt to make use of the prevailing passion for gambling: its chief merit in his eyes seems to have been not the profit finally made on it, but the fact that the money came in some time before the prizes had to be paid out. The use of this balance before prize day helped to meet the government's temporary shortages of cash and so to reduce the issue of exchequer bills.[1]

It was, however, not enough to save expenditure and experiment with loan machinery. Income had to be increased. Ever since 1774 Lord North had been looking for new taxes; indeed, successive heads of the treasury since 1760 had been seeking means of diverting a fair share of the rising national prosperity of the country into the exchequer. All so far had been experimental and trivial. Between 1779 and 1781 most existing taxes had been increased by 5 per cent. Fancy imposts were produced whose yield often failed to justify the irritation they caused. Pitt, in his turn, played with such taxes, usually directly assessed. In 1784 he imposed taxes on horses used for sport and those for carriage work. In 1785 he brought in a graduated tax on personal servants which was imposed at a higher rate on bachelors than on married men (it was repealed six years later). In 1786 hackney carriages, pedlars, pensions, and official salaries were made to bear heavier burdens. In the 1790's hairpowder, dogs, clocks, and watches were all taxed. Meanwhile Pitt's tax on maidservants was intended to supplement his unsuccessful tax on shops. Yet to the detriment of all these taxes it must be admitted that they were broken into too many separate parts, too easy to evade and too costly to collect.

[1] Exchequer bills were anticipations of revenue secured upon particular taxes and put into the market by the Bank of England as a kind of short-term loan bearing interest at about 3 per cent.

Pitt's real reconstruction of the tax system was begun with his Commutation Act of 1784. The high tax on tea was a temptation to smuggling and the source of high expenditure on customs enforcement. Pitt therefore reduced the tea duty from the level of 112 per cent. to 25 per cent. *ad valorem*. The rewards of smuggling were thus lowered. At the same time the customs service increased their fierceness. Pitt congratulated himself that the destruction of boats drawn up on the shingle at Deal away from storm tides, would show that he was in earnest. To supply the revenue lost by the dramatic cut in duties, Pitt made a correspondingly large increase in a direct tax, that upon windows in houses. Pitt did not, as is sometimes supposed, invent a window tax. But he made it really important in the scheme of national finance. The tax was graduated, beginning at the rate of 1s. per window, and rising steeply in its rate per window over ten.[1] The tax was easily assessed and difficult to escape. It fell upon the wealthy with large houses while the benefit of cheaper tea was felt by the whole community. A further advantage of the reliance upon a direct tax on houses was, as North had seen, it would increase in its yield as Englishmen converted their newly made fortunes from trade into bricks and mortar. It had thus some of the moral and practical advantages of an income tax, while it was not so inquisitorial; the assessor could calculate from outside the liability to tax.

With his Commutation Act, Pitt aimed at increasing revenue by the only painless method—by associating it with a stimulation of trade and prosperity. So the commercial treaty with France can be regarded as a logical continuation of this policy. Pitt did not believe that free trade was a theory which could speedily be put into effect. He was, however, prepared to work for freer trade. After the failure of his Irish trade proposals[2] he turned to France. Adam Smith had argued that France would prove a better market for British commerce than American allies for it was eight times as populous and its propinquity trebled the importance of these consumers. Eden was employed as negotiator; the chamber of manufacturers, so hostile in the Irish negotiations, was used by Pitt on this occasion to supply him with technical information and advice. France was willing

---

[1] In 1792 Pitt did away with taxes on any house with less than seven windows. In 1797 (see below, p. 375) the tax on windows was trebled.

[2] See above, pp. 276-8.

to treat. She wished to keep England friendly while she pursued a forward policy in the Netherlands. Economic arguments, similar to those accepted by Pitt, also moved her. France, like England, had increased her national debt during the war in America; like England she sought relief for overstrained national finances in stimulation of mercantile trade. In the treaty it was agreed that the staple products and manufactures of each country should be allowed on easier terms into the other. The duty upon imported hardware was in either country to be 10 per cent. Cottons, woollens, muslins were to pay 12 per cent.; so were pottery, porcelain, and saddlery. The duty on beer was higher at 30 per cent. The duty on French wines was reduced to the lowest charged on any other nation. The duty on brandy was halved. Silk was excluded from the treaty. This last point is the main justification for regarding the treaty as a victory for England over French interests. In textiles, pottery, and hardware, England would at least hold her own or gain greater benefit. The English silk of Spitalfields hand-weavers could not compete with Lyons: and here the doctrine of letting manufactures find their own level was given up. French silk was to be kept out of England. On balance it may be said that English industry and French vineyards were the main beneficiaries.

It was still regarded as essential that expanding trade should be carried in British ships. The revived Board of Trade, under Jenkinson's lead, made the perpetuation of the navigation laws one of its main concerns in order to maintain in the peace the number of seamen, as expanded by the war. British shipping, which in 1774 had, including America, amounted to 701,000 tons, was in 1784, though all American ships were then naturally excluded, 869,259 tons. The loss of America had damaged the old triangle of trade across the Atlantic.[1] Strenuous but unavailing efforts were made to develop Nova Scotia as a grain supplier to the West Indies so as to replace New England in the imperial system. But Nova Scotia and Canada generally were not able to export corn. Illicit trade with alien America was a necessity to the West Indies. Pitt's government in 1787 made free ports in Jamaica, Dominica, New Providence, and Grenada. But their purpose was to open up trade with the Spanish colonies, not with the United States. For these ports were open only to foreign vessels which did not exceed 70 tons burden and

---

[1] See above, pp. 21, 22.

which were owned by subjects of a European state; the list of permitted imports was made up of those raw materials useful for British manufactures and for the island's agriculture. The carrying of provisions was reserved for British ships.[1] But Pitt nevertheless cherished the idea of mutual prosperity springing from the re-entry of the United States of America into an economic partnership. To this end he encouraged negotiations with America. In 1794 negotiations with Jay resulted in the plan of a treaty which, however, was still-born. In the last analysis the obstacle was still the navigation laws. Trade with America expanded all the time. But British statesmen were unwilling to allow ocean-going American ships to operate freely in imperial trade. The Americans would not submit to limiting themselves to coastal trade while relying upon Britain for carrying services on the high seas.

The result of Pitt's economies, of his stimulation of trade, and of shifting the bases of taxation were, he claimed, quickly visible in the accounts of succeeding years. He believed he could give members of parliament striking proof of the progress made and a pledge of relief to come. He proposed to reduce the burden of the national debt. North, it will be remembered, had aimed at devoting £1 million annually to debt redemption. But his surplus had disappeared and other calls had taken precedence of the scheme. Pitt had a parliamentary committee appointed which, in 1786, reported that there was now—and would continue to be in future—an annual surplus of £1 million. Pitt therefore appointed commissioners of the sinking fund; they were to be a public body operating apart from the treasury. To them £1 million was to be paid, in quarterly instalments, each year. With this money they were to buy government stock, below par when possible. The interest on this stock would be paid to them in the normal way and the money applied in turn to the purchase of more stock. Thus these public trustees would, in addition to their annual million, be enabled to apply the magic of compound interest to the redemption of loans. Pitt calculated that at the end of twenty-eight years their income would amount to £4 million.

---

[1] By a further act of 1788 foreign coffee and sugar were admitted in foreign ships to islands which did not themselves raise these crops. In 1793 the admission of tobacco to free ports in Jamaica, Antigua, and Grand Corcas was regarded as a blow to the United States.

Pitt's sinking fund owed a great deal to the ideas of Lord Shelburne's protégé, Dr. Price. It was a modified version of that nonconformist arithmetician's less practical project. No portion of Pitt's financial work has been more contemptuously criticized. Its later history has brought it into derision. For after 1793, in the frantic expenditure and widespread borrowing of the years of war, the government continued to make its annual million available to the commissioners. They could only do so by borrowing. The terms on which they borrowed were less favourable than in the past. There is obviously an absurdity in borrowing money at high rates of interest to repay loans at lower rates. Pitt is blamed for making his sinking fund so much a fetish that it was respected even to this point of absurdity. But the defence which his admirers made throws light upon the whole scheme. Pitt's object was from first to last to prevent his sinking fund suffering the fate of Walpole's.[1] It would always be a temptation to a hard pressed financial minister to sacrifice debt-payment to the needs of the hour. Hence the fund was made inviolable under independent commissioners. The payments to the fund were made a first and inescapable charge on revenue. In a lean year the chancellor must raise more revenue or he must undertake a short-term loan. To any such new loan a sinking fund of its own, a device of self-liquidation, was to be attached. Thus a minister's good intent would be held firm by the iron stays of statute. Thus, again, fat years would be made to pay for the lean and the process of debt redemption steadily pursued. Even in war the new loans would be funded and in the following peace the redemption of debt would proceed with heavier charges equitably spread out upon the nation. So long as war was an exceptional and passing interruption of normal life, this argument was sound. It was the length of the wars with France, twenty-two years long, which, making war the normal state and peace the exceptional condition, made borrowing to repay an habitual (and hence ridiculous) feature of the finances.[2]

---

[1] See B. Williams, *The Whig Supremacy* (O.H.E., vol. xi), p. 178.

[2] J. C. Herries (1778–1855), a good exponent of Pittite finance in the next generation, said (1828) that Pitt, in 1793, calculated that war would not last more than four years, and therefore made the inviolability of the fund his creed. Herries also argued that the action of the commissioners buying stock on the market helped to keep up the price of stock and so enabled new borrowing to be done more cheaply.

The steady reduction of debt by automatic rules depended of course upon the million pounds annual surplus really being available over an average of years. It implied, that is, that Pitt really had succeeded in solving the long-standing budgetary problem. In 1784 revenue was increased by £3 million, the increase being almost entirely from Customs. Expenditure was reduced by £10 million, the decrease coming from the slashing of naval and military expenditure at the end of the war. The surplus for the year was £¾. But in 1785 Pitt was not able to keep naval expenditure at the unnaturally low level of the previous year: an increase of £3½ million converted a surplus into a deficit of £2¼ million. In 1786 the revenue improved, rising by £¼ million to £18,300,000: expenditure on the navy fell, to give a total surplus of £1½ million out of which the first half year's payment (£½ million) to the sinking fund could be made. In 1787 heavy expenditure on the ordnance, plus a sudden (but temporary) decline in customs receipts on reorganization, produced a deficit of £1¼ million which was increased to £2¼ million by the payment to the sinking fund. In 1788 and in 1789 customs had revived; there were no special military expenses; the books, after paying the sinking fund, balanced. In 1790 there was no true surplus available for the sinking fund, but in 1791 there was £½ million surplus even after paying to the fund, and in 1792 the situation seemed to have been securely stabilized. Customs were yielding £½ million more than in 1784, direct taxation £¾ million more. £19½ million was the total revenue. On the expenses side, revenue collection cost £¼ million more, the Debt cost a steady £9½ million, the sinking fund was taking £1 million (plus receipts from the old sinking fund, £¾ million in 1792), civil government cost £1¾ million, and the armed forces required £5 million, £2¾ million of which was for the navy.

Thus from a review in some detail—as Pitt would himself have begged us to make—it did appear that Pitt had worked his miracle.[1] The burden of debt (half the annual expenditure) was in process of being liquidated without unfair or penal taxation. For if the situation in 1792 is compared with the

---

[1] The figures were not so clear to Pitt, indeed, as they can be to us. At the time of the introduction of the sinking fund he thought he had a surplus which was not in fact there; for the admiralty had issued navy bills and not made its full charge known. However, the future justified his introduction of the fund.

situation in Lord North's last good year, 1774,[1] it is clear that
more than three-quarters of the rise in income was derived from
increased customs yield on an expanding trade. At the same
time it is quite clear that Pitt's system of finance worked only
so long as there was neither war nor rumour of war. Expenditure on the navy had to be kept at a low level—though fortunately not so disastrously low as had been the case under
George Grenville. Every rearmament scare destroyed the budgetary balance.

Pitt, then, as a minister of financial reconstruction, needed
peace and cheap armaments: as a minister who rose to power at
the end of the disastrous American war he inherited the problem of British isolation in the face of a hostile western Europe.[2]
The basic facts were still the same. So long as the storm
centres of European diplomacy lay in the east—on the Danube,
in Poland, or round the Black Sea—and so long as France
declined to be embroiled in them, Pitt's hopes of finding allies
were remote. In 1784 and 1785 the Emperor Joseph II was the
trouble maker. His scheme for exchanging his Belgian provinces for Bavaria roused against him the self-interest of 300
little German rulers. The aged but great Frederic of Prussia
put himself at their head and so quickly forced the emperor to
abandon his scheme, that there was hardly any opportunity for
Britain and Hanover to play any effective part. Joseph II's
other project in the west was that of redeveloping these Belgian
provinces as he could not rid himself of them. He planned to
make a great trading centre there and to bring them fully under
control from Vienna. To achieve the first object he had to
force the Dutch to open the Scheldt for free transit to Antwerp.
In 1784 shots were fired on an imperial brig by the Dutch
troops at Lillo fort, all but opening war between Austria and the
United Provinces. England did not welcome the development
of Ostend and Antwerp as commercial rivals; she could not
therefore take Austria's side. But neither were the Dutch her
friends. To France, therefore, they addressed their appeals for
help and Maillebois was sent to take command. Pitt watched
hopelessly the struggle of two forces, both of them opposed to
his interests. The emperor gave up his ambition to open the

---

[1] See above, pp. 153 f.   [2] See above, p. 241.

Scheldt, but in 1785 France and the United Provinces bound themselves by a treaty of alliance.

Inside the United Provinces the aristocratic party, who were in the ascendant, valued the French alliance for its assistance in ejecting the stadholder from all influence in their affairs. Through the bad winter of 1785-6, with its floods and famine, excitement and francophil spirit increased in the United Provinces. The states of Holland suspended the stadholder from all his offices. The French were converting Cherbourg into a naval base. The opposition at Westminster assailed Pitt for sitting back and watching France wax stronger and more malevolent, imperilling British trade routes and markets in Western Europe. This was the background of Fox's attack upon the commercial treaty with France in 1787. Soon, however, developments inside the United Provinces began to assist Pitt. The aristocratic party were alarmed to find themselves not merely supported, but pushed along, in their attacks on the stadholder, by a popular party. It might be that the assault upon the House of Orange would be followed by a revolutionary upheaval in which all aristocratic privileges would be assailed. Thus in 1787 a reaction in favour of the stadholder was clearly visible. In this situation the French alliance counted for less. The princess of Orange, wife of the stadholder, was the sister of Frederic William III of Prussia.[1] The popular party, which had power in Utrecht, had stopped her, on a journey at Schoonoven, and had sent her ignominiously back whence she came. Prussia demanded amends for the House of Orange after this insult. The aristocratic party was not prepared to resist by calling in France. The Prussian army moved into the Netherlands, coercing the provinces of Utrecht and Holland. By October 1787 Amsterdam had been taken. The prince of Orange was fully restored as stadholder. England hastened to show her approval in a practical form. In 1788 alliances were made between England and the United Provinces and between England and Prussia for mutual defence and the maintenance of the *status quo*.

England had thus emerged, luckily, from twenty years of isolation. At last she had a value both to the United Provinces and to Prussia for the aid she could give in European affairs: possibly, she would need to help also in countering the schemes of Joseph II. For Joseph II was once more active in Belgium.

---

[1] He had succeeded in 1786.

In an attempt to centralize his power he issued edicts for Belgium which roused a revolution. The trading companies of Brussels, in language reminiscent of Locke, declared that the abolition of traditional privileges left them 'discharged from all duty and service to him, until due reparation shall be made for such infringements'. The university of Louvain was purged by the Austrians. Fighting broke out between Flemings and Austrians and dragged on until 1790. Then Joseph II's troops returned to their fortresses. The Belgians were assured of the restoration of all those ancient rights known as the 'Joyous Entry'.[1]

The reason for Austrian faintheartedness in Belgium was that the centre of interest was once again shifting from the Low Countries to the east. In 1786 Catherine the Great was fighting the Turks in the Caucusus and was in occupation of the Crimea. The emperor was determined to take part in a partition of the Turkish empire in Europe in collaboration with Russia. France offered her mediation and was rebuffed by the Turks. In 1788 Joseph fought the Turks along the Danube. He made small gains in Moldavia which did not compensate for the concessions which, in the stress of war, he was forced to make to his rebellious Hungarian subjects. Russia, at the same time, fought vigorously in the Black Sea and Caspian areas. Potemkin with 150,000 men laid siege to Oczakov near Odessa. There was a warm naval action on the shallow waters of lake Liman. The Turkish fleet retired from the mouth of the Dnieper back to a base at Varna.

This shift in interest was alarming to England. In such a war she was once more on the sidelines. But she feared a Russian advance towards the Mediterranean. It seemed possible that Russia might draw Austria and Prussia once more into her orbit and leave England alone in face of France. English sailors were forbidden to seek service with Russia while Pitt waited apprehensively the outcome of the Turkish war. The war was soon extended. Sweden chose this opportunity to reopen the struggle for supremacy in the Baltic with an attack on Russia in Finland. She was defeated at sea at Sveaborg. Denmark then joined the Russian side and invaded Sweden. When the Danes reached Göteborg the English were at last enabled to take

---

[1] The privileges of Brabant and Limburg which their dukes were obliged to swear to maintain before being allowed to enter the ducal residence.

action. In the interest of the *status quo* in the Baltic the Triple Alliance of England, Prussia, and the Netherlands intervened. They forced an armistice upon Denmark by the threat that otherwise they would take arms against her. Denmark betook herself to neutrality once more. The king of Sweden,[1] after defeat by Russia in Finland, made peace in 1790 on the basis of the restoration of the *status quo ante bellum*.

England had made herself felt in the Baltic by the alliance made in Holland. Yet the war with Turkey went on its menacing course without hindrance. In 1789 the Austrians took Belgrade, while the Russians under Suvorof took Bucharest. These events were, however, hardly noticed in the excitement aroused in England by the outbreak of the revolution in France. For this seemed to rob any other European event of dangerous significance. France, bankrupt and in disorder, ceased apparently to be a threat or to be able to take part in hostile combinations. In the very next year, 1790, this good fortune seemed to be emphasized. English fishermen in the Pacific had made a settlement on shore at Nootka Sound in what is now Vancouver Island, British Columbia (but which was then referred to as California). The Spanish, claiming the whole western American coast from Cape Horn to latitude 60° (Alaska), had seized the English ships. In great excitement parliament voted £1 million as a military credit and prepared for war. Spain, unable in the new circumstances to count on French support, gave way. British possessions at Nootka were returned; it was conceded that the British had a right to peaceful exploitation of Pacific fisheries provided that they did not come within ten leagues of any Spanish settlements on the coast.

Meanwhile the French assembly renounced territorial ambitions. Any British government was bound to approve such sentiments. More solid satisfaction was derived from the evident incapacity of the French to play any part in diplomacy. Thus freed from care, Pitt began to extend the sphere of his European activity. In 1790 the Triple Alliance stepped in to settle Austria's difficulties. Joseph died in this year leaving a rebellious Hungary, Belgium mutinous, and armies on the Danube who were fighting more for Russian than Austrian benefit. Leopold the

---

[1] The king of Sweden had pressing domestic preoccupations; he had just imprisoned the leaders of the nobility and begun to play the part of a popular king, opening careers to plebeian talents.

new emperor had reason to fear Prussian opposition to his accession. By the treaty of Reichenbach he gained Prussian support in return for allowing the triple alliance to wind up the adventures of Joseph II. Austria was repossessed of Belgium on condition that she guaranteed its ancient liberties. Peace was made between Austria and Turkey on the basis of things as they had been before the war: if Russia disagreed, Austria would desert her. The triple alliance tried to mediate between Russia and Turkey, but Catherine rejected their overtures.

Catherine's rebuff to the triple alliance raised for Pitt the question whether it was advisable to strengthen his foreign policy yet further. His foreign secretary, the duke of Leeds, argued in the cabinet that the triple alliance was England's only refuge from isolation. Therefore Prussia must at all costs be encouraged in activity against Russia. Leeds accordingly helped draw up an ultimatum to Catherine in March 1791; unless she would at once make peace with Turkey, restoring conquered territory, Britain and Prussia would take action against her. Catherine replied that she was not willing to return the city of Oczakov, which she valued as a base on the Black Sea. On 28 March the house of commons was invited to agree that an augmentation of naval forces would be required to enforce their will upon Russia. The address was carried by 93, the opposition resolutions condemning the policy were defeated by 80. Yet on 15 April Pitt drew up new dispatches which conceded to Catherine that Russia might keep Oczakov. The duke of Leeds refused to agree to such a surrender and resigned. In August Russia concluded peace on her own terms with Turkey.

The duke of Leeds saw in these events the failure of the whole of Pitt's policy up to that date.[1] The opposition rejoiced that the executive had given way to the legislature. It may be doubted whether the arguments in parliament really decided Pitt. He weighed the financial cost—'tho' they may support me at present, I should not be able to carry the vote of credit'.[2] Moreover, even if the money were available, how could such strength be asserted against Russia? It was not possible, now that Sweden had made peace, for the triple alliance to find a base to attack Russia in the Baltic. The Black Sea was 3,000 miles away and Prussia could not assist the British navy there. Pitt

---

[1] A view shared by Professor D. G. Barnes, *George III and William Pitt*, pp. 229 f.
[2] Ibid., p. 231.

also must have felt that action involving a European war, with the re-entry of Austria into hostilities, was only worth while if it countered the menace of France and Spain. But here was France obviously disintegrating, as the national assembly and the king drifted into strife. He would not, in the end, risk his political position by gambling on a war to avert a danger which was melting away.

It is true that the triple alliance began to collapse from this time forward. Prussia was discouraged and found it difficult to keep Leopold of Austria faithful to the Reichenbach agreement. Yet it is doubtful whether Prussia would not in any case have become cooler towards England. For the alliance was born in the Netherlands: the climate of eastern Europe did not favour it. In March 1790 the Poles had made an attempt to put their diminished territories in order. In 1791 they made a new constitution (with a hereditary monarch) hoping to prevent further seizures by Russia. The Poles asked Prussia for help. The king of Prussia, while promising it, made demands for Danzig and Thorn. It was clear that once Russia was clear of a Turkish war, she would turn to destroy Poland. It was equally clear that Prussia would be inclined to join Russia in a further partition and that Austria could once more be drawn in. The Polish question, in short, in 1791 as in 1772, drew the three eastern powers together to the exclusion of England. The alliance of England and Prussia could be animated by French attacks on the Netherlands and dissolved by Russian designs on Poland.

Lord Hawkesbury (formerly Charles Jenkinson), in his maiden speech in the Lords in 1792, declared that 'the strength and influence of France being at an end, we had no further danger to apprehend from that once formidable rival', but that the restless and ambitious views of Russia made her 'no less deserving of attention' as a rival of this country. Even if this were so it was not apparent how allies could be found to deal with this distant danger. In the past, in 1730, for example, France had been involved in Polish questions. In 1791 she did indeed complicate the settlement in Poland, but only by providing a counter-attraction of her own weakness to the German powers. The *emigrés* meeting at Pilnitz in August 1791 with the elector of Saxony, the emperor of Austria, and the king of Prussia, produced a counter-revolutionary programme to support the royal authority in France. In December the Imperial forces began a march to Trèves to implement these words with armed force. Thus a pattern of a Prussian–Austrian alliance against France was superimposed on the Prussian–Russian alignment against Poland. No English interest called for intervention. In the event of Austrian ambitions growing with success over France, it was safe to reckon on the automatic revival of Prussian co-operation with England in the Netherlands.

Pitt might well feel in Feburary 1792 that he had lost a foreign secretary but been presented with an easy policy. In his speech in committee he optimistically predicted a permanent surplus of revenue over expenditure[1] of some £400,000. He therefore proposed to begin at once on reduction in taxes to absorb half this anticipated surplus. There was no need to doubt the wisdom of this. The finances were steady, France was no longer a menace, his foreign policy was a success: 'unquestionably there never was a time when a durable peace might more reasonably be expected than at the present moment.' The opposition did not seriously dispute this statement, which prefaced twenty-two years of war; they questioned instead the morality of raising money by lotteries.

---

[1] Expenditure, that is, which included the fixed payment of £1 million to the sinking fund.

XII

THE COLLAPSE OF THE OPPOSITION
1784–93

IN 1784 Pitt stood alone, the champion of a new government free from the factions of the past. By 1792 he could point to a purer administration, to a record of steady purpose, and point forward to the prospect of tax reliefs. To the king, as to the squires, Pitt had proved his worth. Pitt was conscious of his personal ascendancy and of his lack of intimate association with his admirers. Hence he became increasingly a man who relied upon the magic of his reputation: he rarely confided in any one. Inscrutability was part of his stock in trade, for it enabled him to preserve his ideas for reform, free from argument, until a suitable occasion.

Under Pitt the idea of cabinet government developed.[1] In theory the king and ministers could still believe in departmental government and count the cabinet no more than a regular meeting of ministers individually responsible to the monarch. But Pitt's hold on the purposes of government, his will to power, his remoteness, and his prestige, all meant in practice that everything that was done required his assent; or at least, for Pitt was prepared to compromise with the king, it meant that no other minister could pursue any important line unless the king knew Pitt's views upon it. Pitt did not over-strain his power. On questions like parliamentary reform, the repeal of religious tests, the prosecution of Warren Hastings, or the abolition of the slave trade, Pitt was careful to deny that he wished to command his ministers. His influence on these questions seemed to grow despite his will. It did so because respect for his political acumen and fear of thwarting so powerful a figure increased year by year. In 1789 he rid himself of Lord Sydney, in 1791 of the duke of Leeds, in 1792 of Lord Chancellor Thurlow: he preferred to ditch a colleague rather than to dispute with him.

The cabinet, summoned by any ministers who felt the need

[1] On cabinet development see, particularly, below, p. 574.

of the advice of colleagues, gradually became an executive committee with a collective responsibility. It did so, not as Fox would have had it, from the party and friendly links binding its members, but from their common deference to one man; and that one man used it rather as a sounding board than as a place for discussion. For Pitt often enough decided policy outside the cabinet with Dundas or his cousin Grenville.[1] In cabinet he would then listen and reveal decisions. On at least one occasion he wrote the cabinet minutes in advance of the meeting.[2] This is not to say that Pitt had supreme power. In these private discussions with Dundas, or in the even more secret debates in his own mind, he had always to calculate how far he could use his prestige without rousing revolt from court or cabinet. Everything was a matter of timing and experiment: this was the reason why some called him dilatory and others deplored his lack of open intelligible policy: this was the reason, again, for the attacks upon his consistency.

Pitt's friend, Wilberforce, for instance, threw his whole political life into the cause of slave-trade abolition. In April 1792 he moved resolutions for ending the trade. Pitt had begged Wilberforce not to bring in the resolutions then: he had made no effort to stop Dundas from moving a wrecking amendment. Yet on that night Pitt's own speech against the trade—'that noxious plant by which everything is withered and blasted; under whose shade nothing that is useful or profitable to Africa will ever flourish or take root'—was the most splendid of all. His advocacy was not insincere, but it was not carried to the point of disrupting his political system. He was still a reformer yet he resisted both relief for dissenters[3] and reform of parliament. In view of his advocacy of the latter in 1785 his opposition to Grey's proposals in 1792 is the more striking. Pitt explained that reform was still desirable at some time so as to increase the

[1] William Wyndham Grenville (1759–1834), youngest son of George Grenville; privy councillor, 1783; vice-president of the board of trade, 1786–9; Speaker of the house of commons, 1789; home secretary, 1789–90; foreign secretary, 1791–1801, and president of the board of control, 1790–3; after 1801 stood fast in favour of catholic emancipation and allied with Fox; first lord of the treasury, 1806–7; leader of the conservative wing of the whig opposition, 1807–15.

[2] See A. Aspinall, 'The Cabinet 1784–1835' in *Proceedings of British Academy*, xxxviii (1952), pp. 243–4.

[3] Pitt opposed motions to modify the Test and Corporation Acts, so as to legalize the full participation of dissenters in civil government, in 1789 and 1790; he opposed Fox's bill to relieve unitarians in 1792.

prestige of parliament. But it was essential that the basis of English constitutional life should not be cracked in efforts to add a few improvements. When reasonable reforms were proposed by violent men they became dangerous. Reform, in short, was not expedient in 1792. Pitt enthusiastically supported Windham's picturesque argument, 'Who would repair their house in a hurricane?'[1]

No doubt the rise of a revolutionary wind in France did contribute to Pitt's caution. But a more important key to his actions lies in his conviction that he must stand or fall as the national minister, the embodiment of patriotic causes. Therefore, even when he was percipient and the majority (or the king) obtuse, he must only persuade; he must never go ahead to a point of no return, never use a big stick when a compromising speech would win universal respect and leave the future open.

One result of Pitt's attitude was a scarcity of memorable legislation in this decade of supreme power: apart from acts which were really part of the administrative reorganization there was, after the India Act, only his Canada Act. Everyone wanted to prevent Canada going the way of the United States. In the Act of 1791 Pitt's government divided Canada into upper and lower provinces, following rough racial divisions between French Roman catholics and English protestants. The assemblies of Canada were to be modelled on those of Britain. An upper chamber was to be created. It was hoped that the governor general with the royal power of creating peers would strengthen the executive (of which he retained effective control) by infusing into all departments of social life a respect for rank and privilege. The antidote to that radical breeze ever stirring across the Atlantic was to be an imitation aristocracy.[2] This act apart, it can be said that the most important statutory change of the time was promoted from the opposition benches. Fox's Libel Act of 1792 was passed in time to save many men from condemnation for seditious libel in the ensuing years of war. Until this act juries could only find whether the words complained of had, as a matter of fact, been published by the accused. The judge then ruled, as a matter of law, whether they were criminal

---

[1] Speech of 30 April 1792.
[2] For the end of this constitution for Canada see Sir E. L. Woodward, *The Age of Reform*, p. 363.

libel or not. Fox's act, however, gave to the jury the responsibility of pronouncing both on fact and law in libel cases.[1]

As Pitt avoided controversial change and concentrated upon his great and daily work of financial reconstruction, he presented few fronts for the opposition to attack. On the great issues ventilated in parliament it was difficult for the opposition to dissent from his personal views. Pitt and Fox were divided, until the 1790's, not by principle but by personality and past history. They both took a liberal view of Ireland, believed in state supervision of the East India Company, favoured reform, both economic and political, opposed the slave trade, and feared French rivalry. Even Pitt's growing conservatism was only really forced upon him by the need to keep the support of those who drifted to him from the old party of Lord North: in office, to gain exactly this support, though more formally, Fox had been obliged to promise to 'go slow'.[2] Pitt was unlike Fox in declining to express his views with passion in season and out of season; he was also unlike him in having the responsibilities of government upon him. The fact that he had this government authority was his offence in Fox's eyes. Never could his capture of power by a palace plot be forgiven him.

'There was no address at this moment', Fox shouted with an oath in 1792, 'Pitt could frame he would not propose an amendment to and divide the House upon.' The 'at this moment' was an unnecessary qualification. The opposition pursued Pitt with unremitting vigilance. But it was also with growing despair as Pitt consolidated his power and declined to give battle on general issues. In consequence the Foxites began to play all the old and stale tricks of opposition earlier in the century. They became, for instance, the party of the prince of Wales against the king, basing their hopes of power upon the person to sit on the throne and not on any principle.

It was a complaint of George III against Fox that he had led the prince of Wales from paths of virtue. Fox, said George Selwyn, had three interests which were, in order of priority, gambling, women, and politics. The prince of Wales almost inevitably became his companion in all three. For Fox's personal charm, the obvious and rough power of the man, was as potent in society as in the house of commons. Whereas Pitt drank heavily on occasion to relieve, one suspects, the strain

[1] See above, p. 57.   [2] See above, p. 259.

of constant alertness and tension, Fox drank his port out of bonhomie, out of expansive energy. So Fox was the shaper of London life for young men of fashion. His gambling away of his father's inheritance set the standard for play. His recklessness was satisfied in crowded rooms with high stakes by candlelight. Into this world the prince escaped from the uncomfortable propriety and etiquette of Windsor or Kew.[1] In this world the prince could be a king, even if his father thought him king of the damned. Kept from power by his father, it was a comfort to the prince to look forward to the day when he should be supreme. In that day he would reward all his jolly companions of the bottle and the dice-box.

The day seemed to dawn in November 1788. George III fell into a depressed and violent insanity. Pitt could not deny to himself that if this state were permanent, then his political enemies would displace him. Part, after all, of his claim to represent a national policy depended upon his approval by the king, for he would have agreed that 'The Regal power is that part in the Constitution which being detached from, and superior to, all the local parts, parties and interests in the Nation, exerts itself to preserve a constitutional equipoise and general interest in all the parts.'[2] A new ruler would have at least the initiative in proposing new men to seek general support in parliament. But Pitt hoped that George III would recover. Therefore he proposed that the prince of Wales should be regent under conditions. In particular his power of appointing to offices or peerages—and thus of entrenching his favourites —should be limited by parliament for at least twelve months, in the hope that the king would resume his functions. In answer to this Fox and Burke insisted upon the automatic right of the heir to full royal power once the incapacity of his father was known.

In this regency crisis both sides were driven to desperate arguments and changed constitutional places as in some fantastic minuet. Fox appeared to champion the throne against parliament; Pitt to decry it. The opposition denied that parliament was sovereign against the voice of reason. Pitt while contending for the supremacy of statute had to admit that his Statute of

[1] How uncomfortable and cold it was, Fanny Burney, that enthusiastic royalist, bears witness.

[2] From a fragment on the regency crisis attributed by Mr. Vere Somerset to Burke. Royal Archives, Windsor, Geo. 38403–38411, quoted by gracious permission of H.M. the Queen.

Limitations would only be resolutions and not an act, unless the royal assent could be given by the most obvious of fictions. Cries of treason filled the political world. The queen was made guardian of the king's interests against her own son. In a situation which did not admit of a perfect constitutional answer all men delighted in constitutional pedantry and all thought only of political advantage. In the midst of this, in February 1789, the king regained his sanity, resumed his power, and thanked his ministers for loyalty. It had been observed, however, that some had been preparing to desert to the prince. For Fox there was the mortification of seeing the promised land dissolve like a mirage.

Apart from the regency crisis, the opposition, however, could not launch many hopeful attacks. They could not oppose Pitt's financial programme: Fox claimed that he had resisted only the tax on shops. In general, therefore, they could only exploit difficulties over Ireland factiously, or reproach Pitt with failing to live up to his own promises on reform. It was in such a mood that they pursued the question of India. The issue was one to attract them all: the rhetorician Sheridan, the philosophical teacher Burke, the party man Fox, the moralist humanitarians, and those who wished profits from the East. For it was on an Indian question that Fox had lost power. It was in India that war seemed endemic, expensive, and open to French exploitation. Above all, the attack on Warren Hastings in India might embroil Pitt with Dundas or with the former supporters of North around him. Could Pitt be forced to fight and India brought to live in peace by the same shrewd move? With such thoughts the opposition marched into a narrow path, torrid, deceptive, long, and yet leading to no political end. On Warren Hastings the most prodigious efforts of the opposition were expended for seven years (1788–95) while Pitt once more side-stepped—and returned to his desk.

It will be remembered[1] that ever since the early sixties there had been two main complaints about East Indian affairs: the Company failed to make the profits expected of it, which was generally attributed to the corrupt practices of its local agents; the Company found itself drawn into war and the government of Indian provinces, activities beyond the normal scope of a

[1] See above, pp. 22, 23, and pp. 158 f.

trading company. Lord North's Regulating Act which had been intended to meet these criticisms had only intensified trouble. For since that act there had been general suspicion that the immense patronage of the Company was twisted to serve political ends of the government. A further element of criticism had become important by the 1780's: there was a growing humanitarian feeling which led to attacks upon the Company for neglecting—or outraging—the basic rights and decencies of the Indian population in areas of British influence.

Warren Hastings had been bred from a boy in the ordinary service of the Company. Clive had distrusted him for his excessive timidity, his tradesman's caution in handling great issues in Bengal. His experience had, in fact, given him a distaste for grand gestures or doctrinal solutions. He knew more of Indian life and literature than any other Englishman high in the service. From this he derived a distrust of general principles and a belief in personal arrangements to suit Indian conditions. He was at once mild and dictatorial. That is to say, he took account of difficulties, eschewed the role of reformer, and worked through friendships made with his English subordinates and with Indian rulers. But he was dictatorial in that he was never a good committee man, never a politician. He had never really lived in England, apart from childhood, until he resigned: his training was confined to the courts and contacts of a princely Indian society. As a result he was himself like a benevolent Indian despot, personally gracious but grandiosely personal in formulating policy. He was a good, even an indulgent, master, but he did not know how to share thoughts with a colleague. He never forgot a service or an injury, a friend or an enemy.

Hastings was from the first in an impossible position. There were two aspects of the governor general's power in India. He managed trade and had to make a profit by managing the investment: at the same time he represented the king and the majesty of British government. After Pitt's act these two opposing functions were split apart. Lord Cornwallis, the first governor general under the 1784 Act, knew he stood for government, answered to the board of control, could defy the mercenary interests of the Company when they conflicted with state policy. But under North's Regulating Act Hastings was supposed to serve both God and Mammon, or at least George III and the general court of the Company. He had to use the mechanics of an investment house to serve both the high political purposes of England and the welfare of a humble Indian population. He had, said Hastings himself, but 'a delegated and fettered power'.

North's Regulating Act may be said even to have weakened his authority as a public servant. For it was marked throughout with the eighteenth-century belief in the balance of power, opposing to the governor his council, so that the governor was automatically suspect to the council as the embodiment of corrupt Company interests: furthermore the governor could never count on support from the directorate at home, for they were the sport of political pressure groups and domestic quarrels. In such circumstance the strength of Warren Hastings lay not in government backing or in Company support, but in his own will, his own knowledge of the facts, and his own prestige. He decided for himself the correct balance between Company and state. To achieve his ends he relied upon loyal support of those thoroughly immersed in Indian affairs. This meant that he could not impose a new code of morality. He used men who had lived in the world of presents, rake-offs, and sinecures. He insisted that there should be a limit to corruption; it was not to interfere with the job being done or be flamboyant. But he would permit a faithful servant the customary perquisites. Only thus, by accepting the code of the Anglo-Indian, could he get his work done against the opposition of both the doctrinaires and of those who sought profit alone.

As he was aware of the inferior metal with which he worked, Hastings wished to avoid increasing the strain upon it. He tried to limit English activity in Indian life to a minimum. He never believed Clive's dual system was workable. In place of joint control by English and Indian authorities he wished to establish purely Indian states friendly to England around Bengal, while in Bengal itself he accepted the fact that the indigenous Indian government had been displaced. The merits of this course can best be realized by comparing the comparative justice and efficiency of Bengal with the hopeless, squalid, corrupt, inefficiency of Madras, where dualism persisted.

Inside Bengal it was Hastings's hope to leave local government in the hands of Indian officials acting under the supervision of central committees made up of senior English administrators. This freed the junior Englishman from the temptations of tyranny and left him to the cultivation of trade. It merged

Indian and English methods in a system at once understood by the people and checked by the governor. It was part of his attempt to fuse two cultures. He desired to revive Mohammedan and Hindu law. He studied and codified it for himself. The provincial civil courts were to administer native law subject to the control, in revenue cases particularly, of the governor's council. He did this not as a superior being but as one who admired Indian culture and accepted Indians as equals of Europeans in all but military ability.

Under Hastings's encouragement many Englishmen devoted themselves to the study of Indian culture. In 1783 Sir William Jones went out to India as a judge of the supreme court and in 1784 he founded the Asiatic Society as a centre for oriental studies, particularly for religion and law. North's Regulating Act established a new supreme court under Chief Justice Impey.[1] The limits of jurisdiction of this court were not clear. It should certainly have appellate authority over the mayor's court in Calcutta, long ago established to try the disputes of European subjects. But was every servant of the Company, whatever his origins, to be accounted a British subject liable to judgement by this imported English law? Was every revenue dispute to be within its competence? What, then, became of the quasi-judicial functions of the governor's council?

This legal battle was eventually solved by Hastings. By 1781 the new high court had given up its claim to decide revenue disputes. Impey had agreed to link the two systems of law in Bengal by personally serving on Hastings's civil courts for Indians. But this had not been done before at least one rajah had been ordered by the high court to pay, and by the supreme council to refuse payment. The dispute had embittered life in sweltering Calcutta and been reported back to the critical audience in Parliament and the East India Company. Its settlement was followed by the recall and impeachment of Impey because his wish to find a *modus vivendi* with Hastings was taken as evidence of his corruption.

Before Hastings had had time for many internal reforms and before the Regulating Act had come into full operation, he had

---

[1] Sir Elijah Impey (1732–1809), at Westminster School with Hastings; appointed to India, 1774, as chief justice of Bengal; president of the appeal court in revenue cases, 1780; returned home, 1783; impeached, but impeachment dropped, 1788; M.P., 1790–6.

been active in the external relations of Bengal. He desired the neighbouring state of Oudh to be independent and friendly. The vizier of Oudh, Shuja-ud-daula, was menaced continually by the Maratha confederacy which extended from Mysore's frontier in the south up the west coast to Rajputana and across central India to the Jumna and the Ganges. The Marathas by 1773 had the old emperor at Delhi under their control. Hastings had therefore refused to pay tribute any longer to the emperor. He handed the districts of Korah and Allahabad, which the Company held for the emperor, over to Oudh. In return the vizier agreed to pay 50 lakhs of rupees (£500,000) to the Company for the territory granted him and to hire troops from the Company for his own defence. A special representative at the vizier's court was to maintain the new cordial friendship with Hastings. But for Oudh to be militarily secure vizier and governor agreed that it was necessary to impose discipline on the Afghan warriors who, forty years before, had occupied land between the Himalayas and the Ganges. These Afghan soldiers of fortune, called the Rohillas, were suspected of co-operation with the Marathas. Therefore the vizier in one month in 1774 fought, punished, and subdued the Rohillas. He thus gave himself a defensible Ganges frontier against the Marathas.

Hastings was pleased with the new stability of his ally who could be used as a buffer between Bengal and the Marathas. But Englishmen at home were suspicious that he had begun on wars of expansion inconsistent with the trading interests of the Company. Moreover, British troops had been employed purely as mercenaries by an independent native prince. They were not in a position to restrain the vizier if he acted ferociously nor, in any way, to affect his policy. To which Hastings could answer that on a higher level he personally could persuade the vizier to act as a friend and a reasonable man.

The new councillors, however, arriving to act as a check on the governor under Lord North's act were in no mood to listen to his case. They withdrew his representative with the vizier, Nat Middleton, a man certainly not of outstanding probity but one as honest as their substitute Bristow; one, in addition, who was personally agreeable to the vizier as well as trusted by Hastings. The new council proceeded, after a week's Indian experience, to denounce the vizier for cruelty. When, in 1775, Shuja-ud-daula died, they increased the rates of hire for

Company troops: they forced the new ruler, Asaf-ud-daula, to cede the wealthy area of Benares to the Company and, contrary to Mohammedan law, they imposed on him an agreement by which the begums (the mother and widow of the dead vizier) kept three-quarters of the fortune of Shuja-ud-daula.[1] Oudh was weakened, bullied, and reduced to mutinous disorder by these transactions. Hastings's policy of the strong and good neighbour was ruined.

As has been said, the spirit of North's act militated against a strong governor. Hastings had, in addition, as it happened, to deal with men on his council who were fiercely prejudiced against him. On the other hand one, Barwell, was an easy-going experienced man who had made an immense fortune in India by means best left in obscurity. Barwell admired Hastings for his judgement and his courage. He became his ally. But the other three, the majority, came out from England taking for granted that any man who had lived in India for twenty years must be a rogue, a corrupter, and a liar. General Clavering hoped in a short time to replace Hastings himself: Monson was bad tempered and suspicious: the brains of the combination were in the head of Philip Francis.

Francis was a clever man on the make who used ideas as his sword to cut a way through the world. He excelled in the writing of intelligent minutes whose eventual result, if heeded, would be folly. He was a doctrinaire. He believed all Company servants were corrupt. He wished to reduce the power of such men drastically. He believed the Company should have no policy to put before Indian rulers; instead it should sit tight in established bases and avoid expansion by denying itself contact with the interior of India. He erred in supposing that an abdication of responsibility was the same as an improvement in policy. To Hastings, busy with unavoidable choices between evils, Francis must have seemed to resemble Pilate, constantly washing his hands. Francis would boycott all who had personal loyalties which would not let them give unquestioning loyalty to the new majority on the council. Before they had set foot in India, or met the governor, Francis had decided that Hastings must be checked. Francis's power to effect his purpose was great. He had the authority of a new act behind him. Everyone knew how rotten the Company had been in the past and how shady

---

[1] Which amounted to some £2 million.

was the history of many whom Hastings, if he was to have any government, had to employ. Finally Francis excelled in the committee, the clique, the confabulation before a decisive meeting. To all this Hastings could only oppose a wounded hauteur and a well-informed, stubborn, resolve.

Between 1774 and 1777 the majority on council reversed Hastings's policy in Oudh, they abolished the bank he had established to benefit trade, they demoted his agents, they criticized the government salt and opium monopolies, they accused him of extortion in collecting taxes from native zemindars.[1] They tried to prove him personally corrupt. In the course of his service in India Hastings accepted £300,000 in presents from rulers which he turned over to public service of the Company. Later on, in 1784, he was to ask for some of this to be credited to him personally. His conduct was hardly discreet. It is a bad principle to combine public decisions with the acceptance of presents. But Hastings, unlike Clive, passed on the presents to the Company. He published his acceptance of them. It was the custom of India. Francis and Clavering themselves seem to have been willing to accept presents—and to keep them for themselves. In this, therefore, there is little basis for an attack on Hastings's probity. It is much more serious that Hastings only limited and did not stop the private trade of Company officials and their profits out of supplying public needs. He may himself have been sleeping partner in business enterprises which exploited this situation. His private fortune, like those of his subordinates, could be brought home in diamonds and escape investigation. Hastings would have answered that his bank, now abolished, was intended gradually to reform this system. Again, it was the custom. Better to govern well by gradually improving the system than to produce chaos by throwing every Company servant into revolt. If he had taken such a rash course he would have been disowned and dismissed by London.

Francis, Clavering, and Monson chose, in 1775, to attack Hastings on a trumped-up charge of corrupt dealings with the Mani Begum in 1772. Their agents were a Brahmin financier and money-lender, Nandakumar, and a European diamond dealer from the commercial underworld, Joseph Fowke. These two collected evidence from any source in the back streets of Calcutta. As soon as it was rumoured that the governor was

[1] For a discussion of 'what was a zemindar?', see below, p. 313.

falling, a mass of Indian evidence was available from every liar who sought to curry favour with the rising power of Francis. Francis was foolish enough, or headstrong enough, to use all this quite uncritically. Nandakumar had, however, for many years been engaged in a civil law suit in which he had committed forgery. Hastings proceeded to charge Nandakumar and Fowke with conspiracy against him. The governor was evidently fighting back. This encouraged Nandakumar's enemies in his civil suit to gamble on Hastings's eventual triumph. They had the money-lender arrested for forgery. They refused to allow proceedings to be protracted or compromised in the usual Indian way. They had Nandakumar brought before the supreme court, tried by English law, found guilty, and executed. It was enough. The Indian favour-seekers decided that Francis might scream, but Hastings struck. There was a rush to change sides and conciliate the governor.

Francis, of course, accused Hastings of the judicial murder of an awkward opponent. All that had happened, however, was that Hastings's friends had gambled on his eventual success and the governor had not intervened to save Nandakumar from death. The result was a gain in Hastings's position in India. But the fight had been transferred to London. Francis had invited the government to replace Hastings by Clavering or by himself. Lord North was appalled to see how his India Act had produced chaos instead of reform. It was natural he should support the majority against Hastings, who was little known in England but had been put in as a man of experience to initiate the new system. Lord North persuaded the directors of the Company to vote Hastings's dismissal, but they were overruled by a shareholders' meeting. Hastings's agent in London, the reckless financier Macleane,[1] had, in the midst of the Nandakumar affair, been authorized to offer Hastings's resignation. This he now did, hoping to get Lord North out of an awkward position and so earn for Hastings honour in retirement.

One must remember the time consumed in sending messages between India and England. Hastings had given Macleane authority in March 1775. It was used in a letter to the government in October 1776. Hastings did not hear of this until June 1777. By then Hastings was feeling more secure. But on receipt of the news from London General Clavering declared Hastings

---

[1] See his past history, above, p. 166.

already out of office; he summoned a council and declared himself governor. Hastings's reply was to order the troops to stand by under his orders and to appeal for a constitutional ruling to the supreme court. The court ruled that Hastings had not yet resigned and that Clavering's attempted coup was illegal. Hastings now declared he could, after such a show of force against him, no longer resign with decency. He wrote to North withdrawing his resignation. By the time he had this letter North was in such parliamentary difficulties that he could no longer insist on it. Soon he was glad to reappoint Hastings because America claimed all his attention.

Death also favoured Hastings. Monson died in 1776 so that from then, until the arrival of his successor, Hastings plus Barwell and a casting vote could defeat Francis. Then, before Wheler arrived to replace Monson, Clavering also died. 'My antagonists sickened, died, and fled. I maintained my ground unchanged, neither the health of my body nor the vigour of my mind for a moment deserted me.'[1] Hastings resumed his active government. Francis was arguing that the Bengal revenue was erroneously assessed and incapable of collection. He proposed that fixed sums should be required of the zemindars to give a permanent land revenue. This argument assumed that the zemindars were like English landowners and could expect a fixed impost like the English land tax. This was bad finance and worse fact. The zemindars were something between feudal tenants, landlords, and revenue collectors. There was no reason why demands on them should not vary according to circumstances. Moreover, as Hastings pointed out, to leave the peasant unprotected against the zemindar was not a benevolent policy. Hastings therefore organized the Amti office to investigate the worth and taxable capacity of individual holdings in Bengal, with the double purpose of fixing a just rate to demand from the zemindar and to check oppression by him of the cultivators of the soil. Francis fulminated in vain against such open intervention in Indian life. Hastings later followed this up by abolishing the provincial councils; of the displaced Company officials he made local magistrates. Incidentally he thus inaugurated that system of local rule by English magistrates which was the basis of the later English administration of India.

By 1778 the fruits of Hastings's policy were evident in

[1] K. G. Feiling, *Warren Hastings*, p. 345.

London. The crisis produced by the great famine had receded. The Company, at least in Bengal, seemed solvent again. There was still, in fact, jobbery—Hastings gave Impey's cousin Fraser a contract worth £15,000 a year for keeping up bridges in Burdwan—but at least the Company was not bankrupt from it. The investment sent to England was larger than ever before. Only in Madras had conditions grown worse, but there Hastings's authority was only nominal. Hastings needed but a few years' more prosperity to return home to a peerage. Instead he spent the next five years fighting for survival, and then returned home to face impeachment.

The balance of power among Indian states was still precarious. The Marathap pentarchy constantly threatened to expand and, in the south, Mysore was another restless power. The Bombay English settlement favoured intervention to secure itself against the Marathas. The king of the Marathas had ceased to count. The confederacy was headed by a Peshwa or hereditary Prime Minister. From 1773 there had been a dispute for this office between one Raghurath Rao, known as Raghoba, and his infant grand-nephew. The Bombay council in 1775, without Hastings's knowledge, intervened on the side of Raghoba, though they risked bringing down the whole confederacy on them. By the treaty of Purandhar (1776) they gained Salsette and agreed to desert Raghoba. This settlement was forced on bellicose Bombay by Hastings who wished for peace yet, unlike Francis, was unwilling to humiliate the Bombay council.

Hastings agreed with Francis in opposing extensions of territory. But he was anxious to see his influence increase, making Oudh once more a happy ally, working to detach Berar from the hostile confederacy, hoping in time to rectify the disgraceful muddle which spread out from Madras over the whole Carnatic. It was to Hastings therefore a sinister sign that a French agent had been honourably received at Poona, the headquarters of the Marathas. So when Bombay marched against the Marathas (alleging their failure to abide by the treaty of Purandhar) Hastings stood by them. Nana Farnavis, the effective ruler of the Marathas, was accounted an ally of France. It would be well to replace him. Bengal fitted out an expedition to march right across India, east to west, to the aid of Bombay forces.

Bad news reached India. It was learned that Burgoyne had

surrendered to the Americans at Saratoga and that France had declared war on England. Soon the French admiral Suffren swept the sea approaches to Bengal, strong enough for anything except an actual invasion of British-held territory. Hastings seized French settlements, he raised new battalions of sepoys, he laid in stores, he called in money from friendly princes and sent his agents to Mysore and to Berar to counterwork the purposes of France. It was a grievous blow that at this juncture the army of Bombay was surrounded and forced to a shameful surrender at Wargoon. Francis at once blamed all on the militant spirit of the governor and argued for peace at once and at any price. Hastings replied that their existence, not just expansion, depended upon British prestige in India. Disaster was therefore a signal for further heroic efforts. By February Goddard,[1] in command of the east to west march, successfully arrived at Surat on the Bombay coast. It was a task achieved thanks to the concealed friendship of the rajah of Berar.

With his own general in command at Bombay, Hastings now strove to batter the Marathas into quiescence. Goddard attacked Ahmadabad and Gujarah, and made peace with the Gaikwar of Baroda. While this operation drew Maratha attention to the west, Hastings, from the east, invaded the territories of Mahadaji Sindhia, one of the most powerful chiefs. Under Captain Popham a small force climbed the reputably impregnable walls of Gwalior fortress one dark night, and astonished all India by capturing this 'key of Hindustan'. By this and other defeats Sindhia lost heart. He began to negotiate for peace both for himself and for the rest of the Maratha confederacy.

Philip Francis had made, however, one final assault upon Hastings, in the very crisis of the war. He had agreed to allow the governor to carry on military operations and Hastings in return had allowed his solid old voting aid, Barwell, to retire. Then Francis ventured to criticize operations. The governor, in an official minute at council, labelled him 'void of truth and honour', the propagator of fabricated massacres and aggravator of misfortunes.[2] As a result Francis called Hastings out to a duel. Francis was wounded. 'The British Empire in India', he wrote,

---

[1] Thomas Goddard (d. 1783), an active soldier in India since 1759; much trusted by Hastings.

[2] G. W. Forrest (ed.), *Selections from the State Papers of the Governors-General of India*, vol. i, Warren Hastings, p. 188.

'is tottering to its foundation in spite of everything I could do to save it.' He resigned and returned to England—to fight again with pen instead of pistol.

The British rule did seem in 1780 to be shaken desperately, even though the fight against the Marathas had prospered. For in Madras the local government had brought fresh war upon themselves. They had angered the Nizam of Hyderabad by seizing the Guntur Sarkar area and installing a garrison there. Even worse they marched to attack a French trading post at Mahé, inside the territory of Mysore, without the consent of Haidar Ali. Haidar Ali sought and obtained the sympathy of Berar and Hyderabad and then burst furiously across the territory of the Carnatic. British troops fled before him as he burned his way to the walls of Madras. Once more it seemed that all India was rising to force the British into the sea.

Hastings's response was heroic and decisive. He bribed Berar to hold up hostile acts. He promised amends to Hyderabad. He suspended the acting-governor of Madras. He sent the avaricious, irascible, but still splendidly pugnacious Sir Eyre Coote[1] (who had been latterly on the Bengal council) to take military and civil command in the Carnatic. Above all he strained every nerve to give Coote's forces the gold, cattle, rice, and grain on which they depended. So, though the French under Bussy arrived to help Haidar Ali, Coote won victories in 1781 (Porto Novo) and 1782 (Arni) which saved the situation though they did not end the war.

British prestige had been restored. In 1782 peace was made with the Marathas. Peace was not made with Mysore (where Tipu had succeeded his father Haidar Ali) until 1784 and then on terms disliked by Hastings. But the new governor at Madras, Lord Macartney, insisted upon running things his own way, which meant snubbing the nawab of the Carnatic and making peace (at Mangalore) on a basis of the *status quo* with Mysore.

Hastings, in the years when Britain lost heart and empire in America and was obliged to make peace with a successful French government, had not only sustained himself in India,

[1] Sir Eyre Coote (1726-83) had served against the Pretender in 1745; in India distinguished by the victory of Wandewash, 1760; came home in 1762; M.P. Leicester, 1768; returned to India, 1769; commander in chief in India, 1777; died at Madras.

but had enormously improved British standing there without aid from outside.

'I sent forth its armies with an effectual but economical hand . . . to the retrieval of one [possession] from degradation and dishonour, and of the other from utter loss and subjection. I maintained the wars which were of your formation or that of others—not of mine. . . . When you cried out for peace, and your cries were heard by those who were the object of it, I resisted this, and every other species of counteraction, by rising in my demands, and accomplished a peace, and I hope a lasting one, with one great state: and I at least afforded the efficient means by which a peace . . . was accomplished with another.'[1]

This Herculean accomplishment had strained the financial resources of Bengal. So tight was money that in 1784 Hastings's own salary could not be paid but he had to borrow some £30,000 from an unsavoury old moneylender (who had been his teacher in Persian) called Nobkissen. Nobkissen begged him to take it as a gift. He later devoted the money to that encouragement of eastern learning which was, in the most hectic days, still close to his heart. This episode was later used to attack his honesty. Far more serious were the two other crises produced by the Company's need of money. The Company called on its dependent rulers to assist it. The zemindar of Benares (detached from Oudh by Francis on his arrival in India) was rich because Benares was a city of pilgrimage. The zemindar, Chait Singh, was under-taxed. It was rumoured he could pay double the 22½ lakhs (about £230,000) a year required from him. Afterwards his successors certainly found 40 lakhs a year without difficulty. For the duration of the war he was, in any case, given an extra contribution of 5 lakhs to find. These war contributions he delayed. He gave Hastings a present of £20,000, which the governor devoted to war expenses, but he failed to provide 1,000 horsemen required of him. In 1781 Hastings proceeded to Benares in state, having made up his mind to fine Chait Singh £½ million or to depose him. The rajah grovelled at his feet and laid his turban before the inflexible governor. Hastings was not moved by beating of chests or wailings: he was set upon apology and a fine large enough to mark the offence and advance the war. He arrested the rajah. At this point Chait

---

[1] Hastings's Address: 2 June 1791: *Trial of Warren Hastings*, ed. E. A. Bond, vol. ii, p. 521.

Singh's followers in hysterical panic fell upon Hastings's body-guard and slew them, and then besieged the governor. From this situation Hastings recovered by his coolness. He stayed quietly with the inadequate troops he still had, refusing for the sake of prestige to accept aid from Oudh, and waited for British reinforcements. The rebellion was crushed, but Chait Singh escaped with a good portion of his treasure. £230,000 from his hoards was in error dispersed among the British troops in the course of this minor war. So, as a financial expedient, the cowing of Chait Singh was a failure. It had also showed Hastings at his most overbearing and despotic.

At this same time the nawab of Oudh was in arrears with his payments to the Company. The need for ready cash forced Hastings to urge every sort of reform, public and private, upon the weak Asaf-ud-daula. He accepted a present of £100,000 from the thriftless ruler, and applied it to the Company service as a voluntary contribution of his own. He did not therefore slacken in his efforts to reform the government of Oudh. The governor agreed to withdraw costly British troops and to order British merchants, who battened on the nawab's weakness, out of Lucknow. In return the nawab promised to grasp power, rid himself of luxurious favourites, and pay up what he owed. Between them it was soon agreed to take from the begums, his grandmother and mother, what Francis and the majority had weakly granted them six years before. For the begums hated the nawab—his grandmother had any chair he might sit on promptly broken to pieces as unclean. The begums were suspected of having given aid to Chait Singh. Their jaghirs (grants of land revenue) were taken from them. As the two ladies, in their zenana in the palace at Fyzabad, refused to hand over their store of treasure to aid further in the liquidation of Oudh's debts, their two eunuchs, their men of business, were put in irons, kept without food, and punished by the nawab; Middleton stood by to prevent abuse of power or slackening of resolve. Most of this money went to pay what was owing to the British. Yet by 1784 Asaf-ud-daula had again fallen into their debt by as much as £¾ million.

Hastings had disregarded plighted faith in encouraging the robbing of the begums. Yet he pleaded that he did so partly to restore the strength of Asaf-ud-daula's government, partly to meet the war-needs, and partly to punish rebellious intent.

Moreover the begums were, even after this spoliation, left in wealth and themselves continued to regard him as a friend and faithful ally of their family.

To these desperate and rash moves the war had driven Hastings. At its end he hoped to resume the work of stabilizing Company finances. But he still lacked power to order all he would. From home he heard only sweeping (and uninformed) condemnation of Indian government. Pitt's India Act was almost as much a condemnation of the old order, within which he had done his best, as Fox's bill. In January 1785 he resigned and sailed for home, composing on the journey an account of his career which shows only too clearly how authority maintained in such difficulties had killed his powers of self-criticism, and how the sun had burned him stiff and brittle.

Hastings wrote this account of his career in part to answer critics but in part to justify the honours he expected. Yet on his return he was soon the universal scapegoat. 'I gave you all, and you have rewarded me with confiscation, disgrace, and a life of impeachment.' In this Burke was the chief mover. All the Foxite opposition squirmed under the never to be forgotten crushing blow of 1783, which they interpreted as a counter-revolution by a corrupt gang of East Indian directors allied with the court and using Pitt. Philip Francis had convinced Burke that Hastings stood for the corruption of the bad old system. Burke sincerely burned against the tribe of money-grubbers in India. A purified, independent, Company, uncontrolled by Pitt's political friends, was his ideal. To the private fortunes of the 'nabobs' he attributed all the weakness of the Company. He blamed them for the ruin of his friends in business,[1] and the defeat of his allies in politics. That William Burke, paymaster in India, was as corrupt as any, was a member of the Tanjore set against the Arcot set, does not damage Burke's good faith. It was an endearing side of his nature that he refused to see evil in his friends. In passing events he saw great and lasting lessons. The principles he perceived in this way he eloquently taught to his less philosophical hearers. So he had turned Rockingham's American policy into lessons of imperial statesmanship. So he was to use the stories of French émigrés to formulate a conservative philosophy of politics in his 'Reflections on the French Revolution'. So now he meditated on the

[1] See above, p. 166.

shortcomings of Englishmen in India, the losses caused to England and the suffering inflicted on Indians, and enunciated a doctrine for dealing with Eastern races. Unfortunately he also decided to use the figure of Hastings to represent all that was wrong. His play was one of ideas, but it was miscast.

Burke's error can be excused. Hastings worked within a bad system. All Burke's fulminations about Madras were justified. There the English money-lenders ruled all, and when governor Pigot, backed by the Rockinghams at home, attempted to defy them he was imprisoned by his own council. This was not Hastings's work. But he had not supported Pigot. In his last years in India he had enjoyed the support of Sir John Macpherson, one of the richest of the Madras ring. He had opposed Macartney who had controlled the Nawab and his parasites. Burke read the worst of motives in all this. For in truth, before Hastings had returned, Philip Francis had used all his cleverness to feed Burke's imagination with the facts it craved.

Hastings himself increased Burke's certainty of purpose. Hastings's megalomania, his bland self-confidence, his craving for honour and position in England, made Burke strain to pull away his mask and break his stiff spine. Hastings's agent in parliament, Scott,[1] taunted Fox and Burke with their failure to follow up charges against the returned governor. In 1782, in his absence, the house of commons had condemned Hastings. Here he was in England waiting to reply. The answer of Burke, Fox, and Sheridan, assisted by Windham, was to move that Hastings be impeached. Their first charge, concerning the Rohilla war, was rejected by the commons. But on their next two, the treatment of Chait Singh of Benares and the spoliation of the begums of Oudh, the house supported them. In the course of the seven years' trial before the house of lords many other accusations about Hastings's life and finance were ventilated. But the flash point for this long-rumbling explosion was the vote in the house of commons on the Benares charge. It was decisive because Pitt apparently changed his mind.

Pitt had come to power by opposing Fox's India Bill; he might therefore be thought a friend to Hastings when the latter became the target for Fox's fusillade. This was not so, however. For Pitt, perhaps more than Fox, wished to discipline the East

---

[1] John Scott (1747–1819), major in the Bengal army; came to England, 1781, as agent for Hastings; M.P. West Looe, 1784.

India Company. He had now his board of control and Dundas was mastering the art of Indian patronage. But it was still necessary to cow and correct the Company. Hastings—many as his enemies among the factions of the Company were—was the greatest public figure the Company had ever produced. To snub him was to keep the Company in a properly subject spirit; it was a psychological reinforcement of the regulating act. Dundas certainly wished to keep so formidable a rival in Indian affairs out of power, immobilized. That Thurlow approved of Hastings was a further reason why none of Thurlow's colleagues should.

Pitt, as usual, played the role of an open-minded man of judgement. He supported Hastings on the Rohilla war issue with great power of common sense. He sent to Hastings for explanations of the position of a zemindar before the decisive debate on Chait Singh. Most of Pitt's back-bench admirers came to the debate to knock Burke down again. Pitt's speech surprised them. He successfully demolished Burke's main lines of argument because they were founded on errors about the rajah's status and about Indian life. But then he proceeded to declare that, all the same, the fine Hastings had proposed to levy was so vindictively too great that he must record condemnation of him on that account. It was a very clever stroke. Pitt was exercising a right that no politician is entitled to—of judging a question exactly on its intrinsic merits, in isolation, without regard to consequences. It was exactly true that Hastings had intended to be unduly severe. For this intention he must no doubt answer to God on judgement day. Pitt might, as a private individual, therefore refuse to approve him, despite the hundred other ways in which he had earned approval. But as Pitt was not just a private individual his adverse vote meant that Burke's charge would be supported by a majority. It inexorably followed that an impeachment of the whole of Hastings's career—not just of his one thwarted intention—must proceed. So Pitt, insisting on a nice distinction, was responsible, while not appearing to take any responsibility, for allowing Burke to proceed with his frenzy and Hastings to endure his purgatory.[1]

---

[1] Warren Hastings believed Pitt had been persuaded by a last-minute talk over breakfast with Dundas to vote as he did on the Benares charge. This seems evidence of Hastings's failure to understand Pitt's political position, his character, and his subtlety.

Pitt had sidestepped. It would have been preferable for Fox to lose the motion for impeachment if thereby he could saddle Pitt with the duty of defending every mistake made in India. As it was, the charge in respect of the spoliation of the begums was also upheld. Managers of the impeachment, principally Burke, Fox, and Sheridan, opened the trial in Westminster Hall on 13 February 1788. Hastings, aged fifty-three, five feet six inches high, 122 lb. in weight, dressed in a plain red suit, looking, said the sympathetic Fanny Burney, 'pale, ill, and altered', knelt to face his accusers, in the face of the whole of London society which thronged there with enthusiasm compounded of delight in prize-fights, in politics, in play-acting, in rhetorical exercise, and in seeing a human soul stripped bare. They were not cheated by the main actors. Sheridan's eloquence on the subject of the begums caused experienced men of affairs to collapse into one another's arms and society ladies to be removed insensible from nervous exhaustion. What Burke had to say could best have been put in a short pamphlet. Instead it was couched in day-long melodramatic speeches. The trial became a bore as the years passed. The accusers descended to use false witness and cloak it with abuse. The proudly enduring Hastings was portrayed as a wild beast sadistically muttering in corners over corpses or as a libertine sneering in bad prose at the ruin of provinces. When in 1795 Hastings was finally acquitted on all charges, Burke's reputation, rather than his, was in need of repair.

The consequence of all this was that Dundas had increased his hold over the Company. Hastings had exhausted the £100,000 or so which he had brought back from India and had exhausted also his vitality so that he lingered on another score of years a quiet, innocuous, old man. In India reform was on foot before the trial ever started. Lord Cornwallis had insisted upon greater power than Hastings had ever had. He had purged the service. The whole board responsible for contracts found themselves investigated by secret agents, dismissed, and brought to trial or flight. The new order was purer than the old. Yet something was lost. Regarding everything Indian as corrupt, the new British officials kept their skirts clear of the dust and mud. Thus began a racial division unknown to Hastings. The administrator was of a different breed from those he guided. All this, of the emphasis on non-aggressive policy, flowed directly from Pitt's board of control, not from the impeachment.[1] All that can be claimed as constructive for the impeachment is that it was a melodramatic advertisement of the love felt by Foxite whigs for unpopular causes and under-dogs.

It is clear that by the summer of 1789, when the French Revolution began and when the Hastings trial was already boring London, the Foxites were not only friends to under-dogs, they were themselves politically under-dogs. Pitt's finance gave hope to tax-paying squires, and his trade policy was as cautious as the mercantilist section could wish. He was still respected as an independent patriot who would not build himself a con-nexion or play with factions.[2] The king respected him, and the king was more popular since his insanity than at any other point in the reign. Pitt was still sufficiently the reformer in his speeches and his own ideas to hold the support of progressives or humani-tarians like Wilberforce. At the same time his refusal to coerce others into agreeing with him seemed to show a proper con-servative appreciation of the need to weigh all proposed changes very carefully. As a man of business he attracted other profes-sional men of affairs. He had not inextricably involved his credit in Indian or other intractable issues. As a result of all this the opposition were near despair.

The effect of the French Revolution upon England was to animate the opposition politicians once more. The reaction of Burke, Fox, and Pitt to the excitement across the Channel was highly characteristic. Fox declared the fall of the Bastille the greatest and best event in the history of the world. France was at last trying to win some of the treasures of English liberty for herself. This was an addition to human happiness. Equally enamoured of the broad historical view, equally unreserved in exposition, Burke hurried out his *Reflections* on the revolution. He saw in it not the imitation of the English 1688 but its anti-thesis. He would countenance change only when it was in harmony with the broad traditions of a people. He foresaw that from an artificial equality, a wholesale destruction of the past, would come blood, war, tyranny, and a destruction of human

---

[1] The permanent land settlement in Bengal was a mistaken return from Hastings's ideas to those of Francis, made perhaps because of the odium fallen upon all Hastings's work. See S. Gopal, *The Permanent Land Settlement in Bengal*.

[2] Pitt's personal following was estimated at 52 of whom only 20 would follow him if he were out of power: as against this Fox had a following of some 90 even in the blackest period of his career.

rights. While Burke and Fox declared their views and tried to teach them to others, Pitt was almost silent. If he foresaw new currents in European affairs, he kept his visions to himself. There was no practical need to nail any colour to his mast. So he deplored French excesses in words both platitudinous and sensible, but otherwise he reserved his position until there should be some political need to declare it.

Burke's *Reflections* were published in October 1790. In May 1791 he spoke in the commons reiterating his disagreement with Fox. Fox whispered that at least, though they might contradict one another, they might still remain friends. 'Yes,' Burke answered out loud, 'there was a loss of friends—he knew the price of his conduct—he had done his duty at the price of his friend—their friendship was at an end.' Here was a further weakening of the opposition. A silent Pitt would profit by the outspoken differences of two opponents.

For some time Fox seemed to have taken the better opposition line. Societies all over the country who had just been celebrating the centenary of the expulsion of James II remained in being to applaud the French. The movement for reform in England was given an impetus. The Society for Constitutional Information, suspended since 1784, was revived in 1791. The Corresponding Society, for the encouragement of constitutional discussion, was launched in January 1792. In April 1792 young aristocrats formed the Society of Friends of the people, an enthusiastic group of rather innocuous would-be Mirabeaus. The dissenters, with many men of unusual gifts among them, naturally joined in to urge careers open to talent. Both the prince regent and Sheridan made plain their scorn for Burke's cries of woe. But as the revolution in France became more clearly republican and violent, conservative alarm rose in England. The riots in July 1791 in Birmingham showed that excitement could be used against reform. To see that popular effervescence was a dangerous explosive to play with, one only had to look back a decade to the Gordon riots. In May 1792 the government by proclamation encouraged magistrates to be rigorous in controlling riotous meetings or seditious publications. In a little while they would find it necessary to employ spies in industrial areas and to begin tightening up the law.

When blood really began to flow in Paris then popular feeling began to swing back to Burke and to praise him for his wisdom as a prophet. Yet Fox would not trim his sails to this breeze. He was not going to lose sight of a great beneficent force because its early stirring was marred by crime, or because cowards feared easily for their property. With obstinacy, which cost him much in the short run, he refused to abate his praise of the revolution. The consequence was that the party of the duke of Portland, whose distinguishing mark had been its personal loyalties, began to split asunder.

Pitt had always been anxious to attract to himself as many Whigs of this group as possible. From May 1792 onwards, therefore, there was much talk of a new coalition. All those who feared war desired to see a government of national unity. The negotiations were complicated, unofficial, and behind closed doors. But the main issue was simple. Pitt would willingly receive recruits, but he would not step down to lift up his opponents of ten years. The duke of Portland was pressed by his right wing (Loughborough particularly) to accept offices and not to bargain over prestige. Burke wished to support a strong line in face of France. But Fox refused to serve under Pitt. The duke of Portland refused to abandon Fox and break the party. Optimists like the duke of Leeds thought the solution was for Pitt and Fox to hold equal offices under the captaincy of a neutral third party—say the duke of Leeds. Pitt would not sacrifice his position so easily.

In the upshot the negotiations lasted nine months until February 1793, when Portland's right-wing followers began one by one to join Pitt as individuals. But by that time strategic considerations—not ideology—at last drove Pitt into war with France. At once Burke's philosophy became of use as government propaganda; the fears of conservatives were blown up into a patriotic crusade. Gradually Fox's hold on Portland gave way under this new strain, until in 1794 the Portland whigs joined Pitt: Fox was left in opposition with a much diminished group.

Great movements depended on these changing personal relationships. For the war with France began a new chapter in politics. Finance, industry, society, political agitation, literature, all felt the effects of the years of war that were to fill George III's remaining years. It was of the greatest importance for the working out of the new forces that the culmination of thirty years of the old political manœuvres saw Pitt more firmly in power than ever, and Fox hopelessly in opposition. Fox had only a small band of faithful followers, but every man (except Pitt and George III) was his friend: in that lay his magic. Pitt ruled events and cabinets at the cost of having no man or woman who could read his heart.

XIII

A CIVILIZED SECURITY, 1760–90

THE political turmoil of the thirty years preceding 1790, and the emergence at their end of a generally acceptable patriotic line, cannot be fully understood unless the habits of mind of those years are taken into account. The constitution would never have worked without those customary responses which formed the civilization of the age. It was a civilization which in 1793 was on the verge of revolution, both from economic changes within and from the impact of political theory and war from without: yet it can never have seemed more everlasting, integrated, and immutable than at that moment.

In 1776 that percipient historian and agnostic philosopher, David Hume,[1] was in his last illness and made his way to Bath to seek vainly for health from its waters. His fellow Scot, Adam Smith, gravely disapproved. Mineral water, he wrote, was 'as much a drug as any that comes out of an Apothecaries Shop' and must therefore be an unnatural remedy, occasioning itself 'a transitory disease' and weakening 'the power of Nature to expel the disease'. In this belief that stimulants must upset the self-balancing power of Nature he was out of tune with fashionable medicine but very much in accord with the current thinking about the world and society. For it was generally believed that there was a natural order and harmony in human society, a pattern as clear as that of the bee-hive and as little subject to reconstitution by the exertion of human will-power. Nature for the Englishmen of this time was not red in tooth and claw; it was not a mysterious dark force dimly descried; it was a beneficent power whose intentions were clearly evident in the world

---

[1] David Hume (1711–76). His work is a splendid example of the primacy of Scotland in the intellectual and academic field at this period, but he was rejected by Scottish universities for his sceptical views. His life is also an example of the many-sidedness of intellectual leaders of the period for he was in his time a military judge-advocate, librarian, secretary to our ambassador in Paris, a social lion in French society, the benevolent friend of Rousseau, under-secretary to Conway, pensioner of George III, as well as secretary of the Edinburgh Philosophical Society. See also B. Williams, *The Whig Supremacy*, p. 404.

around them, a power tending always to balance and stability. They assumed, in fact, that their world was a natural one, that common sense, not irrationality, was part of the natural order.

It is true that highly sophisticated men often cried out for natural simplicity, in contrast to the life around them. But this was a superficial pose. They assumed that the simple life would not be much unlike the world they knew; they did not seek an existence whose foundations were different: they aimed, at most, to remove incongruous or tedious details from the familiar round. Marie Antoinette playing at being a milkmaid at Versailles was not rejecting the framework of French society, but simply sighing for an idealized version of existing life. So in England an aristocrat might praise rural simplicity, but it was rural life with all its accepted conventions, rural life seen in a haze of sentimentality. When Oliver Goldsmith[1] chose to portray natural virtues uncorrupted by the city in his *Vicar of Wakefield* (1766), the result was the reverse of revolutionary. Natural virtue appeared as a simple-hearted goodwill towards others, a placid acceptance of the orders of society, an absence of torturing ambition. So, too, Boswell pretended to envy an Ayrshire ploughboy, happy as the day is long. Dr. Johnson had little patience with such abnegation of responsibility. It never entered either of their heads to question the naturalness of the status of the ploughboy or the peer. These wistful glances towards simplicity are, indeed, the strongest evidence of the strength of a given pattern of life. Dr. Johnson himself lives in Boswell's pages as a superbly natural man because he expresses himself forcibly and logically. Yet this coherence of expression, in all its eighteenth-century formality, was achieved at the cost of thrusting into the background a jungle of primitive fears and urges. This suppression seemed at that time to make Johnson a more and not less natural being; the dark terrors were irrelevant nonsense because they could not fit into the pattern of reasonable life. Boswell's lack of success in ordering his own life efficiently made him not more natural in the eyes of contemporaries, but simply less of a full human being, because he could not conform to any acknowledged type.[2]

---

[1] Oliver Goldsmith (1728-74), an Irish journalist of feckless but engaging character working in London; a member of Johnson's circle; novelist, playwright (*She Stoops to Conquer*) and minor poet (*The Deserted Village*).

[2] Dr. Samuel Johnson (1709-84) had already emerged from his years of poverty as schoolmaster and hack-writer by the time George III came to the throne, for his

The same strong faith that nature was known and tamed is evident when one turns to examine the great works of political thought of the age. Two economists, Dean Tucker[1] and Adam Smith,[2] attacked the institutions of their day for unnatural interference with the normal course of relations between men. Adam Smith was the more influential in that, while his general approach to economic problems was anticipated by Tucker, his own theories were based upon, illustrated by, and applied to, a mass of concrete facts of his own day. Smith's work, said Pulteney in 1797, 'would persuade the present generation and govern the next'. Both parts of this proposition were correct: Lord North, Shelburne, and Pitt—as has been seen—all appreciated his scientific point of view. As for the next generation, we justly associate the whole revolution in social relationships, the expansion of Britain as the world's greatest industrial power, and the prevailing social philosophy of the early nineteenth century with Adam Smith's influence. So keen is our appreciation of his effects that it has blinded us to his intent.

Adam Smith was not preaching revolution or prophesying change. If left to themselves, he urged, the laws of nature would produce ideally just results. He did not in the least foresee—except possibly in his discussion of the social results of issuing notes of small denominations[3]—that 'natural' freedom would result in the building of a new world and the shuffling of all accepted standards. On the contrary he assumed that the world and certain types of human behaviour were constant; he failed to perceive their historical relativeness. So he surveyed the existing state of things and lamented the minor follies of kings

great *Dictionary* had been published in 1755. He enjoyed at this time a lordship in literary and artistic circles in London. James Boswell (1740–95) only began the important work of his life, his biography of Johnson, when he met his hero in 1763. He was elected a member of the Literary Club in 1773. For his disordered life see his *Journals*.

[1] Josiah Tucker (1712–99), dean of Gloucester and author of many controversial pamphlets; opposed the old colonial system and wrote in favour of American independence and freer trade.

[2] Adam Smith (1723–90), Glasgow University and Balliol College, Oxford; lecturer on literature and jurisprudence in Kirkcaldy; professor at Glasgow, at first of logic and then of moral philosophy; *Theory of the Moral Sentiments* (1759); appointed tutor to the duke of Buccleuch by Charles Townshend which gave him the opportunity of travel abroad and friendship with the French physiocrats, as well as a pension for life; appointed Scottish commissioner of customs by Lord North; his great work, *The Wealth of Nations*, published in 1776, may be taken as the beginning of political economy as a distinct subject.

[3] *Wealth of Nations*, ed. Cannan, 1904, p. 307.

and ministers in whom 'it is the highest impertinence to pretend to watch over the economy of private people'. Governments should cease to impose restrictions on industry and commerce, and leave individuals free to seek their own profit. The result of private profit would be the public wealth. The theory was destructive of the mercantile system of the day; it dealt contemptuously with the human laws which too often obstructed the natural march towards prosperity. The state, he said, had only three proper functions: the protection of its members against violence from without, the administration of justice, and the carrying out of certain public works which were too large to be left to private persons. Thus to limit the operations of the state was to prove dangerous in time of upheaval. But Smith propounded his principles in times of stability. He dealt with classes as they were. His work is an indication of the stability of society in this age.

Something of the same easy—and question-begging—certainty may be detected in the work of Jeremy Bentham,[1] proud as he was of his iconoclasm. In that year of great events, 1776, Bentham produced his *Fragment on Government*: in 1780 he published his *Introduction to the Principles of Morals and Legislation*. Bentham's purpose was to destroy the mystical vagueness with which Blackstone had surrounded the English Law. For Blackstone the spirit of English legal interpretation, rooted in past tradition, was the essence of English life. The common law was like a divine revelation, gradually unfolding, and the smallest details of legal history were therefore to be approached with awe. Bentham, on the other hand, boldly declared that law was quite simply a set of rules to achieve certain ends effectively. When it ceased, by age, to answer its purpose, it should be altered. He proposed a refurbishing, a codification, of the whole legal system. The ultimate end of society was simply the greatest happiness of the greatest number, each counting for one and none for more than one. As attainment of happiness was the good each man set before himself it was therefore the standard by which the whole society should be judged. Every institution might be tested to see if its aim was consistent with the greatest happiness: if it was, then it should be examined to

---

[1] J. Bentham (1748–1832). Student of law; philosopher; famous as the founder of utilitarianism. Author of *A Defence of Usury*, *A Catechism of Parliamentary Reform* (in addition to works above).

see if it achieved its end efficiently: if it was not, then it should be thrown on the scrap-heap.

There is much in all this which admittedly is truly revolutionary. Bentham's use of happiness to explain away moral judgements, his logical extremism, certainly cut at the roots of existing institutions. In the hands of his nineteenth-century heirs utilitarianism was to make a new England with scant regard for old ways of life.[1] Benthamism remodelled law, education, local government, prisons, and schools. In the process it lost some of its early simplicity and clarity. Later utilitarians, such as John Stuart Mill, were more sensitive in the appreciation of the complexity of human nature, but they lost Bentham's dry exactness of argument. It is here that Bentham most clearly shows his kinship with other theorists of the first half of George III's reign. For his argument is made more watertight by the harshness of his concepts. He simplifies human nature to make it fit his pattern. When closely examined the simple hedonistic being he calls man is seen to be a reflection of the common-sense conventional man of the age. Bentham no more than Adam Smith foresees the explosiveness of human beings, for he cannot imagine them released from the straightjacket of the eighteenth-century code. Moreover, his principle of utility, as Sir William Holdsworth pointed out,[2] for all its revolutionary air is something very like the old and hackneyed law of nature once more. The conventional side of Bentham is at once appreciated if we compare him with Robert Owen (who was only five years old in 1776) who appreciated the fluidity of human society and proposed to remake human nature itself instead of accepting it as simple and certain;[3] such faith in the creative possibilities of human energy lay thirty years on. Or, another comparison, there is more similarity than appears at first glance between the minds of the radical Bentham and the conservative Paley.[4] Paley defended Christianity by a profit-and-loss account. His view of God and man has a devitalized clarity, a formal but unreal cogency.

Strong indeed in these years must the confidence of men

[1] See Sir E. L. Woodward, *The Age of Reform*, O.H.E. vol. xiii, p. 34.
[2] *Chicago Law Review*, vol. ii, no. 4, 1935.   [3] See below, p. 533.
[4] William Paley (1743–1805), archdeacon of Carlisle, his *Political Philosophy* (1785) was a Cambridge textbook; his *Evidences of Christianity* (1794), as well as his *Horae Paulinae* (1790) and *Natural Theology* (1802), are the most famous statements of rational Christianity.

have been that they had found their destined place in nature, when this faith could colour the work of men of the originality of Smith and Bentham. To explain its strength one must recall the long period of internal peace enjoyed by England in that century. One must recollect the supremacy of the landed gentry. It is true that economic change was gradually accelerating. But it had not yet cracked—or even been seen to threaten—the secure foundations of English life.[1]

By 1790 developments in industry had begun which were capable of leading on to a completely new order; so the later observer may comment. But it had not progressed far enough to be described as a revolution except in the light of later changes. The abundance of capital, the markets widened by transport improvements, the shortage of labour in the north leading to high labour costs, all these were a stimulus to invention. In the twenty years preceding 1790 the annual average of patents taken out was 41. But in the ten years following the rate increased to $65\frac{1}{2}$. Many ingenious men applied themselves to the problem of making economies in labour and in natural resources. The economy was buoyant enough for capitalists to invest in them. Up in Scotland John Roebuck developed sulphuric acid works near the old salt works at Prestonpans, a vital development for textile bleaching. Roebuck, again, invested in James Watt and his condenser, only to be forced to abandon them as he approached bankruptcy in 1773. In iron and steel the improved accuracy of finish of Wilkinson's metal cylinders (developed for the making of cannon) was the prerequisite of all steam-engine development. Cort's inventions of puddling and of rolling iron bars have already been mentioned.[2] These latter developments only came in 1783 and had not been widely adopted before the outbreak of war.

In the cotton industry the most famous of the inventions concerned with spinning had been made by 1790. Hargreaves's spinning jenny (1765) enabled one man, or woman, to spin on several spindles simultaneously by using a movable carriage on a rectangular wooden frame. This produced a fine thread but a brittle one: it increased production but it did not interfere with the old pattern of the industry, spinning by families in their own cottages. By 1788 there were said to be 20,000 jennies

[1] See above, p. 32.
[2] See above, p. 31, and see, for details of the process, below, p. 505.

at work in England.[1] Arkwright's water-frame (patented 1769) spun thread on to vertical spindles from four pairs of wood and leather rollers by water-power. The thread produced was strong but coarse. The adoption of the water-frame did involve social changes for it necessitated the gathering of spinners together into some sort of factory organization. In 1771 Arkwright had 300 employees, but he trebled this in one decade. Before he died, in 1792 (worth £½ million), he himself controlled ten mills and there were about a hundred mills in England, almost half of them in Lancashire. In 1779 Samuel Crompton produced his 'mule' which married the jenny and the water-frame, using the moving frame of the former and the rollers of the latter. The thread produced was both strong and fine. With it the weavers were in a position to produce muslins superior to those of India.

These processes were not always immediately successful. Though £12,000 was sunk in Arkwright's spinning roller it was some five years before profit began to be made. It was the improvement in the use of water-power by Kelly of Lanark which made the 'mule' of major importance, but this development only dates from 1790. Cotton weaving became a bottleneck which impeded progress. Here mechanization (devised by Dr. Cartwright) was not commercially successful until 1801. In calico printing the important invention was that of Bell's copper cylinder which was produced in 1783 and only gradually superseded the old hand-block printing. As for the older branch of textiles, woollen goods, invention there was always behind that in cotton. The jenny was introduced in Yorkshire about 1790: other improvements belong to the later period of war with France.[2] However, work was already standardized and divided. In the textile industry the list of processes would by 1790 already baffle the lay reader.

Yet so long as invention merely made one man capable of doing the work formerly requiring two or three, or so long as it depended upon water-power, the concentration of industry into large towns, and into great factories within these towns, was unlikely to be rapid. Units were growing larger. The Shropshire

---

[1] P. Mantoux (trans. J. Vernon), *The Industrial Revolution in the Eighteenth Century*, p. 223.

[2] The account of industrial development in its more dramatic stage is resumed below, p. 504.

iron-manufacturing firm of William Reynolds & Co. was valued at £138,000. Thrale's brewery fetched almost as much when he died in 1781. In cotton many processes tended for convenience to be gathered into adjacent buildings round a bridge over a river, as water-power increased in importance. It was the application of steam, however, which really centralized production in great units: steam-power expanded industry to the point that it began to change the whole face of the country, to upset wage-levels, to produce a new class of self-confident industrial masters, and so to disturb the tranquillity of men's ideas.

Watt's development of the steam-engine is closely connected with the immense scientific activity all over Europe in the sixties and seventies. In one year, 1774, for instance, Priestley and Lavoisier, in England and France, succeeded in isolating oxygen; Scheele discovered chlorine and Bergman presented his treatise on carbon dioxide and carbonic acid to the Scientific Academy at Uppsala. Watt's work depended upon two things: Joseph Black's[1] study of steam with his enunciation of the theory of latent heat, and his own skilled training as instrument-maker for Glasgow University. In 1769 he produced and patented his condenser. It was not until after his move to Birmingham and partnership with Boulton that he set to work on a rotative engine with connecting rod and crankshaft. By 1780 there were forty of his pumping-engines in operation. The first steam-engine with rotary motion in a cotton mill was in Nottingham in 1785: there was none in Manchester until 1789 or Glasgow until 1792. The policy of Boulton and Watt was in many ways restrictive. In order to maintain the reputation of their engines they controlled manufacture under licence, insisting upon their standards of workmanship and fitting. 'It would not be worth my while', said Boulton, 'to make for three counties only; but I find it worth my while to make for the world.'

It is clear from this survey of the dates of the discoveries in industry that in 1790 their application could not have been widespread. Statistics confirm the common-sense conclusion. 'After 1782 every statistical series shows a sharp upward turn.' 'More than half the growth in the shipments of coal and the mining of copper, more than three-quarters of the increase of

---

[1] Joseph Black (1728-99). A professor of medicine and a practising physician in Glasgow.

broadcloth, four-fifths of that of printed cloth, nine-tenths of the export of cotton goods, were concentrated in the last eighteen years of the century.'¹ Until 1790 British development does not look any more dramatic than that of France: from that time forward it lurched rapidly into a quite different scale of industrial operation.² What concentration upon her own affairs (after the American separation) had begun, was completed by the application of inventions by Britain under the stimulus of war: her competitors were distracted, her own overseas trade remained. Total exports, which in 1760 stood at £14·7 million, in 1770 at £14·3 million, and in 1780 had fallen to £12·6 million, rose steadily every year thereafter to reach £18·9 million by 1790 and £23·7 million in 1792. In 1797 £27 million was a poor annual figure and exports of over £30 million were expected. The expansion was most marked in capital goods and basic factors of production. Coal output in the forty years preceding 1790 had grown by some 40 per cent.; but in the next five years alone it increased by rather more than a further 30 per cent.³

While, then, this explosive change was preparing, the stability of the old social order remained and with it the feeling of secure values. Industrialists had not yet forced their way up from provincial obscurity into prominent positions in society. At the top of the social ladder were the great lords taking their enormous rent-rolls as the natural tribute to their station. The second Viscount Palmerston drawing £12,000 a year from estates in Ireland and England may serve as a representative figure of this class, though some, like the duke of Newcastle, had incomes more than ten times as great. To describe other income groups we have workable figures only after the first census of 1801. If we remember that war had affected money values by then, we may still use Colquhoun's⁴ classification of society, founded upon the census, to get some picture of the nineties. Next to the great lords come the opulent: 300 families with incomes, mostly from land, of £4,000 or over and 200 families, merchants, and

---

¹ T. S. Ashton, *An Economic History of England: the 18th Century*, p. 125.

² See J. U. Nef, 'The Industrial Revolution Reconsidered', in *The Journal of Economic History*, iii (1943), pp. 1–31.

³ From figures calculated by the Commissioners of 1871 and quoted by W. Cunningham, *Growth of Industry and Commerce, Modern Times*, p. 463.

⁴ P. Colquhoun, *A Treatise on the Wealth, Power and Resources of the British Empire* (1814).

bankers for the most part, with over £2,500. Below this group, which produced the leaders in society, came the rich: perhaps 70,000 people with incomes over £1,500, made up of baronets, knights, and prosperous esquires. Below them were the higher office holders and lesser, but still substantial, merchants; the best guess one can make is ¼ million people in all whose annual incomes were more than £700. In this group, that of the upper middle class, were the leading manufacturers—builders, shipbuilders, warehousemen. Here were *nouveaux riches*, self-made men whose rise was not yet at an end. It will be noted, however, that they had not risen to the first place beside the bankers and contractors.

Below this group again ½ million shopkeepers were doing well at about £150 a year: twice as many farmers thought themselves the substantial backbone of the country on £120 a year. Minor clergy and dissenting ministers had incomes, generally, at about the same level. Two million citizens lived on a line which divided comfort from poverty, that is about £55 a year. Below this line, among the poor, were the 1½ million agricultural workers with their £31 per annum, the labourers in the mines with an average of £40, and the vagrants, gipsies, vagabonds, thieves, prostitutes, and recipients of poor relief (of whom in 1800 there were a million) whose earnings were estimated at some £10. Other groups, of course, may be picked out—¼ million innkeepers and publicans with £100 per annum, ½ million small freeholders with £90, traders' clerks with £75, and even 2,000 university teachers and kindred professions at £60.

The money figures given here are difficult to use. There are so many doubtful elements in them, as for instance the value of the benefits in kind received by the agricultural labourers. But what is clear and definite is the pattern of society, the relationships, and relative importance of classes. This society clearly was one where industry had not destroyed the dominance of a group, small in numbers, but secure in wealth, composed of landed gentry and financial experts. Even those of the politically conscious class who mouthed democratic phrases did so within a convention which assumed the inertness of the poor.

The supremacy of the great proprietors was taken for granted as a natural thing. This is apparent even in their sports. Just at this time cricket emerged from obscurity in villages of the

Weald, and in schoolboys' pastimes, into prominence as a national game. Its rules, first codified in 1744, were established securely under such aristocratic guidance as that of the earl of Tankerville in 1774. It was a game which satisfied the two main passions of the upper classes, for open air exercise (for it was, as yet, a game of rapid movement played in shoes, without pads) and for gambling. In it their masterful patronage was fully displayed. Territorial magnates took their villagers to play each other for side stakes, or they laid bets on single-wicket encounters between their favourites. Sir Horace Mann of Canterbury liked to lead his picked men for a wager of 500 to 1,000 guineas on a game. The duke of Dorset enticed promising bowlers to work on his estates that he might humble the pride of Lord Sandwich. The famous Hambledon club was organized by the duke of Bolton's son, a local parson, to a point where it could challenge the rest of England. On the field through long summer afternoons there was a rough camaraderie between the part-time professionals and their gentlemen patrons, a camaraderie born of aristocratic self-confidence. To suit the convenience of the masters the centre of cricketing soon became London. On the first 'Lords' ground[1] Lord Frederick Beauclerk, the parson son of the duke of St. Albans, established himself as a middle-man between the world of fashion and that of sinew. He made 600 guineas a year as a gambler, thanks to his skill in slow bowling (under-arm, as all bowling was until the 1820's) and to his authority over humbler exponents of the game. With such encouragement cricket had spread to Oxfordshire, Nottinghamshire, and even to Sheffield by the 1770's. It was a sport as typical of the age as horse-racing. Nor was it yet considered any better in its effects on national character. Soame Jenyns[2] lamented England's degeneracy with

> her well-bred heirs
> Gamesters and Jockeys turned, and cricket-players.

What was most attractive, however, in the life of this small knot of 'natural' rulers was their lively intellectual energy. It was a society where everyone knew everyone else and where argument on arts and politics, within the accepted framework, was both personal and pertinent. In it the qualities of true citizens by Aristotle's definition were realized. They had leisure

---

[1] Which was at White Conduit Field, now King's Cross.
[2] Soame Jenyns (1704–87), poet, moralist, and commissioner of trade.

for intellectual pursuits, yet they were sufficiently in touch with practical needs—through the stewards of their estates or their service in parliament—to avoid speculation which was purely abstract. They were rarely professionally competent in any field but possessed sufficient acquaintance with many skills to interest themselves in many forms of excellence. Georgiana, duchess of Devonshire, thought it proper to turn a thought in verse; the young man on his grand tour in Europe would aspire to meet the leading French philosophers, while Gavin Hamilton[1] in Rome did a good trade in ancient marbles or Renaissance pictures with his visiting countrymen.

It would be wrong to idealize the picture of this society. Much of its leisure was devoted to drink or gaming rather than to connoisseurship. Yet few societies have had as living an intellectual life or as strong a common culture. Charles James Fox was so potent a politician because he carried most of the tastes of his contemporaries to a striking extreme. His activities at the gaming table cost his father some £100,000: equally no one excelled him at the choice of an apposite quotation from Aristotle or Blackstone or Montesquieu. His great merit was 'his amazing quickness in seizing any subject, he seems to have the particular talent of knowing more about what he is saying and with less pains than anyone else. His conversation is like a brilliant player at billiards, the strokes follow one another piff puff', reported the young duchess of Devonshire in 1777.[2] In the circle of the Townshends, or Lord North's friends, or Holland House, or even the Bedfords, as in those of Topham Beauclerk, Johnson, or, in more soberly simple a style, that of Clapham Common, in all these, intellectual manysidedness was expected and respected.

The lively society of the capital was honeycombed with clubs. The professional men—politicians like Burke, painters like Reynolds, actors like (but there was nobody like) Garrick—would gather to argue theory over their wine. An amateur like Lord Palmerston[3] went to his Catch Club, or rejoiced that his election to the Dilettanti[4] showed recognition of his standing as a

---

[1] Gavin Hamilton (1730-97), a painter and excavator of Roman remains.

[2] *Georgiana* (*Correspondence of the Duchess of Devonshire*), by Lord Bessborough, p. 32.

[3] See Brian Connel, *A Whig Peer*: the life of the second Viscount Palmerston, *passim*.

[4] The Dilettanti Society, founded 1734 to combine the cultivation of artistic

man of taste. He cultivated the society of Sir Joseph Banks[1] to hear of exploration or that of Sir Charles Blagden[2] to get a formula for fireworks. Members of the Royal Society could dine out on a discovery in astronomy, but would be expected to contribute also to talk of Flemish art or the Irish poor. The habitués of Almack's or Brooks's would, no doubt, be more excited by the turn of a card than a turn of phrase: nevertheless, even here it was a lively interest in national affairs which caused such gambling houses to acquire a party flavour; a wit like George Selwyn[3] was counted a welcome customer. A man of no inherited fortune but great talent like Sheridan drank and gambled in the highest society. The passion for play was indeed extraordinary. Wives entangled their husbands' affairs; mothers lamented, while sharing, the gambling mania of their children. Hard drinking and high stakes were enlivened by conversational gaiety, ranging from gossip about the latest cuckold to the most recent volume of Gibbon, from the illegal marriage of the prince of Wales to Hannah More's tracts for the humble, but having at all times the edge and charm of variety within a fixed convention. Fortunately in Horace Walpole's letters, in Boswell, and in the many diaries of a literate society, we can apprehend its quality.

The supremacy of London in social life gave a certain unity to the culture of England in these years. The squire's lady aimed at dressing in the London style, for the rapid alternation of women's fashions had begun. Feathers rose higher on the head and petticoats varied in thickness. In acting, the most ephemeral of arts, the names and styles of Garrick or Mrs. Siddons were the standard of the provinces. In furniture the great house was restocked with chairs from a London craftsman and the closest possible copies made in the market-town. Taste in furniture

knowledge with conviviality. In 1764 the rapid accumulation of its funds enabled it to send an expedition to Asia Minor to collect details of the monuments of antiquity. Volumes on Ionian Antiquities were published in 1769 and 1797. Egyptian, Etruscan, Greek, and Roman sculpture received its princely patronage.

[1] Joseph Banks (1743–1820), president of the Royal Society; student of natural history; accompanied Cook round the world.

[2] Sir Charles Blagden (1748–1820), physician; secretary of the Royal Society.

[3] George Augustus Selwyn (1718–91), M.P., 1747–80; holder of several sinecures; elected to White's, 1744, and to the Jockey Club, 1767; his wit, whose fame was widespread at the time, must have depended too much on local colour and his manner for it to look well in cold print.

had been growing more refined: the process steadily continued. At the accession of George III Chippendale's *Gentleman and Cabinet Maker's Directory* had set the tone. Furniture was often, by later standards, heavy and fantasticated, solid frames with 'Chinese' ornamentation for instance. During the seventies a further elegance was sought in the rather more austere lines of furniture, such as that designed by Adam: here classical lines and beauty of proportion replaced earlier exuberance. This was, no doubt, part of the general craze for antique simplicities from Greece and Rome. By 1790, however, the popularity of architectural form in furniture was waning. Sheraton's *Drawing Book*, published in 1791, shows a liking for pieces which are more slender and fragile. Their elegance is increased by the greater use of veneers in woods of various colours and by using metal inlays. With this more feminine feeling there came also delight in tricks, hinges, and, in short, ingenuity for its own sake.

There was, nevertheless, for all its delight in novelty, an underlying respect for moderation and harmony among the rules of taste at this time. This is exemplified in architecture. The building or enlarging of great country houses continued to be a favourite method of gratifying creative feelings and displaying opulence. The basic tenets of Palladian architecture were still unchallenged. Once again the most admirable feature of the work was its dignity and sense of proportion. There is also, in contrast with later work of George III's reign, a sense of restraint and decorum. As compared with the earlier part of the century, building appeared, on the whole, less heavy and massive. A builder of a great house tended to rely for effects less upon ponderousness and more upon touches of individual grace. A cupola perhaps here, or a few added pillars there, gave a delicate individuality without sacrificing the unity of the whole. Yet here too, of course, the 'gravitas' of the Adam brothers[1] left its mark; they had a notable concern for the effect of the whole block of building. A building by their school was finished down to the last detail. Not only did the exterior present a balanced whole, but interior decoration matched the lines of

[1] James Adam (d. 1794) and Robert Adam (1728-92), M.P. Kinross-shire, architects to George III, 1762-8. They brought back from their studies in Italy a deep feeling for classical proportion: this they combined with a theory of movement of line in architecture. Between 1768 and 1772 the brothers built several streets of houses on an embankment along the Thames; this was the Adelphi; it involved them in financial difficulties.

the structure. Even the plasterwork had a working place in the
total effect. That effect was noble, rooms full of light, air, and
splendid lines, but cold and formal; palaces of reception rather
than places of rest.

The country houses had new surroundings. The vogue of
Lancelot ('Capability') Brown[1] was at its height. He set the
great houses in a contrasting setting of elaborately informal
charm. He delighted in parkland and great lawns and trees in
place of the old formal patterns of hedges and walks. Water too
was used not for fountains but for lakes and cascades. On the
creation of such opulently pastoral surroundings thousands
of pounds might be spent by the leading county family. Brown
combined landscape gardening with architecture and with
the business of supplying building materials. The patronage of
all the leading men of taste ensured that he had many successors: Henry Holland[2] inherited much of his work as general
adviser on problems of materials and layout to the aristocracy.

It is true that in building at this time the beginnings of a
romantic return to the Gothic (and hence of a breach with
established canons of taste) have been detected by the sharp-
eyed. Horace Walpole's battlemented house at Strawberry Hill,
or the construction of ruins and follies, may be cited as evidence
of a cracking of the old standards. In truth, however, these were
no more as yet than *jeux d'esprit*: they did not represent revolts
against the prevailing taste but a whimsical fling, made the
more amusing because it was executed against the background
of sound and certain common sense. Only in the light of later
changes can these diversions be given greater significance.
Horace Walpole himself at Stowe confessed: 'The Grecian
Temple is glorious: this I openly worship; in the heretical
corner of my heart I adore the Gothic building.' The poet
laureate Thomas Wharton was another, enjoying heresy because
the faith was in no danger. Confiding in the reader his truancy
from true taste he extolled dark and barbarous churches,

> Where SUPERSTITION, with capricious hand
> In many a maze the wreathed window plann'd

only to be recalled by admiration for Reynolds's chastely correct
window in New College Chapel, Oxford, which—

---

[1] 1715–83, laid out Kew and Blenheim; became high sheriff of Huntingdon.
[2] H. Holland (1746?–1806) enlarged Carlton House: F.S.A., 1797.

Broke the Gothic chain
And brought my bosom back to truth again.[1]

The place of Joshua Reynolds in the history of this severe and aristocratic taste is indeed an important one. For Reynolds had as his objectives in life the development of a 'Grand Style' in native painting and the raising of the status of the artist in society. His own career illustrates his success in both respects. The son of a clergyman, apprenticed to a painter, formed by study in Italy, he set up as a portrait painter in London in 1753 charging five guineas a head. By 1760 he had established himself in Leicester Square and his price had risen to £25 for a head, £50 for a half-length and £100 for whole length; prices which four years later he had increased again to £30, £70, and £150. His success with the rich and opulent, the only people (if one refers back to the list of income levels) who could possibly afford such prices, was sufficient to raise him into the heart of the opulent dominant class himself. The whole of powerful London society flocked to his studio. With his three sittings in the morning and three in the afternoon his income in 1760 (when he was thirty-seven) was £6,000 a year. When he died in 1792 he left £80,000.

Reynolds's power over his aristocratic clientele was used to inaugurate a new interest in native art. He was the intellectual force in the opening of a new and splendid age of British painting. The English connoisseur had for long been accustomed to revere the achievements of the Italian school, and to consider the native school as inferior.[2] Reynolds took a leading part in the formation of the Royal Academy in 1768, with the object of raising professional standards. To the schools of the Academy he delivered his celebrated Discourses. Reynolds married the grand classical style of Italy with the native tradition of portrait painting. He would put his sitter, in the contemporary dress of his station, into a pose of classical antiquity, subconsciously to be recognized by patrons educated in that tradition: the background appropriate to the character would not be a mere backcloth, but would be made, by use of light and shade, a vital part of the whole. Thus he brought heroic feeling to his por-

[1] Quoted in Logan Pearsall Smith, 'Four Romantic Words', in *Words and Idioms*, p. 107 (1943 edition).
[2] In the collection made by General Guise which he bequeathed to Christ Church in 1765, there is, for example, no English work: this seems typical.

traits. At its worst this classical style could result in such care
for pose, drapery, and so on, that feeling is deadened by classical
allusions. But Reynolds was usually preserved from this by the
keenness of his interest in character and by the intellectual
energy of his mind. In the handling of masses as in the delineation of character he was supreme. The personalities of his sitters
were keenly perceived and set forth as on a plane of high
drama. With men he was perhaps more successful than with
women because, except in his final phase after 1780, his interest
lay more in fixing an attitude to life than in the patterns of
dress or charms of adornment.

The small world of great affairs—as well as the world of
letters which he painted for the sake of his many friends in it—
thus found an artist to record it heroically yet without romanticism, acutely, and certainly unforgettably. That the years 1760
to 1790 seem so crowded with men of major stature with whom
one can feel human sympathy is in part his achievement. At the
same time this world of the powerful had its taste moulded, its
interest in patronizing native artists sharpened. It was into an
atmosphere developed by Reynolds that Thomas Gainsborough,
the second great figure of the revival, came when he moved to
London in 1774. Gainsborough was a painter less masculine in
intensity, more sensitive to the surface of life, than Reynolds.
He was more lyrical. His interest was in patterns of line and
colour, in a world of his own imagination. Under pressure of
necessity he painted the set portraits of social leaders, yet at
times the charm of the background—painted with a freshness
more Dutch than Italian in spirit—seems more important than
the figure. Women he painted with sentiment, making them
part of his own delicate dream. Gainsborough renders the
mood where Sir Joshua gives the character. Gainsborough in
consequence, though successful and prosperous, was esteemed
a less important painter than Reynolds in this hard-headed
society. It was not until the 1780's that Gainsborough's landscapes and 'fancy pictures' (that is, his charming groups of un-
sophisticated figures from humble life) became popular.

The traditions of Reynolds were more straightforwardly continued by George Romney.[1] Romney lacked Reynolds's depth

---

[1] G. Romney (1732–1802), son of a cabinet-maker; won prizes from the Society
of Arts in the 1760's; settled in London after study in Italy; patronized by duke
of Richmond and others as a rival to Reynolds.

of insight and Gainsborough's elegance of sensibility. But he pleased the world of taste by his composition of a picture, his placing of the figure, his clear colour, and his ability to hit off the salient point in a character directly. His portraits have an attractive straightforwardness and vivacity. By contrast this flowering of a school of portraiture can be seen to have run to seed by the time of John Hoppner;[1] his imitation of Gainsborough and Reynolds was clever but uninspired; his preoccupation with the details of dress is as superficial as his sentimental flattery of the best points of his sitter.

While Reynolds had been giving London a new patrician tradition of portraiture, Richard Wilson had, with less financial success, been endeavouring to do much the same for landscape. His study of examples of Italian landscape painting—which a young man of taste might collect on his grand tour—was employed to help him render the countryside of Wales and England. As Reynolds might show Admiral Keppel every inch an English seaman yet with the reminiscence of the Apollo Belvedere somewhere hidden in the making of his picture,[2] so Wilson hid the structure of Italian scenery behind the bushes and the waters of the greener English countryside. The result is strange and curiously attractive. The most familiar valley has a foreign air; an alien discipline lurks behind the native luxuriance of the scene. By contrast, in the late 1780's the much less distinguished work of George Morland began, when engraved, to command a large public. Whereas Wilson painted for the connoisseur of style, Morland aimed at lush realism, filling his canvas with leafy trees and injecting an easy human interest with his choices of traditionally English sights and characters. A more characteristic product of the hierarchical society of this time— as well as a greater painter—was George Stubbs. His lifework was the delineation of this society not in its seasonal activity in London but amid the rural life in which it was rooted. Stubbs preferred horses to men apparently, but his work is wrongly classified an animal painting. It is the exact and factual rendering of landscape, squires, and horses, under the distinctive canopy of English clouds. There is a discipline behind his paint-

J. Hoppner (1758–1810), chorister in the Chapel Royal; exhibited in the Royal Academy from 1780.
[2] For discussion of this picture see E. Waterhouse, *Painting in Britain, 1530–1790*, p. 166.

ing; it is the discipline of equine anatomy and of a sense of rhythmic appropriateness in grouping.

The other type of painting which gives to this period the air of an English renaissance is known as history painting. Here Reynolds was not an innovator but a reactionary. He chose subjects from classical mythology and presented them in full classical costume. But the fashionable approach to history was deflationary. Favourite historians of the day—Hume, Gibbon, Voltaire—excelled in the searching for truth behind poses and in a shrewd, if conventional, assessment of motives. There was thus a conflict between the pictorial presentation of statesmen in togas and the literary investigation of their weaknesses. At the same time Chatham's victories had inspired a general enthusiasm for Britain's historical role, an enthusiasm which ignominious experience in America did not quench. The mood of the time was thus at once realistic and proud, enthusiasm overlay cynicism.

In response to these curious currents of feeling a new—and not the least profitable—vogue of 'narrative' painting found exponents. Edward Penny, with his 'Death of Wolfe', began painting historical scenes in contemporary instead of conventionally classical costume. But he underplayed the drama in his scenes and seemed dull or pedestrian. The outstanding exponent of the new style was Benjamin West. West was the favourite painter of the king,[1] who paid him some £34,000 in forty years for historical paintings. West combined patriotic fervour, conventional grouping, and realistic trappings. The appetite for this more vivid representation of events of the time was brilliantly catered for by the American J. S. Copley, who was prepared to provide pictures of any striking story, not just great historical events. His canvases were vast and highly coloured and their main virtue is their stirring enthusiasm and good composition.

These achievements in painting were among the chief glories of this age of opulent patronage. Something of the self-assurance of the patrons makes itself felt in the rules by which painting was judged. For between all the variations of three decades there is an agreement to render life, as a man of common sense viewed

---

[1] George III was more interested in art patronage than any other king since 1688. Even if his taste was below the best standards, it was at least a further instance of his reflection of his age that he shared his subjects' renewed interest in native painting.

it, but with its heroic significance heightened. In the most radical of changes of style in these years there is not yet to be found that desperate rejection of old values, the frantic topsy-turvy-dom of the Romantic movement. At most the owner of a Gains-borough girl with pigs may have envied her quiet life on the farm. He did not dream that her values might be as good as his own, or that she should be consulted about her choice of occupations. The world was clearly made of English parklands, mountains in less important corners, and admirals, generals, secretaries of state at the directing centre of the universe. To artists the task was given of using easily comprehensible symbols to convey the vital force of this straightforward world.

Few outside the opulent or rich could influence the course of artistic taste. For the most part the well-to-do merchant with the new industrialist and the middling squire took their cue from the West End: they were usually, however, a little behind-hand. The middle-class family, as we can observe in Goldsmith's *Vicar of Wakefield*, still delighted to be painted as groups of graces or Greeks rather than in the more realistic manner of Sir Joshua. Moreover, they had a liking for the small conversation piece rather than the portrait: it required only one frame to surround all the family, and, if kept small, cosily suited the drawing-room. But in the 1760's the innovations of Hogarth at length began to be widely followed. The marketing of engravings made from history pictures became a very lucrative trade. West's 'Death of Wolfe' was engraved by Woollet and marketed by Alderman Boydell. By 1760 the engraver had netted £6,000 and the business man £15,000 on the transaction. The engraving, the print, and the cartoon, dispersed among an ever wider circle the more obvious of the artistic tricks which had found favour among the great. The coloured print, indeed, did more than take the aesthetics of the governing class to a bourgeois audience; it circulated their arguments as well.[1] About 1780— just at the time when Rowlandson[2] turned from portrait painting to his true vocation as a caricaturist—Gillray began to use political themes for his cartoons.[3] Cartoons played their part

---

[1] At a guinea a set or at 2s. each they were indeed a very expensive form of popular journalism.

[2] Thomas Rowlandson (1756–1827) exhibited at the Royal Academy from 1775; was a regular caricaturist for Ackerman's *Poetical Magazine* from 1809.

[3] James Gillray (1757–1815), a letter-engraver who took up caricature; produced some 1,500 caricatures from Miss Humphrey's shop in St. James' Street, Piccadilly.

in discrediting the Fox–North coalition and in ridiculing the amatory adventures of the prince of Wales.[1]

It was probably in the popularity of history paintings with a story that aristocratic and common taste most emphatically coincided. The truth of this is attested by Vauxhall. Vauxhall was the meeting place of all orders in an age with few organized entertainments: it was the place for all in search of ostentation for clothes or of obscurity for flirtation, for music, gluttony, drink, a place, as Henry Fielding said, 'where the finest women are exposed to view and where the meanest person who can dress himself clean may in some degree mix with his betters and thus perhaps satisfy his vanity as well as his love of pleasure'. In the combination of a sturdy—at times rough—independence shown by the lower orders with an acceptance of differences of rank, Vauxhall was a fair sample of English society. And among the most uncritically admired attractions of Vauxhall were the more florid pieces of patriotic academy painting.[2] When in 1792 Boswell deplored the raising of the price of admission from one to two shillings because it would exclude common tradesmen from the elegant gaiety of the entertainment, such educational advantages were no doubt in his mind. Certainly the standards of the artistic revival affected commercial design speedily and advantageously. The able painter Joseph Wright (famous for candle-light pieces), as well as Stubbs, were employed by Wedgwood as advisers in production. Arkwright was another rising middle-class industrialist who patronized Wright.[3]

Nowhere is the masterful certainty of this society clearer than in its literature. The achievement of Edward Gibbon[4] is characteristic of the age. His genius lies in his ability to see so vast a subject as the decline of Rome as a whole; he combined this vision with a keen critical sense as he explored scholarly details. The defect of the achievement is connected with its strength:

[1] Mrs. George's splendid *Catalogue of Political and Personal Satires* in the British Museum is, in consequence, a detailed (and racy) social and political history, particularly of the years 1780–1815.

[2] See C. P. Moritz's *Travels in England in 1782* (modern ed. by P. E. Matheson, 1924).

[3] Joseph Wright (1734–97), known as Wright of Derby, where he practised; refused election to the Royal Academy 1784.

[4] Edward Gibbon (1737–94), an M.P. and commissioner for trade; a member of Johnson's Club; formed his plan for a history of the decline of Rome during residence in Italy. It was published between 1776 and 1788.

the standpoint is so sure, so firmly held, that to those not in
Gibbon's world it appears automatic. Life is cut to a pattern.
Gibbon's style, again, is complicated, artificial, yet in his hands
easy. His fluency, as Porson[1] unkindly commented, was like that
of the auctioneer who can be as eloquent on ribbons as on a
Raphael. Every part of page-long sentences is balanced internally and with the context. He can rival Burke in majesty of
exposition. Both, indeed, are supreme in perceiving great principles in passing events and in relating them to firmly held basic
philosophies, but whereas Burke is warmly persuasive Gibbon is
cold and cynical.

It is not by chance that two other historians, Hume and
Robertson,[2] should follow Gibbon in any list of literary achievements of the age. For both the style and spirit of the age were
seen at their best in compilation and criticism. Dr. Johnson
himself, the centre of a middle-class group of intellectuals, is
memorable for the sturdiness of his critical power. His *Lives of
the Poets* exemplify a clear-headed application of simple canons
of judgement, set forth in a formal prose and enlivened, as
everything about this doctor was, by quirks of idiosyncrasy
which gain effect from the conventionality of their context.
Boswell admired this self-disciplined security while he himself
was incapable, for all his efforts, of imitating it. For this reason
his picture of the age in his *Life of Johnson* is the most vivid that
exists.

Among novelists two great talents were reaching their end.
The Reverend Laurence Sterne published *Tristram Shandy* between 1760 and 1768; in that year came his *Sentimental Journey*
and his own death. Both books depend for their success upon
the same elements. Sterne is among the most intellectual of
novelists in the sense that everything comes from the head. He
is sentimental, obscene, paradoxical, fantastic, all with an elegance of sophisticated ingenuity. Everything is contrived with
the greatest cleverness, even the humours of Uncle Toby or the
death of a donkey; he sports with ideas and conventional clichés.

---

[1] Edward Porson (1759–1808), the greatest Greek scholar of the age, renowned
alike for his memory and his thirst for alcohol. In 1792 he lost his fellowship at
Trinity, Cambridge, and entered on the most influential period of his life.

[2] For Hume see above, p. 327. William Robertson (1721–93), principal of Edinburgh University, 1762; his *History of Scotland* (1759) and *History of Charles V* (1769)
demonstrate his method of building generalization upon an extensive groundwork
of facts laboriously assembled.

He depends upon that sober common sense he affects to despise, as with brilliance he cuts his insane capers, laughs, whines, elicits sympathy, and jeers at it, all in a triumph of self-confident art. The other great novelist, Samuel Richardson, died in 1761 and had greater influence probably in France than in England. Richardson on the face of things was a snob and a hypocrite. But in all his vulgar dramas about seduction in high society there is displayed a great analytical ability. He takes for granted (and with gusto) the merits of rank and proceeds to dissect, within this passing framework, the elemental problems of human desires, with a minuteness almost Proustian.

The only other considerable novelist with a vogue in these years was Fanny Burney. She was the daughter of Dr. Burney, a composer, performer and historian of music in the Italianate style popular at the time; for a while she was employed at court and moved in the best literary circles. Her novels show her interest in such social problems as a young girl's entry into society. Her acceptance of the pattern of the day is as complete as Richardson's, though she permits herself to be a little more critical; even the titled may be ridiculed by shrewd common sense. She is, however, less profound than he in her search after fundamental passions and appetites. Her view of life seems superficial, but it is made entertaining by her liking for caricature and for ironic comment. In all this she seems to anticipate, though less keen-edgedly, the work of Jane Austen thirty years later.[1] The startling success of her *Evelina* on its appearance in 1778 was certainly gained by her knack of combining keen observation of character with a plot which is set forth in plain prose.

In writing for the theatre the two great names are Sheridan[2] and Goldsmith. Sheridan wrote with a fine sense of public demand. His mannered comedies are full of simple verbal tricks. His plots are reminiscent of late seventeenth-century plays, such as those of Wycherley. Once that comparison is made, however, the bloodlessness of Sheridan's characters must be felt—and the watering down of the wit. He has no passion behind his tricks,

[1] See below, p. 538.
[2] Richard Brinsley Sheridan (1751–1816), politician, theatre manager, dramatist, and drunkard; a faithful member of the entourage of the prince of Wales; one of the most rhetorical of the orators of the age. For his part in politics see the narrative.

not even the force of disgust or sensuality; the intellectual dexterity sparkles but it does not burn: he is merely playing pretty tricks with a few well-known counters. Goldsmith, too, is a playwright with little original creation in him. His figures are equally stock types familiar to every man and woman in the audience. The moods he skilfully arranges are as conventional as the paradoxes of Sheridan. Neither asked an audience to adjust its habits of thought or startled it with a novelty. The articles they dealt in were very different but they both came in well-known packets. This is as true of *She Stoops to Conquer* as of *The Rivals* or *The School for Scandal*. There is more native force in Foote's farces, but these were too dependent on passing allusions to read well to later generations. Arthur Murphy was another lesser playwright who had his scenes of real power, but he, lacking the verbal felicity of Sheridan or the control of atmosphere of Goldsmith, tried too hard to please and had to emphasize his meaning in heavy, moralizing, final acts. On the stage, in short, this was a period of a few accomplished pieces in a shallow convention and of many Shakespearian revivals in which the text had to be tailored into fashionable shape.

In these years everyone seemed able to turn out verses and none to achieve great poetry. The couplets of Pope were used with competence by a hundred successors. The style lent itself particularly to making an argument more forceful, and so to political satire. Charles Churchill was the most effective in this field: the formality of his verse gave emphasis to the unbridled ferocity of his language. But even less anguished souls—John Wolcot ('Peter Pindar') or the politicians who compiled the *Rolliad*,[1] for instance—could produce witty and entertaining effects in this genre. The more serious poets of repute, Gray,[2] Warton,[3] Goldsmith, were neat, conventional in feeling, tending to easy sentiment. There was too great an acceptance of clichés, of emotion denoted by stock symbols such as owls, towers, ivy, and so on. When arranged with discrimination, as in Gray's

---

[1] A series of verses about members of the house of commons produced by a group of lively members of the whig opposition in 1784.

[2] Thomas Gray (1716-71), professor of history and modern languages at Cambridge 1768; published *Ode on a distant prospect of Eton College*, 1747, and his *Elegy in a Country Churchyard*, 1751.

[3] Thomas Warton (1728-90), professor of poetry at Oxford, 1757-67; Camden professor of ancient history; poet laureate, 1785-90; attacked the Chatterton forgeries, 1782; published *The Triumph of Isis*, 1749, *The Oxford Sausage*, 1764.

best work (which was almost over by this time) these counters could be made to express a real poetical effect—but a limited one. The sentiment of Gray is as remote from romantic excitement as wistful age is from yearning youth. In Crabbe,[1] indeed, who was just becoming known in the early 1780's, a more personal note was played on the old pipes. But even here there is no throwing over the traces. Rather Crabbe comments sourly on human fortunes from the point of view of common sense. Only William Cowper[2] wrote in old measures with a new spirit. Cowper had failed to steel himself for worldly success. The prospect of responsibility threw him into mental breakdown. The only escape from this which he attempted was through faith in an extreme form of fundamentalist protestantism. This in itself put Cowper outside the assured world of the dons, Gray and Warton. Though he was outside he did not despise, or attempt to overthrow, the values of that world. He simply knew that by its standards he was lost. Just so, he accepted the doctrines of calvinist predestination, and recognized that he was predestined to damnation. Something of this makes itself felt in his poetry. The comfortable metre contains in it some uncomfortable despair: the gentle humour has an undertone of tragedy. The result is sometimes great poetry.

North of the border Robert Burns was certainly remote from the stylized certainties of English academic poetry. Yet one cannot therefore rank him as a rebel against the stable world of his day. In the first place the Scottish tradition in poetry was less conventionalized: the school of Ramsay and Ferguson preserved a simplicity in the expression of real country scenes. This tradition Burns crowned with his own tragic dignity and power. The secret of Burns's poetry lies in his personality. He was a man of good heart who respected the virtues of the world in which he was reared: but he was also a man of strong, direct, feelings and appetites, to which he yielded. He observed the working of these same forces in the world around him and set it

---

[1] George Crabbe (1754–1832), a self-taught Suffolk poet; worked as a servant to a doctor and then, after study, practised as a doctor himself; published *The Candidate*, 1780, *The Village*, 1783, *The Borough*, 1810; became a non-resident rector of livings in Leicestershire.

[2] William Cowper (1731–1800), a solicitor and commissioner of bankrupts; victim of melancholia; in an asylum, 1763–5; lay reader for the evangelical curate of Olney; suffered recurring fits of madness; published *Olney Hymns*, 1779, *John Gilpin*, 1782, *The Task*, 1783, *The Castaway*, 1798; recipient of a government pension.

all down with zest. He respected equally his vision of the humble
man and of the leading man. In one inspired six months during
1785 and 1786 he wrote nearly all that is valuable in his work.
He was a success, a hero of educated Edinburgh society. He
delighted in this. He liked to be petted by a painted society
lady, though he did not cease to see her as an unvarnished
woman. He did not break with high society: it, or physical
exhaustion, broke him: after his inspired half year he was
capable of no more than polished trifles. Burns's pictures of ordinary life are so vivid as to make the radical reader suppose that
he must have wished to advance the humble characters whom
he understood so well. It is true that he sympathized with the
French Revolution because it asserted the dignity of man. On
the other hand must be set his acceptance of the imperfect world
around him and his study to advance his family along its conventional paths. Struggling between appetite and duty he put
himself into his poetry; there even his common sense acquires a
moving eloquence. The world acclaimed him for what he was,
a unique phenomenon. There was no sequel. A few rebels
warmed their hearts with the poems, but the established interests were no whit disturbed by them.

On examination, many of the so-called signs of a rising radical
romanticism prove to be further signs of snug security. Beckford's *Vathek*[1] (an imitation of the Arabian Nights written in
French) or Horace Walpole's *Castle of Otranto* (a medievalist
horror story) were tricks of very bookish men. The wealthy
dilettante and the statesman's son both collected bric-à-brac:
they also created these two specimens of it. Those who lived by
common sense enjoyed a safe glance at other worlds, eastern
and magniloquent, or gothic and incoherent. So, too, a generation without doubt that its own values were eternal derived a
little scholarly enjoyment from the study of remote traditions.
There was the charm of novelty in medievalism. Hence the
excitement created by Macpherson's reconstructing pieces of
Gaelic verse to form a fraudulent opus of a great poet 'Ossian'.[2]

---

[1] William Beckford (1759–1844) was the son of the wealthy lord mayor of
London (see p. 96 n. 1). *Vathek* appeared when he was 22. Beckford with Fonthill
Abbey, as Walpole with Strawberry Hill, chose to put his fancies into bricks and
mortar.

[2] James Macpherson (1736–96) was a scholar, a versifier, and a politician. In
the latter capacity he was a champion of Lord North's American policy. His
Gaelic poems were a skilful mixture of real originals with his own work.

Thomas Chatterton, trying similarly to catch an easy market, invented the medieval poetry of Rowley and added to its meretricious interest by his own suicide.[1] Dr. Thomas Percy, a good and honest scholar, gave the literary world genuine work of interest with his *Reliques of Ancient English Poetry* in 1765.[2] The market for these discoveries was the same that the bookseller Dodsley catered for with his edition of English plays of the previous two centuries. In the more troubled future such survivals might seem to afford inspiration to men of creative power who sickened of the polished style of the eighteenth century. But such a response was not possible so long as the social order remained unchallenged. Up to about 1790 an interest in remote cultures was the hobby of a circle whose own culture was as urbane as it was unquestionable. Such an interest was merely a relief from tedium. It may be compared to that 'gloom' which was so much the pose of young Englishmen that it was regarded on the Continent as one of the national characteristics. This gloom was the balancing side to an existence too clearly mapped, too calculated, and lit with steady lights: beginning as a psychological relief it had become a fad.[3] C. J. Fox had a happier mode of escape. When the world was too much with him he read his Latin or just sat in the sun until his natural equanimity returned.

The French Revolution, both in itself and in its economic consequences, marked the end of a social and cultural as well as a political epoch in England. In all spheres the more profound effects took time to show themselves. But even at the outset some significant changes appeared. Miss Hannah More, hitherto a facile playwright, a blue stocking, a lively companion at literary dinner-parties, turned in 1789 to good works. Convulsions across the channel made her aware of the seamier side of life at home. An earnestness, hitherto the monopoly of the dissenting groups outside the main stream of English life, invaded governing circles and the church of England.[4] At Clapham by 1793 there was gathered round the Reverend Joseph Venn's church a most powerful evangelical group. Pitt's friend,

[1] In 1770 when he was but eighteen years old.

[2] Thomas Percy (1729–1811), bishop of Dromore; in addition to the *Reliques* published other antiquarian work including *Northern Antiquities*, 1770.

[3] Dr. Johnson may serve as an example of the first stage, Boswell of the second.

[4] Philanthropy was not new, of course; see the work of Raikes and Howard, described above, pp. 38, 39. What is new is the spirit with which it was now pursued and organized on a broad front.

Wilberforce, Thornton of the Bank of England, Granville Sharp (a seasoned radical campaigner for philanthropy) and, later on, the returned Indian administrator Lord Teignmouth, these were the powerful 'Saints' of Clapham. They re-examined their own bases of conduct and argued to others that 'the author of all moral obligation has enjoined us to renounce certain actions, without any enquiry as to reason or consequences'.[1] Yet they were not negative abstentionists. With them self-examination was soon followed by self-expression. Their faith had a new vigour and practical expression. Charles Simeon,[2] who owed much to the influence of Venn, forced his evangelical views upon his Cambridge congregation. He was a founder of the Church Missionary Society (in 1797) and a champion of the interdenominational British and Foreign Bible Society (founded 1804), both notable as expressing a new confidence in propagandist purpose. In such organizations, as well as in governing Sierra Leone as a home for freed slaves, Zachary Macaulay,[3] the father of the historian, found an outlet for his purposeful energy.

The Claphamites were, however, intensely conservative and they by no means rejected the social pattern of their day. The limit of their innovation was to urge a greater seriousness in self-discipline within that design. In their dealing with negro slavery, to take the most famous of their activities, they first attacked the trade and it was long before they condemned the institution. This was much more than tactics. Slavery was not bad in itself, but the trade was iniquitous because it involved the brutal alteration of status and domicile (often to the next world) of West Africans. The Claphamites never exhorted a slave to revolt[4] because they did not want to interfere with the obedience due from one section in society to their natural superiors. Yet the conduct of some slave owners might be bad: therefore they should be exhorted to behave better. So at home the evangelicals were increasingly conscious of social evils and deplored them. But they opposed the formation of unions of

---

[1] Wilberforce in the *Christian Observer* (April 1807).

[2] Charles Simeon (1759-1836), Fellow of King's College, Cambridge, and vicar of Holy Trinity, Cambridge: set up trustees to secure and administer Church patronage on evangelical principles.

[3] Zachary Macaulay (1768-1838) was also editor of the *Christian Observer*.

[4] Except for one rash statement by Wilberforce's brother-in-law, the barrister, James Stephen (1758-1832).

working men: to them such energized self-help seemed as immoral as a slave insurrection. Their reliance was upon the
voluntary benevolence of converted employers. Hannah More,
as an associate of the Claphamites, set herself the task of educating
the poor both through her Mendip schools and through cheap
tracts. But it is significant that she would teach them to read
while refusing to encourage them to write. For writing was too
active a skill for their station. They should be made receptive
to good ideas whose framing was divinely entrusted to other
heads than theirs.[1]

That the existing order of their world was natural was a belief
as strongly held by the Claphamites as by any of the writers or
public figures in the palmy days before 1790. They saw it
threatened. They believed an attack on authority anywhere
might open the flood-gates to chaos. As representatives of
authority they were, however, prepared to scrutinize their own
behaviour with greater consciousness of sin than their fathers
had done. This was an interim reaction to the upheaval in
France.

The first consequence of the new forces released after 1790
was to solidify the surface of the established order. But as widespread changes proceeded beneath this surface it became brittle.
To doubt the virtues of the established order became dangerous.
But for the young to do so was almost inevitable. In every
department of thought and expression a new passion began to
show, the product of uncertainty and conflict. Economic changes
forced on the intellectual battle. In social life, when the leadership of the country gentlemen was in danger, their conservatism,
their conviction that they followed the only patriotic course,
became aggressive where before it had been only an unconscious assumption. So in politics, the old enemies of Pitt were
faced with problems both long-term and immediate. In the
long run they were called upon to decide their attitude to the
new radicalism in its intellectual and its practical development.
More pressingly, as a matter of tactics once war with the revolution began, they had to contrive how any sort of opposition
to Pitt could survive in face of blind but powerful patriotic
emotions.

[1] On this see the *Life of Hannah More*, by M. Gladys Jones (*passim*).

XIV

THE FIRST STAGE OF THE WAR
1793–8

THE war which began in 1793 in the long run gave an entirely new character to Pitt's régime. Within a year the duke of Portland, as a realistic patriot, forgave the way in which Pitt had supported the king in seizing power in 1783; for Pitt alone could lead the country in resisting France in 1794. Equally important was the change in outlook of back-bench squires: when every loyal man of respectability feared not only the French but their 'agents' in England, the squires perforce cried out for stronger government action. But these recruits to Pitt inevitably made their leader in a new image. He personally was still the man of day-to-day practicabilities, interested mainly in economic reform: but his significance to the country was now his resoluteness as an opponent of France and French ideas. From this it followed that the party of Mr. Pitt, whose origins have already been explored,[1] acquired in its maturity a philosophy. This was a new sort of conservatism, one not contentedly rooted in the past, but one fiercely on the defensive. Within the leadership of the coalition of groups in the government were divergent views on most problems of the day: but they were all united in this, that they put victory in war before the success of any of their own views while they feared radical upheaval more than they supported any scheme of reform.

This unity in fundamentals, combined with variety in everything else, gave the government great strength: but it was strength which was derived from crisis and which encouraged hysteria. There was a witch-hunt in the countryside. The opinions of the village might be checked by a house to house inquiry. The suspect notables might expect local ostracism. Only in areas under the domination of some great landed proprietor who had thrown in his lot with Fox were radical opinions unthreatened by popular excitement. The new enthusiasm for the king's government was matched, though unevenly, by a new excitement against it. The centre of this was not found

[1] See above, pp. 267 f. and 273 f.

among Foxites in parliament. The role of Fox's friends was, indeed, one of aloofness. They stood outside the conflict and excitement, refusing to step down into the arena, maintaining at all costs an old-fashioned devotion to unemotional radicalism. Fox, in the midst of war, in 1797, bade the house of commons 'be as ready to adopt the virtues, as you are steady in averting from the country the vices, of France'. Fox confessed it gave him pleasure to see France gain advantage over England, so long as our policy remained so mistaken. He felt no need to defend the bad against the worse. He was quick to attribute the admitted evils of the government of revolutionary France to the mistaken hostility of conservative Europe. This was enough to make Fox seem, to all but his close friends, either a mountebank or a traitor. In a reformed electorate the champions of parliamentary reform would have been swept away. Fox's friends, to the number of ninety or so, secure in their hold on unreformed boroughs, were able to advocate reform whatever the political climate. But they were vague in their notions of it. They defended the victims of repression at home without leading them.

The real leadership of the new radicalism was outside the old political circles; it rested with intellectuals like Thelwall, closely backed by 'artisans, shopkeepers, dissenting ministers, schoolmasters'.[1] Support came not from the poorest nor from the unorganized labour of the industrial towns: rather it was dissenters of the middle class, men of skill either handicraft or professional, men conscious both of ability and of lack of privilege or opportunity, who gave strength to radicalism. The character of the movement was indicative of the as yet unbroken firmness of the social system against which it agitated. For it was a movement of political theory not of economic organization, of a political theory, moreover, looking back to Locke and 1688 though stimulated by French contemporary rhetoric. In many ways the radical societies of 1793 had more in common with Wilkes than with those born in industrial conditions after 1800: they were more old-fashioned than the machine-breakers. Where they differed from Wilkes was in their seriousness of purpose; this was reflected in the proliferation of their societies.

[1] C. Cestre, *John Thelwall*, p. 159. Thelwall (1764–1834), a tailor and attorney's clerk; joined Society of Friends of the People; arrested, charged with treason but acquitted, 1794; pamphleteer and poet; lectured on the cure of defective speech.

All political organization seems to have made great strides at this time. The respectable propaganda against the slave trade, for instance, anticipated some of the methods of the Anti-Corn-Law League.[1] With the support of men of means they showered pamphlets about slaving horrors on the public. With the aid of dissenting churches they organized meetings in every locality, and initiated petitions to the house of commons. They had indeed a sort of bureau for information and propaganda. Wilberforce was their parliamentary spokesman whose brief came prepared by the back-room experts of the anti-slave headquarters. The radical politicians lacked the means to imitate this. But they had the more easily copied, if more dangerous, example of the French clubs to inspire them.

The Society for Constitutional Information tried to extend its ideas at least among the literate by sponsoring editions of radical pamphlets. The Corresponding Society of London had, like the Jacobins, its daughter associations. By 1793 it was linked with Manchester, Stockport, Norwich, and Sheffield. It was the most serious attempt to seize control of the forces of discontent (which had found expression hitherto only in endemic riots) and use them not for passing political advantage but to make a more egalitarian society. The Corresponding Society was not an innovator in ideas; its doctrines were those of Locke spiced with Rousseau. Their basis was the idea of government as a trust given by the majority of the people. In detail this was translated into manhood suffrage, annual parliaments, cheaper government, the end of unjust land enclosures, and a simpler legal system. It was certainly more radical than any proposals hitherto submitted to parliament. Equally important was the fact that the Corresponding Society was founded by a shoemaker (Hardy) and charged only 1d. a week for membership, with an entrance fee of 1s., as compared with 5 guineas a year demanded by the Constitutional Society. Moreover the Corresponding Society had an apparatus of general committee and executive committee, changing monthly, thus training its members in administration.

Inevitably the Corresponding Society looked to France for inspiration. In November 1792 Frost[2] (a qualified attorney) and

[1] See Sir E. L. Woodward, *The Age of Reform*, pp. 113, 114.
[2] John Frost (1750–1842), secretary (and a founder) of the Corresponding Society: struck off the roll of attorneys, 1793.

Barlow had presented addresses from the Society to the French Convention, with assurances that the British people would never support war against liberty. In theory one might no doubt, after 1793, support the British war effort while praising the political ideas of the enemy: in practice such activity seemed dangerously disloyal. In February 1793 Frost was sent to prison for six months as a result of a seditious conversation in a tavern. In August 1793 Thomas Muir, another lawyer and a founder of the Scottish Friends of the People, was sentenced to fourteen years' transportation for seditious speeches. The Scottish judges, particularly Lord Braxfield, showed themselves more in touch with the panic of the ruling class and less scrupulous of the traditions of their impartial office than their English counterparts. Braxfield took up a line of argument which had not been heard in English courts for almost a century. The constitution, he held, was perfect. Therefore anyone proposing change was prima facie an enemy of the state. Moreover the constitution lodged authority in the hands of a limited number of people: to encourage others, not given such power, to interest themselves in questions of state was, by inevitable practical consequence, an incitement to violence. Violent pressure for change was only slightly removed from open war against the king's government. On such reasoning another victim, a leading Scottish unitarian, a former fellow of Queens' College, Cambridge, Thomas Palmer, was sentenced in September 1793 to seven years' transportation.

The effect of such savagery in Scotland was to make reformers everywhere more desperate. It was feared that Hessian troops might enforce military discipline on the populace. Fears of government spies increased. At the end of 1793 a convention met in Edinburgh where delegates from popular societies made preparations for secret meetings of delegates to deal with a foreign landing or to resist government interference. For this three of the leaders, including Margarot the president of the London Corresponding Society, were transported. The response of the radicals was to issue appeals in 1794 for a further national convention. In doing so they obviously challenged the authority of parliament. However moderate their proposals for reform, they were, in proposing to meet on a national scale, claiming to be a rival body expressing the will of the community better than the house of commons. Moreover they were set upon petitioning the king for an end of the war with France. In Scotland the usual arrests were followed by the usual—except that there was even a death sentence this time—punishments. In England, however, the leaders arrested—Hardy, the veteran agitator Horne Tooke, Thelwall, and ten others—were indicted for high treason. They were acquitted. The government had overplayed its hand. The charge of high treason had to be supported by evidence of intent to use armed force which was extremely flimsy: a lesser charge might have succeeded. As it was the reform clubs entered 1795 in a mood of jubilation and a spate of mass meetings which, in London, caused such alarm that the cavalry were held in readiness for open conflict. Mass support for the agitators was increased by the bad harvest of 1794 with high food prices and dislocated trade during the wet cold summer of 1795.[1]

Pitt, faced with the possibility of invasion, determined to recover by legislation the authority lost by haphazard prosecution. Already in 1794 parliament had temporarily suspended the Habeas Corpus Act so as to allow political suspects to be held without trial. Following peace demonstrations, during which a stone was thrown at the king, parliament passed two acts to restore order. The Seditious Meetings Act prohibited, for the next three years, meetings of more than fifty people except under licence of the local magistrates and under their control. No lectures (outside the universities and schools) were allowed except under similar licence and supervision by magistrates. The Treasonable Practices Act redefined the law of treason. Those who devised evil against the king, those who plotted to help invaders, and those who sought to coerce parliament, were all brought within its scope: those who dared to attack the constitution were made liable to seven years' transportation. Foxites bitterly complained that these acts made it an offence to do what Pitt himself had done only ten years before: criticism of the constitution had carried him to the cabinet, but now it would bear a poor wretch away to Botany Bay.

Much depended in 1796 on the way these acts were administered. Severe but consistent action was preferable to the irregu-

---

[1] The summer of 1795 does not appear in the records as an exceptionally bad one. But poor weather followed a hard winter lasting into March with frost damaging the wheat when it 'bloomed'. Moreover, in 1793 rain had damaged the harvest and there was a drought in 1794. 1795 was thus one of a series of poor years.

lated ferocity of Braxfield. It was an advantage that since 1794 Portland had replaced Dundas as home secretary, for the duke was neither a zealot nor a Scot. Much was left to the discretion of local magistrates. Inevitably this was so, for the weakness which made the government ferocious was its lack of any agents of central authority save the armed forces. But in consequence knowledge of local conditions and men was, under the advice of the Home Office, important in the administration of the law. The effervescence seems quickly to have subsided. The societies were cautious and kept their meetings to less than fifty people. It is perhaps the best argument that the government were unnecessarily alarmed that the repressive legislation was accepted with docility by most of the population. It was not possible to prove a connexion between the naval mutinies (at the Nore and at Spithead in 1797)[1] and the revolutionary clubs. By 1798 the London Corresponding Society was debating a motion that it should form a loyal corps to resist French invasion, so disillusioned were they by the progress of events across the Channel. Thelwall, the most spirited and pugnacious of the propagandists, gave up the struggle in 1797, concluding that his countrymen were 'enslaved because degenerate'.

At the very end of this first period of popular agitation, as the fire went out of the clubs, the whig grandees made their most positive gesture. Up to this point the 'Friends of the People' had been too languid or too alarmed or too divided to do more than protest at the violence of contending parties. In 1796 Fox posed their problem: if the court triumphed there would be no place in English life for men of his liberal principles; if the democrats won then there would be a 'state of things which can make a man doubt whether despotism of a monarchy is the worst of all evils'.[2] His aim was still to restore a balanced constitution of the old type with a parliament mediating between Crown and people. Experience had convinced him that the whigs of his group must lead and control popular passion so as to win power and save the Crown. In 1797 his disciple Charles Grey,[3] the future prime minister, moved resolutions for reform. He proposed a uniform household franchise for boroughs, the substi-

---

[1] See below, pp. 372 f.   [2] C. J. Fox, *Correspondence*, iii. 135.

[3] Charles Grey (1764–1845), later Viscount Howick and second Earl Grey; the prime minister who passed the 1832 Reform Bill; at this date he had acted with Fox on the regency question, helped with the impeachment of Hastings, and joined the Friends of the People.

tution of more county members for corrupt borough nominees, and triennial parliaments. In doing so he defended the French Revolution—'in the end it will tend to the diffusion of liberty and rational knowledge all over the world'. Fox went further. He claimed that the French had discovered a new motive force in human affairs. England should not assail but adapt their work. These proposals were a first step towards making every man feel his part in the state so that he could feel 'he is fighting for himself and not another; that it is his own cause, his own safety, his own concern, his own dignity on the face of the earth and his own interest on the identical soil which he has to maintain'. Pitt replied flatly that the hazard was too great, and that the abuses of the constitution were an integral part of its charm. In debate Fox soared and Pitt sat heavily upon the ground, but in action Pitt remained heroic, defying all odds in a chosen course, while Fox declined into a pettish refusal to attend parliament for some months. After a vote of 256 to 91 had rejected Grey's plan the Foxites 'seceded' from both houses.

The renewal of agitation out of doors in 1798 was more industrial in character: already the war was having its disturbing effect upon the economy. It was met therefore not only by the Newspaper Publication Act, which put publishers under the close supervision of the magistrates, but also by the acts against combinations. In 1799 the Corresponding Society and other such bodies with linked branches, oaths, or secret offices were suppressed. In that year, and the following, all combinations of workmen to harass their employers by shortening hours or increasing wages were made punishable by summary jurisdiction.[1] This legislation marked a further stage in the growing militancy of the conservatives behind Pitt. The acts of 1795 had dealt with a particular crisis in war effectively if fiercely. The acts of 1799 showed a deep-seated fear of the new form of society. The provision for the trial of industrial offences before two magistrates simply made the masters judges of their own men in many cases. The answer to such legislation was bound to be sporadic violence by men who felt themselves outside the law. It is significant that the whigs hardly noted the passage of this

---

[1] These statutes were a reinforcement of the law. Active unions of workmen could also be repressed under the common law doctrines of conspiracy. But the acts of parliament were intended to intimidate the men and to make their punishment more speedy and more certain.

legislation; only Hobhouse, Sheridan, Burdett, and Lord Holland[1] made any opposition. These acts were indeed no part of the struggle over French or radical ideas. They were the first signs of a rising class struggle, of a new age of conflict which marked the nineteenth century.

It should not be supposed that because Pitt supported repressive legislation at home he had entered the war with France in any ideological spirit. He entered it in 1793 with very limited aims. He thought, as his father had, that Britain's true interest lay outside Europe. She had certain spheres of interest, the Netherlands, the Baltic, the Mediterranean, where her security could be threatened. Apart from these she had no real areas of European policy, only an interest in engaging her trading rival France in Europe so as to outstrip her overseas. In 1793 the French invasion of the Austrian Netherlands had touched on one of the vital areas of interest. It had also robbed Austria of one of her possessions. Pitt's policy was therefore to help Austria recover her territory, thereby automatically restoring British security. He had to work with Austria, but would avoid committing himself to the general policy of the allies, their royalist campaign in particular. The main British activity would be the capture of French islands overseas. The course of the war was to convince Pitt, within four years, that he could not work with allies without framing a European policy in co-operation with them; the disasters of the allied arms speedily made all Englishmen aware that they fought not for profit but for survival.

In 1793, however, most men shared Pitt's view both that they should not be principals in the war and that it would be short. The army and navy were not on a war footing after the ten years of economy which had followed peace with America, but the navy at least had been improved in efficiency since Lord North. It was easily expansible by pressing the men and resources of mercantile shipping into the king's service. One hundred and thirteen sail of the line were available of which three-quarters were ready for service once they had crews. But economy had consciously been allowed to reduce the army to a

---

[1] Henry Richard Vassall Fox, third Baron Holland (1773–1840), nephew of Charles James Fox; lord privy seal, 1806–7; urged abolition of death penalty for stealing; chancellor of the duchy of Lancaster in Grey's reform ministry; wrote *Memoirs of the Whig Party* and other contributions to political history.

skeleton. Grenville considered that once the French Revolution broke out the greatest danger to the state lay in the revolutionary clubs. But they would be formidable only if bad times gave them mass support. The surest defence therefore was to reduce military expenditure in order to keep up standards of domestic ease, an argument with a very modern ring. It was in this spirit that, only nine months before war, Pitt had made fresh reductions in the army from 17,000 to 13,000 men. However, when France declared war on 1 February 1793, it was possible to send the duke of York with three battalions, of very poor quality, over immediately to assist in the defence of Holland.

The allied powers, Prussia, Austria, and the *emigrés*, had embarked on war nominally to defend the French monarchy. Their hesitant invasion of France in 1792 had failed because they lacked determination. Their objectives were still, in 1793, extremely doubtful. For in January 1793 Prussian troops had entered Poland. Further partitioning of that country between Prussia and Russia was advanced in plan. Austria resented the attempt to leave her a loser in the east: increasingly her aim was not to restore the French monarchy but to gain some resounding territorial success in the west to compensate for falling behind in the race to the east. In February 1793 Austrian statesmen were anxious to recover their Netherlands mainly in order to persuade the elector of Bavaria to surrender his country to them in exchange for Belgium. By March the Austrians were more anxious to conquer Alsace as part of a similar exchange bargain. In each case they discussed the use of prizes before they had them. While the allies were distracted and mutually suspicious Doumouriez dashed with the French army into the Netherlands. His threat to Holland produced the need for the duke of York's expeditionary force under the supreme command of the Austrian general Prince Frederick of Saxe-Coburg.

Pitt still supposed nevertheless that his rôle in Europe would be that of paymaster. In March 1793 a subsidy treaty was negotiated with Russia. By the end of August Britain had agreed to finance Austria, Prussia, Sardinia, Hesse-Cassel, Spain, and Naples, in war on France. At British insistence the allies had dropped their demands for a royalist restoration—which must involve unconditional surrender—though the ultimate war aims were not thereupon defined. It was exceedingly difficult for Britain to do more than exert herself financially and diplomatically. Apart from the troops sent with the duke of York she could count upon 14,000 men from the king's Hanoverian electorate. Eight thousand Hessian mercenaries were as usual taken into British service. There remained a need to increase the size of the British army. The method of doing this was deplorable. The militia was called up for home defence in order to release regular troops for service overseas. But a system of paid substitution for militia service was allowed. Thus many evaded service by substituting for themselves others who would have been the natural reserve from which to draw regular troops for overseas. Secondly, encouragement was given to anyone who would raise an independent company or a company of fencibles. The latter were regular troops raised for home service for the duration of the war. In the independent companies the offer of rank was used as encouragement; the nomination of officers by private recruiting agents resulted in bad officers and in disgruntlement among regular officers who were passed in promotion. One of the few good things arising from this individual enterprise in recruitment was the formation of the Seaforth Highlanders. Yet given the social system, the supremacy of the squire in the countryside, it was difficult to avoid decentralizing recruitment in this way. The dislike of the standing army made Englishmen instinctively distrust expansion of armed forces under the control of the Crown: the idea of conscription for service overseas was beyond imagination. Even the French did not have conscription until 1798. Meanwhile the regular army not only had its potential recruits taken away for home service: the navy, with its traditional right of pressing, stole as much untrained manpower as it could.

The chaos of recruitment was matched by confusion in direction. There was no commander-in-chief. The secretary-at-war was concerned with the equipment and supply of armies and was not necessarily senior enough to be in the Cabinet. In the cabinet the minister with the greatest authority in military planning was the secretary of state Dundas, but the secretary of state for foreign affairs, Grenville, was sometimes his rival. In truth the war had to be run by a committee of the king, Pitt, and Dundas, carrying with them the rest of the cabinet, and there was, for the first twelve months, no war minister. Even when,

---

[1] The office was held from 1783 to 1794 by Sir G. Yonge, later an unsuccessful governor of the Cape of Good Hope. Windham became Secretary-at-War in 1794.

in 1794, Dundas was given particular charge of war, in the new office of Secretary of State for War, he was not relieved of all his other ministerial jobs nor, for that matter, of interference from colleagues.[1]

The result of these inadequacies at the top and bottom of the military machine, when combined with a mistaken idea of the strength of the French, may be seen in Pitt's schemes in April 1793. He entered into negotiations with French colonials in the island of Haiti with the purpose of capturing their half of the island: simultaneously he devised raids on the French Brittany coast: these were to be attempted at the same time as an offensive expedition in the eastern Mediterranean: but none of this was to prevent an intensification of the British effort in Flanders. Yet to undertake these worldwide military campaigns he had an available British army of only 20,000 effectives.

The British cabinet indeed believed that the war was almost over. Doumouriez had been defeated at Neerwinden in March 1793. When he fled his own camp and deserted to the allies there seemed a possibility that the revolution would be crushed. But Coburg preferred the classical war of advance by sieges to that of the thrust past fortified towns. He sat down to take every French strong point in the north. By July he had captured Valenciennes while farther south Mainz also had fallen. France seemed to be yielding to steady pressure around her frontiers. The allies withdrew their proclamation which had promised that they did not intend annexation. But the answer of France was total war. Carnot appeared at the Committee of Public Safety in August. The French prepared to resist with every man, the *levée en masse*. The secret of French victory was for the future to consist in their adopting first the practice and then the full principle of conscription. Enough of the old French army remained to give shape and elementary training to the masses of men thus made available. The French hurled hordes of half-trained men against the small professional armies of the allies. Amateur soldiers were more expendible than mercenaries. With ruthless generals, the French were able to force their enemies to retire on all sides.

---

[1] Dundas continued to be Treasurer of the Navy (until 1800) and President of the Indian Board of Control (until 1801). He prophesied 'constant wrangling' with 'the various Executive Boards' while 'the Master General of the Ordnance, the First Lord of the Admiralty, the Commander in Chief and now the Secretary at War are all of the Cabinet,' as well as the new Secretary.

In the summer of 1793 the duke of York with his 6,500 British, 13,000 Hanoverians, and 15,000 Dutch troops moved towards Dunkirk while waiting for 8,000 Hessians to arrive. He was repulsed by the French at Hondschoote. It was evident that a combined operation with the navy was necessary. But the navy was elsewhere, part of it at Nantes supporting an unsuccessful rising against the ruthless Jacobins in the Loire valley, part of it in the Mediterranean. Nevertheless, Pitt was hopeful of a French surrender which should ensure British interests in the Netherlands: the capture of Dunkirk was intended to provide a bargaining unit for discussion with the allies. He hoped that the allies would soon reinforce their Flanders armies. Instead the defeat of the Austrians at Wattignies by Jourdan involved the duke of York in a general retirement. The first British campaign in Flanders ended with the army entangled near Ostend.

But if the possibility of a direct attack at the heart of France through Flanders came to nothing, there was still hope farther south. In August 1793 a royalist rising in Toulon enabled Admiral Hood to establish an allied force there. The navy by itself was in no position to hold a land-locked base of this sort. The stroke could only have significance if Toulon were used as a land base for a campaign to split France. But for this the allies needed to perceive the first essential of strategy, striking blows at a vital spot. As it was, less than half the expected troops arrived. The Austrians in Milan never moved at all; one-sixth of the Sardinian forces arrived, while a British force (originally intended for Brittany) did not stir from England until it was too late. At the end of December 1793 the republicans, with the artillery commanded by young Napoleon Bonaparte, 'found means once more to penetrate between our posts . . . and in a very short space of time we saw that with great numbers they crowned all that side of the mountain which overlooks the town'.[1] There was nothing for it but to blow up thirty-four French ships of the line, crowd as many refugees on transports as possible, and leave Toulon and the remaining royalists to republican vengeance.

The Toulon episode had one lasting effect. Pitt had hitherto been steadfast in refusing to commit his country to a crusade against the form of government adopted by France. Co-operation with the royalists at Toulon had involved the British in the

[1] J. H. Rose, *Pitt and the Great War*, p. 160.

ideological conflict. This process was carried further by the accession of Burke's friends, the Portland whigs, to the ministry in July 1794. Windham[1] became in practice the minister for co-operation with the *emigrés*. To him no peace could possibly be made with any revolutionaries in control at Paris, for their purpose must always be aggression. Yet while war aims were expanding, operations were being contracted. Pichegru and Hoche pushed allied armies back against the Rhine. Prussia was in a sad state, her treasury exhausted and her peasants rioting. Her normal subsidies were used not for operations against the French but for consolidating her hold on Poland— to the indignation of the British who disapproved of the whole Polish affair. Austria meanwhile suspiciously opposed any Prussian activity on the Palatinate front. Pitt, advised by Lord Malmesbury,[2] his agent for negotiation with north Germany, decided to hire the Prussian army of 60,000 men as simple mercenaries.[3] On the advice of George III it was then resolved to march them more than a hundred miles across the Saar to the Meuse so as to assist the duke of York. For sixteen days in May, however, the British cabinet was too preoccupied with home affairs to give the necessary orders for the payment and for dispatch of the Prussian troops. In those days the unfortunate duke of York, already the victim of ministerial disparagement as he struggled with inadequate and ill-organized troops to co-operate with distrustful allies, had joined the main Austrian armies and had been involved in their defeat at Turcoing. The battle began appropriately in thick fog, rising from the Scheldt and the Lys. It ended with the duke of York, conspicuous from the star he wore, being hunted across country and thanking God for the speed of his horse. It was significant that two-thirds of the allied force stood, or counter-marched purpose-

---

[1] William Windham (1750–1810), a friend of Dr. Johnson and a disciple of Burke; joined Pitt with the rest of the Portland whigs; secretary at war, 1794–1801; adhered to Grenville after Pitt's resignation; assisted Cobbett to found his *Political Register*; introduced a new system for recruiting military forces, 1806.

[2] James Harris, first earl of Malmesbury (1746–1820), an active diplomat from 1770; played a large part in negotiating the Triple Alliance (see above, p. 294); created Baron Malmesbury, 1788; took Fox's side on the regency question but went over to Pitt with the Portland whigs; negotiated with Prussia, 1794, and also the marriage of the prince of Wales with Princess Caroline of Brunswick; British negotiator in abortive peace talks, 1796–7; he left *Diaries* which are a valuable primary source for the history of foreign policy.

[3] In addition Prussia was still obliged, under the treaty of 1792, to supply 20,000 men to the support of Austria.

lessly, while the rest of their comrades were being annihilated. This did not arise simply from incompetence: the Austrians were already, under the influence of their chancellor Thugut, thinking how best to disengage their army from the Netherlands so as to use it to bargain with Russia and Prussia in Poland.

The return of the emperor from Brussels to Vienna at the end of May marked the decision of Austria only to feign action in the west so as to retain a British subsidy while using it—*à la Prusse*—to co-operate in the suppression of the Polish patriot Kosciusco. The Austrians had steeled themselves to abandon their Netherlands. The British would eventually have to contrive some fresh means of keeping this vital area out of French hands. The great French victory at Fleurus was followed by a general retreat. Valenciennes and other fortresses were left to fall into French hands. The duke of York with the English army was swept back by the general retirement of the allies. All through the early summer the retreat continued until, in late July 1794, after passing through Ostend, Nieuport, and Antwerp, the British army was parted from the Austrian. The indiscipline of the British army in retreat can be excused only by their shameful lack of ordinary medical and transport services. As they passed through Holland they found little help from the armies of the stadholder and a great deal of opposition from the pro-French party amongst the Dutch. Behind them the French swept in hordes into Holland, fighting prodigiously in a fervour of new confidence. The end of the whole campaign came in March 1795 when, after a ragged march, forced back into Germany, without aid from Prussia, and reproached by the Hanoverians whom they left to their fate, the remains of an army, 6,000 fully effective fighting men and more invalids, was embarked at Bremen to return to England.

The Pitt government had thus clearly failed to achieve the object for which it had gone to war, the security of Flanders. The French were now all along the coast of the Low Countries and preparing for invasion of England. The defeat had been so swift that it exposed the folly of all the peripheral activity of the English war-planners. In November 1793 Sir John Jervis[1] had

[1] John Jervis (1735–1823), created earl of St. Vincent, 1797; served with Wolfe in the capture of Canada (1759) and with Keppel during the American war; promoted admiral after the capture of Guadeloupe in 1794; commander-in-chief Mediterranean; defeated Spanish off Cape St. Vincent, 1797; sent Nelson to Aboukir. In navy a severe disciplinarian; first lord of the admiralty, 1801; reformed

sailed with 7,000 men, soon to be sorely needed in Europe, to assault the French West Indies. During 1794 this force captured Guadeloupe, St. Lucia, Marie Galante, and the Saints, and established itself on Haiti. Command of the seas, preventing French reinforcement across the Atlantic, was maintained by Lord Howe's naval victory off the Brittany coast on 'The Glorious First of June'. But two elemental forces worked against Britain in the West Indies. The revolutionaries in Paris had proclaimed the equality of black and white men. All over the islands of the West Indies the slaves were stirring. In Haiti the black followers of Toussaint l'Ouverture (500,000 against 40,000 white settlers) rose to expel French and English alike. The second force was yellow fever. By 1796 British troops in the West Indies had lost 40,000 dead and 40,000 unfit for service.[1] Possession of all the islands—and Guadeloupe had been regained by the enemy—would not have been worth half this price in men.

The basic errors were still the same. Pitt and Dundas thought in terms, when they were optimistic, of a short war in which it was vital to have overseas gains to bargain with at a conference; when they were pessimistic they believed that a long war could be won by economics and that France would be beggared and broken by loss of her overseas possessions. It is true that Britain was economically relieved by gains across the Atlantic. New opportunities for trade were provided as an alternative to European markets disrupted by war. But France, like Attila, did not fight on a book-keeping system.[2] She could only be reduced by a blow at Paris, not at Port-au-Prince (Haiti).

From the military point of view there was therefore much to recommend Windham's scheme, undertaken in June 1795, of an invasion of the Vendée. But there were insufficient forces to launch this as a major operation. 3,800 *emigrés* were landed to join the royalist rebels of the area. But for just over a month they quarrelled with one another on the Quiberon peninsula and then were overwhelmed and massacred by Hoche's republicans. It was becoming impossible to find a foothold in Europe to resist France. In April 1795 Prussia made peace with France; Holland

admiralty administration; fiercely criticized by Pitt; resumed command of the Channel fleet, 1806-7.

[1] Wellington later lost fewer than 40,000 men from all causes in the whole of the vital Peninsular War.

[2] This is a paraphrase of the percipient remark of a guest at Wilberforce's dinner-table.

followed in May. In July the Spaniards, angry with the allies and anxious about their failures in frontier fighting, also made friends with the French. Against all this Pitt could only set, in Europe, the occupation of Corsica whose utility was not, for the moment, readily apparent. Perforce he concentrated his attention on overseas activity; not only were the West Indian forces strengthened but, following on Holland's change of sides, Britain captured the Cape of Good Hope on the Indian route and then Pondicherry, Trincomalee, Ceylon, Malacca, Amboyna, and Banda, lording it in the East but powerless to affect the balance of force in Europe. Meanwhile, however, a measure of military reorganization gave hope for the future. The duke of York, appointed to the new office of commander-in-chief, was as successful in an office as he had been unhappy in the field.

Pitt, urged by Wilberforce and the Foxites, made overtures for peace. Grenville and the king rejoiced that these were fruitless. France insisted upon keeping all her conquests up to the Rhine, regardless of British security. War could be no worse. But for war the only ally of weight was now Austria. Agreement was maintained, on the surface, with Russia: but Catherine had her eyes on Turkey and Persia, not on western Europe. Austria had played England false, but she alone had a comparable stake in the war with France: for she felt she had to make gains in the western war which would compensate for her disappointment in seeing Russia and Prussia take the lion's share of Poland while she was left only the jackal's.

To reopen the war in Europe Pitt pressed Austria to attack France along the Rhine. Britain would finance this. The French for their part had solved the problem of raising armies but were still grappling with that of paying them. To this Napoleon Bonaparte had an answer. 'Soldiers,' he addressed his new command, 'you are ill fed and ill clothed. The Government owes you much but can give you nothing.' He proposed to make war pay for itself. He would lead the soldiers into Italy, 'the most fertile provinces of the world', to 'support themselves by war at the cost of the enemy's territory'. So before Austria could move on the Rhine, Napoleon advanced from Nice, forced Sardinia to abandon her hesitant friendship with the allies, took Milan, plundered Lombardy, traversed Tuscany, taxed the papal states at the bayonet's point, and entered Leghorn. Naples agreed to withdraw her ships from the British navy and to sue for peace. Thus by July 1796 Austria had fresh loss of territory, Italian following Belgian, to bemoan, while Britain was endangered in the second of her areas of particular concern, the western Mediterranean.

The gloomy picture was completed by the action of Spain. She had long been angry because she construed British activities in the West Indies as a covert plot against her own interests in the South Atlantic area. In October 1796 Spain declared war on Britain. The Mediterranean position, already dangerous, now seemed hopeless. The cabinet perforce ordered the evacuation of the Mediterranean: Corsica and Elba were given up. Only Gibraltar was to be retained and there a Spanish assault was expected. Fortunately, in February 1797 fifteen sail of the line under Sir John Jervis encountered a Spanish fleet of almost twice the size off Cape St. Vincent. In the ensuing action Nelson distinguished himself: he broke from the line, sailed through and across the Spanish force so as to divide them, and finished the job by his dash in boarding operations. The result was a complete victory for Jervis which removed, for the time, any threat from the Spanish navy.

Nevertheless Britain was now everywhere on the defensive. Austria was in 1797 forced to make peace at Campio Formio. A French invasion fleet had sailed in December 1797 for Ireland. They met with no interference from the British admiralty. Only bad seamanship and bad weather prevented their landing in Bantry Bay: instead they returned to Brest. The Dutch were preparing another invasion of Ireland where the temper of the inhabitants was growing steadily more rebellious during 1797. The army in Ireland was said (in 1798) by its commander Abercromby 'to be in a state of licentiousness which must render it formidable to everyone but the enemy'. The Bank of England was forced to suspend cash payments in February, and all Pitt's skill was needed to meet the financial crisis. True it was that the activity of the radical clubs was throttled down by sedition acts. But a far more serious sign of discontent showed itself in April 1797. The Channel fleet under Lord Bridport lying at Spithead mutinied and refused to put to sea. The English sailors were not much better cared for than French soldiers, and had no alien provinces on which to feed themselves. The naval mutineers asked for fair wages, sufficient food and that of decent quality, security against embezzlement, better medical service, and some shore leave at the end of a voyage. The organization of the sailors was splendid. They gave calm obedience to their chosen leaders and these leaders were both firm and restrained. They declared that they would put to sea if the enemy appeared, but that otherwise they would remain on strike until their demands were granted and guaranteed by act of parliament. Within a week the cabinet had acquiesced. Even so it required the personal visit of Lord Howe, rowing round from ship to ship with George III's pardon in his hand—for these were the only two men the sailors trusted—before normal work was resumed. The army was granted a corresponding increase in pay.

No sooner had the Spithead fleet returned to duty and sailed to its station off Brest than the sailors of the North Sea fleet at the Nore mutinied in their turn (May 1797). But here the excitement was more political. Led by Richard Parker they did indeed frame demands for a more equitable division of prize money and modification of the brutal rules of discipline: but these did not seem to be the real cause of the unrest. The men hardly seem to have known the extent of their demands or the distance they were prepared to go in fighting for them. They threatened to blockade the Thames, but instead began fighting among themselves. Their mutiny was soon sternly suppressed and Parker was hanged. That was in July. In October this same fleet, under Duncan[1] who had had to bluff the Dutch at Texel during the summer, met and destroyed de Winter's Dutch invasion fleet at Camperdown.

In spite of mutiny, therefore, the navy had by Christmas 1797 locked the enemy fleets in their ports in the Netherlands, in Cherbourg, Brest, Cadiz, and Toulon. Invasion was impossible until the shipyards of western Europe could refit these enemies. Pitt, nevertheless, was downcast. His third overture for peace had been a confession of this, for he offered to allow France to retain her natural frontiers, including the vital Low Country area. The French refusal to treat showed their determination to dominate Italy and Germany as well. This confirmed George III and the Portland group in the belief that the revolution had to be crushed before there could be peace.

---

[1] Adam Duncan (1731–1804), created Viscount Duncan, 1797; he had prevented the mutiny from spreading to his own ship, the *Venerable*.

Pitt's conception of a limited war was unpopular and out of date. Even Fox admitted that the French attitude was bellicose, though he traced this evil back to the hostility of Europe since 1789. Pitt, though gloomy, was convinced he still had a work to do. If Britain had no allies, then she could not be betrayed by them. She could endure and resist and hope. Meanwhile she could refurbish her strength, particularly her financial strength. To the congenial task of reorganization Pitt therefore set himself while waiting for some great turn of fortune.

If Pitt had been mistaken in supposing originally that the war with France was a war for trade, he was none the less clearly right in believing that the means of surviving lay in Britain's economic resources. Great efforts were made to increase food supplies by the new board of agriculture: the improvements earlier in the century were extended, under royal encouragement, to backward areas. To keep down high bread prices, which in the years of dearth about 1795 provoked social disorder, the government encouraged the milling of whole-meal flour and members of parliament pledged themselves to eat less bread and abjure pastry. More important and effective were Pitt's efforts to extend trade even in the darkest days of military failure. In 1794 the Americans were persuaded to enter into a treaty by which they sent more raw cotton and some corn in return for manufactures. Dundas was a powerful advocate both for the textile interests and for the sugar importers. Clearly a trade expansion would increase potential strength in war. The problem was how to convert the potential into the actual. How could the government command a fair share of new wealth in order to use it for subsidies and supplies?

Pitt had always been anxious to avoid running the war on a basis of debt. If war is financed by loans it means, in effect, putting the burden on unborn generations. For a great war of survival, such as this had proved, there is a strong case for making the future pay a considerable share of the cost at which the foundations of its way of life are preserved. Yet if the whole cost of the French wars (£831 million) had been met by loans the whole income of future governments would have been swallowed up in debt payments, leaving no room for economic manœuvre. In 1791 Pitt faced a deficit of £19 million. He decided to meet £12 million of this from loans and voluntary gifts and £7 million from new taxation. Such new taxation must be direct. He wished to base revenue more evenly on the two pillars of direct and indirect taxation, each sensitive to changes in well-being among the citizens. But the proportion supplied by indirect taxes, which were most felt by the less wealthy, was too high: in 1792 it was 75 per cent. Yet Pitt had come to the end of fancy methods of getting direct taxation. He proposed a radical remedy. He trebled the existing assessed taxes, on such things as windows, houses, servants, carriages, and so on, and introduced into them the principle of a differential rate, so that the wealthy man with four carriages paid more than four times as much as his humbler neighbour with one.

Yet Pitt was not satisfied that these taxes were effective in tapping new wealth efficiently or fairly. The only answer was a tax upon all incomes. However, it was impossible even to talk of such a tax so long as the old and uneven land tax remained one of the main elements in direct taxation. The land tax could not be abolished without favouring certain sections of the population. For this tax having become fixed not only on a seventeenth-century assessment but also on particular properties, land had been bought and sold for a century with liability to the tax as part of many private bargains. Pitt therefore produced his plan to redeem the land tax. First the tax was made legally—as it already was in fact—perpetual at the rate of 4s. in the £1. Then those who were liable were encouraged to redeem each £1 of tax due annually by the payment of a capital sum which would give the exchequer relief in debt interest of £1. 4s. As the 3 per cent. loan then stood at 50, this meant that the obligation could be redeemed at 20 years purchase. If the stocks rose, the redemption would cost more.[1]

By this means the government obtained ready money from land tax payers at 5 per cent. so long as the general interest rate was 6 per cent. Nevertheless, taken by itself it might well have seemed an expedient for getting ready money at the cost of decreasing future revenues. But Pitt was not mortgaging the future, he was burying the past. For the operation of his new tax, the income tax, was made simpler by this operation; the

---

[1] Other parties were given permission to redeem the tax if the landlords failed to do so. According to Dr. Ward, half had been redeemed by 1800, according to others, only a quarter. As by his act parliament lost control over the land tax, Pitt made up for this by making a corresponding part of taxes servicing the Consolidated Fund subject to annual vote in parliament.

civil servants of the old land tax office took over administration of the new system. To replace the old conventional charges, a realistic survey was made in the autumn of 1798 of national income. Landed incomes were estimated at a taxable value of £25 million, house rentals at £6 million, mines and canals at £3 million, incomes from overseas at £5 million, annuities at £12 million, internal trade at £28 million, and the total national income at £102 million. All was to contribute to the war-time revenue. Incomes under £60 a year were exempt. Between £60 and £200 there was a graduated rate. Incomes of £200 and over were to pay 2s. in the £1 or 10 per cent. Pitt hoped soon to collect £10 million a year, an estimate almost twice as great as the reality.

There could be no greater proof of the change in political conditions since 1790 than that a nation which had resisted the excise now swallowed an income tax. It was criticized for being inquisitorial, for being radical, and for bearing too heavily on the upper classes, but, nevertheless, it was accepted as the price of war. Pitt had remodelled the whole fiscal system and succeeded in making Britain's economic successes pay for her military trials.

There was clearly a new vigour in Pitt's mind at this desperate hour. Even when he had to deal with the rebellion in Ireland,[1] aided by a French invading force, he was not content just to send over troops to encourage the lord-lieutenant. He was already planning a great change in the relationship of Ireland and England. So too he busied himself once more on the improvement of army recruitment. He needed 40,000 men. The militia system was sacrosanct, localized and almost autonomous, yet it locked up manpower for home service only. Pitt hoped to proceed on a voluntary basis and an act of parliament provided for taking 10,000 militiamen into the regular army. But the lords-lieutenant did not co-operate in encouraging their men to transfer. So in the end the government raised recruits by offering ten guineas bounty to any militiamen enlisting for service in Europe only (and not for the dreaded West Indies). This scheme produced the numbers but not disciplined armies. To make effective battalions of these men enlisted for drink required hard work by their commanders; it also required time. Time, unfortunately, was not Pitt's to command. But one other means of remedying the manpower shortage could be adopted at once.

See below, p. 398.

In the West Indies in 1797 men were found, men who did not sicken and die; negro regiments were raised. To prevent the Caribbean consuming strength needed for Europe, moreover, the annual expenditure there was limited to £300,000. Commitments in the area were also reduced when, on the responsibility of the colonel on the spot, Thomas Maitland, St. Domingo was given up to Toussaint L'Ouverture, who was left to fight for himself against French and Spaniards.

Yet with all this it was still necessary to attack France. Pitt had to start collecting allies once more. His efforts in 1798 show clearly that a great change had come over his attitude to Europe. The government adopted, for the first time since William of Orange, a truly European standpoint. Objectives and interests remained constant but Pitt saw that to achieve the security of the Netherlands he had to have a scheme for Italy, for Switzerland, for, in a word, the satisfaction of other great powers. So Russia, where the Tsar Paul had succeeded Catherine, was lured on by the prospect of suzerainty over the Knights of St. John at Malta and of a share in the supervision of the Germanic states. In return she agreed to join in the battle against France both in the north and in the south. To achieve the independence of the Netherlands, Pitt propounded, in 1798, the idea that Belgium should be joined to Holland under the House of Orange, thus forming a strong little buffer state.[1] In the central area of French expansion, the powers newly allied were to protect the independence of Switzerland. To the south, Sardinia was to act as barrier against France: but behind her Austria was to stand master of new Italian possessions. In return for giving up Belgium, which she did not want, Austria was to gain Lombardy, which she coveted. The further beauty of this plan was that it avoided irritating Prussia, a power of whose intentions Pitt found it impossible to make any sure prediction.

These conversations were admirable for forming an alliance, praiseworthy for mapping a peace settlement, indicative of the plan of military operations, but in no way a substitute for victory over Napoleon and the directory. The second coalition looked good on paper but it had to be tested in campaigns.

[1] Not at this time, but soon after, Britain proposed that Holland, in payment for gaining Belgium, should cede the Cape of Good Hope and Ceylon to her—thus the sea route to India would benefit by the same operation which secured the position in Europe.

XV

THE BATTLES OF THE SECOND
COALITION AND THE FALL OF PITT
1798–1801

ALL the allies of the second coalition looked, with bland confidence, to Britain for subsidies. Yet they also expected that Britain should take the initiative in opening up the fight. Pitt's courage was never more apparent than in his acceptance of this responsibility. He accepted Grenville's advice that they must re-enter the Mediterranean to make certain of the aid of Austria and Naples. The admiralty complained that—unless a further 8,000 sailors could be found—it was impossible to do more than guard the Channel and keep contact with the scratch army which had been put into Portugal to protect her against Spain. Despite this advice and despite the threat of invasion at home the cabinet ordered Lord St. Vincent to detach a squadron from his Lisbon fleet and to send it forward under Nelson into the Mediterranean. It was a decision whose boldness was matched by its good fortune. For Napoleon had decided that invasion of England was not yet possible. So he sailed from Toulon with a French army destined for Egypt. He, too, saw the war in a wider framework than Europe and aspired to recapture France's empire in the East.

Once it was known that Napoleon had captured Malta it was generally supposed that he would seek to occupy Naples for this was the link point for British co-operation with Austria. Nelson hurried into the eastern Mediterranean and back to Naples in a vain search for him. Returning eastwards once again he found the French fleet at anchor in Aboukir Bay, at the mouth of the Nile, the troops having already landed. It was 1 August 1798. Nelson decided upon immediate action despite the hazard of shoals and batteries. He ran his thirteen ships of the line (and a 50-gun ship) in among the French fleet of roughly equal numbers. The result was that nine French ships were captured and the rest destroyed. Thereafter though Napoleon might remain master of Lower Egypt, he did so not as a general of a great power but as the isolated captain of a roving and self-contained army of adventurers. At one blow Britain not only re-entered the Mediterranean but subdued its waters. She proceeded to establish herself for further prosecution of the war against both Spain and France. General Charles Stuart,[1] taking part of his force from Portugal, captured Minorca. Nelson, for his part, hurried back to excite still more the effervescent spirit of the Neapolitans.

The Neapolitans would have been well advised to wait for Austria rather than to fight with Nelson. Their first onrush carried their 15,000 men up into the Roman Republic. Yet within three weeks the French army from the north of Italy had pushed them, almost contemptuously, back on to the defensive within their own territory. The court of Naples, and Nelson, were obliged to take refuge across the water in Sicily. To their aid came the redoubtable Charles Stuart who made Sicily a base for defence or offence. He turned this reverse, indeed, into an advantage. From Sicily, disciplined and prepared, it was possible to direct attacks against either the western or eastern shores of southern Italy. The French remained uncertain of the main direction of a major British offensive.

Britain had played her part in opening up the war. One French army was on the alert in southern Italy, another was advancing towards Sir Sidney Smith's holding force in Acre. It was time for the full coalition to complete the confusion of the enemy by simultaneous action on the vital points of their extended lines in 1799. Pitt had, naturally, great hopes of a decisive blow in the Netherlands: he had, as usual, insufficient men trained for the expedition. At midsummer he was promised the assistance of 17,500 Russians receiving pay from England. He expected 8,000 Swedes and received none. He hoped for the assistance of Prussia which remained immobile. He estimated he might send 25,000 British and 12,000 finally embarked. Between 10 September and 15 October the allied army under the duke of York, Abercromby, and Hermann, moved forward, through pouring rain, from the Helder to the line of the Zype. The Dutch failed to stir a finger to help their would-be liberators. The armies stuck fast in the mud and sickened. Finally the

[1] Sir Charles Stuart (1753–1801), the fourth son of George III's friend the earl of Bute; M.P. Bossiney, 1780; knighted, 1799.

expedition was withdrawn. Its only results had been, on the credit side, the destruction of the Dutch fleet, and, on the debit side, the destruction of all good feeling between British and Russian colleagues.

Meanwhile, however, the coalition had also been brought into the fight in the Italian theatre. The Austrians had, despite all Pitt's diplomatic plans, evaded definite promises of action; they feared what lay behind the heavy, sullen silence of Berlin. In March 1799, however, they were brought into action by French movements in Switzerland and Italy. The Austrians and the Russians under Suvorov captured Milan and Turin. The French withdrew from Naples. Soon they were driven from all Italy save for a strip of the Genoese coast. This sweeping victory was only marred by quarrels among the allies. It became clear that Austria—always panting for gains to offset her meagre share of Poland—planned to annex Piedmont as well as Lombardy and Venetia. Her relations with Russia speedily grew worse. While Suvorov climbed through the St. Gothard pass to rescue the Swiss who were locked in a desperate struggle with the French, the Archduke Charles withdrew the Austrian forces for service in Suabia. As a result the French led by Soult restored their power in Switzerland. More serious still was the anger of the tsar. He resolved to leave treacherous friends and to listen to the blandishments of Paris.

Nevertheless Napoleon, who had returned from the East and seized power as first consul in November 1799, was not in a triumphant mood. Pitt's plan for attacks on many fronts had miscarried partly from lack of men to carry them out effectively and partly from the disunity of the powers. In spite of this the allies now held Italy, and had regained confidence in their ability to master French armies. At the end of 1799 the Austrians had 70,000 men ready to renew the work of driving the French northwards away from Italy. This was twice the force the enemy could muster against them. In addition the British fleet could harry the Riviera and co-operate in an invasion of France from the south-east. For the British fleet had again emphasized its crushing superiority. The losses of Holland and France at sea could not be replaced for some years even by the work of all the shipwrights of western Europe. In this danger Napoleon made overtures for peace in December 1799.

Napoleon's peace proposals never advanced beyond preliminaries. Pitt had long been the advocate of a settlement, though he was opposed within the cabinet by the Portland group and by Grenville. But seven years of war with revolutionary France had impressed upon him the essentially aggressive nature of that country. Peace he still wished, but a peace which should guarantee Britain's vital interests in the Netherlands and the Mediterranean. Such a settlement could only be reached with a government which had so permanent a basis in France that it would not need to elicit support at home by seeking adventures abroad. Pitt did not believe that Napoleon had such a power. Therefore the overtures were rudely rebuffed with a letter from Grenville which seemed, on the face of it, to suggest that the whole cabinet had come to agree that the restoration of royal rule would be if not the only, at least the most likely, method by which France could come to peace with England. 'If peace', said Pitt in the house of commons, 'affords no prospect of security: if it threatens all the evils which we have been struggling to avert . . . then I say it is prudent in us not to negotiate at the present moment.' To this Fox and his friends, not yet realizing that Napoleon was the betrayer of those elements which they favoured in the revolution, opposed heated arguments for peace. But the house of commons supported Pitt by 260 to 64.

It is clear that the intransigent attitude of English ministers arose in part from their expectation of speedy success in 1800. These hopes soon dissolved. Napoleon, denied peace, carried war to his enemies. He took the Austrians, who had been methodically preparing to push the French from Genoa, in their rear. By mid-June 1800 Bonaparte's victory of Marengo had turned the tables once more. The Austrians were no longer meditating a thrust northwards but were, on the contrary, concerned to hold on to fragments of their gains. To this débâcle the British had contributed. So confidently did they expect a great Austrian drive that Pitt and Dundas had once more erred by dispersing their strength. Instead of staking all on the Riviera offensive they had planned to distract and disintegrate France by many small affrays. Thus Windham had proposed to use the royalists in La Vendée once more, while Dundas supported the idea of reinforcing Minorca as a base for attack on the south of France. A compromise, the worst course of all, was finally accepted. Six thousand men were sent to capture Belle Île off the coast of Brittany while 5,000 were sent to Minorca. A project against Brest, a landing in Quiberon Bay, an encouragement to the disaffected in Provence, and an expedition to Ferrol, were all undertaken at the same time. This was to fight with pinpricks against an enemy who delivered a hammer blow. Too late the men intended for Minorca and Belle Île were brought together to go to the aid of the Austrians. Too late the forces in the Mediterranean were increased to 20,000 men: by then Marengo had been two months past.

Only in the Far East did Britain act in good time and with striking success. Since Warren Hastings left, the main interest had been in internal reform of the Company's service. Yet Tipu, the sultan who succeeded Haidar Ali in Mysore, looked down from the central tableland of south India with covetous contempt upon the Carnatic to the east. There the welter of debt and corruption, of Company influence and the Nabob's patronage, persisted despite Cornwallis's reforming zeal. In 1790 Tipu attacked. Cornwallis took personal charge of the war. Mindful of the India Act, however, he did not follow victory in 1792 by destroying Mysore. The territorial gains were small and they were distributed among the Marattas and Hyderabad in an effort to gain the goodwill of these independent neighbours. Tipu did not meet Cornwallis's forbearance with gratitude. On the contrary, he devoted all his energy to plotting revenge. The whole administration of Mysore was geared to a future war: commerce was run by the state, taxes piled high to prepare a war-chest. In 1795 Tipu intervened in the war between the Marattas and Hyderabad, not so much for territorial gain but in order to play a decisive part in the internal affairs of Hyderabad whose nizam lay dying. His aim was to undermine the position of Azim-ul-Umara, the pro-English minister there. At the same time, such was the range of his views, he entered into negotiations with Zennan Shah, the Afghan ruler at Kabul, negotiations designed to precipitate trouble for the Company in northern India.

This was the position in India when Cornwallis resigned in 1793. His resignation, it is significant, arose simply out of his reforms and not from anything in Indian foreign affairs. The officers of the Bengal army were obstructive and he failed to find the full support from London which he demanded. The

Marquis Wellesley[1] was appointed to India in 1797: his mind was stored with quite different ideas. Cornwallis had acted in the light of Pitt's India Act; he was a reformer who had studied the career of Hastings. Wellesley saw India as a theatre in the world war with France; he was a statesman who feared the conquests of Napoleon. By temperament he was, in any case, imperious, arrogant, and splendour-loving. It is said that he wore his decorations even on his night-attire. He was aware, as everyone was, that the East India Company had not yet solved the problem of balancing its books. But whereas Charles Grant[2] urged that honest administration and no expansion was the best course morally, legally, and for the dividends, Wellesley and Dundas seem to have decided that the intentions of Pitt's India Act should now be disregarded. It seems likely that their unconfessed objective was to expand British rule and to make this larger empire pay for itself by opening up the trade to interests outside the old Company. The expansion of the Lancashire cotton industry was radically altering the possibilities of trade with India. A new export to India would be provided and the balance of trade revolutionized, once the old restrictions were removed. For this, however, it was also desirable to take a position as the leading power in India. For the moment, bullion still had to be exported to India to pay for imports as well as for troops.

The war of France and England was bound to reopen trouble in India. In 1797 an adventurer Ripaud de Montaudevant masqueraded as an ambassador from France to Mysore. Tipu welcomed him and sent messages to the French in Mauritius. He asked for military aid which would enable him to invade Bengal as well as the Carnatic. He planned to expel the English from India. The governor of Mauritius, however, had no troops. His last

[1] Richard Colley Wellesley (1760–1842), from 1799 Marquis Wellesley, a supporter of free trade and an opponent of parliamentary reform; member of the India board, 1793; governor-general of India, 1797; disregarded orders to restore French posts at the time of the peace of Amiens; quarrelled with the directors at home; recalled 1805. From that time began to play an important part (for which see below) in home politics. In spite of his talents he rarely achieved the success which he thought his due.

[2] Charles Grant (1746–1823), a philanthropist, advocated missionary activity in India. He was influential in the board of trade at Calcutta; he became chairman of the Company. He continued his crusade against Wellesley's ideas and supported a move to impeach him. After his return to England Grant's counter-policy was to continue the internal purging of the Company: for this end he proposed the establishment of Haileybury School to train its future servants.

reserves had been sent to Batavia. He punished Montaudevant for misleading Tipu and sent to the Sultan only 99 men and a formal alliance. British naval dominance of the approaches to India seemed to guarantee security from this threat. Wellesley, even on his voyage out, had been preparing for aggressive action. He reported to Dundas that he would make a defensive treaty with the Marattas and then expel French influence from Hyderabad. Tipu's correspondence, which was intercepted by the British, prompted a more direct and dramatic course. Mysore should be destroyed.

Napoleon's expedition to Egypt in 1798 did not cause, it merely accelerated, the war in India. It seemed to Dundas that co-ordination between Mysore and Paris was even closer than had been supposed. The governor of Mauritius, he believed, must have had orders from Paris. From Egypt Napoleon could strike towards India either by the Red Sea or Arabia or down the Euphrates. Four thousand troops were therefore dispatched from England to reinforce India in late 1798. The Persian Gulf was policed by British men-of-war. Though the news of Aboukir relieved the immediate anxiety, Wellesley continued to plan the destruction of Mysore: he decided to send a force from Bombay down the west coast to match the march of his other armies from Madras and Bengal. The time chosen was February and March 1799, after the mud and before the drought. Despite some misgivings from young Arthur Wellesley[1] the campaign went according to plan. Seringapatam, Tipu's capital and fortress on its island river site, was most brilliantly besieged and taken. Tipu was killed. Arthur Wellesley became a commissioner to control the future of Mysore. Grants of territory were made to Hyderabad and a piece retained for bribing the Marattas. Some of the richest areas were annexed for the East India Company. All that remained was completely within British control. Immediately after this triumph the governor-general accused the ruler of the Carnatic of treachery. Correspondence discovered in Tipu's palace was used as an excuse to put an end to the old and unsatisfactory dual system. A new puppet ruler was put on the throne and given one-fifth of the land

---

[1] Arthur Wellesley (1769–1852), the younger brother of the governor-general and later to outshine his glory as the duke of Wellington. His later career appears in the narrative below and in that of Sir E. L. Woodward, *The Age of Reform* (O.H.E. vol. xiii).

revenues. The Company took the Carnatic and assumed in Madras the full control they had long enjoyed in Calcutta. Under Colonel Read the foundations of a new school of administration had been laid. The land was surveyed to ascertain the revenues that should be derived from it. At the same time a serious study was made of local languages and conditions. An attempt was made to adopt in the Carnatic the Permanent Land Settlement which Cornwallis had mistakenly riveted on Bengal.[1] Later, in 1803, when Lord William Bentinck[2] was governor of Madras, it was realized that this system was unsuitable for the peasant communities (*ryotwary*) of Madras.

Wellesley the expansionist might, by 1801, claim to have ousted French influence from southern India. For in addition to gaining the Carnatic and destroying Mysore he had reduced Hyderabad to a subject state. The French troops there had been surrounded and disarmed. The Nizam had been forced to disband his own army and to cede territory to pay British costs in defending him. Then the governor-general turned his eyes to the centre and the north. Oudh was treated like Hyderabad. Advantage was taken of the endemic quarrels of the Mahratta confederacy. The British championed the cause of the Peshwa against Holkar, Sindhia, and the rajah of Berar. The climax of the ensuing wars came when Arthur Wellesley, aged thirty-four, assumed command as major-general. By characteristic attention to the details of staff work, by particular care for bridge-building materials and for victualling, General Wellesley outmarched and out-manœuvred the Mahrattas until he destroyed the military power of Sindhia at the battle of Assaye in 1803. As he sat exhausted among the corpses on that most bloody field, he could reflect that he had achieved the supremacy of Britain as a territorial power in India. In 1804 Holkar was in turn overwhelmed. In 1805 the Grand Mogul, Shah Alam, accepted British protection. Wellesley's diplomacy extended west to Persia and east to China.

The old eighteenth-century conception of the British role in

---

[1] See above, p. 323 n. 1.

[2] Lord William Cavendish Bentinck (1774–1839), soldiered with the duke of York and with Suvorov; recalled from Madras after a mutiny at Vellore for which he was held responsible; served with Wellington in Spain; in 1827 returned to India as governor-general in Bengal and initiated a great era of liberal reform; 1833 the first governor-general of India under the new constitution. See Sir E. L. Woodward, *The Age of Reform* (O.H.E. vol. xiii), p. 18.

India was brought to an end in these four years. Wellesley was recalled but his conquests could not be cast on one side. Yet such imperial acquisitions, though they coincided with the period of Pitt's second coalition, could not, at the time, outweigh its disasters nearer home. What could it profit the prime minister to gain a sub-continent and lose the whole of Europe? For as the year 1800—which was to have been so glorious—went on, disaster continued to fall upon the coalition in Europe. All Italy came to terms with the French. The British could do no more than delay the process. For this sorry end had Pitt raised 80,000 men at the cost of £10 million. The Russians had now gone over definitely to the French. Other powers, either irritated by British interference with trade on the seas, or anxious to join the victors, adopted a hostile attitude. Before December 1800 the Austrians had been so decisively beaten by Moreau at Hohenlinden that they were obliged to sue for peace; Spain had joined France to put pressure on Portugal; the Baltic powers were discussing with Russia the formation of a Northern League of armed neutrality to take measures hostile to Britain. The capture of Malta was a poor off-set to such calamities.

The end of the war of the second coalition came in 1801. Britain rescued something from the wreck. Nothing could be done to prevent Austria making an abject peace at Lunéville. But in the Middle East Abercromby, with a British army of 18,000 men, defeated at Alexandria that French army which Bonaparte had once led and then deserted; success was achieved in spite of the British intelligence service which had estimated the French force to be half its actual strength.

Up in the Baltic, Denmark, Sweden, and Russia laid an embargo on British ships. Grenville in return encouraged the capture of their shipping by British captains. Then Prussia entered this northern league and invaded Hanover to force that state to abandon the cause of its elector, the king of England. The Danes occupied Hamburg the more effectively to prevent England trading with north Germany. To this, at least, a stern reply was made. Eighteen ships of the line and auxiliaries were dispatched under Hyde Parker to Copenhagen. His second in command, Lord Nelson, on 2 April 1801 took twelve ships of the line and all the smaller vessels into Copenhagen harbour under the shore batteries. Disregarding signals to return, heedless of the fact that three ships of the line had gone aground and lay motionless targets for the cruel fire of the shore gunners, he persevered until he had sunk, burnt, or taken, all seventeen of the Danish first-line ships cooped within their own harbour. The carnage, Nelson admitted, was the most dreadful he had ever witnessed. The result of this action was an armistice and a convention dissolving the Northern League; its armies withdrew from areas they had occupied, and a code was agreed to govern the searching of ships and the definition of contraband of war.

The moving spirit behind the Baltic belligerency had in any case disappeared. The tsar Paul was murdered in March 1801, and under his son, Alexander I, Russia reverted for the moment to a watchful and less adventurous policy. While this lively last act of the drama of the second coalition was being played out, the control of British policy had ceased to lie in Pitt's hands. Long disappointed in war, but inexhaustible in expedients at home, he had at last stumbled on his chosen ground. In his reorganization of the home front, Pitt had at length destroyed the basis of widespread, non-sectarian acceptance of his leadership. Not he but Addington received plaudits for victory in Egypt and Denmark. The short-lived peace that marks the change from a struggle with revolutionary France to that with the Napoleonic empire was negotiated while Pitt languished as a bystander.

The war with France had brought the Irish problem, like so many others, to a new intensity. But it is impossible to understand Pitt's policy here unless one appreciates the fundamental, as well as the new, causes of unrest in Ireland. Irish settlements and Irish crises have appeared from time to time in this narrative already; it is time to see the problem as a whole: for under Pitt it reached a dramatic crisis.

The source of unrest in Ireland was, as always, poverty. Ireland possessed neither wood nor coal nor iron on which to develop industrially. Her resources were land, linen, and cheap labour. Irish agriculture had swung backwards and forwards between arable and pasture during the century with the consequent damage to established human interests. It had not, on the whole, kept abreast of the agricultural improvements in England. This in part arose because the legacy of past disputes had been a population so discontented and prone to senseless disorder that there was no security for a capitalist to sink his money in improvements. In part it arose from the fact that the greatest landlords were absentees living in England who drew what they could from Ireland without nursing its capacity. It must also be remembered that English agriculture was a competitor for investment. The main development of Irish agriculture had therefore been the increased cultivation of the potato. This meant a more intensive cultivation of the soil; it fostered an increase in population, but it was a population living near subsistence level and resistant to change. The Irish peasant looked on the land as his by prescriptive right. The changes of the seventeenth century had substituted in some southern areas an English for a native overlord; while, in the eyes of an English lawyer, this had been a change in ownership, in the memory of the Irish village there had only been a change in due-collectors. The peasant still thought the soil was his whatever the lord or the English law might say. Thus the Irish countryside, outside of Ulster, was both poor and antagonistic to interference. Irish commerce had certainly been damaged by English laws. Irishmen had been prevented from competing with English rivals inside the empire. Only Irish linen had been encouraged and, to a lesser extent, the export of Irish provisions.

These economic facts underlay the political problem. There were three main parties in Irish society, all of them, in the first part of the eighteenth century, opposed to England. The Roman catholic majority were aliens in their own country, deprived of all political rights and, in theory, of the rights of property and education as well. They were, however, in 1760, inert. Up in Ulster a presbyterian population was also excluded, like the dissenters in England, from political influence though exempt from the harsher religious laws affecting the papists. Both these sections, however, regarded the established church as the club of a small minority in whose hands all power was lodged. Yet even this third party, that of the protestant episcopalians, was not thereby made pro-English. So long as it felt secure in Ireland it was, on the contrary, anti-English. For it felt as a grievance—as an impediment to its own prosperity—all the constitutional and economic limitations imposed by England. Political power in the Irish parliament was securely in its hands. Of the 300 Irish members of parliament a majority represented rotten borough seats controlled by a few great Anglican Irish families. These parliamentary anglicans were traditionally grouped in interests and sold their support to the lord-lieutenant. They were pro-English only so long as their services were rewarded.

The financial difficulties under which every English government after 1763 laboured gave the anglican leaders of Ireland their chance. The attempt of the lords-lieutenant, as has been explained,[1] to replace the 'Undertakers' with new parliamentary managers simply drove the former to take up popular causes against England as a means of increasing their own bargaining power. When in 1768 England had wanted an increase in Ireland's military contribution it had to be bought by endorsing an Octennial Act, as well as distributing jobs. In 1775 Lord Harcourt as viceroy held his own with the turbulent groups only by creating eighteen barons and awarding twelve steps in the peerage. The war with America did not create a new problem in Ireland but it raised excitement to a new pitch and produced, in Grattan and Flood, leaders of new stature. What had been the exploitation of personal advantage became a constitutional battle. 'The King', said Grattan to his countrymen, 'has no other title to his Crown than that which you have to your liberty; both are founded, the throne and your freedom, upon the right vested in the subject to resist by force of arms, notwithstanding their oath of allegiance, any authority attempting to impose acts of power as laws, whether that authority be one man or a host, the second James or the British Parliament'.

In the face of such arguments, backed by force, England gave ground first in allowing the Roman catholics to inherit property and hold long leases (1778), second by allowing Irish ships to sail as British (1779) and finally by allowing complete legislative independence to the Irish parliament (1782).[2] To the problems thereby created no solution had been found. Though Pitt had made no overt move since the failure of his trade proposals in 1785, the outbreak of war in Europe had gravely increased the need to find a solution. For it was more than ever necessary to keep the policy of the two countries, now with one king but separate and independent parliaments, in harmony in face of a

[1] See above, pp. 221, 222.
[2] For these steps see above, pp. 222, 224, and 245.

hostile world. The link between them was that their common king was the head of the executive. Yet it is just here that the weakness of Grattan's system lay. A king who was a figurehead would not hold both countries to one line of policy. No one in either country supposed, in any case, that the king should be anything less than an active figure in his executive government. It was English constitutional theory, accepted wholeheartedly by Grattan, that the legislature checked this royal executive. The theory of the balance was made workable in England because an executive team was always found which was acceptable to—not chosen by—the legislature. It was not easy to extend the same system to Ireland. An executive trusted by the English parliament might be anathema to that of Ireland; or vice versa: but the executive had to be the common element. It was optimistic to hope to find two separate legislatures, planted in such different soil, with exactly the same tastes. One parliament or the other was likely to find itself in a head-on collision with the royal ministers.

In practice the viceroy and chief secretary were representatives in Ireland of a king's government which stood or fell by the will of the English parliament. Deprived of the chance of playing a part in the selection of the executive, the Irish politicians developed the idea of a balance of forces until it became a parody of the English system. 'Let the kingly power', said Grattan in 1796, 'that forms one estate in our constitution, continue for ever: but let it be, as by the principles and laws of these countries it should be, one estate only—and not a power constituting one estate, corrupting another, and influencing a third.' This sounded well as an attack on corruption: said by an English politician it would probably have concealed a desire to upset one set of ministers in favour of the orator's own group: said in Ireland, by Grattan, it should be read as a refusal to assume any responsibility for administration. For the Irish could not compete in pulling power with the English and as yet they did not urge the separation of executives and parliaments, as in modern dominion status. To do so would have made an abstraction of monarchy: it would also have meant that Irish critics would have had to forsake their opposition mentality. Grattan always refused to contemplate taking office. He was a good friend to Charles James Fox because Fox was usually in opposition also. The Irish fought the executive

even when the issues were not Irish. It was not a predilection
for the prince of Wales but simply the love of a fight with the
holders of power which made Grattan oppose Pitt on the
regency issue.[1]

While Grattan's parliament continued to be so negatively
critical of English authorities it was inevitable that Englishmen
should view the sister country with suspicion and read sinister
motives into all its actions. There was a general failure in England to appreciate the efforts which Grattan had to make in
order to control the many strains and stresses in Irish society.
Nevertheless in the two decades in which Ireland had an independent parliament she enjoyed prosperity. The government
was obliged to concede that a protectionist policy should be
followed: in this instance, in contrast to what has been said
above, the Irish politicians were prepared to put forward a
responsible official. John Foster,[2] as chancellor of the exchequer
in 1784, encouraged corn production by bounties which kept the
marginal farm and the weaker producers in existence. More
healthy was the revival of Irish trade and industry. The linen
industry was thriving. Irish wool exports, it is true, continued
to decline for the good reason that they were poor in quality.
Yet thirteen Irish mills supplied the calicos and muslins needed
by the Irish market. It was a prohibitive duty on the raw
material which handicapped the Irish cotton industry. Irish
glass, on the other hand, being free of the excise duty which fell
on their English rivals, was exported from Cork and Waterford
to the United States. The sugar refiners also made great progress though they did not get the full protection they asked
against English competition. This general revival of trade
helped to conceal the weakness of Irish public finance whose
taxation system was fossilized and feeble.

The Irish politicians attributed all this prosperity, naturally
enough, to the measure of independence they had gained.
Grattan believed that they could still further increase their independence, their authority, and hence their own power of
opposition. The gaining of an independent parliament had not
brought a new status to the presbyterians or to the Roman

---

[1] For which see above, p. 304.

[2] John Foster (1740–1828), lawyer who entered the Irish house of commons in
1761; chancellor of the exchequer; protested against the union of parliaments;
opposed relief of Roman catholics; created Baron Oriel, 1821.

catholics. There was therefore still discontent—vocal among the protestants and latent among papists—which weakened the claim of an Irish parliament to speak for their country to alien governors. Within the ranks of the old volunteers a split between radicals and conservatives had been apparent. Grattan agreed with the radicals that parliamentary reform was the logical conclusion of his own campaign. At the same time he had to reassure his more conservative friends that the anglican leadership—upper class leadership—was not in danger. He called for emancipation of the Roman catholics in order to broaden the basis of his authority in battling with the executive. 'The Irish Protestant', he had declared, 'can never be free until the Irish Catholic has ceased to be a slave.' The corollary was his pledge—'I shall never assent to any measures tending to shake the security of Property in this Kingdom or to subvert the Protestant ascendency.' In this there was no contradiction. Like Fox's friends in England, he had sufficient confidence in the leadership of his class to believe that it would be strengthened by bringing in a popular vote; political change was not bound, in this view, to result in social revolution.

Revolutionary activities, nevertheless, increased in Ireland with the stimulus of the French example: the Irish radicals in Ulster formed a 'United Irishmen' society. This organization was the admiration of English extremists and the bogy of the government. At a time when England was in mortal danger there seemed a likelihood—every viceroy gloomily reported it —that French invaders would be welcomed by considerable sections of the Irish population, by protestants in the north and by catholics in the south. Grattan's talk of reform and emancipation seemed suddenly more dangerous to Englishmen fighting the revolution. The Roman catholics were, after all, in the main poor, discontented, and given to bloodthirsty, if hitherto aimless, violence. Furthermore the Irish leaders in their chosen role of checkers of the executive seemed as lacking in realism or public spirit as Charles James Fox.

Pitt's approach to the problem of Ireland was more constructive and less openly declared than that of the majority of his supporters. His lord-lieutenant, the earl of Westmorland, was content to play the traditional role of the chief of state in Dublin. He made a few concessions and corrupted as many members as possible. But he profited also by the fact that some Irishmen felt, as the English did, great fear of the social forces roused by the revolution. Fitzgibbon,[1] the Irish chancellor, played on these fears to weaken Grattan's influence. The officials in Dublin Castle, men like John Beresford,[2] began to use arguments in which religious and class elements were blended together. An appeal was made to the wealthy Anglican minority to cease opposition to England in face of the gathering threat from peasant catholics and petty bourgeois nonconformists. The fight of protestant against catholic, quiescent for a century, seemed likely to recommence.

Pitt never accepted in its entirety the view of Dublin Castle. He was searching for a permanent settlement, not a perpetual feud: he was more impressed by the danger from Ulster's radicalism, less afraid of the doctrines of Defenderism[3] of the catholics. To cure the latter he relied upon prosperity and the strengthening of local government. He also agreed with Langrishe[4] and Grattan that there was need for concessions. Indeed, Pitt's policy of relief came very close to that of Grattan. It was tragic that past history, Fox's alliance, and constitutional theory, prevented real co-operation between Pitt and Irish reformers. Nevertheless, between January and April 1793 Westmorland, acting on Pitt's orders, used full official pressure to get the Irish parliament to pass a Catholic Relief Act. By this reform, pushed through in the first months of war, Roman catholics were not just given relief, they were given rights, and some political power. The papist population was given the vote on the same basis as the protestant. From this time forward, therefore, the mass of the electorate in Ireland was of an outlook alien to England. The papists were also allowed to sit on juries,

[1] John Fitzgibbon, earl of Clare (1749–1802), a distinguished lawyer, was, until 1785, a moderate nationalist; supported Pitt on Regency Bill, 1789; lord chancellor of Ireland, 1789–1802; one of the leading architects of the Act of Union; stressed catholic danger and was said, by his enemies, to have exacerbated relations between protestants and catholics in Ireland.

[2] John Beresford (1738–1805), first commissioner of revenue; a leading figure in the building of eighteenth-century Dublin; Pitt's adviser on local conditions of Irish politics; dismissed by Lord Fitzwilliam but afterwards reinstated; supported the Union and retired in 1802.

[3] The underground peasant organization for arson and destruction.

[4] Sir Hercules Langrishe (1731–1811), an office holder from 1766 to 1781 who eventually supported the Act of Union. Though so different in views from Grattan he agreed with him on the need for relief for the catholics and introduced a bill to that end, 1792.

to hold minor civil posts, and junior commissioned rank in the army. True, catholics of higher rank were still debarred from top places in administration, and they were still debarred from sitting in parliament. From the Irish point of view it was probably an error to start at the lower rather than higher levels with concessions, but the English political situation determined these tactics. For Pitt was pushing on with this plan single-handed; he had to carry king and country with him by keeping his own counsel as to the end of it all.

In 1794 Pitt gained reinforcement for a liberal campaign in Ireland, for his new colleagues, the Portland whigs, as much as Fox, had associated themselves with Grattan's movement. Yet they were from the start an embarrassment to Pitt. For his intentions were kept in his head; theirs had been shouted around London. Their coming to his side revealed to his older supporters the possible extent of his innovations. Pitt might be counter-working Fitzgibbon, Beresford, and the Irish conservatives, but he did it all without personal quarrel or even battle of principle. His method was to fight on practical proposals step by step; his new whig allies liked to announce a new order. But it was part of the terms of the Portland union that Westmorland should go from Dublin and be replaced by Fitzwilliam,[1] an adherent of Portland. The young Fitzwilliam, even before taking up his appointment, had written to Grattan announcing that the system was to be changed and asking for his support. This gave a warning to the enemies of a liberal policy. Pitt had to face discontent in his cabinet. A special cabinet conference was held to clear the air before Fitzwilliam's formal appointment as lord-lieutenant in December 1794. Fitzwilliam appears to have agreed to drop talk of 'a new system' and, while adhering to his own view that full catholic emancipation and a purification of the executive were needed, to use his first months in Ireland to inform himself of the facts and report to the cabinet on them.

Fitzwilliam's tenure of office in Dublin was only from January to March 1795. In that short time he brought the Irish problem to a head and seriously increased Pitt's difficulties in timing

---

[1] William Wentworth Fitzwilliam, second Earl Fitzwilliam (1748–1833), nephew and heir of the marquis of Rockingham; after his failure in Ireland he fought a duel with Beresford; lord president of the council in Ministry of All the Talents; except for this brief experience he spent the rest of his life in opposition.

any reforms. In the first week of January, Fitzwilliam dismissed John Beresford, the head of the revenue department in Dublin, second in importance only to chancellor Fitzgibbon as leader of the conservative 'pro-English' conservatives. To all Irish politicians this could only mean 'a new order'. Grattan promptly introduced a bill for catholic emancipation. Fitzwilliam, following his instructions in form at least, gave it no government backing. But it was guessed that he must agree with it and must be prepared to argue for it in the cabinet. George III complained that Fitzwilliam 'after no longer stay than three weeks in Ireland' condemned 'the labours of ages' for the defence of religion and property. The king in his excitement went even farther. He declared that any such change as Fitzwilliam envisaged was 'beyond the decision of a Cabinet of Ministers', on the ground that the exclusion of papists from parliament was a fundamental part of the political order and that he was bound by his coronation oath to resist any alteration of it.

Pitt and Grenville believed that the king would find much support among their colleagues. They were not prepared to fight on this issue at this time. Fitzwilliam was forced to resign. So precipitate had been his conduct that not even colleagues of the Portland group, who shared his aims, would give him any support. Consequently he left Dublin amid ovations from the populace and returned to London to find a stony silence among politicians. The premature discussion of emancipation had bad effects in Ireland and England. Grattan was now clamorous against the Beresford–Fitzgibbon anglican alliance. The English government appeared to be identified with one small reactionary faction. Outside the Irish parliamentary circles the presbyterians argued that the Fitzwilliam episode showed that Irish parliamentary independence was only a façade screening English reactionary control. In this year, 1795, a young lawyer from Belfast, Theodore Wolf Tone, left Ireland first for America and then Paris, to fight actively to throw off English control. Even the Roman catholics were roused from their apathy by having hope held out and then withdrawn. Meanwhile in England the enemies of Irish reform had been put on the alert. Pitt continued to aim at two objectives: first he wished to cure the Irish malaise by healing the breach between her anglican, presbyterian, and papist sections so as to give her a secure social order; second, he wished to secure co-operation between this healed

Ireland and an England at bay before France. But after the Fitzwilliam fiasco internal reform in Ireland seemed likely to endanger partnership with England. About this time Pitt may probably have seen that his two purposes could only be combined if Rockingham's legislation were reversed. The Irish parliament could not be increased in strength and independence if it used them to organize anti-English sentiment.

The difficulties of Grattan's party should be understood. They began to take a more outspoken line against England and thus they lost the support of English moderate opinion, for they had to attack Pitt as much as Chancellor Loughborough or the archbishop of Canterbury, condemning them all as reactionaries. Yet if they had attempted to understand Pitt's attitude they would have lost all hope of guiding the excited Irish masses. As it was, the most sinister feature of the scene in Ireland after 1795 was that both sides tended to regard parliament as irrelevant and to transfer the struggle to the streets and fields. Napper Tandy,[1] for instance, a protestant who had once helped to secure Grattan's election, was now active in giving the United Irishmen a military organization in armed battalions. He was no longer a champion of protestantism or even of nationalism: he fought instead for a revolutionary social and political idea, the principles of the French Revolution. This was true of the United Irishmen as a whole. Many of their presbyterian but respectable supporters fell away. The minority who were left were the more efficient as a dedicated revolutionary party of the kind which Lenin approved a century later and in another country. These professional agitators conducted their propaganda not only among the presbyterian business men but widely among the hitherto aimless catholic peasantry of the south.

The French were aware of this. When Hoche threatened invasion in December 1796 his expectation was that a small number of French troops would suffice because they would only be required to stiffen the local mass rising. It seems probable that he would not in fact have received the welcome he expected.

[1] James Napper Tandy (1740–1803), a 'Volunteer'; defended the French Revolution; arrested, but successfully sued the viceroy for wrongful imprisonment; on the failure of military schemes fled to America and then France; made abortive landing with French troops in Donegal; took to drink; arrested in Hamburg and imprisoned in Ireland; released to return to France, on intervention of Napoleon, at time of peace of Amiens.

But in 1797 the new lord-lieutenant, Lord Camden,[1] and his chief secretary, Thomas Pelham, drew the attention of the cabinet to the great strides made by the organization of the United Irishmen. The French in February 1797 had been able to embark 1,400 men in four vessels which, after anchoring off Ilfracombe, sailed on to land at Fishguard in South Wales. Their force was a ragged, half-trained one. It was easily captured by the Pembrokeshire militia. But if it had landed in Ireland it might, in the view of Dublin officials, have been just the spark to detonate the explosive situation. When it is remembered that within three months of this exploit the sea defences of Ireland were temporarily suspended by the naval mutinies, it is not surprising that the lord-lieutenant should have felt that he had, without delay, to take decisions upon which would depend the issue of the war and the continuance of English rule in Ireland.

Lord Camden resolved upon strong measures. He would destroy the apparatus of revolt in good time. Accordingly General Lake was instructed to disarm presbyterian Ulster which was still, despite the growing papist scare, the centre of really formidable revolutionary preparation. The followers of Grattan showed their impotence; after commending, with equal futility, conciliation to the government and restraint to the people, they seceded from parliament. General Lake found that the regular troops at his command were insufficient to subdue the six northern counties. He therefore called up the yeomanry to his assistance. But the volunteer soldiers who made up this force were the local defenders of property and the established religion, the core of extreme conservative enthusiasm. A disarmament carried out by such a force resembled a civil war; it afforded opportunity for the payment of private grudges, for religious bigotry, and for class persecution. 'Murder', said Lord Cornwallis, 'appears to be the favourite pastime' of the Irish militia. The yeomanry certainly believed in flogging on the flimsiest suspicion.[2]

The coercion of Ulster may have been ruthless but it was also effective. The United Irishmen saw their underground

---

[1] The second earl and first marquis of Camden (1759–1840), the son of Chatham's lord chancellor.

[2] For an example, though not in Ulster, see *Wright* v. *Fitzgerald* where a school teacher was flogged because he knew French and therefore must be a potential rebel. Costin and Watson, *The Law and Working of the Constitution*, ii. 241.

organization being crippled. They therefore decided to strike while they could. This meant that they could not synchronize their movements with the French. This in turn meant that the majority of their rank and file supporters lacked arms. However, they hoped to compensate for this by striking a blow in Dublin itself and capturing or paralysing the directing forces of the government. The plot made in February 1798 was suppressed in March with the arrest of fourteen of the delegates in a house in Dublin. Both sides became more ferocious. The government undertook the pacification of Leinster on the lines of that completed in Ulster. The revolutionaries came into the open with attacks on Naas, Carlow, and Wexford. By the end of May 1798 a force of 15,000 men captured Wexford with its garrison and went on to take Enniscorthy also. The army of revolt was ill organized. Inevitably religious passion, under the stimulus of a revolutionary priest, had to take the place of arms or discipline, just as the government used terror where they had not numbers.

The insurrection gradually acquired the character of a religious rebellion. This—as well as the recent pacification—prevented effective co-operation from revolutionary but protestant elements in the north. The rebels revenged themselves for a repulse at New Ross by the massacre of a hundred protestant prisoners. By mid-June, however, General Lake had mobilized a powerful force for the suppression of the rebellion. He attacked the main rebel force near Enniscorthy. On 21 June 1798 their wild but untrained force broke at Vinegar Hill. Wexford was retaken and soon nothing remained of rebellion in the south but pillaging bands rapidly degenerating into that sporadic gang disorder which was too regular a feature of Irish life. Meanwhile, forces which had come out to fight in the north, mainly in Down and Antrim, had been separately crushed in an action on 12 June near Ballinahinch.

The precipitation of open rebellion by the discovery of the plot had prevented the French from giving assistance when it was needed. The victory of Duncan over the Dutch at Camperdown had, in any case, prevented any full-scale naval expedition from sailing to Ireland. Nevertheless on 22 August 1798 a French force, 900 regular troops under General Humbert, landed up in the north-west at Killala, County Mayo. They were too late. Not only had Vinegar Hill and Ballinahinch destroyed the spirit of the Irish people, but a new viceroy, Lord Cornwallis, had been appointed who was also commander-in-chief and brought fresh regular troops. Even so, the small French force, gathering a fringe of rebellious driftwood as it moved, advanced to Castlebar and repulsed General Lake. They then crossed the Shannon only to be caught between Cornwallis at Carrick and Lake coming up in their rear to Ballinamuck. The French then surrendered. Even less successful was the small French squadron which brought the hot-spirited Wolf Tone back to his native shores. It was captured by Commodore Borlase Warren in Lough Swilly. Tone was condemned by a court-martial for treason and cut his own throat in prison.[1]

So the Irish rebellion closed. But the Irish question was still pressing. It was essential for success in war to solve it. Cornwallis, the new viceroy, was a man instinctively in sympathy with Pitt's policy; the chief secretary, Lord Castlereagh,[2] was active in propaganda for it. This policy was brought into the open during 1799. To prevent Ireland from acting as a thorn in England's side the two countries must be united under one legislature as well as having one executive. At the same time—and just as vital—it was the view of Cornwallis, Castlereagh, and Pitt that, in the words of the first of these, 'until the Catholics are admitted into a general participation of rights (which when incorporated with the British Government they cannot abuse) there will be no peace or safety in Ireland'.[3] Yet the difficulties in the way both of catholic emancipation and of the Union were many. To their settlement Pitt, already fully engaged in conducting the war of the second coalition, already harassed by his private financial troubles, had to devote a great deal of time and of negotiating skill.

The Irish parliamentarians were not likely to relish the loss

---

[1] By his suicide he prevented some interesting constitutional issues—about the power of the court martial to try him—being fully tested in the ordinary courts of law.

[2] Robert Stewart, Viscount Castlereagh, marquis of Londonderry; best known as Viscount Castlereagh (1769–1822), chief secretary 1799, having been acting chief secretary since 1797; steered the Act of Union through the Irish parliament; a believer in the necessity for catholic emancipation and resigned on this issue in 1801; president of Indian Board of Control, 1802; war and colonial secretary in addition, 1805. For his later career and his greatness as foreign secretary, 1812–22, see narrative below. See also Sir E. L. Woodward, *The Age of Reform*, p. 52.

[3] 15 November 1799: *Correspondence of Charles, 1st Marquis Cornwallis* (ed. C. Ross).

of their little world of power. Two arguments could be used with them. Their blood could be chilled by dwelling on the insecurity of their position in Ireland. Could they hope to continue to enjoy control of a rebellious country merely by manipulating a narrow and corrupt franchise? The second means of persuasion was more direct. It was proposed to pay the owners of borough seats or of offices for the loss of kudos they would suffer. Peerages were promised, jobs offered, and straight cash (£7,000 for a seat) made available. A further argument had to be used on both those who supported Grattan in his advocacy of catholic emancipation and on those who fought against it. To the former it could be represented that it would be impossible to emancipate the catholics inside the Irish parliament. The protestant passion, after the late rebellion, was too strong. But a united parliament could take a broader view of this reform. To the latter, on the other hand, it had to be urged that emancipation might be dangerous in Ireland on its own: but if the steadier weight of England were brought to bear then emancipation would lose half its dangers, for the catholic peasant would then remain a minority voter instead of becoming three-quarters of the electorate. A final inducement could be held out to the whole commercial community: under Union there would be free trade and the enterprising men of Ulster would be able to push their linen as a British product within every province of the British empire.

It was a mixture of all these arguments which eventually induced the Irish parliament, by 158 to 115, to vote away its own existence in the spring of 1800. It is clear that catholic aspirations played a great part in the decision. In 1799, when the project was first introduced, the viceroy had been glad to let his plan wait over until it came forward again successfully in 1800. In the interval the government played for catholic support. In Castlereagh's view they could not have passed the Union without soothing catholic opposition.[1] While the Union Act was passed under the implied promise of emancipation, it was not openly accompanied by any such measure or guarantee of it. For that would have frightened away the right-wing protestant supporters. It was a game such as Pitt knew well how to play.

Pitt knew that English politicians would welcome the Union

[1] *Memoirs and Correspondence of Castlereagh* (ed. Londonderry), iv. 8 et seq.

but dislike emancipation. He hoped to put it to them as a necessary sequel to the Union, one, moreover, which could be regarded as part of the disagreeable but necessary consequence of war. He himself believed emancipation to be just; he also believed that it was necessary for the war effort to quieten Ireland. When Cornwallis's son was asked who would succeed his father as ruler of Ireland, supposing emancipation to be rejected, he replied 'Bonaparte'.[1] This was a witty précis of Pitt's view. But to get his way Pitt had to carry the cabinet with him, for it was essential to present the conservatively minded backbenchers with little choice. In this he failed. From the beginning some of his colleagues, such as Lord Chancellor Loughborough, were listening to Irish die-hards like Lord Clare (as Fitzgibbon had become) rather than to him. Within three months of Pitt's opening his mind to the cabinet, Portland, Westmorland, Liverpool, and Chatham, had turned against his scheme. In January 1801 George III himself took a decisive part. He felt very much as most of Pitt's ordinary supporters did. He felt that Pitt was being too clever by half. How could it be useful to the war against revolution to put political power into the hands of a turbulent lower class who had alien loyalties? The king also sincerely felt that emancipation meant the ruin of the church of England which he stood pledged to govern and guard. So at his levée on 28 January 1801 the king blurted out to Dundas: 'The most Jacobinical thing I ever heard of! I shall reckon any man my personal enemy who proposes any such measure.'

Pitt must have expected difficulty with the king. What made it serious was the failure of the cabinet to reach a clear and united decision in the previous September. Instead of meeting an angry king with the backing of all those ministers on whom he relied for the prosecution of the war, Pitt had to face a king who had information from Loughborough of the arguments used against emancipation in the cabinet. The king's strength was that he was still regarded as head of his own executive and that his view on this issue was a popular one. Pitt seemed to be sinning as Fox sinned, that is, in pushing a particular partisan point to the detriment of national unity in time of war. It could be argued that he was abandoning the national, agreed, coalition spirit on which he had rested ever since 1784. Pitt's

---

[1] *Diaries of Sylvester Douglas, Lord Glenbervie*, ed. F. Bickley, i. 170.

strength, against this, was that he had been right for so long that his judgement automatically was respected; in addition, it might prove difficult for the king to replace him with any minister capable of running the war and facing the house of commons. Yet such a head-on collision with the king was what Pitt most desired to avoid. At the worst he must have hoped that the king would permit him the same liberty as he had had in moving for parliamentary reform fifteen years before.

Pitt tried to persuade the king by rational argument as he had persuaded the majority—but not all—of the cabinet. His main claim was that the papists no longer constituted a political danger provided they were given a stake in the state: 'The grounds on which the laws of exclusion now remaining were founded, have long been narrowed, and are since the Union removed.' George III was not to be persuaded. His objection was emotional rather than rational. He had courage to be obstinate because he had found a substitute for Pitt. As early as 29 January 1801 he had seen Henry Addington,[1] the Speaker of the house of commons, and used him as an agent to persuade Pitt to yield: on 31 January he had asked Addington if he would form a ministry: 'Where am I to turn for support if *you* do not stand by me?' On 14 March Addington formed a government and Pitt left office after seventeen years, being accompanied in his resignation by Dundas, Grenville, Windham, Spencer, Cornwallis, and Castlereagh.[2]

Pitt, said the king, had behaved like himself throughout this business and, 'Nothing could possibly be more honourable.' His kindness towards his sovereign, his desire to make all concessions short of the main one, his promise that out of office he would still support the government, and even more his never raising the subject again even when, four years later, he resumed office, all these considerations made the king praise his honourable course. They have, in contrast, led historians to attack Pitt for duplicity. Pitt has been accused of tricking the Roman catholics in Ireland into supporting the Union as part

[1] Henry Addington, first Viscount Sidmouth (1757–1844), son of a court doctor and childhood friend of Pitt; Speaker of the house of commons, 1789–1801; first lord of the treasury, 1801–4; lord president of the council 1805, and again 1812; home secretary 1812, when he severely repressed radical agitation. A man of clear common sense who had to contend with more talented but less reliable rivals.

[2] Loughborough, though opposed to Pitt, was not included in the cabinet of Addington.

of a bargain and then only feigning to struggle to fulfil his part
of it, of accepting a brief spell in opposition as a purging of all
promises so that he might resume power unencumbered. Such
an analysis is false to the facts of the situation. Pitt often had to
coax his friends by inches towards the solutions he favoured.
Usually he knew when he could advance, when he must wait.
He misjudged the political climate on emancipation. This he
not only promised but believed in. But there were always limits
to the lengths to which Pitt would push an argument. He
believed in firm government before he believed in particular
measures. In war he believed that no difference of opinion on
minor matters should interrupt operations. He also considered
that the support of the Crown—even if reluctantly given—was
essential to a good government fit to conduct the war. Therefore,
when he found George III stubborn, he hoped to push him
into a decision which he would hate for a time but which he
would eventually realize was right. Pitt found he had not sufficient support in cabinet or parliament to do this. As a man of
honour he had then to resign. But as a patriot he had still the
duty to promote the war effort. This he could only do by supporting the new government. Furthermore, once he had failed
to move the king, there could be no chance of carrying catholic
emancipation through parliament as a non-party if unpalatable
necessity. Pitt had never, in war-time, been prepared to carry it
in any other way. If he had revived the issue after 1801 the
result would have been that parliament would have dissolved
into warring parties and George III would have gone mad
again in his agitation. Both results would have been as bad as
military defeat. Pitt did not forget his promise to Ireland but
he always regarded it as subordinate to—or a subordinate part
of—his duty to help win the war.

The fall of Pitt from power seemed almost an impossibility.
Politicians suspected a trick, some shabby manœuvre. But it
marked in fact a logical stage in political development as well
as in the war struggle. To take the latter first: it was clear that
the second coalition had failed, but equally clear that Britain
was undefeated. There opened up a new sort of conflict, between a triumphant land power and an untamed sea empire,
with neither able easily to grapple with the other. Pitt drew
back from such a clumsy and protracted encounter. He was
once more in favour of peace even though such a peace could

mean little more than an armistice, even though the original war aims of his country would have to be abandoned. Grenville and Windham deplored this compromising weakness in their leader. Thus the ministerial team which since 1793 had fought France was not sufficiently united to continue or to close the war. It was therefore as well to let others take their place. This feeling contributed to their lack of will in the emancipation crisis.

Politically, also, the fall of Pitt closed one chapter and began another. When Pitt had first taken the highest office, the maintenance of any executive had been imperilled by the spasmodic 'oppositionism' of independent country gentlemen. His own leadership, then fear of Jacobinism, then the perils of war, had changed all this. It was now generally felt to be a clear patriotic duty for ordinary members to support the government of the day. But in return the government of the day should abstain from fancy plans and concentrate on those clear national necessities which everyone could see. Pitt, while remaining in popular esteem the best man for saving his country in war, had at length pushed a personal crotchet to the front so that it marred the common effort. The position thus was that there were plenty of political troops, but their captain was deserting them. The back-benchers wanted a new no-nonsense leader. The days when talent was demanded in a leader, because it was needed in the house, were over for the while. The opposition had declined in effectiveness partly out of habitual wrong-headedness and partly from Fox's lazy disinclination to make any effort.

The country gentlemen wanted a sound government, one 'without those confounded men of genius in it'. As Speaker of the house of commons, Addington had made his character well known to them all. He believed that the war was just; but he had come to the conclusion that it should be ended as a draw in order to save expense. He thought the abolition of the slave trade too hazardous an experiment to be undertaken. He thought parliamentary reform would open up the way to revolution. He believed that catholic emancipation was another such dangerous experiment with the foundations of the constitution. More positively Addington was a tidy-minded and a tolerant man in personal relations. He might be a good administrator. He would certainly not exclude from a share of power anyone who was prepared to work in his humdrum conservative government. It seemed that only a brilliant offensive in parliament or defeat in war could shake such a ministry. Against the first he had the promise of Pitt's aid; against the second he could insure by pushing on peace talks. All in all it seemed once again that George III had acted as the barometer of the feelings of ordinary members of parliament, and that the new order would last, despite the shaking of heads among professional politicians.

XVI

FROM AMIENS TO TRAFALGAR

ADDINGTON did not replace Pitt in February 1801 simply because he was the enemy of concessions to Roman catholicism. He represented also the war-weariness which made many an Englishman feel that Pitt's courage was as dangerous as it was admirable. As early as 1797 Addington had been passing on to Pitt the strong, though damped-down, defeatism of many back-benchers. Pitt, too, was a man for peace—but his desire for it was never unconditional. Yet by 1801 many arguments were advanced for peace at any price. The treaty of Lunéville marked the complete collapse of the continental alliances and, said Addington, 'there was not the least prospect of obtaining any such alliances'[1] for the present, so complete was the exhaustion of Europe.

Britain's own strength was, at this time, shaken though not exhausted. It consisted in the ability to keep up the war by paying heavy subsidies to maintain the armies of other powers. These payments could only be made either in gold—which was limited in supply—or in goods. The inflation, which followed the bank's abandonment of cash payments,[2] had helped to stimulate industrial expansion. Pitt's financial policy, that of keeping taxes high to pay for the war, had kept this inflation within limits and so it had not ended in a giddy collapse of confidence. The stimulation of industrial expansion meant that it had been possible to arm the forces and yet offer goods—particularly cotton textiles—to the world.[3] In addition England, with control of the oceans, had no real competitor for colonial re-exports. Europe had no other merchant to supply coffee, sugar, raw cotton, or the spices and dyes of the East. Taken together these lines of exports exceeded in value the goods obtained from Europe. The difference between the figures was available for making presents to allies. The healthy state of

[1] See report of Addington's Table Talk, *Diaries of Sylvester Douglas, Lord Glenbervie*, ed. F. Bickley, i. 267.
[2] See above, p. 372.   [3] See below, p. 509.

English banking and credit arrangements in every commercial centre of the world made the necessary transformation of a trade surplus into a subsidy quite easy.

Ever since 1798 the Directory had been doing their best to damage this economic weapon of England. The Rhine was blocked as a trade route. England, nevertheless, pushed its goods into Europe from north Germany, from the Baltic and from the Adriatic. It was therefore a great disaster economically when the Northern League took sides with France, for it at once closed an avenue for exports and dried up the sources of corn and wood imports.[1] Nelson at Copenhagen removed the military but not the economic menace. As the allies had dropped away, it might be said that there was no longer need of an export surplus. Unfortunately England, for a while, had not even a balance but a deficit in trade. The harvest of 1799 was very bad. The need to import grain required exports to pay for it. Between 1800 and 1801 £23¼ million had to be paid to the Continent to cover the subsidies (£5½ million), garrison expenses (£2¾ million), and the increased grain purchases. It could only be done by making payments in gold. The Bank of England's reserves were draining away. The pound was depreciated on continental exchanges (by 13 per cent. at Hamburg, by 16 per cent. in Spain).

Bread in England was scarce and dear. Riots were the result. Some feared that the ultimate cost of fighting the French Revolution would be the victory of agitators in England. Short of food, with timber supplies threatened, in the midst of a financial crisis, without any allies, the reasonable men of politics cried not for success but for rescue. It was their mood of desperation which made many members of parliament particularly hostile to Pitt's advocacy of catholic emancipation. They wanted not an architect for constitutional rebuilding but someone to rig up a shelter. Such a patcher-up of peace was Addington.

Addington's administration was as strong in general support as it was weak in combative debating power. Addington had no party in any modern sense. Estimates of the numbers of his following in parliament are puzzling because they vary from 12 to 60. The solution is that he had a dozen close friends, many of them his relations, who had personal obligations to

[1] Seventy-five per cent. of the corn imported, which was about 16½ per cent. of British bread consumption, came from Danzig.

him, while beyond these an unorganized body looked to him with greater confidence than they did to any other notable politician. He had few friends or admirers among the ablest politicians. His ministerial appointments were in consequence not impressive. St. Vincent (as Sir John Jervis had become) brought to the admiralty naval talents proved at sea. At the foreign office Lord Hawkesbury (the son of Charles Jenkinson, now earl of Liverpool) had a chance to demonstrate skill which was to loom large in British politics for the next twenty years. But Hobart,[1] Chatham,[2] Westmorland,[3] Yorke,[4] and Pelham,[5] were but second-rate stuff. The appointment of his brother Hiley Addington, his cousin Golding and his brothers-in-law Bragge and Adams, to minor offices exposed him to jeers from Canning.[6] It suggested that of the three tests on which Addington professed to make his appointments—'character, talents, and their being his own personal friends'—the third was the most potent. All the same, a ministry might begin with a weak team and gain stronger recruits once it showed itself secure: had not Pitt done just this? Castlereagh joined the government

[1] Robert Hobart (1760–1815), Irish secretary, 1789; governor of Madras, 1794; Baron Hobart, 1798, and active in arranging Irish Union; succeeded his father as earl of Buckinghamshire, 1804; under Addington he was secretary of state for war and the colonies; subsequently he served under Grenville as postmaster general and under Liverpool as president of the board of trade.

[2] John, second Earl Chatham (1756–1835), had previously held office as first lord of the admiralty, lord privy seal, and lord president; he now became master of the ordnance. His reputation was to be ruined by his command of the Walcheren expedition in 1809 (see below, p. 478).

[3] John, tenth Earl Westmorland (1759–1841), had been recalled by Pitt from office as lord-lieutenant of Ireland, 1795, as an avowed opponent of catholic emancipation; from 1798 to 1827 he peacefully occupied the office of lord privy seal.

[4] Charles Philip Yorke (1764–1834), grandson of Lord Chancellor Hardwicke and son of Lord Chancellor Yorke (who died before his patent of nobility was completed, see above, p. 146). He became secretary at war and then home secretary; after the fall of Addington he served only as teller of the exchequer in 1810 and first lord of the admiralty, 1810–11.

[5] Thomas Pelham (1756–1826): as a Portland whig he had been Irish secretary 1795–8; he now became home secretary until his removal to the chancellorship of the duchy of Lancaster in 1803; for nineteen years (1807–26) a postmaster general; succeeded his father as second earl of Chichester in 1805.

[6] George Canning (1770–1827), brought up in a whig milieu, had attached himself to Pitt on the outbreak of the French Revolution; Pitt made him under-secretary for foreign affairs (1796), a member of the India Board (1799), and pay-master general (1800). Canning was already noted in parliament, in society, and in journalism, for his wit and brilliance. His intolerance of Addington's dullness was characteristic of his temperament. For his later career, as foreign secretary in 1807, as rival of Castlereagh up to 1815, see the narrative that follows.

after it had been in existence a year. There was hope of gaining adherents from Fox's group; Erskine and Tierney[1] were willing; Sheridan spoke in defence of the new ministry. Addington agreed with their pacific policies. He was, said Canning, 'a sheep calling wolves to his assistance'. In truth Addington was not such a sheep, such a man of infirm will, as was alleged. He advanced the status of prime minister. The king agreed not to see ministers or deal with them except through Addington—'This is the notion of a Prime Minister as known formerly sometimes under the French government.'[2]

The two planks on which the government had to stand were peace and retrenchment. The estimates for secret service were at once reduced from £35,000 to £12,000, a specimen of the new policy. To achieve greater reductions Hawkesbury negotiated with the French diplomat Otto;[3] peace preliminaries were concluded on 1 October 1801, to be turned into a definite peace treaty at Amiens on 27 March 1802. Definite is perhaps the wrong adjective for this truce. For the basis of the peace was undermined by unspoken differences in the minds of the French and English negotiators. Addington had at first used Pitt's notes of 1800 as his brief; these proposed that the English hold of Malta, Ceylon, Cochin, and the Cape was to be kept and some satisfactory arrangement to be reached about the Netherlands and Egypt. But, in his haste for peace, he had scrapped this plan and had proposed a settlement on *uti possidetis* principles. France had been unwilling to concede the loss of her overseas territories and had resumed belligerency. So finally the British government agreed to restore all its conquests to France, to Spain, and to Holland (now the Batavian republic), with the exception of Trinidad (taken from Spain) and Ceylon (taken from Holland). Cochin, the Cape, and the Spice Islands were returned to Holland; Minorca was handed back to Spain, and the captured Indian and African stations were to be restored

---

[1] Thomas Erskine, first Baron Erskine (1750–1823), intimate friend of Sheridan and Fox. A great barrister noted for his contributions to commercial law and his defence of the radicals during the war-time prosecutions for sedition and treason. Appointed lord chancellor in 1806 despite his ignorance of equity.

George Tierney (1761–1830), a Foxite who had offended his own political friends in 1798; fought a duel with Pitt, who had accused him of obstruction; president of the board of control, 1806.

[2] *Diaries of Sylvester Douglas, Lord Glenbervie*, ed. F. Bickley, i. 220.

[3] Louis Guillaume Otto, Comte de Mosloy, who became minister to the Court of St. James after the conclusion of peace.

to France as well as St. Lucia, Tobago, Martinique, St. Pierre, and Miquelon.[1]

Malta, it was agreed, should be returned to the Knights of St. John of Jerusalem, into which order no English or French knights were to be admitted. British troops were to evacuate Malta within three months, allowing Neapolitan troops to en-sure its security until the Knights of St. John were ready to assume full control. The independence of the order in the island was to be guaranteed by Great Britain, France, Austria, Spain, Prussia, and Russia. The last power, it was believed, would welcome this responsibility.

To balance these surrenders by Britain, France agreed to help to find compensation for the House of Orange, whose expulsion from Holland was formally admitted. France also agreed to evacuate southern and central Italy, Naples, and the Roman states. These seem small enough concessions. So they were. But this did not trouble the British government which believed that guarantees, more important to its position, had already been given, not at Amiens but in the Treaty of Luné-ville, made in the previous year between France and Austria. To this treaty Britain was not a party, but in it she had a vital interest. At Lunéville Napoleon had, while taking the whole left bank of the Rhine for France, agreed to respect the indepen-dence of the Helvetian (Swiss), Batavian (Dutch), Cisalpine, and Ligurian republics. Britain considered the peace of Amiens tolerable only because she believed the independence of Hol-land, Switzerland, and northern Italy had already been secured. With these provisos she would accept the new and greater France. To which the French soon replied that these stipulations were not in the treaty with Britain; they were the concern of France, Austria, Spain and the republics involved, and of no one else.

Peace after nine years of war gave a chance of relaxation. Fox and the whig notables dashed off to Paris to meet the first consul and examine the manners of an egalitarian nation. Lady Elizabeth Foster[2] was one such, a typical English traveller to the new Paris. She noted that there was indeed a new society in

---

[1] Wellesley in India ignored orders from home and refused to hand back French posts.

[2] A woman of admirable intelligence but whose private life—she was the mistress of her best friend's husband, the duke of Devonshire—was less praiseworthy.

France, for the lower orders had grown impertinent and a common postilion dared to peer into the ladies' coach to remark 'Diable, au moins elles sont jolies.' 'Very good to hear,' she commented, 'but odd.' Those who met the first consul himself found him in a mood of restless bonhomie; but behind the 'things which were good to hear' from his mouth, they suspected that there lay more than oddity or impertinence. Some of them began to debate seriously how far Napoleon was a pacific democrat, how far a parvenu and expansionist dictator.

Fox's friends gained from these contacts a more realistic view of the revolution and of Napoleon. Grey, recognized as Fox's eventual successor, came from this time onwards to admit that the war was just and necessary. It had not taken a tour to convince Grenville of this. He had condemned the peace from the start as unsound and dangerous. Windham called it a disaster. Yet Pitt himself gave powerful support to Addington, saying publicly that no better terms were possible and privately declaring that he would have been glad to sign them himself. Yet he too implied that while France was to be conceded great new gains she was to rest content with them and to cease expansion.

Even before the peace was made definitive, however, France had, by private negotiation with Spain, acquired in addition Louisiana, the isle of Elba, and the duchy of Parma. The French fleet sailed from Brest to reconquer St. Domingo from the negroes—a perfectly legal proceeding, sanctioned in London, but one which nevertheless underlined France's determination to re-establish her colonial empire and which therefore caused uneasiness to the British. Much worse followed, even as the peace was honoured by illumination of the streets of London. The Cisalpine republic professed its inability to exist without Napoleon's patronage. He accepted the personal presidency of the republic. At the same time 'many political reasons' were said to prevent the evacuation of the republic by French troops. The result clearly was that Napoleon had taken over northern Italy. This might be a breach of what Addington expected, but it could not be shown to have any inconsistency with what he had formally agreed.

Before the end of 1802 France showed her expansionist spirit even more clearly. Piedmont was annexed to France; this confirmed Napoleon's supreme position in Italy. By treaty with the

bey of Tunis France secured economic privileges which suggested her ambition to control the southern shores of the Mediterranean as well. France meddled in the internal disputes of
the Swiss and ended by enforcing her control of Switzerland by
armed intervention. Napoleon's control of Holland, though less
dramatically signalled, was no less apparent. Even in Germany
the resettlement of the empire, made necessary by the indemni-
ties imposed at Lunéville, was guided by France and Russia,
whose 'preponderance might remove all obstacles', as the
French minister admitted. Spain, a client state of France, in
October 1802 seized the property of the Knights of St. John in
Spain; the king of Spain assumed the mastership of the order in
his dominions. This seemed to threaten that the knights would
hold Malta only as French agents at one remove. In these
circumstances it was natural that Britain should delay her restitution of Indian posts and her evacuation of Malta. She broke
the letter of the treaty of Amiens, pleading as her excuse that
Napoleon was breaking its spirit. She was paying for haste and
carelessness in peace-making.

The peace, though it never looked secure, gave Addington a
chance to bid for popularity through economy. The regular
army establishment was reduced to 95,000 men (double that of
1784), with 48,000 militia and 24,000 in reserve, as well as
18,000 in Ireland. More striking were the navy reductions. In
spite of the mutinies, Pitt's first lord, Lord Spencer,[1] had had a
fine record of achievement. Dockyards and fleets were in first-
class fighting order. St. Vincent axed this service remorselessly.
Artificers were laid off and stocks of material sold. Manpower
was reduced at once from 130,000 to 70,000 men, with the hope
of getting down to 30,000 by 1803. Such speed in disarmament
aroused Pitt's friends to protest but was supported by the
Foxites. By the end of 1802 Addington could claim a saving of
£25 million, thanks to the peace. It is to his credit that he
undertook the reform as well as the reduction of the finances
of the country. He began the practice of making a complete
annual survey of the national accounts, the budget in its
modern sense. He continued the work of setting the civil list
expenditure on a modern footing. Parliament took over direct

---

[1] George John Spencer, second earl of Spencer (1758–1834), a Portland whig;
while first lord of the admiralty singled out Nelson; resigned with Pitt but did not
rejoin the ministry with him; home secretary in the Talents ministry, 1806–7.

responsibility for the departmental salaries, colonial and consular services, instead of letting the king provide for them.[1] Public burdens were thus publicly recognized.

Pitt's income-tax had been bringing in £6 million annually, much less than the estimated amount. £1¾ million of this had been reserved to meet the interest on the 3 per cent. loan. Addington raised a new loan and abolished the income-tax. To meet necessities—and the expenditure was still high—he perpetuated the war-time high rates of export and import duties as well as Pitt's excise and stamp duties. The abolition of income-tax indeed was likely to be more popular with men of wealth than with the poor. It could be argued for this relief, on the other hand, that the income-tax was an administrative nuisance. To complete his organization of peacetime finance Addington consolidated all the provisions of the sinking funds so as to repay his loans within forty-five years.

By the time of the general election of 1802 Addington's popularity in the country was strong. The country gentlemen approved his businesslike attention to detail: the trading classes thanked him for a trade revival (for in the first nine months of peace exports had increased by £4½ million). Among parliamentary leaders, on the other hand, opposition was growing. Pitt was urged by his friends to assert himself. But Pitt was not willing to work his way to power; he wanted a unanimous call for his return. This could not be. Grenville stood firmly against Addington's peace policy but also for catholic relief. Fox approved disarmament but supported the catholic relief. Pitt himself, like Dundas, would abandon the catholics but opposed the government's reckless disarmament. The leading politicians were split into many groups. The unity of national feeling, for which Pitt looked, did not exist inside parliament: feeling outside was against him. Criticism of Addington, however, mounted and uneasiness increased everywhere. By December 1802 the economic effects of Napoleon's expansionist policy began to be felt as he blocked exports to Italy or Holland.[2] Yet at this moment the government opened an inquiry into the navy

---

[1] See above, pp. 247, 248, and 286.

[2] J.-A. Chaptal (the distinguished French chemist and minister of the empire) had urged on Napoleon that the Peace of Amiens should be consolidated by a trade treaty on the lines of Pitt's pre-war one. Napoleon, heeding the business men of Lyons, decided instead to close France and her areas of influence to all British competition.

management with the twin purpose of reflecting on its predecessor's wastefulness and of making new economies. Addington made offers of office to Pitt; the latter, while still claiming that he was not in opposition nor tied to any other politician, would only serve if he were given *carte blanche*, making clear his intention of dismissing St. Vincent, Hawkesbury, Pelham, and Hobart.

Criticism of Addington was whipped into fierceness by the failure of the peace. It had been impossible to abandon Malta while France continued to expand, particularly as Egypt and the Cape had been given up. French preparations for war were obvious. She had a programme for increasing her vessels of the line from 43 to 66: this it was expected would be completed by 1804. With sudden resolution, on 17 May 1803, the British government declared war before France could complete her preparations. But though Addington opened war, it was not to be the all-out war of Pitt. He planned a war which should be purely defensive and therefore cheaper. The navy would hold the high seas. Napoleon would control the continent. To win Napoleon would have to cross the Channel. The defeat of that invasion would mean victory for England.

In parliament all was confusion. The Foxites, still advocating peace, seemed to muster about 70: the Grenvillites, anxious for a real war, about the same number. Pitt, who wanted to conduct the war himself, had some 58. Addington seemed secure with 230 supporters, but of these many had no confidence in him but voted for any government in being at such a time of crisis.

As a war minister Addington was pre-judged. No one believed he had the heroic energy for his situation. He reintroduced the income-tax at 5 per cent. and greatly improved it by simplifying its collection: he made an attempt to deduct it near the source. As a result he could count on £4½ million from his tax as against Pitt's £6 million even though the new rate was one-half that formerly imposed. His credit for this was submerged in the blame cast on his handling of the armed forces. Even Nelson, a faithful friend to Addington, lamented that he had had to sail from Portsmouth with a ship half-manned—his suggestions having been shelved in Whitehall—to reach a Mediterranean fleet, every ship of which was in need of docking repairs. Windham could reasonably assert that in the raising of the army there was no real direction at all.

Just at this time, however, the reforms of the duke of York were beginning to bear fruit in the regular army. The duke had, since 1799, won his battle with the secretary-at-war; much to the benefit of discipline the commander-in-chief now controlled numbers, discipline, and efficiency. He had initiated a system of making returns and confidential reports to the central office. The old system by which colonels clothed their own regiments had been modified: there had even been an issue of greatcoats to the troops at the public expense.[1] Improved drill and manœuvre had been put into force. On the duke of York's orders in 1800 the 95th Regiment—later known as the Rifle Brigade—had been formed and trained. These men were armed not with the standard small-bore musket but with the Baker rifle which, though clumsy, was accurate at 300 yards. Dressed in uniforms which put concealment above ostentation, given a regular course of lectures and of exercises, they were a picked body in which the relationship between officers and men was closer than had ever been known before. In its stress upon the duty of an officer to be father to his men, to maintain discipline by efficiency instead of flogging, the Rifle Brigade was the first manifestation of that new spirit in military officers which also produced the Royal Military College in 1802.

The regular army was therefore rapidly improving in morale. But it was sadly deficient in numbers. The consequence of Addington's decision to fight a war of home defence was that, in his eyes, the regular army seemed less important than the militia and volunteers. Yorke, secretary-at-war, praised his own moderation in asking only for a trivial increase in the size of the army in June 1803. The government's main effort was to increase the militia. The Militia Act of 1802 provided for raising 51,500 men by ballot for home defence. As the execrable system of substitutes was still permitted this act would, as Pitt's had done, lock up the manpower for which the army appealed in local, better rewarded,[2] and much less trained, operations round a parish pump. A second Militia Act in 1803 provided for raising another 25,000 men without removing any of the flaws in the original act. After the militia came the volunteers. As the

[1] For this system, and the old organization of the army in general, consult R. Whitworth, *Field Marshal Lord Ligonier*, particularly p. 43.

[2] The current rate for which a substitute could ask for serving in the militia was £20 or £30, while the bounty given him for entering the regular army was only £7. 12s. 6d.

situation grew worse, as invasion grew more likely, Addington's government appealed for volunteer companies to defend their country. The patriotic response was great. It was indeed so great that the government had no idea how to manage it: they had no arms to equip the companies nor instructors to teach them military discipline. Moreover, the government belatedly realized that men who were accepted in these self-regulating bodies would not be available for the militia or the regular army. The patriotic volunteers found, therefore, that when they rushed to help their country they were coldly received, their expense allowances reduced, and a pike at most put into their hands. Not unnaturally there were loud cries against such ineptitude.

Addington did his best to undo the impression made so far by further acts; there were those, for instance, setting up an army of reserve, or compelling men to become volunteers. But the new acts further entangled the position. No one even knew whether a volunteer could legally resign or not. The lords-lieutenant and the local parish authorities only too often gave up all attempt to do anything systematic in face of the conflicting instructions which fell upon them. Several systems of cash allowances and different training requirements overlapped. The chief critic of the muddle was Pitt's former secretary-at-war, Windham. He argued that it was more important to recruit the regular army and to train it than to assemble a rabble of part-time soldiers. He usefully suggested that it would help army recruitment to allow men to volunteer for a fixed term of years instead of committing themselves to indefinite service. But to these arguments Addington was deaf. He thought not of the eventual final defeat of France but of the immediate prospect of a landing some night on Egdon Heath while the little groups of squires and labourers would gather in the dark cheering themselves by muttering 'we be the bravest of the brave in natural jeopardies, or the little boys wouldn't run after us and call us the "Bang-up Locals" '.[1]

The period of suspended animation at Westminster lasted until April 1804, largely because Pitt refused to take an outspoken line. It was prolonged also by the king's illness: he had another period of madness lasting from February to mid-April, and this increased men's reluctance to upset the existing arrange-

[1] Thomas Hardy, *The Dynasts*, Act II, Scene v.

ments. At length, on the Irish Militia Bill, Pitt, Grenville, and
the Foxites were able to vote on the same side. The government
still had a majority of 21 (128 to 107) but Addington decided to
resign. By 7 May Pitt was forming his new—and last—administration. Addington had failed: he had refused to make a fight
for the survival of his government. Many, like Southey or
Warren Hastings, felt that his sensitiveness to the feeling of the
country, his calmness—as shown for instance in the Despard
affair[1]—made him, in spite of military confusion, the best possible leader. But just this very sensitiveness made Addington
feel it was wrong for him to stay in office at the cost of a factious
fight. In exactly the same spirit Pitt had carefully refused to
co-operate with other groups in opposition—though he profited
by their efforts to replace Addington—and now negotiated to
make a government of complete national unity for a great
struggle. He wished to include his own particular friends,
Addington's group (without their chief), Grenville, and Fox.
But this was a daydream. The king was opposed to Fox's being
given office, partly on personal grounds, partly because he did
not believe national unity in war would be advanced by the
promotion of one who had so bitterly opposed its prosecution.
Grenville the king would tolerate. But in opposition Grenville
had done what Pitt had refused to do. In his devotion to the
catholic cause and his contempt for Addington he had entered
into a common plan of campaign with Fox. He declined now to
abandon those with whom he had this understanding, or to
abandon the advocacy of catholic emancipation. This was, in
Pitt's eyes, to put the lesser loyalty before the greater. It broke
for ever the old alliance of Pitt and Grenville.

Pitt did not fight against, and fully test, the king's ban on
Fox. He had achieved much in persuading the king to allow
offers to be made to Grenville and Fox's friends; the way those
two groups stood together and refused any service except on
their own terms, angered Pitt and made him wish to tame them.
Moreover, in the courting of the other interests whom he wished
to include it became obvious that the comprehensive ministry
was impossible. Spencer Perceval, for instance, a rising man

[1] Colonel E. M. Despard, an officer on colonial service and unjustly suspended,
became frantic in his struggle to win justice from officials and hatched a crazy plot
to overthrow and murder the government. For this he was executed in 1803.
Addington wisely did not exaggerate the affair.

brought on by Addington, would not serve unless Fox were
excluded.[1] In the end, therefore, Pitt made a ministry of his own
particular friends and Addington's ministers: Portland, Eldon,
Chatham, Castlereagh remained of the leading figures in the
old ministry. By January 1805 Addington himself was back
in office under Pitt, only to resign at the end of June. This
resignation was one sign of the unsatisfactory nature of Pitt's
last ministry. The events since 1800 had gravely damaged the
basis of his power, patriotic common agreement. Feelings were
so sore that men could not agree to differ without quarrelling.
Pitt's majority for his own act raising armed forces (the Additional Forces Act, which had many of the defects for which
Windham had castigated Addington) was only 29. Grenville
and Fox acted together against him as much as against Addington. Yet Tom Grenville, a Pittite, thought it was better to be
defeated than to buy Addington's aid and 'tie up with such a
crowd'. Nor did Pittites and Addingtonians forget past provoca-
tions. These came to a head over the navy. St. Vincent had
been dropped by Pitt, and Pittites blamed his economies for
every defect in the navy. On the other hand, the committee of
naval inquiry, set up while Addington was in office, reported
in February 1805 and its report made grave allegations against
Dundas (who had become Lord Melville and replaced St. Vincent) in his former capacity as treasurer of the navy.

Pitt would have liked to return a flat negative to all proposals
to pursue the matter. This would have cost him every Addingtonian supporter. Yet to allow the hunting of Melville was to
allow the Addingtonians to restore their own credit in naval
matters at the expense of one of his oldest and closest friends.
What Melville had indeed been guilty of was negligence. Burke's
Act had obliged public moneys to be lodged in the Bank of
England and had prevented their being treated as private
accounts of ministers.[2] But officers of spending departments
could still draw moneys from the Bank of England on imprests
to use for current needs, accounting for the expenditure in
detail afterwards. One Trotter, working under Dundas as
treasurer, had in fact drawn large sums in this way, had put
them in Coutts's Bank which was nearer to the West End and

---

[1] Spencer Perceval (1762–1812), a younger son of the second earl of Egmont.
For his later career see the narrative below.
[2] For a fuller account see above, p. 247.

Somerset House, where they had been mingled with his own personal account as completely as ever the two accounts of Henry Fox had been mingled in the bad old days. Dundas's sin was not only that he had failed to stop this. Thomas Raikes,[1] the governor of the Bank of England, had protested to Pitt about it in 1798. Pitt had spoken to Dundas, and the latter, with his usual dour insouciance, had convincingly maintained that everything was in order.[2]

In April 1805 the charge against Melville was, however, not one of negligence, of which he was guilty, but of malversation, of which he was not. Whitbread,[3] a rising radical whig, forced the house to vote on resolutions which were obviously intended as the basis of an impeachment. Pitt moved the previous question, that is the shelving of the matter, on the grounds that whatever irregularities there might have been there was no public loss. In the division there voted 216 for Whitbread and 216 against. Amid tense silence Mr. Speaker Abbot[4] gave his casting vote for Whitbread's side and against Melville. Pitt was overwhelmed. His oldest political friend and adviser was ruined. More than this, the alliance to prosecute the war was riven; the fight between his friends and Addington's must now come into the open to the detriment of common policy. It was a victory for Fox at last. The house of commons had refused to accept, as they had been doing ever since 1785, Pitt's own picture of himself as the man above petty personal intrigue, the man who subordinated his own aims to a general will, the soul of patriotism. So great was the blow to Pitt that his self-control was snapped. Tears ran down his proud face and he was, for the moment, defenceless. His friends gathered round him to shield him from view and to protect him from the taunts of victorious enemies.

[1] Thomas Raikes (1774–1848), a nephew of the philanthropist (for whom see above, p. 39 n. 3), a merchant and financier who was also a dandy mixing in the circles of the prince regent and Beau Brummel.

[2] Dundas may have been moved in part by resentment of treasury control through the bank. He admitted spending money on naval purposes without bothering to get the consent of anyone else when he decided to change plans of development.

[3] Samuel Whitbread (1758–1815), a brewer, M.P. for Bedford; a leader of the radical wing of the whigs from 1790. For his later career see below: he killed himself in 1815.

[4] Charles Abbot, first Baron Colchester (1757–1829), clerk of the rules in king's bench, 1794; M.P., 1795; promoted the Census Act, 1800; Irish secretary, 1801; Speaker, 1802.

Pitt rallied his powers. He announced not only that Melville had resigned but that the idea of his ever returning to office was completely annihilated. The impeachment,[1] in due course, naturally failed. Fox and Grenville introduced a motion for catholic relief not only because they believed in it, but also to animate known differences between Pitt and Addington. Pitt met this by saying that he favoured the change in proper circumstances but that for the moment he must oppose. The house supported Pitt by 336 to 124. But though he still stood, it was as the leader of one group only of the four into which politicians were divided; nor could he hope that independent backbenchers would give him the automatic confidence that he had enjoyed in the past. After a little while his methods of raising army recruitment seemed worse than Addington's. With the navy he had a brilliant success. The appointment of Admiral Charles Middleton, Lord Barham,[2] to replace Melville brought talents of the highest administrative order into full play. Yet even this appointment had its disadvantages, for the Addingtonians felt that one of them should have had the place. After the open break with Addington in June, Pitt negotiated with Fox and Grenville and, in consequence, with the king. But the situation had not changed. Fox, as in 1784, insisted that he would never join as a subordinate but only as an equal. The king opposed offers to Fox. He might, though he did not say so, have consented to Fox's inclusion in a coalition if he had thought Pitt's situation desperate. But he believed Pitt had only to persist to persuade all reasonable men to rally to him. He refused to heed George Rose's[3] argument that too much was being made to depend upon Pitt's personal good health and activity.

Without allies from any other group, therefore, Pitt had to persevere. He stood as a national leader conducting a desperate war but much of his energy had to be devoted to a grim struggle with politicians simply to keep himself in power and to keep the national need from being submerged in a hundred cross-eddying streams. And this strain fell on him most heavily just as the war of the third coalition moved through a decisive stage.

---

[1] Melville's trial in the house of lords took place in May and June 1806 and he was acquitted on all the ten charges brought against him.

[2] Charles Middleton (1726–1813), created Baron Barham 1805.

[3] G. Rose, *Diaries*, ii. 196.

The consequence of Addington's plan for limiting England's effort to insular defence was that the French had been free to concentrate all their strength for an invasion. Camps were prepared at Boulogne, Flushing, Nieuport, Ostend, Dunkirk, Gravelines, and Calais. For a while Napoleon hoped simply to push his army across in troop-carriers on one calm tide and one dark night. But the boats were so numerous that, to get them across together, they would have had to be pushed out in detachments and assembled together in the Channel, an operation spread over more than one tide. Such a protracted operation would have given the British frigates a chance to attack, and British ships of the line time to hurry towards the fishing-boat armada. Moreover, the building of barges and invasion boats, the alterations to harbours, the conversion of boats to carry large numbers of horses, all these technical preparations had been mismanaged; Napoleon's own interventions in his admiralty's plans had been anything but helpful. So by January 1804 Napoleon had changed his invasion scheme. Hitherto he had hoped to profit by surprise, sending over his army in one great wave in vessels built to fight light opposition as well as to transport heavy military equipment. Now he decided that he must use transports as transports only: the protection of his invasion force must be provided by regular French and vassal naval forces. But he had wasted resources which might have been devoted to strengthening that navy on the light-armament of the vessels now considered purely as transports.

This mismanagement by the French gave England time to breathe. Poor use was made of it in the preparation of the army. Moreover, the emperor of France, as Napoleon became in 1805, had the initiative so long as England stood purely on the defensive. He might send his fleet off from Toulon to the West Indies so as to draw ships away from the Channel. Or he might plan a break-out with his Brest fleet to rouse rebellion in Ireland. That Ireland remained a weakness in the defences was demonstrated in 1803 by the ridiculous yet alarming 'rising' of Robert Emmet.[1] Emmet had plotted to paralyse Ireland with a handful of men by seizing the viceroy and government offices: Emmet was too gentle a man to steel himself to the ruthlessness required to make up for small numbers. Nevertheless he had the

[1] Robert Emmet (1778–1803): he obtained Napoleon's promise of aid when he visited France in 1802.

sympathy of many Irishmen, perhaps including such leading whig orators as John Philpot Curran,[1] and had the French been at hand the insurrection might have succeeded.

The king's speech on 31 July 1804, Pitt's announcement of a programme on his return to power, said that

the benefits to be derived from our successful exertions will not be confined within ourselves but that, by their example and their consequences, they may lead to the re-establishment of such a system in Europe, as may rescue it from the precarious state to which it is reduced; and may finally raise an effectual barrier against the un-bounded schemes of aggrandizement and ambition which threaten every independent nation that yet remains on the Continent.

These words were the keynote of Pitt's work. In a more emotive way he was to echo them in a speech at the end of his life, saying England would save herself by her exertions and Europe, he trusted, by her example. But the earlier form though less dramatic was the more realistic. England needed Europe if she was to survive: her example alone would not animate Austria. Pitt had fully grasped the interdependence of all those threatened by Napoleon.

His first aim therefore was to create a diversion to prevent Napoleon completing his preparations for invasion. Direct attack seemed out of the question, apart from a few unsuccessful raids on the French coast. England had no great forces nor any foothold on the Continent save in Sicily. Pitt therefore employed diplomacy, seeking to bribe or convince other powers to fight. This was by no means easy. Prussia seemed to have resolved to remain neutral. She was indeed most interested in acquiring Hanover, declared neutral by George III but invaded by France. Austria was disposed to bear all Napoleon's breaches of the spirit of the Treaty of Lunéville as long as possible, hoping to repair her army, her finances, and her system of government. As for Spain, she was Napoleon's ally in all but name. In October 1804 Captain Moore[2] with the *Indefatigable* and three other frigates fell in with Spanish frigates escorting

[1] John Philpot Curran (1750–1817), an Irish lawyer and orator who supported Grattan's plan for catholic emancipation and parliamentary reform; defended the United Irishmen when they were brought to trial in 1798; appointed master of the rolls in 1806; Emmet was in love with his daughter.

[2] Sir Graham Moore (1764–1843), the sailor brother of General Sir John Moore; he later provided the escort to take the Portuguese royal family to Brazil; served in the Walcheren expedition.

the main Spanish treasure convoy from the American mines to Cadiz. The escort was sunk and all the bullion seized, this without declaration of war. This action, reminiscent of Drake, was justified by the claim that the gold would have ended in the service of France. It helped to drive Spain into open war.

The only power with whom Pitt was able to establish any fruitful contact was, oddly enough, Russia. Oddly enough because Russia had lost less, and had been less deeply involved, by French action so far than any other power. But the new tsar, Alexander I, was nursing schemes for expansion. He wished to complete the work of his vicious grandmother Catherine and destroy Turkey, so that Russia might reach Constantinople. At the same time he shared the interest of his maniac father in the Baltic as a sphere of Russian expansion. In the torn Europe of 1804 he saw a chance of achieving both his ends—and even more—if he could intervene in all disputes as a powerful mediator. In England the opposition urged Pitt to use Alexander's mediation in a hope of peace with France. Pitt was never willing to agree to give up Malta even to Russia. Napoleon was, on the face of things, more ready to accept Alexander's intervention without conditions. But Alexander was worried by Napoleon's sustained interest in Egypt and Turkey. He too felt that there was a spirit of expansion in the new French empire which had to be tamed if any Russian ambition was to be realized.

Napoleon seemed to delight in increasing the tsar's uneasiness. In March 1804 a party of French cavalry crossed the Rhine into Baden and dragged off the duc d'Enghien, who lived there as a private citizen. He was accused of espionage and shot within the week. This affair outraged every aristocrat in Europe, for Enghien was the duc de Bourbon's son and the prince de Condé's grandson; it angered all humane men, for they saw in it Napoleon's contempt for law and justice. It had the further significance, to the tsar, that it showed that Napoleon treated south Germany like his own estate. France was indeed drawing Baden, Bavaria, Württemberg over to her side by offering them the estates of the smaller princes of Germany. Neither Prussia nor Austria was disposed to do anything for the victims. The tsar began to pose as the kindly elder brother of the Germans. As France extended her influence into Germany she was bound to collide with Russia. Distrust of Addington seems to have delayed the tsar's co-operation with England. But by 29 June

1804 Pitt had achieved the first of his positive counter-strokes to Napoleon's invasion, an understanding with Russia which was to become a full alliance ten months later.

Though there was an alliance there was no action, for want of a suitable field of operations. Russia was almost as cut off as England so long as Prussia and Austria remained neutral. To secure their co-operation Pitt and Alexander devoted their efforts. Napoleon clearly had, in these years, the best chance ever offered to a French government of consolidating the internal régime in France and of fixing its expanded frontiers. No European power between 1801 and 1805 any longer possessed the will to pursue an ideological crusade against the revolution. In their exhaustion they would permit France to keep her natural frontiers. Pitt, in his alliance with Alexander, stipulated that France should be forced out of Belgium but it is doubtful whether Russia had her heart in this. As for Austria and Prussia, it seemed impossible to bring them back into the struggle. Napoleon brought this about, nevertheless, by his erratic gestures. It was not enough to be crowned emperor of France. In May 1805 he had himself also crowned king of Italy. At last Austria moved. She might just bear the loss of her influence in Germany or of that she enjoyed in Italy. Both at once was too much. In August 1805, for self-preservation, she joined the Anglo-Russian alliance.

Pitt had thus achieved his counter-strokes to the invasion. Armies were to threaten Napoleon from the south and east. The aims were declared to be the securing of independence for Naples (now under French control except for Sicily), of Holland, of Switzerland, the evacuation of French troops from Italy and from north Germany. Russia was to provide 500,000 men for whose upkeep England would provide £6¼ million. The coalition was not yet fully in movement. Both Pitt and Alexander thought it most important to strike into northern Europe, occupy Hanover, and march back to the battlefields of 1793, Holland and Flanders. There was much to be said for the plan, for it threatened France at a vulnerable spot. It was indeed a plan to march across the great flat plain of northern Europe and across the rivers of the Netherlands into France and on to Paris. Yet it had a fatal flaw. Sweden's assistance was useful and was given; that of Prussia was indispensable and was withheld. Prussia held the key and would sell it to the highest bidder. Alexander could not persuade Frederic William to allow even transit to his army.

It was therefore necessary to think about attack in another quarter. With Malta and with Sicily as bases, with Austria as an ally, Britain and Russia could hope to bring converging forces upon the French in north Italy; if the first plan was, in its later stages, to resemble the campaigns of Marlborough, this was to follow those of Prince Eugene. The fatal error was to hesitate between the two. Pitt's preference for the first prevented his going wholeheartedly for the second and practicable one. Five thousand men were sent to Malta once Naples had joined the allies. This was too small a force to launch a real Italian offensive. Twenty-six thousand men were sent to the Weser, large enough for a German offensive if only there had been a place for it to happen. Pitt clearly gambled unsuccessfully upon Prussia being moved to action by the sight of troops even when the force of argument had failed.

Yet though pregnant with great disaster, Pitt's plans had by August 1805 produced one clear victory. The invasion of England had failed. In July Napoleon was still watching his opportunity to push the 90,000 men near Boulogne across the Channel—and claiming, incidentally, that they were 150,000 men. He had his 2,000 transports ready also. He trusted that the chaos of mismanagement which had prevented the co-ordination of men and boats for the past year had been remedied. His fleets in Brest and Toulon were keyed-up for greater activity. The British fleet was shown to be incapable of bottling up all his fleets all the time. Admiral Villeneuve took the Toulon fleet out in January 1805 but was forced back by bad weather. Admiral Missiessy, with a small force from Rochefort, came out and sailed across to attack the West Indies. At the end of March Villeneuve slipped out of Toulon, dispersed the British blockading force at Cadiz and so liberated Admiral Gravina there, and finally sailed away westwards. Napoleon had ordered this activity to provide a side-show in the West Indies. Once it was under way he realized its further use. He ordered the admirals to assemble and return to Europe for a massed blow in the Channel against any English ships which remained there undispersed by the feint. With this manœuvre he might gain control of the Channel for long enough to get his army on to English soil and at the throats of the English militia. His plan was completely destroyed by the movements of Austria and Russia. As late as 3 August 1805 when the emperor heard that Villeneuve was back at Vigo, he at once ordered him to put to sea again, to liberate more ships from the blockade, and to hasten to clear the British from the Channel. Six days later, however, Austria entered the war against France. Four days after that the emperor told Talleyrand that he was giving up the invasion in order to march against Austria. By 1 September the camps at Boulogne were deserted. The French army was on its way to meet the third European coalition on the Danube.

The allied effort in northern Europe under the tsar and the mad king of Sweden was still-born. In the Tyrol the Archduke John, with 25,000 men, prepared a defensive campaign. In Italy the British planned to land in Naples and meet a Russian expeditionary force from the Black Sea, while, farther north, the Archduke Charles, with 65,000 men, pressed Massena back on the Adige as the Italians rose in anti-French insurrection. Napoleon, having summoned Marmont and Bernadotte from Holland and Hanover, made swift progress towards the Danube. To prevent this French army from piercing through the Black Forest into Austria, General Mack concentrated his men at Ulm, hoping for speedy reinforcement from the Russians. The rapidity with which Napoleon brought the grand army upon him through rain and snow bewildered the Austrian. By 7 October 100,000 French troops were on the Danube in his rear. In scrappy but bloody engagements the Austrians were prevented from breaking out of their chosen centre. Two French corps occupied the Austrian line of communications with Vienna. On 20 October Mack surrendered and there was no longer an Austrian army on the Danube.

The result of this rapid blow was to set the Austrian armies in Italy in reverse. The Archduke Charles had to fall back with his army towards Vienna, though Napoleon from the Danube was sure to race him. The French had withdrawn from Naples but the British and Russian force there, lacking cavalry, were unable to come north in time to give aid to their allies. The coalition was no longer aggressive. Its object now was to unite all the Austrian and Russian forces near Olmütz (for Napoleon entered Vienna on 13 November) in order to fight a final desperate battle to prevent the complete overrunning of Austria.

Thus, though the coalition had forced Napoleon to abandon his attack on England, it was now itself, under the violence of the French reaction, on the brink of extinction.

Meanwhile the naval war, which had been initiated while the invasion was still in contemplation, had been brought to a dramatic conclusion. Until the invasion had been in prospect the French fleet had been content to concentrate upon raiding and to allow the British fleet to patrol their coasts. The French navy had been much more disorganized than their army by the revolutionary purging of aristocratic officers. Having in consequence been unable to act in the early stages of the war, having been pinned down in home harbours, their younger men had had little experience of deep-water action. The decline in their naval effectiveness was thus cumulative. To add to this, the disorganization of work in their dockyards had never been set right by clear direction from Paris. Nevertheless, by 1805 their numbers were considerable. They had 20 ships in Brest, 11 in Toulon, 5 in Rochefort, plus 15 Spanish ships. It was always clear to the British admiralty that if these forces could escape the blockade and unite there was a serious danger of their gaining control of the Channel by surprise or even by a great naval action. The general plan of the admiralty, therefore, was that in the event of a break-out the ships of the blockade should hasten to make rendezvous off Ushant to prevent disaster.

It was one of the necessary consequences of the blockade that British forces had to be dispersed in small groups: another was that ships had to remain at sea for long periods without refitting. It followed that a breaking of the blockade could never be securely prevented and that in each crisis a very great deal had to be left to the initiative of the commander on the spot. When Villeneuve first came out of Toulon (December 1804–January 1805), Nelson, commanding there, was guided by his own general views on the war strategy and on 'the character of Bonaparte' whose 'orders given . . . on the borders of the Seine would not take into consideration either winds or weather'; in other words, Nelson guessed—wrongly—that the French would be most likely to hit at the rear of the Italian offensive of the third coalition, a supposition at which he may have arrived the more easily because he himself had been associated with Neapolitan campaigns in the past and placed the highest value on an Italian offensive. So Nelson, though his ships had been twenty-two months at sea without attention, hastened through storms to the east to safeguard Sardinia and Sicily. Not finding the French, who had put back into Toulon, he thought it possible they had gone to Egypt to reopen a front there. Pressing on all sail he made his way to Alexandria and then rapidly turned and came back to Toulon. The main ships of the blockading fleet were at all times dependent upon their frigates for intelligence reports. So when Villeneuve came out the second time on 31 March 1805 Nelson, cruising between Barcelona and Palmas, was made miserable because his frigates had entirely lost contact with the French. He lay off Sardinia losing valuable time while he considered whether he should again dash to the east. Orde,[1] off Cadiz, when Villeneuve's force descended there had, prudently, hurried north to join the fleet in the Channel. Nelson, on the other hand, had by May 1805 come to the conclusion that Villeneuve was bound for Jamaica. 'I cannot very properly run to the West Indies, without something beyond mere surmise; and if I defer my departure Jamaica may be lost.' Yet on surmise and conversation with Portuguese friends he reached a gambler's decision. He was bound for the West Indies. 'If they are not gone to the West Indies, I shall be blamed: to be burnt in effigy, or Westminster Abbey is my alternative.'[2]

This decision to go to Jamaica and risk the loss of the Channel was a characteristic one. Nelson was a great commander because he aimed always at a decisive result, was prepared to take calculated risks for it, and because the ships and men under his orders were well-attuned to such decisive control. In all Nelson's career the same reckless coolness is apparent, under the guns of Copenhagen, landing in Teneriffe, urging on the Neapolitan armies to their defeat, acting triumphantly on his own initiative to break the line of the enemy at Cape St. Vincent. It emerges, again particularly at St. Vincent, in his liking for the locking of his ship alongside the enemy and boarding with a neck-or-nothing impetuosity to overpower the opposing commanders. This personal impetuosity was combined with an unremitting

---

[1] Sir John Orde (1751–1824), served in America and West Indies; complained of supersession by Nelson when both served under St. Vincent; M.P., 1807–24.

[2] A. T. Mahan, *Life of Nelson*, ii. 294.

interest in the science of his profession, a close study of text-books and history.

Nelson was in many ways a typical man of the class from which he came, the gentry of Norfolk.[1] Like the majority of country gentlemen he preferred Addington to Pitt as a man and a politician, yet, again like them, at the supreme moment of crisis he acknowledged that there was no one else but Pitt to command a great nation. Nelson had a simple confidence in God's care for England, an instinctive conservatism, and an impatience with the talk of any who doubted the justness of the cause. Where, of course, he differed from other parsons' sons, or squires', was in his professional dedication. In this he went far beyond, say, the simple service of any other officer of his day, of men like Admiral Collingwood.[2] Collingwood was capable, like Nelson, of maintaining discipline without severity, of making his men trust and admire him. In seamanship, in gusto for hard blows, in dash, in confidence that one English vessel was a match for two French, Collingwood might at least claim some comparison. But Nelson had a quality in addition which accounts for his ability to inspire others with his own successful initiative. This was his ambition, his intense conviction that he was the agent of great purposes, or more than a conviction, an assumption apparent in all his actions. This quality which imparts simplicity to the character but forbids introspective self-criticism made him appear an exhibitionist and a cultivator of influential contacts; it gave a rather unpleasant atmosphere to his private relations with his wife, a rather comic air to his intrigue with Lady Hamilton.[3] But it also gave its sweetness to his friendship with his colleagues and its nobility to his leadership of a ship's crew or a great fleet.

[1] Horatio Nelson (1758–1805), Viscount Nelson. His father was vicar of Burnham Thorpe, his mother a distant connexion of the Walpoles. He entered navy, 1770; served in the West Indies between 1778 and 1787; married Mrs. Nisbet, 1787; unemployed, 1787–93; lost his eye in attack on Corsica, 1794; lost his right arm at a battle in the Canary Isles, 1797; for the actions of St. Vincent, the Nile, Copenhagen, and Trafalgar, see the narrative.

[2] Cuthbert Collingwood, first Baron Collingwood (1750–1810), entered navy 1761; saw service in West Indies (censured for petulance) and served with Nelson; took command of fleet on Nelson's death; better in command of a ship than a fleet.

[3] Emma née Lyon (1761?–1815), after living with various men of fashion became the mistress and then (1791) the wife of Sir William Hamilton, British ambassador at Naples; became intimate with Nelson on his return from the Nile; gave birth to a daughter, Horatia, in 1801; pursued by her creditors after the death of her husband and of Nelson; died in obscurity in Calais.

With Nelson in command his men felt their personal welfare was in sympathetic hands and it seemed a just return to follow his star unquestioningly with him.

Nelson seemed the embodiment of that patriotic enthusiasm which found expression in the popularity of historical painting.[1] It was appropriate that he should himself take pleasure in paintings of the 'Death of Wolfe'. Yet at the heart of this hot enthusiasm the man himself was clear and steady; he was friendly and informal but a fanatic. He could permit his officers more liberty of visiting and dining and calling ashore than Collingwood thought wise: yet as the decisive moment approached his nerves would not permit him to sleep but he paced his ship all night in a thin overcoat and bootless until, when at last action arrived, he gave his orders unhesitatingly in a sort of happy trance.

The risk he took in sailing west after Villeneuve was never criticized by his officers or the Admiralty. Yet Jamaica was clearly a secondary theatre and the Channel still the area for vital decision. Nelson passed Gibraltar on 7 May 1805, a month behind Villeneuve. But whereas the French took thirty-four days, Nelson took only twenty-four to cross the Atlantic. On his arrival he found that Villeneuve, contrary to his instructions to wait long enough for all French detachments to rally to him, had sailed back to Europe once he knew Nelson was hard on his heels. Nelson took up the return chase. 'We are all half-starved, and otherwise inconvenienced by being so long away from a port, but our full recompense is that we are with Nelson', wrote one of his captains, 'the fleet', on Nelson's own evidence, 'having received not the smallest refreshment, or even a cup of water', in the hastily visited West Indies. When he finally arrived off Tetuan and the Straits it was two years since Nelson had set foot on shore or even had his foot out of the *Victory*.

Coming back to Europe, Nelson had once more to speculate on Villeneuve's objectives. His fears for the Mediterranean still obsessed him. So instead of making for Ushant, even now, he made for Cadiz and Gibraltar whence he could sail quickly into the Mediterranean once more, or, if needed, could turn north with Collingwood's Cadiz force up to the Channel. Villeneuve, however, had crossed the Atlantic farther north, making for the

[1] See above, p. 345.

Bay of Biscay. The promptitude of Barham in London prevented the French from appearing off Brest while the fleet was so dispersed. The admiralty sent Sir Robert Calder[1] with fifteen ships to block Villeneuve's twenty on their route towards Brest. On 22 July, the day after Nelson had reached the Straits of Gibraltar, Calder fought the French off Cape Finisterre. The action was indecisive: the French lost two of their Spanish ships but fog prevented pursuit. Nevertheless the French retreated back into Ferrol. Calder was bitterly criticized for failure to destroy them, though Nelson doubted whether he could have done better. But in any case the immediate crisis was over. The importance of this, of course, in retrospect can be seen to be that only a month remained before Napoleon was to be forced to abandon Boulogne and chase the Austrians.

During that last month the British forces were once more dispersed, for Admiral Cornwallis[2] feared for the safety of Craig's expedition in the Mediterranean as well as for the Indian convoy, so long as the French ships from Rochefort were still at large wandering who knew where upon the oceans. Nelson was meanwhile back on leave in England. Villeneuve was still under orders to emerge and unite French forces in the Channel. But the condition of his ships forbade his doing more than moving to Cadiz on 14 August. It was impossible for the French admiral to remain there. In the first place there were no supplies to feed or refit his crews: in the second, Napoleon was at last issuing the orders which Nelson had expected six months earlier, he was instructing Villeneuve to sail out and into the Mediterranean so that an attack on Naples might pin down allied forces there while he advanced in central Europe.

Nelson in London received command once more of naval operations in the Mediterranean and the Atlantic coast oi Spain; he was ordered to take over Calder's fleet. He had an opportunity to discuss with the ministers responsible for the war the grand plan to be pursued. Nelson pressed upon them the importance of developing the Mediterranean theatre and rode excitedly upon his old hobby-horse, the value of Sardinia. He felt sure that the enemy would be drawn in that direction. He

---

[1] Sir R. Calder (1745–1818), entered navy, 1759; knighted after battle of St. Vincent; admiral, 1810.

[2] Sir William Cornwallis (1744–1819), brother of second Earl Cornwallis; he was in command of the Channel fleet at this time.

urged upon ministers that this was no time for half-measures. The opportunity offered and everything should be staked on a decisive blow. The object should be not just the defeat but the annihilation of the French fleet. Ministers decided to give Nelson *carte blanche*. He chose his personnel and issued the orders. He already had sketched out new tactics. It was, he said, impossible to meet, arrange the fleet, and annihilate the enemy in the course of a single day on the old system of tactics. His proposal was to divide his fleet into three. Two parts of it should advance in double line to pierce through the enemy and split his force into sections roughly two-thirds and one-third. The enemy should then, while disorganized, have each section ruthlessly handled. Meanwhile, the remaining third of the British fleet, made up of fast two-decker ships, should be available as a swift-moving reserve, sailing at need to deliver blows in any part of the battle and able to pursue fugitives or stragglers, a kind of light cavalry of the sea. 'I think it will surprise and confound the Enemy. They won't know what I am about. It will bring forward a pell-mell Battle, and that is what I want.'

Nelson, full of confidence in his destiny, full of flamboyant talk about 'the Nelson touch', arrived off Cadiz in the *Victory* on 28 September 1805, his forty-seventh birthday. It was a 'Nelson touch' certainly, that, contrary to his instructions (which were to shame him before the navy by curt dismissal), he sent Calder home in decent style aboard his own 90-gun ship, which might well have been invaluable in action,[1] and this because Calder had ever been his enemy and now 'finds me one of his best friends'. After this Nelson sent away further ships partly that they might refit and partly also in the hope of enticing the French out of harbour. On 20 October Villeneuve at last came out with thirty-four ships of the line. On 21 October, off Cape Trafalgar, the British fleet of twenty-seven ships came up with them. The enemy were extended in a half-moon. Nelson carried out his original plan to the extent that the British line split one-third of the French fleet off from the rest: ten of their ships took no real part in the action. But then it was simply a 'pell-mell Battle', in which the gunnery and determination of the British in fighting at close quarters, ships locked together, carried the day. Eighteen of the French fleet were

---

[1] Sir Robert Calder was found guilty by the inquiry at home of an error of judgement and was reprimanded.

accounted for on the day of battle: none of the remainder ever
fought again. In men the enemy lost in killed and wounded
5,860 against the British 1,690. But in this latter total was included the commander. Nelson believed that explosives carried
aloft cost more in danger of damage to sails than it gained in
firing power. It was a British tradition to concentrate upon
damaging the enemy hulls. But it was a sniper on the mizzen
mast of the French ship *Redoubtable* who picked out the commander as he strode across his cleared twenty-one feet of quarter-
deck wearing his four orders of knighthood.

The first and obvious result of the victory of Trafalgar was to
prevent any French attack by sea on Naples. The second was
not to prevent the invasion of England, which had been abandoned over two months before, but to make any revival of that
threat impossible. From Trafalgar onwards it was clear that not
only was Napoleon without the ships but neither had he the
sailors or the spirit ever to dream again of controlling the Channel while an army was ferried across. Following from this was a
third consequence: to break the deadlock of an invincible naval
power and an all-conquering land empire, experiments had to
be made on both sides for fighting opponents who could not be
directly reached. Finally, Trafalgar also suggested the means
by which Britain might tackle France: for the completeness of
British sea-mastery invited statesmen to seek some point on the
Continent from which to fight, some point where the navy
might serve as a means of supply and as a last line of defence or
as a bridgehead to offence.

The news of Nelson's victory and death reached London on
5 November, received with mingled 'transport and anguish'. It
stirred the prime minister as it did his countrymen. But close
upon the heels of victory at sea came news of the crushing of
the alliance on land. The combined army of Austria and Russia
did not wait at Olmütz for reinforcement by the Archduke
Charles coming up from Italy. Nor did they seek to avoid action
until Prussia could distract the French. The Prussian court had
been antagonized by the French marching across their territory
to the rendezvous on the Danube: Prussia had made a convention with Russia at Potsdam to impose peace upon the French.
The Russian commanders waited for nothing. They attacked
the French at Austerlitz on 2 December 1805. The French army
of 73,000 smashed the centre of 87,000 opposed to them, and

then rolled up the left wing. The Austro-Russian losses were 26,000. Austria was left helpless. On 6 December 1805 she signed an armistice which, by the 26th, became the Treaty of Pressburg. Austria gave up all possessions and all influence in southern Germany. Bavaria, Württemberg, and Baden became independent of Austrian overlordship and fell under French domination. Austria surrendered the Tyrol, the Vorarlberg, and everything in Italy and Dalmatia. The linking point in Pitt's Triple Alliance had been smashed to pieces.

The effect upon Pitt was the heavier because of his weakened condition under the disillusionment and wearying labours of the past twelve months. At the age of forty-six he was dying of a general wearing-out of his body. His friends hoped that rest, a spell at Bath, perhaps some good news, might revive him. As all along it was his splendid self-assurance (George Rose was right in seeing the same qualities of selflessness—which viewed by enemies seemed arrogance—in both Pitt and Nelson) which bore him up, so now the extinction of the third coalition and the growing disbelief in his leadership snapped the only thing by which he lived. On 23 January 1806 Pitt died. He died as he had not, except latterly, lived, the centre of outspoken criticism. Windham, once his colleague, opposed the address for his monument in Westminster Abbey. The Common Council of London decided by only 77 votes to 71 to erect a monument to him in the Guildhall.

XVII

THE FAILURE OF THE TALENTS AND THE PROBLEMS FACING PORTLAND
1806–9

PITT's death laid bare the weakness of his last cabinet. Though it had the support, if not the confidence, of a majority in the commons, it was quite unable to face the criticisms of Foxites, Grenvillites, and Addingtonians. Hawkesbury thought that it would be foolish to go on. The king, *faute de mieux*, appealed to Grenville and raised no objection to Fox. The new ministry, misleadingly known as the 'Ministry of All the Talents', was in truth only another narrow-based one, for past squabbles would have prevented the re-creation of a comprehensive government of national unity even if the Foxites had not, from habit and principle, clung closely together against the rest of the political world. The ministry was therefore predominantly Foxite. Fox himself was a secretary of state along with Spencer and Windham, both of whom had, in anger at Pitt's conduct in his last years, returned from the Portland group to that of Fox. Erskine was lord chancellor, Howicke (Grey), first lord of the admiralty, Lord Henry Petty (Shelburne's son, but now, and later when Lord Lansdowne, an influential leader of moderate whig opinion), chancellor of the exchequer: Fitzwilliam, driven to pure whiggery by his humiliation in Ireland, was lord president of the council: Lord Moira,[1] as master of the ordnance, represented the entourage of the prince of Wales. Grenville nominally headed these friends of Fox as first lord of the treasury.

To these was added, as privy seal, Addington, now Viscount Sidmouth, who distrusted his new associates but in conscience felt it his duty to serve, principally no doubt because the need for a solid administration was desperate, but in part too, perhaps, because he hoped to act as a conservative influence, a

---

[1] Francis Rawdon-Hastings, first marquis of Hastings and second earl of Moira (1754–1826), fought with distinction in the American war; fought in Flanders under duke of York; general, 1803; governor-general of Bengal, 1813–22.

voice sympathetic to the king within the cabinet. The other members of the cabinet were glad to have him for they hoped that he would keep the king inclined favourably towards them. To make Sidmouth feel a little less like a hostage, his friend Ellenborough,[1] the lord chief justice, was also made a member of the cabinet: this appointment aroused complaints that it was an unconstitutional breach of the independence of the judiciary.

This new government had as enemies all the Pittites, men for the most part apprenticed to power. When in unhabitual opposition these men began to act as clannishly as their opponents. Offers were made to Canning but he refused to serve unless all his friends were taken in as well. Canning, the darling of fashionable dinner parties and the disciple of Pitt, was a striking, though erratic, example of the force arrayed against the Foxites. For the strength of this group was talent. In the twenty years which had passed since Fox had last seemed likely to enjoy power the young men entering politics who were ambitious for office had naturally been drawn to Pitt's side. It was possible to take this side whether one's views were 'liberal' or 'reactionary' —it was only necessary to believe that the war emergency came before any other interest. Family connexion, borough influence, could still make Foxite recruits in these years, but the superior pulling force of possession of power had already affected the distribution of talent between the rival alliances, though it was to be much more clearly felt after a further twenty years had lengthened whig exile in the wilderness to almost half a century.

It is true that a few young men had lately been entering politics who resisted the allurements of office-holders because they were disgusted by the whole system. To them Fox's refusal to accept conventional judgements on the revolution and the war was his chief merit. But such radical young men, of whom only Whitbread was already prominent in 1807,[2] represented a new development of Foxite whiggery which was not pleasing to the majority of its old exponents. Romilly, Brougham, and

---

[1] Edward Law, first Baron Ellenborough (1750–1818), counsel for Warren Hastings; M.P., 1801; lord chief justice, 1802; councillor to the queen during the regency.

[2] Whitbread resented the failure to find an office for him in the Talents cabinet. His hostility to the Grenville group accordingly became more marked thenceforward.

(in rather a different style) Horner, were to be a powerful and exceedingly disturbing influence in the future.[1] With their concern for reform of the penal system, of the poor law, for popular education, for reform of the fiscal system, they were to give a new colour to politics. For the moment they were only on the verge of parliamentary careers, their talents as yet unrevealed. They could not strengthen the old cause of Fox and Grey. Only Mackintosh,[2] outside parliament, gave a philosophical freshness and depth to the ideas of that long-enduring, rather tired, band of brothers.

Fox himself obstinately determined to test the unpopular beliefs of fifteen years. He negotiated to end hostilities: he quickly found that it was impossible to arrange a secure peace with Napoleon, whose appetite increased with every victory. Fox admitted that Grey and Grenville—if not Pitt—were right to regard war as unavoidable. Therefore, as Napoleon profited from Austerlitz, ministers gradually became resolved to fight on, though they were not very happy in their conduct of operations, and though Grenville took a more positive view of their eventual aims than Grey. That they put negotiation first did not, however, make back bench independents any more convinced of their wisdom.

Windham boldly swept away Pitt's system of army recruitment. In its place he enacted that men might enlist for a short period: they were to enjoy higher rates of pay if they chose to re-engage. The volunteer system was ended. In its place the whole male population were to be given short periods of military training and no one was to be able to buy his way out with a substitute. These reforms were admirable in conception but were wretched in execution. Windham, as Wilberforce said, was a poor creature when it came to detail. The administration

---

[1] Sir Samuel Romilly (1757–1818), a law reformer and barrister; now appointed solicitor general; effected reforms in criminal punishment; supported the abolition of slavery and emancipation of the catholics.

Henry Peter Brougham, later Baron Brougham and Vaux (1778–1868), a barrister associated with reforming causes and with the *Edinburgh Review*; M.P. for Camelford. For his later history, including his appointment as lord chancellor, see Sir E. L. Woodward, *The Age of Reform* (O.H.E. vol. xiii).

Francis Horner (1778–1817), a barrister who made himself the whig expert on financial reform.

[2] Sir James Mackintosh (1765–1832), philosopher and historian; published *Vindiciae Gallicae* (1791) as a reply to Burke's *Reflections on the French Revolution*; accepted a legal appointment in India for the seven years from 1804.

of the new system made it seem worse than the old. Once he had launched his plan, Windham's main interest seemed to lie in the conduct of operations, and here he had a fatal predilection for numerous, scrappy, side-shows.

Despite these weaknesses the government had its sources of strength. The most obvious was, of course, that there seemed to be no alternative to it. It might lack able young men in its middle reaches but it had the great names of Fox and Grenville. Against these the talents of the Pittites seemed those of majors and captains against generals. In the second place, Fox himself proved a source of unexpected strength. He was a good man in the office. Even more he was, on Sidmouth's testimony, the best of colleagues. His authority was not questioned. His fairness gave confidence to the most suspicious of ministers. He seemed likely to settle his team in office and to conciliate many who had held his past against him. Unfortunately Fox, in this flowering of his powers, was near his end. In July 1806 his health began to fail. In September he was dead. Both the king and Sidmouth, despite or because of past hostility, seemed to mourn him more than they had mourned Pitt.

In the rearrangement of offices to fill Fox's vacancy the friends of Sidmouth gained greater influence. But the unity which Fox had been able to secure by his personality had now to be sought painfully by elaborate discussions and bargains. It was with the idea, nevertheless, of giving greater coherence to the ministry in parliament that, in October 1806, Grenville decided upon a general election. It was ordinary practice to choose a new house of commons to suit a new ministry. It enabled the 'official men' to be reshuffled properly. In the Talents election treasury pressure was exerted in the traditional way in favour of the ministry's men. The estimated gain of the government was 46 and the loss to Pittites 31. But such figures mean little because still, as in the previous century, there was no tight party list, no clarity on the affiliations of most members of parliament. All one can say is that 46 more members of parliament were returned who were, for the moment, on good terms with Grenville, in place of some who were at odds with him; but it was quite possible that his friends of this sort would take an independent line on occasion or transfer their favours if circumstances changed.

The most interesting point in the election was the losses

suffered by Sidmouth's personal following of some thirty politicians. For Grenville gave preference in finding government boroughs to the Foxites and there were not safe seats left for Sidmouth. Facing independent-minded constituencies, the Sidmouth group found that they had lost their chief advantage, their reputation as ordinary unofficial men. Power, intrigue with Pitt, their link with Fox, these rapid changes had made them look like typically unscrupulous politicians; as such they were inefficient: they fell between two stools. The effect of this loss of support was to make Sidmouth a much more difficult colleague. Sidmouth now felt that he must, for self-protection, insist upon his particular point of view and refuse to be treated as a negligible wasting asset.

On their side the Grenvillites and Foxites also felt the need to emphasize those ideas which marked them out from Pittites. To run the war was not enough, nor was war news encouraging.[1] But in emphasizing policy they were not a very happy family. They regarded parliamentary reform as a dead issue. It had been possible for Grey to move motions for reform ten years previously. But it was clear that such proposals would be intensely unpopular among the politically powerful. Moreover, the social changes which had resulted from war had made parliamentary reform an issue with changed significance.[2] A mild increase in the country representation plus representation of new urban conglomerations might now rouse the sleeping Jacobinism crushed for the moment in 1798.[3] Only a few insignificant radicals hankered after such a leap in the dark. Lord Grenville and his friends would have parted from Grey rather than join in such a violent upheaval. The ministry was seeking a unifying idea; this one would have been the most dividing of all.

Economic reform, the cutting away of sinecures and influence, had not been a Foxite speciality since Burke had left them. It had rather been Pitt's quiet achievement. Yet Pitt's former friend Grenville was now the strongest opponent of carrying such reform further. The Grenvilles had a personal stake in sinecures. In 1806, it was later calculated, the Grenville family were drawing £55,000 a year from public sources.[4] Lord

---

[1] See below, pp. 451 f. [2] See below, pp. 503 f.
[3] See above, pp. 361 f.
[4] Leigh Hunt in the *Examiner*, 10 May 1812.

Grenville believed that it would soon be difficult to reward any official services or to keep any government in a position of requisite influence for its day-to-day operation. Grey was indifferent. This too, then, remained a dead issue as long as office made it necessary for the younger whig generation to remain on terms with Grenvillites.

Romilly found, under the Talents, that it was difficult to advance any of the Benthamite ideas of efficiency and rationalism to whose spread he had determined to devote himself. As for Whitbread, advocate of minimum wage scales, a revised poor law and freer general education, he continued a rough John Bullish career on the back benches, slightly impeded in advocacy by having his friends in office.

The only remaining Foxite principles which could be cultivated, because they found universal support in the ranks of government and were points of division among the opposition, were the two cries on behalf of those underdogs, the Roman catholics and the negroes. The latter were, of course, the particular concern of Wilberforce and 'the Saints'. The small group of earnest evangelical Christians in the house of commons, notably Wilberforce, Bankes, Grant, and Thornton, had been admirers of Pitt. His businesslike character and dedicated service made a strong appeal to the serious-minded bankers and professional men who felt the call of practical Christianity. Pitt had disappointed them in failing to crush opposition to their crusade. Now Grenville and Grey (who had not been sympathetic in the past) offered to put the whole power of government behind a bill to abolish the slave trade. Sidmouth was opposed: he preferred to instruct the captured blacks in the virtues of Christian marriage. But Sidmouth could not resist his colleagues effectually. There was no political deal made. Grey did not ask, or receive, the political adhesion of the Saints in return for backing their gospel. They simply aided the government bill on this issue and consequently looked with a little more charity on the activities of the ministry as a whole.

The votes of government men in the commons plus those of the liberal-minded Pittites were sufficient to overcome the West Indian interest and what grumbling, general, and unorganized opposition there was. In the lords Grenville was able to defeat obscurantist resistance by the force of his own efforts. So the slave trade was abolished by Britain just as the Talents ministry came to an end.[1] It was hoped that other countries would follow this example. England was ready, once others had been persuaded to legislate in their turn, to use the navy for enforcement of the ban. This was to lead foreign critics to suggest that the whole campaign was a hypocritical attempt to increase her naval authority upon the high seas. On the contrary, it is clear that the banning of the slave trade was the first product of the new evangelical conscience allied with Fox's advocacy of depressed minorities. Its timing owed most to the desire of the Talents to have some striking success to mark their administration.

The emancipation of the Roman catholics was the other issue on which it was possible to rally a powerful whig party. One may begin to call Fox's heirs 'the Whigs', for Pitt was dead, who had called himself a whig, and his disciple Canning used the name tory—for the first time in a century—to denote principles both practical and respectable, principles in which he himself exulted. But Catholic emancipation presented great difficulties. Stick-in-the-mud squires might think slave trade abolition foolish: they would deem catholic emancipation criminal frenzy, the putting of power into the hands of traitors supported by lower class Irish voters. The king, too, stood as resolutely opposed as ever to such proposals. The Talents therefore did not propose to fight so desperate a battle. Yet they wanted a token victory for their principles.

Pitt's Irish Act of 1793 had given Roman catholics the right to hold commissions in the army up to, and including, the rank of colonel. But this only applied to Ireland. This was most inconvenient when Irish troops were moved to England. It would be some help to army recruitment to offer the papists a career in the armies of England. It was proposed therefore to give catholics everywhere the rights given in the limited Act of 1793. To this proposal his colleagues secured the assent of Sidmouth. The king expressed 'strong dissent'. By 12 February 1807 the king had been persuaded by Sidmouth to permit the measure to be brought into Parliament.

There then arose a question of interpretation, whether the new clauses of the Mutiny Act were to allow Roman catholics merely to hold ranks up to colonel or whether at the same time

[1] For the abolition of slavery in its turn see Sir E. L. Woodward, *The Age of Reform*, p. 354.

as extending the concessions to England and Scotland it was intended to broaden them so as to allow catholics to hold staff appointments. Howicke (formerly Charles Grey) and Grenville interpreted the clause in this way, for so they hoped to please Ireland: furthermore they believed that the king's assent covered this interpretation. Sidmouth protested that if this was its meaning he would himself resist the clause in parliament. He denied that the king realized that his consent had been asked for any such change. Grenville on 2 March commented triumphantly that the king had had his dispatch and returned it without comment. But the king was almost blind. On 4 March Sidmouth explained to the king the significance of the proposals and his own opposition to them. Despite the king's emotional expression of disapproval, Howicke brought the bill into the commons on 5 March. By 14 March Sidmouth had offered his resignation and had been commanded by the king to remain in office but to resist this measure in parliament.

It would seem that the king wished to defeat the proposals but to keep his ministerial team together. The ministers made an attempt to strengthen themselves against attack. They tried to persuade Canning to join them as a friend to the catholic cause. But he was also Sidmouth's personal enemy, since his jeers at the Addington administration. These overtures made Sidmouth angrier. He would insist on resigning if Canning came in. By 14 March Canning had decided not to join so leaky a ship. Thus ministers were bound to see that the king could beat them in this dispute. Once again on the catholic issue he had on his side the great majority of rank and file sentiment. The Pittites would back him to dish the whigs. The revelation of cabinet business would make the minister appear to have attempted to hoodwink the king in order to ride roughshod over back-bench opinion. Just at this point too Howicke was obliged by the death of his father to leave the house of commons for the lords. Having failed to win Canning the cabinet would have no commanding leader in that house.

The ministers therefore met without Sidmouth or Ellenborough and sent an offer to the king to drop their bill. But, in order to save their faces and rally enthusiasm among their stauncher friends, they demanded the right to extol the beneficial results which would have proceeded from their abortive and abandoned reform. The king took this as a threat to disturb him in future. Ministers who lauded the merits of a proposal might be expected to return to it. He could not forget that he had almost allowed them to succeed without his noticing it. He met the request with a demand that they should give him a written promise never again to raise the question. By so doing he brought the whig ministry to an end. He already knew Portland was willing to serve, and on 19 March Eldon and Hawkesbury were summoned to form the new government and on 24 March 1807 the whigs surrendered their seals, never to hold office again under George III.

The king's request for a promise of future conduct was a very doubtful constitutional propriety.[1] It was made because he had already lost confidence in his ministers: it was carried off successfully because the house of commons had lost this confidence also. The whigs had not succeeded in their double duty, that of putting enthusiasm into their own ranks while keeping Sidmouth, their badge of respectability, happy. On the slave trade he had opposed them: on catholic relief he accused them of trickery and broke them. It must be remembered that these controversial measures of party policy were introduced in wartime and when the war was not going well. Napoleon had stamped on Prussia and slaughtered a Russian army in Poland: England had no fighting ally left on the Continent and was declared in a state of blockade.[2] The general belief that perilous times called for national unity was potent enough to bring a whig ministry of experiment to an end: it was not able, however, to conjure up a better one. The groups were miserably divided. The issue was not a simple one between 'the Talents' and the rest. The followers of Sidmouth were still sore against those of Pitt. Personal differences between Pitt's own disciples prevented their presenting any common front. There was no man anywhere, since the deaths of Pitt and Fox, of sufficient stature to subdue the petty quarrels of ambitious and able men. Sidmouth and Canning would never serve together. Canning would serve with Castlereagh or with Perceval or with Hawkesbury (Liverpool), but not under them.

The administration gathered together under the duke of

---

[1] The king's action revived the whole whig theory, started by Burke and fed by the events of 1783, of George's plot against the constitution.

[2] See below, pp. 464 f.

Portland was therefore loosely organized. It had no cabinet policy but staggered along like a motor firing intermittently on different cylinders as first one then the other of its members took the initiative. Portland himself was both dull and ill. It was exactly his lack of force which constituted his title to conciliate the diverse and ambitious ministers. 'It is not', said Perceval, 'because the Duke of Portland is at our head that the Government is a Government of Departments, but it is because the Government is and must be essentially a Government of Departments that the Duke of Portland is at our head.'

Lord Eldon, as pompously patrician as only a self-made man can be, was the senior of the effective leaders in the necessary coalition. He was fifty-six. He represented the purest conservatism. Having risen to greatness in the law he would permit no feature of the order in which he had found so exalted a place to suffer change. He was alien to all Pitt's tradition except in hostility to revolutionary France. Next in age came Spencer Perceval at forty-five. He was another lawyer, not this time a pundit of the constitution but a workmanlike practitioner in the courts. His clear head was his greatest asset in politics, along with his courage. Everyone knew him to be both honest and good. He had worked unremittingly to support his thirteen children. His only eccentricity was his protestant fervour. With energy he fought against emancipation of the papists and against the godless forces of continental revolution. And in his fighting, while he never dazzled an audience, he often convinced it. Pitt had seen in him the most effective of his allies against Fox. Lord Castlereagh, at thirty-eight, was a truer exponent of Pitt's policy, however. He wanted to complete the broken bargain of Irish Union. But a man of such attention to detail found that his post at the war office left him little time for domestic causes. At the home office the thirty-seven-year-old Hawkesbury (soon to be Liverpool) was rapidly overcoming his early faults of irresolution and procrastination.[1] He was achieving a tensed but unshakable calmness: self-mastery aided him in dealing with the tantrums of colleagues. There was in him a reserve of strength not yet fully realized.

The youngest member of the team was George Canning. At thirty-five Canning's ambitions were well known. He thought of himself as the only true heir of Pitt. Indeed, he dramatized

[1] For evidence of these faults see B. Perkins, *The First Rapprochement*, p. 133.

himself in that role with a flamboyance unknown to the master and with a recklessness equally alien. Canning had been the cleverest boy of his time at Eton and at Christ Church, Oxford. That he was known as the cleverest man in the house of commons was a disadvantage to him. For power is not won like a university prize. Brilliance and liberal views might win him applause from the whigs. Vehemence in support of the war effort kept him support among the tories. But for all this he could never unite a national party. His personality was a catalyst in politics. It was his enmity with Sidmouth which made it impossible to reunite all Pitt's old followers. Lord Grey would never admit into his confidence anyone so obviously not a gentleman.[1] He could not conceal his contempt for his rivals. The foreign office could not absorb all his energy. He was active as a friend of the princess of Wales in her squabble with her husband. He intrigued in matters of military promotion. He worked with Wellesley to build a new political connexion. He openly criticized the work of cabinet colleagues. In short, the luxuriance of his talent earned him distrust.

The Portland ministry, thus uncomfortably assembled, dissolved parliament. The corporation of London had already sounded the main note of the electioneering literature. It had voted an address to thank George III for the 'decided support and protection given by him to the protestant reformed religion as by law established'. Here was the old radical city applauding the royal prerogative and decrying the whigs. The cry of 'No Popery' was a powerful one among independents. To it the whigs had no very satisfactory answer. For the whigs were being hanged not for a sheep but for a lamb. They had not proposed full emancipation. In Ireland the democrats and the catholics had been roused by the activity of the Talents ministry, but roused only to derision. What difference would the opening of staff appointments have made to Ireland? But if the whigs denied that they had made important proposals they condemned themselves for obstinacy over a trifle. The alternative, to rouse and lead a real movement for altering the position of the catholics, was unacceptable to their own cautious leaders. So

---

[1] It was not only that Canning's mother had been an actress which made men think of him as 'no gentleman'. Of Canning's maiden speech, the duchess of Devonshire reported that her brother said it 'was good but in bad taste, outré, and not seeming at all afraid of himself. He is certainly however very clever.'

men like Ponsonby,[1] from 1808 the official but disregarded leader of the whigs in the house of commons, laboured to find a solution which would be judged safe in England but which would yet satisfy Ireland. This seemed to have been found in the scheme for a veto. It was proposed to recognize Roman catholics as full citizens if in return the king was given a veto on the appointment of their bishops. It would have been an arrangement comparable to Napoleon's concordat with the papacy. For a while it seemed possible that Rome and the Irish would accept the suggestion, which was clearly welcome to English papists. All such hopes proved illusory. The negotiations ended in misunderstanding, discord, and embittered abuse of the go-betweens employed. For six years this will-o'-the-wisp distracted the whigs from rallying to the one proposal which was able to unite them all, from right to left, from Grenville to Brougham, the proposal of simple catholic emancipation. In those years O'Connell rose to take the lead of Irish feeling away from them;[2] the liberal tories, too, such as Canning, also began to urge emancipation and so to rob the whig campaign of its effect.

Once a 'No Popery' election had confirmed the Portland government in power it was the task of the whigs to find issues on which they could fight. Here the record of the Talents' administration was an encumbrance. The Insurrection Act for muzzling Ireland might, indeed, be dangerous in driving legitimate discontent into traitorous courses underground. But this measure of Portland's had been prepared by the Talents government. On the issue of reform, how could Grey and Grenville unblushingly lead a campaign when, owing no doubt to political exigencies, their own government had made no step whatsoever in that direction?

The best that could be done was to reply to 'No Popery' taunts with the cry 'No corruption', a slogan equally effective in arousing echoes from the independent back-benchers. In February 1807 a committee was set up to inquire into sinecures. This committee, after various changes in size and membership

[1] George Ponsonby (1755–1817), the son of a Speaker of the Irish parliament; resisted the Irish union; chancellor of the exchequer in 1782; lord chancellor of Ireland under the Talents.

[2] Daniel O'Connell replaced the elder Keogh as leader of the Catholic Committee in 1808. For O'Connell's career see Sir E. L. Woodward, *The Age of Reform*, p. 325.

from session to session, produced a string of reports which are comparable to those produced by the committees of North and Pitt on whose work so much reorganization had already been based.[1] They gave the statistical basis for many projects of reform. Thus in 1809 they revealed that seventy-six members of parliament at that time were holding offices of some sort costing £150,000 (two-thirds of these being held during the king's pleasure); of these members of parliament twenty-eight held sinecures or pensions costing £42,000. The attack upon places and gifts was not exclusively controlled by a whig opposition. One of the leaders was Henry Bankes, a tory and member of Wilberforce's evangelical group. From 1808 to 1812 Bankes laboured to make grants of office in reversion illegal and succeeded in having them suspended until 1814.

Speeches for economic reform could be countered by praise of what Pitt had already achieved; they were sustained by abuse of the government of the day and its means of retaining power. But a campaign in general terms was traditional rather than exciting. The public took more pleasure—it was the spread of newspapers and even more of obscene cartoons which enabled it to do so—in attacks upon the morals of the ruling classes and of the royal family. All George III's sons, except the eccentric duke of Cambridge, lived irregular lives. The prince of Wales was not content, like his brothers, to disregard his wife; he hated her. For her part she lived sluttishly. From 1801 onwards rumours circulated of the princess having borne an illegitimate child. A committee of the privy council was set up to make a 'Delicate Investigation'; as ministers took different sides on the matter this did not make for ministerial harmony. To the radicals it was an occasion to abuse the court. Even more explosive was the unearthing of a scandal in which there was a suggestion of administrative as well as a personal corruption, a revelation which involved the bureaucracy in these bedroom stories.

In January 1809 the radical member of parliament Wardle[2] brought before the house the squalid tale of the duke of York and Mrs. Clarke. Mrs. Clarke, an extravagant actress, was the duke's mistress. It was proved that she had taken money from

[1] See above, pp. 284 f.
[2] Gwyllym Lloyd Wardle (1762?–1833), yeomanry officer in Ireland; M.P. Okehampton, 1807–12; died abroad after escaping from his creditors.

those who wished to buy promotion or favours in the war organization. It was alleged that the duke of York knew of her sales of office, and even that he took a share of the proceeds. For two months the house examined witnesses from the underworld of London society. In the end it was carried, by 278 to 196, that the duke of York was not guilty of personal corruption or of connivance at corruption. But as he had clearly been guilty of allowing his mistress to know too much of official business he was obliged, in spite of his services to the Army, to resign his official appointments.[1] To this débâcle private jealousies had contributed, but a public consequence was the lowering of the prestige of the administration. Grey disapproved of the radical joy in this: he stood aside declaring: 'It is not by such means that I wish to see the influence of the Crown reduced.'

Perceval, for the government, was certainly shocked by the revelation of public belief that places were for sale. Striking at once, therefore, he carried an act making it penal to solicit money for procuring offices. But this did not rob the opposition of their initiative. A select committee brought before the house allegations of corruption in the East India Company, and the use of its patronage for government purposes contrary to Pitt's Act.[2] This charge was brought home, with chapter and verse, against Castlereagh. He had wanted a seat in parliament for his friend Lord Clancarty. To do this he had used his influence (as president of the board of control) with the East India Company to obtain a writership for someone who had paid £3,500 for the position to intermediaries: the money was to be used for Clancarty's election expenses. The government defeated the motion of censure on Castlereagh by 216 to 167, but they were further damaged in the eyes of the country. Mr. Madocks[3] followed with allegations, against both Perceval and Castlereagh, of corruption in using treasury influence to control Irish elections. Once again the government exerted itself and defeated a motion in the house, but at the cost of seeming to depend on pressed majorities. It was alleged, and generally believed, that the influence of government was increasing, an increase which whigs equated with the influence of the Crown.[4]

[1] He was reappointed commander in chief in 1811.   [2] See above, pp. 274-5.
[3] William Alexander Madocks (1774-1828), a philanthropist and agricultural improver; M.P. Boston (Lincolnshire), 1802-20, and Chippenham, 1820-8.
[4] In 1811 John Ranby tried to answer this with his *Inquiry into the supposed Increase of the Influence of the Crown.*

A whig country gentleman, one who, in his paternal care for his tenantry and his social standing, had a great deal in common with the most solid of the independent country gentlemen, Mr. Curwen, the member of parliament for Carlisle, followed up this agitation. He introduced a bill to prevent the sale of seats in parliament. Elected persons were to take oaths against bribery and corruption: the bribery laws were to apply to all agents of candidates and were to apply at any time and not just in the weeks preceding an election. Heavy penalties were prescribed for selling seats. The government felt the force of opinion behind the whig move. And it was emphasized to them when the Speaker of the house of commons, Charles Abbot, with all the immense prestige of his office as guardian of the constitution and with all the interest attaching to him from his respectable past as a staunch Addingtonian, spoke emphatically in support of the bill. Perceval, for the cabinet, secured some amendments. The amended bill prohibited 'express' treasury bargains for electoral support, but ignored the knotty problem of 'implied' bargains. With such modification the government accepted the bill and helped eventually to pass it into law. Curwen's act, together with the internal reforms of administration, decreased the number of seats which a government could manipulate for its regular supporters. Lord Henry Petty, for the whigs, confessed that royal influence in the commons was diminished. Lord Liverpool in 1812 told an applicant that 'Mr. Curwen's Bill has put an end to all money transactions between Government and the supposed proprietors of boroughs'; government had to rely upon 'general influence' and the efforts, financial and personal, of its would-be adherents.[1]

As the ministry flinched under these assaults, the radical wing of the whigs began to develop their campaign. At a Westminster meeting in March 1809 called to thank Wardle for his exertions in uncovering the Mrs. Clarke scandal, the field was not left free to Sir Francis Burdett and his wild friends. Whitbread also attended. He tried to draw a lesson and a programme from these excitements. It was that only a general reform, political as well as economic, would give the country the cheap, efficient, pacific, and prosperous régime that it needed. 'What I hope now is that the People will be thoroughly convinced of the necessity of Parliamentary Reform' and would

[1] C. D. Yonge, *Lord Liverpool*, i. 444.

apply a steady pressure to secure it. Thus for the first time for twelve years the movement for electoral reform entered politics again.

At this juncture also Jeremy Bentham[1] was drawn out of his academic studies of law and philosophy into political activity. The principle of 'the greatest good of the greatest number' can in theory be as easily used to defend despotism as democracy. The point of decision comes when to it is added the rider that as each man knows his own happiness best, the greatest happiness can only be reached by allowing the majority to prevail, with each man counting for only one. This point Bentham made in 1809 when he wrote his *Parliamentary Reform Catechism* and circulated it privately.[2] Here he declared his support for 'the democratic interest (which is no other than the universal interest)', identifying the good of all with parliamentary reform. His clear, unsentimental arguments were applied to support annual parliaments, equal electoral districts, a household franchise, full reports of all parliamentary speeches, and compulsory attendance by members of parliament.

Under this mounting pressure, Lord Grey, the veteran of the last reforming agitation, had to declare himself. As leader of the party he said, 'To temperate, intelligible, and definite reform . . . I have always been, and still continue, a friend.' But he also showed his hostility to wild men like Burdett. This hostility was even more strongly felt in Lord Grenville's wing of the alliance. It was clear that the whigs could not smash their way to power as a party of reform, given the attitude of the squirearchy in war-time, unless they were resolute, united, consistent, and long-enduring. Burdett, and a section of the left wing, in 1810 tied themselves up in an attack on the privileges of parliament which ended in Burdett's imprisonment and in litigation reminiscent of Wilkes.[3] On this the leadership of the party looked with frigid disapproval. Nevertheless, on 21 May 1810, Thomas Brand[4] introduced the first whig reform bill since 1797. It proposed triennial parliaments and an extension of the franchise to householders in boroughs and to copyholders in the counties. It did not propose equal electoral districts but was

---

[1] See above, pp. 330 f.
[2] It was not published until 1817.
[3] This is the case of Burdett *v.* Abbot (Costin and Watson, ii. 243).
[4] Thomas Brand (1774–1851), twentieth Baron Dacre; M.P. Helston, 1807, for Herts., 1807–19.

content to suggest changes in polling districts. Brand's motion was defeated 234 to 115. It was reassuring to its champions to find that Tierney and Ponsonby, representing the official and respectable leadership in the commons, voted with Whitbread for the bill. Nevertheless, this move was of importance rather for the future—in keeping the whig record consistent and by bridging the years between 1797 and 1830—than for any immediate gain in strength by the opposition at the expense of the ministry.

There were two reasons for the whig failure to make a more effective assault upon the ministry. The first, and less important, was their own internal divisions and the poverty of the parliamentary tactics displayed by Ponsonby. More important was the continuing effect of the war. Whatever the faults of the Portland administration, it was at least unremitting in the fight against Napoleon. By contrast the whigs, with their unpatriotic past to live down, appeared defeatist.

The Portland government inherited grave military difficulties from the Talents. After the smashing of Austria and the Treaty of Pressburg in 1805, England and Russia remained in a somewhat perplexed state of hostility towards France. A possible point for common action was the central Mediterranean. The Russians occupied Cattaro and Castel Nuovo. But the French spread along the Dalmatian coast and occupied Ragusa (Dubrovnik) so that the Russian garrisons became isolated and useless. Meanwhile British forces from Sicily, the fleet under Sir Sidney Smith, and 4,800 men under Sir John Stuart, made an attempt to restore the queen of Naples to possessions on the mainland from which Joseph Bonaparte had driven her.[1] Sir John Stuart landed in Lower Calabria and attacked the French to the number of 7,000 who were encamped at Maida on 4 July 1806. The British troops withstood the rushes of the enemy by their firm use of the bayonet. This victory was a heartening foretaste of the success of well-disciplined troops against the impetuosity of the French. But it was barren of

---

[1] Sir William Sidney Smith (1764–1840), entered the navy, 1777; fought at St. Vincent; captured off Le Havre, 1796; escaped, 1798; commanded the successful defence of Acre, 1799; much service in the Mediterranean theatre; an energetic, capable, and boastful admiral.

Sir John Stuart (1759–1815), fought in American War of Independence and was at Yorktown (1781); prominent in battle of Alexandria (1801); resigned command in protest against lack of support from the government.

strategic result. Though the Calabrian peasantry rose they were left to the punishment of the enemy, for Stuart, judging the situation hopeless, withdrew to Sicily.

In the north of Europe the obstacle to any effective co-opera-tion between England and Russia was still the manœuvres of Prussia. That power had occupied Hanover as its reward for standing aside from the struggle with Austria. The king of Prussia was, however, suspicious of the French. Napoleon quickly proceeded to goad him into disastrous action. In his peace talks with Fox, Napoleon had been willing to promise the return of Hanover to George III. In his negotiations with Russia, Napoleon had agreed to resist Prussian designs upon Sweden. Murat, the emperor's brother-in-law, had been in-vested with the duchies of Berg and Cleves on Prussia's frontiers. The grouping of Bavaria, Württemberg, Ratisbon, Baden, Berg, Hesse Darmstadt, and minor princedoms in a Confederation of the Rhine under Napoleonic protection and military control, was distasteful to Prussia. Finally, Prussia was told to desist from exerting pressure on north German states and informed that Napoleon would be the protector of the Hanse towns. At length, therefore, Prussia was provoked into war single handed despite her earlier refusals to join the allied effort. From mid-summer 1806 troop movements had been in progress, though Prussia did not admit the inevitability of war until 1 October. Within a fortnight the French army had destroyed the Prussian forces in a massive conflict of a quarter of a million men and 700 cannon at Jena. By 25 October the French were in Berlin.

At the end of 1806 the French crossed Prussia into Poland and drove the Russians east of Warsaw. Thus with Holland now a kingdom ruled by Louis Bonaparte, with Prussia abject, and Saxony a client state, there was no opening for Anglo-Russian initiative in the north unless, improbably, Sweden could be persuaded to gamble her future. In the south the decadent ruling house of Spain was disgruntled, but was supplying the French with men; Italy was French controlled, as was Dalmatia. Russian appeals for active English assistance were not easily met. The poor best that could be done was to help maintain Russian influence in the eastern Mediterranean. Ships of the British fleet were sent to the Dardanelles to reinforce the Rus-sian pressure upon Turkey, for the Turks were refusing to allow a Russian interest in Wallachia and Moldavia and were in negotiation for alliance with France. This naval expedition (three ships of the line and four frigates) was useful only in taking on board the Russian and British ambassadors. Five thousand men were at the same time dispatched to Alexandria where they were roughly handled before they were recalled in failure.

The Talents ministry, in short, could not prevent Napoleon reasserting his control of the Continent. Russia alone—and at a distance—remained as a threat to him, and Britain's relations with Russia were certainly not close. But while attempting in vain to arrest the collapse of Pitt's European plan, the Talents had tried their hand also at war in Addington's style, the war which disregarded Europe. Sir Home Popham[1] having captured the Cape of Good Hope had then sailed with 1,500 men under Beresford[2] to South America. In June 1806 he arrived at the River Plate. By a bold attack upon the Spaniards he then captured Buenos Ayres. The elated commander made haste to trumpet his success back to England. He announced that the whole of the golden continent, from which England had always been excluded, was now open to trade: he wanted London merchants to recoup themselves after the vicissitudes of war. Before the first ship could sail, the inhabitants of Buenos Ayres, helped by Spanish forces under a French officer who crossed the broad river in mist, had risen and captured the British garrison. Popham blockaded the river and battered at Buenos Ayres for a while. From such operations he was called home to face a court martial.

Nevertheless, Windham and his colleagues in the Talents ministry did not despair of South America. From it they would restore the gold balance of the Bank of England, so drained by

---

[1] Sir Home Riggs Popham (1762–1820), entered the navy 1778 but engaged, while on special leave, in Far Eastern trade, 1787–93; served with the duke of York in Flanders; reprimanded for his actions in South American expedition; served in Copenhagen expedition, 1808; rear-admiral in West Indies after the war.

[2] William Carr, Viscount Beresford (1768–1854), illegitimate son of marquis of Waterford; commanded Connaught Rangers in reconquest of West Indies, 1795; served in Channel Islands, India, and Egypt, before this expedition to the Cape and Buenos Ayres; governor of Madeira in name of king of Portugal, 1807; fought at Corunna; reorganized the armies of Portugal; won battle of Albuera, 1811; wounded at Badajoz; under Wellington at Vittoria and the Pyrenees; created viscount, 1823; master general of the ordnance, 1828–30; involved in controversy in defending his conduct at Albuera.

the fallen European allies. It was a greater prize than the sugar islands upon which Pitt had expended his energies when shut out from Europe. It was supposed that Popham's fault was in raiding a river instead of planning the conquest of a continent. Not only was Buenos Ayres to be recaptured, but then an assault was to be made on Chile, on the west coast, and a continuous line a thousand miles long to be established from Valparaiso to Buenos Ayres over the Andes. When General Whitelocke[1] arrived to take command in the Plate area he had some 10,000 British troops under his command. He had hopes, moreover, of assistance from the Spaniards. That party of the colonists who wished to establish their independence from Spain would, it was believed, welcome the British as liberators. At the end of June 1807, 7,800 men were landed to the east of Buenos Ayres and marched resolutely towards the city. On 5 July, when the city was surrounded, a general attack was launched on every entrance simultaneously. In hand to hand fighting two strong points were captured at the cost of almost one-third of the attacking troops. Then General Whitelocke's heart failed him. He withdrew from the attack and from the area, being convinced that local hostility would make any military gain of no significance. For this he, too, was court-martialed and he was dismissed the king's service in disgrace.

The Portland ministry began therefore with the news of one military failure after another. There was the report of the disaster at Buenos Ayres, of the failure of a second naval expedition to the Dardanelles, of a mutiny in the forces at Malta, and of a sanguinary mutiny of Indian troops at Vellore. They heard of the final extinction of Neapolitan resistance to the French. The expedition to Egypt, after heavy casualties in taking Alexandria, and heavier in an attack on Rosetta, was glad to accept an offer to evacuate and sail away to Sicily in order to escape being besieged. When Castlereagh in his first months at the war office reckoned up the forces which he had available, he came to a gloomy conclusion. This was that there were less than 12,000 troops of the regular army ready to strike an aggressive blow to reverse these calamities over the globe. In addition, the failure of Windham's schemes for replacing the volunteers with a nation trained to arms meant that if the

---

[1] John Whitelocke (1757–1833), served in San Domingo, 1793–4; lieutenant-governor of Portsmouth, 1799.

enemy could get into a position to strike, regular forces would be required for defence at home. Castlereagh's first task was to re-equip the army with a system of transports to make the small force available for rapid service where it might be needed. A slower job was the increase in the numbers available. His methods had to be drastic and to override old prejudices. Thirty thousand men were to be torn out of the militia and trained as first-rank troops with the regular army. This gap in the militia was to be more than filled by the raising of another 44,000 militia men from the mass of the population.

The remnants of the European alliance had to be patched up. In southern Europe activity had come to an end. England's only point for attack, Naples, had, to all intents and purposes, been abandoned. The queen of Naples was no longer content just to 'wear the trousers' in the exiled court, she now proposed to 'turn her coat'. British suspicion of her precluded any further action for the moment. To the north and east lay the only interesting possibilities. The Russians in February 1807 had fought a drawn battle with the French at Eylau. This encouraged Prussia to continue her disastrous struggle. It brought more intense appeals for English aid. The place for this was the Baltic. France, refusing to allow Sweden to lurk in neutrality, invaded Swedish Pomerania and prepared to take Stralsund. This port had great importance for England as a means of economic entry into Europe and for the shipment of raw materials in return. By June of 1807 the German legion (8,000 men) had been sent by Britain to aid Sweden and thus, indirectly, Russia. But an end was put to this by Napoleon's destruction of the Russian army at Friedland on 14 June 1807. By the end of the month, which had opened so hopefully, Napoleon and Alexander had met on the raft on the Niemen at Tilsit and by 9 July had not only made peace, but had entered into an aggressive pact for the ruin of England.

At Tilsit Russia promised to shut her ports, and those under her control, to English ships: that control was to be extended. It was not enough for Russia to influence Dalmatia, she must also govern Turkey: more immediate was her plan to dominate the Baltic. By secret articles, Napoleon and Alexander agreed to force Denmark and Sweden to join their condominium of Europe and to make Portugal a client like Spain. The Portland cabinet obtained full information from secret sources of the blow about to be struck in the Baltic. It was a blow whose most serious consequence, British isolation, was inescapable. But it threatened also subsidiary, yet important, evils which could be averted. If Denmark was taken over entire by the French, Napoleon would gain an increase for his fleet and a further stretch of coastline for its secure preservation. This would make England not only isolated but in renewed danger of invasion.

The British acted with speed, while Denmark remained entirely passive, awaiting her fate without moving a gun or assembling her forces. The German legion, now in danger of complete encirclement, at Stralsund, was ordered to make for the island of Zealand, on which Copenhagen stands. A British fleet of twenty-seven ships of the line, with bomb vessels, under Admiral Gambier,[1] sailed up to the Sound. On 12 August 1807 a British envoy, Francis Jackson,[2] called upon the prince regent of Denmark, stressed his peril, and demanded that Denmark should hand over her fleet to Great Britain who promised to restore it at the end of hostilities with France. Denmark, not surprisingly, refused. Thereupon a British force landed on Zealand and besieged Copenhagen on the land side. At the same time the bomb vessels were brought in by the fleet. A rain of fire was inflicted upon Copenhagen from both sides simultaneously. 'The flames', reported Gambier of the action beginning on 2 September, 'were kept up in different places till the evening of the 5th, when a considerable part of the city being consumed, and the conflagration threatening the speedy destruction of the rest, the general commanding the garrison sent out a flag of truce ... to treat for a capitulation.' The British sailors swarmed into Copenhagen's dockyards and hastily rigged up eighteen Danish ships of the line, their fifteen frigates and brigs and gunboats: then, packing in all available naval stores, they sailed them back to England at the end of the six weeks' stipulated period.

This attack upon Denmark, so much more violent than that carried out by Nelson in 1801[3] and unprovoked by any positive action by the Danes, inevitably aroused hostile criticism not

[1] James Gambier, first Baron Gambier (1756–1833), later commander of the Channel fleet; a commissioner for peace negotiations with United States, 1814.

[2] Francis James Jackson (1770–1814), ambassador at Constantinople 1796; British plenipotentiary to France 1801, to Prussia 1802–6, and to the United States 1809–11.

[3] See above, pp. 386–7.

only from other powers but from the opposition at Westminster. The gain in ships, argued Grey, was but 'a poor compensation' for the loss of national character and the enmity of every other power in Europe 'which, I fear, must be the result of this act of violence and injustice'. The government defended itself the less convincingly because, while it had in truth acted in desperate self-defence, it was anxious to conceal its sources of information about the plans of Napoleon. There was, too, a further embarrassment on the government benches. Their policy of removing Danish ships before Napoleon seized them—and the French had only been slower, not less ruthless, in bullying the Danes—could be justified as a necessity for survival in war. But this policy had, at the last moment, almost been revised by Canning. He had proposed to break the truce terms arranged at Copenhagen and to turn the episode not into a salvage operation, but into the beginning of an offensive campaign. He would, but for the firmness of commanders on the spot, have tried to make a new front in Denmark, to hold the Sound, and deny the Russian fleet any exit from the Baltic. Such offensive action would have been worse than a breach of an engagement. It would have necessitated a major campaign without adequate preparation and resources. As it was, the suggestion only further impeded the ministry's defence of itself.

It was but natural that a man of restless energy such as Canning should scheme to keep a British base in northern Europe. Indeed, all hope was not yet lost in the Baltic. Sweden, under its lunatic king Gustavus, was still continuing to prevaricate in face of the Franco-Russian menace. When at length Russia marched into Finland the Swedes, albeit crazily, entered upon war again with British support. In 1808 Britain provided a subsidy of £1,200,000 for Sweden and in May sent 12,000 troops to Göteborg under the command of Sir John Moore.[1] Moore was an officer of experience which went back to the American war. He was accounted in politics a Foxite. While this did not endear him to the Portland government, his claims to a high command were hotly backed by the war office—and Castlereagh spoke for professional opinion—while his competence in

---

[1] Sir John Moore (1761–1809); son of a Glasgow doctor and brother of Admiral Sir Graham Moore; had served in the West Indies, Egypt, and the Mediterranean; a studious and technical soldier; introduced a new system of drill and manœuvre; for his death see below, p. 461.

the world of diplomacy further recommended him for authority in the tangled affairs of Sweden. For all his tact, his courtesy, and his powers of decision, Moore failed in the Baltic. Gustavus, losing Finland to Russia, attacked now by Prussia and Denmark in addition, nevertheless insisted on a war of conquest in Norway. Instead of arguing with Moore, Gustavus ordered his arrest. Moore was obliged to escape in disguise, bringing his men back home without ever having landed them. Ministers who saw only their last foothold in Europe lost, and who did not realize that it had in fact gone before Moore sailed, vented their exasperation upon him.

Even while they lamented their loss of northern Europe a new opportunity for intervention against the French was afforded them. As part of the plan for completing his mastery of western Europe, Napoleon had delivered an ultimatum to the regent of Portugal. This miserable man wavered for as long as he could. From London he was advised to quit Lisbon and to establish his rule in Brazil; there in co-operation with the English fleet and English commercial interests he might live perhaps to fight another day, or at least to preserve a counterpoise to France across the ocean. A vital part of this plan was that the Portuguese fleet should sail with the regent and escape Napoleon. Happily threats—and not bomb-ships as with Denmark—were sufficient to persuade the Portuguese government to follow the British plan. Napoleon declared war on Portugal but General Junot and the French army arrived in Lisbon only in time to see the fleet sailing away (November 1807).

The struggle in the Peninsula did not stop with this defensive success. To send his army through to Lisbon Napoleon had had to concern himself more intimately with the squalid politics of the Spanish court. He was not the man to rest content with any merely nominal control of Spain and Portugal. He was determined to exploit his control of the Iberian peninsula to the full in war with England. It was accordingly necessary to administer both countries with French efficiency. In Spain there was a popular fear that their king might sail across the Atlantic like the regent of Portugal. In truth he was but an imbecile, a pawn in a struggle for power between the queen, with her favourite Godoy, and the heir apparent Ferdinand. In March 1808 Ferdinand forced the abdication of his father. In April Napoleon, after hearing the queen herself deny Ferdinand's legitimacy, compelled all the parties to sign away their rights. The Spanish throne was given to Joseph Bonaparte. The French had taken care to occupy Madrid with Murat's army before this announcement. 'Your nation', Napoleon proclaimed, 'is old: my mission is to restore its youth.' Paradoxically the promise was fulfilled. Spain became once more a fighting force as revolt against the French *diktat* broke out from Bayonne to Seville and to Cadiz. In Portugal too independence was declared. The British were presented not only with allies—allies whose enthusiasm exceeded their military effectiveness—but with the use of ports on the European coastline and with a terrain too broken to be effectively held by forces of the size which the French could at first deploy.

In Spain the fighting began with a series of local actions. At Cadiz the insurgents gained possession of the town and established contact with Admiral Lord Collingwood at Gibraltar. The French fleet in Cadiz harbour, five ships of the line, a frigate and 4,000 men, remnants from Trafalgar, were then compelled to surrender. The French from Madrid marched through Andalusia, regained Cordoba and pillaged it. But this army was shortly in difficulties at Anduyar and beaten into capitulation by the Spaniards at the battle of Baylen in July 1808. Navarre and Catalonia were strongly held by the French. But in Aragon, after three months of street fighting and siege operations, they were forced to leave Saragossa in the hands of the Spaniards. So general was the effervescence that it was clearly impossible to reduce Spain to order by isolated repressive acts. In preparation for a full scale reconquest from France, the new king Joseph began to evacuate Madrid. In Portugal too the French drew back in order to concentrate for a decisive blow.

From London 10,000 men were rushed out to help either the Spanish or the Portuguese. Their commander, Sir Arthur Wellesley, went first to the Spanish at Corunna and then to the Portuguese at Oporto. Wellesley landed in Mondego Bay and marched on Lisbon, being joined by reinforcements as he went. The main reinforcements, however, were expected to come later under the command of Sir John Moore. Junot decided to attack the English while they were yet weak. On 21 August 1808 he attacked at Vimieiro, a battle in which the French were entirely defeated, losing 13 cannon and 3,000 men. This happy opening to the drama was followed by farce. Wellington was superseded in his command by Sir Harry Burrard; twenty-four hours later he was, in turn, succeeded by Sir Hew Dalrymple.[1] These ridiculous changes in the command had their origins in personal squabbles and questions of seniority. The result was to put decisions into the hands of those who lacked the spirit of victory. Junot's position was so bad that he asked for an armistice. By the Convention of Cintra (30 August 1808) the French forces in Portugal gave up the fight but they were to be returned to France with all arms and equipment. This provoked an outcry of indignation in England where the victory of Vimieiro had excited all the hopes of a nation long starved of military success. The cabinet sought to escape the responsibility by casting all blame upon the soldiers, upon Dalrymple, Burrard, and Wellesley. Ultimately it was possible to let Dalrymple alone carry the stigma of the king's most serious disapprobation.

While Englishmen debated the reasons for the failure to humiliate the French in Portugal, Napoleon devised the means to restore French control of the peninsula. He arranged peace with Prussia and withdrew his veteran troops for a massive blow in Spain: 160,000 conscripts were summoned to the colours in France. The French army moved quickly down to Bayonne and then on to a headquarters at Vittoria. The Spanish supreme junta, under the presidency of Count Florida Blanca, divided its forces in three large armies, an eastern under Palafox, a north-western under Blake, and the army of the centre under Castanos. The French under Ney broke Blake's army and pushed the remnants of it on one side into Asturias; they then went on to defeat Castanos completely at Tudela. This opened to them the road through the Guadalajara into Madrid. On 5 November 1808 Madrid surrendered to Napoleon. The south of Spain lay open before the French.

The British scheme had been to push forces under Sir John Moore out eastwards from Portugal to come to the aid of the Spanish in Madrid. But Moore heard of the collapse of the Spanish central resistance when he had only reached Salamanca. He at first prepared for a general retreat back to Portugal. But information about the French lines of communication as

---

[1] Sir Harry Burrard (1755–1813), soldier since 1775; M.P. since 1780; had served in America, Flanders, and Denmark; after his court martial, at which he was acquitted, his service was limited to commanding the guards in London.

Sir Hew Whitefoord Dalrymple (1750–1830), grandson of the first Viscount Stair; lieutenant, 1766; commander at Gibraltar, 1806–8; general, 1812.

well as most urgent pleas from Frere,[1] the English agent with
the Spanish government, caused Moore to change his mind.
He determined that this time he would not take the negative
line of prudence. He made a junction with forces under Baird[2]
and then struck north-eastwards in the direction of Burgos and
the French communications running through the western end
of the Pyrenees. Thirty thousand English troops thus appeared
valiantly at the rear of a quarter of a million men of the Napoleonic invasion. Facing Soult across the river Carrion, Moore
heard that his manœuvre had succeeded in causing Napoleon
to detach half the main force from Madrid and to turn back to
obliterate him. Moore at once retreated, not back on the line
he had come, but more directly westwards to Corunna and the
British fleet. This operation involved a march in the bitter cold
of December 1808 and January 1809 over 250 miles of mountainous country, with troops whose discipline disintegrated
once they turned backwards, with a local population made
hostile by the looting of this disorderly band, and with constant
attacks to the rear by Soult's pursuing force. It says much for
Moore's personal authority that when he had brought his men
to Corunna, they were capable of defending the town. Of his
30,000 men, 24,000 were successfully embarked behind the
rear-guard screen. The commander himself was mortally
wounded in the final operation.[3] This impertinent sally in
northern Spain had prevented an immediate French subjugation of the south. Northern Spain itself, it is true, was gradually
reabsorbed. Saragossa fell on 14 February 1809 and the French
steadily improved the security of their communications with
Madrid. They were unable to proceed to a systematic subjugation of the whole country because events in Europe had taken a
disturbing turn. On 22 January 1809 Napoleon left Spain to
deal with the Austrians.

Though Moore's action had thus, by the happy coincidence

---

[1] John Hookham Frere (1769–1846), poet and scholar; a friend of Canning's
who contributed to the *Anti Jacobin* (1797–8) in which the intellectual opposition to
revolutionary principles was conducted with wit and spirit; M.P. 1799; a special
diplomatic agent, 1800–18; then returned to classical scholarship.

[2] Sir David Baird (1757–1829), served with distinction in wars in India, 1780–
1802; second in command to Moore.

[3] His death was made to live in the minds of generations of schoolchildren by
the famous lines beginning 'Not a drum was heard, not a funeral note', written by
the Irish clergyman Charles Wolfe (1791–1823), first published in the *Newry
Telegraph* in 1817.

of events, been fortunate in that it kept Spain and Portugal in an unsettled condition, it appeared at the time to be only another example of a British retreat to the sea. It was by no means decided that the British main effort in Europe would be made in the peninsula, or that that area could long be kept open for operations. Even after Wellesley landed a second time in Portugal, on 22 April 1809, it was indeed doubtful how far Britain was going to be capable of making a major military effort, there or anywhere else. The persistent pessimism of the whig opposition about the war was based upon more than distrust of the war office: it seemed justified by the new turn of events, the distress and disorganization arising from the economic war.

XVIII

ECONOMIC WARFARE, 1806–12

NAPOLEON did not invent a system of economic warfare after Jena and Tilsit. One of the immediate—and, in France, welcome—results of the outbreak of war in 1793 was the ending of the trade treaty of 1786. French industrialists hoped to profit by the war. The directory tried actively to damage British commerce, and in 1798 ordered the seizure of neutral vessels if they had called at a British port. It was, after all, the common mercantilist view that a favourable trade balance, an influx of gold, was the secret of the power of a nation. It was natural therefore that the British should seek to destroy French strength by using sea-power to take her colonies from her: it was as inevitable that the French should try to deny Britain the profits of exporting to Europe. What was new after 1806 was Napoleon's immense power and his recognition of the changed character of the war. France, with Russia bludgeoned into co-operation, controlled the whole continent. Britain sought a toe-hold in vain. Yet the emperor realized that, since Trafalgar, he was incapable of mounting an invasion of the desperate island. Therefore he sought to turn the economic war into a major operation which should break the spirit of England and bring on a negotiated settlement. For their part, the English cabinet fought hard in this field which their enemy had selected. They tried to provoke uprisings of French vassals and to build a new economic power outside Europe. Neither side, it must be added, followed out a consistent, much less a fully effective, system to achieve these ends.

Great Britain exported to Europe colonial produce, raw materials (which her mercantile marine gathered for her), and manufactures, principally textiles and iron. From Europe her most vital imports, in war-time, were corn and timber. French efforts to exclude British trade were countered by the development of other trade channels. The exports going to Bremen and Hamburg increased sixfold between 1789 and 1800 and the import trade from Prussia and Russia also expanded. France needed the colonial re-exports. In 1800 25 per cent. of French imports were colonial produce. The failure of early French trade restrictions can be seen in the comparison of 1790 with 1800. This shows that English total exports more than doubled while her imports increased by some 64 per cent.[1]

In his determination to break this economic power, Napoleon had two objectives. His first was to increase France's favourable trade balance, his second was to produce distress in England. The two were not identical. To produce a crisis in Britain, for example, it would obviously be expedient to deny her corn and timber so that she should have high bread prices and scanty ships. To cut off timber did not conflict with the mercantilist plan for it meant only impoverishing the Baltic countries. To cut off foodstuffs, however, involved French farmers as well as Polish ones: such a policy was always likely therefore to be relaxed in favour of French trade. Indeed, any policy of favouring French exports was inimical to a blockading policy. The internal communications of Europe were simply incapable of providing a means of absorbing French exports rapidly. Once it was admitted that ships must take goods from France, it was inevitable that they would also, even if it involved extensive smuggling, bring cargoes back. Napoleon cared little for French commercial interests, something for the manufacturers, and most of all for his farmers. He seems completely to have disregarded the bankers. This was a grave error. For the strength of England to maintain her trade abroad, as well as her ability to subsidize allies, or pay her armies, depended upon her strength as the centre of international credit and banking. Yet inside French-dominated Europe, the Rothschilds and others quite freely negotiated English bills.

On 21 November 1806 Napoleon issued his Berlin Decree. By this he declared that the British Isles were now in a state of blockade and that no vessel coming directly (this word should be noted) from Britain or her colonies would be received in the ports under his control. The fact that the decree was issued in Berlin is appropriate, for its efficacy depended upon the emperor's control of the coastline and river routes of northern Europe. Napoleon had insisted that all goods imported by

---

[1] See T. S. Ashton, *Economic History of England in the Eighteenth Century*, table xiv, p. 252.

Holland, Spain, Italy, or Switzerland should bear a certificate of their origins. As early as 1803 he had forbidden the trade in British goods. But as long as imports through the Baltic and the Adriatic were unchecked, the prohibition was unenforceable. Hence the significance of the agreement with Russia at Tilsit. Alexander's ambition to control Sweden and Constantinople would close both British routes of free entry into Europe.

The reply of the British was not to seek to stimulate trade, but rather to bring it under strict control. In March 1807 Perceval introduced legislation which delegated power to the ministry, by orders in council, to confine Europe's trade with neutrals. It had for some time been a grievance of short-sighted patriots that neutral shipping profited by the war. In 1802 28 per cent. of shipping clearing British ports had been under a neutral flag: in 1807 the corresponding figure was 44 per cent. The trade with British sugar colonies had, for lack of native ships, been thrown open to the United States. Behind the orders in council was a wish to check the neutrals, as well as to retaliate upon Napoleon. In practice, however, more practical objectives were accepted. The system was not applied as a means of prohibiting Europe from trading with neutrals but of directing, taxing, and controlling that trade. Neutral vessels going or coming from enemy ports were to proceed by way of Britain, paying customs there and buying licences. In theory, neutrals might export their own primary products to the enemy, or trade with enemy colonies, though quinine and cotton were forbidden as exports to France. The general issue of licences was a source of profit to Britain. It could also be used to impose a pattern upon world trade.

Napoleon answered in his turn when, on 23 November 1807, he issued the Milan decrees. In place of the prohibition of goods 'coming directly' from England, he now commanded that all ships touching in English ports were to be confiscated. Many commodities were to be deemed English (and seized when found) unless it could be proved that they were not. Any neutral who obeyed the British orders in council was thus punished by the French. The unfortunate neutrals—of whom the United States was the most important—had to risk detention by the British navy, or confiscation in Napoleon's ports. The United States tried to find a way of escaping the dilemma, and bringing the parties to a reasonable state of mind, by placing an embargo on trade with both of them in 1807. As the French had no mercantile trade in their own ships, the British were the major sufferers by this.[1]

The economic situation of Britain grew very serious in the course of 1808. Exports which in 1806 had been £40·8 million (declared values) had dropped in 1808 to less than £35·2 million. Liverpool's raw cotton imports fell from 143,000 sacks in 1807 to 23,000 in 1808, while grain imports fell to one-twentieth of the level of the previous year. As a result of this dislocation, corn went up in price (from 66s. a quarter in 1807 to 94s. in 1808) while slackening demand produced low wages and short-time in factories. Manchester was disturbed by frequent and violent strikes. To maintain shipbuilding meant a constant search for timber: Canada could not replace the fall in Baltic shipments. It became difficult to keep stocks in naval dockyards. The merchant marine suffered the most. Its consumption in 1810 had been reduced to five-ninths of that of 1804.

This was the desperate situation which explains the enthusiasm of the Portland administration in following up those military adventures in South America which the Talents administration had bequeathed to them.[2] For they saw in this area hope of a new market into which hard-pressed British traders could be diverted. Despite the bitter criticisms of later historians[3] their South American policy can be counted a partial success. In spite of the hostility of the United States, British sales to America increased from £8 million in 1805 to nearly £20 million in 1808. This was a very substantial crutch at this time of crisis. France's quarrel with Portugal and Spain aided this diversion of British trade to South America by making enterprise there both safer and more respectable. The other area for British expansion was the Levant. There Russia's ambitions had the effect of making both Turkey and Persia friends to Britain. Through Turkey, British exporters found a tedious but practicable road into Europe. Spain and Portugal were also points of entry. Altogether, exports to the Mediterranean countries quadrupled in the years 1805 to 1811.

Despite these encouraging developments, the general picture

---

[1] Napoleon took advantage of the prohibition of trade with the belligerents by the president to declare that all American ships in his ports must be liable to seizure as prizes.

[2] See above, pp. 453 f.

[3] For example, J. W. Fortescue, *British Statesmen of the Great War*, p. 214.

viewed from the board of trade was very black in 1808. There seemed the possibility that Napoleon might succeed in driving England into peace by the efficiency of his customs house officers. But instead his system began to be relaxed. One reason for this was that Austria had revived sufficiently to show her resentment of French domination of Europe. Renewed war on the Danube distracted Napoleon from the superintendence of the blockade. By July 1809, however, he had destroyed Austria once more by the battle of Wagram. More serious in weakening the system was its constant strain upon the vassal states and upon France itself. French customs receipts were declining, those of 1809 were only a little more than one-sixth of 1808. The exports of the empire fell, taking 1806 as 100, to 83 in 1807, then to 73 in 1808 and 1809. French manufacturers, who had at first enjoyed their freedom from English competition, were feeling their need of raw materials. France needed colonial products and was being starved of them. Life without sugar, coffee, cotton, and soda was not only miserable, but uneconomic. Attempts to find substitute sources of supply in Europe were too slow. Grape sugar and linen in place of cotton were elements in siege economy hardly tolerable in France and quite unbearable in conquered countries where there were no compensating advantages. In 1809 Holland opened her ports to American ships provided the imports were stored in state warehouses to be controlled by the government under French guidance. This partial opening was enough to let all smugglers and black-market dealers flourish once more. Napoleon himself decided to allow some trade over the seas provided each ship clearing a French port exported from France more than it imported to her.

Once the exchange of goods was permitted, it was impossible to maintain the system. By 1810 Frankfurt was full of colonial produce and Leipzig had become an English distribution centre for trade with central Europe. The system of licences which the French as well as the English had now adopted became notoriously inefficient. Licences were bought and sold on an enormous scale in all great commercial centres. French consuls in European ports looked on the licences not as a means of regulating trade, but as a means of revenue for France and for themselves. Napoleon himself had, at this stage, two fixed ideas: to allow licences for corn export (so as to pacify the farmers) and to make certain that more was exported than was imported.

The figures supplied to him suggested that in 1809 and 1810 this aim was being achieved, but they were quite unreliably calculated. Even if they had been correct, Britain would have been assisted by this development. She could compensate for her adverse balance with France with her trade with the new world: in trade with Europe she had the means of supplying herself with agricultural produce and of sustaining her financial links with continental powers.

By the early summer of 1810 the dangerous advantages accruing to Britain from the relaxation of the system were evident to the Emperor. In July 1810 he decreed that a new system of licences should come into operation, more limited in scope and more directly under his control.[1] Then in a bid to win the favour of the United States he offered to cancel the decrees as they affected neutrals if Britain would repeal the orders. But his greatest energy was put into a drive against smugglers. Stricter enforcement damaged commercial firms all over Europe. 1811 was the second peak of economic war, 1808 being the first. It was a year of bankruptcies all over the Continent. Napoleon's fiercer police measures goaded his allies and vassals to revolt against him. As he had then to march on them with his grand army he needed more urgently to enforce his customs control in order to collect the money for war. Thus in 1812 he estimated that the Trianon and Fontainebleau decrees, improving the system, would bring him not only American sympathy, but 150 millions of francs. Russia deserted France in part because of the unfortunate effects of a blockade upon her trade. As the grand army marched to Russia it enforced control of the north German ports. As it disappeared eastwards, the smugglers reappeared. The system and the need for more conquest became a vicious circle.

1811 was the worst year for Britain economically. Sweden was brought into the French system. Six hundred vessels caught by wind in the narrow seas tried to make the coast: 240 of them suffered seizure, a loss of some £2 million. British exports to northern Europe (including France) fell in 1811 to only 20 per cent. of the level in 1810.[2] In the same period, exports to the

---

[1] It was intended that licences should be given only to Frenchmen for French ports.

[2] G. Lefebvre, *Napoléon*, pp. 363, 64; a comparison with 1810 seems to me more useful than that with 1805 made by Professor Lefebvre.

United States declined to about 76 per cent. of the level of
1810. Trade with South America also declined to 65 per cent.
of that of 1810. Total British exports which had been approximately £48·5 million in 1805, £40·8 million in 1806, £35·2
million in the bad year 1808, had then risen to almost £61 million in 1810,[1] now fell suddenly in 1811 to £39·5 million. Nor
was this the whole story. The trade to South America, on paper
so valuable, was an irregular and undependable affair with
many delays in payment by the Latin American customers.

The trade crisis of 1811 was the more ominous because it
came on top of monetary troubles. The continuous inflation of
the war period had stimulated expansion. A contraction of
demand could not but put severe strain upon the monetary
system. The adverse trade balance with Europe had, as early as
1808, caused the pound to depreciate in terms of French francs.
From 1809 David Ricardo,[2] the most forceful of all economists
of the day and a radical critic of the government, had been
arguing that economic troubles were due to a recklessly in-
flationary banking policy. In 1811 a committee of the house of
commons gave a report in support of his views. On top of this
break in confidence came the need to pay out gold for the support of the war in Portugal and Spain, as well as for the purchase
of heavier amounts of grain after bad harvests in 1809 and 1810.
Gold payments to Europe went up from 6 to 9, to 14 million
pounds in the years 1808 to 1810. Further depreciation of the
pound followed and a drain of the gold reserves of the Bank of
England. Here was a threat to Britain's ability to fight at all.
Ricardo frankly wanted peace at any price as part of economic
reconstruction.

Following on the bankruptcy of five Manchester firms in
August 1810, a wave of failures and stoppages spread across the
country. Napoleon's tightening of his embargo only intensified
a crisis which was already serious. The effort to reorientate
trade was bound in any case to be perilous; the loss of confidence was cumulative and disastrous. Lancashire by May 1811
was working a three-day week. The remedy of the working man
was machine smashing, that of the radical economists was

[1] The erroneous belief in 1809 that agreement had been reached between
America and Britain about neutral trade set going a temporary rush of shipping
between the two.

[2] David Ricardo (1772–1823); for him see below, p. 531, and Sir E. L. Woodward, *The Age of Reform* (O.H.E. vol. xiii), p. 56.

capitulation and reform, that of the government was simply fortitude. The government's remedy was a greater tribute to their
character than to their brains. They despaired of thinking out
a real answer, but they would not give up the fight. And because
at bottom the immediate crisis was a matter of confidence in
the future, this firmness triumphed. The government succeeded
in obtaining ever greater loans. Matters began to mend.

Napoleon, for his part, failed to take the maximum advantage
of the partial collapse of his enemy in 1811. Food shortage, for
instance, would obviously have intensified English social distress. The harvests for two years had been bad. Imports from
Europe, even though they had to be paid for in gold, were vital.
The French not only allowed these purchases, they rejoiced in
these very sales which were relieving the English position. By
the autumn of 1811 it was clear that the French were feeling
the strain of the trade war as much as the English. The question
was which of them would bear it the longer. Lyons and Rouen
were at a standstill: Paris financial houses were breaking: relief
was sought in opening semi-official relations with the smugglers'
organizations.

With mutual relief therefore the tension was eased in November 1811. Licences were granted on both sides of the Channel
which made possible beneficial exchanges. England lifted the
ban on cotton and quinine. Foreigners were allowed to establish
offices in London from which to negotiate the grant of licences.
Coffee was once more allowed into France: wine was exchanged
for sugar. Trade revived swiftly in 1812. In that year English
exports at £50 million were 28 per cent. up on the levels of
1811. Once again the opening of a small legitimate trade made
possible a widespread illegal commerce.

In 1812 the English cabinet, with many new worries, could
at least congratulate itself on having survived this new form of
warfare. It might, truly, have been not a final victory but only
a respite, like that after 1808. Napoleon was rushing to his
great war with Russia. If he had triumphed he might well have
used his increased control of the Baltic and the Levant to make
a further, and most intensive, effort to force England to peace
through the dislocation of her economy. As it was, economics
took second place in cabinet interest from this time to the movements of armies and fleets, to new alliances and new wars.

War between England and the United States was directly

the product of the expiring economic conflict. In 1793 the
United States had been sympathetic to France. Both gratitude
and radicalism inclined Americans to oppose England. This
feeling gradually changed in face of the excesses of the terror—
which made the name revolution less respectable. French privateers and French doctrines of the rights of black men were
equally irritating. Meanwhile, Pitt had never lost sight of those
objectives which he had first followed as an apprentice to Shelburne.[1] He wished to clear outstanding issues with America so
as to create an economic partnership and a common foreign
policy. In the decade 1795 to 1805 this seemed possible of
achievement. In 1795 the Jay[2] treaty was negotiated. England
evacuated the posts along the frontiers of the United States.
American shipping was allowed into the Indian Ocean where it
competed strongly with the East India Company. American
shipping—if the ships were no larger than 70 tons—was allowed
into the British West Indies on condition that it served only
America: tropical produce was not to be exported to Europe in
competition with England. The disputes about frontier lines
and about American debts were to be settled by arbitration.
The issues on which there was no agreement were those of
escaped slaves and of the rights of neutral shipping on the high
seas. The American government rejected the conditions (in
article X of the draft treaty) attaching to trade in tropical
produce. Here the shortage of British shipping in war-time was
to force the solution which the Americans desired. In 1795 the
United States was re-exporting 21 million lb. of sugar; by 1801
the figure was 50 million lb.: 88 per cent. of the grain and 90
per cent. of the dried fish carried to the British Caribbean by
that date came in American ships.

Under the Jay treaty, England and America traded, in effect,
under a most-favoured-nation agreement. The duties imposed
by America on foreign ships were balanced by countervailing
British duties. A compromise solution was accepted by Britain
on the dispute about the boundaries of Maine and New Brunswick, by following the Chaputneticook River and the Lakes.
On the issues raised both by Toussaint's rebellion in Haiti and

---

[1] See above, p. 256.
[2] John Jay (1745–1829), New York lawyer; negotiated peace with Britain at
the end of the War of Independence; worked with Hamilton and Federalists;
secretary of state; chief justice, and governor of New York.

by Miranda's activities in Latin America,[1] there was identity
of views between London and Washington. So by 1798 Great
Britain and the United States were practically in alliance. Joint
convoys were operated by their naval forces to guard against
French privateers. America was waging an undeclared war
against France.

Three issues remained in dispute between England and
America, though they were submerged for the moment under
the greater conflict with the French. The first was static: no
agreement had been reached for settling the money owed to
private British citizens since the American revolution. The
other two were explosive. The British navy was constantly short
of men. Who would voluntarily enlist to serve for the duration
of the war at half a crown a week under a discipline depending
on lashes? Numbers were kept up by impressment and menaced
by desertion. Any English-speaking, able-bodied, man on leave
in a port might find himself swept up in the press. Any American
ship on the high seas might be boarded and combed for English
deserters. The British government refused to recognize the easy
laws for naturalization passed in the United States.[2] By English
law 'no British subject who was not an Inhabitant of America
on or before the separation of that country can be regarded as a
Citizen of the United States if liable to be impressed'. Many
men shouting they were Americans were swept into the silence
of service in King George's fleet. The British were obdurate in
refusing to regard an American vessel as immune from inspection or an American protective passport as proof of citizenship.
It happened that the need for impressment was less stringent
between 1797 and 1802 so, for a while, the dispute was left to
official correspondence. The other, and kindred, issue was that
of freedom of the seas. The English worked on two clear principles. A belligerent had a right to seize contraband of war
going to an enemy port. Here the difficulty was that there was
no agreed definition of what constituted contraband. Next, no
neutral—this was the rule of war of 1756—could carry on a
trade in time of war which had been closed to it in peace. In
accordance with these principles an order in council in 1794
authorized the seizure of any vessels proceeding from the French

---

[1] Toussaint was the independent negro leader; Francesco Miranda (1754-1816)
was the leader of the independence party in Spanish America.

[2] Nor indeed did the United States formally request that they should.

West Indies to Europe, as well as the seizure of any French-owned goods coming from the West Indies, whatever their destination.

The United States was less positive on the point of international law. She was very peremptory in requiring that her own ships be left undisturbed. She was feeling her way to the doctrine that the freedom of the seas meant that a neutral flag must be respected, cover what it might. In this case, again, the last few years of the century were years of a slackening of tension. The British courts allowed the re-export of French West Indian produce from the United States. Sir William Scott[1] in the *Immanuel* case in 1799 threatened to be severe on fictitious or nominally 'broken' voyages, but by implication he confirmed the validity of a genuine broken voyage, that is, the transport of goods to America and their re-shipment as American property to Europe. The *Polly* case (1800) may illustrate the point. The *Polly* was taken by the British in mid Atlantic bound for Spain from Massachusetts. Her cargo was mostly Massachusetts fish but she had also sugar which, only a month before, the *Polly* had fetched from Spanish growers in Havana, and which she was now taking to a Spanish merchant. It was argued that this was a device to carry a Spanish cargo. Scott held, however, that as the sugar had been landed on American soil and had paid duties, it had become American and was not subject to seizure on the high seas. The burden of proof of fraud rested upon the captors. This was so until 1805 when Grant[2] decided in the *William* case that in a broken voyage the neutrals must make real proof of import and re-export. Though this was a change merely in legal interpretation of the rule of 1756 it had for Americans all the force of a new order and was correspondingly resented.

Up to 1805, however, co-operation between Britain and the United States continued. The French, with no effective naval forces to make a blockade, in 1800 accepted the full American doctrine of the freedom of the seas. This brought peace between the two countries but it did not disrupt the Anglo-American

---

[1] William Scott, Lord Stowell (1745–1836), brother of Lord Eldon; Camden reader in ancient history at Oxford, 1773–85; a friend of Dr. Johnson; a judge of the High Court of Admiralty, 1798–1828, whose judgements on maritime issues had lasting importance; a member of parliament of conservative attitude of mind from 1790; created Baron Stowell 1821.

[2] Sir William Grant (1752–1832), master of the rolls, 1801–17.

understanding. The replacement of the federalist Adams[1] by the republican Jefferson as president of the United States meant that a party traditionally hostile to England had ousted friends in power. But Jefferson continued the foreign policy of his predecessor. The period of peace after Amiens naturally removed for a few months all the sources of discord. Between 1800 and 1804 important agreements were reached on the subject of United States debts and of British maritime seizures. The United States agreed to pay £600,000 on behalf of her citizens. The British agreed to settle claims for American property seized in war for £1,300,000.

Many circumstances combined to worsen relations from 1805 onwards. There was the stricter control of broken voyages. There was also the fact that the French by acquiring Louisiana from Spain and then selling it, in 1803, to the United States had won Jefferson's warmest gratitude. Moreover, a further frontier agreement had just been negotiated between England and America. That part of it which drew the frontiers of Maine between Deer Island and Campobello island in the Bay of Fundy was unexceptionable. But a further section drew a boundary for Canada between the Lake of the Woods and Lake Superior. This portion, the American senate argued, would prejudice the advocacy of claims to territory associated with Louisiana. In consequence the agreements were not ratified and tempers on both sides grew warm. The reopened war with France made England reassert her claims to impressment: it exposed the American captains once more to the indignity of being stopped and searched. It was against this darkening background that England began, with her orders in council, to tighten up her blockade in answer to Napoleon's continental system.

The very completeness of the English control of the seas was likely to make America resent England's part in the economic battle more than France's. The completeness of the control steadily improved as may be seen from Lloyd's insurance rates which at 12 per cent. in 1806 had by 1810 been lowered to 6 per cent., less than those of the earlier part of the war. The American answer to the situation was Jefferson's embargo on trade with the belligerents, followed by the Non-intercourse

---

[1] John Adams (1735–1826), a very legally minded Massachusetts politician; though a federalist he was not 'a party man'; president of the United States, 1796.

Act in 1809. This was unsatisfactory to many Americans. It avoided incidents only at the cost of denying the possibilities of a very lucrative trade. How much trade was stifled could be seen by the mad rush of merchants and shippers to take advantage of the brief lifting of the ban in 1809. It became the object of the American government, therefore, not to sit quietly by, but to force the belligerents to cancel their restrictions upon neutrals. At the very time that Napoleon was pondering an attack upon Russia to force her to apply his restrictions to British trade, he was ready to proclaim his willingness to give full freedom to the Americans. In 1810 France declared her willingness to relax her decrees if the English would annul the orders in council. In reality, the French were making no concession. They needed neutral shipping in their ports and they had never been in a position to control it on the high seas. Driven to take a dramatic line by the exigencies of domestic politics, President Madison[1] sternly summoned England to relax her orders. His demand was made in February 1811. The English government was slow and reluctant to give a definite answer in that year of economic crisis. It demanded that the French should take the first step. This was done. Under whig pressure the government at length agreed—in June 1812—that it would cancel the restrictions on American trade. It finally did so in July. This was too late. Nor had the problem of impressment been disposed of. By mid-June 1812, in ignorance of the British relaxation of control President Madison, in response to a congressional vote, declared war on Great Britain.[2] Thus the consequence of following plans to win the war by trade restrictions had been to draw France first into exhausting campaigns in Spain and now into a disastrous struggle with Russia: Britain, for her part, had slipped into a tragic, navally embarrassing, conflict with the United States.

[1] James Madison (1751–1836), fourth president of the United States; trained in theology at Princeton; Virginian politician; ally of Jefferson.

[2] For a fuller account of the circumstances of this declaration of war, see below, pp. 550 f.

XIX

PORTLAND, PERCEVAL, AND THE PENINSULA, 1809–12

IN spite of economic and military crises the Portland administration retained office until 1809. They were attacked not only by the whigs, but by many respected tories. Sidmouth's friends disliked their high-handed action against the neutrals, both in ravishing Copenhagen and in issuing the orders in council. Sidmouth himself attacked their financial arrangements: Mr. Pitt had always kept inflation in check by meeting war expenses with new taxes, so redeeming old debts as he incurred new ones: the government's expenditure was not now so backed. At the same time he condemned the war effort in the peninsula as feeble. Yet to expand it would have been possible only by increasing the financial burden. Sidmouth's dilemma—as always—was that of many solid country gentlemen: he did not want to support either a ministry which seemed to him so inept, or an opposition which he thought so unpatriotic. Therefore he quarrelled with both and increased the general political uncertainty.

The general dissatisfaction was balanced, however, by the impossibility of seeing a better alternative. What crumbled the Portland régime was not outside pressure, but inner dissension. Portland's bad health kept ambitious colleagues constantly thinking of the succession: the misfortunes of war made it difficult for any of them to build a spotless reputation. At the war office, Castlereagh had made one decision big with future consequence. He had, in the summer of 1808, taken the advice of Arthur Wellesley, then acting as chief secretary in Ireland, upon the affairs of the peninsula. Wellesley was not only appointed to take command of the forces in Portugal, but to advise on long-term policy in that area. His memorandum was prophetic. He sketched the outlines of the plan upon which the French were eventually to be defeated there. On this plan he was soon to act with singleness of purpose. As Wellesley (by then Lord Wellington) himself said, looking back on 1809, 'I went abroad and took command of the Army, and never returned, or even quitted the field, till the nations of the Peninsula . . . were delivered from the French armies: till I had invaded France . . . till the general peace was signed at Paris; and the British cavalry, sent by sea to Portugal, Spain, and the south of France, marched home across France, and embarked for England in the ports of France in the British Channel.'[1] But this lay in the future. More immediately important was the fact that Wellesley convinced Castlereagh that it was possible and profitable to defend Portugal with 30,000 men. Wellesley's arrival at Lisbon in April 1809 was an indication that England was to make a long and determined effort to establish herself in Europe at this point.

It was not clear that this was to be the main effort, however. On this, as on all subjects, ministers each had their own ideas. In the spring of 1809 war was probable between France and Austria. How could England profit by this? How could she aid the Austrians? There were two propositions before the government. One was for sending a force to northern Europe to join in a general anti-French rising in Germany. The other was for an expedition on the Scheldt which should destroy French installations and ships there, and divert French attention from the Danube. In March 1809 the war office was professing itself unable to undertake either of these schemes. This provoked Canning into writing to Portland to complain of the inefficiency of his colleagues. He threatened to resign himself if the ministry were not reconstructed. When Portland took Canning's letter to the king, George III saw clearly that Castlereagh was the colleague particularly attacked and suggested an exchange of offices for him. Canning was certainly determined to eject Castlereagh from the war office. Behind his personal animosity worked the irritable impatience of a clever man. He was too clever either to be satisfied with the destructive and critical role of the whig opposition, or with the pedestrian pace of those who retained power by their repute among steady men. Therefore he itched to command himself. Castlereagh had to be removed from his path.

Portland was not quick-witted, but he could see the disastrous consequence of breaking up the ministry. He requested Canning to keep his views secret until the end of the session. That would

[1] Wellington to Croker in *The Croker Papers*, ed. L. J. Jennings, iii. 124.

give time to arrange changes without ruining the basis of a war ministry. Lord Wellesley (Arthur's elder brother, the former governor-general of India) might then be put into the war office. This would suit Canning, who was building a personal connexion with the Wellesley brothers. It might perhaps be made tolerable for Castlereagh. So the ministry continued, a façade almost as fiercely assailed from behind as in front. Canning, at no wish of his own, was put in the position of secretly planning a colleague's ruin. His criticisms of Castlereagh—for failing to push the peninsular war as well as for inaction in Germany—were given a sinister appearance.

In this same spring of 1809, however, several items of news raised English spirits. At sea, Lord Cochrane,[1] the most unorthodox of seamen and politicians, demonstrated that the Nelson touch had not perished with Nelson. In a minor but lively little action at the mouth of the Charente, near La Rochelle, he, with five ships, defeated nine French ships of the line, followed them right into the shore, and put them out of action completely. More important was the news of an Austrian victory over the French at Aspern in May 1809, for this gave Britain a second chance to intervene effectively in the war. The Austrians wished for a landing near the Weser which might bring Prussia back into the fight. The British cabinet, from bitter experience, disliked the idea of any operation which made the security of their troops depend upon Prussian action. It was decided instead to descend by the Scheldt upon Antwerp and to inflict quick, ruinous, blows upon a distracted Napoleon. The combined operation, the army under Lord Chatham, the navy under Strachan,[2] was to start in July. This plan, made in June, provided a reason for further concealment of Canning's delayed ultimatum. Portland plausibly contended that it was impossible to change control at the war office in the middle of so complex an operation. Meanwhile, however, dramatic marches had been

---

[1] Thomas Cockrane, tenth earl of Dundonald (1775–1860), a man of lively mind and rebellious spirit who, as a member of parliament from 1806, played an independent radical role attacking admiralty administration; unjustly accused of a stock-exchange fraud in 1814 and expelled from parliament; as a naval officer he was unorthodox and successful in many small enterprises; claimed to have a plan for destroying the enemy's fleets and shore defences, 1811; served after 1815 with navies of Chile, Brazil, and Greece; the first to employ steam power in warships; claimed another secret war plan to defeat Russia in 1854, having been reinstated (as rear admiral) in British navy in 1832.

[2] Sir Richard John Strachan (1760–1828) entered navy 1772; admiral 1821.

made in Spain. Wellesley, or as one may call him for convenience in advance of his ennoblement, Wellington, had fought the campaign of Talavera.

As a younger, and rather despised, brother of a distinguished Irish family, Wellington combined in his character the rigid class feeling of an eighteenth-century aristocrat with the professional spirit of a careerist. He had long ago cast aside the social graces which marked him out in youth: they could no longer help him up the ladder. He was established as high in the army as connexions or favours could take him. To achieve more could only come from science. So, while advising Castlereagh, he had studied to achieve success in each field which the revolving fortune of war had brought into light. From his books he had made himself a man of information on Mexico, Nicaragua, Venezuela, Chile, Denmark, Sweden, and now, at last and most usefully, Portugal and Spain. He travelled to the peninsula with a book-box containing a Portuguese Grammar, traveller's letters on Portugal, and a Spanish prayer book for linguistic rather than devotional use. He confessed that from Sir Charles Stuart's[1] correspondence with regard to Portugal in 1797 he had learned not only about the country but also 'how to treat the [English] Secretary of State like a dog'. It is to Wellington's credit that, in fact, he showed a long-suffering understanding of the problems of his political masters rare in a soldier.

Wellington had studied not only his allies. He had views on the weakness of the enemy. The French had conquered Europe by the speed of their advances and the audacious fierceness of their onslaughts in battle. Their speed derived from their abandonment of eighteenth-century orthodoxy with regard to the supply and servicing of an army. The new French armies lived off the country and slept in branch-woven bivouacs. Travelling light, they could appear where they were not expected: requisitioning their food they could make the occupied territories support them. The weakness which Wellington perceived in the heart of this brilliance was that the new-style French army paid for its marching prowess by an inability to stay still. A massive army speedily cleared all movable food in an area of twenty miles around it, and could not reach farther afield without moving its whole body. Therefore one answer to French tactics would be to compel them to undertake drawn-out

---

[1] See above, p. 379.

operations. Relying upon the old method of establishing depots for supplies, Wellington's army would be better able to play a waiting game. Two further advantages he would have in the matter of supply. He had the support of Spanish and Portuguese armies, with their local knowledge: he had also the good-will of village populations whom, unlike the French, he paid promptly for goods and to whom he came as a deliverer. Command of the sea also enabled him to supply his armies from a line of ports parallel to that of his advance when he finally moved northwards.

Wellington did not hope to defeat the French by playing only on their need to be ever moving. He wished to be able to move himself so that his small force might constantly threaten the lines of communication of the unwieldy mass opposed to him.[1] This again depended upon the organization of his food supplies. British soldiers could not advance without rations, 1 lb. of meat, 1½ lb. of bread, and a pint of wine per man per day. Nor were British soldiers, in his view, capable of carrying rations for several days: at most a couple of days' supply could be distributed at any one time. But if thus regularly fed his troops would then possess a manœuvrability which might embarrass the French. In fact the troops, when advancing, marched in the morning until noon. They would have covered some 15 miles. The bullock carts would catch up with them at their halt: then came dinner and the preparation of a camp, with staff conferences for the officers. At their most pressed pace the army could not exceed 20 miles in a day. This was slow. But their object was rarely to try and catch the main enemy forces and overwhelm them. On the contrary, Wellington proposed to engage in a war of delicate manœuvre whose object was to strike hard blows at any unguarded spot in the enemy's defence. The merit of this method of supply was that, given exact planning, it made it possible for him to concentrate a hard striking force for an attack at any time whereas the French had to disperse to live and were gathered together for fierce battles for a short period of time only. Thus Wellington three times won tactical struggles simply by waiting until the French had to disperse: often concentration more than counterbalanced his smallness in numbers.

For manœuvre, more is needed than food and ammunition. Wellington's organization of his staff was a vital part of his plan.

[1] On this subject see S. G. P. Ward, *Wellington's Headquarters, passim.*

Only two[1] of them were ever of his own selection. He would have had a more aristocratic staff if he had had a free choice. The war office gave him men from the duke of York's training establishment for officers (at High Wycombe) whom he often despised. But he made them work, and he made them completely subservient to himself. These young men (Wellington at forty was several years older than his senior assistants[2]) were set to organize routes for the army in the peninsula. By 1812 there were thirty-seven supply depots with officers posted-out to administer them. Further outposted officers worked with Spanish and Portuguese friends to establish a web of espionage which brought to the British commander details of the enemy activity. To move armies in Spain is always dangerous because of the mountainous nature of the interior. But man had not, until Wellington, reduced this hazard by careful map-reading. His Portuguese allies had few maps. The pitiful state of their mathematical studies in the eighteenth century had resulted in a poverty of cartography. Wellington's officers were set to exploring, calculating, and sketching. By the end of his first eighteen months he had had the whole of Portugal accurately mapped at four miles to the inch. In every advance into Spain the collection of geographical information proceeded. This was to give him an impressive advantage over opposing commanders.

Of his troops Wellington himself sometimes spoke with contempt. But it was the essence of the plan he had formed in 1809 that they should be a more tightly organized force than those which they opposed. The problem, Wellington himself once said, was that in Spain a large force would starve and a small one be beaten. He had a small one, some 30,000 British troops with aid from the Portuguese under British control and some Spanish soldiers as allies. By skilful manœuvre he could avoid being beaten; but to win he must also be able to oppose the French élan with steady resistance, to assault and break troops accustomed to victory all over Europe. By fierce discipline and careful nursing he made his army a highly trained professional team which obeyed him in all emergencies.

When Wellesley landed in 1809, his long-term plans for defeating the French were already forming. But his immediate objective was simply the defence of Portugal. Portugal, he had

---

[1] Colin Campbell and Pakenham.
[2] Murray was 37, Pakenham 35, Fitzroy Somerset 22.

assured the cabinet, though it 'is all frontier' could easily be defended. From Spain, the French would have to follow the desolate
defiles of the rivers Tagus and Doura from west to east. These
invasion routes were commanded by fortresses, Ciudad Rodrigo,
Almeida, and Badajoz. To establish themselves there and advance to the coast the French would need forces three times the
size of the defenders. They could collect such large forces only
at the cost of denuding their armies in Spain and exposing their
communications to the Spanish rebels. But before they could
feel this danger they had to be driven back from northern
Portugal. On 12 May 1809 Wellesley faced Soult across a
ravine on the Doura river. Carelessness by the French enabled
the British to cross unperceived and make a surprise attack. Soult
made a precipitate retreat through the mountains, losing his
guns and 6,000 men. Oporto, and the whole of Portugal, was
thus cleared of the French by one sharp blow.

Wellesley might then reasonably have put into practice his
ideas about holding Portugal's frontiers while he perfected his
plans for further operations in Spain. He decided, however, to
advance into Spain at once. He hoped to take Madrid. This
might have put the French on the defensive everywhere south
of the Pyrenees and have seriously handicapped them in the
war with Austria. The defect of this scheme was, however, that
Wellesley had not had time to make full supply arrangements.
He had to depend upon those of the Spaniards. One Spanish
commander, Cuesta, was aged and self-willed: the other Spanish
general, Venegas, who was required to aim a simultaneous blow
at Madrid from the south-west, was dilatory. The only hope of
the English was that the French would find it impossible to
concentrate their armies in time to parry the first blows. Joseph,
however, did bring a portion of their forces to bar Wellesley's
path, as he came eastwards up the Tagus. At Talavera, July
1809, the battle was bloody, but the victory was British. Nevertheless, Wellesley was halted by it. He now faced the head-on
collision with the main French armies which it had been his
intention to avoid. Ney and Soult were coming down on him
from the north. Already the right bank of the Tagus was closed
behind him by French armies. He would be overwhelmed by
numbers if he did not retreat at once. So he crossed the Tagus
and retired quickly into Portugal, sheltering his despondent and
hungry men behind the fortress of Badajoz. Wellington, for

Talavera earned him his title, had proved to himself that sudden offensives would not do. The Spanish allies were no substitute for food depots. His men were half-starved and blamed the Spanish population. He himself resolved never to rely for his own security upon Cuesta or other Spanish generals. Nevertheless, he had drawn 100,000 French troops to the Tagus and in their absence the north-west of Spain had again risen in arms.

The month of Talavera was also that in which the expedition sailed to the Scheldt. It, too, retired, but without the consolation of a victory. Truly they captured Flushing, but only after a fortnight's siege. This had given time for the defence of Antwerp to be fully prepared. The English landed their troops on the islands of Walcheren and South Beveland. The commanders considered that to throw them on to Antwerp would be suicidal. Chatham embarked most of his men for England in mid-September 1809. The rest remained on Walcheren principally to keep the river open to British trade. Fever decimated them on the marshy island. The British cabinet showed nervous indecision. The expedition had been intended as the opening of a second front in the west against Napoleon. But in July 1809 Austria had been defeated at Wagram and at once opened negotiations for peace. She accepted humiliating terms in September. Thus the British landing lost its original purpose. Were the British to consolidate or evacuate their muddy foothold in the Low Countries? In September they were gathering Flemish peasants to fortify Flushing. In October, building labourers arrived from England with bricks and lime. In November, however, demolition was in full swing. Finally, on 22 December Walcheren was evacuated; nearly half of the force had died or sickened.

The full tide of popular disappointment was aroused against Portland's ministers. Portland himself had a fit and, before the end of the year, was dead. Canning could argue that the events of the summer merely demonstrated the truth of his letter of the previous March. He had opposed both the Walcheren plan and Castlereagh. The latter now at last discovered the plot against him. He called Canning out to a duel on 22 September 1809. Both men resigned their offices. All seemed dissolved. At this dark moment of the war there was no Pitt to ride the storm; only plucky little Perceval trotting down to Windsor, desperately consulting the king about means of making a ministry after this outburst of recrimination and bad temper.

Perceval's aim was to rebuild a government of national unity. Castlereagh and Canning had eliminated each other for the moment. Sidmouth's men were still not favourably regarded by true Pittites after the events of 1800 to 1805; nor did Sidmouth pant to join the dull rump of a ministry which had brought the war into so sad a state. Perceval decided that he must woo the talent—and the parliamentary votes—of the whigs. Lords Grey and Grenville were invited to come and discuss a coalition. But Lord Grey refused even to enter discussions; Grenville, who at first seemed interested, decided to adhere to his ally and turn down the tempter. For this refusal there were several reasons, among them resentment at the king's treatment of the Talents ministry. The king, for his part, had been forced by events to permit an invitation to be extended, but he would never repudiate his demand for silence on the catholic issue. The most that could be hoped was that this issue might be ignored. But behind all points of principle there was a political instinct guiding Grey. He was afraid to join in partnership with men who were stronger than he in their hold on the king, for that way lay either a future quarrel or insignificance. It might even have happened that in office the Grenvillites would have renewed their Pittite friendships: then Grey would have been left to retire, or throw himself into the flailing arms of Whitbread.

All Perceval's ideas of a broader-bottom failed. There was nothing left but to continue on a narrower base even than that of Portland. The vacant ministries were filled with the second-class men who would take them. Lord Wellesley replaced Canning as foreign secretary, Liverpool moved to the war office, and Richard Ryder[1] became home secretary. Perceval himself combined the posts of first lord of the treasury and chancellor of the exchequer. This administration was made up in time to celebrate the 50th anniversary of George III's accession. But the new situation in Europe had a more pressing call upon their attention. Austria had accepted all French demands; after a revolution Sweden had joined the continental system; Russia had taken Finland; the pope was a French prisoner at Avignon. The opposition groups vied with one another in attack on the

---

[1] Richard Ryder (1766–1832), judge advocate general, 1807; held the home office, 1809–12; brother of first earl of Harrowby.

campaign in Spain. The government were told both that it was a silly side show and that they were failing to run it with enough vigour. If any other administration could have been invented, that of Perceval would not have existed. As it was, ministers settled in their offices and were more united, more of a team than hitherto, because they felt their unpopularity and felt, increasingly, how much they depended upon Perceval's courageous skill in the house of commons.

Lord Liverpool showed from his first days at the war office his faith that the peninsular war offered the greatest hope of success. From this no opposition jeers moved him. He asked Wellington, in the autumn of 1809, how many men he would require to hold Portugal. Wellington replied that he needed 3,000 more to make up his requisite 30,000. Liverpool promised him 6,000, but dilated upon the expense of maintaining this force while paying the Portuguese army as well. Wellington was satisfied of his good intentions, yet like everyone else he doubted the capacity of his masters. 'I am convinced that the Government cannot last', he wrote to Liverpool in the spring of 1810, and again, 'I have pressed the strengthening of the Government much against their inclinations'. The government was negotiating all this time with Canning, Sidmouth, and Castlereagh. All these, however, were also convinced that it would not last, and no one boarded the waterlogged ship. The old crew therefore remained and Wellington had to rely upon them.

After a winter of fox-hunting, officers in the field and troops snugly stowed in sound buildings, Wellington prepared to face a major French offensive on Portugal. Peace with Austria had released great quantities of Napoleon's troops for action elsewhere. Many were intended for that massive subjugation of Spain which Sir John Moore had interrupted. Soult went down into Andalusia and ran riot over the south. A large force began the siege of Cadiz, which received British reinforcements. But Masséna in addition was given 70,000 men to reconquer Portugal. Wellington's first concern was to delay this enemy until the harvest had been gathered and stores completed. On the frontiers of Portugal therefore Ciudad Rodrigo and Almeida were told to fight to the end. Craufurd and the Light Division meanwhile skirmished along the frontier to prevent any enemy patrols from ranging ahead and preparing the way for the main forces. By this means Wellington successfully prevented Masséna from making a push into Portugal until late in the summer of 1810. The combined efforts of Ney and Junot, under Masséna, caused the fall of Ciudad Rodrigo in July 1810. Almeida was next invested. The explosion of the main powder magazines in the fort compelled its surrender at the end of August. Wellington the while had his army near enough to keep the French alert but refused to come to the help of the fortress, for that would have meant joining battle on terms which the French desired. After its fall he retired towards Lisbon. As he went his army systematically scorched the earth over which they moved. This operation was grievous to the Portuguese, but was designed to take advantage of the French dependence upon requisitioning.[1] Little was left in the countryside upon which the enemy might live. Nevertheless it was necessary to give the Portuguese hope. A successful engagement would do this. So Wellington halted upon the top of some heathery downs, the Sierra Buzaco, inviting Masséna to try his luck. Up the slope the French obligingly hurried. From the crest they met close volleys. The survivors were jabbed down the slope again by a bayonet charge. It was only a check to the French. But they had lost 4,500 men to Wellington's 1,250.

Masséna tried to hurry on to Coimbra and Lisbon. A second element in Wellington's technique became apparent. He too marched towards Lisbon. But he did so by the shortest route, mapped by the English during the last eight months. The French had no guide in their possession, though they had been in the area before in 1807 to 1808. Using ordinary maps they went by the worst roads and arrived to find Wellington in the best positions before them. The French lost all their wounded and their stores at Coimbra by action of irregular Portuguese bands—a third element in the British strength. Across the Lisbon peninsula Wellington's positions were prepared. The lines of Torres Vedras barred Masséna's advance to the city. The third, innermost line was simply fortifications to cover the harbour for an embarkation in case of need. The two outer lines were really worked as one system. They consisted of natural difficulties elaborated by man. Every hill had been made formidable on its eastern face. Tracks had been barred, stone walls built across the valleys, and water dammed everywhere to flood lines of approach. In October 1810 Masséna sat down in front of these

---

[1] See above, p. 479.

lines of whose existence he had been unaware. It was impossible
to turn them, for they extended to the sea. He never launched
any effective attack upon them. All the difficulties of supplying
a large army began to tell against the French once they were
stationary. To requisition anything in a countryside which had
been devastated demanded detective skill as well as ruthlessness.
The French endured a winter of torment. By March 1811 there
was no course open to them but to drag their way back to the
frontier again through the hills and the marauders. They had
lost 25,000 men.

Throughout this trial by ordeal Liverpool had supported
Wellington manfully. Often he appeared to think that his critics
must be right, that this would be but a protracted evacuation by
gallant but unsuccessful British forces. But whatever he thought,
he always left the military decisions with Wellington. He continued to labour at his desk to find the supplies for him. Political
fortitude as well as military cunning had by 1811 cleared
Portugal.

Portugal though cleared was not secure. The French still held
the three great fortresses, for Soult had found time from plunder-
ing Andalusia to come and take Badajoz. In 1811, therefore,
Wellington's game was to keep in movement, eluding the
efforts of the French to bring him to action when their forces
were combined, seeking the opportunity to fight when he had
local superiority, and aiming all the while at the recapture of
the fortresses. In this country dance of armies the French were
obliged to imitate the English use of food depots. Wellington's
men themselves, on one occasion, outran their camp-followers
and were forced to wait half a week hungrily straining their ears
for the cheerful clatter of the mule trains. In May, Wellington
was blockading Almeida. His force was weakened by his having
detached Beresford to block Soult's army at Badajoz. Masséna
thought he had his opportunity. He fell upon the British at
Fuentes d'Onoro. The battle was Wellington's worst. His right
wing was left unguarded and was driven in. Nevertheless, the
infantry fought in a style which did credit to their training.
They retreated soberly for several miles in formal squares, in
face of the French cavalry. The end of it was that Masséna
gave up pursuit: the British army remained unbroken and
before Almeida. As the French withdrew the fortress fell.
Fuentes d'Onoro therefore was counted a Wellington victory.

He himself preferred to call it an example of French incompetence.[1] Masséna was now replaced by Marmont, the duke of Ragusa.

Within a fortnight of this battle, Beresford was in action with Portuguese troops against Soult away to the south before Badajoz. The battle of Albuerra lacked skill on both sides. In a muddled way the two armies lurched into one another and slogged it out bloodily. The British losses were their heaviest in the peninsula, a quarter of Beresford's force. Both sides lost between 7,000 and 8,000 men. Soult, like Masséna, showed once more that the weakness of the French was in their inability to stand still after a drawn battle. Soult marched off towards Seville. The British tightened their ring around Badajoz and Wellington himself arrived to command the assault. But Badajoz stood massively upon the rocks of the Guadiana. The cannon balls of the besiegers rattled against the castle walls and no breach was made.

The French determined to make another effort to smash opposition with one massive blow. A letter of Soult's was intercepted ordering the assembling of all the force of Estremadura and the advance of Drouet from Toledo. Only Suchet with the army of Catalonia continued undisturbed, systematically reducing the north-east, employing terror, as in the massacre of Tarragona, to cow the Spanish resistance. As Marmont and Soult marched up the valleys into Portugal, Wellington began once more to retire before them. He went across the Agueda and prepared winter quarters for his men in cantonment. This gave the marshals pause. They had no wish to endure another winter in the open in front of a foe who rolled up like a hedgehog. They could not see how to force a fight in the open. They therefore allowed their plan to peter out and made no attempt to reconquer Portugal. Thus at the end of the campaign of 1811, though Wellington had recaptured only one of the frontier fortresses, he still had all Portugal to use as a chess-board, or as a base for offensive operations.

By this time the war-policy of the Perceval government had become firm. They groaned at the cost of keeping the British and Portuguese forces on this basis of perpetual war, but they had resolved to bear it. They had at last put away from them the mirage, which had beckoned on all their predecessors, that

---

[1] 'If Boney had been there, we should have been beat.'

the French might be beaten by one great and sudden master-stroke. Instead they hoped to win by steady and unremitting exertion in the one theatre where there had been any success. They would raise Wellington's force from 30,000 to 40,000: they would send him funds to meet his overdue and depreciated bills to the great Portuguese stores merchants. For the rest, he must wear out the French and give them success in the end. It was a policy which made heavy demands on the loyalty of their supporters, when every retirement was used by the opposition as proof of the folly of the war. In the autumn of 1810 Grey was at his most pacific and was well supplied by Sir Robert Wilson[1] with expert military information. Officers returning to Portugal from leave often told Wellington that either the government would abandon him or would fall. Only in 1811 did the whigs begin to admit that operations in the peninsula might be profitable. But they continued to assume that the French would make no mistakes and that Wellington would only play a waiting role.

In facing the economic crisis of 1811[2] Perceval could be consoled by the knowledge of some success in the European battle. Expansion overseas, moreover, continued, a side-show but an important one for the maintenance of mercantile confidence. All the West Indies were now in British hands or those of friendly Spaniards, except for the negro territory of Haiti. In India in 1811 a palace revolution put the state of Travancore under British influence. A more splendid acquisition was that of Java. Lord Minto in Madras successfully planned the sweeping up of the last vestiges of Dutch power in Indonesia, so long the object of envy. In August 1811 Sir Sam Auchmuty[3] fought his way into Batavia and vigorously asserted control of the whole of Java.

Yet even as the progress of the war seemed to consolidate the Perceval administration, all was thrown into jeopardy by the illness of the king. Princess Amelia, George III's youngest daughter, died in November 1810. The illness of this cherished child reduced the king to the deepest gloom. His madness came upon him once more. The doctors gave optimistic reports, but

[1] Sir Robert Wilson (1777–1849), served in Peninsula, A.D.C. to the King.
[2] See above, pp. 469 f.
[3] Sir Samuel Auchmuty (1756–1822), born in America and volunteered for service as a loyalist; served in India, 1783–97 and 1810–13; commander-in-chief in Ireland, 1821.

he did not emerge from his mania. So on 20 December 1810 Perceval introduced a regency bill, copied from Pitt's bill of 1788.[1] Equally imitative Ponsonby, for the whigs, proposed that the prince of Wales should be accepted as regent by hereditary right. The Regency Act finally passed on 5 February 1811, the royal assent being signified by a commission.[2] The regent was the prince of Wales. For twelve months his powers were to be limited so that no action of a long-lasting character might be taken to which the king might object on his recovery. The king was to resume active power once the queen and her council had notified the privy council of his recovery.

It was expected by everyone that the prince would follow his eighteenth-century predecessors and bring in his friends to re-place those of his father. 'We are all', said young Palmerston, 'on the kick and go.' The prince himself had endured years of political impotence looking forward to the day when he would be revenged upon the court. But there were new factors in the situation since the last change of sovereign. Real issues of prin-ciple existed in politics, principally those of the war and of catholic emancipation, with the reform issue itself only a little below the surface. On the great arguments of the day the prince regent was now on the side of tory thinking. He might attack the tory ministers when he was not in charge of affairs, but once he was in a position where words led to action it was clear that in affairs of state—though not in private life—he had come round to the point of view of any solid country gentleman. He wanted the war to be energetically pushed. He did not want to try experiments at that stage with rights for catholics. He did not feel his old friends were as likely to be sound on these points as his father's ministers. At the same time the prince was not dead to feelings of friendship or at least to the conventional decencies of apparent friendship. His conscience would trouble him if he went straight over from his old friends to those for whom he felt dislike even as he acknowledged the force of their common sense.

All this was but incoherent in the prince's mind. Indeed, he tried to convince himself of his own consistency. So he began by allowing it to be assumed that there was to be a change. There

[1] See above, p. 304.
[2] The authority of the commission itself would not bear a too punctilious legal scrutiny, but that was part of the inherent difficulty of the position.

were difficulties. Grenville's group did not want to serve along with Whitbread. Grenville himself wanted to retain his sinecure post as auditor at the exchequer even if he became first lord of the treasury. The prince uneasily watched the preparations for a complete change. This was more serious than the ejection of a few men, like Perceval, for whom he had a particular dislike. Then on 29 January 1811 the queen sent him a letter with favourable news of the king, who, it was reported, 'gave perfect attention' to a report made to him by Perceval on public business. This was an opportunity to defer action.[1] In spite of the advice of his particular friends, Moira and Sheridan (the latter now a figure of painful fun, politically), the prince informed the whigs that he was going to continue with Perceval's ministry unchanged. This could be defended as filial piety and public-spirited sense. There was no point in making a change if the king's return to activity would reverse it all. Meanwhile the prince satisfied his feelings by being rude to ministers he had decided to retain.

The king did not recover, however. By the autumn of 1811 the prince was weary of Perceval. Relations could not be easy between the puritanical head of the exchequer and a man of taste and tantrums, an aesthete decayed into grossness by habitual self-indulgence. To keep the government respectable and yet to avoid reproach of faithlessness the prince now thought of a new administration which would take in whigs but discipline them. Lord Moira consulted Grey about a reunion but was rebuffed. Then Lord Wellesley, who had always felt himself a cut above his cabinet colleagues, was thought of as head of a Grenvillite government; but Grenville attacked Wellesley's view of the war. By December 1811 the prince, with his debts, his old friends, and his new views, seemed almost as broken as his father: he lay flat on his stomach, bemoaning his physical ills and refusing to do any business.

The restrictions on the regent came to an end on 18 February 1812. After that he had no excuse for not declaring himself. He wanted, as his father had often wanted, a broad-bottomed administration. He did not know, any more than any politician of the time knew, how that could be achieved. On 13 February 1812 he at last stated his intentions in a letter to his brother,

---

[1] The importance of this letter, found in the Windsor archives, is demonstrated by Michael Roberts, *The Whig Party 1807–1812*, p. 368.

the duke of York, which was for the information of Lords Grey and Grenville. His first point was: 'In the critical situation of the war in the Peninsula, I shall be most anxious to avoid any measure which can lead my allies to suppose that I mean to depart from the present system . . . I cannot withhold my approbation from those who have honourably distinguished themselves in support of it.' After this came what can be interpreted either as a gesture to the past, or as wishful thinking for the future—'I cannot conclude without expressing the gratification I should feel if some of those persons with whom the early habits of my public life were formed, would strengthen my hands and constitute a part of my government.' The effect of this letter was to sever the prince's friendship with the whigs. Policy counted for more than persons. All they were offered was a few places on condition that the stiff-necked and unimaginative tories were acknowledged to be right after all. The whigs saw that they must continue to live on locusts in the wilderness after having had their glimpse of the promised land. Wellesley too was a casualty. His dream of leading a new team gone, he resigned his place. This enabled Castlereagh to re-enter the cabinet. In April 1812 Sidmouth (with his friends Vansittart[1] and Bragge) gave the cautious man's verdict on the new look of things: he joined the administration. Only Canning, Grey, Wellesley, and Grenville headed groups locked out, rich in debating points and poor in prospects. Perceval and Liverpool were confirmed in position even if they were neither loved nor admired.

The skill of Perceval was displayed early in 1812 when he piloted the bills for increasing the income of the prince regent through the house of commons.[2] At a time of economic unrest and high costs it was no simple matter to submit as uncontroversial business an increase for a ruler as flamboyantly extravagant as the prince. The opposition on this were led by Tierney, a man who longed for office. But they were handicapped by their past advocacy of the prince's cause. The opposition raised the

---

[1] Nicholas Vansittart, first Baron Bexley (1766–1851), a younger son of Henry Vansittart the governor of Bengal; Irish secretary, 1805; chancellor of the exchequer, 1812–23.

[2] Only on the point of compensating Colonel M'Mahon, formerly the prince's private secretary, so as to keep his mouth shut after his dismissal, did the house revolt. On Wilberforce's motion he was left to the bounty of the prince and not allowed a shameful sinecure (paymaster of widows' pensions) at the public expense.

question of Roman catholic relief in both houses. Here again, though Canning expounded his middle-way between the diehard and the radical solution, the treasury had almost a two to one majority. The progress of war in the peninsula eclipsed all such issues in the eyes of the politically powerful classes, little effect though it had upon the merchants fearing war with America, or the starving frame-breakers in Nottingham.

Wellington had rested his men during the autumn of 1811 while he bombarded ministers with demands for supplies. In December he had received the most important of these, a siege train for his projected offensive. In the heart of winter, on 1 January 1812, he put his army into motion. The enemy garrison was under-manned and unsuspecting, as Wellington rushed forward to the siege of Ciudad Rodrigo. His own men, in wet or icy uniforms, dug away remorselessly at the frozen ground to entrench themselves under the walls. The bombardment then battered two breaches in the walls. On 19 January the British forces stormed their way in through the breaches to capture the second of the key points of the Portuguese frontier. A thousand men were lost, including the dashing Craufurd, whose dying words to Wellington only provoked from him the comment that it was stuff 'one had read of in romances'. Wellington himself wasted neither words nor time. After Ciudad Rodrigo he marched instantly to Badajoz. By March he was attacking it. Here he was not as happy. In April he lost 5,000 men under a downpour of masonry, steel, lead and fire as he vainly tried to storm the great breach. The main attack failed completely. The fortress fell to a surprise move, intended only as a diversion. Picton and the 3rd Division climbed their 20-foot ladders up the walls of the castle. The attackers on the main front were sullenly acknowledging defeat when the shrilling of the British bugles from within announced that the place was theirs. The French troops were treated as honourable prisoners. But the British troops behaved with sickening savagery to the Spanish inhabitants. They burst out from the discipline of their icy commander into a carnival of greed and lust, relieving all their feelings of resentment of the local population and, no doubt, the local weather.

While Wellington had been conducting his two sieges, 80,000 Frenchmen under Marmont and Soult had been trying to collect themselves together. The process was not yet complete by May 1812. The two French armies had the Tagus between them. Hill,[1] on Wellington's command, destroyed the bridge of boats at Almaroz which linked them. To communicate with one another they had to proceed eastwards as far up river as Toledo. Wellington had now achieved his aim of preventing a French concentration. He set about the destruction of his foes in detail. First he wished to deal Marmont a decisive blow. But Marmont was not easily outplayed in manœuvre. From May to late July the two commanders marched and countermarched. French speed forced Wellington to turn back from the Douro to Salamanca. For two days of this operation the two armies were moving feverishly within cannon-shot of one another, a military pageant in choking dust and heat. Then on 22 July Wellington deployed his men for battle south of Salamanca. He watched to see if the French would continue to outflank him, preparing in that case to resume his backward march towards Ciudad Rodrigo. Marmont, in his turn, anticipated such a retirement and pushed out his leading units to cut the line for retreat. This extended his front very dangerously. Wellington perceived the French weakness. Pakenham was ordered to attack the isolated division. Thus the battle of Salamanca opened piecemeal. The French never recovered from their opening disadvantage: their flank was shattered, their centre driven in and Marmont wounded. After weeks of elaborate manœuvre a decisive result had been reached by one direct blow in 40 minutes' fighting. The French lost 14,000 to the British 5,000. The broken enemy remnants straggled back towards Burgos, the Pyrenees, and France.

After this triumph the road to Madrid was open. Joseph was driven from the capital and Wellington entered Madrid as a liberator. Soult was in Andalusia, Joseph had retired to Catalonia, the army of Portugal was being regrouped at Burgos. Wellington had triumphantly demonstrated how a compact force might disintegrate the great masses of the French. The Spanish irregulars had their chance to gnaw at them in their sprawling dismay. Wellington hoped that in Catalonia and Andalusia the French would be fully occupied. He turned north-east to Burgos leaving the dependable Hill with a garrison in Madrid. His purpose was to destroy the French guard upon

[1] Rowland Hill, first Viscount Hill (1772-1842).

their main route through the mountains into Spain and win the peninsula by isolating the other armies so that they might be withered and chipped to pieces. This attempt at a decisive stroke was not sufficiently prepared. The men outran the transports. The mules with guns and ammunition were left behind as he came up to the castle at Burgos. Nor did he find that he could make up for material shortage with disciplined courage. The best men had been left at Madrid. The futile siege of the small castle continued until Wellington had lost the advantages of his mobility. By October the French in the area had recovered their spirits. Soult, from Andalusia, and Joseph from Catalonia, were approaching Madrid and it seemed possible that the French might yet force on the sort of grand engagement which best suited them. Hill, however, was recalled from Madrid in time. He joined Wellington and the reunited army worked a weary way back through Salamanca and Ciudad Rodrigo into Portugal. There Wellington settled them in cantonments for the winter. The retreat had cost them 4,000 lost stragglers. Wellington roundly condemned his army. Its decline in discipline he declared was the greatest ever known because its officers had been habitually inattentive to their duty.

Wellington's harsh general order relieved his feelings of disappointment. He had seen final victory in Spain in sight and had then had to winter once more in Portugal. But his own comments were not a true assessment of the situation. Immediate victory had eluded them, but as surely ultimate victory was now prepared. The French had lost 20,000 prisoners, 3,000 guns, and all their piled stores in Madrid. The French, in the efforts against Wellington, had given up all the country south of the Tagus. Everywhere the Spanish were on the move, not only as guerrillas, but as an organized country in arms. Wellington had been appointed commander-in-chief of the Spanish armies and the Cortes in session at Cadiz had promised him that he should appoint and dismiss the officers of their army. More important than this was the fact that the French were no nearer solving the problem of strategy which they had been set. They had discovered no means of organizing their numbers so as to deal a mortal blow: nor had they discovered how to keep those numbers on any organized basis which could prevent Wellington from inflicting such a series of defeats upon them as to bring on their collapse.

Napoleon at the very outset of this year, January 1812, had shown by his movement of 20,000 men into Swedish Pomerania that he was about to quarrel with Russia. By April he had addressed his formal letter of complaint against Russian failure to abide by the Treaty of Tilsit. Before Wellington had fought Salamanca, Napoleon was busy on the crossing of the Niemen for the most grand-scale of his wars, the Moscow campaign. It is therefore true that the French could not hope for reinforcement in Spain unless there was first a triumph in Russia. But this was not the whole of the story. Napoleon himself, by personal genius in direction, might have been able to give events in Spain a new shift and dent the British victory. But it would, in that case, be Napoleon and not numbers that would make the change. As clearly as military events ever can be foretold, it could be said by 1812 that Wellington had made eventual victory in Spain only a matter of time. Their very size was exhausting the French, like a heavyweight boxer, unable to punch, wearily sagging in the ring. If they were forced back into France it remained to be seen whether a beaten army, living on its own villages, might not undermine the basis of that régime against which England had fought so long.

Napoleon offered peace once more in the early summer of 1812. It was to be on the basis that France would renounce all influence in Spain: that country should be ruled on constitutional lines with her Cortes but that 'the present dynasty' should remain on the throne. Lord Castlereagh firmly declined to discuss any proposal that Joseph should remain in Spain. Napoleon made his overture as part of the preliminaries for war with Russia, the event of 1812 which was to make the greatest difference to the long English struggle. The agreement for France and Russia to hold a condominium over the world had never worked because neither party could see the other make any gain without fearing for its security. Russia complained that French interference in central Europe was aggressive. She demanded that France should cease to control Prussia, to influence Poland, to intrigue in Sweden. Napoleon for his part complained of Russian hostility in Oldenburg: he was never willing to see Russia gain control at Constantinople. He never forgave the ukase of 1810 by which the tsar, for the sake of the luxury of Russian trade and contacts with the outside world, allowed English goods (in neutral ships) into Russian ports and so back into European circulation. Napoleon determined to win his war with England by humbling the only other great power still possessing independence. He assembled the grand army 700,000 strong, 400,000 of them collected from Italy, Poland, Germany, and the subject peoples. He had hoped to fight in Poland but the Russians, by waiting, forced him to invade. He was unopposed as far as Smolensk. After a victory here, and an indecisive slaughter at Borodino, he occupied Moscow on 14 September 1812. By refusing to parley or to fight in the open the Russians forced Napoleon to his nightmare retreat. In this French defects in supply were once more, and catastrophically, apparent. By 5 December Napoleon was back in Paris. He had lost 400,000 men dead or wounded and 100,000 prisoners.

In the course of the campaign Alexander had, naturally, made peace with England and he had handed over his fleet to co-operate with her. The opening of a new front, the gain of a friend in the struggle, these in themselves would have given new hope to the English cabinet. But by the end of 1812 there was this additional and overwhelming fact, that the grand army had ceased to exist. Napoleon dreamed of making a new army. But he had to begin by shooting French officers in Paris who had intrigued, in his absence, to overthrow him. The new and final stages of the war with France had begun. The outlook in Europe was more promising for England than at any time since 1793.

The hold-fast policy of Perceval and George III had been justified by events. But neither of them was able to rejoice in the fact. Perceval, from February of 1812, was becoming generally acknowledged for what he was, the undramatic exponent of the policy upon which the English ruling class were agreed. So during March and April he grew in strength. Then on 11 May 1812, at about 5 in the evening, Perceval was making his way through the lobby of the house of commons when a man called Bellingham came up to him and fired a pistol. The bullet entered the left breast and pierced the heart. Bellingham was a commercial agent, ruined by the economic war, who had been pestering government offices vainly for redress and now crazily attempted to revenge himself. The death of Perceval did nothing to expedite the repeal of the orders in council. It simply produced yet another ministerial crisis.

The prince was put into the position in which his father had been so often earlier in the reign. There was a generally accepted, if imperfectly expressed, patriotic line among independent members of parliament. With this line the prince himself was in agreement. But to express such an agreed policy in actual executive government required the co-operation of many group-leaders among the men of ministerial calibre. From this class, past quarrels and future ambitions made it difficult to fit together enough leaders to form a durable cabinet. As Lord Wellesley told the house of lords, 'the most dreadful personal animosities, and the most terrible difficulties arising out of questions the most complicated and important . . . interposed obstacles to an arrangement so essential to the public welfare'. The truth of this was clearly revealed in the prince's first overtures. He tried to persuade Canning and Wellesley to rejoin the government which would then be a blend of all types of toryism. But Canning disliked Castlereagh and Sidmouth too much to work with them on any terms but those of a master. He gave as a more official ground for refusal that he did not believe that Liverpool's attitude to the catholic cause was a tenable one. Wellesley would not weaken his friendship with Canning, not at least unless he was given a chance of the highest place.

The cabinet jogged on, after this rebuff to the regent, for a few days. But the house of commons was not satisfied with this situation. The whigs naturally cried that the death of Perceval had made a foolish cabinet into an imbecile one. They mocked at Vansittart as the new chancellor of the exchequer. And those who had admired the steadiness of Perceval's rule also joined in the attack. In a great war the independent member was not going to complain of the power of the executive: just the opposite. On 21 May 1812 Mr. Stuart Wortley, an independent member who had been a follower of Perceval and an admirer of Canning, as far as he had accepted any leadership, moved that an address should be presented to the prince regent, begging him to take steps to form an efficient administration. The house went on to decide that this address should be presented not by privy councillors, but by Mr. Wortley and Lord Milton. This was a revolt of the back-benchers who wanted efficient administration against the men of ministerial rank, who alone could supply the want but whose intricate quarrels prevented action. Even great masters of influence and acres, like Lord

Grey, would fail to take notice of this sentiment at their peril. The Liverpool administration, in deference to this vote of no-confidence, resigned.

For a fortnight there was busy negotiation between all leaders. Canning asked for two planks in any programme—the active prosecution of the Peninsular War and an immediate tackling of the catholic question. Grenville asked for catholic relief and a cut in public expenditure, even if it meant looking more narrowly at war expenditure. Wellesley hoped to form a government with Canning, the whigs and some tories: but he needlessly wounded tory feelings by publishing criticism of Liverpool and the deceased Perceval. The regent did not relish the idea of opening the catholic question at once and for some time avoided giving Wellesley any authority to carry on negotiations. At length, however, Wellesley made offers to Grey and Grenville. They were turned down, in the main because the whigs, as the largest compact group in parliament, did not feel that they were obliged to take part in a coalition which would cramp them and in which the regent, with all the initiative of the Crown, would throw his weight against them in any dispute. They also resented the indirectness of the approach through Canning and Wellesley. 'This is capital,' wrote the whig gossip Creevey,[1] 'two fellows without an acre of land between them . . . condescend to offer to Earl Grey of spotless character, followed by the Russells and Cavendishes, by all the ancient nobility and all the great property of the realm and by an unshaken phalanx of 150 of the best men in Parliament . . . four seats in the Cabinet to him and his friends.' It is easy to condemn the whigs for their stiff-necked attitude. But the coalition with Sidmouth in the Talents was a warning of the difficulties of coalesced cabinets. Canning might be co-operative on the catholic question. But on cancelling the orders in council the whigs feared—needlessly as was to be proved later in the year—to be in a minority.

After Wellesley, Moira, the ex-governor general of India, a prince's friend and an independent whig, essayed to unite Canning, Wellesley, Eldon, Erskine, Liverpool, the whig Lords, and Whitbread. With Whitbread he sketched a more radical

[1] Thomas Creevey (1768–1838), an indefatigable politician about town and scribbler of political gossip, selections from whose letters and papers have been published by Sir H. Maxwell and by John Gore.

programme than any yet outlined. The orders in council were to be revoked, America would be conciliated, and parliamentary reform explored. Much of this was sensible. It was of the highest importance to amend the blockade before the Americans declared war. It would have been of the greatest value to embark on reform before bitterness had grown with distress. But it was irrelevant to the problem of politics at that moment. Moira's conversations broke down nominally because the whigs believed that the prince would not agree to change some officers of the household—though apparently he had in fact agreed to do this. But this was a symptom of the real disease. The whigs did not trust the regent: he did not, in his heart, want them. Moira could have swept away this mutual suspicion only if he had been a man of dynamic purpose and courage who could command both parties to work with him in the national emergency. As it was, he mildly retired from the argument.

By 8 June 1812 many patterns had been sketched but none had been accepted. The prince regent therefore asked Liverpool to resume with his ministry as it had been before the crisis began on 21 May: as it had been, that is, in matters of personnel. In parliamentary strength it had become immensely stronger. There was much to be said for the whig point of view as for that of Canning. But it was not clearly said at the time. To the unattached observer it appeared that Liverpool alone had acted with patriotic reasonableness. The other leading politicians appeared to put particular projects—or their own pride—above the real national interest. It seemed to be clearly demonstrated that so long as this was so there was no alternative to Liverpool, none at least which would continue the war on the right lines while leaving all else undisturbed. The back-bencher who had supported Wortley's critical motion in May now, out of the same desire for the best administration, would support Liverpool. He had resigned as a man blocking the way with an inferior cabinet: he came back as the indispensable co-ordinator of a cabinet of national effort. As such he was to remain in power until his stroke fifteen years later.

There were, indeed, two elements in Liverpool's policy as it was formulated in the testing weeks following Perceval's assassination and in his next years in power. On foreign policy, including the war, he remained the symbol of decision. Without counting the economic cost overmuch, the cabinet drove on

with the war, rejoicing in Wellington's exploits, welcoming the
titanic Russian war, enduring the outbreak of hostilities with
the United States. Already by the end of 1812 they could find
encouragement in the results. In the domestic field, on the
other hand, Liverpool stood not for decision, but for drifting.
On the great issues of the day he came, encouraged thereto by
the regent, to adopt an easy-going attitude. He believed that
men of very different opinions could serve together if only they
retained a sense of proportion. On the catholic question, on
reform, on economic distress, this government had, as such, no
policy: all depended upon the strength of the ministers of the
several departments concerned. Thus the government combined fixed aims with vagueness, and each contributed to its
success: it combined a positive effort to win the war with a
negative attitude to home affairs. For in the eyes of those who
served in it, the composition of parliament, or destitution in the
north, were alike minor questions when put alongside the defeat
of Napoleon and the preservation of orderly society in England.
It was the success of this conservative attitude which marked
the politics of the concluding years of George III.

It might well be argued that George III's reign was already
over when Liverpool formed his cabinet. From his madness at
the end of 1810 he did not recover, save momentarily and in
private. The unrestricted regency seemed to release many pent-
up forces, to make a new period in politics, in social life, as well
as in the war. Characteristically the regent celebrated his new
status with style but bad taste. On 18 June 1811 a grand party
in Carlton House marked—prematurely—the change in power.
All the royalty of Europe—such easily available guests, as they
were all in exile—crowded round the long tables down whose
centre a miniature canal, banked with flowers and moss and
filled with gold and silver fish, reflected all the feathers, the
jewels, the gestures, and the lights. Out of mind was the world
of rigid etiquette, draughty rooms, grotesque piety, early rising,
and painful endurance. That was the world of a poor old mad-
man who reviewed imaginary troops in the darkness and wept
or gnashed his gums in rage, a rage no longer rooted in events
of the real and unkind world. The old king was in his strait
jacket: the prince in his corsets seemed to rule a new kind of
England. Indeed this was not mere seeming. For in the years
since the war had begun in 1793 England had, in manners, arts,

economics, and thought, been revolutionized. The frothy exuberance, the shocking wildness of the regency, just like the desperate movements of discontent, were all simply the surface manifestations of the profound changes which had been taking place.

XX

THE TRANSFORMATION OF ECONOMIC AND CULTURAL LIFE
1793–1815

B Y 1813 the end of the war was coming into sight. Britain had succeeded in her twenty-year task of resisting the ideological armies of revolutionary France. Yet while doing so she had herself entered upon a process of transformation. The economic changes which had been gathering force in the eighties[1] had gained momentum until their effects could be detected over a field wider than the economic. Outwardly the world of politics looked resistant to change. The cabinet of Lord Liverpool was almost as aristocratic as that of Lord Rockingham: neither the madness of George III nor the profligacy of the regent imperilled the security of the throne. Nevertheless it could be claimed that England had been reorientated by economic forces more radically than France by the guillotine and the Code of Napoleon. Merchants of Liverpool did not underestimate their own contribution to the war effort. Manufacturers of Manchester, whatever their attitude to parliamentary reform, were no longer content to accept the opinions of their social superiors. Numerically the hard-faced business men were a minority in the community; statistically the industries which had been mechanized were a small part of the whole; over most of the country the system of local government was unshaken as in 1760: Colquhoun's classification of society[2] revealed that the hold of the old ruling classes had not been broken. Nevertheless new economic developments had an effect greater than statistics can reveal. The sense of the future magnitude of the new powers affected the imagination of men in advance of their full realization. So the foundations of social life, mirrored in the way men approached literature, philosophy, in their religion, manners, and dress, were already under drastic revision before the end of the war. France for long enjoyed a

---

[1] See above, p. 332.   [2] Discussed above, see pp. 335 f.

reputation as the home of revolutionary ideas of government. But it was in England that forces which were to reshape all the rest of the world were generated. The new attitude to life was, save in literature, little more than a vague feeling in 1815. It was felt in uneasy hearts, mirrored in hectic gaiety or sullen misery; it was marked boldly on the face of some areas of the countryside, but it was not fully understood. Even in retrospect while its progress may be charted its causes remain difficult to assess.

The causes of any such change are likely to be manifold. England's advantages—good transport facilities, accumulated capital, expanding overseas trade, cheap money, inventiveness[1] —had already resulted in advances in the eighties. A snowballing effect was produced. With confident expectation of future gains the changes were ever accelerating. The end of Lord North's American war had shown that both business men and the government were resourceful. The difficulties of going from war to peace had been met by finding new markets and opportunities. Pitt's commercial treaty with France and the beginning of the building of iron bridges may be taken as symbols of this elasticity of mind. In the decade before 1793 there was ample capital available and a shortage of labour. Nothing would be more encouraging to the use of labour-saving inventions. Not that all inventions were labour-saving. Some economized with power or materials, as when the steam-engine made factories less dependent on running water. Many inventions saved circulating capital. Instead of having a large amount of money permanently locked up in a fund for paying labour it could be an advantage to sink money in a down payment on a machine which would release money as well as labour.

When all is said about these forces for change already operating before 1793 it must still be admitted that the war with France gave a jerk to the economy. For many manufacturers it presented a crisis, a loss of old markets: they were forced to devise swift remedies or to cease business. The rise in food prices as a result of war drove up the demands of labour. This in turn increased the stimulus to efficiency in production. If wages, subsistence wages, of unskilled labour became higher the employer would find it a better bargain to employ fewer, more highly paid, possibly more skilled, men on a mechanized

[1] Discussed above, see p. 332.

process. The wage bill would be reduced even while wage-rates were increased. It was in machine-minded Lancashire that wages, by the end of the eighteenth century, had most rapidly increased.[1] In general British producers and merchants showed initiative and resourcefulness in meeting war-time changes. Given such a spirit difficulties could be turned into advantages: men were forced to do quickly what might otherwise have seemed a hazardous experiment to be undertaken only after much delay.

More particularly, however, war immediately stimulated one industry, that of iron and steel. This had great consequences for all the rest. The demand for munitions at once encouraged an increase in output of iron. The output of pig-iron in Great Britain in 1788 was 68,000 tons. In 1796 it was, for England and Wales alone, 125,000 tons, and a few thousand tons must be added for Scotland's contribution. In 1806 the British total had swollen to 258,000 tons. The extraction of such quantities from the ore was possible because the use of coke in blast furnaces was already known and the whole industry took it up as demand increased. Similarly the addition of limestone as a reagent during smelting, to improve the product, became universal. Expansion of the industry was also aided by improving the bellows of furnaces with the application of a double-acting blowing cylinder driven by Watt's steam-engine. With such progress in pig-iron the multiplication of cast-iron products from the foundries was made possible.

In the further process, that of refining to produce bar-iron, Cort's system (as has been mentioned above[2]) had already solved the main technical problems. The iron, under his process, was first heated and then put into a reverberatory furnace together with clinkers containing oxides of iron; when the carbon had been driven out the purified metal was collected, hammered, and passed through a rolling mill. Technical men such as Watt had supported him as early as 1782. But men of business were slow to take up his 'puddling' process. Even so from 1786 contracts were being made for the use of Cort's method, paying a royalty to him of 10s. a ton. At the end of

---

[1] Admittedly scarcity of labour, the newness of Lancashire industry, had their effects in producing this rise. Admittedly also a considerable amount of unskilled labour was employed in setting up and operating the mills. See T. S. Ashton, *Economic History of England in the Eighteenth Century*, p. 232.

[2] See above, p. 332.

1789 disaster befell Cort personally. His partner's father was found to be guilty of embezzlement in the government service and brought to ruin and suicide. Cort's own finances were involved with those of the dead man. He lost everything including his patent.[1] Disastrous for him, this was good luck for the industry. Manufacturers no longer had the cost of royalties to deter them from general adoption of the process. Once it was in extensive use—and it quickly became general in Wales—important improvements were made in it, particularly by the Homfrays of Pen-y-Darran. At Richard Crawshay's works at Cyfarthfa the output of good bar-iron rose from 10 to 200 tons a week.

The development of the steel industry was less dramatic. Here too, however, the use of the latest process, Huntsman's crucible,[2] was rapidly taken up in the 1790's. It was from 1793 that Boulton's firm placed a regular order for cast steel and it appears that from 1799 onwards steel was being bought to make the cutting and boring tools for Watt's new machines.[3]

It was not only by increasing demand that war contributed to the advance of iron and steel; it also diminished the supply from abroad. Earlier in the century bar-iron from Russia and Sweden had been essential to England. It had been superior to the home-produced. But in 1796 the price of iron coming from the Baltic rose by 30 per cent. Russian iron soon doubled in price. The supply, at any price, was uncertain, and imports fell spasmodically. The amount of foreign iron retained for home consumption fell in 1803 to 18,682 tons (as compared with figures of 30,000 to 45,000 in previous years): after 1805 the figure only once exceeded 18,000 tons and fell as low, on occasion, as 7,361 tons.[4] Forty-seven new blast furnaces came into operation in Britain between 1801 and 1803. By 1812 it was claimed that she had become a net exporter of iron. From 1803, for the first time, government departments used British iron instead of Russian even for the most exacting requirements of the services. This was official recognition of the ability of the home industry to meet all demands as regards quality as well as quantity.

[1] Cort was given a small pension by Pitt: a public subscription was later raised for his widow which brought in £871. 10s.
[2] Perfected about 1750, see above, p. 31.
[3] T. S. Ashton, *Iron and Steel in the Industrial Revolution*, pp. 58, 59.
[4] Ibid., p. 147.

The anxiety of the iron-masters was not whether they could meet the demand but about the danger of over-production. War cut off foreign competition but it also intermittently blocked markets for the export of metal manufactures. Iron and steel goods for Europe had to be smuggled in through Hamburg in 1807 and through Malta in 1811. The most serious crisis, of course, for iron as for all other products, was that of 1811. In 1800 it has been estimated that iron was made up in Birmingham into articles worth £2 million in the year. Of these £1 million worth were sold at home, £200,000 worth went to Europe, and £800,000 worth (nails being an important item) were shipped to the United States.[1] The non-intercourse period, following disputes about the orders in council,[2] therefore had the immediate effect of putting 9,000 Birmingham workers on to poor relief in 1811. By 1812 the ironmasters, in their turn, experienced a slackening of demand for their material. The Coalbrookdale company decided to extinguish a furnace. The Sheffield steel industry worked through 1812 at half capacity.

That the iron industry could continue its general expansion despite such set-backs—as it had survived the cessation of war demand in the period of the peace of Amiens—can be explained by its wise cultivation of the home market. It is at this point that the importance of iron to the expansion of all other industry becomes clear. The use of iron for bridges was the most famous example of selling the product for new uses. The 1776 Severn Bridge was followed by those at Sunderland in 1796 and at Brossley on Severn in 1797. In 1787 the first boat built of metal plates was completed and went into service in inland navigation. John Wilkinson made himself a one-man exhibition of the possibilities of a material which was now available in such quantity and so cheaply (for increasing efficiency had lowered the price from £20 to £12 a ton). Wilkinson made himself iron chairs, he talked of iron houses, he made pipes and vats of iron for breweries, he was buried in an iron coffin. From 1812 the infant gas industry was supplied with iron pipes. Iron wheels, successfully made by Rennie, were brought into general use. Wilkinson improved the reverberatory furnace with a cupola and produced iron which was less liable to break and hence more

---

[1] T. S. Ashton, *Iron and Steel in the Industrial Revolution*, p. 150 (the estimates are those of Attwood).
[2] See above, pp. 474 f.

suitable for machine-making. The invention by Maudsley of a carriage lathe in 1797, and his development of a machine for cutting screws, increased yet further the use of iron products. So too did Clifford's nail-maker of 1790.

Hence when Watt's patents for his steam-engine expired in 1800 the iron industry stood ready to serve all industries requiring the new power. The revolution in economic life was made possible by the use of the steam-engine: this in turn depended upon good metal in cheap supply. As textiles expanded, so new forges—for example, those of Bateman and Sherrett at Salford —opened up all over Lancashire to supply the tools of the mills. In 1800 there were 84 steam-engines in Lancashire (32 of them, total horsepower 430, in Manchester), but this number was soon multiplied many times. Perhaps the most significant use of the new machinery was in the iron industry itself. For when machines were used in the making of machines a new era had arrived. The mechanical hammer, striking 150 blows a minute by steam-power as it turned out metal from which other machines might be made, was a symbol of a revolution begun.

The iron and steel industry had always been on a larger scale than most industries. The Carron and Clyde works consumed as much coal as the whole city of Edinburgh. Metal-working Birmingham, on the other hand, remained in 1815 an area of small workshops. Yet the use of steam-power was felt here as in the great forges. By 1815 half the power in the area came from the new engines. The uses of the steam-engine to turn a wheel or a belt were apparently inexhaustible. Nowhere were the effects more striking than in the new cotton industry.[1]

The cotton industry was, to all intents and purposes, new in England. Its expansion was therefore unhampered by prejudices and vested interests. At the accession of George III about 3 million lb. of raw cotton was being imported.[2] Ten years later 4¾ million lb. were annually imported. In 1781 the figure was 5,300,000 lb. There then began the first great expansion. In 1789, 32½ million lb. were imported. This first stage of development was concerned neither with steam nor metal. The produc-

---

[1] Boulton and Watt had built 289 engines up to 1800, 104 of them for the textile industry, 58 for mines, 31 for canal and water pumping, 30 for metallurgy, and 23 for breweries.

[2] Raw cotton, until 1790, came to England mostly from the West Indies and South America. It was Elias Whitney's invention of the cotton gin in 1793 which enabled the United States to become the main supplier.

tion of cotton goods is, of course, in two parts, the spinning of
the thread and the weaving of the fabric. It took five or six
spinners with the old spinning-wheels to produce the thread to
keep one weaver employed. It was not possible to expand the
production without increasing the amount of thread. Furthermore the chief handicap of England in competition with Indian
muslins was the inferiority of the English thread. The first improvements, Hargreave's jenny, Arkwright's water-frame,
Crompton's mule—which have been described above[1]—were
therefore all concerned with spinning. The mule had not been
patented. Arkwright's patent for the idea of the water-frame
was upset in the courts in 1785 when it was forcefully urged
that the invention was not his at all.[2] From 1785 onwards,
therefore, all manufacturers were free to use the machines of
Arkwright or of Crompton. From 1783 the use of metal rollers
and wheels in the mule greatly increased its reliability. The
final stage, the application of steam instead of water-power,
followed quickly. Thus high imports of raw cotton in 1789 were
a response to the demand of the new spinning capacity. So great
was the change in balance of the industry that weavers were
now unable to deal with the supply available. By 1790 wages of
weavers had risen because there was a shortage of them. Some
cotton thread had to be exported for weaving abroad because
there was not enough capacity at home. The Bolton weavers, exploiting this position, were the aristocrats of the street corners,
sticking £5 notes in their hatbands to show off their wealth.

The outbreak of war at first affected cotton harshly. The loss
of markets, a break in confidence for the future, was enough to
shake the fortunes of many new spinning mills. There was a
financial crisis in the industry and much talk of over-production.
Yet by 1798 imports of raw cotton were up again to 32 million
lb. They then rose steadily to 43 million lb. in 1799, 56 million
lb. in 1800 and 60½ million lb. in 1802. The same story appears
in export figures for made-up cotton cloth. Here the main
expansion is all subsequent to 1785. Before that date exports
had not been more than about £⅓ million. From £1 million
worth in 1785 they mounted to £5½ million in 1800, and over
£7¾ million in 1802.

---

[1] See pp. 332, 333.
[2] Arkwright's talent was for the organization and exploitation of ideas, he was
a business man not an original genius.

The continental system, as has been described,[1] drove British merchants to seek markets in such areas as South America to compensate for difficulties in Europe. The Lancashire cotton manufacturers were particularly prominent in such a move. 1810 more than doubled the imports of raw cotton of 1806; 123 million lb. were imported: after that the figure fell back to a steady level of rather more than 50 million lb. for the rest of the period. The exports of finished cotton rose to almost £13 million in 1808, to £18½ million in 1809, remained at £18 million in 1810 and then receded to £11¾ million in 1811.[2] Meanwhile the effects of mass production were seen in prices; at the time of generally rising prices, 1792 to 1799, the price of muslins fell from 3s. to 1s. 2d. a piece.

The explanation of these figures is that the disequilibrium between spinning and weaving had been corrected. The ingenious Dr. Cartwright, a Leicestershire rector, after discussion with friends in industry, set to work and in 1785 patented a machine for power weaving. After successive improvements this power loom, worked by steam, became a commercial proposition when Monteith opened a factory with 200 looms at Pollockshaws near Glasgow in 1801.[3] From 1803 Horrocks of Stockport were opening up factories with all-metal, steam-operated, power looms. Weavers' wages declined from the scarcity rates found at the end of the eighteenth century: the average Lancashire weaver's wage-rate in 1800 was 13s. 3d. a week, in 1802 13s. 10d.; in 1806 10s. 6d.; in 1808 6s. 7d.; and in 1812 6s. 4d., and this was before the effects of the post-war slump were felt.[4] Weaving, even so, was still less clearly a factory occupation than spinning in 1815. The number of those working the old hand looms did not decline. The employer only mechanized weaving to meet the steady demand which could be calculated when budgeting to meet loan charges and overhead costs. For special lines of exceptional quality, and for exceptional demand of all sorts, in an industry where consumption was always seasonal and subject to the vagaries of fashion,

---

[1] See above, pp. 463 f.

[2] Figures from W. Smart, *Economic Annals of the Nineteenth Century*, i (1801–20), pp. 13, 127, 203, 361, 395, 396.

[3] Dr. Cartwright himself opened a factory at Doncaster, shortly after becoming prebendary of Lincoln in 1786, but it did not prosper.

[4] Figures from W. Smart, *Economic Annals of the Nineteenth Century*, i (1801–20), p. 595.

he preferred to make use of hand-loom labour which could be employed by the job. The great firm of Horrocks, Miller & Company of Preston in 1816 employed 700 spinners in four factories while their weavers, to the number of 7,000, were spread over the whole countryside. This peculiarity of weaving was seen in silk as well as cotton. The old-established hand-loom weavers of Spitalfields enjoyed new prosperity while war protected them from French competition: even in the new and thrusting silk industry in Macclesfield, a man like Ayton had half his employees in his factory, the other half at home weaving by hand.[1] The lot of hand-loom weavers became wretched directly any change in the market forced them from their normal role of complimenting to that of competing with the machines.

Cartwright's invention—which ruined him personally—nevertheless completed the building up of the modern cotton industry. The new methods of bleaching (1790), the new dyes (1790) and mechanical printing (1783), like Bramah's[2] hydraulic press for packing (1795) were but additions to the strength of the industry. It was still possible for a man of vigour to rise from nothing to be a great entrepreneur, as witness Robert Owen's beginnings on £100 of borrowed capital in 1789;[3] but already some great business kings had made themselves supreme in new towns of Lancashire—Oldknow in Stockport, Horrocks in Preston, Robert Peel in Bury. Peel employed almost the whole population of Bury spinning, dyeing, and printing in his factories: surrounding villages were busy weaving for him. Already in 1802 he employed 15,000 people in all and paid £40,000 in excise duties to the government. Such men ruled the lives of a new population. Lancashire (and even more Lanarkshire) was like a frontier colony being rapidly opened up and populated. Manchester had 50,000 inhabitants in 1790, but by 1815 there were over 100,000. Oldham grew from between 300 and 400 inhabitants in 1760 to some 12,000 in 1801—and 20,000 more

---

[1] J. H. Clapham, *Economic History of Modern Britain, The Early Railway Age* (1950 edn.), pp. 185 and 197.

[2] Joseph Bramah was the most versatile of inventors and his discoveries ranged from those in metal engineering, through locks for safes to the beer engine and the water-closet. Against this his rival in ingenuity, Dr. Cartwright, can claim power-weaving, wool-combing, and agricultural experiments for the duke of Bedford.

[3] For Robert Owen see below, pp. 533 f.

were just outside the town limits. With such development all over Lancashire the new men of power could not but be conscious how much of it was due to their enterprise. In their lives there was little ostentation: solid comfort and future profits were what they looked for. They felt themselves to be alien to the old England. Their self-confidence was great. Arkwright proclaimed that he had only to live long enough to pay off the national debt.

The expansion of cotton was the most dramatic economic episode in the twenty-two years of war. But other industries showed hints of similar development on a smaller scale. Silk has already been mentioned as having weaving conditions similar to those in cotton. It must be remembered that the Spitalfields Act of 1783 protected wage-rates, and the employment of weavers outside the district was prevented. This arrested development in the London area. The competition of the finer cotton goods damaged the sales of silk. Nevertheless Spitalfields about held its own, though all expansion was in the more mechanically minded Macclesfield area.

The woollen industry was the leading English industry in 1793, as for centuries past. As late as 1800 its exports, at £7 million, were greater than cotton and iron (the next two) combined. It was partly this old-established position which retarded the development of the woollen trade so that it was passed by cotton before the end of the war. The industry was scattered over the country from Wiltshire in the south-west, Norfolk in the east and the West Riding of Yorkshire in the north. The many small producers in the west and east were loathe to revolutionize their methods or to take the risks involved in expansion with new equipment. Up in Yorkshire at the end of the 1780's people like Benjamin Gott in Leeds were willing to imitate from Lancashire the use of the mule, of water-power, and then of steam. Even in Yorkshire, however, many vested interests were opposed to change. One technical process, that of combing in the making of worsted, demanded considerable technical skill. The wool-combers, with wages as high as 28s. a week, the highest in the trade, naturally tried to preserve their position of strength. It was eventually broken by the use of another invention of the ingenious Dr. Cartwright. Cartwright's combing machine enabled an overseer with ten children under him to comb a 240 lb. pack of wool in twelve hours. Its output was finer as well as cheaper. Though invented in 1790 this machine was not brought into general use until after 1815. Where it was used, as, for example, in Bradford by Ramsbottom, it was, with the mule brought there by Garnett, sufficient to turn what had been a little market town in 1794 into an industrial centre of 6,000 inhabitants ten years later.

In the West Riding generally, before 1815 carding was mechanical but slubbing was not: the flying shuttle was in general use but power weaving was still uncommon. Therefore factory production was not the rule; indeed only one-sixteenth, it was estimated, of Yorkshire's cloth output in 1813 came from factories. The general rule was still for cloth to go to factories only for some small part of the process of production. Yet while Yorkshire lagged behind Lancashire in modernization it was, in its turn, far beyond Norfolk or Wiltshire. In consequence new urban conglomerations round Leeds, Huddersfield, Bradford, Halifax, mushroom towns already almost as startling as those in Lancashire, came into existence. The industry became concentrated there and died away in the southwest even in the earliest epoch of industrialization.

It was not only conservatism that held back woollen expansion—though conservatism was strong and made itself felt in Westminster where Yorkshire members of parliament, such as Wilberforce in 1806, tried to defend the small producers: in addition the problems of raw materials and markets were still unsolved. It was less easy to find other openings when the European market was closed for woollen cloth than for cotton. As to raw materials, whereas raw cotton was improving in supply, that of wool was being throttled. The coarser wool still came from British sheep, from 19 million of them, it was said, in 1800. But these sheep were, by developments in agriculture, becoming better as food and worse as wool producers.[1] For centuries England had depended upon Spain for the finer wool. Spanish wool had cost 9s. a pack in 1785: in 1795 it cost 19s. 10d. War made supply more difficult. It was in 1803 that Captain Macarthur reported that sheep would flourish in Australia. It was the end of the war before the first wool cargo from New South Wales set out for home. Thus the effects of abundant raw material could not be experienced before 1815. The figures

---

[1] See above, p. 33.

of exports reflect all these difficulties: £7 million in 1800, £5¾ million in 1810, £4⅓ million in 1811. It was an industry expanding in Yorkshire only by the amount it declined elsewhere; yet it was equipping itself for a greater development.

It is indeed a mistake to suppose that many industries followed iron, the metal trades, cotton, and wool, in a great wave of invention and mechanization. In linen, the old hand methods of flax spinning flourished alongside the machine production being tried in Leeds. In pottery there was a greater concentration of the industry geographically, as Staffordshire under-sold the products of old firms in such places as Chelsea and Derby. The main factor in Staffordshire's success was enterprise and large-scale units of production. Wedgwood's Etruria works employed 387 people at the end of the war. Even here, however, sub-contracting and out-work were mingled with the factory system. Of new developments in these years the chief was the more general use of transfers in place of special hand-painting for the pots. English pottery by such means had become so famous for cheapness and reliability that a Frenchman could assert that every inn from Paris to St. Petersburg fed its guests on English earthenware.[1] In the glass industry, also famous in Europe, the most noteworthy development was in the size of the firms; this encouraged mass production rather than startling innovation. In the leather industry, still, in 1800, second of all English manufactures, if one measures by the value of the annual products, the output was estimated at £10½ million, nearly all of it absorbed by the home market. The excellence of English leather was said to depend entirely upon the great length of time which the tanners allowed for the tanning process; this suggests that it must have been due quite simply to the monetary resources of producers who could patiently lock up their capital in this way. Salt production or tin-mining, to take two other examples of leading industries, were large-scale but not markedly inventive: salt was important by the luck of having rock-salt to mine in Cheshire; tin, apart from the use of steam pumps, remained faithful to methods known for two centuries. Such industries profited by the expansion of

---

[1] The observation is that of M. Saint Fond who made a survey of English life in 1784 (*A Journey Through England and Scotland*), quoted W. Smart, *Economic Annals of the Nineteenth Century, 1801–1820*, p. 20.

others but, apart from a tendency to increase in size, showed few radical changes.[1]

Expanding commerce, selling the increased product of industry, needed more shipping. In the first decade of war, in spite of the acute timber shortage in Britain, the size of the mercantile marine registered in Britain or her dominions increased by 33⅓ per cent. In 1802 there were 19,772 vessels representing 2,037,000 tons.[2] The annual rate of building in this decade was at least 1,000 vessels, or rather more than 100,000 tons. From 1803 ship-building slackened and did not reach the 1802 level again until 1815. This was often attributed to the competition of the United States. Some old yards, particularly those on the Thames, were closed down as the cross-Channel trade declined. But the revival which began in 1814 showed the soundness of the newer yards. The application of steam to ships began with Symington's experiments in 1788 and with Lord Stanhope's patent in 1790. The *Charlotte Dundas* was, in 1802, the first successful steam-operated canal boat, yet she was laid aside: it was from this experiment that Fulton[3] adopted the ideas which he successfully carried out in navigation on the Hudson. By 1814 steam navigation on canals, though still a marvel, was advanced enough for a boat to carry 200 passengers on the Limehouse canal: a steam packet was being built to carry 500 passengers from London to Calais at 12 miles an hour. These, however, were but glimpses of the future mercantile marine of Great Britain: present proof of her activities upon the waters was to be found in the great development of docks. Between 1789 and 1815 the system of London docks—East India, West India, London, Commercial, and Surrey docks[4]—had been built. Liverpool was extending her docks on each side of the Mersey and using iron in the place of wood. Bristol diverted the Avon, built locks and a dock basin, in a vain attempt to hold her own against Liverpool's challenge. Hull was just beginning to equip herself as a great port. All along the coast harbour works and safety lights witnessed to a new activity on the seas.

[1] For the argument that the size of industrial units has been exaggerated by regarding a few monsters as typical, see J. H. Clapham, *Economic History of Modern Britain*, vol. i: *The Railway Age*, p. 185.
[2] For comparable figures in 1760 see above, p. 14.
[3] Robert Fulton (1765–1815): engineer, inventor, and artist.
[4] St. Katherine's docks were not completed until 1828.

None of this expansion would have been possible without an increase in coal production. It was abundant coal which made it possible to use iron in the docks more cheaply than wood and to apply power in cotton mills. The coal-mining industry had a barbaric life peculiar to itself. Scottish miners were still, in effect, serfs bound to the pits in 1799: in Somerset they were like an alien community planted in the countryside. The location of the coalfields helped to make the prosperity of Lancashire, of Yorkshire, and of South Wales. But Northumberland and Durham were the leading coal producers. Only there had the working of coal at depth begun. The Yorkshire pits which supplied Sheffield were only about 300 feet deep. In much of the country coal was worked from drifts, or scraped off when it outcropped by small groups of men with primitive equipment. The use of wood props to support the roof was an innovation only introduced about 1800. Much coal had therefore to be left as support pillars. In the deep Tyneside pits (300 to 1,000 ft. deep) only about 40 per cent. of the coal could be extracted. As the Davy safety lamp was not introduced until 1815 dangerous mines could not be worked; even the circulation of air was secured only by burning fires to stimulate air currents. In spite of this slow technical development coal was so abundant in Britain that the supply could be stepped up to meet the rapidly rising demand. About 1770 the annual output of coal in Great Britain was some 6¼ million tons (or about the output of a week and a half in the twentieth century). In 1780 it was still approximately only 6½ million tons. After 1790, however, output rose more rapidly to reach 16 million tons by the first year of peace.[1] Coal, during the war, had emerged as a vital industry: the miners, less menaced by imported labour or machines than were the cotton operatives, had begun to form unions and fight their grim battle for wages against the coal owners and royalty-lessees.

The expansion of Britain's trade was necessary to supply armies and to pay allies. The ups and downs of trade have been discussed earlier in connexion with the strategy of war.[2] When one takes a more general survey of the figures of foreign trade they abundantly testify to the reality of the expansion in

[1] J. H. Clapham, *Economic History of Modern Britain*, vol. i: *The Railway Age*, p. 431.
[2] See above, particularly chapter XVIII, pp. 463 f.

production which has just been sketched. In 1792 the official values of imports were £17¼ million and of exports £22⅓ million. In 1801 imports were valued at £31¾ million and exports of goods produced in the United Kingdom were almost £25 million to which should be added almost £10½ million for the re-export of colonial produce.[1] In 1812 the comparable figures were £26⅛ million imports, £29½ million exports of United Kingdom products, and £9¾ million re-exports of colonial produce. In 1815 imports were £29¾ million, and exports £25½ million with colonial re-exports £12¾ million.[2] These are the statistics of a country which cannot live without international trade and which has already become a manufacturer for a good part of the world. Raw cotton from the United States or Egypt was paid for, and more, by the export of finished goods. The lead obtained over war-disturbed Europe was invincible. Amid all the problems of war there lay at the back of British minds a pride in this leadership.

The growth in population—in part the cause, in part the result of the great expansion—gave an expanding home market to industry. The birth-rate probably rose a little while the death-rate fell after 1790. At the census (the first taken) in 1801 the population of England was 8,331,434, of Wales 541,546, of Scotland 1,599,068, a total (when seamen and so on are added) of 10,942,646.[3] The eight greatest towns of Britain were London with 864,000, Manchester 84,000, Edinburgh 82,500, Glasgow 77,300, Liverpool 77,000, Birmingham 73,000, Bristol 68,000, and Leeds 53,000.[4] In 1811 the corresponding statistics were England 9,499,400, Wales 607,380, Scotland 1,804,864, and the total for Great Britain 12,552,144. England had shown a 14 per cent. increase, Wales 12 per cent., and Scotland 13 per

---

[1] Between 1792 and 1800 British exports to the United States rose from about 17 per cent. to 20 per cent. of the whole, that is, £3¼ million to £7 million.

[2] These figures are extracted from the financial blue book Customs Tariffs of the United Kingdom, 1800 to 1897 (c. 8706), by W. Smart, in *Economic Annals of the Nineteenth Century, 1801–1820*, pp. 11, 47, 336. They are all figures of official values. They are useful for comparative purposes therefore, but as they were based upon scales of prices more than a century old, they do not give market value. It is argued that even the appearance of a favourable trade balance may be deceptive and that the favourable balance of accounts of Britain depended upon her invisible exports such as shipping and financial services. (See G. Lefebvre, *Napoléon*, p. 50 n.)

[3] At this time the United States had 6 million inhabitants and France 24 million (though 50 to 60 million Europeans also came under French rule).

[4] Compare the situation in 1760; see above, p. 13.

cent.[1] London's population had become 1,009,546, Edinburgh
and Leith 103,000, Glasgow 100,750, Manchester and Salford
98,573, Liverpool 94,376, Birmingham 85,700, Bristol 76,500,
and Leeds 62,500. Old England was growing within her ancient
coasts almost as fast as the United States with its new lands,
its immigrants, and its expanding frontiers. The urban con-
centrations, moreover, were a phenomenon hitherto unknown
in the world. The world-conquering industries were well based,
having many home consumers within a small space.

Within that space, in addition, the movement of goods and
people continued to become easier. The roads, long admired as
the best in Europe,[2] benefited by the extension and consolidation of Turnpike Trusts. About 20,000 miles of important roads
were maintained by these bodies in 1815.[3] The great days of
Telford[4] and Macadam[5] had only just begun: Macadam in
1811 put to Parliament his scheme for establishing roads upon
a bed of stones broken into inch-long pieces: he was given
charge of the Bristol roads in 1815. Telford was commissioned
in 1802 to suggest measures for improving Scottish roads.
Nevertheless the provision of better surfaces with the use of
stone chippings was already practised before the two great
road builders brought the method to perfection. To relieve the
roads for the transport of heavy goods short stretches of iron rail-
tracks were in use. Between 1810 and 1816 it was thus made
possible to draw coal from Gloucester to Cheltenham. These
lengths of rail, usually 15 or 20 miles each, were most common
in the iron or coal districts: Tyneside had 225 miles of such
tracks; by others Cardiff was linked to Merthyr.

Both rail-tracks and roads were operated in conjunction with
canals. Canal building reached its peak in these twenty years.
Between 1793 and 1805 the Grand Junction canal linked London with Warwickshire, with a side line to Oxford. The Leeds
and Liverpool canal was being pushed up 600 feet to cross the

---

[1] The United States now had nearly 7¼ million. There were 28 million French
speaking people in the French Empire. Paris had ½ million inhabitants.

[2] See above, p. 27.

[3] Out of some 120,000 miles of road: 33⅓ per cent. of Middlesex roads were
under turnpike and only 10 per cent. of those in Essex.

[4] Thomas Telford (1757-1834), perhaps the greatest civil engineer of the age
or bridges, canals, and roads. But such great works of his as, for example, the
Menai bridge, belong to the period after 1815.

[5] John Loudon Macadam (1756-1836), who gave his name to Macadamized
road building.

Pennines by locks and so, via the old Aire and Calder navigation, linked up with the Humber. Birmingham was connected
with the Severn. The Gloucester and Berkeley system was half
finished. Up in Scotland the Firth and Clyde canal began
operations in 1790, the Crinan canal opened in 1801, and the
Caledonian Canal was being built from 1803. The system
represented a great investment of capital in the war years: by
1815 it was paying a return in cheap transport over the whole
country, the cost being about one-third that of road transport.
It was particularly important to London. The raw materials
from the London docks could be moved by canal to all points
of the Midlands while finished products poured back into
metropolitan warehouses for distribution. Faster barges carried
passengers. Mr. Pickford operated a day and night service for
urgent cargoes along the whole of the Grand Junction. The
main defect of the system was the lack of uniformity in lock-
sizes and channels. Against this may be set some remarkable
technical achievements. Among the most striking was Telford's
all-iron aqueduct at Port Cyslltau, opened in 1805, which enabled barges to sail slowly through the heavens, 127 feet above
the river Dee, on the Ellesmere canal.

From the examination of so many novelties of industry it
should not be concluded that agriculture had become of less
importance in the national economy. The most labour was still
employed in it. It was still the key to the problems of periodic
slump. The feature of the trade cycle normal in an industrial
capitalist society can be faintly detected in examining the de-
pressions of the period,[1] but more obvious are the effects of the
harvest. Agriculture still regulated the home market. With poor
crops and exceptionally high food prices the demand for manufactured goods was reduced: when the population had money
to spend after feeding itself the demand for manufactures increased again.

The war diminished the supply of foreign corn just when the
demands of an increasing population were being sharply felt.
The inevitable result was a rise in agricultural prices. In the
years immediately preceding 1764, according to the committee
of the house of commons which examined the question in 1813,
the average price of wheat had been 33s. 3d. a quarter. In the

[1] See Lord Beveridge, 'Trade Cycle in Britain before 1850', in *Oxford Economic
Papers*, iii (1940), 74–109, and iv (1940), 63–76.

period 1764 to 1794, on the same authority, the average price
was 44s. 7d. Burke's Corn Law of 1773 took 48s. as the top price
at which home farmers could expect protection: after that
foreign corn was allowed in at a nominal 6d. duty. The revised
corn law of 1791 lifted this level up to 54s. Actual prices, as
ascertained by parliament, were for 1794 60s. 9d., for 1795
91s. 8d., for 1796 90s. 4d., for 1797 69s. 9d. In 1800 the price was
at the extraordinary level of 142s. 10d. and a 4 lb. loaf in London
cost 1s. 3¼d.[1] Without imports coming easily from abroad prices
were irregular, for they depended on the English weather. The
1804 Corn Law pushed the figure at which foreign corn might
enter at a nominal duty up to 66s. The average price between
1804 and 1812 was said, in fact, to be 88s. 11d. The 4 lb. loaf in
London fell to 8½d. in 1803 and was steady at about 1s. in the
years 1805 to 1809 but was 1s. 5d. in 1812, 1s. 3d. in 1813, only
cheapening to 11½d. in 1814. In a period of inflation the rise in
agricultural prices was higher than in others.[2]

One result was to produce hardship and discontent among
the labouring poor. But another was to encourage expansion in
farming. The enclosure movement, which had been active in
the central wedge of England earlier in George III's reign,[3]
had slackened in the 80's. But between 1793 and 1803 (when
the General Enclosure Act simplified procedure) there was a
hectic period of enclosure. There were only half a dozen
counties in England, at the end of it, with more than 3 per cent.
land unenclosed. It is roughly true to say that all reasonable
agricultural land was enclosed. Some unreasonable land was
also under cultivation, unreasonable that is in any but a siege
economy. The margin at which it became worth while to cultivate a field was pushed back by high prices. Farmers enjoyed
the prosperity of inflation: but their life was based upon insecure foundations: too many small men were cultivating areas
which would not be worth while with ordinary harvests, once
peace restored the normal markets.

The enclosures did not, as has sometimes been supposed,
destroy the small producers. At the end of the war the average
agricultural unit was one employer with 2¾ hands to assist

[1] J. H. Clapham, *Economic History of Modern Britain*, i. 602.
[2] The price of oats was quadrupled, it was estimated, between 1773 and 1800,
while that of hay was trebled.
[3] See above, pp. 34, 35.

him.[1] But the enclosures were fatal to the independence of those who lived in a cottage with customary rights. The farmer, however small his holding, could, with compensation and high prices, continue to farm. The cottager had moral rights which were usually ignored. Even if he did receive compensation it was not enough, as his former privileges had been, to keep body and soul together. So the cottager became the hired hand. For him, with enclosure, there was more work in ditching and hedging than before. The villages were not deserted: the rural population continued to increase. In a Berkshire village such as Mapledurham the more pushing young men might go to Reading or London, but enough remained to increase the size of this purely agricultural community.[2] The countryside, that is, in a period of swelling population, lost only its proportion of the increase compared to the towns, but still had an absolute increase.

In the prosperity of the times improvement in agricultural methods was not forced upon the farmers: on the other hand the means were readily available for technical improvement. Up in the north of England the threshing machine was introduced in the 1790's and its use spread slowly southwards. The adoption of the best farming practices[3] was no longer dependent purely upon the unaided initiative of individuals. In 1793 Sir John Sinclair[4] and Arthur Young[5] organized the setting up of the board of agriculture. This board, by the collection of information and the publication of many reports, did much to spread knowledge among farmers and to prod on the less efficient of them. In England, the traveller Louis Simond reported after his exploration in 1810, every gentleman's conversation was taken up with turnips, clover, enclosures, and drains. He added that, though rents had trebled in fifty years,

---

[1] Such an average figure conceals, of course, the wide variation of different parts of the country. Northumberland, for instance, was the area of very large farms indeed.

[2] Evidence from the unpublished thesis of M. H. Long.

[3] For an account of these see above, pp. 32 f.

[4] Sir John Sinclair (1754–1835), M.P., 1780–1811; president of the board of agriculture, 1793–8 and 1806–13; a critic of the Pitt ministry in 1798; carried Enclosure Bill of 1796 through the commons; a commissioner of excise, 1811; a scientific agriculturalist and collector of statistics, particularly concerned with improvement of northern agriculture.

[5] Arthur Young (1741–1820), journalist who turned to farming; numerous writings including *Farmer's Letters* (1767), *State of the Waste Lands of Great Britain* (1773), *Political Arithmetic* (1774), *Annals of Agriculture* (47 volumes, 1784–1809), and *Travels in France* (1792); secretary of the board of agriculture, 1793.

England was the only country in the world where a man might make his fortune by agriculture.[1]

Another peculiarity of the British rural scene (as compared with Europe) was its lack of forests. They had been eaten by the demand for ships and charcoal. Entry into an age of iron and coal relieved some of the strain. But the navy was increasing its demands. To build a ship of the line required 4,000 grown trees.[2] At the outset of the war there were less than 3,000 such trees left in Epping Forest. In north-west England and in Scotland the forests had been cleared almost completely. As a result Britain depended upon imports of timber in bulk. In the early stages of the war 200,000 loads of timber were imported from the Baltic. As the continental system became effective for northern Europe after 1809, it became necessary to seek more supplies from North America. Despite all encouragements this was a poor substitution. An effort was made to increase home-grown supplies. Under an act of parliament of 1808 5,000 acres in the New Forest were planted with oak. Scotch firs and larch were planted, with the blessing of the Commission on Forests, in many parts of England, Wales, and Scotland. Trees grew slowly, however, while timber prices shot up. From the beginning of the war to 1810 timber prices increased by 300 per cent. This had widespread social effects. In areas away from coal and denuded of trees, such as Cornwall, it became a luxury to eat cooked food. Cobbett, a few years after the war, tells of Cornishmen paying 3d. to cook mutton on another man's fire. The construction of the Caledonian canal was delayed by the shortage and high price of wood. The more universal evil was that houses for the rapidly expanding population were increased in price and lowered in quality by the shortage of the wood to make them.[3] To this, as well as to the unscrupulousness of builders, can be attributed jerry-building— where there was building at all—which made the slums of the new towns.

The effect of the great economic changes of the war-years upon the lives of the ordinary people has been a subject of dis-

[1] W. Smart, *Economic Annals of the Nineteenth Century, 1801–1820*, p. 311, quoting Louis Simond, *Journal of a Tour and Residence in Great Britain*.

[2] J. H. Clapham, *Economic History of Modern Britain*, vol. i, p. 10.

[3] In 1810 a new duty was imposed upon European timber which made the situation worse even though its purpose was, by encouraging colonial exports to a protected market, to overcome chronic shortages and high prices.

pute among historians.[1] This matter of housing conditions is but
one example. It is undoubted that before industrialization,
housing for the labouring classes was very bad. The one-room
cottage of the Lowlands of Scotland—without ash-pit or drain—
which was often only a hovel built of sods, was as bad or worse
than any house built for habitation after 1790. Better housing—
two lower rooms and two bedrooms—was, however, to be found
in the East Riding of Yorkshire. In general the houses in the
south were more commodious than in the north. The growth of
new towns did not therefore introduce new bad standards in
housing. But it did intensify old evils. The old city of Edinburgh,
with its high buildings, was dirty and insanitary in 1760. The
growth of population by 1815 had turned its tenements into a
nightmare of overcrowding and odorous horror. A group of
families living in a village may all have thrown their refuse out
of windows: if that village became a town of many streets in
which all the inhabitants continued to eject filth in the same
way, it might be claimed that there had been no deterioration
in sanitary methods. Nevertheless the result would be to substitute for life in a malodorous lane, life in an intolerable rookery
of humanity established on a dunghill. In Glasgow there were
no sewers in 1790 and only just over 40, for a population of
more than 100,000, in 1815. In Bethnal Green, London, the
new houses after 1800 were built without sewers. They were
houses of a superior kind, by earlier standards, having two
stories: but they had poor foundations and the water of the
growing settlement, the oozings of cesspools, penetrated under
the floors. It is not in housing standards or architects' drawings
that the evils of the new age will be found, but rather in the
effect upon men of crowding so many houses of the old type
together. There were still, however, wide differences in housing
between one area and another, even between one section of the
labouring classes and another.

Even for the skilled man, in a decent house, with some sort of
drainage, life in the enlarged northern towns had new problems.
The old social landmarks had disappeared. He necessarily felt
himself for a while lost in his novel environment. In time new
forms of organization, new churches, trade unions, clubs, and
so on, established a new framework for existence. But in war-

---

[1] Compare the books of J. L. and B. Hammond, on the one hand, with those of
J. H. Clapham or T. S. Ashton on the other.

time, when clubs were regarded as revolutionary centres, such reinforcements of the life of the individual man were slow to rise,[1] and he lived without landmarks. At the time this was most remarked by censorious moralists: the godlessness of the workers, the threatened disappearance of the institution of matrimony among Staffordshire potters, the drunkenness in Lancashire, these were deplored by superior observers. In retrospect historians have been mostly struck by the forlorn state of the human beings of which these things were symptoms. It must again be remembered that such conditions still, in 1815, only operated among a minority of the population. An even smaller minority were affected by the new stresses of factory life. It was not the long hours or poor pay or physical conditions which made the factory detested. In the domestic system working families worked long hours in hovels for pittances. What was detested in the factory was a feeling of servitude and discipline. In a man's own home he could work twenty hours and be drunk for four: in the factory he worked to a time-table and was not his own master even to sweat himself. Though this organization of labour which goes with factory life was the great hope for future improvement,[2] it was at the start its most unpopular feature. This helps to account for the blind animosity sometimes felt towards the machines, the inanimate but powerful agents in a system which seemed to grow ever more inhuman.

Against this black picture of a population plunging into misery there are some powerful and practical considerations to be set on the other side. The diet of the mass of the population was becoming a little more varied. However insanitary the towns, it is a fact that the death-rate declined after 1790; it was better to be born in 1800 than in 1760. Iron pipes were used in attempts to improve sewage disposal, however unscientifically. Even on a less material plane there were some vigorous attempts to lift the clouds from the minds of the poor. The nonconformist churches found new energy. In 1810 Joseph Lancaster[3] and his

---

[1] In spite of the atmosphere of suspicion and repression there were, nevertheless, 820 registered societies for mutual welfare among the working class in Lancashire in 1801.

[2] By making possible control of working conditions by factory acts and state inspection. The factory act of 1802 was a very modest beginning. It applied only to children from poor law institutions who were apprenticed to work in factories; it limited their hours to twelve a day. See also Sir E. L. Woodward, *The Age of Reform* (O.H.E., vol. xiii), p. 11.

[3] Joseph Lancaster (1778-1838), son of a Chelsea Pensioner. His system was

quaker friends formed the Royal Lancasterian Association to push on with the provision of a general educational system in all parts of the country in place of previous intermittent private efforts. In emulation members of the church of England founded, in 1811, the National Society for the Education of the Poor in the Principles of the Established Church. In so doing they hoped not only to repair the ill effects of movement and expansion upon the level of literacy among the population but also to bring instruction into a respectable channel.[1] The earnest and hopeful among the adults sought enlightenment from Sunday schools or charitable ventures. Some adult education was probably going on in the clubs of labouring men. But such activities were driven underground by a repressive government. The old Spitalfields mathematical society, for example, was frightened away from open work by a prosecution for daring to hold unlicensed public lectures. Even so the Corresponding Society, by lending pamphlets and books, must have stimulated an educational as well as a political thirst. All such organizations were ladders to climb out of the state of crowded but isolated savagery.[2]

Man cannot, however, live by books alone: education, cultural, social betterment depended ultimately upon the filling of stomachs and the clothing of backs. With war prices the cost

that of employing half-trained children under the eye of a master to drill the younger children in the rudiments of reading, writing, and arithmetic. This 'monitorial' method was economical. Lancaster estimated the cost of educating a child in this way at 5s. a year. It enabled large numbers to be taught at one time. It aroused enthusiasm not only among philanthropists but also, strangely enough, among the children too. The monitorial method was also used by the National Society who claimed that it had been invented in a Madras orphanage by Andrew Bell (1753–1832), an anglican parson who was their chief propagandist. They therefore called it the 'Madras system'.

[1] Whitbread had attempted in 1807 to make education truly national by making it a state system. His bill had been defeated.

[2] In the period up to 1815, however, it would seem likely that the chief activity of this sort was among the threatened craft-workers of the south rather than among the bewildered new inhabitants of northern towns. In 1815 there were adult schools in Bath, Bristol, Bungay (Suffolk), Bury, Edgbaston, High Wycombe, Ilfracombe, London, Norwich, Plymouth, Rangeworthy (Gloucestershire), Salisbury, Southwark, and Yarmouth. The total numbers in such classes exceeded 4,008 in 1815 (J. W. Hudson, *The History of Adult Education* (1851), pp. 6 and 7). The founder of this movement for adult education was William Smith of Bristol, a doorkeeper in a methodist chapel, who excelled in enlisting benevolent support from the well-to-do. The list of centres confirms the view suggested by common sense that it was easier to set adult education going in settled areas than in those disturbed new centres where the need for it was greater.

of living by 1795 had risen to 130 per cent. of the level of 1790.
Wages, however, had also risen. Agricultural wages were up to
125 per cent. and industrial wages to 112½ per cent. These
figures[1] at once reveal, however, that the lot of the working
class had become harder. Agricultural wages had more closely
kept up with rising costs than those in industry, but this was to
be expected, for the agricultural labourer had started from so
much lower a level, so close to subsistence level, that he would
have starved unless his wages followed bread prices. As one
traces the cost of living and wage levels through the war a
certain pattern becomes apparent. After the bad year of 1795
the cost of living fell slightly so that in 1797 and 1798 it was only
120 per cent. to 121 per cent. compared with the pre-war level:
the rise in wages, however, continued: agricultural wages were
140 per cent. and industrial about 125 per cent. At this stage
therefore one might expect to find the working classes rather
better off than before the war. After this there was a steep rise
in living costs. By 1800 they were 170 per cent. compared with
pre-war, by 1801 they were 174 per cent., then came a sharp
fall to 154 per cent. in 1805, a rise again to 176 per cent. in
1810 and a further drop to 150 per cent. in 1815. The first rise
to 1801 went faster than the rise in agricultural wages which
only climbed to 160 per cent. of 1790 rates. But that was the
last time at which the rise in the cost of living exceeded the rise
in agricultural wages. For in 1805 the labourer's rates were
180 per cent., in 1810 190 per cent., and in 1815 187 per cent.,
and all these figures show a clear gain in real benefits, that is in
wages compared with costs. The industrial worker's average was
not quite so quick to exceed living costs: there the corresponding figures were for 1801 about 130 per cent., for 1805 142 per
cent., for 1810 172 per cent., and for 1815 158 per cent. It was
not until 1810, in short, that industrial wages had approached
parity with the rises in food prices and not until 1815 that they
had passed them.

Such figures are useful only as a very general guide. Not only
are the statistics difficult to ascertain with certainty, but they
relate only to averages. Such averages conceal the wide differences between sections of the working class. While, for example,
one can clearly see that agricultural wages followed food prices

---

[1] These figures, and those which follow below, are adapted from Clapham,
Economic History of Modern Britain, and from the sources which he cites.

closely, there was in fact a great discrepancy between wages
paid in the south and in the north. North of the Trent the need
of industry for labour tended to tempt the ploughman away
from his plough. To keep him the farmer had to pay higher
wages than were common in the south. One should therefore
picture the labourers in the north doing considerably better
than before the war. To balance this the southern labourer had
a worse time than the average figure suggests. Not only were
his wages slow to rise but he lost many contributions to his
purse which are 'invisible' to statisticians. In the enclosures
area, as has already been pointed out, there was a loss of the
products of grazing. With the increase in mechanical spinning
in northern factories the agricultural labourer had lost the
money his wife could bring in to the house by spinning and
now, as weaving in its turn became part-mechanized, the
returns from hand-loom weaving also were cut down. The sums
lost might seem small, perhaps 3s. a week, but they were a vital
supplement when the head of the family might be earning only
10s. a week.

There were therefore depressed areas among the rural poor
even when the national average had become better than pre-
war. In the early years of the war when even the national average showed deterioration compared to peace-time, the condition
of those in the bad patches was catastrophic. But these bad
patches were also, fortunately, those in which the old social
framework[1] was least shaken, where therefore some responsibility might be felt by those in authority for those who suffered.
Berkshire was one of the counties most affected by enclosure: it
was also a county on the fringe of the south-west textile industry
which was going into decline. It was an area therefore where
one might expect particular distress. Meeting in 1795 the Berkshire justices talked over the social problems of this particularly
grievous year at Speenhamland, on the outskirts of Newbury.[2]
They decided that it was necessary, both in the interests of
humanity and to prevent riotous disorder,[3] to supplement their
wages from the poor rates. They agreed, that is, on a minimum
level which would enable a family to survive and further that

[1] Described above, chapter III, pp. 39 f.
[2] A town famous in the sixteenth century for the large-scale textile operations of
'Jack of Newbury' and still noted for silk mills in the mid-nineteenth century.
[3] See J. L. and B. Hammond, *The Village Labourer*, p. 121.

they would make up the pay of those who were below it. When the 8 lb. 11 oz. loaf cost 1s. they reckoned that every man needed 3s. a week for himself and 1s. 6d. for each of his family to survive: for every penny that the loaf rose above 1s. they reckoned that a man would need 3d. more for himself and 1d. for each member of his family. On this basis outdoor relief became widespread in Berkshire.

The system of supplementing wages from parish funds to a minimum figure was soon adopted in other counties where the pinch of want was worst.[1] In 1824—and presumably the situation before 1815 was similar—returns revealed that the system was generally in operation in Dorset, Sussex, Suffolk, Norfolk, Bedford, Cambridge, Huntingdon, Northampton, Nottingham, Berkshire, Buckinghamshire, Leicester, Oxford, Wiltshire, and (surprisingly) the East and North Ridings of Yorkshire.[2] When Arthur Young analysed typical Suffolk labouring class budgets for 1801 he showed a wage of 9s. a week and poor relief of 6s. a week, so large a proportion of the weekly income had by then become a gift from the public. Thus a measure taken to meet a particular sharp rise in the cost of living, in a county particularly hard hit by economic changes, became a general system of supplementing wages on a means test.

To cushion the blow of an acute shift in economic organization was praiseworthy, a recognition of the duty of the community to assist the unfortunate. But the continued use of wage-supplementation as a normal thing had unfortunate consequences for all. It tended to keep wages low. The farmer could underpay because his labour would be kept alive by the parish. The need to press for higher wages, the urge to migrate to areas where labour was more in demand, both these were lessened by the Speenhamland system. Yet both had to be strong if the maximum economic progress was to be made. The object of a benevolent state should be to assist the movements necessary for economic progress while preventing these changes from inflicting unfair hardship upon those who are most closely affected. With the full mechanism of the welfare state it is still hard to combine a mobility in labour with insurance

[1] In 1796 the statute of 1722 restricting the payment of outdoor relief was repealed.

[2] See Clapham's analysis of the Report of the Select Committee on Labourers' Wages, 1824, in *Economic History of Modern Britain*, vol. i, pp. 123, 124.

against unfair hardship. In the primitive state of governmental machinery in the 1790's it was impossible. With all their faults the south midland magistrates at least acted as men of social responsibility. And Canning held that by their action they had saved the state. Economists might agree that pressure upon the distressed labourer was necessary to produce radical reorientation in organization. Canning, however, as a politician, believed that such pressure, if unrelieved, would have resulted in rioting, perhaps revolution, capable of destroying both the bases of the economy and of the war effort. It may well be that the action of the Berkshire justices was taken at the critical moment, at the height of the hardship for the poor, before rising wages and repressive legislation had quelled the rebellious phase of discontent.[1]

When one turns back again from agricultural to industrial wages a similar reservation has to be made about all average figures. The average conceals the great disparity between the fortunes of different trades and areas.[2] The true picture is not, as might have appeared from the statistics quoted, of a whole urban population only just recovering after 1810 the standard of living enjoyed before 1790. Instead it is of a patchy development, some sections of urban communities with wages racing the cost of living, other sections declining calamitously in their standards. Those whose wages failed to rise were, in the first place, the completely unskilled, the navvies digging canals alongside the first wave of immigrant Irish labour which competed with them for jobs. A second class was that which had an old skill which was either replaced by machinery or had to be employed in competition with machinery: of this class the hand-loom weavers may serve as an example by the end of the period. Those who prospered, despite rising costs, in an age of expansion were those who worked in the developing industries with their great demand for labour (and within this group particularly those who had some skill), or those skilled men

---

[1] Compare above, p. 360.

[2] In the case of industrial wages it may also be objected that wage-rates are not the same as actual earnings. If it could be shown that industrialization increased the periods of unemployment, for instance, a rise in rates might take place without the worker being any better off. When wage-rates are related to such indexes of activity as can be constructed (e.g. by Lord Beveridge, *Oxford Economic Papers*, iii, p. 74, and iv, p. 63), there is no significant change, however, in the general picture given by the statistics quoted on p. 526.

who were not replaced by machinery. Thus a fine spinner in
Lancashire about 1815 could earn 44s. 6d. a week. A brick-
layer's wages rose from about 3s. 9d. a day at the end of the
eighteenth century to 5s. 6d. a day before the end of the war.
All around the factories wages were higher than in the declining
areas of the south.

Whereas the farm labourers had been losing their supplementary sources of income, the urban workers in the north tended to
increase theirs. The wives and children of the male operatives
could also find work in the mills, or workshops, or even mines.
The demand for such unskilled labour was so great that the
workhouse authorities of the London area sent their orphan and
destitute children in batches to work in the cotton mills.[1] After
1802, by Peel's Act, certain minimum standards were laid down
for the treatment of these pauper apprentices. It was difficult to
enforce this act. Nevertheless to the extent that it was a nuisance
to the ruthless employer it increased the likelihood that the
children of resident local families would be employed instead.
Child and female labour was a social evil. It was not the result
of the growth of factories: all the evidence would suggest that
in the older domestic system children were made to work just
as long hours by their fathers and were a support of the home
from their infancy. With the development of industry, however,
their employment became more general. Thus the urban family,
in good times, had a larger real income than the available
figures suggest.

So far, then, from mechanization steadily depressing the
standards of the whole working class it raised the real incomes
of those sections which were most closely involved with it. The
impoverishment of other sections was a harsh method of compelling them to adjust themselves to change, to force them to
move jobs or learn skills. A Speenhamland for the temporarily
hard-hit—or even better any sort of labour-exchange to give
information and make labour more mobile—would indeed have
humanized the system. But such a thing was unthinkable in the
urban areas. There were neither means nor will to ameliorate
the processes of change. Nor, when a crisis such as that of 1811

---

[1] One firm, Smalley's in Flintshire, had 300 parish apprentice children living
and labouring in the mill in 1795: this was a model firm treating the children with
firmness but philanthropy. When Robert Owen went to the New Lanark Mills in
1799 he recorded that there were 436 boys and girls working there.

plunged whole areas into unemployment and temporary but intense distress, was there anything but grim fatalism.

The failure of rising entrepreneurs to feel responsibility for the state of their less fortunate employees owed something to theory. In 1798 Malthus[1] produced the first edition of his famous *Essay on the Principle of Population as it affects the Future Improvement of Society*. In this he set out ideas which purported to be universal but which were, in truth, the product of a reaction against eighteenth-century optimism combined with the experience of the first five, particularly bad, years of war. Malthus argued that the lot of the majority of men could never be bettered. Any rise in productivity would be followed quickly by an increase in population; for greater plenty would encourage men to breed more freely. Population, indeed, would outrun subsistence, for the latter can only expand in an arithmetical ratio while population increases in a geometrical ratio. Accordingly, after any improvement men would return to bare subsistence levels, or worse, in a generation. The balance in population was only kept by misery and vice. In his second edition of the *Essay* in 1803 Malthus dropped much of his attack upon perfectability: he admitted that moral restraint might check the population. All the same, what men of affairs learnt from Malthus was what they were predisposed to accept, that the unfortunate were so by their own feckless fecundity and that misery was a medicine by which society was kept in health.[2]

Not only Malthus but the whole trend of up-to-date economic discussion confirmed the manufacturer in his resolute individualism. Adam Smith's principles of free competition were being worked out in detail in the light of recent developments by such men as David Ricardo. Ricardo had not reached the height of his influence by 1815, though his book *The High Price of Bullion* (a plea for a metallic currency and deflation) brought him into prominence in 1810. Ricardo had a dynamic view of economics. He laid stress upon the necessity for the economy to

---

[1] Reverend T. R. Malthus (1766–1834).

[2] The neat logic of Malthus is upset once it is noticed that subsistence levels are to some extent conventional and can be altered: men of the modern world, for example, could not subsist at levels which were tolerable in the middle ages. Even within a few years of 1798 a maintained improvement in working-class standards of life demonstrated that birth-rates need not swamp betterment. The idea of 'moral restraint' (if understood to include birth control) opened a great hole in the theory. In western Europe since Malthus's day rising standards of living have tended to diminish and not to increase the rate at which the population increases.

expand by an increase in fixed capital employed in production. He damned the rent-charges of monopolistic landowners as a drag upon the community. He feared that the investment of capital would be retarded by any interference by the state with the 'natural' wages of labour. The doctrines of Bentham[1] also were growing in influence among the rising middle classes. What they liked about him was his practical no-nonsense approach, his contempt for most of the trappings or traditions of old England. They liked to run their lives, as he proposed, on a profit and loss account. They, too, wanted facts. One of the most striking instances of a Benthamite innovation was the taking of the census in 1801 which for the first time gave facts about population, a necessary basis for businesslike government.

The man behind the census, Rickman,[2] lived his life on a Benthamite calculation. Of Charles Lamb's pathetic protégé George Burnett, Rickman, though an intimate of that little circle of friends, wrote that he should commit suicide. 'As a cosmopolite it is moral to wish him dead': for he had balanced the nourishment Burnett consumed (which might otherwise have gone to others) against the achievements of this hopeless writer, and had decided that Burnett's absence would be a gain to the sum of human welfare. A letter like this was, in Southey's phrase, 'a cruel dose of yellow gambooge'. It was also significant of a new attitude of mind. Utilitarians and classical economists alike felt that the welfare of the whole community depended upon each individual using his native wit and hard common sense in his own interest. The only rule of life suitable for an expanding England, they said, was that the economically fit should survive.

Fitness for survival meant an ability to adjust oneself to changing conditions, a self-reliance, and—to give due credit— a self-denial for the sake of investing in the future. In the homes of better-off working men, and in those of the great entrepreneurs, a new earnestness, almost a new morality, began to make itself felt. The great nineteenth-century virtues of thrift, family solidarity, and grave self-confidence, were hammered

---

[1] For Bentham see above, p. 330.
[2] John Rickman (1771–1840), a clerk in the House of Commons. He was also active in collecting returns about the poor law. For him see O. Williams, *Life and Letters of John Rickman* (1908).

out in the new towns along with the nineteenth-century vices of hardness, narrowness, and self-satisfaction. But above all there was a growing consciousness of power to master nature: this was the natural consequence of recent changes and it was to be the cause of rabid optimism later in the century. Most of the population, it is true, went on in its old ways. But those in the minority were aware of their own significance and the part they were to play in the world.

Among this minority Robert Owen[1] was an exceptional man for his philanthropy. He believed that the employer had a duty to shorten the hours his employees worked, to concern himself with their housing and recreation: he believed, even more exceptionally, that the model employer could still make a fortune. This he proved in his own mills up in Scotland. But extraordinary as all this was, in one thing Owen was typical of his class, in his sense of power. In a small way this appears in his philanthropy; for in ruling the lives of his employees he was as dictatorial as any hard-fisted mill boss. He forced them to live on his lines.[2] In a larger way also Owen shared with his more conventional competitors the confidence that in a rapidly changing world all problems were soluble by clear-headed business methods. In 1813 and 1814 Owen produced his book, *A New View of Society*. There he argued (on the basis of his own experience) that all the evils of the world could be attributed to bad environment. Change the environment of children in their earliest years and you would change human beings. Human nature was but wax ready for stamping: character in its great variety derived from inborn peculiarities, but that this produced conflict rather than co-operation was the result of bad moral training. The millenium could therefore quickly be reached. Set up, as in New Lanark, an educational system, diminish the squalor and anxiety surrounding children, feed them, draw

---

[1] Robert Owen (1771–1858), son of a saddler; manager of a cotton mill at 19; married the daughter of David Dale the banker and factory owner; successful as a manager and part owner of the New Lanark Mills; regarded as a founder of modern British socialism—see Sir E. L. Woodward, *The Age of Reform*, p. 124.

[2] In New Lanark, Owen controlled the whole new village, mills, houses, and even places of refreshment. Emulation was encouraged among the employees by a system of coloured badges for good work and by whipping up public sentiment against slackers. The drunkard was woken by the employer himself with a lecture on the evils of excess. The children were taught on the employer's plan. It was a closed society under benevolent despotism.

upon their need of human affection, and then in a generation
or two the country would be full of well-balanced, prudent,
industrious, amiable people. What distinguishes this view of
the millenium from that of writers of an earlier world-bettering
tradition[1] is its dynamic sense of movement. It is the work of a
practical man habituated to great enterprises even if, as so often
when the man of action turns to theory, there is a crazy over-
simplification about it. Like other middle-class men of the age,
Owen recognized himself as a member of a new-created society.
The masterful ambition common to such a class, but by most of
its members reserved for their private schemes, he extended to
cover social welfare—a strong father whose dependants were
the whole labouring population.

It was not only among economists, political theorists, men of
public affairs, or Brummagem bosses, that a new spirit moved
in the years after 1790. Everywhere the firm horizons were
dissolving, the classical stability was giving way to 'inexhaustible
discontent, languor, and homesickness', as Walter Pater put it,[2]
but to experiment also, to confident reconstruction, or even to
the feverish pursuit of novelty for its own sake. What inspired
so general a mood? It can be discerned in fashions of dress as
well as in metres of verse, in buildings as well as in novels. It is
only part of an answer to say that conventions break by their
own accumulated weight. There was much more than a revolution in forms in progress. 'Gibbon's style is detestable', said
Coleridge, 'but his style is not the worst thing about him'.[3] The
worst thing about him, from the new Romantic viewpoint, was
his superficiality, his comfortable urbanity. Perhaps the first
thing to shake the hold of the old ideas upon the young had been
the French Revolution. Wordsworth and Southey, as well as

---

[1] William Godwin (1756–1836), author of *Inquiry concerning Political Justice*,
published 1793, may serve as an example of this earlier tradition even though,
through Shelley and the literary circles of the early nineteenth century, his influence long persisted in radical thinking. Godwin sees men as passionless, appetite-
less, reasonable beings. Evil therefore for him is the result of mistaken ideas. Ideas
find concrete form in stupid institutions. A few simple constitutional reforms would
therefore put the world to rights—provided everyone will read Godwin and be as
sensible as he is. Godwin believed that the abolition of matrimony would somehow
purify human affections. Owen, in contrast, realized that men do not live by
reason or institutions alone.

[2] W. Pater, *Appreciations*, ed. 1910, p. 104 (on Coleridge).

[3] S. T. Coleridge, *Table Talk* (15 Aug. 1833). For Gibbon see above, p. 347.

Blake, believed that the collapse of the greatest monarchy in the world opened up an exhilarating prospect for all men. Yet this emotion was, for many, only transitory: it was followed by disillusionment. Even so a question once opened is not closed by the failure of the first solution. The French continued to demonstrate resources and variety in human nature hitherto unsuspected. Then, following the impulse from France, there came the disturbing social changes in Britain whose psychological effects spread, like ripples on a pond, far beyond the first small area of impact. To the new world struggling to be born the habits of mind of the old seemed artificial. This was not a matter of politics; staunch upholders of the existing constitution were affected in their ways of thought and methods of expression as much as any radical. Sir Walter Scott[1] was in politics a sentimental tory, in his private life a would-be wealthy country gentleman, and in his mental training he had been conditioned to respect the complex antiquities of the law. Yet Scott was to be hailed all over Europe as the leader of a new romantic attitude of mind.

Romanticism is, at bottom, a mood of discontent with the accepted rules of expression, a feeling that the expression of human nature has been cribbed and confined by dead laws. This discontent issues in an excited attempt to discover fresh means by which the artist may explain himself to others, means more appropriate to new experiences. It is therefore exploration, a search for new values. Rejecting authorities the Romantic will refuse to respect anything but his own heart. Thus Keats who first burst into song in 1815 (at the age of twenty) declared: 'I am certain of nothing but the holiness of the heart's affections and the truth of imagination.' With a cultivation of the feelings quite alien to the eighteenth century (so suspicious of enthusiasm) goes a luxuriance in wild and sensuous detail, a delight in the rich and curious for its own sake. In the quest for new standards the Romantic artist may be inspired by casting his eyes to the future in apocalyptic enthusiasm, or he may, equally well, look back to forgotten far-off things, contrasting the past with the world of which he has wearied. Or yet again he may seek his solution in identifying himself with 'humble and rustic' men who have never suffered the corruption of sophisticated

---

[1] Sir Walter Scott (1771–1832), pursued an official life in the Scottish law courts while practising as a poet, novelist, and historian.

society; or, for that matter, he may go to nature itself, to streams, hills and clouds, pantheistically invested with significance. All these types of experiment, found in the writers who came forward after 1790, bear witness to one common feeling, that the old conventions had shrivelled, had lost relevance to problems now thrusting forward, were denying expression to human energy. In the work of the young men of this period there is at its best passion and curiosity, at its worst sentimentality and frivolity.[1] Taken all in all it was the beginning of one of the greatest periods of our literature.

In Walter Scott the Romantic impulse was not fully developed. He himself was no theorist, no rebel. But Scott's love of the past was intense and was the love of the day-dreamer not the scholar, even though he approached his work with studious care.[2] Scott's characters are often dummies: few of his men and none of his women are more than pegs on which to hang costumes.[3] It is in both the action and the setting for his dramas that there is vivid life. Scott by 1815 was not yet using his talent to re-create the past to full advantage. *Rokeby* appeared in 1813 and *Waverley* in 1814 but up to that point he had been expressing in verse (*Minstrelsy of the Border* 1802, the *Lay of the Last Minstrel* 1805, *Marmion* 1808, the *Lady of the Lake* 1810) an affection for the Scottish past which was to find better expression in the great historical novels. Scott is a romantic because he scorned the universality of the classical view and absorbed himself completely in the ancient customs of a small corner of Britain. In his infectious affection for local peculiarities rooted in the past can be traced one of the elements in nationalism. In the popularity of

[1] Even sentimentality as in the *Irish Melodies* of Thomas Moore (1779-1852) or flippancy as in the same author's *The Twopenny Postbag* seems to have a vigour and freshness in this period of emancipation from the old conventions. The contrast between the old and the new is best felt perhaps in comparing the work of competent versifiers rather than that of men of genius. Erasmus Darwin (1731-1802) may be read as representative of the eighteenth-century world: his *Loves of the Plants* has a controlled and attractive sobriety. By contrast in some of the work of Samuel Rogers (1763-1855)—a man with small talent for poetry but much for benevolent friendship—the excited spirit of the regency contrives to make itself felt, though incoherently.

[2] Scott did serious work as an historian, e.g. editing the papers of Sir Ralph Sadler and later writing a life of Napoleon. In such work he is competent but cramped.

[3] It may be objected that he left a great gallery of Scottish characters. Admittedly his Scots are more real than the rest, but even they tend to be types embodying aspects of national character.

his work can be seen the growth of a reading public whose emotional needs were satisfied by such sentiment.

A much more obvious example of the Romantic movement, and one where the influence of the social history of these years can be seen directly, is the work of William Blake.[1] Blake was a craftsman, an engraver, of only indifferent fortune, who depended upon the patronage of more fortunate artists such as Fuseli[2] and upon indulgent clients. In the 1780's he had mixed in turbulent radical circles in London. The outbreak of the French Revolution stirred him to excited literary composition in the cause of liberty. In 1804 he was tried (but acquitted) at Chichester assizes on a charge of uttering treasonable and seditious expressions about the king and the army. His radicalism was of the crudest: 'Give us the Bread that is our due and right, by taking away Money, or a Price, or Tax upon what is common to all in thy Kingdom.' But when, from this simple premise, he went on to brood over human destiny he brought a rich and confused imagery into play. His earlier poems (*Songs of Innocence*, 1789) are simple in language. Indeed, in freshness of effect he seems to anticipate and excel the efforts of the young Wordsworth. His verses are apparently as direct as folksong. But contained within them is a symbolism which adds to their force by an undercurrent of strangeness.

Over the next thirty years Blake laboured on great prophetic books, often turgid, made difficult by a private mythology, with symbols of shifting significance, but speckled with patches of shining clarity. In these works can be traced an old nonconformist influence going back to the seventeenth century: Blake is the radical working man who has pored over the Bible. But mingled with this strain is that of the Romantic poet whose mind dwells upon metallic giants and tortured flesh. Blake rebelled directly against the industrial changes of the time. His imagination fastened upon the shapes of the new towns and introduced them into nightmares where

> Scotland pours out his Sons to Labour at the Furnaces
> Wales gives his Daughters to the Looms.

[1] William Blake (1757–1827), in both pictures and poems gave expression to his mysticism and his belief that 'all things exist in the human imagination alone'.

[2] H. Fuseli (1741–1825), a native of Zurich: professor of painting at the academy from 1799 to 1825; excelled in sketches where he showed subtlety of line and composition.

Through the prophetic books there is the sound of whirring machines and 'the anvils of Death thunder incessant'. As a painter and engraver he has, with a more consistent control of his technique, the same power to move us into protest by strangeness and horror. Blake struggled to express his own vision of humanity, man defenceless in the new world and alien to the old.

Of course not every writer was as conscious as Blake of changes around them, nor even as hurried along by heated feelings as Sir Walter Scott. Jane Austen[1] was as unromantic as it is possible to be. Her first published novel, *Sense and Sensibility*, was a tart attack upon excessive emotionalism and a defence of sturdy good judgement. *Northanger Abbey* was begun with the purpose of poking fun at the 'gothic' mysteries of romantic fiction. Jane Austen is a great novelist for her exquisite sense of proportion and the delicacy of her sarcasms—all that is unlike the Romantic movement. Yet there is a difference between the rationalism of Jane Austen and that of the eighteenth century. It is tempting to describe it simply in terms of class. Her ground is that of the sensible upper-middle-class woman. Her mind is as rational as that of, say, Johnson or Fielding, but she is at once less robust and less abstract than they. Again, her psychology (as compared with that of Richardson, whom she carefully studied) is closer-knit, is more embedded in 'domestic life in country villages', as she herself said. She is less of a snob, because more self-assured, than Fanny Burney. Unaware as she seems to be of the events of the outside world—as witness the small part the wars play in her chronicles[2]—yet she is in accord with the times at least in her assumption of the independence of her own class: thus she pokes fun at Mr. Collins for his servility, a quality expected of chaplains in the eighteenth century. When all this is said, however, it must still be admitted that Miss Austen lies outside easy generalizations about the spirit of the age.

Byron,[3] too, though in his life he was to be the type-figure of Romantic excess, was in his best work closer to the old than to

---

[1] Jane Austen (1775–1817), a clergyman's daughter. Her major works are *Sense and Sensibility* (1811), *Pride and Prejudice* (1813), *Mansfield Park* (1814), *Emma* (1816), *Northanger Abbey* and *Persuasion* (1818). The dates are those of publication. She had begun writing the books in 1796.

[2] In spite of her having sailor brothers.

[3] George, Lord Byron (1788–1824); for his later history, Sir E. L. Woodward, *The Age of Reform* (O.H.E. vol. xiii), p. 30.

the new world. Before 1815 he had produced *English Bards and Scotch Reviewers*, a work which is in the satirical tradition of Pope and in which both the new school in poetry and its critics are impartially savaged. He had also won great fame with *Childe Harold, The Bride of Abydos*, and *The Corsair*, all in the latest Romantic manner. But though Byron was clever in his use of paint and scenery to catch the taste of the moment, his true genius was but rarely active in such work. He turned out these pieces as B. R. Haydon or Wilkie turned out their historical paintings. Colour was splashed across the canvas, dramatic feeling was emphasized to the point of sentimentality or tedium. Byron's greatest work was done just after the end of the wars, in *Don Juan*. Here the core is not romantic but elegantly cynical. What it owes, apart from the songs inset, to the zeitgeist is an easy informality of style, a style which expresses its intellectual content with greater force (and for a wider audience) than was possible with the old-fashioned couplets.

When Jane Austen and Byron are set on one side it is possible to see in all the other great writers of the epoch a common impulse away from classical order and over to the irregularities of the movements of the imagination. Perhaps the most significant date is 1798. In that year Wordsworth and Coleridge[1] issued *Lyrical Ballads*, poems written not in language hitherto thought poetical but 'as far as was possible in a selection of words really used by men'. The subject-matter was humble 'because in that condition the essential passions of the heart can find a better soil in which they can attain their maturity'. In everyday life, Wordsworth went on, there 'could be found a far more permanent, and a far more philosophical language than that which is frequently substituted for it by poets'.[1] This declaration, with the poems which adorn the theme, though not well received at first, marked the end of the old poetry. There is about the early

---

[1] William Wordsworth (1770–1850), son of an attorney, educated at Cambridge; in France at the beginning of the revolution; after a period in Germany settled in the English Lake district; poet laureate, 1843.

Samuel Taylor Coleridge (1772–1834), son of a schoolmaster and clergyman; educated at Cambridge; by turns a trooper in the dragoons, a unitarian preacher, newspaper editor, a student of German philosophy, a planner of a communistic settlement to be formed in America, and opium addict; but he was also the author of *The Ancient Mariner, Kubla Khan*, and *Christabel*, and the most famous conversationalist of the day.

[2] The quotations here are all from the Preface to *Lyrical Ballads*, the *thèse raisonnée* of the new movement.

poems of Wordsworth and the best poems of Coleridge a magic honesty. In their approach to nature they were not, like poets earlier in the century, superior persons willing to beguile an hour with something picturesque, but men abandoning themselves to—

> that blessed mood
> In which the burthen of the mystery,
> In which the heavy and the weary weight
> Of all this unintelligible world
> Is lightened.

Wordsworth, after he had been disillusioned by the French Revolution, turned to men as he imagined them to be in nature and so to nature itself, which never could betray him. Coleridge was the cleverer and the weaker man: at times he was more artificial and then, as though to balance this, his surrender to dreams and impressions was the more complete. His private life, with its matrimonial difficulties, with its opium clouds, its feckless drifting amid continual bubbling of evanescent talk, was romanticism in an extreme form. He discovered no stays or standards to keep him from disintegration. But before Wordsworth became a bore or Coleridge an encumbrance they had, with *Tintern Abbey* or with the *Ancient Mariner* and *Christabel*, opened up new paths for poetry.

Coleridge in religion, in philosophy, in criticism, in aesthetics, could not desist from teaching. To his influence must be attributed in large measure the replacement of French ideas on aesthetics, which had dominated the eighteenth century, by those of German origin. He was obsessed by the idea of releasing the urge to creation. Much of eighteenth-century literature was, at its best, in his view only the work of fancy. Fancy, he explained, was the ability to see a link between two objects, a link which might be obscure but which could be logically established. The true poet, however, worked by the imagination. The imagination enabled him to fuse together objects hitherto unconnected, and so to create new truths undiscoverable by ratiocination.

Such a theory prepared the path for the second generation of romantics of whom only Shelley[1] matured quickly enough to have revealed some part of his powers before 1815 (his best work was published after that date). These were poets who

[1] See Sir E. L. Woodward, *The Age of Reform* (O.H.E. vol. xiii), p. 30.

elevated beauty like the Host to give help to a troubled world. Shelley hated the past; it shackled him like a stupid father. He gaily dismissed the rules and regulations of ordinary life in the name of the freedom of the spirit. In politics he was a revolutionary radical. He sometimes seemed, in his own life, to lose grip on reality altogether and to suffer persecution mania. But his poetry rose on an imaginative vision both of nature and of an ideal future flowering of the human spirit. Taking his ideas from Godwin[1]—from whom he also took a daughter to be his second wife—he owed the freedom of his verse to the pioneer work of Coleridge.

This outbreak of new artistic energy was a symptom of a restlessness and adventurousness which is the complement to the stirrings in social life. But social changes also had their effect upon thought in a more direct and simple way. The rise of the middle-class public with interest in the discussion of ideas was bound to change the tone and techniques of literature and journalism. The young men, to take one example, who launched the *Edinburgh Review* in 1802 found 10,000 readers who welcomed its forthrightness as a change from the stiff old periodicals. It was progressive whig in its politics and sternly conservative in its views on literature. Seven years later the *Quarterly Review* broke into the same market to counter this virulent whiggery with tory arguments.[2] Many ephemeral publications arose to cater to the demand for news and for up-to-date comments on a world of so many changes. The circulation of *The Times* rose to close on 5,000 in the early years of the war.

In response to a quickened interest in human beings and their feelings a crowd of essayists began to find employment in the journals and newspapers. Southey[3] though a dull poet—a spiritual hanger-on of Wordsworth up in the Lakes—knew exactly how to please readers who wanted prose which would be easy to read and yet dignified, light but yet serious. Prolifically, and in a tory patriotic vein, he gave it to them. The new generation of men of letters rarely attempted to fit books or events into appropriate places in a canon of values. They were romantics and relied upon their feelings and not systems. They used them-

---

[1] See above, p. 534 n. 1.

[2] The *Edinburgh Review* was written largely by Jeffrey, Brougham, and Sidney Smith. The *Quarterly* began with John Murray, Scott, and Southey: it was not at first so successful as its rival, but soon became influential in the hands of Lockhart.

[3] Robert Southey (1774–1834), author of *The Life of Nelson* (1813).

selves as thermometers, they recorded the impact made upon their nerves. Their impressions were set out in an intimate, flowing, style which made even the *Edinburgh* appear stiff. In this genre Leigh Hunt gossiped away on any subject under the sun. To this taste Lamb appealed, filling the pages of Leigh Hunt's *Examiner* with his delicate sentiment and simple jokes through the grim year 1811.[1]

Charles Lamb, indeed, exploited the cult of personality with peculiar brilliance, for he was not content to offer the public one face only but slipped from one shape to another with quicksilver ease. Lamb, the son of a clerk and a farmer's daughter, with a sister periodically overcome by violent insanity, himself laboured away as a clerk of the East India Company. To his friends he was a solid support and refuge. His pleasures were bourgeois, his preferred milieu suburban. But in the public prints he could play the mocking spirit, the sentimental poseur, the sensitive teacher. Hazlitt,[2] by contrast, offered always the same self to the public, pugnacious, self-educated, self-assertive, enthusiastic, and transparently honest. As a critic Hazlitt has the soundest instincts. As a writer he carries the argument along at a manly, easy, stride. His gusto is infectious. His directness which was so admirably suited to his audience (the readers of the *Morning Chronicle* from 1813) would have seemed crude to the taste of only thirty years before. In eighteenth-century work he appreciated only virility—when it could be found beneath the mannerisms. Burke's eloquence he hailed as the greatest imaginative triumph of that age.

It is not the least of the achievements of this group of volatile writers to have rediscovered Shakespeare. They all set to work scraping away the prim façade with which the actors and critics of the eighteenth century had obscured him. In Shakespeare they found a genius to their own taste, a turbulent and adventurous poet of undisciplined force speaking to them from another disturbed age. Coleridge fitted him into his philosophy, Hazlitt gave glimpses of the plays by lightning flash, Lamb (and his sister) introduced new readers to the master with their simple expositions. The success of these writers demonstrates, what would be difficult to prove otherwise, the broadening of

[1] Charles Lamb (1775-1834): *Tales from Shakespeare* (1807): *Essays of Elia*, 1820-22, reprinted in 1823. James Henry Leigh Hunt (1784-1859): editor, agitator, essayist, and talker.

[2] William Hazlitt (1778-1830).

the audience for intellectual and imaginative work. There obviously was a public interested in experiment, with much to learn, and little prejudice in favour of the old conventions.

The rebellion against the old rules is also apparent in painting. The work of the history painters, growing ever larger and more violent, has already been referred to. In portrait painting the only great figure, as Romney faded away, was Sir Thomas Lawrence.[1] Lawrence abandoned the principles of Reynolds,[2] preferring to make an immediate impression with the picture as a whole. The intent was to use the dress and setting as much as the face or poise to establish a mood. Indeed, the detail of the face is sometimes careless. There is a liveliness, a dash, about Lawrence's painting rare in official portraiture, albeit it is combined with great elegance. This same abandonment of the classical framework was beginning in landscape painting also. Here the great master was Turner.[3] Turner appealed to the new taste in part by his subject-matter—paintings to illustrate Byron, Scott, and Rogers's poems and also topographical surveys such as his *Rivers of England* or *Scenery of the South Coast*. His landscapes, even when they did not—as they often do—frame some story of action, are painted with a feeling of movement very different from the serenity of Wilson.[4] Turner in these years was working his way through experiments in rendering nature with intensity in the effort to express Wordsworth's 'something far more deeply interfused . . . that . . . rolls through all things'. After 1815 this pursuit was to lead him on to experiments in painting light in an impressionistic style. These later canvases were thought by many people to be unmeaning splashes of colour: up to 1815, however, Turner successfully met the general taste for feeling and animation in the depicting of natural scenes. Constable, on the other hand, painting with naturalism that, Fuseli said, made him call for his umbrella, was still unsuccessful. He had been sending canvases to the academy from 1802 onwards but had failed to sell even one until 1814.[5]

Music alone of the arts showed no sign of being revivified by

---

[1] Sir Thomas Lawrence (1769–1830); his success was brilliant from the beginning; painter to George III, 1792; knighted in 1815; died in poverty though his income had been over £10,000 a year for many years.   [2] See above, p. 342.

[3] J. M. W. Turner (1775–1851), the son of a hairdresser; professor of perspective at the academy 1807.   [4] See above, p. 344.

[5] For John Constable therefore, though born in 1776, only one year after Turner, see Sir E. L. Woodward, *The Age of Reform* (O.H.E. vol. xiii), p. 569.

the experiments of a shifting society. That the taste of the English public was perceptive would seem to be suggested by the enthusiastic reception given to Haydn on his visits to England in 1790 and 1794. No new English composer worthy of note, however, made his appearance. The most significant figure was probably that of Charles Dibdin.[1] Dibdin wrote patriotic and pathetic pieces about the sea some of which (like 'Tom Bowling' produced in *The Oddities* at the Lyceum Theatre in 1790) attained enormous vogue because they chimed in with middle- and lower-class enthusiasm for Nelson's navy.

As one would expect, architecture was quickly affected by social developments. 'Even men of inferior rank', wrote the architect Sir William Chambers in 1791, 'aspire to taste in the fine arts',[2] and the nature of architecture, in providing halls and homes to commission, enables men of all but the lowest class to have their say in it. From the 1790's onwards the middle-class men of improved fortune were everywhere demanding new homes on the outskirts of the growing towns. James Watt, for instance, when he retired busied himself in directing his architect (Samuel Wyatt) in the building of his house Heathfield outside Birmingham: soon he was building another near Rhayader.

One strong current in architecture therefore was the provision of substantial villas in moderate gardens for the successful business man. These ranged from the large ornamental cottage[3] to the small country house. A new style, the fake antique, grew up with them and imitations of Tudor buildings were popular. Those who eschewed this and inclined instead towards the dignity of the great eighteenth-century palaces, but could not afford to build on sufficient scale, were met by the simple device of building two separate houses masquerading as one from the exterior by a uniform front and linking pediment. Thus the semi-detached house came into popularity out of a middle-class deference to the grandeur of their betters. This at least preserved elegance better than the decorated blown-up cottage.

---

[1] Charles Dibdin (1745–1814); composer and author of many songs and musical plays; a lecturer on music though he lacked training or fitness.

[2] Quoted J. Summerson, *Architecture in Britain, 1530 to 1830*, p. 306.

[3] Cf. Coleridge, *The Devil's Thoughts*, 1799.

> He saw a cottage with a double coach-house.
> A cottage of gentility
> And the Devil did grin, for his darling sin
> Is pride that apes humility.

Romantic interest in the past naturally stimulated the Gothicism which was mentioned in connexion with Strawberry Hill.[1] James Wyatt[2] between 1800 and 1807 built the most extraordinary of all such houses for William Beckford, Fonthill. This was an enormous building in four arms (almost cruciform) with a high central octagonal tower,[3] the outlines of the design being intentionally confused by a loose collection of additional rooms. Superficially it resembled a great cathedral. The Gothic style was as yet only a foible of eccentrics like Beckford and a few villa builders. No close study of medieval building, to enable it to be seriously imitated, had yet been made.

Architects were moved, in general, by two not necessarily compatible ideas. There was first a movement towards simplicity of line, almost to the point of functionalism, as well as that towards a purity of classical style. Secondly there was a wish to make buildings lighter in appearance, more graceful, and particularly more picturesque. Sir John Soane[4] was the greatest of those who broke away from the Adams school. In his Bank Stock Office (1792) as in his Dulwich Art Gallery (1811–14) he dispensed with the traditional pillars and roof ribs in favour of grooved strips. He reduced rooms nearer to the primitive four walls and gave relief in a flatter type of decoration on the surface. As he yielded to the picturesque movement he experimented with planes and with light. In his own house the eye is led from plane to plane until it is difficult to realize exactly where this flat wall, the exact termination of the room, really is. Lighting from above by squat domes or concealed windows enabled him to combine simplicity in line with subtlety of effect. Soane's originality was in his treatment of interiors. Lesser men, notably Smirke[5] and Wilkins,[6] were less scientific in their conception of simplicity of line. The movement showed itself in them as a

---

[1] See above, pp. 341 and 352.

[2] James Wyatt (1747–1813); a master of many styles, great in none. His classical buildings, such as Oriel College library and the Canterbury Gate of Christ Church, are solidly splendid.

[3] The steeple in the centre was badly built and collapsed some twenty-five years after it was built.

[4] Sir John Soane (1753–1837), son of a Berkshire builder; awarded Travelling Scholarship by George III in 1776 and studied in Italy; surveyor to the Bank of England 1788; professor of architecture at the academy, 1806; his house became a museum by his will.

[5] Robert Smirke (1781–1867), son of an academician painter.

[6] William Wilkins (1778–1839), son of an architect and sixth wrangler at Cambridge.

demand for 'pure' designs based on the study of Greek and not Roman models. Downing College Hall in Cambridge (Wilkins, 1807) is an example of this unadorned Greek revival.

The other movement, that towards the picturesque, was probably the more characteristic of the age. Its greatest exponent was John Nash,[1] but the landscape gardener Humphrey Repton[2] must be reckoned of equal significance. For gentry everywhere felt the need for a change from the principles of Capability Brown.[3] They were bored by his pastoral platitudes. Repton believed that every estate should be different, that nature should be encouraged to show the peculiarities of each local setting. To add to the variety he, with Nash and others, would stud the grounds with dairies, cottages, and such outbuildings, in a variety of styles, Indian, Chinese, French, Italian, or Gothic. They imitated the picturesque quality of Morland's[4] paintings, and the honeysuckled bower became a feature of the small country estate. In this trade Nash gained his experience. From 1806 as a government architect he carried the lessons of this experience into building on a greater scale. His designs for the prince's palace at Brighton (the banqueting and music rooms were being built in 1815) were a curious mixture. The convex ceilings and the inverted funnel silhouette suggested a great tent of a medieval king on some field of battle: there was a mixture of Chinese ornament with Gothic trimmings.[5]

Nash's greatest opportunity came in 1811. The whole area from Marylebone to Carlton House was to be laid out to include a new metropolitan thoroughfare, Regent Street, as well as a garden suburb in Regent's Park. Nash rose to so splendid an occasion. He produced a plan which combined the features of Bath—crescents, terraces, and so on—with his new doctrines of movement and the use of trees and grass. There were groups of many-pillared blocks separated from one another by open spaces, the heaviness of massive blocks was relieved by the

[1] John Nash (1752–1835), son of a millwright; built stucco-fronted houses as a novelty until he went bankrupt in 1783; started in London practice again after 1795; became a member of the prince of Wales's entourage; 1806 surveyor to the office of woods and forests; responsible for the regent's town planning schemes; discredited by his chaotic rebuilding of Buckingham Palace.

[2] Humphrey Repton (1752–1818), an 'estate improver'.

[3] See above, p. 341.

[4] See above, p. 344.

[5] To this Chinoiserie the Indian-inspired parts of the pavilion were added after 1815, though Repton had proposed to copy Indian examples as early as 1806.

breaking of the lines of frontage, by smaller semi-detached groups and, always, by open spaces. The whole is a brilliant blend of the formal and the picturesque in which economic needs—the access roads, the use of the new Regent's Canal—have been skilfully met. With the start of Regent Street in 1813, where the curve of the street was emphasized by the gay use of Ionic pillars, Nash could claim to have made the West End of London the most delightful urban prospect in the world.[1]

Regency building is distinguishable from that of the pre-war period by its gaiety and lightness—sometimes, as with Nash's detail, by a shoddy slipshodness. The exteriors of houses were relieved by fretting straight walls, by adding balconies and trellises, often in the metals which industrial expansion had cheapened. This fanciful decoration gained in effect because it often merely overlaid the basic simplicity and fine proportion of the classical design which was traditional. Thus the charm of the style of the period is like that of a woman of natural beauty of bone-structure who frivolously adorns herself with jewelled gegaws and cosmetics; the combination of formal dignity and lightheartedness produced, for the moment, a captivating effect. But the lightheartedness was a symptom of restlessness. The balance of taste was precarious. The success of the regency period was the prelude to a disastrous decline in architecture as novelty and pastiche swamped the sense of form, and the adornments became an end in themselves.

Restlessness might indeed be taken as the key to the cultural history of 1793 to 1815, taking the form of an inspired discontent in literature and of a lightness of touch in architecture. Restlessness also showed itself in the lives and manners of the aristocratic society which ruled England. A symptom of this was the increase in ostentation in society, the competition to give ever more magnificent parties in the style set by the prince regent himself.[2] It amused the leaders of this society to admit into it on familiar terms those who amused them, so that there existed a disreputable fringe of glib men with no visible means of support, devotees of the turf and dice-box. Much of this hectic amusement was vulgar. The regent himself was a man of taste, but no fixity of affection. As a result his sudden and

---

[1] Nash's Regent Street has been demolished. His buildings in Regent's Park were threatened with demolition but seem to have been saved.

[2] For an example see above, p. 501.

passing enthusiasms, his preciosity, left a general impression of shallowness and sordidness. He dabbled in too many styles and had too many friends to be faithful to any. In 1794 the prince met George Brummel[1] who at the age of sixteen had just inherited £30,000. For the next twenty years Brummel enjoyed the princely favour; in 1814, deserted by his prince and too closely followed by his creditors, he fled to France. While his favour lasted he gave himself the airs of the dictator of fashion.[2] Brummel's world was one both of elaborate etiquette and of rowdy familiarity: the art of living consisted in knowing when which was appropriate. In it the ageing Sheridan exhausted himself like some tipsy moth blundering around the phosphorescent prince, while pimps, languishing ladies, a confidential physician or secretary, artists, and a politician or two, joined in the dance.

Old fashioned people deplored the changing of old standards. They saw a reflection of feverish decadence in the dress of fashionable women. Up to about 1810 the well-dressed woman was still lacing herself up tightly in corsets to hold the bosom high, and keeping warm with several petticoats, the whole being finished with a dress of simple lines. About the time of the beginning of the regency all this was changed. Corsets were discarded. A woman was to be as nature made her—for even the dressmaker felt the spirit of Wordsworthian romance. The petticoats too were thrown away, until the lady of fashion went out in one simple dress, cut exceedingly low over the bosom, and practically nothing else.[3] As Byron, for once a conservative in morals and as ever ironically, remarked

> Like Mother Eve our maids may stray unblam'd
> For they are naked—and are not ashamed.

On her feet the smart lady wore sandals or Roman boots. Her head was covered not now with feathers but with simple crown hats very tight on the temples and often completed with tassels. The latest craze was for a new dance, the waltz. The waltz was thought particularly decadent because the partners were enlaced unlike the older formal figures. Byron, again, was shocked:

---

[1] George nicknamed 'Beau' Brummel (1778–1840). Died in extreme poverty.

[2] Among Brummel's innovations was the wearing of trousers instead of breeches in fashionable society.

[3] With the rejection of petticoats women of fashion began to wear knickers, hitherto the undergarment only of professional dancers. Thus both men and women experienced a revolution in nether garments.

Terpsichore—too long misdeem'd a maid—
Reproachful term, bestow'd but to upbraid
Henceforth in all the bronze of brightness shine
The least a vestal of the virgin nine. . . .
Through the full veins thy gentle poison swims
And wakes to wantonness the willing limbs.

Middle-class people were apt to regard most of these changes as signs of debauchery. But one restless habit which they were quick to adopt was the new fad for holidays at the seaside. George III had popularized Weymouth and his son had given immense publicity to Brighton. Other watering places were popular by 1815; middle-class families walked by the sea, gossiped in tea shops, and patronized the circulating library. Even the hard-working Lamb found time, he said, to be dull at Worthing, duller at Brighton, and dullest at Eastbourne, but happy for a brief week at Margate.

England had, then, after twenty years of war, two faces, the one bacchanalian the other businesslike. A new creative energy in industry and in literature was matched by an uneasy activity in the old ruling classes. The old institutions went on working, bringing the country successfully through crises to peace. But they were defended where before no defence had been necessary. A clever young man like Canning could dazzle his admirers by his skill in using a very modern mind to justify old ways which before had been taken for granted. The professional cleverness—and the carelessness—of Canning as a politician is reminiscent of the tricks of Nash as an architect. Both were expert in enlivening old plans with novel touches and so of pleasing both the aristocracy and the pushing businessmen. But in their reckless ingenuity they typify the end of an epoch, the exhaustion of a style. Conflict and confusion were only postponed as men waited for the end of the war. In 1815 the shape of society and the currents of thought clearly indicated changes to come. Meanwhile the new moon held

the old Moon in her lap foretelling
The coming-on of rain and squally blast.[1]

[1] S. T. Coleridge, *Dejection* (1802).

XXI

THE END OF THE WAR, 1812–15

THE years from 1812 to 1815 formed an epilogue to the
effective reign of George III; in them the great struggle
with France, which had dominated the latter days of the
obstinate old king, was brought to a triumphant conclusion; but
now that it at length arrived he was oblivious. There was also
a tragi-comic pendant to another of the great issues of the reign,
the conflict with America.

The federalist party in America, with its interest in commerce
and its support in New England, had naturally co-operated with
England on the general lines sketched out by Shelburne and by
Pitt.[1] The defeat of this party by the Jeffersonian democrats had
meant that America had become less co-operative. The policy
of President Madison, up to the end of 1811, had been to coerce
England peacefully by such measures as an embargo on trade.
At the end of 1811 a new force came to the front in American
politics, that of western nationalism which was as much the
enemy of Jeffersonian ideas as of those of the federalists. It was
equally opposed to the Jeffersonian idea of limited central power
and to the federalist use of such power in the interests of conservative financiers or commercial men. The spokesmen of the
frontier states were exponents of the 'Manifest Destiny' of
America (though that phrase had not yet been invented); they
were hungry for the virgin lands of the west and for the settlements of Spain and Britain. The spirit of the West had already
rendered all treaties made with the Indians inoperative. In
1811, despite the settlement reached at Fort Wayne two years
before, Governor Harrison[2] of Indiana picked a quarrel with
the greatest of the Indian chiefs, Tecumseh, and fought the
battle of Tippecanoe in order to open up the lands beyond the
Mississippi. The Indians were ripe for destruction. But, Americans alleged, they were supported and maintained by the
British. The old dispute between Whitehall and the frontiers-

[1] See above, pp. 253 f. and also pp. 276, 290.
[2] William Henry Harrison (1773–1841), later to be ninth president of the
United States.

men was still alive even after Independence. To obtain the western lands it was necessary to destroy British influence which percolated down the rivers from Canada into the unmapped areas between the United States and the Rockies. In addition the purchase of Louisiana from Napoleon had tempted land-speculators to look across into Spanish Florida with covetous eyes. And in 1811 Spain and Britain were allies. Therefore the western nationalists wanted the might of the whole United States to be used for the ejection of European powers from North America, thus clearing the way for the wagons and axes of the restless pioneers.

In the Congress which met in November 1811 Henry Clay[1] of Kentucky was a spokesman of this movement: he obtained the key position of Speaker of the house of representatives. Peter B. Porter of South Carolina (but whose business interests were in expansionist road projects in the Niagara region) became chairman of the foreign affairs committee. Together these two pushed the president towards a breach with England. The committee on foreign affairs reported that there must be a war with England. The object should be to destroy British fishery controls on the northern shores, to shatter the British control of the United States trade with the West Indies and to conquer Canada. 'I feel anxious', added Felix Grundy of Tennessee, 'not only to add the Floridas to the South but the Canadas to the North of this Empire.'[2] These warlike words synchronized with the warlike actions of Harrison at Tippecanoe: such words and deeds overbore the protests of New England. In May 1812 a motion in the house of representatives—'That under the present circumstances it is inexpedient to resort to a war with Great Britain'—was negatived by 62 votes to 37. On 1 June 1812 President Madison sent a message to Congress setting out the grievances of the United States against Great Britain.

Madison's message grouped his complaints under five heads. The first four dealt with the maritime quarrels which had so long been the subject of diplomatic exchanges and which had been intensified by the orders in council.[3] Yet the groups most

[1] Henry Clay (1777–1852), of Virginian stock: he was later to be a notable secretary of state but to fail, for all his political astuteness, to become president.

[2] Quoted in G. Dangerfield, *The Era of Good Feelings*, p. 37. Felix Grundy (1777–1840), an ally and rival of Andrew Jackson in politics.

[3] Which were on the eve of repeal, see above, p. 475, and below, p. 552 n. 3.

affected by blockade, impressment, and search, were against war. They were flourishing happily on the evasion of rules, enjoying prosperity by supplying the deficiency of British shipping caused by the wars. Madison's fifth point was 'the warfare just renewed by the savages on one of our extensive frontiers . . . among tribes in constant intercourse with British traders and garrisons'. Here was a more powerful theme. Yet the British were not guilty of encouraging Tecumseh. On the first four points the American case was strong in law but weak in their hearts: on the fifth their case was as weak as its potency to move men was strong. Certainly the maritime grievances had their effect. They added a sense of emotional fervour to a practical decision, they cloaked acquisitiveness with morality. 'We are going to fight', said Andrew Jackson,[1] 'for the re-establishment of our national character, misunderstood and vilified at home and abroad . . .',[2] in other words to remedy pride hurt on the high seas by an acquisition of prairies and forests. On 18 June 1812[3] the house of representatives voted, by 79 to 49, that war existed between Great Britain and the United States; the Senate took the same decision by 19 to 13: the votes for peace were given by the states extending from New York to the north and east: the south, starting from Pennsylvania, was for war. War was formally declared by the president the next day.

The obvious way to open up free expansion along the 3,000 miles of frontier, which stretched from Maine to the Old North West and slanted south from there to the mouth of the Ohio and Spanish Florida, a rough and mysterious area of forest and rivers, was for the Americans to drive the British from Canada. Upper Canada was the most tempting area for it jutted down by the Great Lakes towards the heart of the United States. The most effective method of conquering this area was by attack upon the St. Lawrence supply route upon which it depended for all its British stores. But the Americans chose instead the superficially easier strategy of the direct assault upon its frontiers. At the very start of the war General Hall moved into Upper Canada by Detroit. But he was driven back by Brook

---

[1] Andrew Jackson (1767–1845), later seventh president of the United States.

[2] Quoted in Dangerfield, *The Era of Good Feelings*, p. 39.

[3] Lord Castlereagh had declared two days earlier that the orders in council would be repealed if all corresponding acts of interdiction against England were given up, but this news, of course, had not reached America. The formal cancellation of the orders, as regards America, was effected on 23 July 1812.

and forced to surrender with his 2,500 men. General Wadsworth was no luckier in his push farther east towards Queenstown, near Niagara: he, with 900 men, surrendered to Major General Sir Roger Sheaffe. Thus in land operations in 1812 the British stood successfully on the defensive.

On the seas the Americans began with small forces. A motion to build a bigger fleet was defeated in Congress. But the 165 gunboats and the 16 frigates (most of them larger than British frigates and almost the equivalent of ships of the line) with which America began the war were very effective in privateering, thanks to the preoccupation of the British navy with other parts of the world. The Americans did build new ships of war but they were intended for service on the Great Lakes, serving the master plan of the conquest of Canada.

In 1813, after talk of an armistice had come to nothing, the Americans began once more to tap away along the frontier on the lakes. General Winchester led 1,000 men to attack Detroit, but he led them only to disaster. On the other hand General Dearborne succeeded in capturing York,¹ the capital of Upper Canada on Lake Ontario. A British counterthrust, under Proctor, was attempted at the Miami rapids near Lake Erie but had to be abandoned. Perry with his American lake fleet overcame Canadian opposition on Lake Erie. On Lake Ontario the American Commodore Chauncey fought vigorous but indecisive actions against Sir James Yeo. By September the Americans had achieved their first objectives. Having pushed across the border near Niagara they were on Canadian soil along the whole frontier. The British had lost all their posts in Michigan save Machilimackinac. In the late autumn therefore the Americans believed that the time had come when they might subdue this province of loyalists completely. A double attack was launched on Montreal. Hampton advanced by land and Wilkinson started down the St. Lawrence from Lake Ontario. Both attacks were defeated and in consequence the Americans were forced back again on their own side of the frontier. The British seized the initiative, cleared Niagara, and burned the town of Buffalo in revenge for damage done in Upper Canada. By the

---

¹ York was so named in honour of the second son of George III when General Simcoe made it the capital in 1794. Subsequently (in 1834) its name was changed back to that given it by the Indians, Toronto. It was twice burned by the Americans during the war.

end of the year therefore the Americans were even less advanced than they had been the previous winter.

On the ocean it became a war of dashing commanders. The Americans rejoiced in the victory of their frigate *The Constitution* in a fight with the British *Java*: against this British sailors chuckled over the daring with which their *Shannon* had destroyed the enemy's *Chesapeake* right under Boston lighthouse. There were signs of a more serious British naval effort as the frontier war settled down into a see-saw affair of raiding parties. English commanders began to raid the Carolina coasts. In April 1814 Cockrane, well trained in European waters, proclaimed a blockade of the whole American coastline. In July Moose island, a fishing centre in Passamaquody bay, was seized by the British. In August Cockrane took General Ross[1] from Chesapeake Bay up the Patuxent on a dramatic raid: landing his soldiers within striking distance of Washington Ross brushed aside the 9,000 Americans who defended the capital, burned the Congress buildings, the presidential house,[2] the treasury, the arsenal, the dockyards, and the bridge across the Potomac, and then returned to Cockrane. A similar raid destroyed stores in Alexandria, but that attempted against Baltimore was abortive. Such enterprises bore witness to the British power to wound if not to conquer.

On the Canadian frontier, in 1814, it became clearer that there was a stalemate. American attacks round Lake Erie were gallantly repulsed by de Watteville. British attacks in the area of Lake Champlain were brought to naught by Macdonough's victory over Downie's flotilla on the Lake near Plattsburg. By October 1814 it was clear that the Americans could not attempt invasion of Canada. Equally the British could only hope to slice off a section of Maine and to harry the coasts. The chief sufferers from the war were the New England merchants who had opposed it from the first. So bad were the finances of the American government that it could only discharge its obligations abroad in bills drawn upon those engaged in illegal trade with the enemy. Governor Strong of Massachusetts openly spoke against the war and was suspected of planning in secret to take his state

[1] Robert Ross (1766–1814) had served with Moore at Corunna, at Walcheren, and with Wellington in Spain; he died of wounds received at Baltimore.

[2] Which was whitewashed to hide the marks of flames and thus acquired its nickname of the White House by which Americans reminded themselves of their indignation at this exploit.

over to the British side. In October 1814 the Hartford Assembly, with representatives from Massachusetts, Connecticut, Rhode Island, and from counties in New Hampshire and Vermont, proclaimed that the union had, thanks to Madison's war, failed 'in the greatest objects of its formation'. It seemed that the United States might be threatened by northern secession. Yet from American troubles Britain could gain nothing. Soldiers were brought from Europe and there was talk of sending Wellington to command them. But no one in Britain wanted to fight the War of Independence over again. Britain's interest, every year made clearer, was to trade with and not to fight with the United States.

In the last months of 1814, therefore, peace was painfully negotiated. Its terms were that both sides should revert to their position before the war, except that Britain kept the disputed islands in Passamaquody Bay. After much discussion of frontier lines (the United States proposed the 49° latitude from the Lake of the Woods across the Rockies) these, like the problem of fishing rights, the navigation of the Mississippi, and the great question of the freedom of the seas, were left in doubt and silence. It was appropriate to this war which began after its stated cause had been removed, and during which diplomatic relations had been maintained between the belligerents, that its operations went on after peace was signed. Peace came on 24 December 1814, but it was in January 1815 that Pakenham, in ignorance of the signature of peace, made a full-scale but unsuccessful attack on New Orleans,[1] and in February that Cockrane and Lambert captured Mobile.

The American War was, for Britain, always a side show, a distraction from the conflict with France. As the American War began, the greater struggle had entered its last phase. At the end of 1812 Napoleon was returning from Russia and Wellington was preparing to advance in the peninsula. In the first weeks of 1813 the Russians, pouring after the wreck of the grand army, occupied Königsberg in East Prussia. If a new offensive operation in north Germany was to follow the successful defence of Russia then the co-operation of Prussia was vital. The Prussian general Yorck, left in charge of the force guarding Napoleon's flank, showed the way to his king. By the convention of Taurog-

---

[1] It was here that Andrew Jackson began to establish his personal legend in American history.

gen, on the first day of the year 1813, Yorck declared his army
neutral. It was soon co-operating with the Russians. By the end
of January the king of Prussia was calling his subjects to take up
arms for the defence of their country—against whom was left,
for the moment, diplomatically vague. By 8 February the Russians were in Warsaw: France's ally Austria promptly retired
into Galicia and announced a truce. By the end of February the
king of Prussia was, at last, bold enough to proclaim that he
was against Napoleon. 'We bent under the superior power of
France. That Peace which deprived me of half my subjects
procured us no blessings, on the contrary it was more injurious
to us than war itself.' Prussia, as ever, was not only self-interested
but slow to perceive her best course. The Russians reached
Berlin on 4 March and Hamburg on 18 March. Sweden, under
the guidance of the Gascon Bernadotte, declared that she was
co-operating with Russia and expected in return to be given
Norway at the expense of Denmark.

In these months Napoleon had managed to gather a new
army. By April 1813 the contingents of this force had been
united near Jena. By the end of May it had retaken Hamburg.
Half of Germany, including Saxony, was either coerced or
attracted into Napoleon's camp for the decisive operations
which followed. Twice Napoleon defeated his enemies, at Lützen
and then at Bautzen. To maintain the new coalition in face of
such discouragement Great Britain entered into negotiations
with Prussia and Russia at Reichenbach. It was agreed that the
fight must be intensified. Prussia was to be restored to her position in 1806. Russia's rewards were not yet defined. Britain
would pay £2 million to enable Russia to keep 150,000 and
Prussia 80,000 men in the field. The new allies agreed to Castlereagh's request that none of them should open negotiations with
the enemy without consultation with the rest.

Austria, still dubious about the chances of war, now came
forward as a mediator. Metternich negotiated an armistice
between the opposed armies which lasted from 4 June to
10 August 1813. In that period Austria conveyed to the French
suggestions for peace about which Britain was kept in the dark.
Napoleon was offered peace if he would agree to the dissolution
of his duchy of Warsaw, to enlarge Prussia, to return Illyria to
Austria, and to restore Hamburg and Lübeck as free cities. At
the famous interview in Dresden Napoleon scorned this pro-

posal. The result was that the allies reopened the war and were joined by Austria. As they took up their swords again the allies admitted Britain—for whose interests they had shown no care in their Dresden overtures—back into their confidence. Britain was not averse to treating with France, was not yet set upon an unconditional surrender, but she intended to impose upon her friends certain principles of negotiation.

The risk of treating with France is great [Castlereagh declared], but the risk of losing our continental allies and the confidence of our own nation is greater. We must preserve our own faith inviolate to Spain, Portugal, Sicily, and Sweden. We must maintain our most important conquests, employing others to improve the general arrangements . . . and with respect to the Continent we must sustain and animate those Powers through whose exertions we can alone hope to improve it, taking care, in aiming at too much, not to destroy our future means of connexion and resistance.[1]

British authority in the councils of Europe, so recently scorned, was not derived only from her payment of subsidies. It gathered strength also in late June and July from the news which arrived from Spain.

At the beginning of 1813 Wellington was in Portugal refitting his men to achieve what he had so narrowly failed to do the previous year. The French had one army at Salamanca and Valladolid: another, under Soult, was at Toledo, close to King Joseph at Madrid. The demand for troops for Napoleon caused the French to draw in their outposted men and to concentrate in the centre and in the vital areas of the north. Along the east coast Suchet, with fair success, strengthened their hold as far south as Valencia. In May Wellington moved out on his prepared path into Spain marching north-eastwards from Freynada to Salamanca, and then on to Valladolid; at each river, the Douro, Tormes, Esla, Pisuerga and Carrion, he crossed westwards of the demoralized enemy, outflanking them and forcing them to retire before him. By early June he was at Burgos, the scene of his check the previous year;[2] but this time no serious

[1] Reported to Metternich on 21 June 1813; C. K. Webster, *The Foreign Policy of Castlereagh, 1812–1815*, p. 146. Britain had recently acquired special treaty obligations to Sweden; those to Spain and Portugal were part of the peninsular campaign: Lord William Bentinck was still maintaining British influence with the Neapolitan court in its refuge in Sicily and, in the intervals of quarrelling with them, was planning to use Sicily as a base for clearing Italy, a dream which had obsessed Englishmen ever since the time of Nelson.

[2] See above, p. 495.

opposition was attempted and on 14 June he began crossing the
Ebro. By this time the French had concentrated their armies of
the south and of the centre: these, under King Joseph and
Marshal Jourdan, took their stand before Vittoria. On 21 June
Wellington captured the heights commanding the river Zadora
in some severe fighting, brought his men across it, and drove in
the French centre. The Anglo-Spanish army had broken the
French hold of Spain, except on the east coast where Suchet
still kept Sir John Murray out of Tarragona. But in the north-
west of Spain the main French army streamed back across the
Bidassoa and so, through Irun, re-entered France. Soult with
some 30,000 to 40,000 men vainly tried to bar the gateway into
France on the west. But by mid-September the castle of San
Sebastian had fallen: by the end of October General Don
Carlos d'Espana received the surrender of Pamplona. On the
night of 10 November, having gathered together the troops
released from the sieges, Wellington forced the French defences
near St. Jean de Léon and penetrated to the rear of the French
right wing. This compelled the French armies to retire to
Bayonne, leaving the British firmly encamped on the French
side of the Pyrennees.

The news of the battle of Vittoria and of the collapse of the
French rule in Spain was a stimulus to the allies as they confronted Napoleon in central Europe and reopened hostilities in
mid-August. The allied aim was to drive the French from Silesia
and back across the Elbe by a series of attacks on the front and
flanks of their position. By 27 August the main armies faced
one another at Dresden. After a head-on collision with Napoleon's 130,000 men the allies had to scramble back from Saxony
into Bohemia. It took many small but severe actions over the
next six weeks before the allies recovered from this set-back.
Nevertheless by mid-October the French had been forced back
once more to the Elbe. Blücher and Bernadotte had cleared
Silesia of the French. Bavaria had entered the war against
France with 55,000 troops. Austria had re-emerged from her
defensive positions in Bohemia. On 16, 17, and 18 October at
Leipzig the great armies once more pushed bloodily against
one another. Napoleon could claim to have shown himself
superior in this battle considered as an exercise in military art,
but its consequence was that he had at once to commence a
retreat westwards towards the Rhine. He had 40,000 casualties

and, during the action on the 18th alone, seventeen battalions of deserters had left him. With his retreat many more units were forced to capitulate until, on his own showing, only a little over half his army of 180,000 men remained to him.

The allies, in contrast, gathered strength as it became clear that Napoleon was no longer irresistible in Europe. Württemberg joined the alliance. Hanover was speedily cleared of French troops. In November the population of Holland rose in revolt against the French occupying forces and welcomed the government of independence which the prince of Orange established at Amsterdam. Thus by the end of 1813 the allies were approaching the Rhine and Wellington was working on his maps of south-west France. France was at bay. The allies were successful enough to begin to dispute about the shape of a new Europe. Castlereagh once more implored them to remain united and to agree upon a common basis of peace, for 'the only safety for other Powers of Europe is to impose upon the ambitious propensities of France that constraint in time of peace, to which alone they will owe the concessions, which may by war be extracted from the enemy'.[1] The reminder was needed; the ancient jealousies between Austria and Russia threatened the alliance with disruption; nor could Britain herself be unaware of the disregard for her vital interests manifested by her three partners.

In December 1813 the powers decided to put forward the Frankfurt proposals as a basis for peace with Napoleon. France was offered her natural frontiers (that is the Rhine, the Alps, and the Pyrennees) but was to give up all influence in Germany and Italy. Holland was to be absolutely independent but its frontiers were not specified. Colonial questions were left vague except that on the high seas England should 'reconnaître la liberté du commerce et de la navigation, à laquelle la France a droit de prétendre'—a phrase of sinister possibilities to an English mind. To these terms the English representative at allied headquarters, Lord Aberdeen, guilelessly consented. Castlereagh disapproved when he heard of them. Not only had maritime questions been raised before the European problems were solved but, much more important, nothing had been proposed which would remove Antwerp from French control. Belgium had received no consideration. Yet constraint here

[1] C. K. Webster, *The Foreign Policy of Castlereagh*, p. 186.

upon the French was, in his view, the first necessity. The Frankfurt terms were, indeed, Metternich's terms. He wished to
arrive at a quick settlement in the west, where Austria had no
interest now that she had abandoned her Netherlands, in order
that all Austrian effort might be devoted to the settlement of
Poland, Saxony, Bavaria, and eastern Europe. Already the
Dalmatian coast had been cleared by Austrian troops; their
army was poised for action in northern Italy. To Austria the
dangers remaining were the ambitions of Russia and Prussia.
Castlereagh was not on the spot to prevent peace on the Frankfurt basis being urged upon Napoleon. Fortunately—in English
eyes—Napoleon did not accept at once: moving constantly to
strike blows on the allied armies, he scored some successes
against Blücher. He still had hopes of retaining influence in
Germany and Italy. In the period of delay the tsar became more
hostile to the idea of peace of any sort with this Corsican. The
Frankfurt terms ceased to be available to the French once Castlereagh, in January 1814, had himself arrived in Europe to
co-ordinate the aspirations of the allies.

The cabinet of Lord Liverpool was in a strong position;
success in the war justified it at last against the criticism of
whigs and independent tories. Nevertheless, as experience soon
showed, Castlereagh's authority as leader in the house of commons was indispensable for the smooth conduct of business. Yet
the Cabinet released him for service in Europe and trusted him
with great discretion in the management of policy. His fellow
ministers saw that this was the moment for which he had prepared himself, that he was, in the next few months, to play a
part in settling Europe never equalled by any British statesman.

Castlereagh insisted that in future parleys the French must
be told of the general lines of settlement for all Europe. This
he did as much to force his friends into accepting a system of
making peace as to enlighten the French. At the talks at Châtil-
lon he successfully committed the alliance to the idea of a
general European settlement and not to a series of hand-to-
mouth treaties. Further he secured the control of the eventual
settlement for the four powers England, Austria, Russia, Prussia
with the conditional addition of France. He dissuaded the tsar
from the idea of bringing the Americans into discussions and
himself repulsed the protests of the Spanish allies. Thus
emerged the modern concept of the great powers.

The idea of a European peace agreed among the great powers was carried further by the Treaty of Chaumont. England's three allies agreed to keep 150,000 men each in the field to fight the war. England agreed to split up a subsidy of £5 million between them and herself to provide 150,000 men.[1] 'What an extraordinary display of power', exclaimed Castlereagh. 'This I trust will put an end to any doubts as to the claim we have to an opinion on Continental matters.'[2] The first opinion which he successfully pushed was that the powers should agree to continue their co-operation after the war so as to guarantee the preservation for twenty years of 'the order of things'. What maintaining 'the order of things' meant, whether a rigid preservation of frontier settlements or simply the maintenance of peace by collective action against aggression, had to be left for discovery in the future.

When the Chaumont agreement was made it was possible that the war might still be a long one. It still seemed that it might be impossible to make a treaty with France unless she was left under Bonaparte's rule. The tsar, it was said, favoured other aspirants, Orleans or Bernadotte. Castlereagh looked cautiously for some sign in France of a willingness to accept any change in government; treaties, after all, could be made only with authorities who had some hope of stability. In March 1814 Wellington produced the sign for him. In his hard fought advance in south-west France he was striking up to Toulouse and to Bordeaux. When one of his advanced parties reached Bordeaux the inhabitants, on 12 March, rose to proclaim the restoration of the legitimate Bourbon line. This was enough to satisfy Castlereagh that it was safe to gratify the desires of the prince regent and his cabinet colleagues at home by restoring the Bourbons. On 28 March the allied leaders drank to Louis XVIII: their war aim was now the expulsion of Napoleon Bonaparte from France. They had been encouraged by the failure of Napoleon's attack on Blücher at Craone and Schwarzenberg's victory at Arcis-sur-Aube. To forestall Napoleon's aim of slipping between the two armies and defeating them separately, both pressed on rapidly towards Paris and the knock-out blow. On 30 March 1814 the allied armies were fighting on the slope of Montmartre. On 31 March Paris capitulated.

---

[1] Many of these, of course, would be hired, not native, troops.
[2] C. K. Webster, *Diplomacy of Castlereagh*, p. 228.

Once it had been decided that Napoleon should be sent off to
Elba, and that Talleyrand should be allowed to set up a Bourbon government on constitutional lines, Castlereagh concentrated his attention upon the making of a peace treaty with
France. By the treaty of Paris of 30 May 1814 France was given
her frontiers as they had been in 1792 with the addition of a
piece of Savoy and the recognition of her incorporation of
Avignon. Her overseas possessions were restored to her with the
exception of Tobago, St. Lucia, and Mauritius. She promised
to abolish the slave trade but not until the lapse of five years
had permitted the re-stocking of her colonies. To the indignant
slave-trade abolitionists in England Castlereagh's reply was
the same as that he gave to those who wished to punish France
for her past aggressions: the only settlement which would be
durable would be one which France could regard as just and
workable. For this reason also he joined with the tsar in check-
ing the revengeful spirit of the Prussians.

The choice of the frontiers of 1792 implied the exclusion from
French control of Belgium and the left bank of the Rhine up to
that boundary. The future destination of that territory might
well have been left over for future discussion. But Castlereagh
inserted into the treaty with France the provision that Belgium
should belong to Holland. Thus this question was settled at
once. Britain, therefore, alone of the powers, had secured what
was vital to her in advance of any general settlement, and without any bargaining or compromise. This was important not
only because Antwerp and the Scheldt were in safe hands[1] but
because British influence in discussion of all other problems was
immensely increased. Castlereagh, with his immediate objectives secured, could move freely as a mediator in all the ensuing
wrangles between his allies.

The main lines of English policy remained strong and coherent from this time until the end of the Vienna Peace Congress.
Castlereagh's first aim was to set up a peaceful France and then
to erect barriers against any possibility of future expansionism.
In the north the new kingdom of the United Netherlands should
stand like a small watchdog capable of self-defence against
French attack. The United Netherlands should have at their

---

[1] The Scheldt, Castlereagh agreed, should be open to trade; he thus gave up
the older British policy, to which Liverpool had wished to adhere, of shutting this
river.

back, for their support, an expanded Prussia and Hanover, now become a kingdom, so that in stage two of any future war with France considerable forces would be available to fight for the defence of the Scheldt and Rhine. Contact with the policy of the Netherlands government, it was hoped, would be made closer by the marriage of Princess Charlotte, the regent's daughter, with the heir of the prince of Orange.[1] In the south, Piedmont, which despite Bentinck's promises to the Genoese was compensated for the cession of a slice of Savoy with the acquisition of Genoa, was to play the role of the small watchdog. For their reinforcement Austria was to stand firmly in the rear. Thus Castlereagh welcomed the Austrian claim to Milan and Metternich's garrisoning of the whole of Lombardy and Venetia. The working of this system of guards against a French break-out either in the north or the south clearly depended upon the satisfactory settlement also of Prussia and Austria. Castlereagh founded his system upon a strong central Europe with Prussia and Austria, looked upon as stabilizing powers, working in co-operation to safeguard the new order. He successfully pushed therefore for the cession of the Rhineland as far south as Baden to Prussia.

The settlement with Holland was sealed, as that with France had been, by using the colonial conquests of Britain to bolster up the European arrangements. Britain retained the Cape of Good Hope (hers since 1806) and the Guiana settlements. These acquisitions, like the few taken from France, and the retention of Malta, represented the consolidation of a strategic control of trade routes[2] in the Mediterranean, the West Indies, and the route to India. The protests of those who had sunk capital in lands not needed for these purposes, and therefore relinquished, were brushed aside by the British cabinet. Castlereagh, indeed, feared that he had been induced to take too much from the Dutch, for 'I am sure our reputation on the Continent as a feature of strength, power, and confidence is of

---

[1] In 1814, however, the princess showed that she was unwilling to marry the Dutchman and Castlereagh had to apply his efforts more negatively to see that the prince at least did not marry an enemy of this country.

[2] The protectorate over the Ionian islands which Britain acquired at the end of the Congress had no special purpose. It was the result of efforts made by the tsar's adviser Capo d'Istria (born in Corfu) to keep them out of the hands of Naples or Austria and to make possible junction with Greece if Greece ever gained her independence.

more real moment to us than an acquisition thus made.'[1] On such arguments the Dutch East Indies, where Stamford Raffles[2] had been governing Java since 1810, with all the fabulous riches of the spice trade, were unhesitatingly handed back to Holland. To soothe the feelings of the Dutch about losing the Cape they were given £2 million: this £2 million was to be spent on the fortification of their Belgium frontier against France, a further neat interlocking of colonial and European issues.

The idea of basing peace upon a satisfied Prussia and Austria was not derived simply from the requirement to confine France. From the start of discussions Castlereagh found the Tsar Alexander an unreliable partner. No Englishman could overlook the fact that Russia, with her ambitions in the Black Sea and Baltic areas, threatened British interests almost as did France. To this fear the tsar had given point by his acquisition of Finland in 1812. Consequently the tsar had only to show signs of co-operation with French leaders for Englishmen to be haunted by the nightmare of Tilsit, by the prospect of the two restless powers at either end of Europe combining to squeeze the rest. Therefore the concept of the predominance of the central powers was advanced as much to restrain Russia as to hold France. Castlereagh wished to keep Russia away on the extremity of Europe, to cultivate the independent Baltic powers, particularly Sweden (to whom Norway was attached by a Union of Crowns), and to prevent either Austria or Prussia playing the tsar's game. The key points in this policy could not be settled at Paris in the spring of 1814, however, but had to be referred to the autumn Congress in Vienna. It was enough for the first stage to have settled France and Holland.

When the powers, in September 1814, came to discuss the rest of the map of Europe two great questions threatened Castlereagh's schemes. The tsar, by demanding the whole of Poland as a Russian subject kingdom, was claiming that Russia must enter Europe and come within striking distance of Berlin and close to the Carpathians. To this claim Castlereagh hoped to oppose a united front of Austria and Prussia. But Prussia wished to annex the whole of Saxony, a claim which, as it weakened Austrian influence among the German states, Metter-

---

[1] Castlereagh to Liverpool, 19 April 1814, quoted C. K. Webster, *Diplomacy of Castlereagh*, p. 273.

[2] For Stamford Raffles see Sir E. L. Woodward, *The Age of Reform*, p. 395.

nich was loath to accept. By acting as intermediary in these
discussions Castlereagh persuaded Austria to agree that Prussia
should be given most of Saxony: he then made himself the fierce
spokesman of the three powers in telling the tsar that his army
must evacuate Poland. In taking so prominent a part in the
dispute he showed great boldness. For parliament did not look
with favour upon his deciding the future of Saxony. Nor did
either parliament or Liverpool's cabinet wish to see Poland
partitioned. Yet though Castlereagh, duty bound, spoke up for
a free and independent Poland he knew that the most likely
substitute for a Russian Poland would be a partitioned Poland;
this was, indeed, the result expected by his two allies. At the end
of 1814 disaster befell Castlereagh's diplomacy. The king of
Prussia was persuaded to agree that the tsar should take Poland.
This released the Austrians from their undertaking to allow
Prussia to have Saxony. All was now in the melting-pot with
the exception of the one point, and that the most unwelcome,
that Poland would certainly become a Russian puppet state.

It was bad that Russia, with Poland added to her gains of
Finland and Bessarabia, would have a foot in every European
quarrel. It was worse that the unity of the two great Germanic
powers, upon which the western as well as the eastern settlement depended, had disappeared. Accepting the inevitable success of Russia, Castlereagh set himself to impose agreement in
central Europe. He had instructions from the cabinet that these
questions were not sufficiently close to Britain for it to be possible to risk war over them. Nevertheless he made an agreement
with Austria and with France—who thus found her way back
into the ranks of the great powers—to oblige Prussia to give up
her claim to Saxony by the threat of force being used against
her. In face of this Prussia gave way. The tsar was persuaded to
detach from his Polish prize Cracow, which would remain a
free city under Austrian supervision, and Thorn which should
be ceded to Prussia. With this, with her great gains on the
Rhineland, with some small sections detached from Saxony,
with transfers from Sweden in the area of Pomerania, Prussia
had to remain content. She had good defensible frontiers
against France and even against Russia. Her weakness was that
her territories were in two wings, one in the east and the other
in the west, and that she was vulnerable to a thrust from the
south. This, in England's view, was no real defect, for it imposed

upon Prussia the necessity of playing a reasonable part in the Confederation of German States (which was being formed) and of co-operating with the Austrians.

On 1 March 1815 Napoleon landed on the Riviera coast on his return from Elba. The whole of Castlereagh's work seemed to be rendered vain. The abject exodus of the Bourbons seemed to suggest that France refused to settle down to the life Castlereagh had intended for her. There was little agreement as to what should be done. In England Lord Grey and Whitbread spoke for a considerable section of the whigs when they argued that the only sensible course was to recognize Napoleon and to live with him, as most European rulers had been prepared to do only twelve months before. Lord Wellesley, Wellington's brother, surprisingly echoed these sentiments. Lord Grenville and Grattan, on the other hand, had some whig support in calling for the extermination of Bonapartism. This war party, which included of course the Liverpool cabinet and their tory supporters, wanted to punish France vigorously for her contumacy. Castlereagh, whose aim was immediate war, but war only to reinstate the moderate settlement which had been agreed at Vienna, was therefore almost alone and unsupported in the country whose representative he was.

The European allies agreed to contribute 150,000 men each to the army for suppressing Napoleon. Castlereagh found it more persuasive to tell his countrymen that they must fight in order to keep in step with Europe than to specify war aims: Britain agreed once again to supply a £5 million subsidy to the allies. The tsar was disinclined to restore the Bourbons though anxious to expel Napoleon. Prussia aimed at a salutary punishment of France and at further frontier changes. Metternich seemed to have been persuaded that an agreement must be reached with the Jacobin party in Paris. Castlereagh and Wellington were determined to restore the Bourbons and recommence as before. To this end Castlereagh laboured to impress upon Louis the need to adapt himself more fully to a constitutional role: that France must have constitutional liberty was proved by the fact that even Napoleon had, on his return, to play the liberal and to deal out freedom as urgently as muskets to his Parisian supporters. So Louis was persuaded to accept Talleyrand and, eventually, Fouché as his temporary mentors.

Wellington was in command of the allied forces in the Netherlands. By assembling the British forces from garrisons there, with
urgent reinforcements from home (though many British soldiers
were away in America), he could find some 40,000: the remaining 100,000 had to be hired from the smaller powers in the
usual way. To join this army in the Netherlands the Prussian
quota came up in May. The Russian and Austrian forces
wended their ways more slowly towards the French frontiers.
Napoleon did not intend to wait to be attacked. It had always
been his way to fly at his opponents when they were divided and
overwhelm them one by one. So on 12 June 1815 he left Paris
intending to drive a wedge between the British and Prussian
forces, master them, regain Belgium, and then face the other
pair of allies: would they then pursue their crusade against him?
The Prussians were duly attacked on the Sambre on 15 June and
driven back to the north-east. Then a brigade of the army of
Belgium was pushed northwards towards Brussels as far as a
farm-house named Quatre Bras. Wellington began moving to
the east to support the Prussians. But on 16 June part of
Blücher's forces were engaged by the French and forced to
retire after a sharp engagement lasting the afternoon. Wellington had made Quatre Bras the meeting-point for his forces as he
gathered them to aid Blücher, but was himself attacked and
had to struggle to hold his position. Blücher fell back to Wavre
during the night of 16th to 17th. On the morning of the 17th
Wellington therefore had in his turn to draw back: he established himself at Waterloo, on the junction of the roads from
Charleroi and from Nivelle to Brussels, while he tried to keep
communication open with the Prussians away to his left. On
the 18th the main action frothed up around the British posts in
the farmhouses of Hougomont and La Haye Sainte. Napoleon's
aim was to smash Wellington quickly while Blücher was at a
distance. Once more the contest was between the hammer tactics of the French and the dour discipline of Wellington's army
on the defensive. Napoleon sent column after column against
the British line, disdaining all manœuvre. Wellington had
leavened every unit with British soldiers trained in his defensive
technique. From ten in the morning until evening Wellington's
army withstood a furious cannonade and the attacks of cavalry
and infantry. By evening Blücher's guns firing announced that
he had evaded the French forces which had been detached to

keep him from the field. With this certainty of aid Wellington advanced his whole line of infantry under the support of artillery and cavalry. The French were driven in confusion from the scene. Napoleon's power was broken. He fled to Paris and then made his way to surrender to the British and to imprisonment on St. Helena.

The solution of one problem in the peace-making had been facilitated by the hundred days of Napoleon's power. Naples could now be returned to the Bourbons, so long penned in Sicily: Murat had forfeited all claim to it by joining Napoleon. Everything else was for a while in confusion. Prussia proposed that France should make further territorial sacrifices to the United Netherlands while, in return, the House of Orange should cede the grand duchy of Luxembourg to the Hohenzollerns. The British cabinet, too, expected severe terms to be imposed upon France. But Castlereagh in the next five months doggedly adhered to his own ideas. The throne he immediately secured for Louis: he hurried him to Paris with the British command and presented the tsar with a *fait accompli*. Then he proceeded to isolate Prussia among the great powers. The Prussian attempt to appeal from the big four and to involve all the smaller powers in the argument was easily defeated. In the end therefore Castlereagh succeeded in saving France from harsh retribution. The changes made by the second peace of Paris were that instead of the frontiers of 1792 France was left with those of 1790, that she was to suffer an occupation by 150,000 men for five or three years, that she was to pay a war indemnity of 700 million francs, that she was to meet private and some public claims for war damage, and that she was to restore the art treasures collected in the Louvre during twenty years of war. The substitution of the frontiers of 1790 meant that France yielded the Saar, Landau, a small area along the Belgian frontier, and the strip of Savoy which she had gained.

This final settlement was signed on 20 November 1815. On the same day the victorious powers also signed an agreement to bind themselves to act together to maintain the settlement in the event of any further French eruption. To this Castlereagh added another clause, that they agreed to meet together in regular conference to discuss the working of the European settlement. On this Castlereagh now based his hopes of stability in Europe. He scoffed at the tsar's mysticism on the same subject, the declaration by the sovereigns of Europe that they would work together to enforce the operation of Christian principles everywhere. Castlereagh thought of his own plan as a practical arrangement for the government of international relations. A weakness of his scheme was that he had not really convinced his own country of the need to operate it.

In the protracted making of peace all the frontiers of Europe had been guaranteed except those between Turkey and Russia. In addition the free navigation of the Rhine as an international waterway had been settled. The powers had been persuaded to declare the slave trade immoral and most of them induced, by profuse expenditure of English money, to fix a limit to the time they would allow their nationals to traffic in this guilty commerce. In most of this labour Castlereagh and England had played a leading part.

The settlement was not simply a pushing back of the clock to the early days of George III. The sentiment of democratic nationalism was not, as has sometimes been supposed, ignored by Castlereagh and the Liverpool cabinet.

It is impossible not to believe [wrote the British foreign secretary in 1814] a great moral change coming on in Europe, and that the principles of freedom are in full operation. The danger is that the transition may be too sudden to ripen into anything likely to make the world better or happier. We have new constitutions launched in France, Spain, Holland, and Sicily. Let us see the result before we encourage further attempts. The attempts may be made and we must abide the consequences; but I am sure that it is better to retard than accelerate the operation of this most hazardous principle that is abroad.[1]

Castlereagh aimed at a compromise between the new principle and the old legitimate princes. The settlement with France, to take an example, was designed to satisfy a people as well as to settle a dynasty; in the projected German Bund, again, there was to be a balance between the traditionalists and those whose influence had risen in the decades of disorder. One might go further and see principles of the future as well as of past and present in the Vienna settlement. For in slave-trade regulation and the programme of congresses there lay the germ of an international system which might temper the exercise of full

---

[1] Castlereagh to Lord William Bentinck, 17 May 1814. Printed in *British Diplomacy, 1813–1815*, ed. C. K. Webster, p. 181.

sovereignty by princes or peoples. The public law of Europe was at last given some substance.

Castlereagh himself embodied the contrasting forces in this changing world. He was at home with the cosmopolitan aristocracy and argued with Metternich or Alexander from common assumptions. Yet this grandee of Vienna was equally in his element discussing trade in the rough and tumble of Westminster. He appreciated, indeed, that a country whose total pre-war expenditure rarely exceeded £18 million and which had spent over £830 million in withstanding France, was in need of a generation of stable peace if the energies of her traders were to pay the bill. Castlereagh used his skill in the old diplomacy to make a world fit for a new England to expand in.

To profit by the opportunities before her England needed self-assurance and firm purpose. At the end of the war these seemed singularly hard to find. Only in dealing with the Far East was an assured advance made. In 1813 the Charter of the East India Company was revised. Parliament took away from the Company its monopoly of trade with India (but not with China). This was welcome to Liverpool shippers and the Manchester businessmen behind them. At the same time, to the joy of Wilberforce and his group, a church establishment was officially made for India. The way was prepared for cargoes of cotton-goods and missionaries, for the expansion of English exports and ideas. But this was a solitary act of confident preparation for the future. For the most part parliament temporized in the face of domestic problems.

Since the years 1810 and 1811 there had been a recrudescence of discontent. The commercial difficulties of the economic war were passed back to industry.[1] This came on top of problems produced by changing methods of production. Machinery had been quietly installed in Lancashire because there it served a new industry. But it met with opposition from skilled men once it invaded the older industries in Yorkshire and the Midlands, particularly in Nottinghamshire. Every deterioration in conditions could be attributed to the new machines. So in the winter of 1811 organized machine-breaking, to be known as Luddism, broke out in Nottingham. Men fearing unemployment tried to defend themselves by destruction. The magistrates groped in the dark to find them. The government tried to make up for the

[1] See above, pp. 469 and 507.

inefficiency of local control by making the penalties for the offence more ferocious. To smash frames, to damage property, to take Luddite oaths, became capital offences. Troops were moved to the affected districts. In the month of January 1813 seventeen men were executed at York and six more were transported. This cowed but did not crush the Luddites. They persisted in greater secrecy swearing 'to punish by Death any Trater, or Traters, should any arise among us . . . to persue with unceacing vengence' should he fly to the verge of Statude'.[1] The brutish conflict between frightened workers and indignant authority continued into the post-war period.

This struggle was between the labourer and the middle-class manufacturer. But the atmosphere of mounting discontent nevertheless aroused the ardour of the middle-class men to do battle also with the old aristocracy. Sir Francis Burdett[2] had made his name in 1810 by a melodramatic defiance of the Speaker of the house of commons and of parliamentary privilege. Now in 1811 he became chairman of the first Hampden Club. These clubs were intended to continue the agitation of the old Corresponding Society and the Society for Constitutional Information. The law against societies with branches had throttled previous organizations. This law was now evaded. Each Hampden Club was nominally a separate body. Their petitions and propagandist meetings were unobtrusively coordinated by the itinerant activity of the veteran agitator Major Cartwright. Membership was confined to men of substance (£300 a year in land in the case of the London Club); they worked for the extension of the franchise to all taxpayers. When this moderate programme seemed to arouse insufficient enthusiasm William Cobbett[3] began to spice it with warmer items, attacks upon the regent's way of life, or on government spending, or on interest payments on the national debt, for example. But whether flat or flamboyant the propaganda failed to canalize popular discontent, nor did it gain the support of any considerable group in parliament. The whig party of Lords

---

[1] From the Luddite Oath quoted in S. Maccoby, *English Radicalism, 1786–1832*, p. 521.

[2] Sir F. Burdett (1770–1844) was a wealthy radical who linked the age of Horne Tooke, at whose feet he had sat, with that of Young England and romantic reforming toryism (for which see Sir E. L. Woodward, *The Age of Reform* (O.H.E. vol. xiii), pp. 108–13).

[3] For him see Sir E. L. Woodward, *The Age of Reform* (O.H.E. vol. xiii), p. 20.

Grey and Grenville was deflated by the success of Lord Liverpool abroad. It was just as worried as the tory cabinet by the
dangerous situation at home. It had no solution to the problems
of the day, save for the catholic problem. Lord Grenville was
moving back to the conservatism of his youth while Lord Grey
was hoping that memories of his early radicalism might lie
dormant. Even Brougham and the energetic younger men in
the party saw little advantage in co-operation with the Hampden Club theorists.

Political toryism was given a momentary fillip by the victory
over France. But for the future it had no clear course. There
were admitted social evils developing, with which the existing
machinery of government could not deal. The country gentlemen were uneasily aware of the growth of new powers in the
state. Lord Liverpool's policy was to wait for better times;
while waiting he would improve the influence of the church by
his care in appointing bishops; he would build churches in new
centres of population in the hope of improving the morals of
the leaderless workers; he would ask all responsible men to give
loyal support to the regent's executive. But the landed gentlemen feared for the future, particularly the immediate future.
For peace might mean ruin to war-inflated agriculture. In 1813,
therefore, a Corn Bill was introduced which was calculated to
keep marginal farms in production at the cost of raising bread
prices almost to famine level. Against this proposal at least the
rest of the country could unite. Manufacturers, shopkeepers,
and working men joined in meetings and in sporadic riots
which went on all through the months in which the peace of
Europe was being painfully reconstructed.

Castlereagh returned home therefore to a country in which
the end of war had inevitably relaxed unity and common purpose, where the government was strong in votes but weak in
policy. Economic dislocation was likely to accompany peace
and to intensify all problems. In England a great battle was
preparing. The opposing sides were gradually forming up and
exchanging preliminary shots. But it was not yet clear on what
issues they were to fight nor did they yet know in what cause
they believed. Battles in war are often confused and inglorious
in their execution but they begin with the meeting of two
opposed forces. In this social conflict the muddle was at the
beginning and the sides only became clearly distinguishable as

it proceeded: only after much clashing of groups and squadrons in useless anger could the forces sort themselves into contestants for power. Victory in Europe was the beginning of a long and confused struggle in whose course the England over which King George III had ruled was to be battered into a new shape.

LIST OF THE HOLDERS OF GREAT OFFICES OF STATE, 1760–82, AND OF CABINETS, 1782–1815

[IN the previous volume of the *Oxford History of England* Professor Basil Williams printed Lists of Office Holders; in the volume which follows this Sir Llewellyn Woodward prints Lists of Cabinets. This difference corresponds to a change in the operation of cabinet government which was proceeding during the reign of George III. The operation of an inner or efficient cabinet which can be distinguished from the formal cabinet was no new thing. But this efficient body of ministers, regularly transacting business together, only slowly acquired precise definition of membership. To print lists of cabinets it is requisite that there should be some certainty about those entitled to attend and a sense of a collective cabinet opinion—even if the agreement to which members are faithful may only be an agreement to allow some questions to remain open. The emergence of a cabinet in the nineteenth-century form therefore depended much upon that other subtle development, the growth of party. In George III's reign the question of whether a minister was of the cabinet depended as much upon his own strength as upon the office he held: the importance of the rising but still second-rank post of chancellor of the exchequer, for instance, depended upon whether the first lord of the treasury was in the lords and upon whether the cabinet had other leading members to represent it in the commons.

Any abrupt beginning of cabinet lists is bound to appear arbitrary. The process of change has been discussed with more subtlety in the text above than it can receive in a tabular exposition. Nevertheless the advent of the second Rockingham administration in 1782, which was marked by replacements in nearly all the major offices, and when a point of policy sharply divided the administration from its predecessors, seems the most defensible point at which to change the style of the lists. After this administrations fall and are succeeded by others instead of melting into new shapes: the right to attend is more strictly watched.

The information given in these lists is derived from R. Beatson, *Political Index* (1806 edition), F. M. Powicke, *Handbook of British Chronology* (1939), the *Annual Register*, the *Parliamentary History*, Fortescue's edition of the *Correspondence of George III*, and (for the period after 1783) from A. Aspinall, *The Cabinet Council, 1783–1835*.]

A. Holders of Great Offices of State, 1760–82

First Lord of the Treasury

Duke of Newcastle

Earl of Bute (from 29 May 1762)

George Grenville (from 16 April 1763)

Marquis of Rockingham (from 13 July 1765)

Duke of Grafton (from 2 August 1766)

Lord North (from 10 February 1770 until 27 March 1782)

Lord President of the Council

Earl Granville

Duke of Bedford (from September 1763)

Earl of Winchelsea (from 12 July 1765)

Earl of Northington (from 30 July 1766)

Earl Gower (from 23 December 1767)

Earl Bathurst (from 24 November 1779 until 27 March 1782)

Lord Privy Seal

Earl Temple (in commission October 1761)

Duke of Bedford (from 25 November 1761)

Duke of Marlborough (from 22 April 1763)

Duke of Newcastle (from 25 August 1765)

Earl of Chatham (from 30 July 1766, with a brief period in commission in February 1768)

Earl of Bristol (from 2 November 1768)

Earl of Halifax (from 26 February 1770)

Earl of Suffolk (from 12 January 1771)

Duke of Grafton (from 1 June 1771)

Earl of Dartmouth (from 4 November 1775 until 27 March 1782)

Secretaries of State

For Northern Department	For Southern Department	For American Colonies
Lord Holderness	W. Pitt (later Earl of Chatham)	
Earl of Bute (from 25 March 1761)	Earl of Egremont (from 9 Oct. 1761)	
G. Grenville (from 29 March 1762)		
Earl of Halifax (from 14 Oct. 1762)		
Earl of Sandwich (from 9 Sept. 1763)	Earl of Halifax (transferred from N., 9 Sept. 1763)	
Duke of Grafton (from 12 July 1765)	General H. S. Conway (from 12 July 1765)	
General H. S. Conway (transferred from S., 23 May 1766)	Duke of Richmond (from 23 May 1766)	

Secretaries of State (cont.)

For Northern Department	For Southern Department	For American Colonies
	Earl of Shelburne (from 2 Aug. 1766)	
Viscount Weymouth (from 20 Jan. 1768)		Earl of Hillsborough (from 20 Jan. 1768)
Earl of Rochford (from 21 Oct. 1768)	Viscount Weymouth (transferred from N., 21 Oct. 1768)	
Earl of Sandwich (from 19 Dec. 1770)	Earl of Rochford (transferred from N., 19 Dec. 1770)	
Earl of Halifax (from 22 Jan. 1771)		
Earl of Suffolk (from 12 June 1771)		
		Earl of Dartmouth (from 14 Aug. 1772)
	Viscount Weymouth (from 10 Nov. 1775)	Lord G. Germaine (afterwards Viscount Sackville) (from 10 Nov. 1775 to February 1782)
Viscount Stormont (from 27 Oct. 1779 to 27 March 1782)		
	Earl of Hillsborough (from 24 Nov. 1779 to 27 March 1782)	Welbone Ellis (from Feb. 1782)
		Office abolished 1782

Lord Chancellor

Lord Henley (created Earl of Northington 1764)
Lord Camden (from 30 July 1766)
C. Yorke (from 17 January 1770) in commission from 20 January 1770

Lord Apsley (became Earl Bathurst in 1775) (from 23 January 1771)
Lord Thurlow (from 2 June 1778 until 9 April 1783)

First Lord of the Admiralty

Lord Anson (from 21 March 1761)
Earl of Halifax (from 19 June 1762)
G. Grenville (from 1 January 1763)
Earl of Sandwich (from 23 April 1763)
Earl of Egmont (from 10 September 1763)

Sir Charles Saunders (from 16 September 1766)
Sir Edward Hawke (from 13 December 1766)
Earl of Sandwich (from 12 January 1771 until 30 March 1782)

Commander-in-Chief

Earl Ligonier
Marquis of Granby (from 1766 to 1769)

Lord Amherst (from 1778 to March 1782)

Master General of the Ordnance

Earl Ligonier
Marquis of Granby (from 1763)

Viscount Townshend (from 1772 to March 1782)

Lord Lieutenant of Ireland

Duke of Bedford
Earl of Halifax (from April 1761)
Earl of Northumberland (from April 1763)
Viscount Weymouth (from June 1765)
Earl of Hertford (from August 1765)
Earl of Bristol (from October 1766)

Viscount Townshend (from August 1767)
Earl of Harcourt (from October 1772)
Earl of Buckinghamshire (from December 1776)
Earl of Carlisle (from November 1780 to 8 April 1782)

Chancellor of the Exchequer

H. B. Legge
Viscount Barrington (from 12 March 1761)
Sir F. Dashwood (from 29 May 1761)
G. Grenville (from 16 April 1763: combined with first lord of the treasury)

W. Dowdeswell (from 13 July 1765)
Charles Townshend (from 2 August 1766)
Lord Mansfield (from 12 September 1767)
Lord North (from 1 December 1767: combined with first lord of the treasury from 10 February 1770)

Paymaster of the Forces

H. Fox
C. Townshend (from 1765)
Lord North ⎱ (from 1766)
G. Cooke ⎰

G. Cooke ⎱ (from 1767)
T. Townshend ⎰
R. Rigby (from 1768 to March 1782)

Secretary at War

Viscount Barrington
C. Townshend (from 1761)
Welbore Ellis (later Lord Mendip) (from 1763)

Viscount Barrington (from 1765)
C. Jenkinson (later Lord Liverpool) (from 1778 to March 1782)

Treasurer of the Navy

G. Grenville
Viscount Barrington (from 1762)
Viscount Howe (from 1765)

Sir Gilbert Elliot (from 1770)
Welbore Ellis (later Lord Mendip) (from 1775 to April 1782)

President of the Board of Trade

Earl of Halifax

Lord Sandys (from 21 March 1761)

C. Townshend (from 1 March 1763)

Earl of Shelburne (from 20 April 1763)

Earl of Hillsborough (from 9 September 1763)

Earl of Dartmouth (from 20 July 1765)

Earl of Hillsborough (from 16 August 1766)

R. Nugent (later Earl Nugent) (from December 1766)

Earl of Hillsborough (from 20 January 1768)

Earl of Dartmouth (from 31 August 1772)

Lord George Germain (from 10 November 1775)

Earl of Carlisle (from 6 September 1780)

Lord Grantham (from 9 December 1780)

Office suppressed in June 1782, but revived later.

Lord Steward

Duke of Rutland

Earl Talbot (from 1761)

Master of the Horse

Earl of Huntingdon

Duke of Rutland (from 1761)

Earl of Hertford (from August 1766)

Duke of Ancaster (from December 1766)

Duke of Northumberland (from 1778)

Duke of Montagu (from 1780 to 1790)

B. LISTS OF CABINETS FROM 1782 TO 1815

The Second Rockingham Administration (formed March 1782)

First lord of the treasury	Marquis of Rockingham
Secretary of state (home and colonial affairs)	Earl of Shelburne
Secretary of state (foreign affairs)	Charles James Fox
Lord president of the council	Lord Camden
Lord chancellor	Lord Thurlow
Lord privy seal	Duke of Grafton
First lord of the admiralty	Admiral (now created Viscount) Keppel
Commander in chief	General Conway
Master general of the ordnance	Duke of Richmond
Chancellor of the exchequer	Lord John Cavendish
Chancellor of the duchy of Lancaster	John Dunning (now created Lord Ashburton)

(Outside the cabinet were Edmund Burke as paymaster, Colonel I. Barré as treasurer of the navy, Thomas Townshend as secretary at war, and the duke of Portland as lord-lieutenant of Ireland.)

The Shelburne Administration, *1782–3* (formed July 1782)

First lord of the treasury	Earl of Shelburne
Lord president of the council	Lord Camden
Lord chancellor	Lord Thurlow
Lord privy seal	Duke of Grafton
Secretary of state (home affairs)	Thomas Townshend (created Lord Sydney in 1783)
Secretary of state (foreign affairs)	Lord Grantham
Chancellor of the exchequer	William Pitt
Master general of the ordnance	Duke of Richmond
First lord of the admiralty	Viscount Keppel
Commander-in-chief	General Conway
Chancellor of the duchy of Lancaster	Lord Ashburton

(Outside the cabinet were: as lord-lieutenant of Ireland Earl Temple, as paymaster colonel Isaac Barré, as treasurer of the navy Henry Dundas, and as secretary at war Sir George Yonge.)

Changes. In January 1783 Viscount Howe replaced Viscount Keppel as first lord of the admiralty. In February 1783 the duke of Rutland was added to the cabinet as lord steward of the household.

The Fox–North Coalition Administration, *1783* (formed April 1783)

First lord of the treasury	Duke of Portland
Secretary of state (home and colonial affairs)	Lord North
Secretary of state (foreign affairs)	Charles James Fox
Lord president of the council	Viscount Stormont
Lord privy seal	Earl of Carlisle
First lord of the admiralty	Viscount Keppel
Chancellor of the exchequer	Lord John Cavendish

(Outside the cabinet were: as lord chamberlain the earl of Hertford, as lord steward the earl of Dartmouth, as master general of the ordnance Viscount Townshend, as paymaster Edmund Burke, as treasurer of the navy Charles Townshend, as secretary at war Richard Fitzpatrick, as attorney general J. Wallace, as solicitor general John Lee, and as lord-lieutenant of Ireland the earl of Northington.)

William Pitt's First Administration, 1783–1801
(formed 19 December 1783)

FIRST PERIOD, 1783–94

First lord of the treasury and chancellor of the exchequer	William Pitt
Lord president of the council	Earl Gower
Lord chancellor	Lord Thurlow
Home secretary	Earl Temple—replaced on 23 Dec. 1783 by Lord Sydney

William Pitt's First Administration (cont.)

Foreign secretary	Earl Temple—replaced on 23 Dec. 1783 by marquis of Carmarthen (created duke of Leeds 1789)
First lord of the admiralty	Viscount Howe
Lord privy seal	Duke of Rutland (took office 23 Dec. 1783)
Master general of the ordnance	Duke of Richmond (took office 13 Jan. 1784)

Changes. The duke of Rutland left the cabinet on becoming lord-lieutenant of Ireland: the earl of Gower (created marquis of Stafford in 1786) became lord privy seal in November 1784: Lord Camden (earldom 1786) succeeded as lord president of the council. The earl of Chatham replaced Viscount Howe as first lord of the admiralty in July 1788. William Wyndham Grenville (peerage 1790) replaced Lord Sydney as home secretary in June 1789. In April 1791 Lord Grenville took the place of the duke of Leeds as foreign secretary and in April–June 1791 Henry Dundas became home secretary while Lord Hawkesbury joined the cabinet as president of the board of trade. Lord Thurlow left office in June 1792 and, after a period in which it was in commission, the great seal was given to Lord Loughborough. Lord Amherst joined the cabinet as commander-in-chief in January 1793.

SECOND PERIOD, July 1794 (on the junction of the Portland whigs) to 1801

First lord of the treasury and chancellor of the exchequer	William Pitt
Lord privy seal	Earl Spencer
Lord president of the council	Earl Fitzwilliam
Lord chancellor	Lord Loughborough
Home secretary	Duke of Portland
Foreign secretary	Lord Grenville
Secretary of war	Henry Dundas
First lord of the admiralty	Earl Spencer
Master general of the ordnance	Duke of Richmond
Chancellor of the duchy of Lancaster and president of the board of trade	Lord Hawkesbury (created earl of Liverpool in 1796)
Secretary at war	William Windham
Commander-in-chief	Lord Amherst
Minister without portfolio	Earl of Mansfield

Changes. The earl of Chatham exchanged office with Earl Spencer in December 1794 and the earl of Mansfield replaced Earl Fitzwilliam as lord president of the council. The marquis Cornwallis replaced the duke of Richmond as master general of the ordnance in February 1795 and the cabinet was made smaller by the exclusion of the commander-in-chief. In September 1796 the earl of Chatham became lord president of the council in place of the earl of Mansfield and the privy seal was left in commission until it was taken by the earl of Westmorland in February 1798. In June 1798 Earl Camden entered the cabinet as minister without portfolio but the master general of the ordnance ceased to be a member.

The Addington Administration, 1801–4 (formed February 1801)

First lord of the treasury and chancellor of the exchequer	Henry Addington
Lord privy seal	Earl of Westmorland
Lord president of the council	Earl of Chatham
Lord chancellor	Lord Eldon
Home secretary	Duke of Portland
Foreign secretary	Lord Hawkesbury
Secretary of war (with responsibility for colonies)	Lord Hobart
First lord of the admiralty	Earl of St. Vincent
Chancellor of the duchy of Lancaster and president of the board of trade	Earl of Liverpool

Changes. In July 1801 the earl of Chatham became master general of the ordnance, the duke of Portland replaced him as lord president of the council and was himself replaced at the home office by Lord Pelham. In October 1802 Viscount Castlereagh was added to the cabinet as president of the board of control. In August 1803 Charles Philip Yorke succeeded Lord Pelham as home secretary. In November 1803 Lord Liverpool ceased to hold the chancellorship of the duchy of Lancaster.

The Second Pitt Administration, 1804–6

First lord of the treasury and chancellor of the exchequer	William Pitt
Lord privy seal	Earl of Westmorland
Lord president of the council	Duke of Portland
Lord chancellor	Lord Eldon
Home secretary	Lord Hawkesbury
Foreign secretary	Lord Harrowby
Secretary for war and colonies	Earl of Camden
First lord of the admiralty	Viscount Melville (formerly Dundas)
President of the board of control	Viscount Castlereagh
Master general of the ordnance	Earl of Chatham
Chancellor of the duchy of Lancaster	Lord Mulgrave
President of the board of trade	Duke of Montreal

Changes. In January 1805 Viscount Sidmouth (Addington) replaced the duke of Portland as lord president, Lord Mulgrave replaced Lord Harrowby at the foreign office, the two replaced ministers remaining in the cabinet as ministers without portfolio: the earl of Buckinghamshire took the chancellorship of the duchy of Lancaster. In May 1805 Lord Barham replaced Lord Melville as first lord of the admiralty. In June–July 1805 the earl of Camden became lord president in the room of Viscount Sidmouth and Viscount Castlereagh took the secretaryship of state left vacant by the Earl of Camden's move, while retaining his presidency of the board of control.

The 'Ministry of All the Talents', 1806–7

First lord of the treasury	Lord Grenville
Chancellor of the exchequer	Lord Henry Petty
Lord privy seal	Viscount Sidmouth
Lord president of the council	Lord Fitzwilliam
Lord chancellor	Lord Erskine
Home secretary	Earl Spencer
Foreign secretary	Charles James Fox
Secretary for war and colonies	William Windham
First lord of the admiralty	Charles Grey (became Viscount Howick April 1806)
Master general of the ordnance	Earl of Moira
Lord chief justice of the king's bench	Lord Ellenborough

Changes. T. Grenville joined the cabinet as president of the board of control in July 1806. In September–October 1806 Lord Holland became lord privy seal in place of Viscount Sidmouth who became lord president of the council, while Earl Fitzwilliam, in his turn, became a minister without portfolio. At the same time Viscount Howick became foreign secretary and Thomas Grenville replaced him at the head of the admiralty.

The Portland Administration, 1807–9

First lord of the treasury	Duke of Portland
Chancellor of the exchequer and chancellor of the duchy of Lancaster	Spencer Perceval
Lord privy seal	Earl of Westmorland
Lord president of the council	Earl Camden
Lord chancellor	Lord Eldon
Home secretary	Lord Hawkesbury (became earl of Liverpool 1808)
Foreign secretary	George Canning
Secretary of war and colonies	Viscount Castlereagh
First lord of the admiralty	Lord Mulgrave
Master general of the ordnance	Earl of Chatham
President of the board of trade	Earl Bathurst

Changes. The cabinet was enlarged by the addition of Lord Granville Leveson-Gower as secretary at war in June 1809 and by that of the earl of Harrowby as president of the board of control in July 1809.

The Perceval Administration, 1809–12

First lord of the treasury and chancellor of the duchy of Lancaster	Spencer Perceval
Lord privy seal	Earl of Westmorland
Lord president of the council	Earl Camden
Lord chancellor	Lord Eldon
Home secretary	Richard Ryder
Foreign secretary and president of the board of trade	Earl Bathurst

First lord of the admiralty   Lord Mulgrave
President of the board of control Robert Saunders Dundas (became
              Viscount Melville 1811)
Master general of the ordnance Earl of Chatham
Ministers without portfolio   Duke of Portland until his death,
              30 October 1809
              Earl of Harrowby from November
              1809

Changes. The marquis of Wellesley succeeded Earl Bathurst as foreign secretary in December 1809 but the latter remained in the cabinet as president of the board of trade. In April 1810 Charles Philip Yorke became first lord of the admiralty while Lord Mulgrave took the place of the earl of Chatham as master general of the ordnance. In March–April 1812 Viscount Sidmouth became lord president of the council but Earl Camden remained in the cabinet as another minister without portfolio: Viscount Castlereagh became foreign secretary, Viscount Melville first lord of the admiralty, and the earl of Buckinghamshire president of the board of control.

Lord Liverpool's Administration (formed June 1812)

First lord of the treasury   Earl of Liverpool
Chancellor of the exchequer   Nicholas Vansittart
Lord privy seal   Earl of Westmorland
Lord president of the council   Earl of Harrowby
Lord chancellor   Lord Eldon
Home secretary   Viscount Sidmouth
Foreign secretary   Viscount Castlereagh
Secretary for war and colonies and (until Sep- Earl Bathurst
 tember 1812) president of the board of trade
First lord of the admiralty   Viscount Melville
President of the board of control Earl of Buckinghamshire
Master general of the ordnance Lord Mulgrave
Chancellor of the duchy of Lancaster C. Bragge-Bathurst
Minister without portfolio   Lord Camden

Changes. The earl of Camden left the cabinet in December 1812. W. Wellesley-Pole joined it, with the office of master of the mint, in September 1814.

BIBLIOGRAPHY

BIBLIOGRAPHIES AND WORKS OF REFERENCE

FOR the first half of George III's reign bibliographical information has recently been made readily accessible in two admirable works. Stanley Pargellis and D. J. Medley, *Bibliography of British History, the Eighteenth Century 1714–1789* (1951), produced under the direction of the Royal Historical Association and of the American Historical Association, is invaluable. B. D. Horn and Mary Ransome in *English Historical Documents Volume X— 1714–1783* (General Editor David C. Douglas) (1957) have prefaced their illustrations of each topic with lists of books and articles and a most judicious commentary upon them. Since the present history was in proof the publication of volume xi, 1783–1832, in this series, edited by A. Aspinall and E. Anthony Smith (1959), has provided a convenient source of information for the years from the younger Pitt to 1815. It will be only a small number of students therefore who will now find it necessary to have recourse to the *Subject Index* and the *Author Catalogue* published by the London Library and then to proceed to the wider field covered by the *British Museum Catalogue of Printed Books with Supplement* (of which a new edition has reached the letter D) and to the *Subject Index of Modern Works added to the Library of the British Museum*. For those who require only highly selective lists the *Cambridge Bibliography of English Literature* (4 vols. ed. F. W. Bateson 1940, supplementary vol. ed. G. Watson 1957) ranges more widely in the field of social, political, and constitutional history than the title might suggest. Mention should also be made, for those who seek to set George III's England in a wider context, of a very useful guide by J. S. Bromley and A. Goodwin, *A Select List of Works on Europe and Europe Overseas 1715–1815* (1956). The defect of all bibliographies, that they are no sooner published than they are out of date, can be remedied by use of the *Annual Bulletins of Historical Literature* issued by the Historical Association.

For the exploration of articles and essays on the period there is at present no satisfactory alternative to a search in the index sections of the major periodicals, in particular the *Transactions of the Royal Historical Association*, the *English Historical Review*, the *American Historical Review*, the *Economic History Review*, the *Journal of Modern History*, *History*, and (for constitutional points) the *Law Quarterly Review*. There is, however, in the Bodleian Library a cumulative index to the articles in all these periodicals, except the last named, prepared by R. G. Chapman; this simplifies the work of any student in Oxford. The Catalogue of English Newspapers and Periodicals in the Bodleian Library 1622–1800 is a most useful guide to these contemporary sources. *Volume V* of the *Catalogue of Political and Personal Satires* by D. M. George does more than list cartoons; it is a vivid survey of the history of the period.

The *Twenty Second Report* (1946) of the *Historical Manuscripts Commission* forms an index to the many collections of manuscripts which have been printed by the Commission. The *Bulletin* of the Institute of Historical Research supplies further information about the movement of these and other manuscripts. Exploration of such primary sources is daily going forward, particularly at the headquarters of the History of Parliament Trust under the direction of Sir Lewis Namier. The publication of the late eighteenth-century section of this great enterprise should therefore enlighten us on sources as well as supplying a rich field of biographical detail. The manuscripts in public possession may be tracked down with the aid of M. S. Guiseppi, *Guide to the Manuscripts Preserved in the Public Record Office* (1932–4), with the later and supplementary *Lists and Indexes*, with the *British Museum Catalogue of Additions to the Manuscripts* (1843–1933), and with the guides issued by local museums and record societies.

Though it is not free from error, no historian could easily dispense with the *Dictionary of National Biography*, or at least its epitome the *Concise Dictionary*, close to his hand. It is a pity there is no such epitome of the *Dictionary of American Biography*. Only a little less important as a tool of the trade is G. E. C[okayne], *The Complete Peerage* edited by the Hon. V. Gibbs and others. With these should be grouped Gerritt P. Judd, *Members of Parliament 1734–1832* (1955), a book which is valuable not for its arguments (which are questionable) but for its appended lists of members and sources of information. *Byran's Dictionary of Painters and Engravers* edited by G. C. Wilkinson

(1903/4) is much criticized but remains the most useful work in its field. Beyond carping criticism is H. M. Colvin, *Biographical Dictionary of Architects 1660–1840* (1954). For literature the *Cambridge Bibliography* has already been mentioned and for music the standard reference works are Sir George Grove, *Dictionary of Music and Musicians* (4 vols. and appendix 1879–89), and P. Scholes, *The Oxford Companion to Music* (1938). Articles on a miscellaneous collection of topics for this period will also be found in the various editions of the *Encyclopaedia Britannica* and the 1950 edition of *Chambers' Encyclopaedia*.

Two contemporary works needed for reference are *The Parliamentary History* and *The Annual Register*. *The Parliamentary History* was produced by Cobbett until 1812 when it was taken over by T. C. Hansard. Its reports are based on a variety of sources but are defective. Nevertheless they are indispensable. For the House of Commons 1768–71 they may be usefully supplemented by the Cavendish debates (edited J. Wright 1841–3). The *Annual Register* begun in 1758 by R. Dodsley and Edmund Burke gives a useful summary of the events of each year. It falls into a partisan tone from the outbreak of the Revolution in France but for its first thirty years it maintains both vitality and fairness to a surprising degree.

POLITICAL HISTORY

There is a dearth of satisfactory chronological accounts of the political development of this period as a whole and an embarrassingly rich crop of special studies of short periods or of particular aspects. Early attempts to write histories of the period were made by W. Bisham, *Memories of the Reign of George III to the Session of Parliament ending in A.D. 1793* (4 vols., 1795), John Adolphus, *The History of England from the Accession of King George III to the Conclusion of Peace in 1783* (3 vols., 1802), and John Aikin, *Annals of the Reign of King George III, 1760–1815* (2 vols., 1816). All three have still some use—Adolphus because he writes with moderation as a conservative sympathizing with the established order, Bisham because he gives a dissenter's viewpoint, and Aikin for his systematic, if prosaic, summary of the main events of each year. *The History of England from the Peace of Utrecht to the Peace of Versailles (1713–83)* by P. H. Stanhope, Viscount Mahon (later Lord Stanhope) (7 vols. 1836–54) gives a remarkably clear and well-balanced account of the early part of the reign; it is Whiggish but it is not partisan. Compared to this the eight volumes of W. E. H. Lecky, *A History of England in the Eighteenth Century* (1879-90) seem crude and mechanical in judgement though they are remarkable for their comprehensiveness and for the sustained narrative power. Sir Charles Grant Robertson's *England under the Hanoverians* (1911, revised 1930) made a simplified version of Lecky's story available in one volume.

Two books by Sir Lewis Namier, *The Structure of Politics at the Accession of George III* (2 vols., 1929; rev. ed. 1957) and *England in the Age of the American Revolution* (1930), challenged the basis upon which Lecky and those who followed him had written of the reign. Once these two books had appeared it was impossible to write usefully on the political history of the reign without taking account of this brilliant scholarly achievement. But though they provide ideas for the reinterpretation of politics, and though they examine a few years microscopically they were not intended, of course, to be a consecutive history of the period. *England in the Age of the American Revolution* is at present being expanded by Sir Lewis Namier and by others under his supervision. Two detailed studies of key episodes have so far been published: J. Brook, *The Chatham Administration 1766-68* (1956) and G. R. Christie, *The Fall of North's Ministry* (1958). Sir Lewis Namier himself has discussed 'Monarchy and the Party System' and 'Country Gentlemen in Parliament 1750-85' in his *Principalities and Powers* (1955).

The ideas of these scholars of 'the Namier school', particularly their stress upon the mechanics of politics, have been criticized by H. Butterfield in *George III and the Historians* (1957) with particular attention to the beginning of the reign. More widely ranging, and in harmony with Namier's ideas, is the work of a scholar who, but for his long and mortal illness, would have written this volume in the Oxford History, Richard Pares: his *George III and the Politicians* (1953), the fruit of his preliminary work, displays his radiant intelligence playing upon many problems over the whole period. But the only major attempt made since Namier's intervention to give a vista rather than brilliant *aperçus*, to tell the story chronologically for the whole reign, is Sir Keith G. Feiling, *The Second Tory Party 1714-1832* (1938) and here, as is clear from the title, a particular (and elusive) thread is followed.

For political history, therefore, the reader must make his way among a multitude of studies. For the period 1760–80 original material is to be found in R. Sedgwick, *Letters of George III to Bute* (1939), which is most valuable, both for the light the letters throw on the king's character and for the stimulating essay— upon the significance of a change of monarch—which introduces them. There is evidence of great value also about the early years (though less entertaining) in *The Grenville Papers* edited by W. J. Smith (4 vols., 1852–3). Politics from the point of view of an ambitious working man of affairs are presented in N. S. Tucker, *The Jenkinson Papers 1760–66* (1949) and in *The Parliamentary Papers of John Robinson 1774–1784* edited by W. R. Laprade (1922). Some of the events seen from an aristocratic height can be appreciated in *The Correspondence of John, Fourth Duke of Bedford* selected by Lord John Russell (3 vols., 1842–6). Information for the first twenty years can also be found in Newcastle's narrative of changes in the ministry 1765–7 edited by M. Beatson (1898), in the *Chatham Correspondence* edited by W. S. Taylor and J. H. Pringle (4 vols., 1838–40), though this is a disappointing selection of surviving originals, in *The Autobiographical and Political Correspondence of the Duke of Grafton*, edited by Sir W. R. Anson (1898), where the duke puts forward his own case in a curiously faint fashion, and in the Duke of Albemarle's poorly edited *Memoirs of the Marquis of Rockingham* (2 vols., 1852): much material is also to be found in *The Works and Correspondence of Edmund Burke* edited by Earl Fitzwilliam and Sir R. Bourke (8 vols., 1852), though the new edition of *Burke's Correspondence* (edited by T. W. Copeland and others) of which volume I appeared in 1959, will supersede this, and in Lord Edmond Fitzmaurice's *Life of William earl of Shelburne* (3 vols., 1875–6) which includes an autobiographical fragment. *The Correspondence of George III 1760–83* edited by Sir J. Fortescue (6 vols., 1927–8) and *Additions and Corrections to Sir John Fortescue's edition*, L. B. Namier (1937), are obviously a vital aid to study. A contemporary source which has to be handled with care because the author combines partisan prejudices, an appetite for exact information, a taste for the malicious, and great literary skill, to produce his beguiling effects is Horace Walpole. His *Letters* were edited by Mrs. Paget Toynbee (16 vols., 1903–5, with supplement by Paget Toynbee, 3 vols., 1918–25); a new edition is being produced from Yale under the editorship of W. S. Lewis (1937 ff.). His *Memoirs of the Reign of King George III* edited by G. F. Barker (4 vols., 1894) cover the years 1760 to 1771. His *Last Journals* edited by A. F. Steuart (2 vols., 1910) cover 1771 to 1783. Almost equally strongly marked with the author's personality—in which cynicism and common sense predominate—are *The Historical and Posthumous Memoirs of Sir Nathanial Wraxall* edited by H. B. Wheatley (5 vols., 1884): these are enjoyable for the shrewdness of their views and for the wealth of information they provide about the minor politicians of the time.

For the period from the fall of North to 1815 original materials have been printed in many books, including those biographies, so popular in the nineteenth century, which consist of extracts from letters and diaries strung together on thin links of editorial comment. A most useful quarry is Lord John Russell (ed.), *Memorials and Correspondence of Charles James Fox* (4 vols., 1853–7). This part of the story is continued in Lord Holland, *Memoirs of the Whig Party during my Time* ed. by his son, Henry Edward Lord Holland (2 vols., 1852–4) and *Further Memoirs of the Whig Party 1807–1821* ed. by G. Fox-Strangways, Lord Stavordale (1905). P. H. Stanhope, 5th Earl Stanhope, *Life of the right honourable William Pitt* (4 vols., 1861–2; ed. 3, 3 vols., 1879), a work of literary merit based upon careful editing of the correspondence, Lord Auckland's *Journals and Correspondence* ed. by the Bishop of Bath and Wells (4 vols., 1861–2), *Life and Letters of Sir Gilbert Elliott, first Earl of Minto* ed. by the Countess of Minto (3 vols., 1874), and the *Diaries* of that exceedingly snobbish and foolish man *Sylvester Douglas, 1st Lord Glenbervie*, ed. F. Bickley (2 vols., 1928) all contain much interesting information. There is original material printed in the very flaccid *Life and Correspondence of the Right Hon. Henry Addington, First Viscount Sidmouth* by G. Pellew (1847). A great deal of political evidence as well as administrative gossip is to be found in *The Diaries and Correspondence of George Rose* ed. L. V. Harcourt (2 vols., 1860) and in *The Diary and Correspondence of Charles Abbot, Lord Colchester* ed. by his son Charles, Lord Colchester (3 vols., 1861). A more important quarry, for it is stuffed with all the news and ambitions of the Grenville family, is Richard Plantagenet Temple-Nugent-Brydges-Chandos Grenville, duke of Buckingham and Chandos's *Memoirs of the Court and Cabinets of George the third* (2 vols., 1853–5): it is unfortunate that so much valuable material should be so poorly presented. The *Correspondence of Charles, first Marquis Cornwallis* ed. C. Ross (3 vols., 1859) covers a field wider than that simply of political history. Mention must also be made of R. W. Ketton-Cremer, *The Early Life and Diaries of William Windham* (1930), of the dull *Memoirs* of J. Mackintosh, ed. by his son, P. J. Mackintosh (2 vols., 1835), of the *Works* of J. Bentham ed. J. Bowring (11 vols., 1838–43), of the rhetorical *Memoirs of the Life and Times of the right hon. Henry Grattan* by his son (5 vols., 1839–46), of Spencer Walpole, *The Life of the Rt. Hon. Spencer Perceval* (2 vols., 1874), of H. Twiss, *The Public and Private Life of Lord Chancellor Eldon* (3 vols., 1844), and of C. D. Yonge's very disappointing *The Life and Administration of Robert Banks, second Earl of Liverpool* (3 vols., 1868), as well as, on the fringes of the world of high politics, C. Wyvill, *Political Papers* (6 vols., 1794–1802). The *Memoirs and Correspondence of Viscount Castlereagh* ed. by his brother, the third Marquess Londonderry, fill 12 volumes (1848–53) with material on home as well as foreign politics. Earl Stanhope's *Notes of Conversations with the Duke of Wellington* (modern ed. 1938) are enlightening on peace as well as war. The *Portrait of a Whig Peer, compiled from the Papers of the 2nd Viscount Palmerston* by B. Connell (1957), *A Portion of the Journal kept by T. Raikes from 1831 to 1847* (4 vols., 1856–7), and *Georgiana. Extracts from the Correspondence of Georgiana, duchess of Devonshire* ed. by the Earl of Bessborough (1955) contain a great deal of information about the social and cultural life of those in the centre of political activity.

It may be well, when turning from these sources of evidence to secondary works containing more guidance to the reader, to consider the field in two chronological parts. The first two decades of George III's reign are discussed in D. A. Winstanley, *Personal and Party Government 1760–66* (1910) and *Lord Chatham and the Whig Opposition* (1912). These two books are still useful if they are read critically, bearing in mind that their conception of party and of the role of the king was formulated before Namier's work had opened up new interpretations. Other useful studies for the years 1760–80, in addition to those like Brook and Christie discussed above, are in the main biographical; they include: the Earl of Ilchester (G. Fox-Strangways), *Henry Fox, 1st Lord Holland* (1920), Basil Williams, *William Pitt, Earl of Chatham* (2 vols., 1913) where hero-worship leads the author into error in dealing with Pitt's opponents (the opposite tendency appears in A. von Ruville, *William Pitt Earl of Chatham*—English translation, 3 vols., 1907), P. H. Fitzgerald, *Charles Townshend* (1866), a collection of anecdotes with some crude judgements, and Sir P. Magnus, *Edmund Burke* (1939). A study of one aspect of Burke is Dixon Wecter, *Edmund Burke and his Kinsmen* (University of Colorado, series B, i, 1939): the atmosphere of murky suspicion which this creates will, one suspects, probably be dissipated by the meticulous new edition of Burke's correspondence (see above). It is striking that there is no scholarly biography of Lord North and that the political history of his twelve years of power has been, on its English side, comparatively neglected. R. Lucas, *Lord North* (1913) is old fashioned in its approach to politics, and W. B. Pemberton, *Lord North* (1938) is a piece of book-making rather than a contribution to knowledge but there is nothing else available covering the subject. These books should be corrected by C. R. Ritcheson, *British Politics and the American Revolution* (University of Oklahoma Press, Norman, 1954) and G. H. Guttridge, *English Whiggism and the American Revolution* (University of California Publications in History xxviii; 1942). H. Butterfield, *George III, Lord North and the People, 1779–1800* (1949) explores in detail the collapse of the North administration and the Yorkshire petitioning movement.

For the radicalism of these two decades the most easily available book is S. Maccoby, *English Radicalism 1762–1785* (1935) and *1786–1832* (1955): H. Bleakley, *Life of John Wilkes* (1917), and R. Postgate, *That Devil Wilkes* (1939) are two very different but unsatisfying attempts to write this biography; A. Stephens, *Memoirs of John Horne Tooke* (2 vols., 1813) gives a better insight into radical politics. The politics of London are etched by Lucy [S.] Sutherland, 'The City of London in Eighteenth Century Politics' in *Essays Presented to Sir Lewis Namier* (1956), pp. 49–74. Use can also be made of J. P. de Castro, *The Gordon Riots* (1926) and a paper by G. F. E. Rudé, 'The Gordon Riots: a study of the Rioters and their Victims' in *Transactions of the Royal Historical Society*, 5th series, vi (1956), pp. 93–114, for examination of London turbulence. The most useful of the editions of *The Letters of Junius* is that of C. W. Everett (1927).

The years following the fall of North are of course dominated by the contest of Pitt and Fox. Pitt has been well served by—in

Also g. Rudé, *Wilkes & liberty*.

addition to Stanhope's *Pitt* mentioned above—J. H. Rose, *William Pitt and the National Revival* (1911) and the same author's *William Pitt and the Great War* (1911) and *Pitt and Napoleon*, essays and letters (1912). D. G. Barnes in his *George III and William Pitt 1783–1806* (1939) hits some nails on the head but he hits them with unnecessary reiteration, nor does he show much subtlety in developing his arguments. Fox has not yet had an adequate modern biography: that by E. C. P. Lascelles (1936) is perhaps the least bad, but it is advisable to ignore all of them and to use the originals in Lord John Russell's work (above). For Dundas, H. Furber (1931) and C. Matheson (1933) have both provided serviceable accounts. For Sheridan the choice is between W. S. Sichel's rather dull *Sheridan* (2 vols., 1909) and the rather too light *Harlequin Sheridan* of R. C. Rhodes (1933). If it is read with a critical eye, as much for appreciation of the author's career as for his subjects, there is still much enjoyment to be derived from Lord Brougham's *Historical Sketches of Statesmen who Flourished in the Time of George III* (3 parts, 1839–43).

The changing atmosphere of politics after 1789 is very well dealt with in P. A. Brown, *The French Revolution in English History* (1918) and in the first half of H. W. C. Davis, *The Age of Grey and Peel* (1929). For the political situation on the death of Pitt and Fox the indispensable guide is the detailed history of *The Whig Party, 1807–12* by M. Roberts (1939). The biographies of *George Tierney* by H. K. Olphin (1934) and of *Sir Samuel Romilly* by C. G. Oakes (1935) are of assistance. Though the main interest of W. R. Brock, *Lord Liverpool and Liberal Toryism, 1820–27* (1941) is obviously outside this period it is nevertheless so good an essay in the understanding of Toryism and of Liverpool that it must be mentioned for the light it casts on the end of George III's reign. Similarly it is worth using A. Aspinall, *Lord Brougham and the Whig Party* (1927) even though it is really concerned with the years after 1815.

The rising radicalism of the last years of the reign may be studied in some of the books already listed and also in M. W. Patterson, *Sir Francis Burdett and his Times, 1770–1844* (2 vols., 1931), G. D. H. Cole, *A Short History of the British Working Class Movement*, vol. i, 1789–1848 (1925), in the same author's *The Life of William Cobbett* (1924), in M. Cole, *Robert Owen of New Lanark* (1953), in A. Cobban (ed.), *The Debate on the French*

Revolution 1789–1800 (1950), while theoretical ideas of the discontented are reviewed in M. Beer, *A History of British Socialism*,
vol. i (1919). The broadest survey of the impact of the new
ideas upon the old political system is G. S. Veitch (who was the
author originally commissioned to write the present volume
but who, like Richard Pares, died before he could proceed far
with it), *The Genesis of Parliamentary Reform* (1913). A. Briggs's
The Age of Improvement (1959) appeared after the present work
had been completed in proof.

LEGAL AND CONSTITUTIONAL

There is no better general survey of the working of English
government in the eighteenth century than vol. x of Sir William
S. Holdsworth, *A History of English Law*, while scattered in all
the 12 volumes (1922–38) are the most enlightening items of
information (a new edition, under the editorship of A. L. Good-
hart and H. G. Hanbury is in process of publication, 1956 ff.).
This is a work which may challenge comparison with Sir W.
Blackstone's famous *Commentaries on the Laws of England* (4 vols.,
1765–9). On one aspect of the law L. Radzinowicz, *A History
of Criminal Law and its Administration from 1750* (3 vols., 1948–56)
is very helpful. For a biographical approach there is still great
pleasure to be found in Lord John Campbell's *Lives of the Lord
Chancellors* (8 vols., 1845–69) and his *Lives of the Chief Justices of
England* (3 vols., 1849–57). R. Gore-Browne, *Chancellor Thurlow,
the Life and Times of an XVIIIth Century Lawyer* (1953), though
not a profound or original work, will also give pleasure and
information.

For Parliament E. and A. G. Porritt, *The Unreformed House of
Commons* (2 vols., 1903) provides a clearly arranged picture of
the composition and election of the lower chamber: the move-
ment for its reform is most clearly set out in G. S. Veitch (see
above on this page). The only considerable studies of the
Upper House are A. S. Turberville's *The House of Lords in the
Eighteenth Century* (1927) and his *The House of Lords in the Age of
Reform* (1958).

Relations between the Crown and Parliament are dealt with
(apart from works already mentioned in the previous section)
in Betty Kemp, *King and Commons, 1660–1832* (1957) and in A. S.
Foord, 'The Waning of "The Influence of the Crown"' in

English Historical Review, lxii (1947), pp. 484–507. On the election of 1784, which is particularly important to this subject, the views of W. T. Laprade, 'Public Opinion and the election of 1784', ibid. xxxi (1916), pp. 224–37, should be compared with those of Mrs. E. George, 'Fox's Martyrs: the General Election of 1784' in *Transactions of the Royal Historical Society*, 4th series, xxi (1939), pp. 133–68.

The development of the Cabinet is considered in entertaining detail by A. Aspinall, 'The Cabinet Council, 1783–1835' in *Proceedings of the British Academy*, xxxviii (1952), pp. 145–252. It is a pity that the preceding twenty years can still be examined only through the posthumous second volume of E. R. Turner, *The Cabinet Council of England, 1622–1784* (2 vols., Baltimore, 1930–32) which is vague where one seeks precision. As a guide to an understanding of the principles involved E. T. Williams, 'The Cabinet in the Eighteenth Century' in *History*, N.S., xxii (1937–8), pp. 240–52, with further note, pp. 332–4, is most useful.

The background of constitutional theory may be derived from a contemporary source by study of J. L. de Lolme, *The Constitution of England* (1775) or in a modern and stimulating study F. T. H. Fletcher, *Montesquieu and English Politics, 1750–1800* (1939).

Investigation of local government must be based upon the nine bulky volumes of S. and B. Webb, *English Local Government from the Revolution to the Municipal Corporation Act* (1906–29) but it is also worth consulting J. Redlich and F. W. Hirst, *Local Government in England* (2 vols., 1903). Those who seek a contemporary, copious, and classic account will still turn to R. Burn, *The Justice of the Peace and Parish Officer* (23rd ed., 6 vols., 1821). E. G. Dowdell's *A Hundred Years of Quarter Sessions* (1932), though it ends nominally in 1760 nevertheless is most helpful for understanding of the special problems of Middlesex after that date.

The best modern constitutional history in outline is Sir David L. Keir, *The Constitutional History of Modern Britain, 1485–1937* (1938) while original materials are assembled for illustration of the main themes in W. C. Costin and J. S. Watson, *The Law and Working of the Constitution: Documents 1660–1914* (2 vols., 1952).

ADMINISTRATIVE AND FINANCIAL

Recently there has been a growth in interest in the machinery of eighteenth-century government. The fruits of this are to be seen in such works as M. A. Thomson, *The Secretaries of State, 1681–1782* (1932) and Margaret M. Spector, *The American Department of the British Government, 1768–1772* (New York, 1940), K. Ellis, *The Post Office in the Eighteenth Century* (1958): there are also articles by Mary P. Clarke, 'The Board of Trade at Work' in *American Historical Review*, xvii (1911–12), pp. 17–43, E. Jones-Parry, 'Under Secretaries of State for Foreign Affairs 1782–1855' in *English Historical Review*, xlix (1934), pp. 308–20, and G. R. James, 'The Admiralty Establishment, 1759' in *Bulletin of the Institute of Historical Research*, xvi (1938–9), pp. 24–27, as well as a discussion of the whole question of the significance of Administrative reform in Sir David L. Keir, 'Economic Reform 1779–87' in *Law Quarterly Review*, i (1934), pp. 368–85. Particularly useful for financial problems are E. Hughes, *Studies in Administration and Finance, 1558–1825* (1934), which is mainly concerned with the salt tax, W. R. Ward, *The English Land Tax in the Eighteenth Century* (1953) and J. E. D. Binney, *British Public Finance and Administration 1774–92* (1958), a work of the greatest detail and acumen. *The History of Taxation and Taxes in England* by S. Dowell (4 vols., 1884) remains a useful reference book as does H. Hall, *A History of the Customs Revenues in England from the Earliest Times to the Year 1827* (2 vols., 1885): C. H. Wilson, *Anglo-Dutch Commerce and Finance in the Eighteenth Century* (1941) helps to relate the problems of the Treasury to wider issues of trade and economics. A particularly dark corner of financial history is illuminated by Lucy S. Sutherland and J. Binney, 'Henry Fox as Paymaster General of the Forces' in *English Historical Review*, lxx (1955), pp. 229–56, with appendix, pp. 256 f. While the outline of administrative history after the rise of Pitt will be found in works listed under political history in this bibliography these may usefully be supplemented by an article by C. B. Cone, 'Richard Price and Pitt's Sinking Fund of 1786' in *Economic History Review*, 2nd ser., iv (1952), pp. 243–51, and by a book by A. Farnworth, *Addington author of the modern Income Tax* (1951).

On financial business generally, besides books listed under economics, it is useful to consult *The Paper Pound of 1797–1821*:

a reprint of the bullion report [8 June 1810] ed. E. Cannan (1919), and N. J. Silberling, 'Financial and Monetary Policy of Great Britain during the Napoleonic Wars' in *Quarterly Journal of Economics*, xxxviii (1924), pp. 214-33, 397-439. Banking history is clearly expounded in E. V. Morgan, *The Theory and Practice of Central Banking, 1797-1913* (1943). J. H. Clapham, *The Bank of England* (2 vols., 1944) and L. S. Pressnell, *Country Banking in the Industrial Revolution* (1956) are both works of great authority. To this list should be appended T. Tooke, *A History of Prices, and of the State of the Circulation 1793-1837* (2 vols., 1838).

ECONOMIC AND SOCIAL HISTORY

For the years 1760 to 1800 the best outline is T. S. Ashton, *An Economic History of England: the Eighteenth Century* (1955). This supersedes earlier economic surveys and has very valuable statistical tables. For the years 1800 to 1815, however, there is no such steady guide. J. H. Clapham, *An Economic History of Modern Britain*, vol. i, The Railway Age (1926) has 1820 for its starting-point: its numerous retrospective glances, however, are enlightening on the period back to 1800. It does not, however, enable the student to follow chronologically (as he can in Ashton for the period 1760 to 1800) the progress made in the first fifteen years of the new century. Yet, as the dating and extent of the industrial revolution has become a controversial subject this is important (see Sir G. N. Clark, *The Idea of the Industrial Revolution*, 1953, J. U. Nef, 'The Industrial Revolution reconsidered' in *Journal of Economic History*, iii (1943), pp. 1-31, as well as Ashton and Clapham above). One is forced back to W. Smart, *Economic Annals of the Nineteenth Century* (2 vols., 1910-17) for chronological information: use can then be made of a host of other books which take surveys of the period as a whole and make generalizations which have to be checked against Smart's facts. These include the works of J. L. and Barbara Hammond, *The Village Labourer* (1911, ed. 4, 1927), *The Town Labourer* (1917; new ed. 1925), *The Skilled Labourer* (1919), and *The Rise of Modern Industry* (1925). Their gloomy view of the consequences of economic change upon the condition of the people has been challenged: the opposing views will be found summarized in T. S. Ashton, 'The Standard of Life of the Workers in England, 1790-1830' in *Journal of Economic History*, ix (1949), Supplement, pp. 19-38, and in F. A. von

Hayek (ed.), *Capitalism and the Historians* (Chicago, 1954) but it is defended by E. J. Hobsbawn, 'The British Standard of Living, 1710–1850' in *Economic History Review*, 2nd series, x (1958), pp. 46–61. Other useful secondary works are T. S. Ashton's small *The Industrial Revolution 1760 to 1830* (1948), W. H. B. Court, *A Concise Economic History of Britain from 1750 to Recent Times* (1954), C. R. Fay, *Great Britain from Adam Smith to the present day* (1928), P. Mantoux, *La Révolution Industrielle au XVIIIe Siècle* (1905; English tr. of ed. 2, *The Industrial Revolution in the Eighteenth Century*, 1928) and W. Cunningham's *The Growth of English Industry and Commerce* (1882; ed. 4, 2 vols. in 3 parts, 1905–7, part separately issued as *The Industrial Revolution*, 1908). A. P. Usher, *A History of Mechanical Inventions* (New York, 1929) describes a multitude of inventions in understandable language. The attempt to use statistics for a general survey, *The Growth and Fluctuations of the British Economy, 1790–1850* by A. D. Gayer, W. W. Rostow, and A. Schwartz (2 vols., 1953) has to be used with care and T. S. Ashton's review of it, 'Economic Fluctuations 1790–1850' in *Economic History Review*, 2nd series, vii (1955), pp. 377–81, is useful as a guide in interpretation. E. F. Heckscher, *Mercantilism* (orig. Swedish ed. 1931; Eng. tr., 2 vols., 1934) is the standard exposition of the old system of trade at the onset of this industrial change.

There are a multitude of studies of particular areas and of particular industries. Reference should be made to J. B. Williams, *A Guide to the Printed Material for English Social and Economic History 1750–1850* (2 vols., New York, 1926) and to the annual bibliographies of the *Economic History Review* for works published since 1926. Notable among studies of particular areas, however, are H. Hamilton, *The Industrial Revolution in Scotland* (1932), A. H. John, *The Industrial Development of South Wales 1750–1850* (1950), A. H. Dodd, *The Industrial Revolution in North Wales* (1933), W. H. B. Court, *The Rise of the Midland Industries 1600–1838* (1938). For particular industries the most generally useful are J. H. Clapham, *The Woollen and Worsted Industries* (1907), G. Unwin, A. Hulme, and G. Taylor, *Samuel Oldknow and the Arkwrights* (1924), A. P. Wadsworth and Julia de L. Mann, *The Cotton Trade and Industrial Lancashire 1660–1780* (1931), which can be supplemented by G. W. Daniels, 'The Effect of the Napoleonic War on the Cotton Trade' and 'The Cotton Trade at the close of the Napoleonic War' in *Transac-*

tions of the Manchester Statistical Society, 1915–16, pp. 53–82, and
1917–18, pp. 1–29, respectively, Sir F. Warner, *The Silk Industry
of the United Kingdom* [1921], T. S. Ashton's invaluable *Iron and
Steel in the Industrial Revolution* (1924), H. W. Dickinson, *A Short
History of the Steam Engine* (1939) and *James Watt, Craftsman and
Engineer* (1936), T. S. Ashton and J. Sykes, *The Coal Industry of
the Eighteenth Century* (1929), W. Burton, *Josiah Wedgwood and
his Pottery* (1922), A. and N. L. Clow, *The Chemical Revolution*
(1952): E. A. Pratt, *A History of Inland Transportation and Communication in England* (1912) is still a standard authority but it
may be supplemented by Roy [Margaret R. R. P.] Devereux,
John Loudon McAdam (1936) and L. T. C. Rolt, *Thomas Telford*
(1958): C. N. Parkinson, *The Rise of the Port of Liverpool* (Liverpool, 1952) is well done. The comprehensive account of canals
is in U. A. Forbes and W. H. R. Ashford, *Our Waterways*
(1906). For business organization it is best to use A. B. Du Bois,
The English Business Company after the Bubble Act, 1720–1800
(New York, 1938) with B. C. Hunt, *The Development of the
Business Corporation in England 1800–67* (Cambridge, Mass.,
1936), but it will still be useful to hunt for further information
in the biographies of the business men of the day: of these
Boulton has received most attention, and views such as those
expressed in his biography by W. H. Dickinson (1937) have
been usefully criticized by J. E. Cule, 'Finance and Industry
in the Eighteenth Century: the Firm of Boulton and Watt' in
Economic History, iv (1940), pp. 319–25. *The Early Factory
Legislation* is considered in a book of that name by M. W.
Thomas (Leigh-on-Sea, 1948), but the standard work for
reference is B. L. Hutchins and A. Harrison, *A History of
Factory Legislation* (2nd ed. 1911).

When one turns from the industrial field in which there is an
embarrassing abundance of material to the agricultural a great
contrast is felt. Many historians have sharply criticized the
book of R. E. Prothero, Lord Ernle, *English Farming Past and
Present* (1912; revised ed. 1936) but there is no other comparable
work: it is moreover very good reading. It may therefore be
commended provided it is read with caution and corrected by
specialist studies, e.g. J. D. Chambers, *Nottinghamshire in the
18th Century* (1932), R. A. C. Parker, 'Coke of Norfolk and the
Agrarian Revolution' in *Economic History Review,* 2nd series,
viii (1955), pp. 156–66, or Olga Wilkinson, *The Agrarian*

Revolution in the East Riding of Yorkshire (East Yorkshire Local History Society Publications No. 5, 1956). Arthur Young's eye-witness accounts of conditions—to be found in *Annals of Agriculture* (46 vols., 1784–1815; selections in London School of Economics Reprints of Scarce Tracts 14, 1932) or in *A Six Months Tour through the North of England* (4 vols., 1770) or in his *Autobiography* ed. Matilda Betham-Edwards (1898)—are of course the most splendid contemporary source for this subject. Comparison can be made with W. Cobbett's *Rural Rides in the Counties of Surrey, Kent, Sussex* (1830; modern ed. by G. D. H. and Margaret Cole, 3 vols., 1930) for the later part of the period. Enclosures and rural society are expounded in E. C. K. Gonner, *Common Land and Enclosure* (1912), A. H. Johnson, *The Disappearance of the Small Landowner* (1909), G. E. Fussell, *The English Rural Labourer* (1949) and, no doubt from a different ideological standpoint, U. M. Lavrovsky, Parliamentary Enclosures of Common Lands in England in the late Eighteenth and early Nineteenth Centuries (in Russian, Moscow, 1941). D. G. Barnes, *A History of the English Corn Laws from 1660 to 1846* (1930) is invaluable as a reference book.

For population a general study was made by G. Talbot Griffith, *Population Problems in the age of Malthus* (1926) but the figures and conclusions of this work were challenged by T. H. Marshall, 'The Population Problem during the Industrial Revolution' in *Economic History*, i (1929), pp. 429–56. The controversy has been considered by H. J. Habakkuk, 'English Population in the Eighteenth Century' in *Economic History Review*, 2nd series, vi (1953–4), pp. 117–33. Wages are dealt with in Elizabeth W. Gilboy, *Wages in Eighteenth Century England* (Cambridge, Mass., 1934) and A. L. Bowley, *Wages in the United Kingdom in the Nineteenth Century* (1900). Mention must also be made of two attempts to deal with questions of costs and prices: N. J. Silberling, 'British Prices and Business Cycles, 1779–1850' in *The Review of Economic Statistics*, prelim. vol. v, supplement 2 (1923), pp. 219–61, and T. S. Ashton, 'Changes in Standards of Comfort in Eighteenth-Century England' in *Proceedings of the British Academy*, xli (1955), pp. 171–87. For nutrition the most easily manageable book is Sir J. C. Drummond and A. C. Wilbraham, *The Englishman's Food* (1939) which draws on many sources. A more specialized taste is catered for in R. N. Salaman, *The History and Social Influence of the*

Potato (1949). For dress C. W. and Phyllis Cunnington, *Handbook of English Costume in the Eighteenth Century* (1957) is authoritative. The picture of life in high society given by Brian Connell from the diaries of the second Viscount Palmerston (see above) may usefully be compared with that in Gladys Scott Thomson's *Family Background* (1949) and her other works on the Russell family. A wider range of classes are depicted in *Johnson's England* (ed. A. S. Turberville, 1933): the life of the lower classes is depicted in Dorothy Marshall, *The English Poor in the 18th Century* (1926), and Mrs. [M.] Dorothy George, *London Life in the 18th Century* (1925).

RELIGION, PHILANTHROPY, AND EDUCATION

The authoritative survey of the history of the Established Church is N. Sykes, *Church and State in England in the Eighteenth Century* (1934): this is a readable and well-balanced account. The same ground is covered in chatty, but much less profound, style by S. C. Carpenter, *Eighteenth Century Church and People* (1959). For particular topics it is useful to consult the articles in S. L. Ollard and others, *A Dictionary of English Church History* (1912; 3rd ed., revised, 1948) and, for shorter but meticulously well-ordered information (and bibliographies), F. L. Cross, *The Oxford Dictionary of the Christian Church* (1957; reprint with corrections, 1958). To gain an impression of the life of a parish clergyman reference should be made to *The Diary of a Country Parson 1758–1802* (J. Woodforde) ed. J. Beresford (5 vols., 1924–31). For the evangelical movement Sir L. Stephen, *Essays in Ecclesiastical History* ii (1849), pp. 287–382 ('The Clapham Sect'), E. M. Howse, *Saints in Politics* (1953), and W. K. Lowther Clarke, *Eighteenth Century Piety* (1944), are all useful: M. Gwladys Jones, *Hannah More* (1952), deals lucidly with one on the fringe of this circle. *Wilberforce: a narrative* by R. Coupland (1923) is more manageable than the five-volume *Life* produced by his sons (1838): E. Williams, *Capitalism and Slavery* (1944) is a modern attempt to assess the anti-slave-trade campaign; Granville Sharp's life of good causes may be traced in the *Memoirs* by Prince Hoare (1828 ed.).

The Roman Catholic Church in England is examined in B. Ward, *The Dawn of the Catholic Revival in England 1781–1803* (2 vols., 1909). There are a considerable number of books on Protestant nonconformity, particularly as considered from the point of view of its social origins and effects. Many of them are, however, marred by excessive generalization unchecked by relation to precise economic or political facts. Among the most useful are E. D. Bebb, *Nonconformity and Social and Economic Life, 1660–1800* (1935), and A. H. Lincoln, *Some Political and Social Ideas of English Dissent 1763–1800* (1938). Maldwyn L. Edwards, *John Wesley and the Eighteenth Century* (1933) is continued by the same author's *After Wesley: a Study in the Social and Political Influence of Methodism in the Middle Period 1791–1849* (1935); the two works form a very interesting study of Wesley's influence: less useful, but adding a few points is W. J. Warner, *The Wesleyan Movement in the Industrial Revolution* (1930). Two other biographies of nonconformists which are useful to an understanding of their importance are Anne Holt, *A Life of Joseph Priestley* (1931) and R. Thomas, *Richard Price* (1924).

H. McLachlan, *English Education under the Test Acts 1662–1820* (1931), is the best history of dissenting academies. The appropriate chapters in S. J. Curtis, *History of Education in Great Britain* (1948; ed. 4, 1957) give a fair but rather bald account of the educational position generally. A splendid study of elementary education is M. Gwladys Jones, *The Charity School Movement: A Study of Eighteenth Century Puritanism in Action* (1938). For educational reform see D. Salmon, *The Practical Parts of Lancaster's Improvement and Bell's Experiment* (1932). A. Gregory, *Robert Raikes, a History of the Origins of Sunday Schools* (1880) is informative. R. K. Webb, *The British Working Class Reader 1790–1848* (1955) is not very full on the period before 1815. A difficult, because not well defined, subject is handled with moderate success in *Public Schools and British Opinion 1780–1860* by E. C. Mack (1938). The universities are broadly surveyed in D. A. Winstanley, *The University of Cambridge in the 18th Century* (1922), in the same author's *Unreformed Cambridge* (1935), in A. D. Godley, *Oxford in the 18th Century* (1908) and in the appropriate section of Sir C. E. Mallet, *A History of the University of Oxford*, iii (1927); the bewildering complexity of University politics is explored in parts iv and v of W. R. Ward, *Georgian Oxford* (1958).

LITERATURE AND THE ARTS

It is impossible to supply a select bibliography of literature in its change from eighteenth-century classicism to romanticism without its appearing ridiculously skimpy. It is therefore better to refer the reader to the biographies (and to the works) of the writers in whom he is interested and also to the *Cambridge Bibliography of English Literature*—with the passing reminder, however, that J. Nichols, *Literary Anecdotes of the Eighteenth Century* (9 vols., 1812–15) and *Illustrations of the Literary History of the Eighteenth Century* (8 vols., 1817–58), which have all the appearance of a disorganized encyclopaedia, are in fact mines of information about politics and society as well as literature, while Leslie Stephen, *Hours in a Library* (1874) has enduring value in its appreciation of the writers of the early nineteenth century.

For painting the contemporary starting-point is Sir Joshua Reynolds, *Seven Discourses delivered in the Royal Academy* (1778) and with this F. W. Hilles, *The Literary Career of Sir Joshua Reynolds* (1936) is very useful. H. Walpole, *Anecdotes of Painting* (3 vols., 1762–3; vol. 4, 1771 [1780]; numerous later eds.) is a contemporary source of miscellaneous information and catalogues. For literary value if not for the study of painting B. Haydon, *His Life from his Autobiography and Journals*, ed. T. Taylor (3 vols., 1853) is a major work. W. Sandby, *The History of the Royal Academy* (2 vols., 1862) still has some use. There is much that is interesting in Sir L. [H.] Cust and Sir S. Colvin, *History of the Society of Dilettanti* (1898; reprinted with supplementary chapter, 1914). A stimulating and scholarly study is C. Mitchell's paper on 'Benjamin West's "Death of General Wolfe" and the Popular History Piece' in *England and the Mediterranean Tradition* (ed. by The Warburg and Courtauld Institutes, London, 1945), pp. 179–92. Probably the most readily available summary for the earlier period is E. K. Waterhouse, *Painting in Britain 1530 to 1790* (1953).

For architecture J. [N.] Summerson, *Architecture in Britain 1530 to 1830* (1953) and R. [S.] Dutton, *The English Country House* (1935) open up the way for further study. J. Lees Milne, *The Age of Adam* (1947), A. T. Boulton, *The Works of Sir John Soane* [1924], A. Dale, *James Wyatt, Architect, 1746–1813* (1936), Dorothy Sirond, *Henry Holland* (1950) and J. [N.] Summerson, *John Nash, Architect to George IV* (1935), all are helpful in tracing the development of styles and the social circumstances within which this took place. There is no clearly outstanding work on furniture and interior decoration. H. Cescinsky,

English Furniture of the Eighteenth Century (3 vols., 1909–11) and
O. Brackett, *An Encyclopaedia of English Furniture* (1927; revised
ed. as *English Furniture Illustrated*, by H. C. Smith, 1950) are
useful guides. H. F. Clark, *The English Landscape Garden* (1948)
is the best work on its subject. For music, in addition to works
already listed above, it is only necessary to mention P. A.
Scholes, *The Great Dr. Burney* (2 vols., 1948).

MILITARY AND NAVAL

For naval history it is logical to begin with the books of the
American A. T. Mahan which have moulded much subsequent
thought: they are *The Influence of Sea Power on History, 1660–1783*
[1890], *The Major Operations of the Navies in the War of American
Independence* (1913), *The Influence of Sea Power upon the French
Revolution and Empire, 1793–1812* (2 vols., 1892), *The Life of
Nelson, the Embodiment of the Sea Power of Great Britain* (2 vols.,
1898; revised ed. 1899), and his *Sea Power in its relation to the
War of 1812* (2 vols., 1905). A short account of the whole subject
is M. [A.] Lewis, *The Navy of Britain* (1948). Sir H. W. Richmond's Ford Lectures *Statesmen and Sea Power* (1946) give
admirable surveys of problems of naval strategy.

Studies of the navy in particular wars are J. S. Corbett,
England in the Seven Years' War (2 vols., 1907), Sir W. M. James,
The British Navy in Adversity (1926), J. S. Corbett, *The Campaign
of Trafalgar* (1910), P. [G.] Mackesy, *War in the Mediterranean
1803–10* (1957), J. H. Rose's article 'Napoleon and Sea Power'
in *Cambridge Historical Journal*, i (1925), pp. 138–57, and C. N.
Parkinson, *War in the Eastern Seas 1793–1815* (1954). Two very
different types of commanders who felt the Nelson touch can
be studied in G. L. N. Collingwood, *A Selection from the Public
Correspondence of Lord Collingwood* (2 vols., 1828) and Thomas
Cockrane, 10th Earl of Dundonald, *The Autobiography of a
Seaman* (2 vols., 1860). The story of the naval mutinies in 1797
is well written up in G. E. Manwaring and B. Dobrée, *The
Floating Republic* (1935). The direction of the Admiralty may
be studied in *The Private Papers of John, Earl of Sandwich*, ed.
by G. R. Barnes and J. H. Owen (4 vols., 1932–8), *Private
Papers of George, Second Earl Spencer*, ed. by J. S. Corbett and
H. W. Richmond (4 vols., 1913–24) and the *Letters and Papers of
Charles, Lord Barham*, ed. by J. K. Laughton (3 vols., 1907–11).
Finally the foundations of naval strength are fascinatingly

discussed in R. G. Albion, *Forests and Sea Power* (Harvard Economic Series xxix, Cambridge, Mass., 1926).

For the army the first, but not the most interesting, work is C. M. Clode, *The Military Forces of the Crown* (2 vols., 1869). Sir J. W. Fortescue, *A History of the British Army* (vols. i–x, 1899–1920) has many full descriptions of battle but disappoints on larger issues. For the War of American Independence E. E. Curtis, *The Organisation of the British Army in the American Revolution* (1926), and an article, 'American versus Continental Warfare' by R. Pares in *English Historical Review*, li (1936), pp. 429–65, are very useful. For the War in Spain Sir C. Oman, *A History of the Peninsular War* (7 vols., 1902–30) is the most reliable. There are of course a multitude of secondary works on Wellington's methods and career. Among the most useful are S. G. P. Ward's study of staff work, *Wellington's Headquarters 1809–1814* (1957), D. [H.] Bell's rather light but enjoyable biographical sketches, *Wellington's Officers* (1938), G. Davis, *Wellington and his Army* (1954), C. [A.] Mercer, *Journal of the Waterloo Campaign*, with introd. by J. Fortescue (1927). Two of the most interesting of the military figures of the period can be studied in B. Willson, *The Life and Letters of James Wolfe* (1909) and Beatrice Brownrigg, *The Life and Letters of Sir John Moore* (1923). For a humble soldier's view of war there is *The Letters of Private Wheeler 1809–28* ed. B. H. Liddell Hart (1951).

IRELAND AND SCOTLAND

W. E. H. Lecky, *A History of Ireland in the Eighteenth Century* (8 vols., 1878–90; revised ed. 5 vols., 1892) is history on a grand scale and is still the most important work in the field and a readable narrative. A shorter general history of merit is E. Curtis, *A History of Ireland* (1936). The economic side is covered only very generally by Lecky, and here G. O'Brien, *The Economic History of Ireland in the Eighteenth Century* (1918) is useful for reference: K. H. Connell, *The Population of Ireland 1750–1845* (1950) is a model work of its kind. Much information of interest has been assembled in two books by R. B. McDowell, *Irish Public Opinion 1750–1800* (1944) and *Public Opinion and Government Policy in Ireland, 1801–46* (1952). Books dealing with the Union will be found in the Political Bibliography but two biographies may be added; S. [L.] Gwynn, *Henry Grattan and his Times* (1939) is popular in manner but reliable and well-proportioned: D. [R.] Gwynn, *Daniel O'Connell, the Irish Liberator* [1930] (revised ed. 1947) is rather slight but is particularly interesting for those early years which are relevant here.

Most of the books dealing with Scottish economic or political history will be found in the general lists above but some few more may be added. P. Hume Brown's *History of Scotland* (3 vols., 1899–1909) is the standard work but is uninspiring. Agnes M. Mackenzie, *Scotland in Modern Times, 1720–1939* (1941, revised ed. 1947) is more likely to provoke further reading. J. Galt, *Annals of the Parish* (1821; many subsequent editions) is deservedly famous because it provides, in fictional form, much accurate social history. Another book not by an historian but by a minister and a novelist, J. Watson, *The Scot of the Eighteenth Century. His Religion and his Life* (1907), does not pretend to scholarship but nevertheless gives an attractive outline of the place of the kirk in Scottish life.

COLONIAL POLICY

For a general view of the purposes and policies behind the overseas expansion of these years the soundest guide is V. T. Harlow, *The Founding of the Second British Empire 1763–93* (1952 ff.); his work is more convincing though less eloquently presented than R. Coupland, *The American Revolution and the British Empire* (1930). V. T. Harlow and A. F. Madden, *British Colonial Developments 1774–1834* (1953) is a good selection of documents. For an examination of contemporary ideas K. E. Knorr, *British Colonial Theories 1570–1850* (Toronto, 1944) is dependable. *The Cambridge History of the British Empire* (7 vols., 1929–40) is an invaluable work of reference, though J. A. Williamson, *A Short History of British Expansion* (1922; ed. 3, revised, 2 vols., 1943–45) is certainly more easily readable. An introduction to the economic side of the matter may be found in Lilian C. A. Knowles, *The Economic Development of the Overseas Empire 1763–1914* (3 vols., 1924–36). Fuller consideration of the subject will be found in G. L. Beer, *The Old Colonial System* (2 vols., New York, 1912; new edition, 1933) and *The Commercial Policy of England towards the American Colonies* (ibid., 1893; reprinted 1948) and in R. L. Schuyler, *The Fall of the Old Colonial System* (1945): the interpretation offered in these works should be critically compared with that in O. M. Dickerson, *The*

Navigation Acts and the American Revolution (Philadelphia, 1951) and that in the essay on the causes of the American revolt in W. J. Ashley, *Surveys Historical and Economic* (1900). For the course of exploration there are J. C. Beaglehole, *The Exploration of the Pacific* (1934), A. H. Carrington, *Life of Captain Cook* (1939), W. J. L. Wharton (ed.), *Captain Cook's Journal during his First Voyage round the World* (1893) and J. A. Williamson's short study, *Cook and the Opening of the Pacific* (1946). For the West Indies L. J. Ragatz, *A Guide for the Study of Caribbean History, 1763–1834* (Washington, 1932) opens up many new avenues: the same author's *The Fall of the Planter Class in the British Caribbean 1763–1833* (New York, 1928) is full of stimulating ideas. More limited in its interests, but useful, is Frances Armytage, *The Free Port System in the British West Indies 1766–1822* (1938); R. Pares, *War and Trade in the West Indies 1739–1763* (1938) and *A West Indian Fortune* (1950) are also useful in linking the colonial question to England's domestic history.

For Africa Eveline G. Martin, *The British West African Settlement 1750–1821* (1927) and H. L. Hoskins, *British Routes to India* (1928) should be consulted.

INDIA

The Cambridge History of India volume v (1929) and V. A. Smith, *The Oxford History of India* (ed. 2, 1923) with P. E. Roberts, *History of British India under the Company and the Crown* (1923) supply the general picture of India in this period. Lucy S. Sutherland, *The East India Company in Eighteenth Century Politics* (1952) provides a definitive account of the exceedingly complicated story of the Company to Pitt's Reform Act. For the opening years of this period H. Dodwell, *Dupleix and Clive* (1920) sets the scene competently. For the drama of the Warren Hastings period H. Furber, *John Company at Work* (Cambridge, Mass., 1948) is a rather involved but very informative account of the Company's trade. E. P. Moon, *Warren Hastings and British India* (1947) though brief is a brilliant account of the facts from an interesting point of view, while G. R. Gleig, *Memoirs of the Life of Warren Hastings* (3 vols., 1841) is valuable for the letters it prints but is abominably and uncritically written. It is a relief to turn to the unassertive edition of Hastings's dispatches in G. W. Forrest (ed.), *Selections from the State Papers of the Governors General of India. W. Hastings* (2 vols., 1910). The most recent life of Warren Hastings is that by Sir Keith G. Feiling (1954), a book written with affection both for India and for Hastings, full of erudition which is lightly carried, though its allusive style makes it less easy for unskilled readers. Sophia Weitzman has excellently analysed the quarrels of the Bengal Council in *Warren Hastings and Philip Francis* (1929). C. C. Davis, *Warren Hastings and Oudh* (1939) is clear and cogent. Other special studies for the Hastings epoch are M. E. Monckton Jones, *Warren Hastings in Bengal, 1772–74* (1918), J. Strachey, *Hastings and the Rohilla War* (1892), H. W. Richmond, *The Navy in India, 1763–1783* (1931), A. P. Dasgupta, *The Central Authority in British India 1774–84* (London thesis, Calcutta, 1931), R. B. Ramsbotham, *Studies in the Land Revenue history of Bengal, 1769–1787* (1926). A vivid impression of the social life of the English in India at this time may be found in the pages of the *Memoirs of William Hickey, 1749–1809* (4 vols., 1913–25) though it could be wished that the editor, A. Spencer, had made clearer the degree of reliance which can be placed upon the manuscripts.

For the period from Pitt's India Act the best guide is undoubtedly C. H. Philips, *The East India Company, 1784–1834* (1940). G. W. Forrest (ed.), *Selections from the State Papers of the Governors General of India. Cornwallis* (2 vols., 1926) may be used with A. Aspinall, *Cornwallis in Bengal* (1931) as a commentary. Further raw material for this period has been edited by C. H. Philips in *The Correspondence of David Scott . . . relating to Indian Affairs, 1787–1805* (Camden third series lxxv and lxxvi; 1951), and by H. Furber, *The Private Record of an Indian Governor-Generalship, the Correspondence of Sir J. Shore with H. Dundas, 1793–1798* (1933). P. E. Roberts, *India under Wellesley* (1929) presents the facts of imperialist expansion with admiration but with shrewd judgement: it should be read with S. J. Owen (ed.), *A Selection from the Despatches, Treaties and other Papers of the Marquess Wellesley* (1877). J. C. Sinha, *Economic Annals of Bengal* (1927) and S. Gopal's little book, *The Permanent Land Settlement in Bengal and its Results* (1949) direct attention to economic factors often left vague.

AMERICA

In addition to books already mentioned under Colonial, Naval and Military, and Political History, there are a great number of works of importance dealing with the establishment of the independent United States. J. C. Miller, *Origins of the American Revolution* (1945; shortly to be reissued) and *Triumph of Freedom, 1775–1783* (Boston, Mass., 1948) are the most useful short accounts: Miller has summarized in an attractive narrative much of the recent work of American scholars on the American side but he is much less good (at times indeed misleading) on the English side: but his virtues far outweigh his defects. G. H. Van Tyne, *The Causes of the War of Independence* (1921) is now less useful but this author's *The Loyalists in the American Revolution* (1902) is certainly worth reading: the subject is one which has not usually been given its due prominence. A short summary of many of the themes in the Revolution is to be found in Eric Robson, *The American Revolution in its Political and Military Aspects, 1763–1783* (1955). L. H. Gipson, *The Coming of the Revolution, 1763–1775* (1954) is extremely thorough. An admirable collection of documents (and no less admirable prefatory essay) is *Sources and Documents illustrating the American Revolution, 1764–1788, and the Formation of the Federal Constitution* by S. E. Morison (1923). S. E. Morison and H. S. Commager, *The Growth of the American Republic* (New York, 1930; ed. 4, 2 vols., 1950), is marked by the same freshness and common sense. The problems of expansion and the frontier were notably expounded in C. W. Alvord, *The Mississippi Valley in British Politics* (2 vols., Cleveland, Ohio, 1917) and have been further explored in T. P. Abernethy, *Western Lands and the American Revolution* (New York, 1937). The problems of an expanding society are also the theme of J. F. Jameson, *The American Revolution considered as a Social Movement* (Princeton, 1926). On one economic factor A. M. Schlesinger, *The Colonial Merchant and the American Revolution, 1763–1776* (New York, 1918) is interesting. Jane Clark deals with one of the most disputed incidents of the war in her article 'Responsibility for the failure of the Burgoyne campaign' in *American Historical Review*, xxxv (1930), pp. 542–59. For American leaders the obvious first step is to consult *Benjamin Franklin's Autobiographical Writings* selected and edited by C. [C.] Van Doren (1946), the monumental new edition of *The Papers of Thomas Jefferson* now being produced under the editorship of J. P. Boyd (vol. i, 1950), Thomas Paine, *Common Sense* (1776), and D. S. Freeman, J. A. Carroll and W. M. Ashworth, *George Washington* (7 vols., 1948–57). Of

English sources D. Bonner-Smith (ed.), *The Barrington Papers* (2 vols., 1937–41), C. E. Carter (ed.), *The Correspondence of General T. Gage with the Secretaries of State, 1763–1775* (2 vols., New Haven, 1931–33), William Knox, *Extra Official State Papers* (1789), and the Knox papers in *Hist. MSS. Com. Various Collections VI* (1909) should be added at this point to previous lists of political papers.

FOREIGN POLICY

Foreign policy has been rather neglected by historians for the first twenty years of the reign: thereafter it becomes almost inextricably intermingled with the problems of the direction of the war. *The Cambridge History of British Foreign Policy, 1783–1919*, ed. A. W. Ward and G. P. Gooch, vol. i, 1783–1815 (1922) is reliable, and R. W. Seton-Watson, *Britain in Europe 1789–1914* (1937) is a clear outline. The problems of policy in Central Europe are temperately discussed in Sir A. W. Ward, *Great Britain and Hanover* (1899) and in Sir R. Lodge (whose *Studies in 18th Century Diplomacy*, 1930, provide good background knowledge), *Great Britain and Prussia in the 18th Century* (1923): also useful are Z. E. Rashed, *The Treaty of Paris* (1951) and D. B. Horn, *British Public Opinion and the First Partition of Poland* (1945). One episode in relations with Spain, *The Struggle for the Falkland Islands*, is very adequately covered by J. L. Goebel (New Haven, 1927). For Russia it is possible to follow up ideas in F. W. Reddaway, 'Macartney in Russia' in *Cambridge Historical Journal*, iii (1931), pp. 260–94, but the only comprehensive account is in German, D. Gerhard, *England und der Aufstieg Russlands* (1933). A. Sorel, *La Question d'Orient au XVIIIᵉ Siècle* (1878; English tr. as *The Eastern Question in the Eighteenth Century*, 1898) is still the best survey of British policy for that area. For the Netherlands S. T. Bindoff, *The Scheldt Question to 1839* (1945) and, for a more limited period, G. J. Renier, *Great Britain and the Establishment of the Kingdom of the Netherlands, 1813–15* (1930) are very useful. C. H. Wilson in his exposition of finance, *Anglo-Dutch Commerce and Finance in the Eighteenth Century* (1941), also casts light upon problems of foreign policy.

For the period of the wars with the Revolution and Napoleon H. W. V. Temperley and Lilian M. Penson (ed.), *Foundations of British Foreign Policy from Pitt, 1792, to Salisbury, 1902* (1938) provides an admirably balanced introduction. Sir J. W.

Fortescue, *British Statesmen of the Great War, 1793–1814* (1911) is a sustained vituperative commentary on the ineptness of all statesmen before Perceval and some after him: its effect is dulled by over-emphasis. A. J. P. Taylor, *The Trouble-Makers, Dissent over Foreign Policy, 1792–1939* (1957) has some interesting points to make about the attitude of Foxites to the world but it is uneven, sometimes facile, occasionally stimulating.

Economic considerations in foreign policy during the war are most fully considered in E. F. Heckscher, *The Continental System: an economic interpretation* (1922): there are very interesting chapters on England with relevance to this aspect in G. Lefebvre, *Napoléon* (1935; ed. 4, revised, 1953). Relations with the United States between 1795 and 1805 are explored in great detail by Bradford Perkins, *The First Rapprochement, England and the United States, 1795–1805* (Philadelphia, 1956): W. A. Phillips and A. H. Reede, *Neutrality*, vol. ii, The Napoleonic Period (New York, 1936), L. M. Sears, *Jefferson and the Embargo* (Durham, N.C., 1927), and G. Dangerfield, *The Era of Good Feelings* (New York, 1952) are also useful for the events leading up to and the conclusion of the war of 1812 with the United States.

For the final stages of war diplomacy C. S. B. Buckland, *Metternich and the British Government from 1809 to 1813* (1932) will be found useful, but the outstanding contribution to knowledge in this field has been made by Sir C. K. Webster with his *British Diplomacy, 1813–15* (1921) together with his masterly *The Foreign Policy of Castlereagh* (2 vols., 1925–31) and his succinct but scholarly *The Congress of Vienna* (1919; revised ed. 1934).

Among original materials which have been printed are *The Journal and Correspondence of William* [Eden], *Lord Auckland* [ed. G. Hogge] (4 vols., 1861–2), the *Diaries and Correspondence of James Harris, first earl of Malmesbury*, ed. by his grandson (4 vols., 1844) and *Britain and the Independence of Latin America 1812–1830. Select Documents from the Foreign Office Archives*, ed. C. K. Webster (2 vols., 1938). Books bearing upon foreign policy will also be found in the lists for America, the Colonies, Naval affairs, as well as in the general Political list.

INDEX

For discussions of policies of countries in Europe see under foreign affairs

626   INDEX

INDEX 635

M.P. for Yorkshire, 271, 513; support
of abolition of slave trade, 301, 354,
358, 440; member of Clapham sect,
354.
Wilkes, John (1727–97), 64, 270, 357;
North Briton, 81 n. 1, 99–102, 133;
character, 98 f.; lack of support, 114;
1768–74 elections, 131–43, 148–50;
and identity of Junius, 145 n. 1;
1780 reform movements, 230; and
Gordon Riots, 238 f.
Wilkie, David, 539.
Wilkins, William (1778–1839), biog.
545 n. 6, 545 f.
Wilkinson, John (1728–1808), iron-
master, 32, 332, 507 f., 553.
Willes family, 61.
William case (1805), 473.
Wilson, Richard, painter (1714–82),
344.
Wilson, Sir Richard (1777–1849),
biog. 489 n. 1, 489.
Winchelsea, earl of, lord president of
council (1765–66), 575.
Winchester, American General, 553.
Winchester School, 39.
Windham, William (1750–1810), biog.
368 n. 1, 302, 320, 411, 414, 416,
434; secretary at war (1794–1801),
365 n. 1, 368, 370, 381, 402, 404, 580;
secretary for war and colonies (1806–
7), 435, 437, 453 f., 582.
Window tax, 115, 288, 375.
Wolcot, John, 350.
Wolfe, James (1727–59), 25, 369 n. 1;
pictures of death, 86, 345 f., 430.
Wolfe, Rev. Charles (1791–1823), 461
n. 3.
Wood, Robert, under-secretary of state,
100.
Wood, Thomas, M.P., 228 n. 1.
Woollen manufacture, *see under* Textiles.
Woollet, William (1735–85) 346.

Wordsworth, William, biog. 539 n. 1,
539 f., 534.
Worsley, royal surveyor, 97.
Worthing, 549.
Wortley, *see* Stuart-Wortley-Mac-
kenzie.
Wray, Sir Cecil, 275.
Wright, Joseph (1734–97), 347.
Wright v. *Fitzgerald*, case of, 397 n. 3.
Wyatt, James (1747–1813), architect,
544 f., with biog. 545 n. 2.
Wyatt, Samuel, architect, 544.
Wyndham, Charles, *see* Egremont,
earl of.
Wyvill, Christopher (1740–1822), 228–
31, with biog. 228 n. 4, 278.

Yale, 149.
Yeo, Sir James, 553.
Yonge, George, secretary at war (1783),
579.
Yorck, Prussian general, 555 f.
York, Canada, *see* Toronto.
York, duke of, military campaigns, 364 f.,
367–9, 379, 385 n. 2, 435, n. 1, 453
n. 1, 492, 415; commander-in-chief,
371; Mrs. Clarke affair, 447 f.;
training establishment, 481.
Yorke, Charles (1722–70), 85, 117, 146,
576.
Yorke, Charles Philip (1764–1834),
biog. 408 n. 4; secretary at war, 415;
home secretary (1803–4), 408, 581;
first lord of the admiralty (1809–12),
583.
Yorke, Philip, *see* Hardwicke, 1st earl of.
Yorktown, 217 f.
Young, Arthur (1741–1820), biog. 521
n. 5, 12, 27, 521, 528.

Zemindars, 311, 313, 321.
Zennan Shah, 382.
Zuylestein, William Henry, *see* Roch-
ford, earl of.